Complete Curriculum

Grade 4

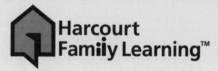

Harcourt Family Learning™

© 2006 by Flash Kids
Adapted from *Comprehension Skills Complete Classroom Library* by Linda Ward Beech, Tara McCarthy, and Donna Townsend;
© 2001 by Harcourt Achieve • Adapted from *Steck-Vaughn Spelling: Linking Words to Meaning, Level 4*
by John R. Pescosolido; © 2002 by Harcourt Achieve • Adapted from Steck-Vaughn *Working with Numbers, Level D*;
© 2001 by Harcourt Achieve • Adapted from *Language Arts, Grade 4;* © 2003 by Harcourt Achieve • Adapted from *Experiences with Writing
Styles Grade 4;* © 1998 by Steck-Vaughn Company and *Writing Skills Grade 4;* © 2003 by Steck-Vaughn Company • Adapted from *Test Best for
Test Prep, Level D;* © 1999 by Harcourt Achieve.

For more information, please visit www.flashkids.com
Please submit all inquiries to Flashkids@sterlingpublishing.com

ISBN 978-1-4114-9881-5

Manufactured in Singapore

Lot#:
26 28 30 29 27
09/19

FlashKids

New York

Dear Parent,

Beginning a new grade is a milestone for your child, and each new subject is bound to present some challenges that may require some attention out of the classroom. With this comprehensive fourth-grade workbook at hand, you and your child can work together on any skill that he or she is finding difficult to master. Here to help are hundreds of fun, colorful pages for learning and practicing reading, spelling, math, language arts, writing, and test preparation.

In the reading section, the wide range of high-interest stories will hold your child's attention and help develop his or her proficiency in reading. Each of the six units focuses on a different reading comprehension skill: finding facts, detecting a sequence, learning new vocabulary through context, identifying the main idea, drawing conclusions, and making inferences. Mastering these skills will ensure that your child has the necessary tools for a lifetime love of reading.

Lessons in the spelling section present fourth-grade words in lists grouped by vowel sound, suffix, or related forms, like plurals and contractions. This order will clearly show your child the different ways that similar sounds can be spelled. Your child will learn to sort words, recognize definitions, synonyms, and base words, as well as use capitalization and punctuation. Each lesson also features a short passage containing spelling and grammar mistakes that your child will proofread and correct.

The math section starts with estimation and multiplication skills, followed by techniques to solve complex multiplication and division problems. Next your child is introduced to conversion problems using time, money, and measurement, and finally, basic fractions and geometry. Each section begins with clear examples that illustrate new skills, and then practice drills, problem-solving lessons, and unit reviews encourage your child to master each new technique.

More than 100 lessons in the language arts section provide clear examples of and exercises in language skills such as parts of speech, sentences, mechanics, vocabulary and usage, writing, and research skills. Grammar lessons range from using nouns and verbs to constructing better sentences. Writing exercises include the friendly letter and the research report. These skills will help your child improve his or her communication abilities, excel in all academic areas, and increase his or her scores on standardized tests.

Each of the six units in the writing section focuses on a unique type of writing: personal narrative, how-to writing, fable, comparative writing, descriptive writing, and short report. The first half of each unit reinforces writing aspects such as putting ideas in a sequence and using descriptive details, in addition to providing fun, inspirational writing ideas for your child to explore alone or with a friend. In the second half of each unit, your child will read a practice paragraph, analyze it, prepare a writing plan for his or her own paper or paragraph, and then write and revise.

Lastly, the test prep section employs your child's knowledge in reading, math, and language to the basic standardized test formats that your child will encounter throughout his or her school career. Each unit in the first half of this section teaches specific test strategies for areas such as word study skills, reading comprehension, and mathematics. The second half of the section allows your child to apply these test-taking skills in a realistic testing environment that includes a detachable answer sheet. By simulating the experience of taking standardized tests, these practice tests can lessen feelings of intimidation during school tests.

As your child works through the test prep section, help him or her keep in mind these four important principles of test-taking:

1. Using Time Wisely
All standardized tests are timed, so your child should learn to work rapidly but comfortably. He or she should not spend too much time on any one question, and mark items to return to if possible. Use any remaining time to review answers. Most importantly, use a watch to keep on track!

2. Avoiding Errors
When choosing the correct answers on standardized tests, your child should pay careful attention to directions, determine what is being asked, and mark answers in the appropriate place. He or she should then check all answers and not make stray marks on the answer sheet.

3. Reasoning
To think logically toward each answer, your child should read the entire question or passage and all the answer choices before answering a question. It may be helpful to restate questions or answer choices in his or her own words.

4. Guessing
When the correct answer is not clear right away, your child should eliminate answers that he or she knows are incorrect. If that is not possible, skip the question. Then your child should compare the remaining answers, restate the question, and then choose the answer that seems most correct.

An answer key at the back of this workbook allows you and your child to check his or her work in any of the subject sections. Remember to give praise and support for each effort. Also, learning at home can be accomplished at any moment—you can ask your child to read the newspaper aloud to you, write grocery lists, keep a journal, or convert the ingredients for a recipe. Use your imagination! With help from you and this workbook, your child is well on the way to completing the fourth grade with flying colors!

TABLE OF CONTENTS

Reading Skills

Spelling Skills

Math Skills

Language Arts

Writing Skills

Test Prep

Answer Key

Reading Skills

What Are Facts?

Facts are sometimes called details. They are small pieces of information. Facts can appear in true stories, such as those in the newspaper. They can also appear in tales and other stories that people make up.

How to Read for Facts

You can find facts by asking yourself questions. Ask *who*, and your answer will be a fact about a person. Ask *what*, and your answer will be a fact about a thing. Ask *where*, and your answer will be a fact about a place. Ask *when*, and your answer will be a fact about a time. Ask *how many* or *how much*, and your answer will be a fact about a number or an amount.

Try It!

Read this story and look for facts as you read. Ask yourself *what* and *when*.

The *Titanic*

On April 10, 1912, the *Titanic* left England on its first trip. It was the largest and one of the safest ships ever built. Many rich and famous people were on board. They planned to arrive in New York in six days. But on the night of April 14, the ship ran into an iceberg. The iceberg tore a huge hole in the ship's side. The passengers climbed into lifeboats as the ship began to sink, but there were not enough boats for everyone. Only 711 of the 2,207 people on board lived to tell about the shipwreck.

Did you find these facts when you read the paragraph? Write the facts on the lines below.

◆ What happened to the *Titanic*?

Fact:_____

◆ When did the ship run into the iceberg?

Fact:_____

The kangaroo has a large, useful tail. It is like a chair. The kangaroo leans on its tail to rest. The tail is also good for leaping and landing. It helps the kangaroo to keep its balance. This is important because an adult kangaroo can leap as far as 15 feet at a time.

A fox has a big, bushy tail. This is a good tail to have on cold nights. The fox can put its tail over its nose and paws while it sleeps. The tail is a blanket that keeps the fox warm.

Some animals don't keep their tails with them at all times. One example is the lizard. If an enemy pulls the lizard's tail in a struggle, the tail breaks off. The lizard leaves its tail and runs to safety. Don't worry! The lizard will soon grow a new tail.

_____ **6.** The kangaroo uses its tail as a place to
    A. eat   **C.** lean
    B. grow   **D.** leave

_____ **7.** A kangaroo's tail is also helpful for
    A. jumping   **C.** walking
    B. swimming   **D.** crying

_____ **8.** The fox uses its bushy tail as a
    A. pillow   **C.** chair
    B. cover   **D.** brush

_____ **9.** A lizard's tail can help the lizard escape from
    A. friends   **C.** enemies
    B. kangaroos   **D.** blankets

_____ **10.** The lizard can grow a new
    A. fin   **C.** nose
    B. leg   **D.** tail

Words Around the Nation

Most people in the United States speak English. But they don't all use the same words for the same things. For instance, what do you call a round, flat breakfast food served with maple syrup? Some people call these *flapjacks*. In other places people call them *griddlecakes*. If you live in the hills of Arkansas or Tennessee, you might answer *flitters*. If you live in Mississippi, you might say *battercakes*. Most people in the United States say *pancakes*.

Suppose you are talking about an insect some people call a *dragonfly*. People in Florida wouldn't know what that means. They call this insect a *mosquito hawk*. People in nearby Georgia don't know what a mosquito hawk is. They call the very same insect a *snake doctor*! Still another word for dragonfly is *snake feeder*.

_____ **1.** People describe things using different
    A. works   **C.** plants
    B. words   **D.** sights

_____ **2.** A dragonfly is a kind of
    A. insect   **C.** doctor
    B. pancake   **D.** monster

_____ **3.** Another word that means *flapjack* is
    A. carrot cake   **C.** griddlecake
    B. dragonfly   **D.** slapjack

_____ **4.** A dragonfly is also called a
    A. snake doctor   **C.** snake nurse
    B. snakeroot   **D.** snapdragon

_____ **5** The word *mosquito hawk* is used by people in
    A. Oregon   **C.** Tennessee
    B. Arkansas   **D.** Florida

Do you want to build a fire? Building a fire might not be very easy if you live in the United States. One language expert has found 169 different words for the wood used to start a fire. Some of these words are *lighterd knots*, *kindling wood*, and *lightning wood*.

Let's go shopping. Do you want cling peaches, plum peaches, green peaches, or pickle peaches? It doesn't matter. They are all the same thing. It just depends on where you are.

Once you buy your fruit, you can put it in a paper bag, a sack, or even a poke. You can eat it at home on your porch, veranda, or gallery. You might want to invite your friend or buddy to share the snack, chow, or grub. Don't eat the pits, though. They will make you sick no matter what you call them!

_____ **6.** You use kindling wood to
    A. build a porch   **C.** build a house
    B. start a fire   **D.** plant trees

_____ **7.** A *poke* is a
    A. paper   **C.** sack
    B. plum   **D.** pig

_____ **8.** How many words mean the same as *lighterd knots*?
    A. 196   **C.** 16
    B. 168   **D.** 96

_____ **9.** A green peach is the same as a
    A. cling peach   **C.** red plum
    B. pink peach   **D.** green plum

_____ **10.** Some Americans say *gallery* instead of
    A. porch   **C.** kitchen
    B. pooch   **D.** vessel

Wonder Worker

You have probably heard the saying "busy as a beaver." This saying is really true. Beavers are almost always working.

The beaver is a builder. This furry animal builds dams and tunnels. It builds a home called a lodge. The beaver's tools for this work are a broad, flat tail and strong front teeth.

The first thing a beaver does is build a dam. Beavers build their dams across quiet streams where no other beavers live. They use their powerful teeth to cut down trees. Then they use their teeth to make the trees into logs about 6 feet long. They drag the logs across the stream to the dam. Beavers also use leaves and branches in their dams. They pack them together with mud to make a wall. The beaver's wide tail is handy for slapping the mud into place. When it is finished, the wall of a beaver dam is strong enough to keep out water.

_____ **1.** Beavers are almost always
    A. playing   **C.** sleeping
    B. working   **D.** fighting

_____ **2.** A beaver home is called a
    A. cabin   **C.** lodge
    B. dam   **D.** ledge

_____ **3.** Beavers build dams across quiet
    A. puddles   **C.** streets
    B. oceans   **D.** streams

_____ **4.** Beavers cut down trees with their
    A. paws   **C.** saws
    B. teeth   **D.** tails

_____ **5.** Beavers pack the branches in their dams with
    A. clay   **C.** glue
    B. water   **D.** mud

The beaver's dam holds back the water in the stream. A pond forms behind the dam. Then the beaver builds its lodge in the middle of the pond. This is the beaver's way of keeping its home safe from other animals.

Most of a beaver's lodge is under the water. The beaver dives under the water to get to the entrance. Then it swims through tunnels to get to the upper part of the lodge. This part of the lodge is above the water. It is a safe place where the beaver can raise a family.

The inside of a beaver's lodge is hollow. Here the beavers raise a family. They have as many as six young in April or May. Young beavers stay with their parents until they are two years old. Then they leave the lodge to find a new stream and begin their busy adult lives.

_____ **6.** Beavers build homes in the middle of ponds for
    A. fun   **C.** protest
    B. protection   **D.** enjoyment

_____ **7.** The entrance is
    A. very large   **C.** under the water
    B. under the ground   **D.** above the water

_____ **8.** The beaver swims through the entrance into
    A. stairs   **C.** tunnels
    B. mines   **D.** enemies

_____ **9.** The upper part of the lodge is
    A. on the banks   **C.** under the water
    B. behind the water   **D.** out of the water

_____ **10.** Beavers have as many as
    A. six young   **C.** eight young
    B. seven young   **D.** ten young

Ferris's Wheel

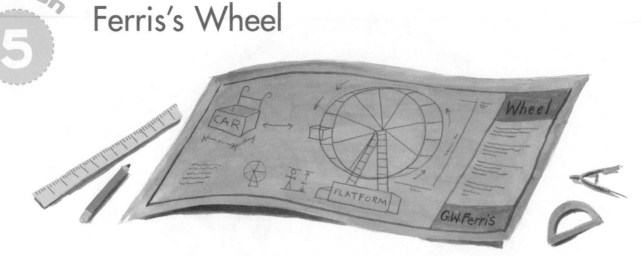

In 1892, Chicago city leaders planned a fair. They wanted it to be the greatest fair ever. It would show the newest ideas in science, business, and art. They also wanted to build something grand at the fair. The Eiffel Tower had been built three years before in France. The Chicago leaders wanted something even grander. So they asked people to send in designs.

G. W. Ferris was a young engineer. He heard about the fair. He designed a huge wheel made of steel. The wheel was 250 feet across. Large cars hung from the end of each spoke. Each car could carry 60 people in a giant circle through the air.

On May 1, 1893, the fair opened. People came from around the world to see the latest inventions. They felt the heat of new electric stoves. They stood in the cool breeze of small fans. They even saw a machine that washed dishes.

_____ **1.** Ferris's wheel was
  A. 1 mile high   **C.** 250 yards across
  B. 250 feet across   **D.** 60 feet tall

_____ **2.** Ferris's wheel was made of
  A. steel   **C.** wood
  B. rubber   **D.** gold

_____ **3.** Ferris designed his wheel so people could
  A. walk under it   **C.** ride it
  B. study it   **D.** learn about motion

_____ **4.** The fair opened
  A. in 1492   **C.** in 1893
  B. in 1892   **D.** in 1983

_____ **5.** People at the fair felt the heat of
  A. a bonfire   **C.** a heated fountain
  B. gas heaters   **D.** electric stoves

Ferris's wheel was the main attraction at the Chicago fair. People stood in line to ride on it. They wanted to see the fairgrounds from the wheel's highest point. As the wheel cranked upward, some people were frightened. Others were thrilled at what they saw below. Fountains glistened in the sunlight. Flags waved in the breeze. A train snaked through the grounds. At night colored searchlights lit the sky. Their beams reflected off the water fountains.

When the fair closed, the newspapers called it "a splendid fantasy." Ferris's wheel was later sold for scrap. Today smaller wheels based on his idea turn at fairs all over America. They are called Ferris wheels.

_____ **6.** Ferris's wheel was an attraction
    A. in France   **C.** in Chicago
    B. in Columbus   **D.** beside the Eiffel Tower

_____ **7.** Ferris's wheel
    A. broke down   **C.** was dangerous
    B. was popular   **D.** came from France

_____ **8.** People who rode Ferris's wheel could see
    A. the Eiffel Tower   **C.** Canada
    B. France   **D.** fountains and flags

_____ **9.** Newspapers called the fair a
    A. disaster   **C.** fantasy
    B. failure   **D.** thrill

_____ **10.** Ferris's wheel was sold for scrap
    A. after the fair   **C.** in 1892
    B. before the fair   **D.** during the fair

Starfish

Starfish of different sizes and colors live in the oceans. Starfish are often yellow, orange, or brown. They can be other colors, too. From point to point, a starfish can be as small as a paper clip or as long as a yardstick. Most starfish are shaped like stars, with five arms extending from their bodies. Some starfish, called sunstars, have a dozen arms. Other types have 25 arms.

Rows of tiny spines cover the top of a starfish's arms. Each spine moves easily when it is touched. Enemies that brush against a starfish may get a surprise. Some starfish spines are very sharp and have poison in them.

Underneath each arm of a starfish are rows of tiny holes. Tube feet extend from these holes. The tube feet can become suction cups to help starfish grip things. These suction cups hold starfish very strongly. Even storm waves will not tear a starfish from a rock.

_____ **1.** Starfish are often
    A. red   **C.** blue
    B. yellow   **D.** green

_____ **2.** From point to point, a starfish can be the size of a
    A. grain of rice   **C.** yardstick
    B. car   **D.** door

_____ **3.** A starfish can protect itself with its
    A. tube feet   **C.** mouth
    B. arms   **D.** spines

_____ **4.** The tube feet of a starfish are located
    A. on its back   **C.** under suction cups
    B. near its mouth   **D.** underneath its arms

_____ **5.** The suction-cup feet of a starfish
    A. are weak   **C.** are very strong
    B. have bristles   **D.** have pointed tips

A starfish's mouth is on its underside. It is in the middle of its body. Starfish swallow small animals whole. Sometimes they eat mollusks. These include clams and oysters, which are protected by hard shells. A starfish attaches its tube feet to each side of the shell. Then it slowly pries the shell open. The starfish next pushes its stomach out through its mouth, into the open shell. There, its stomach begins to digest the soft flesh.

Fishers who collect oysters and clams sometimes try to kill starfish by cutting them into pieces. This does not kill them. Starfish can grow new arms. They can even grow a new body. This can happen when one arm remains attached to a piece of the old body. Even a small part of a starfish's body can become another starfish.

_____ **6.** A starfish's mouth is
    A. on one arm   **C.** on its tube feet
    B. inside its stomach   **D.** on its underside

_____ **7.** Starfish swallow
    A. small animals   **C.** plants
    B. other starfish   **D.** tiny spines

_____ **8.** Oysters and clams are
    A. mammals   **C.** reptiles
    B. seashells   **D.** mollusks

_____ **9.** An oyster has
    A. a shell   **C.** arms
    B. a clam   **D.** spines

_____ **10.** If a starfish loses an arm, it will
    A. die   **C.** grow another
    B. not move   **D.** lose another

Ed's Dream Garden

Ed lives right outside a small town. He has decided to turn his back yard into a water garden with ponds and waterfalls. He wants flowers to grow everywhere, even in the ponds. Because Ed does not know how to begin, he signs up for a tour with his neighbor, Mr. Hall. Mr. Hall is known for his water gardens. He gives tours each Saturday.

On Saturday Mr. Hall greets Ed and takes him through a gate to his gardens. They pass a pond covered with large, green leaves floating on top of the water. Mr. Hall calls them lily pads. To Ed they look like big stepping-stones. Mr. Hall tells Ed about a type of water lily in South America with even bigger leaves. Its leaves can be more than 5 feet across. Mr. Hall explains that the plant is called the Victoria lily. Its leaves look like giant green pie pans because their edges turn up.

_____ 1. Ed and Mr. Hall live
     A. in different states   **C.** on different farms
     B. in the same area   **D.** in a large city

_____ 2. Mr. Hall gives tours
     A. every day   **C.** on Saturdays
     B. on Mondays   **D.** once a month

_____ 3. To Ed the lily pads look like
     A. green frogs   **C.** pie pans
     B. stones to walk on   **D.** waterfalls

_____ 4. The Victoria lily
     A. has enormous leaves   **C.** grows on land
     B. has purple berries   **D.** blooms each Saturday

_____ 5. The Victoria lily's leaves look like pie pans because of their
     A. size   **C.** name
     B. color   **D.** shape

Ed sees blue flowers scattered among the leaves. The blooms stand above the water on stout stalks. Each one has several petals attached to the stem. Mr. Hall explains that these Australian water lilies bloom all day. Other types of water lilies bloom only at night. He also explains that water lilies are not always blue. They can be yellow, pink, or red.

Ed asks if the plants have roots like other flowers. Mr. Hall explains how lilies grow. He says that the fruit of each water lily is like a berry. The berries are filled with seeds. Often the fruit ripens underwater. Then the seeds float away or sink. The roots of the plants grow from the seeds.

When Ed leaves, he thanks Mr. Hall. He tells Mr. Hall that he will plant water lilies in his garden. Mr. Hall shakes Ed's hand and offers to help him. He starts by giving Ed a package of seeds.

_____ **6.** The bloom that Ed sees is
    A. blue   **C.** red
    B. yellow   **D.** pink

_____ **7.** Australian water lilies
    A. make vines   **C.** bloom all day
    B. are white   **D.** don't have roots

_____ **8.** The fruit of each water lily is like a
    A. flower   **C.** stalk
    B. berry   **D.** seed

_____ **9.** The fruit of a water lily ripens
    A. in the mud   **C.** in the spring
    B. near the petals   **D.** underwater

_____ **10.** When Ed leaves, Mr. Hall gives him
    A. stems   **C.** seeds
    B. roots   **D.** flowers

Trail Drives

Millions of cattle roamed on the open range in the Old West. Cattle ranchers rounded them up. They could sell them in Texas for $4 or $5 each. Easterners also liked to eat beef. They would pay from $40 to $50 each. Cattle ranchers hired cowboys to drive their cattle north. In towns like Abilene and Dodge City, the railroads crossed the plains. There the cattle were put on trains headed for the East Coast.

Before each trail drive, several ranchers hired a leader for the long trip. This trail boss hired from 10 to 12 cowboys to round up the cattle. While the roundup was going on, the trail boss hired a wrangler and a cook. The wrangler gathered 50 or more horses for the trip. The cook prepared the chuck wagon for cooking beans, bacon, and biscuits on the trail.

_____ **1.** A cow could be sold in Texas for
    A. $10   **C.** $40
    B. $4   **D.** $50

_____ **2.** Cattle were driven
    A. east   **C.** north
    B. west   **D.** south

_____ **3.** Cattle were taken to the East Coast on
    A. horses   **C.** wagons
    B. trains   **D.** trucks

_____ **4.** The leader of a trail drive was called a
    A. trail boss   **C.** cook
    B. wrangler   **D.** roundup

_____ **5.** Before the trail drive, the cook prepared the
    A. horses   **C.** cattle
    B. saddles   **D.** chuck wagon

Each trail drive lasted for two or three months. The cowboys drove the cattle as far as 1,000 miles. They moved from 2,000 to 3,000 cattle on each drive. Those who were new to the job rode behind the herd. The dust clogged their throats and burned their eyes. At night some cowboys circled the herd, often singing to pass the time. Others slept next to saddled horses, ready for action.

Cowboys faced thieves, storms, and unfriendly tribes on trail drives. They feared stampedes the most. If a single cow was startled and ran, all the others followed. The earth shook with a deafening roar under their pounding hooves. After one stampede, the restless cattle were easily scared into stampeding again. Cowboys knew that they couldn't stop a stampeding herd, but they rode in front of it and tried to turn the cattle into a circle. This did not always help. Herds sometimes ran for days.

_____ **6.** Trail drives lasted two or three
   A. days   **C.** months
   B. years   **D.** weeks

_____ **7.** At times the number of cattle on a drive was
   A. 12   **C.** 1,000
   B. 50   **D.** 3,000

_____ **8.** On the trail new cowboys were positioned
   A. in front of the herd   **C.** next to the herd
   B. behind the herd   **D.** among the herd

_____ **9.** On the trail a cowboy slept ready for
   A. rain   **C.** coffee
   B. action   **D.** a bath

_____**10.** Stampedes were caused by
   A. horses   **C.** a frightened animal
   B. a sick animal   **D.** singing cowboys

Writing Roundup

Read the story below. Think about the facts. Then answer the questions in complete sentences.

Do you know how the sandwich got its name? The name comes from the man who invented it. In the 1700s there lived a man who belonged to the royal class of England. He was called the earl of Sandwich. One day he was too busy to stop for a meal. He asked his servant to bring him two slices of bread and some roast meat. He placed the meat between the bread slices. The first sandwich was invented! The earl named the creation after himself.

1. Who invented the sandwich?

_____

_____

2. When was the sandwich invented?

_____

_____

3. What was the first sandwich made of?

_____

_____

Prewriting

Think of an idea you might write about, such as an important invention or a well-known person. Write the idea in the center of the idea web below. Then fill out the rest of the web with facts.

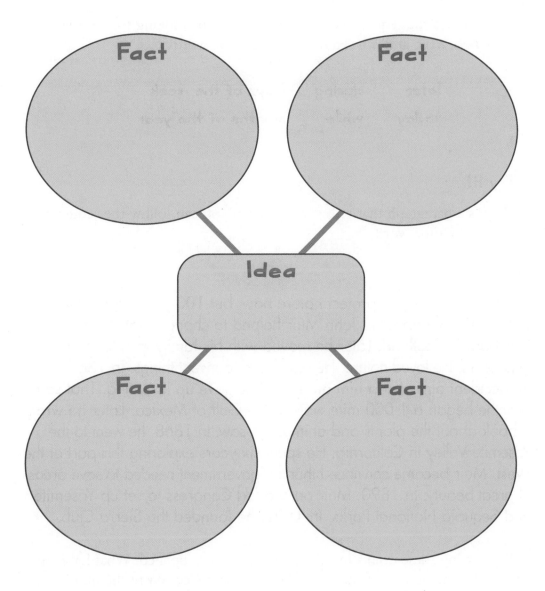

On Your Own

Now use another sheet of paper to write a paragraph about your idea. Use the facts from your idea web.

unit 2

What Is Sequence?

Sequence means time order, or 1-2-3 order. If several things happen in a story, they happen in a sequence. One event happens first, and it is followed by another event.

You can find the sequence of events in a story by looking for *time words*, such as *first*, *next*, and *last*. Here is a list of time words:

later	during	days of the week
today	while	months of the year

Try It!

Here is a paragraph that tells a story. See if you can follow the sequence. Circle all the time words.

John Muir

Many people try to protect nature now, but 100 years ago, few people thought about it. John Muir helped to change that. Muir was born in Scotland. Later he moved with his family to a farm in Wisconsin. He loved nature. He also loved to invent things. In 1867, an accident almost cost him an eye. Muir gave up inventing. That same year he began a 1,000-mile walk to the Gulf of Mexico. Later he wrote a book about the plants and animals he saw. In 1868, he went to the Yosemite Valley in California. He spent six years exploring this part of the West. Muir became convinced that the government needed to save areas of great beauty. In 1890, Muir persuaded Congress to set up Yosemite and Sequoia National Parks. In 1892, he founded the Sierra Club.

Try putting these events in the order that they happened. What happened first? Write the number **1** on the line by that sentence. Write the number **2** by the sentence that tells what happened next. Write the number **3** by the sentence that tells what happened last.

_____ Muir explored the Yosemite Valley.

_____ Muir moved to Wisconsin.

_____ Congress set up two national parks.

Practice with Sequence

This unit asks questions about sequence in stories. Here are some practice questions. The first two are already answered. You can do the third one on your own.

B 1. When was the Sierra Club founded?
   A. before Muir went on the 1,000-mile walk
   B. after Yosemite became a national park
   C. while Muir was an inventor

Look at the question. It has the words *Sierra Club* and *founded*. Find those words in the story. You will find the sentence, "In 1892, he founded the Sierra Club." The sentence before this one says that Muir persuaded Congress to set up Yosemite and Sequoia National Parks in 1890. So **B** is the correct answer. Muir founded the Sierra Club two years after Yosemite became a national park.

C 2. What happened just before Muir walked to the Gulf of Mexico?
   A. he wrote a book about what he saw
   B. he grew up on a farm
   C. he almost lost an eye

Look at the question carefully. Notice the time word *before*. Notice also that the word *just* is there. So the question is asking what happened *just before* Muir walked to the Gulf of Mexico. In the story you will find these sentences: "In 1867, an accident almost cost him an eye. Muir gave up inventing. That same year he began a 1,000-mile walk to the Gulf of Mexico." So the correct answer is **c**.

_____ 3. When did Muir persuade Congress to set up Yosemite and Sequoia National Parks?
   A. when he was exploring Yosemite
   B. before he walked to the Gulf of Mexico
   C. in 1890

Can you find the answer?

Read each story. After each story you will answer questions about the sequence of events in the story. Remember, sequence is the order of things.

Garden Art

Is it a tree? Is it a bear? If you're looking at a tree in the shape of a bear, it's a topiary. A topiary is a tree or bush that is trained into a shape. Topiaries are a kind of sculpture. Growing a topiary garden takes both time and skill.

The first thing a topiary gardener does is make a drawing. The drawing shows the form the gardener would like a tree or bush to take. The gardener then chooses the bush for the topiary. It may be one that was just planted or one that is already in place. Special bushes are used for topiaries. These bushes are yew, privet, or boxwood.

In June of the plant's first year, the gardener looks for new leaves. When the leaves grow, it is time to shape the bottom of the bush. The gardener shapes the bottom of the bush for about five years. The top is not trimmed during this time.

In the fifth year, the bush grows tall enough for shaping. Then the gardener begins to shape the whole bush. Sometimes branches are bent to form a shape. The gardener wires the branches in place.

Once a topiary has been started, it needs care all year. In the summer it must be clipped many times to keep its shape. This cutting also helps the bush grow. In the winter the bushes don't grow. The gardeners have to brush snow off the plants. Snow can hurt the flat parts of the plants.

Topiary gardening is a very old art. The Romans did it in the first century. In the sixteenth century, people in Europe liked topiaries too. The Dutch and French grew very pretty topiaries in their neat gardens. By the late 1600s, topiaries were also grown in America. Today there is a topiary garden in Williamsburg, Virginia. It's much like a garden that grew there hundreds of years ago.

1. Put these events in the order that they happened. What happened first? Write the number **1** on the line by that sentence. Then write the number **2** by the sentence that tells what happened next. Write the number **3** by the sentence that tells what happened last.

_____ The gardener chooses the bush.

_____ The gardener draws a sketch.

_____ The gardener shapes the bottom of the bush.

_____ **2.** When does the gardener look for new growth?
    A. in the fifth year
    B. in June
    C. after the first century

_____ **3.** How long does it take a topiary bush to grow tall enough for shaping?
    A. five years
    B. hundreds of years
    C. one year

_____ **4.** When did the Romans grow topiaries?
    A. in the late 1600s
    B. in the first century
    C. in the fifth century

_____ **5.** When were topiaries first grown in America?
    A. before the 1500s
    B. during the 1600s
    C. after the 1700s

Football Factory

A football has to be tough. After all, it gets kicked around most of the time. Each football is made very carefully. It takes about 50 steps to make a football.

It all starts with leather. About 2 feet of leather are needed to cover a pro football. A machine cuts the leather into four pieces. Another machine stamps the pieces. The stamp tells the name of the company that makes the ball. Workers then sew a cloth lining to each piece. Next they stitch the four pieces together. A small opening is left. The football is then turned inside out. Workers trim the extra leather inside.

The football is turned right side out again. A worker puts a rubber lining into the ball. Now the opening in the ball is sewed up. Each ball is sewed three times by hand. The first time, a worker uses heavy linen thread to close the opening. After that, two sets of leather laces are added. These laces help players get a good grip on the ball.

Once the ball is sewed up, it is placed on an iron mold. A worker pumps air into the rubber lining. Then another worker shines the leather football.

Next workers weigh and measure the ball to see that it is the right size and the right weight. A football should weigh between 14 and 15 ounces. It should be 21 inches around and 11 inches from end to end. A good football must be strong so it stands up to rough play. It must not be too hard or players will hurt their feet when they kick it.

If the football is just right, it goes to the packing area. Workers then put the balls in boxes to send to professional teams and sports stores.

1. Put these events in the order that they happened. What happened first? Write the number **1** on the line by that sentence. Then write the number **2** by the sentence that tells what happened next. Write the number **3** by the sentence that tells what happened last.

_____ Machines cut pieces from leather.

_____ Workers sew in a cloth lining.

_____ Machines stamp the leather pieces.

_____ 2. When are the four pieces sewed together?
   A. while a worker sews in a cloth lining
   B. before the inside is trimmed
   C. after workers check the ball's weight

_____ 3. When is a rubber lining put into the football?
   A. while the ball is turned inside out
   B. after the ball is turned right side out
   C. before the ball is turned inside out

_____ 4. When is each ball sewed up with leather laces?
   A. before the rubber lining is added
   B. while the lining is added
   C. after it is sewed with linen thread

_____ 5. When are the footballs measured?
   A. after they are sent to stores
   B. while they are inspected
   C. while they are used in games

Making Skeletons

Some people make skeletons for a living. Here are the bare-bones facts.

At a factory in England, workers make human skeletons from plastic. The skeletons are sold to hospitals and schools that train doctors. They are sent to more than 40 countries around the world. People study the skeletons to learn about the human body. Some scientists think these plastic skeletons are better and last longer than the real ones.

The workers start with a soft plastic called acrylic. They pour the acrylic into molds. It takes two hours for the acrylic to get hard. Then the workers remove the plastic bones from the molds. The factory has more than 200 molds. That is one mold for each bone in the body.

The next job is to smooth any rough spots on the bones. The workers polish these rough spots with power tools. The finished bones are then placed in special drawers. There is a drawer for each kind of bone.

Next it's time to put the bones together. Each worker puts together a different part of the body. For instance, one person puts together the hands. Each hand has 30 different small bones in it. The worker drills a tiny hole in each bone. Thin wire is then slipped into the holes. The wire holds the bones together in the right position.

Another worker puts together the rib cage. The ribs are made of rubber so they can be bent. Then they are wired together to form a rib cage. The worker joins the rib cage to the spine.

Finally all the skeleton parts are put together. The finished skeleton is hung up on a rack. An expert checks to make sure all the bones are in place. At the week's end, about 20 skeletons are ready for shipment.

1. Put these events in the order that they happened. What happened first? Write the number **1** on the line by that sentence. Then write the number **2** by the sentence that tells what happened next. Write the number **3** by the sentence that tells what happened last.

_____ People study plastic skeletons.

_____ People make plastic skeletons.

_____ Skeletons are sold to hospitals.

_____ **2.** When do workers place the bones in drawers?
   A. after they are smoothed over
   B. before the acrylic is hard
   C. before they are smoothed over

_____ **3.** When are hand bones wired together?
   A. after a worker drills holes in them
   B. while the acrylic gets hard
   C. after they are shipped around the world

_____ **4.** When do workers smooth the bones?
   A. after they are put in drawers
   B. after workers remove bones from molds
   C. after workers put the bones together

_____ **5.** When is the skeleton hung on a rack?
   A. after the bones are joined together
   B. after an expert checks it
   C. before the bones are placed in drawers

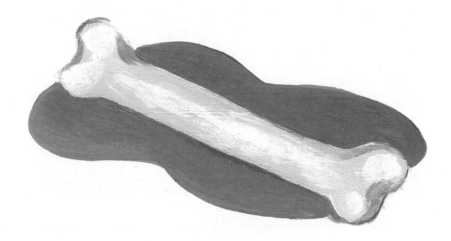

How Mail Is Delivered

The post office has plenty of work to do. It handles thousands of letters per day. Let's follow a letter all the way across America.

Juan lives in New York. He wrote a letter to Dave. Dave lives in Oregon. Juan put the letter in the mailbox on Monday night. On Tuesday morning a truck stopped at the mailbox. The mail carrier put the letters into a large bag and took the bag to a post office in New York.

Tuesday afternoon the letters were sorted. Zip codes were used to sort the mail. A machine picked up a letter and held it. A worker read the Zip code. Then the worker pushed five buttons on another machine. The worker had only one second to do this. After the worker pushed the buttons, the machine put the letter in a box. By Tuesday night the box was on a truck. The truck went to the airport. An airplane took off for Oregon on Wednesday morning. Juan's letter went on the airplane.

By noon the letters were in an airport in Oregon. Mail trucks then took them to post offices. One of these was in Dave's town. Wednesday night people in Dave's town sorted the letters by street name.

Thursday morning the mail carrier for Main Street picked up her pile of letters. She sorted all of them by street address. The people at 1 Main Street got their mail first. Dave lived at 221 Main Street. He got his letter before lunch.

1. Put these events in the order that they happened. What happened first? Write the number **1** on the line by that sentence. Then write the number **2** by the sentence that tells what happened next. Write the number **3** by the sentence that tells what happened last.

_____ The machine put the letter in a box.

_____ A worker read the Zip code.

_____ A worker pushed five buttons.

_____ **2.** Where did Juan's letter travel first?
     A. on a truck that went to the airport
     B. to a post office in New York
     C. to a post office in Oregon

_____ **3.** When did the letter go to Oregon?
     A. Monday night
     B. Wednesday morning
     C. Tuesday morning

_____ **4.** When did people sort the letters by street names?
     A. before the letters went on the airplane
     B. Wednesday night
     C. Tuesday night

_____ **5.** When did Dave get the letter?
     A. Monday after lunch
     B. Tuesday afternoon
     C. Thursday before lunch

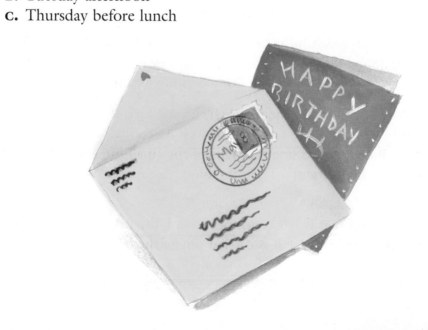

The Digestive System

Have you ever wondered what happens to the food you eat? Most people know that food provides energy for the body. Do you know how food becomes energy? We can find out by studying the digestive system.

Digestion is the breaking down of food into nutrients. Nutrients are the parts of food that the body can use. The nutrients must be small enough so that the blood can carry them to all the cells of the body.

The first part of the digestive system is the mouth. Food enters the body through the mouth. Teeth grind up the food into small pieces. The food is mixed with a liquid called saliva.

Saliva has a chemical that changes starch into sugar. This is the first step in breaking down food. When you swallow, food goes down the esophagus. This long tube leads into the stomach.

In the stomach more chemicals are mixed with the food. More starches are changed into sugar. Stomach juices begin to break down proteins. The muscles of the stomach act like a blender to turn the food into liquid.

When food leaves the stomach, it goes into the small intestine. The small intestine is like a hose. If it were stretched out, it would be 20 feet long. Blood vessels line the walls of the small intestine. These blood vessels soak up the nutrients. Then the blood carries the nutrients to every cell in the body.

The food that is left is not needed by the body. It passes into the large intestine. From there it is carried out of the body.

1. Put these events in the order that they happened. What happened first? Write the number **1** on the line by that sentence. Then write the number **2** by the sentence that tells what happened next. Write the number **3** by the sentence that tells what happened last.

_____ The food that is left goes into the large intestine.

_____ Chemicals mix with food in the stomach.

_____ Teeth grind up the food into small pieces.

_____ **2.** When is food mixed with saliva?
   A. while it is in the stomach
   B. when it is in the mouth
   C. after it is in the small intestine

_____ **3.** When does food go down the esophagus?
   A. after you swallow
   B. after it leaves the stomach
   C. when it leaves the large intestine

_____ **4.** When do juices begin to break down proteins?
   A. when food is in the mouth
   B. after food is in the small intestine
   C. while food is in the stomach

_____ **5.** Where do blood vessels soak up the nutrients?
   A. in the small intestine
   B. in the large intestine
   C. in the stomach

Koalas

Koalas are sometimes called koala bears because they look like live teddy bears. But koalas aren't bears. They are marsupials. Marsupials are mammals with pouches. Most marsupials live in Australia. If you lived in Australia, you could go to a koala preserve and see these cute, cuddly animals for yourself.

After mating, a female koala waits for about five weeks. Then her tiny, blind baby is born. The hairless baby is about 3/4 of an inch long. It looks like a worm with a big head and arms. The baby koala must climb 6 inches to get into its mother's pouch. This is a dangerous journey. If the tiny koala falls off, it will die.

The baby is safe once it's inside the mother's pouch. A strong muscle keeps the pouch closed for the first few months. The baby has plenty to eat. It grows larger, and its fur becomes thick. From time to time, it sticks its head out and looks around.

The baby stays in the pouch for about six months. Then it is ready to come out for short periods of time. By now it is 7 inches long and has its first teeth. The baby chews on young gum leaves, and drinks its mother's milk.

After leaving the pouch, the koala baby rides on its mother's back. The mother's strong arms and claws allow her to climb easily, even with the baby on her back. For the next few months, the baby clings to its mother during the day. At night it returns to the pouch. At about nine months old, the young koala will go short distances from the mother to eat gum leaves by itself.

The mother koala takes good care of her baby for about a year. By then the baby is full grown and can take care of itself.

1. Put these events in the order that they happened. What happened first? Write the number **1** on the line by that sentence. Then write the number **2** by the sentence that tells what happened next. Write the number **3** by the sentence that tells what happened last.

_____ The baby koala stays in the pouch for six months.

_____ The tiny, blind baby is born.

_____ The baby koala rides on its mother's back.

_____ **2.** When does the baby koala look like a worm?
   A. when it's about six months old
   B. after it's a year old
   C. when it's born

_____ **3.** When does the baby koala make a dangerous journey?
   A. when it first tries to reach its mother's pouch
   B. the first time it climbs a tree
   C. when it's 18 months old

_____ **4.** When does the baby koala first leave the pouch?
   A. before it's five weeks old
   B. when it's about six months old
   C. after it's full grown

_____ **5.** How long does a mother koala care for her baby?
   A. about one year
   B. less than six weeks
   C. more than three years

The *Hindenburg*

Have you ever seen a huge, cigar-shaped balloon called a blimp, or airship? They are sometimes used for advertising. Blimps float because they are filled with a gas that is lighter than air. They have engines and can be steered.

In the 1930s blimps were used for passenger travel. The *Hindenburg* was one of the largest airships ever built. It had made 10 trips from Germany to the United States. On May 3, 1937, it left Frankfurt to make another trip across the Atlantic. There were 97 people on board.

The *Hindenburg* was filled with hydrogen. Hydrogen explodes easily. For this reason passengers were not allowed to carry matches or lighters. People wore shoes with rubber soles to prevent sparks. Many safety measures were taken to prevent a fire.

On May 6 the *Hindenburg* neared Lakehurst, New Jersey. This is where it would land. Passengers gathered their luggage. They waved to friends and families waiting below. Just then Captain Pruss felt a jolt. He wondered what it was. He heard screaming on the field below. On his radio someone cried, "The ship is burning!"

People watching from below were terrified. The tail of the ship had burst into flames. The ship was crashing to the ground. Some passengers jumped out the windows. The ground crew ran for their lives.

The fire caused 36 deaths. No one knew what caused the ship to explode. Perhaps it was static electricity. There was no way to tell for certain. After the crash of the *Hindenburg*, airships were never again used for passenger travel.

1. Put these events in the order that they happened. What happened first? Write the number **1** on the line by that sentence. Then write the number **2** by the sentence that tells what happened next. Write the number **3** by the sentence that tells what happened last.

_____ The *Hindenburg* neared Lakehurst, New Jersey.

_____ Airships were never again used for passenger travel.

_____ The *Hindenburg* burst into flames.

_____ **2.** When were airships used for passenger travel?
  A. before balloons were invented
  B. in the 1930s
  C. after the *Hindenburg* crashed

_____ **3.** When did the *Hindenburg* leave Frankfurt?
  A. in the spring of 1937
  B. after the winter of 1940
  C. before the summer of 1935

_____ **4.** When did the *Hindenburg* crash?
  A. on November 1
  B. on April 5
  C. on May 6

_____ **5.** When did Captain Pruss feel a jolt?
  A. before they left Frankfurt
  B. while they were getting ready to land
  C. as soon as they saw the Atlantic Ocean

Great Blue Whales

Blue whales are the largest animals that have ever lived. The tongue of a blue whale can weigh as much as a small elephant. Blue whales can weigh 150 tons and can be 100 feet long. Even though they are huge, blue whales are graceful. They swim fast and make quick turns.

There used to be hundreds of thousands of these giants in the oceans. For many years, they were killed for their meat and blubber. Now most countries have agreed to stop hunting these whales. No one knows for sure how many blue whales are left.

Instead of teeth blue whales have a baleen that looks like a large comb. The blue whale eats small, shrimplike animals called krill. The blue whale opens its mouth to let in water and krill. Then it closes its mouth and forces the water out. The baleen keeps the krill inside. In Antarctica there are so many krill the ocean looks orange. A hungry blue whale can eat 8,000 pounds of krill per day.

Female whales are called cows. Their babies are called calves. Blue whales give birth to their babies in warm waters. Blue whale calves grow faster than any other animal. They gain about 200 pounds per day for the first seven months.

In the spring when the calf is a few months old, the mother and baby begin migrating. They swim south to Antarctica to find food. For about six months, the mother whale has not had much to eat. The baby has been living on its mother's milk. The baby and mother travel alone. It takes the two whales many weeks to reach Antarctica.

When fall comes the young whale is old enough and large enough to take care of itself. It will make the return trip to warm waters alone. In a few years, it will look for a mate.

1. Put these events in the order that they happened. What happened first? Write the number **1** on the line by that sentence. Then write the number **2** by the sentence that tells what happened next. Write the number **3** by the sentence that tells what happened last.

_____ Countries agreed to stop hunting blue whales.

_____ Blue whales were hunted for their meat and blubber.

_____ There once were hundreds of thousands of blue whales.

_____ **2.** When do blue whales migrate to Antarctica?
   A. before the calf is born
   B. when the calf is a few months old
   C. during a full moon

_____ **3.** How long does it take the whales to get to Antarctica?
   A. many weeks
   B. a few days
   C. many months

_____ **4.** When do blue whale calves gain 200 pounds per day?
   A. before they are born
   B. when they look for a mate
   C. during the first seven months of their lives

_____ **5.** When is the young blue whale old enough to take care of itself?
   A. when it weighs 100 tons
   B. when fall comes
   C. soon after it is born

Writing Roundup

Read the paragraph below. Think about the sequence, or time order. Answer the questions in complete sentences.

What happens when you ride in an elevator? First, two sets of doors close and lock. One set is in the walls of the building, and the other set is part of the elevator car. Next a motor turns on. Then cables pull the car up. While the car goes up, a set of weights goes down to balance the load. When the car reaches the chosen floor, brakes hold the car in place. The doors open, and people can get out.

1. When you ride in an elevator, what happens first?

_____

_____

2. What happens while cables pull the car up?

_____

_____

3. What happens when the car reaches the chosen floor?

_____

_____

4. What happens last when you ride in an elevator?

_____

_____

Prewriting

Think about something that you have done, such as eating at a restaurant, baking a loaf of bread, or playing a game of checkers. Write the events in sequence below.

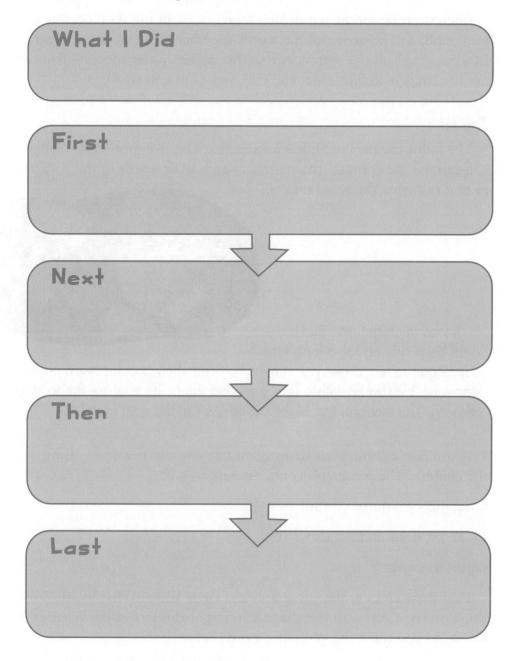

What I Did

First

Next

Then

Last

On Your Own

Now use another sheet of paper to write a paragraph about what you have done. Write the events in the order that they happened. Use time order words.

unit 3

What Is Context?

Context means all the words in a sentence or all the sentences in a paragraph. In a sentence all the words together make up the context. In a paragraph all the sentences together make up the context. You can use the context to figure out the meaning of unknown words.

Try It!

The following paragraph has a word that you may not know. See whether you can use the context (the sentences and other words in the paragraph) to find out what the word means.

It was midnight. Mr. Blake had been driving for a long time. He began to feel **drowsy**. His eyes fluttered shut, and his head nodded forward. He awoke with a jerk a second later. "It's time for me to stop driving," he thought. Mr. Blake pulled over at the next motel.

If you don't know what **drowsy** means, you can decide by using the context. The paragraph contains these words:

Clue: his eyes fluttered shut

Clue: his head nodded forward

Clue: he awoke

Find these clues in the paragraph and circle them. What words do you think of when you read the clues? You might think of *tired*. What other words do you think of? Write the words below:

_____

Did you write *sleepy*? The context clue words tell you that **drowsy** means "sleepy."

Working with Context

This unit asks questions that you can answer by using context clues in paragraphs. There are two kinds of paragraphs. The paragraphs in the first part of this unit have blank spaces in them. You can use the context clues in the paragraphs to decide which word should go in each space. Here is an example:

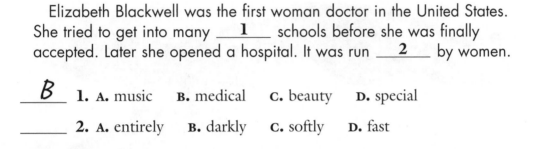

Elizabeth Blackwell was the first woman doctor in the United States. She tried to get into many ___1___ schools before she was finally accepted. Later she opened a hospital. It was run ___2___ by women.

___B___ 1. **A.** music   **B.** medical   **C.** beauty   **D.** special

_____ 2. **A.** entirely   **B.** darkly   **C.** softly   **D.** fast

Look at the answer words for question 1. Treat the paragraph as a puzzle. Which pieces don't fit? Which piece fits best? Try putting each word in the blank. See which one makes the most sense. Doctors don't go to *music* schools or *beauty* schools. Doctors do go to a *special* school. *Special* is a possible answer. But *medical* is even better. The correct answer is *medical*, answer **B**. Now try to answer question 2 on your own.

The paragraphs in the second part of this unit are different. For these you figure out the meaning of a word that is printed in **dark letters** in the paragraph. Here is an example:

Daffodils are a sign of spring. Their bright yellow color and long, thin leaves are easy to spot. Wild daffodils cover hillsides in the country. Other kinds are found in city parks.

The word in dark type is **daffodils**. Find the context clues. Then find the answer words that mean the same as **daffodils**.

_____ 3. In this paragraph, the word **daffodils** means
     A. a kind of bird   **C.** a kind of animal
     B. a kind of flower   **D.** a kind of kite

Read the passages and answer the questions about context. Remember, context is a way to learn new words by thinking about the other words used in a story.

Computers are fun and ___1___ machines. They help us store and work with information. Some people use them to ___2___ math problems. Others like them just for playing games.

_____ 1. **A.** lazy   **B.** helpless   **C.** useful   **D.** awkward

_____ 2. **A.** earn   **B.** solve   **C.** refuse   **D.** destroy

The cheetah is a big cat. It is known for its great speed as it runs short ___3___. It uses its sleek body and long, powerful legs to run fast. This cat's claws help it grab the ground as it races to catch its ___4___.

_____ 3. **A.** days   **B.** evenings   **C.** naps   **D.** stretches

_____ 4. **A.** bath   **B.** water   **C.** quarry   **D.** apple

Lightning is usually seen as a streak across the sky. Lightning in the shape of a ___5___ is called ball lightning. It is rarely seen, and no one can ___6___ why it occurs.

_____ 5. **A.** sphere   **B.** square   **C.** heart   **D.** line

_____ 6. **A.** deny   **B.** recall   **C.** explain   **D.** cure

A telescope is used to make ___7___ stars look closer and larger. It looks like a long tube. The light from a star enters one end of the tube. Two mirrors are used to ___8___ the light to an eyepiece. When you look through the eyepiece, you are able to get a better view of the star.

_____ 7. **A.** remote   **B.** narrow   **C.** late   **D.** wild

_____ 8. **A.** attach   **B.** brush   **C.** tow   **D.** reflect

The ostrich is the largest bird in the world. It can grow to a height of 8 feet and can weigh 300 __9__. The ostrich can't fly, but it can run fast to __10__ from danger.

_____ 9. A. pounds   B. miles   C. bikes   D. insects

_____10. A. remove   B. escape   C. walk   D. block

The tiger lives in parts of Asia. It is the largest __11__ of the cat family. Its fur is brownish orange with black stripes. The tiger __12__ the woods alone as it hunts for large prey to eat.

_____11. A. food   B. member   C. country   D. enemy

_____12. A. prowls   B. eats   C. obeys   D. sleeps

The abacus is a counting __13__. It was invented thousands of years ago. It has beads strung on wires that are attached to a frame. The beads are used to represent numbers. Math problems are __14__ by moving the beads.

_____13. A. time   B. force   C. value   D. machine

_____14. A. failed   B. calculated   C. avoided   D. melted

The castle was once a very important place, and it had many uses. It was a palace for the rulers of the region. Lawbreakers were held in a __15__ that was part of the castle. The castle also served as a __16__ for protection against enemies.

_____15. A. tree   B. prison
          C. closet   D. window

_____16. A. fort   B. curtain
          C. ranch   D. harvest

Stonehenge is a circle of huge stones. It stands on a flat ___**1**___ in England. It was ___**2**___ more than 4,000 years ago. It may have been used for measuring time. There are still many questions about how and why it was built.

_____ **1.** **A.** hug   **B.** plain   **C.** river   **D.** carpet

_____ **2.** **A.** delayed   **B.** taught   **C.** chased   **D.** erected

Although a koala looks similar to a bear, in ___**3**___ it is not a bear at all. This cute, cuddly ___**4**___ is a marsupial. This means a mother koala will carry her baby in a pouch as it grows.

_____ **3.** **A.** object   **B.** fact   **C.** arm   **D.** hunger

_____ **4.** **A.** bear   **B.** insect   **C.** creature   **D.** savage

You know that calculators are well ___**5**___ because so many people use them. This was not always the case. Calculators have gone through many ___**6**___. At first, calculators were large and solved problems slowly. Today they are much smaller and can compute problems quickly.

_____ **5.** **A.** launched   **B.** poured   **C.** accepted   **D.** won

_____ **6.** **A.** keys   **B.** books   **C.** parts   **D.** stages

What animal can eat 50 pounds of food in one sitting? If you said "elephant," you are right, but that little bit isn't dinner. It's more like a ___**7**___. Can you guess how much food an elephant eats in a day? If you said up to 500 pounds, you have an ___**8**___ idea of how much it eats.

_____ **7.** **A.** drink   **B.** friend
         C. snack   **D.** foot

_____ **8.** **A.** apple   **B.** engine
         C. accurate   **D.** ill

The first human-powered airplane crossed the English Channel in 1979. It looked like a bicycle enclosed in a cabin with long wings. It held just one person. The craft's only power came from the ____9____ of a human. The ____10____ pedaled to turn the propeller that was in the back of the plane.

_____ 9. **A.** muscles **B.** eyes **C.** nerves **D.** thoughts

_____10. **A.** engine **B.** pilot **C.** wind **D.** battery

---

Prairie dogs are small, furry animals. They love to play. They live in ____11____ called towns. Prairie dogs build their ____12____ by digging holes and tunnels.

_____11. **A.** houses **B.** colonies
　　　　　C. toys **D.** plants

_____12. **A.** cars **B.** families
　　　　　C. hopes **D.** burrows

People once used pools of water as mirrors. Then they saw that ____13____, polished pieces of metal made better mirrors. Later, metallic film was ____14____ to the back of polished plates of glass. This process made the best mirrors.

_____13. **A.** scratched **B.** smooth **C.** dark **D.** heavy

_____14. **A.** summoned **B.** led **C.** applied **D.** trotted

---

A sea horse is a tiny fish with a long tail. Its head looks like that of a horse. It moves by swimming upright. The sea horse has a single fin on its back that ____15____ it through the water. If the sea horse wants to stop, it ____16____ its tail around a sea plant.

_____15. **A.** lives **B.** propels
　　　　　C. sings **D.** feeds

_____16. **A.** coils **B.** loses
　　　　　C. hits **D.** plants

Geckos are lizards that are good climbers. There are more than 800 varieties of geckos. Many of them make clicking ___**1**___ with their tongues. Others are ___**2**___ and never make any noise.

_____ **1. A.** eyes **B.** bites **C.** sounds **D.** leaps

_____ **2. A.** tan **B.** tired **C.** nervous **D.** silent

Wind power is an old ___**3**___ of energy. The windmills used now are much better than they once were. Windmills can supply ___**4**___ power to run lights, toasters, fans, and radios in homes.

_____ **3. A.** plan **B.** job **C.** trick **D.** type

_____ **4. A.** wave **B.** electrical **C.** solar **D.** no

Flying squirrels have flaps of skin between their hind and front legs. These flaps can be used like a parachute. The squirrels leap from high branches and ___**5**___ their flaps of skin. Then they ___**6**___ through the air to lower branches.

_____ **5. A.** tear **B.** wrinkle **C.** spread **D.** forget

_____ **6. A.** trot **B.** soar **C.** freeze **D.** look

A hedgehog is an unusual animal. It snorts as it ___**7**___ for food at night. If it senses danger, the hedgehog will roll into a ball with its spines pointed out. During the day it stays safe in its nest. Sometimes it will ___**8**___ loudly as it sleeps.

_____ **7. A.** eats **B.** rummages
        C. melts **D.** dresses

_____ **8. A.** type **B.** march
        C. snore **D.** eat

The sea otter can use a rock as a tool. First the otter ___**9**___ in the water on its back. Then it puts a rock on its stomach. Finally the otter takes a clam and ___**10**___ it against the rock to open it.

_____ **9.** **A.** writes   **B.** drifts   **C.** runs   **D.** covers

_____ **10.** **A.** eats   **B.** rubs   **C.** smashes   **D.** fishes

---

Caribou are a type of large deer. The herds migrate long distances. They move across Greenland and the northern ___**11**___ of North America. They eat many types of plants in open ranges when the weather is warm. At the first ___**12**___ of winter, they start to move. They go to wooded regions. There they eat small plants. These plants grow on trees and under the snow.

_____ **11.** **A.** echo   **B.** package   **C.** chain   **D.** territory

_____ **12.** **A.** trails   **B.** indications   **C.** toes   **D.** cans

---

Riding in a hot-air balloon is quiet ___**13**___ for the noise made by the gas burner. This burner is needed to ___**14**___ a flame. The flame stretches up into the nylon or polyester bag. This bag is the balloon. The air inside the bag becomes lighter as it is warmed. This causes the balloon to rise. As the air inside the balloon cools, the balloon floats back down to the ground.

_____ **13.** **A.** above   **B.** except   **C.** below   **D.** in

_____ **14.** **A.** generate   **B.** brush   **C.** hug   **D.** surprise

---

A platypus is an odd animal. It is ___**15**___ at ease on land or in the streams and lakes of Australia. The platypus swims to catch its food. The platypus uses its ducklike, ___**16**___ front feet and its long, flat tail to swim. It sleeps in a burrow on shore.

_____ **15.** **A.** tall   **B.** giant   **C.** equally   **D.** heavy

_____ **16.** **A.** hot   **B.** webbed   **C.** tied   **D.** icy

The sloth lives in the Central and South American forests. Its shaggy, grayish green hair helps it hide in the trees. The sloth has curved claws. It can hang upside down on a branch. It __1__ on fruit, leaves, and twigs. The sloth moves at a very slow pace. It drinks dew or raindrops when it is __2__.

_____ 1. **A.** nibbles   **B.** dances   **C.** winks   **D.** fixes

_____ 2. **A.** asleep   **B.** tired   **C.** brave   **D.** thirsty

---

A rainbow is seen when the Sun's rays shine on drops of rain or mist. It appears in the sky __3__ the Sun. It has seven colors. The amount of space used by each color __4__ on the size of the waterdrops in the rainbow.

_____ 3. **A.** gold   **B.** opposite   **C.** water   **D.** upset

_____ 4. **A.** quits   **B.** blends   **C.** sits   **D.** depends

---

A hovercraft is a vehicle that __5__ on a layer of air above land or water. The air __6__ is made using fans. There is a rubber skirt on the craft's lower edge. It fills with air from the fans. This helps the craft cross rough ground or waves.

_____ 5. **A.** moves   **B.** sews   **C.** feeds   **D.** crashes

_____ 6. **A.** show   **B.** pill   **C.** cushion   **D.** stem

---

A sand dollar is an animal that lives in shallow waters off the coast. It stays partly __7__ in the sand. It crawls and digs using the little spines on its body. The sand dollar finds bits of food to eat while it digs in the __8__ of sand.

_____ 7. **A.** buried   **B.** cut   **C.** neat   **D.** sewn

_____ 8. **A.** hearts   **B.** tins   **C.** grains   **D.** castles

Long ago the giant panda was a common sight. It lived in many parts of China. Then people began cutting down _____9_____ areas of bamboo. The giant panda had a hard time finding bamboo to eat. Now the giant panda lives only high in the mountains of southeastern China. People are working to protect the giant panda. Seeing a giant panda today is very _____10_____.

_____ 9. A. easy   B. slight   C. dangerous   D. immense

_____10. A. purple   B. dry   C. uncommon   D. large

The first American woman to travel in space was Sally Ride. She went in the space shuttle for a six-day _____11_____. Sally helped launch satellites, and she _____12_____ experiments.

_____11. A. mission   B. sleep   C. leap   D. walk

_____12. A. obeyed   B. dyed   C. conducted   D. sealed

The manatee lives in freshwater canals. It's a mammal, but it spends its entire life in the water. The manatee helps keep the canals _____13_____. It eats large amounts of plants that cause _____14_____ in the canal.

_____13. A. happy   B. kind   C. clear   D. loud

_____14. A. blocks   B. signs   C. wagons   D. tables

A robot is a machine. It is built to do certain _____15_____. A computer inside the robot gives it directions about how to complete special jobs. A robot is faster and makes fewer _____16_____ than most people.

_____15. A. flips   B. tasks   C. flowers   D. calls

_____16. A. laws   B. sleeves   C. shouts   D. mistakes

Most people like football because it is full of action. But the ball is in motion only 20 percent of the game. The rest of the time is **expended** in things such as huddles and time-outs.

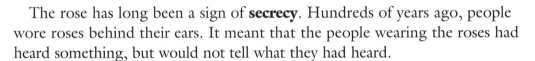

_____ **1.** In this paragraph, the word **expended** means
    A. kicked   **C.** wished
    B. spent   **D.** saved

You can measure yourself. On bare feet, stand with your back to a wall. Put a thin piece of cardboard across the top of your head and mark where it hits the wall. Run a tape measure from the mark to the floor. Now you know **precisely** how tall you are.

_____ **2.** In this paragraph, the word **precisely** means
    A. partly   **C.** exactly
    B. slightly   **D.** fairly

The rose has long been a sign of **secrecy**. Hundreds of years ago, people wore roses behind their ears. It meant that the people wearing the roses had heard something, but would not tell what they had heard.

_____ **3.** In this paragraph, the word **secrecy** means
    A. riddles   **C.** talking
    B. silence   **D.** sharing

The squid is a sea animal with 10 **tentacles**. It uses eight of them to catch its food. The other two are longer. The squid uses them to bring the food to its mouth.

_____ **4.** In this paragraph, the word **tentacles** means
    A. eyes   **C.** nets
    B. arms   **D.** heads

How can anybody remain underwater for 10 minutes? **Ponder** that question no more. Just fill a glass with water. Then hold it over your head for 10 minutes!

_____ 5. In this paragraph, the word **ponder** means
- **A.** swim after
- **B.** think about
- **C.** forget about
- **D.** know of

How do pilots avoid **collisions** with other planes in the air? The sky is mapped into highways just like the land is. Signals are sent up from control towers to mark these "skyways." It's a pilot's job to listen to the signals.

_____ 6. In this paragraph, the word **collisions** means
- **A.** birds
- **B.** crashes
- **C.** insects
- **D.** tires

The trunk of a tree is made up of **annual** rings. Each year a new layer of wood grows to form a new ring. You can tell the age of a tree by counting its rings.

_____ 7. In this paragraph, the word **annual** means
- **A.** yearly
- **B.** large
- **C.** hard
- **D.** weekly

The Venus flytrap is a plant that **consumes** bugs. When there are no bugs, this plant will gladly accept bits of cheese!

_____ 8. In this paragraph, the word **consumes** means
- **A.** eats
- **B.** releases
- **C.** hates
- **D.** grows

Oh Nooooo!

In Rome long ago, only the emperor and his family could wear purple. Others were **forbidden** to wear that color!

_____ **1.** In this paragraph, the word **forbidden** means
    A. chosen   **C.** encouraged
    B. spoken   **D.** not allowed

When a whip is snapped, it makes a loud cracking sound. Whips can **accelerate** to a speed of more than 700 miles per hour. At that speed a whip can break the sound barrier.

_____ **2.** In this paragraph, the word **accelerate** means
    A. maintain   **C.** go slower
    B. speed up   **D.** remain the same

Surgeons wore white uniforms until 1914. A doctor thought that the white uniform showed too much blood from **operations**. He wore green instead. Red did not show as much on the green.

_____ **3.** In this paragraph, the word **operations** means
    A. surgeries   **C.** oxygen
    B. janitors   **D.** straps

There is only one flock of whooping cranes in the world. These **endangered** birds live in Canada. They migrate to Texas for the winter. If all the birds in this flock die, the whooping crane will become extinct.

_____ **4.** In this paragraph, the word **endangered** means
    A. large   **C.** threatened
    B. white   **D.** Canadian

The tortoise is the animal that lives the longest. The Mauritius tortoise had a life **span** of 152 years. Some scientists think it lived for 200 years! The Carolina tortoise is found in the United States. Some of these creatures have lived for 123 years.

_____ **5.** In this paragraph, the word **span** means
- **A.** height
- **B.** weight
- **C.** length
- **D.** thirst

What makes popcorn pop? Popcorn kernels are small and hard. There is water within the kernel. When the moisture heats up, it turns to **steam**. The steam causes the kernel to explode.

_____ **6.** In this paragraph, the word **steam** means
- **A.** dry corn
- **B.** water vapor
- **C.** melted butter
- **D.** sea salt

Only one bird can fly **backward**. It is the tiny hummingbird. The bird flies in front of a flower. It sucks the nectar out of the flower. When it is finished, it simply backs up.

_____ **7.** In this paragraph, the word **backward** means
- **A.** in reverse
- **B.** fast
- **C.** up and down
- **D.** like a helicopter

Many people believe that red makes a bull angry and causes him to attack. They believe that is why a bullfighter waves a red cape, but a bull is colorblind. It is the **motion** of the cape that excites the bull. A bullfighter could wave a white or green cape, and the bull would charge.

_____ **8.** In this paragraph, the word **motion** means
- **A.** color
- **B.** red
- **C.** stopping
- **D.** shaking

How can you tell a vegetable from a fruit? In 1893 the Supreme Court passed **judgment** on the subject. If it is consumed with the main course of a meal, it's a vegetable. If it is served as a dessert or snack, it's a fruit.

_____ 1. In this paragraph, the word **judgment** means
- **A.** properties
- **B.** award
- **C.** decision
- **D.** umpire

Ice cream was first made in China. The explorer Marco Polo described eating dishes of ice **flavored** with fruit. Italians liked it so much they changed the name to Italian ices. The French added cream and renamed it ice cream.

_____ 2. In this paragraph, the word **flavored** means
- **A.** given warmth
- **B.** given taste
- **C.** given cream
- **D.** given dishes

Dragonflies are usually seen flying through the air. This happens during the last stage of a dragonfly's life. It can only fly for a few weeks. It spends most of its life under water. Before becoming an **adult**, it lives underwater as a nymph. A nymph looks like a mature dragonfly, but it does not have wings.

_____ 3. In this paragraph, the word **adult** means
- **A.** baby
- **B.** tame
- **C.** young
- **D.** full-grown

Mistletoe has thick green leaves and white berries. It is never found growing on the ground. This plant does not grow in soil. It grows on the **limbs** of trees.

_____ 4. In this paragraph, the word **limbs** means
- **A.** clouds
- **B.** branches
- **C.** roots
- **D.** flowers

Ping-Pong is another name for table tennis. Ping-Pong and tennis are very much **alike**. In both games a ball is hit over a net. The name Ping-Pong came from the noise made when the ball was hit by a paddle.

_____ 5. In this paragraph, the word **alike** means

    A. different   **C.** hard

    B. sounds like   **D.** the same

Dingoes are wild dogs in Australia. No one knows how they got there. The people who moved to the area long ago might have had dogs. Dingoes may be **descendants** of these dogs.

_____ 6. In this paragraph, the word **descendants** means

    A. details   **C.** parents

    B. offspring   **D.** worlds

The praying mantis is a fierce insect. It **ceases** to move so that it looks like part of a plant. The mantis uses its front legs to trap its prey. It usually catches insects, small frogs, and lizards.

_____ 7. In this paragraph, the word **ceases** means

    A. quits   **C.** feeds

    B. inspects   **D.** whistles

The giraffe is the tallest animal in the world. It can grow to a height of 20 feet. Giraffes **tower** over people and cars.

_____ 8. In this paragraph, the word **tower** means

    A. run from   **C.** knock down

    B. stand tall   **D.** work hard

The pygmy marmoset lives in Brazil's forests. It is the smallest monkey. Its head and body are about 6 inches long. You can **barely** feel its fur because its coat is so fine.

_____ **1.** In this paragraph, the word **barely** means
- **A.** coldly
- **B.** hardly
- **C.** lively
- **D.** sweetly

The cone snail has a beautiful marbled shell. Many people like to collect the shell. They must be careful of a living cone snail because it has poisoned **barbs**. The snail's stab is fatal.

_____ **2.** In this paragraph, the word **barbs** means
- **A.** rounded tips
- **B.** golden crowns
- **C.** sharp points
- **D.** dull edges

Libby Riddles wanted to win a famous sled-dog race in Alaska. She knew conditions would be **brutal**, but the blizzards and freezing weather did not stop her. She became the first woman to win the race.

_____ **3.** In this paragraph, the word **brutal** means
- **A.** simple
- **B.** easy
- **C.** ordinary
- **D.** cruel

The Leaning Tower of Pisa is in Italy. The ground on one side of the tower is so soft that the side is **sinking**. This makes the tower lean a tiny bit more each year. People are trying to save it from falling.

_____ **4.** In this paragraph, the word **sinking** means
- **A.** rising higher
- **B.** walking with
- **C.** dropping lower
- **D.** touching against

Dreaming is an important part of sleep. Dreams occur during a period of rapid eye movement. The eyes move quickly during this stage of sleep. If awakened during this period, a person can clearly **recall** the dream.

_____ **5.** In this paragraph, the word **recall** means
- **A.** remember
- **B.** cure
- **C.** forget
- **D.** escape

The zebra belongs to the horse family. It has black and white stripes. The zebra spends time **grazing** on the African plains. Then it goes to watering holes. The lion is its enemy. The zebra bites and kicks to protect itself.

_____ **6.** In this paragraph, the word **grazing** means
- **A.** drifting in air
- **B.** feeding on grasses
- **C.** walking by mountains
- **D.** swimming in streams

A tornado is a very **fierce** storm. This funnel-shaped cloud does not last long. But it sucks up everything in its path. The strong winds can be very destructive.

_____ **7.** In this paragraph, the word **fierce** means
- **A.** friendly
- **B.** sticky
- **C.** dangerous
- **D.** small

The wolf is a large member of the dog family. It is a good hunter. Hoofed animals are its **normal** prey. The wolf inhabits areas that have few people.

_____ **8.** In this paragraph, the word **normal** means
- **A.** curious
- **B.** delicious
- **C.** usual
- **D.** unusual

Writing Roundup

Read each paragraph. Write a word that makes sense on each line.

Aisha was starting to walk home from school when it began to rain. "Oh, no," she thought. "I forgot to bring my **(1)** _____. Now my **(2)** _____ will get soaked!"

Cody had always wanted to be in the band. He dreamed of playing a big **(3)** _____. He was sure that no one would be able to **(4)** _____ better than he could.

Last spring I tried to build a birdhouse. I used a hammer and some **(5)** _____. When I finished, that birdhouse looked **(6)** _____.

Read each paragraph. Write a sentence that makes sense on each line.

Mrs. Singh was planting flowers when her spade struck something hard. She wondered what she should do next. **(1)**_____. She gasped in surprise when she saw what the object was.

(2)_____.

Mrs. Singh knew just what she would do with it.

(3)_____.

Carmen needed to earn some money. She really loved animals. What could she do? **(4)**_____

_____.

Then her next-door neighbor, Ms. Fielder, rang the doorbell.

(5)_____. Now Carmen has a job, even though it has nothing to do with animals.

(6)_____

_____.

What Is a Main Idea?

The main idea of a paragraph tells what the paragraph is about. The other sentences add details to the main idea. The main idea sentence is often the first or last sentence in the paragraph. But the main idea sentence can be found in the middle of the paragraph too.

The following example may help you think about main ideas:

$$4 \ + \ 6 \ + \ 5 \ = \ 15$$

detail + detail + detail = main idea

The numbers *4, 6,* and *5* are like details. They are smaller than their sum, *15.* The *15,* like a main idea, is bigger. It is made of several smaller parts.

Try It!

Read this story and underline the main idea sentence.

Barbara Jordan is an admired public figure in American history. She was the first African American woman from the South to serve in Congress. She grew up in Texas. Her parents taught her to work hard. Jordan became a lawyer and then entered politics. She tried to make fair laws for everyone.

The main idea sentence is the first sentence in this story about Barbara Jordan. All the other sentences are details.

The main idea could come at the end of the paragraph:

Barbara Jordan was the first African American woman from the South to serve in Congress. She grew up in Texas. Her parents taught her to work hard. She became a lawyer and then entered politics. She tried to make fair laws for everyone. Jordan is an admired public figure in American history.

Practice Finding the Main Idea

This unit asks you to find the main idea of paragraphs. For instance, read the paragraph and the question below.

You've heard of a full moon and a new moon, but have you heard of a blue moon? Once in a while, there are two full moons in one month. We call the second moon a blue moon. A blue moon appears about every 32 months. So if something happens once in a blue moon, it doesn't happen often.

_C_ 1. The paragraph mainly tells
  A. why the Moon looks full
  B. how the Moon moves
  C. what a blue moon is
  D. about the different colors of the Moon

The correct answer is C. "You've heard of a full moon and a new moon, but have you heard of a blue moon?" is the main idea sentence. The paragraph is about blue moons.

Sometimes a story does not have a main idea sentence. You must read the details in the paragraph. Read the following story. Try to put the details together and find the main idea. Write the letter of your answer in the blank.

When lion cubs are born, they have thick, brown, spotted fur. As many as six cubs are born at one time. The mother lion hides her cubs. She wants to keep them safe from hyenas and leopards. When the cubs are one month old, they meet the lion group.

_____ 2. The story mainly tells
  A. the number of cubs born at one time
  B. how hyenas and leopards hunt
  C. how much cubs weigh
  D. about the lives of lion cubs

Read each passage. After each passage you will answer a question about the main idea of the passage. Remember, the main idea is the main point in a story.

1. People do not really use music to charm snakes. Snakes have no ears, so they can't hear a flute. The snake charmer startles the snake by waving a hand near it. The snake lifts its head to look around. The charmer then sways back and forth or moves the flute. The snake moves its head to keep an eye on the movement.

_____ **1.** The story mainly tells
     A. why flute music charms snakes
     B. why snakes can't hear sounds
     C. how people really charm snakes
     D. why snakes have no ears

2. A bat can fly at night or even with its eyes closed. If you cover its ears, it can't fly very well. Bats make sounds that people can't hear. The bats find their way by listening to these sounds as they echo off things. Bats even locate insects to eat by following the sounds that bounce off the bugs. People use their eyes, but bats use their ears to know where they're going.

_____ **2.** The story mainly tells
     A. how bats use sound
     B. what things bats often eat as food
     C. how bats fly toward people
     D. how people can hear the sounds of bats

3. Some people say that the White House has ghosts. The most famous ghost is Abraham Lincoln. He is often seen standing in his room looking out the window. Even Eleanor Roosevelt said that she saw him. There is a legend that old Abe walks back and forth all night before something terrible is about to happen.

_____ **3.** The story mainly tells
   A. what Lincoln's ghost is like
   B. when Eleanor Roosevelt's ghost walked
   C. how many ghosts the White House has
   D. how ghosts show when something will happen

4. Dolphins are very smart animals. They even have their own language. They talk to each other with clicks, whistles, and grunts. Scientists have been studying this dolphin language. They hope that in the future, people and dolphins will be able to talk to each other.

_____ **4.** The story mainly tells
   A. how dolphins talk to people
   B. how smart dolphins are
   C. how dolphins are different from fish
   D. which scientists are studying languages

5. Deer are the only animals with bones sticking out of their heads. Some animals have horns, but horns aren't bones. They are more like fingernails. Deer have true bones. Every year two new bones grow from the top of a deer's head. At first the bones are soft and covered with skin. Later the skin dries up. The deer rubs off the skin. The bones get hard. The deer uses these horns for fighting.

_____ **5.** The story mainly tells
   A. what deer like to use for fighting
   B. how deer grow bones out of their heads
   C. which animals have horns on their heads
   D. why deer have fingernails

1. Do you believe that air is heavy? If you don't, try this. Put a straw in a glass. Fill the glass with water. Suck on the straw. When you do this, you take all the air out of the straw. The air around the glass pushes down on the water in the glass. It pushes hard. The only place the water can go is up the straw. You can drink through a straw because the weight of the air pushes on the water.

_____ **1.** The story mainly tells
- **A.** how heavy air is
- **B.** how much water to drink
- **C.** how water and air are different
- **D.** how we need air to live

2. For years scientists have wanted to know the spider's secret. The threads of spiderwebs are so tiny, yet so strong. How can these threads be so strong? Now scientists have found out. The inside of the spider's thread is soft. It helps the web stretch without breaking. The outside of the web is hard and strong.

_____ **2.** The story mainly tells
- **A.** who makes thread soft
- **B.** how spiders make strong thread
- **C.** how scientists make strong thread
- **D.** why spiders spin webs

3. Camels have adapted well to the desert. The large humps on their backs hold fat that can serve as food. Camels don't sweat very much, so they don't need much water. The camel's broad feet don't sink in the sand. Long eyelashes and big eyelids protect their eyes from the sun.

_____ **3.** The story mainly tells
- **A.** why camels don't sink in the sand
- **B.** what the hump of a camel is for
- **C.** how the camel is suited to live in the desert
- **D.** why camels do not need a lot of water

4. Bees talk to one another by dancing. When one bee finds flowers for food, it flies back to the hive. The movements it makes tell the bees where the flowers are. If the bee moves in a small circle, the flowers are close. A bee moves slowly in a figure eight when the flowers are more than 100 yards away. Bees may tell about food that is as far as 6 miles away.

_____ **4.** The story mainly tells
   A. how far bees may fly searching for food
   B. how bees talk with each other
   C. what kind of flowering plants bees prefer
   D. how bees collect their food from plants

---

5. Papermakers made the first hot-air balloon. They got the idea when they saw ashes rising from a fire. They turned paper bags upside down over the fire. Just as they had hoped, the bags filled with hot air and floated up. Soon they tried bigger bags made of paper and then cloth. Finally in 1783 people took their first ride in a hot-air balloon. The age of flight had begun!

_____ **5.** The story mainly tells
   A. how the hot-air balloon was invented
   B. how paper bags floated up
   C. why ashes rise over a hot fire
   D. how hot-air balloons are made

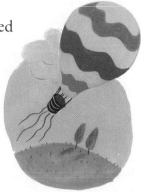

1. People store different kinds of information in different parts of their brains. One area saves only pictures of things we see. Another area remembers how those things are arranged. The area that stores smells and sounds is very close to the area that stores feelings. That's why you sometimes feel happy when you smell homemade bread or sad when you hear a love song.

_____ **1.** The story mainly tells
   A. how we remember pictures
   B. how sounds can affect feelings
   C. when we get different kinds of information
   D. where our brain stores information

---

2. In 1963 someone made a wide ski to ride down snowy hills. That's how the snowboard was invented. The snowboard looks like a small surfboard. It has sharp edges to cut through snow. To ride it you stand sideways, just as you would on a surfboard. Snowboarding is like surfing on the snow.

_____ **2.** The story mainly tells
   A. how much fun surfing is
   B. how surfing was invented
   C. about the sport of snowboarding
   D. how a surfboard and a skateboard are alike

3. If gum ever sticks on your clothes, don't try to wash it off. Otherwise the gum may never come off. Put an ice cube on the gum. That will harden it so you can try to scrape it off with a table knife. Try nail polish remover. It can sometimes melt gum. If the gum is from a burst bubble, try chewing more gum and using it to lift off the stuck pieces.

_____ **3.** The story mainly tells
   A. how chewing gum was invented
   B. how to melt gum
   C. how to use nail polish remover
   D. how to remove gum from your clothes

_____

4. The Richter scale measures the strength of an earthquake. An earthquake measuring 2.0 is a weak one. A quake that measures 8.0 is very strong. A quake measuring 1.0 can't be felt. The earthquake that hit San Francisco in 1906 was very strong. It measured about 8.25.

_____ **4.** The story mainly tells
   A. what to do during an earthquake
   B. about the 1906 San Francisco earthquake
   C. about the Richter scale
   D. how to measure energy

_____

5. Each year a tree grows a layer of new wood just under the bark. When the trunk or a branch is cut, the layers look like rings. Each ring shows one year of growth. To tell how old a tree is, count the rings.

_____ **5.** The story mainly tells
   A. how to tell the age of a tree
   B. how long a tree lives
   C. how to cut a tree
   D. how many rings a tree has

1. Birthdays are celebrated in many ways around the world. In Thailand children give gifts to others on their birthdays. A child may give food to a monk. In Mexico a blindfolded child uses a stick to break open a piñata. A piñata is a hollow, paper figure. It is filled with gifts.

_____ **1.** The story mainly tells
- **A.** about birthday celebrations in different countries
- **B.** about birthdays in Thailand
- **C.** about the best way to celebrate a birthday
- **D.** what a piñata is

2. Twins are born in one out of every 80 births. There are two kinds of twins. The most common twins are fraternal twins. They look no more alike than most other brothers and sisters. One-fourth of all twins born are identical twins. They are the same sex. Identical twins look just alike.

_____ **2.** The story mainly tells
- **A.** how many twins there are
- **B.** about two kinds of twins
- **C.** how fraternal twins look
- **D.** when identical twins are born

3. Garlic was important in the history of Chicago. Jacques Marquette was a French priest. In 1674 bad health forced him to stop his journey for the winter. He stayed where wild garlic grew. Garlic soup and a fire helped keep Marquette warm. In fact, eating the garlic saved him from getting sick. The place where he stayed was called Checagou. *Checagou* is a Native American word. It means "place of garlic." That place is now named Chicago.

_____ **3.** The story mainly tells
- **A.** how Chicago got its name
- **B.** where Chicago is
- **C.** how to make garlic soup
- **D.** about winter in Checagou

4. The gecko, a small lizard, can do something special. It can shed its tail when attacked. When it drops off, the tail wriggles on the ground. The wriggling tail may confuse an attacker. This gives the gecko time to escape. New cells will grow where the tail dropped off. This growth is called a bud. The bud grows into a new tail. After 8 to 12 months, the gecko has a full-sized tail.

_____ **4.** The story mainly tells
- **A.** what a bud is
- **B.** how a gecko gets away from its attacker
- **C.** what a gecko is
- **D.** about a gecko's unusual tail

---

5. The dandelion is a common weed. It has a bright yellow flower. The leaves are shaped like lions' teeth. Its name comes from three French words, *dent de lion*. Those three words mean "tooth of the lion."

_____ **5.** The story mainly tells
- **A.** about common weeds
- **B.** how the dandelion got its name
- **C.** about dandelion flowers
- **D.** about lions' teeth

1. The moon has one-sixth the gravity of Earth. Everything weighs six times less on the moon. One woman weighs 120 pounds on Earth. On the moon, the same woman would weigh only 20 pounds. She could jump higher on the moon than she could on Earth. A blue whale weighs 150 tons. If a blue whale could go to the moon, it would weigh just 25 tons.

_____ **1.** The story mainly tells
    A. how to get to the moon
    B. about weight differences on Earth and the moon
    C. what a woman weighs on the moon
    D. how much a blue whale weighs

---

2. A crazy quilt is a work of art. People sew together odd-sized pieces of cloth. They don't use any special patterns. They use many different shapes and fabrics. After a backing is attached, the quilt is finished. It looks like a large, beautiful puzzle. Maybe a crazy quilt should have a nicer name.

_____ **2.** The story mainly tells
    A. that a crazy quilt is a work of art
    B. how odd-sized pieces of cloth are used
    C. how a backing is attached
    D. how a crazy quilt looks like a puzzle

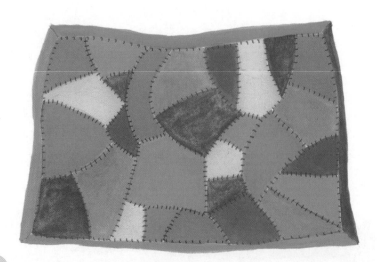

3. The world's greatest traveler is the Arctic tern. This bird migrates from one end of Earth to the other. It flies from the Arctic to the Antarctic and back each year. The round trip is about 23,600 miles.

_____ **3.** The story mainly tells
     A. how an Arctic tern looks
     B. about animal movement
     C. about the migration of the Arctic tern
     D. about the Arctic tern's nest

---

4. Forest fires burn thousands of trees each year. They are unsafe to the people and homes in their path. However, fires in forests are not always harmful. Fire is one of nature's ways of destroying problem weeds. Then native plants can return. When thick trees and brush are gone, animals find it easier to get food.

_____ **4.** The story mainly tells
     A. how forest fires start
     B. how forest fires can be helpful
     C. how fires destroy problem weeds
     D. how animals find food

---

5. Sneakers were invented more than 100 years ago. They were called croquet sandals. They cost five times as much as other shoes, so only rich people wore them. Then a company began to make tennis oxfords. Most people could afford these. They were very popular. Soon special sneakers were made for other sports, such as running. Now we have all sorts of sneakers.

_____ **5.** The story mainly tells
     A. how sneakers have changed through the years
     B. which sneakers are right for your sport
     C. what the difference is between shoes and footwear
     D. who could buy croquet sandals

1. The ocean is 7 miles deep in some places, but scuba divers can go down less than a mile. Below that the water pressure is too strong. Scientists have built special submarines that can go deeper. Some of them are made to hold one person. Others can be controlled from ships on the surface. With these subs people go nearly 4 miles down. The deepest parts of the ocean are still a mystery.

_____ **1.** The story mainly tells
    A. how strong the pressure is in the ocean
    B. which submarines can be controlled from ships
    C. how water pressure affects exploring in the ocean
    D. how people see the bottom of the ocean

---

2. Thousands of years ago, someone was traveling across the desert. For food he carried sheep's milk in a goatskin bag. The hot desert sun turned the milk thick and sour. He was hungry, so he ate the strange stuff. To his surprise he liked it! That's how yogurt was discovered.

_____ **2.** The story mainly tells
    A. which foods to take in the desert
    B. how yogurt tastes
    C. how yogurt was first made
    D. how to stay alive in the desert

---

3. Many green leaves, which are food factories for trees, change color in the fall. Their green coloring makes food out of sunlight, air, and water. When the days grow shorter in the fall, these factories slow down and then finally stop. The green slowly fades away. Where do the yellow, orange, and brown come from? They were in the leaves all the time, but the green was too bright for the other colors to show.

_____ **3.** The story mainly tells
    A. why leaves change color in the fall
    B. how leaves make food from sunlight, air, and water
    C. what the parts of a tree are
    D. what food factories make

4. When baseball was new, players had to throw the ball and hit the runner to make an out. The ball had to be big and soft so the runners wouldn't be hurt. Later, players used the tag as a way to make an out. This made the game more exciting, and it caused some other big changes. The ball could be smaller and harder. The smaller ball could be thrown faster, and batters could hit it farther. Thus the modern game of baseball was born.

_____ **4.** The story mainly tells
  A. how baseball changed
  B. how people used to make an out in baseball
  C. how large old baseballs were
  D. how far a modern baseball can be hit

---

5. If you are going on a picnic, don't wear anything that smells good. Some insects are crazy about perfume. Bees will smell you and come swarming. People have also found that bees like bright, flowery material. It seems that some insects just can't tell the difference between the real thing and a copy!

_____ **5.** The story mainly tells
  A. when to wear perfume
  B. how to dress well on trips
  C. how to avoid bees on picnics
  D. how some things can attract insects

1. It takes practice and skill to throw a Frisbee. Be sure your index finger is lined up on the outside rim. Tilt the edge of the Frisbee that is opposite your thumb downward. The stronger the wind, the more the Frisbee should be tilted. You need a strong wrist. It's the snap of your wrist that sends your Frisbee spinning.

_____ 1. The story mainly tells
    A. how to throw a Frisbee
    B. how important strong wrists are
    C. what to do in a strong wind
    D. how to aim at your target

2. Why do rabbits always seem as if they have itchy noses? Experts say the nose wiggling helps keep their nose tissue damp. This improves their sense of smell. Rabbits adjust their air intake in this way, too. It keeps them cool on hot days. Sometimes nose wiggling simply means rabbits are excited.

_____ 2. The story mainly tells
    A. why rabbits wiggle their noses
    B. how a rabbit improves its sense of smell
    C. why rabbits adjust their air intake
    D. what rabbits do when they are excited

3. Maybe you have seen flamingos in a zoo. These brightly colored birds with long necks look too pink to be real. Wild flamingos get their bright-pink feathers from the plants and fish they eat. However, in zoos they don't eat the same things they do in the wild. They could turn white. To keep this from happening, the zookeepers give these birds a special pill.

_____ **3.** The story mainly tells
    A. how flamingos stay pink
    B. what flamingos eat
    C. what kinds of birds there are
    D. how birds in zoos get pink

---

4. If you sneeze, you'll almost always hear someone say "bless you." Some historians think that people started saying "bless you" more than 1,000 years ago in Europe. At that time the plague was spreading everywhere. One of the first signs of this terrible sickness was sneezing. People thought the blessing might help keep them from getting sick.

_____ **4.** The story mainly tells
    A. how a disease spread across Europe
    B. what happens to the body when people sneeze
    C. how the saying "bless you" got started
    D. why sneezing is a sign of getting sick

---

5. Scientists are studying a sea turtle. She lives in a tank in Boston. The scientists think she can teach them how she uses hearing to sense her world. She is being trained to respond to signals.

_____ **5.** The story mainly tells
    A. about turtle senses
    B. where the turtle lives
    C. how turtles make signals
    D. what scientists hope to learn from the turtle

1. Television was invented in the 1920s. Few people had televisions until the 1950s. Forty years later, 98 percent of the households in the United States had a television. Watching television is a popular activity. Many homes have two or more televisions. Americans watch more than 1,500 hours of television per person each year.

_____ **1.** The story mainly tells
    A. the history of television commercials
    B. when television was invented
    C. what television-watching habits Americans have
    D. how televisions actually work

2. When their enemies chase them, ostriches lie down on the sand. The giant birds stretch their necks out flat on the ground. When they lie there, the loose feathers on their bodies look like bushes. Ostriches don't need to hide often. Their strong legs are good for both running and fighting.

_____ **2.** The story mainly tells
    A. how ostriches stick their heads in the sand
    B. how smart ostriches are
    C. how ostriches avoid their enemies
    D. how strong ostrich legs are

3. Ballet dancers often spin around and around. Why don't they become dizzy? A dancer's body turns smoothly. The dancer holds his or her head still and then jerks it around quickly. This way the head is still most of the time. The dancer does not become dizzy.

_____ **3.** The story mainly tells
    A. why a dancer spins
    B. how to become a ballet dancer
    C. where a ballet dancer practices
    D. why a dancer does not become dizzy when doing turns

4. An octopus gets its name from its eight arms. There have been new discoveries about these sea creatures. Experts have found that an octopus has a memory. It uses that memory to solve problems. An octopus in danger uses a built-in defense. It squirts a stream of ink to help it hide.

_____ **4.** The story mainly tells
    A. that an octopus has eight arms
    B. how an octopus uses its memory
    C. some interesting facts about octopuses
    D. how an octopus can squirt a stream of ink

---

5. It is important to put a return address on mail. Mail with a wrong mailing address goes to the dead-letter office. There postal workers open it to search for clues. If they don't find any, the mail is thrown away. The post office can sell items of value. It keeps the money.

_____ **5.** The story mainly tells
    A. how to write a letter
    B. what can happen to mail with no return address
    C. how mail gets thrown away
    D. how the post office makes money

Writing Roundup

Read each paragraph. Think about the main idea. Write the main idea in your own words.

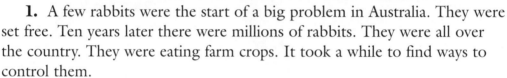

1. A few rabbits were the start of a big problem in Australia. They were set free. Ten years later there were millions of rabbits. They were all over the country. They were eating farm crops. It took a while to find ways to control them.

What is the main idea of this paragraph?

_____

_____

2. Tom Bradley was the first African American to become a lieutenant on the Los Angeles police force. He was also the first African American on the city council. He was the first African American mayor in the city. The people of Los Angeles loved him. They kept him as mayor for almost 20 years.

What is the main idea of this paragraph?

_____

_____

3. Iron Eyes Cody was a Native American actor. In 1971, a tear changed his life. He shed the tear in a TV ad about keeping America clean. The ad became very popular, and Iron Eyes became famous for his tear. He was remembered for it even after his death in 1999.

What is the main idea of this paragraph?

_____

_____

Prewriting

Think of a main idea that you would like to write about, such as an interesting country, what you would do if you were mayor of your city, or what it would be like to be in a TV ad. Fill in the chart below.

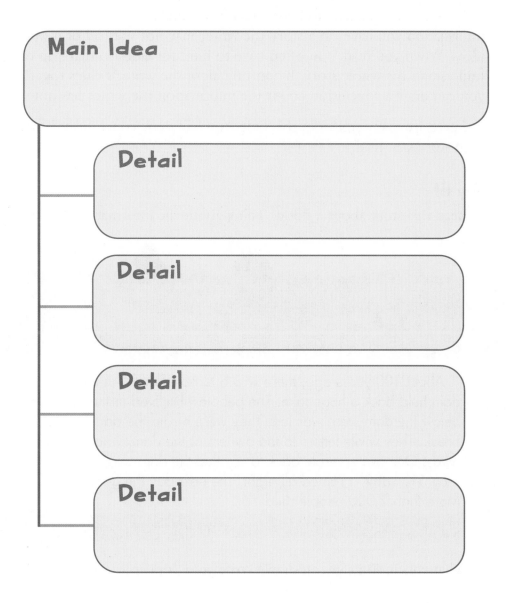

Main Idea

Detail

Detail

Detail

Detail

On Your Own

Now use another sheet of paper to write your paragraph. Underline the sentence that tells the main idea.

What Is a Conclusion?

A conclusion is a decision you make after thinking about all the information you have. In a story the writer may not state all of his or her ideas. When you read, you often have to hunt for clues so that you can understand the whole story. By putting all of the writer's clues together, you can draw a conclusion about the information the writer has not stated.

There are many stories in this unit. You will draw conclusions based on each story you read.

Try It!

Read this story about a flood. Think about the information it gives you.

About 100 years ago, there was a terrible flood. An old, dirt dam held back a huge lake. The people who lived in the valley below the dam were worried. They were afraid the dam would break. They wrote letters to the owners of the dam, who lived far away. One owner wrote back to say that the dam was safe. On May 31, 1889, it rained all night. The next day the dam broke. More than 2,000 people died.

What conclusion can you draw? Write your conclusion on the lines.

_____

_____

You might have written something such as, "The people who lived in the valley knew that the dam was not safe," or "The owners weren't worried about the dam." You can draw these conclusions from the paragraph. The second sentence says that the dam was old and built of dirt. This made the valley people worry that the dam would break. They were worried enough to write letters to the owners, but the owners did nothing to make the dam stronger. The sixth sentence tells us that one owner replied that the dam was safe. From these clues, you can draw the above conclusions.

Using What You Know

Read the stories on this page. Hunt for clues that will tell you the time of year for each.

It's getting too cold to wear shorts and sandals. Now I need warm clothes when I go outside. The colors of the leaves on most of the trees are changing. Instead of green, they are now all shades of red, orange, and brown. I like to collect the beautiful, dried-out leaves.

It is _____.

My mother and aunt have been cooking all day long. My sister and I have been watching a football game on television. It's almost time to eat. Turkey and dressing, vegetables, cranberry sauce, and a pumpkin pie are on the table. When we sit down, we will think about the things for which we are thankful.

It is _____.

Even though it's been a very hot day in the middle of summer, we've had a good time. This morning we watched a parade and listened to a speech. Then we went on a picnic with some friends. We ate hamburgers and watermelon. Tonight we will go down to the river and watch the fireworks. They are supposed to be even better than last year's.

It is _____.

I've been cutting out red paper hearts all day. I'm going to paste them on sheets of white paper that I've folded in half to make cards. Then I'll write a saying inside of each card. I'll also make a small hole on the folded edge of each card so that I can tie some red and pink ribbons. Tomorrow I'll give each of my friends one of my special cards, along with some candy hearts.

It is _____.

Read each passage. After each passage you will answer a question that will require you to draw a conclusion about the story. Remember, a conclusion is a decision you make after putting together all the clues you are given.

1. Serious dancers begin their training when they're very young. By the age of three, these dancers have already begun to learn a few dance steps. Dancers spend years learning how to move smoothly. They practice for hours each day. Still, young dancers must go to school like other children. The only time they can practice dance is after school.

_____ **1.** From this story you can tell that
    A. most dancers never learn spelling
    B. learning how to dance is a secret
    C. dancers have to work very hard
    D. three-year-olds are the best dancers

2. Have you ever tugged on a chicken's wishbone? You might know the custom. The one who wins the larger piece gets to make a wish. Did you know this custom is more than 2,000 years old? The Etruscan people first practiced the custom. They thought that chickens could read the future. They believed a hen could predict the laying of an egg with her squawk. They also thought a rooster could predict the dawn with his crow.

_____ **2.** From this story you can tell that
    A. some beliefs are very old
    B. the Etruscan people liked to eat chicken
    C. wishbones have magical powers
    D. the loser in a wishbone tug will have bad luck

3. Ramesh and Maya were happy. In seven months they would have a child. Maya ate good food and exercised. She saw the doctor each month. Ramesh helped fix a room for the child. Together they read books on raising children.

_____ **3.** From this story you can tell that
- **A.** they wanted to take good care of their child
- **B.** the baby would be born in July
- **C.** Ramesh was good at fixing things
- **D.** Maya loved to cook

4. Dr. Pavlov did scientific tests on dogs. He noticed that hungry dogs drooled when they saw food, so he rang a bell before he fed them. He did this over and over again. After several days he rang the bell, but he didn't feed the dogs then. The hungry dogs still drooled when they heard the bell, even though there wasn't any food. Pavlov found one way that animals learn things.

_____ **4.** From this story you can tell that
- **A.** a ringing bell always makes animals hungry
- **B.** the dogs expected food when they heard the bell
- **C.** Pavlov probably lived a long, long time ago
- **D.** Pavlov loved dogs

5. Computers read signals that travel along wires. These signals move very fast. They move as fast as light. Signals that travel on very long wires sometimes get mixed up. When this happens, the computers don't work anymore. New computers use shorter wires. This keeps them from having so many problems.

_____ **5.** From this story you can tell that
- **A.** computers can read better than people
- **B.** computers move faster than light
- **C.** the length of computer wires is important
- **D.** computer problems can't be fixed

1. Spaceships can go 7 miles per second. That sounds fast, but it's really slow. A trip to Mars takes a spaceship about nine months. Light is much faster. It travels about 200,000 miles per second. Light travels faster than anything else. If people could ride on a ray of light, a trip to Mars would take five minutes.

_____ **1.** From this story you can tell that
    A. spaceships can now move as fast as light
    B. long space trips will need very fast spaceships
    C. a trip around Earth would take five minutes
    D. traveling in space is dangerous

2. People used to ride a bike called the ordinary. The back wheel was about 1 foot high. The front wheel was about 5 feet high. When this tall bike hit a little bump, the bike often fell over. Later people began riding the safety bike. Its two wheels were about the same size.

_____ **2.** From this story you can tell that the safety bike
    A. was probably longer than the ordinary
    B. was most likely made of iron
    C. was probably not as dangerous as the ordinary
    D. was invented 100 years ago

3. There weren't always oranges in Europe. People from the Far East brought oranges to Europe during the Middle Ages. Later, sailors from Europe brought oranges to America. Now the United States grows a million tons of oranges each year.

_____ **3.** From this story you can tell that
    A. the first oranges probably grew in the Far East
    B. orange trees make fruit only in winter
    C. orange trees have blue flowers
    D. there were many wars during the Middle Ages

4. Once dodo birds lived on an island. They ate the seeds of one kind of tree. The seeds had hard shells. Dodo birds had strong stomachs. Their stomach juices broke up the shells. Because of this, the seeds could grow. The last dodo birds died out years ago. Scientists found that the trees were dying out, too. They wanted to save the trees, so they decided to feed the hard seeds to turkeys. Turkeys have strong stomachs. With their help the trees live on.

_____ **4.** From this story you can tell that
- **A.** animals ate all the dodo birds years ago
- **B.** the seeds were the dodo's only food
- **C.** the tree couldn't grow without a bird's help
- **D.** birds can't eat seeds with hard shells

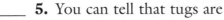

5. Tugboats help link the city of Seattle to the sea. The small, strong tugs guide large ships into and out of the harbor. Without the tugs the big ships could not make the trip safely. To honor the tugs, Seattle holds tugboat races each spring. At that time the harbor is full of stubby boats splashing in the water like playful whales

_____ **5.** You can tell that tugs are
- **A.** used only in the spring
- **B.** unsafe
- **C.** hard to steer
- **D.** necessary

1. When it is hot in India, people have a tasty way to stay cool. They eat mangoes. The mango is a fruit. It looks something like an apple. On the inside the mango is soft and yellow. In India the mango gives relief even when the temperature is higher than 100 degrees.

_____ **1.** You can tell that
- **A.** mangoes grow in cool climates
- **B.** mangoes probably sell well in India when it's hot
- **C.** Indians like apples
- **D.** mangoes make good jams

2. Many American children love peanut butter. Many adults like it too. Peanut butter is served for lunch in many schools. Some people like it for a snack, and others have it at breakfast.

_____ **2.** From the story you can tell that peanut butter
- **A.** sticks to the roof of your mouth
- **B.** is popular with all ages
- **C.** is always crunchy
- **D.** is best as a lunch food

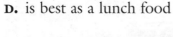

3. In Hawaii people make pretty necklaces called leis. A lei is made of flowers. A single lei often has more than 400 blossoms. The blossoms are attached by the stems. Leis are worn at special events. Important visitors are also given leis to show that they are welcome.

_____ **3.** To make a lei, you would need
  A. to grow flowers
  B. to be an important person
  C. to have many flowers
  D. an invitation to a party

4. Today a book is a stack of printed papers bound in a cover. Today's books are easy to carry, but years ago books were different. Each book was made of heavy clay tablets with carvings on them. The tablets of one book filled a long shelf. It would have taken many trips to carry such a book from the shelf to a reading table.

_____ **4.** One clay tablet can best be compared to
  A. a page in a modern book
  B. a carving in a museum
  C. the cover of a book
  D. part of a library shelf

5. Military ants may be small, but people and animals run when they see them. Thousands of these ants travel together through the thick jungles of South America. The ants swarm over any animal in their path. They can eat birds, animals, snakes, and even humans. The ants are always on the move, and they are always hungry.

_____ **5.** Military ants are dangerous mainly because they
  A. live in the jungle
  B. are always on the move
  C. are so small
  D. eat any living thing in their path

1. Clownfish are small, colorful saltwater fish. They are bright orange with black and white stripes. These fish are found in the warm waters of the Pacific Ocean near coral reefs. They live among sea anemones, which protect them.

_____ **1.** This story does <u>not</u> tell
  A. the colors on the body of a clownfish
  B. where clownfish live
  C. how the sea anemones protect the clownfish
  D. what kind of water the clownfish needs

2. May 6 is a special day for the people of Northville, New York. Every year on that day, a flock of swifts returns to the town. The birds fly to Northville from their winter home in Peru. They circle over a large chimney in a vacant factory. Then they settle into the chimney as the people watch.

_____ **2.** After the swifts arrive, they probably
  A. look for smoke
  B. go back to Peru
  C. build nests
  D. build fires

3. Ranchers in Texas had a problem. Coyotes and other wild animals were killing their sheep and goats, so some ranchers began using donkeys to protect the herds. The donkeys do a good job. The coyotes are terrified of the teeth and sharp hooves of the donkeys.

_____ **3.** You can tell that when donkeys see coyotes they
  A. kick and bite
  B. tell the ranchers
  C. run away
  D. hide the herds

4. What drink do we like on a hot day? Lots of people drink lemonade. This sweet and sour drink cools us off. Children set up stands to sell it. Families take it on picnics. Neighbors sip it on porches. Lemonade is popular in America. It was first made in Paris, France, in 1630.

_____ **4.** From the story you can tell that
   A. most lemonade comes from Paris, France
   B. more lemonade is sold in summer than in winter
   C. lemonade is heated before it is served
   D. lemonade is a healthy drink

5. The man wriggled his toes in the sand and then returned to the towel on the ground. He picked up the pair of binoculars by the towel and looked through them. The ship in the distance didn't have an American flag. But he couldn't tell what country's flag the ship was flying.

_____ **5.** You can tell that the man
   A. is a spy for a foreign country
   B. is standing on a beach looking out in the ocean
   C. doesn't have very much money
   D. is camping in the mountains during the winter

YOU WILL TRAVEL FAR -- SOON.

WHEREVER YOU GO, THERE YOU ARE.

1. Many Americans like to eat Chinese food. At the end of the meal, fortune cookies are served. These folded-up cookies have messages in them. Some messages tell what the future will bring. Other messages give advice. Still others are just wise sayings. All messages are written for Americans. Fortune cookies are never served in China.

_____ 1. From this story you can tell that
   A. the messages are in Chinese
   B. people in China can't read
   C. fortune cookies are an American custom
   D. people in China don't like cookies

2. Weddings have many customs. Cakes are a special part of these customs. Wedding cakes were not always eaten as they are today. Long ago, guests threw small wheat cakes at the bride. Wheat was considered a sign of good fortune. By throwing cakes, guests wished the bride a happy marriage. Later, in the Middle Ages, guests began the custom of eating wedding cakes.

_____ 2. From this story you can tell that
   A. early people did not like to eat cakes
   B. some wedding customs have changed
   C. early people liked to waste food
   D. people today should throw cakes at brides

3. What causes the traffic light to change colors? A timer in a box near the light is set for a certain number of seconds. The number of seconds isn't the same all the time. At night when there's less traffic, the light may change more slowly.

_____ **3.** You can tell that during rush hour
   A. the light stays red all the time
   B. the lights change more quickly
   C. the timer always breaks
   D. the light stays yellow

---

4. These days we find zippers on many products, but there was no such thing as a zipper available before 1893. That was the year Whitcomb Judson designed the zipper. His device often jammed. Twenty years later Gideon Sundback improved the zipper. It was not popular on clothes for another ten years. B. F. Goodrich named it _zipper_ because of the sound it made when pulled.

_____ **4.** The story suggests that the zipper
   A. improved by Sundback didn't jam
   B. was an immediate success
   C. was used on clothes before 1893
   D. was invented by B. F. Zipper

---

5. Farmers have known for a long time that pigs like toys. Research shows that when pigs play with toys, they are less likely to harm one another. What kind of toys do pigs like? Reports say that pigs are fond of rubber hoses. They like to shake them and chew on the ends.

_____ **5.** You can tell that
   A. toys help improve the way pigs behave
   B. pigs like to play with balls
   C. farmers play with pigs
   D. pigs do not share their toys

1. Hockey is one of the oldest games in the world. The ancient Greeks and Persians played it. So did Native Americans. The name comes from an old French word, *hoquet*. It is the word for a shepherd's crooked stick, or staff.

_____ **1.** From this story you can tell that
   A. hockey is played with a ball
   B. the French have played hockey for a long time
   C. hockey is now played by shepherds
   D. hockey will not last much longer

2. Millie frowned as she looked up at the sky. She pulled up the neck of her jacket and hunched down inside it. Despite the heavy air, the wind was rough. As Millie crossed the street, the first drops began to fall. She quickened her pace in the darkening day.

_____ **2.** In this story the weather is
   A. snowy
   B. stormy
   C. sunny
   D. warm

3. He heard the steady drumming sound he made on the pavement. One foot was becoming sore, but he didn't let himself feel the pain. At last he passed the park bench with the broken seat. "One more mile to go," he thought.

_____ **3.** From this you can tell that the man
   A. is running in a gym
   B. is running along a route he often takes
   C. is a stranger to the neighborhood
   D. has broken his foot

4. Miniature horses are becoming very popular. A miniature horse looks like a horse but is only as big as a German shepherd dog. These little horses come in many colors. They can learn tricks and earn ribbons at horse shows. Best of all, they eat much less than regular horses do.

_____ **4.** You can tell that the little horses
   A. can pull big loads
   B. are fast compared to normal horses
   C. can only be brown
   D. cannot be ridden by an adult

_____

5. A steeplechase is a horse race. The path of the race goes through ditches and over hedges. It might also go across streams. The name for this race comes from England. In the 1700s, riders would get together for a race in the country. They would pick out a distant church steeple and race to it.

_____ **5.** From this story you <u>cannot</u> tell if
   A. the riders were English
   B. the riders were in the country
   C. the riders were on horses
   D. the riders were men or women

1. Bob Siekman of Pyote, Texas, has an unusual hobby. He collects old fire trucks. As a youth, Bob watched a man build a fire truck. Young Bob thought fires and fire trucks were very exciting. As a man, Bob continued his interest in fire trucks by collecting them. He has five old fire trucks in his collection.

_____ 1. The story does <u>not</u> tell
    A. where Bob Siekman lives
    B. about Siekman's hobby
    C. how many old fire trucks Siekman owns
    D. where Siekman finds the old fire trucks

2. Do you know about the Seven Wonders of the Ancient World? These structures were built long, long ago. One was the Lighthouse at Pharos in Egypt. It stood more than 400 feet tall. Another was the Colossus of Rhodes on an island near Turkey. This bronze statue was almost 200 feet tall. All but one of these wonders have disappeared. You can still see the Great Pyramids in Egypt.

_____ 2. The story suggests that
    A. the Colossus was in Egypt
    B. six of the ancient wonders no longer exist
    C. the Great Pyramids have disappeared
    D. the Colossus was taller than the Lighthouse

3. Alfred Wegener looked at a world map. He noticed a strange thing. All the continents looked like jigsaw pieces. All the pieces seemed to fit together. Wegener thought about this idea for a long time. In 1912, he offered a new theory. He claimed that all the continents were once a large landmass. Then over time the continents moved apart. Wegener called his theory "continental drift." Other scientists did not accept his ideas until 40 years later.

_____ 3. The story suggests that Wegener's theory
    A. was about jigsaw puzzles
    B. was accepted immediately
    C. did not have a name
    D. explained how the continents were formed

4. You have probably seen a lightning flash, but often you don't hear the sound of thunder until a few seconds later. You can use a simple formula to learn how far from you the lightning struck. When you see the flash of lightning, start counting seconds. When you hear the thunder, stop counting. Sound travels at 1,200 feet per second. Multiply 1,200 by the number of seconds you counted. Then you will know how many feet from you the lightning flashed.

_____ **4.**. You can tell from the story that
  A. light travels at 1,200 feet per second
  B. sound travels faster than light
  C. thunder always comes before lightning
  D. light travels faster than sound

---

5. Trees are very useful plants. They help provide us with air to breathe. Trees take in carbon dioxide and give off oxygen. This action is known as photosynthesis, but this action works only with sunlight. At night the process is reversed.

_____ **5.** This story suggests that trees
  A. grow very tall
  B. like kids climbing in them
  C. give off carbon dioxide at night
  D. sleep at night

1. Have you ever tied a string on your finger? The purpose of the string is to help you remember something. This practice comes from an old European superstition. People once thought that they could trap a wish until it came true. To trap the wish, they would tie a string on one finger. They thought that the string would keep the wish from leaving the body.

_____ **1.** The story does <u>not</u> tell
  A. why people today tie a string on one finger
  B. why people used to tie a string on one finger
  C. where this practice began
  D. on which finger you should tie the string

2. If you look under your kitchen sink, you will see some drain pipes. One pipe is U-shaped. It is called a trap. Harmful gases develop in a sewer line. The curved part of the trap holds a small amount of water. The water closes off the pipe. The trap keeps you safe. The gases can't enter your house and harm you.

_____ **2.** The story suggests that the trap
  A. is a straight pipe
  B. lets harmful gases enter your house
  C. is not part of the drain pipe
  D. has a very useful purpose

3. José was taking guitar lessons. He wanted to join a band when he got older. José's lessons were on Fridays after school. His teacher thought José was a fast learner. She gave him harder and harder things to play. José could play them all.

_____ **3.** This story does <u>not</u> tell
  A. what José wants to do when he gets older
  B. when José goes to his guitar lessons
  C. what kind of music José likes to play
  D. what José's teacher thinks of his ability

4. In 1901, Jagadis Bose talked to the Royal Society in London. Bose thought that plants had senses just like people. As Bose spoke, the scientists there laughed at him. Bose was not discouraged. He returned to his home in India. He began tests to prove his claims. After years of work, Bose had his proof. His tests showed that plants have all the senses except hearing. When Bose returned to the Royal Society, he was cheered. The scientists there soon made him a member.

_____ **4.** The story does <u>not</u> tell
  A. where the Royal Society is located
  B. where Jagadis Bose lived
  C. what kinds of plants Bose tested
  D. what Bose's tests proved

5. Are you familiar with the belief about broken mirrors? If you break one, you are supposed to have seven years of bad luck or ill health. This belief is about 2,000 years old. The early Romans were the first to have this notion. They thought that a person's health changed in cycles of seven years. They believed that mirrors reflected one's health. So to break a mirror was to break one's health.

_____ **5.** The story does <u>not</u> tell
  A. what is supposed to happen if you break a mirror
  B. how old this notion is
  C. what the Romans thought about the cycles of health
  D. what might happen if you fix a broken mirror

Writing Roundup

Read each paragraph. Think about a conclusion you can draw. Write your conclusion in a complete sentence.

1. Jim Thorpe was a Native American. He won fame in track and field in the Olympic Games. He also won fame as a star player in the early days of football. Thorpe had other skills, too. For six years he played major-league baseball. In one of those years, he batted right-handed and left-handed!

What conclusion can you draw from this paragraph?

_____

_____

2. Until 1952, two titles of respect were used before a woman's name. One was *Miss*. This title meant the woman was single. Another was *Mrs*. This title showed that the woman was married. In 1952, another title was added. It was *Ms*. This meant the person was a woman. She might be either single or married.

What conclusion can you draw from this paragraph?

_____

_____

3. The year 2004 marked the twentieth year of the show of a famous TV talk show host. Her name is Oprah Winfrey. When she started, her show was seen only in the Chicago area. It wasn't long before TV stations all over wanted Oprah. Two years later her show was on everywhere. She soon had the most popular talk show on television.

What conclusion can you draw from this paragraph?

_____

_____

Read the paragraph below. What conclusion can you draw? Use the clues in the paragraph to answer the questions in complete sentences.

Paco was glad his grandfather had come to visit. He was glad to share his room with his mother's father. His grandfather told Paco stories about their family. They had come from Mexico. They moved to Texas in 1847. That was only two years after Texas became a state. They may still have some family in Mexico. Paco's grandfather did not know. "It seems like we've always been in Texas," he told Paco. "My father was born here. His father was born here, too."

1. Does Paco's grandfather live with Paco? How do you know?

_____

_____

2. Did Paco have the same last name as his grandfather? How do you know?

_____

_____

3. When did Texas become a state? How do you know?

_____

_____

4. Does Paco's grandfather seem interested in finding more family in Mexico? How do you know?

_____

_____

unit 6

What Is an Inference?

An inference is a guess you make after thinking about what you already know. Suppose you are going to see a movie. From what you know about movies, you might infer that you will wait in line to buy a ticket. You will watch the movie on a large screen in a dark theater.

An author does not write every detail in a story. If every detail were told, stories would be long and boring, and the main point would be lost. Suppose you read, "Jane rode her bike to the park." The writer does not have to tell you what a park is. You already know that it is a place where people go to have fun outdoors. From what you know, you might guess that people who go to a park can play ball, swim, or play on the swings. By filling in these missing details, you could infer that Jane went to the park to meet friends for a ball game. You can infer the missing details from what you know.

Try It!

Read this story about Harriet Beecher Stowe. Think about the facts.

> Harriet Beecher Stowe lived in the 1800s. At that time some people owned slaves. Stowe knew that slavery was wrong and wanted to speak out against it. She wrote a book called *Uncle Tom's Cabin.* It was published in 1852. It was the story of Tom, a good man who was a slave. It told about how badly slaves were treated. This book made many people think about slavery.

What inference can you make about Harriet Beecher Stowe? Write an inference on the line below.

_____

You might have written something such as, "Stowe hoped to help slaves by writing a book about how bad slavery was." You can make this inference by putting together the facts in the story and what you already know. You know that people who have strong feelings about something want to help.

Practice Making Inferences

Read each story. Then read the statements after each story. Some are facts. They can be found in the story. Other statements are inferences. Decide whether each statement is a fact or an inference. The first one has been done for you.

Tim and John played basketball together each day after school. One day Tim started shouting that John was not playing fair. John took his basketball and went home. The next day John didn't show up at the basketball court.

Fact	Inference		
○	●	**1.** **A.**	Tim and John were friends.
●	○	**B.**	Tim and John played basketball together.
●	○	**C.**	John took his basketball and went home.
○	●	**D.**	John was angry with Tim the next day.

You can find statements **B** and **C** in the story, so they are facts. You can infer that the boys were friends, but that isn't stated in the story, so statement **A** is an inference. We don't know for sure why John didn't come to the basketball court, so statement **D** is also an inference.

Alfred Nobel was a Swedish inventor. He invented dynamite in 1867. Nobel was worried about how dynamite would be used. He hoped it would be used for peaceful purposes. He established a fund that gave awards each year. These awards are called Nobel Prizes. They are given for works of writing and of science. They are also given to those who have done special things for peace.

Fact	Inference		
○	○	**2.** **A.**	Nobel was an inventor.
○	○	**B.**	Nobel was a strong supporter of world peace.
○	○	**C.**	Nobel believed that war was bad.
○	○	**D.**	Some Nobel prizes are given for writing.

Read the passages. Use what you know about inference to answer the questions. Remember, an inference is a guess you make by putting together what you know and what you read or see in the stories.

1. Pam and Pat tried out for the soccer team. The coach needed only one more player. She needed a good goalie to block the other team's shots. Last year the team lost every game by more than five goals. During tryouts Pam passed the ball well but couldn't block goal shots. As a practice goalie, Pat saved many shots.

Fact	Inference	
○	○	**1.** **A.** The coach picked Pat to be on the team.
○	○	**B.** A good goalie can help a team win.
○	○	**C.** Pat and Pam tried out for the soccer team.
○	○	**D.** Pam could pass the ball well.

2. It was spring and time to get the garden ready for planting. Chris had a load of dirt delivered to his backyard. For two whole days, Chris shoveled dirt into a wheelbarrow. He put the dirt in the garden. He went back and forth between the dirt pile and the garden. It took many hours and much hard work. On the third day, he saw his neighbor coming over with a wheelbarrow.

Fact	Inference	
○	○	**2.** **A.** Chris needed another wheelbarrow.
○	○	**B.** Chris hoped his neighbor would help.
○	○	**C.** Chris put the dirt in the garden.
○	○	**D.** Chris had the dirt delivered.

3. One rainy day Nan noticed water dripping from the ceiling. That was when she knew she needed a new roof. She asked a few people for their advice. One person told her that putting new shingles over the old roof would make it too heavy. Another person told her that it would be all right to add another layer of shingles.

Fact	Inference		
○	○	**3. A.**	Nan needs a new roof.
○	○	**B.**	Two people gave Nan different advice.
○	○	**C.**	A heavy roof might fall into the house.
○	○	**D.**	Nan can't do the job by herself.

4. Maria's mother gave her a tool kit. It has tools in the lid and in the bottom. The tools fit into molded plastic trays with a place shaped like each tool. On the top are wrenches and sockets. The sockets are both English and metric sizes. In the bottom tray are screwdrivers, pliers, and a ratchet. Maria is excited about using the tools.

Fact	Inference		
○	○	**4. A.**	Maria's mother knows what Maria likes.
○	○	**B.**	The tool kit has screwdrivers.
○	○	**C.**	All the tools fit into one box.
○	○	**D.**	Sockets can come in different sizes.

5. Don had a beautiful lawn. It looked like a thick, green carpet. Don's next-door neighbor Fred's lawn looked awful. It had weeds and patches of brown grass, and there were some places where grass didn't grow at all. Both Don and Fred watered their lawns. They also cut the grass once a week. Don always put fertilizer on his lawn in the fall and spring, but Fred did not.

Fact	Inference		
○	○	**5. A.**	Don and Fred watered their lawns.
○	○	**B.**	Don and Fred cut their lawns once a week.
○	○	**C.**	Don took good care of his lawn.
○	○	**D.**	Grass needs fertilizer to stay green.

1. Frank loved to play tennis, and he was on the tennis court every day. Frank could hit the ball very hard. He was a good player. One day he met his friend Jim for a game of tennis. Jim had just started playing tennis. After the game Frank said, "I will help you with your shots, Jim."

Fact	Inference		
○	○	**1. A.**	Frank loved to play tennis.
○	○	**B.**	Frank and Jim met for a game of tennis.
○	○	**C.**	Frank won the game.
○	○	**D.**	Jim was not a good tennis player.

2. Chicago is one of the few places where people play softball with a 16-inch ball. Most softballs are smaller. The rules for softball are like the rules for baseball, but most of the players don't use gloves or mitts. The pitcher throws the ball underhand. It is hard to hit a softball a long distance.

Fact	Inference		
○	○	**2. A.**	People in Chicago like the 16-inch ball.
○	○	**B.**	Most softball players don't use mitts.
○	○	**C.**	Baseball players need mitts.
○	○	**D.**	Most softballs are smaller than 16 inches.

3. Many young people are interested in the past. They can learn facts about the past from their families. Grandparents can give many facts. Rachel likes to record her grandfather's stories about growing up on a farm in the early 1900s. Rachel shares the stories with her friends. They are always surprised at how people lived during that time. "How could they live without air-conditioning?" one friend asked.

Fact	Inference		
○	○	**3. A.**	Families pass on their past experiences.
○	○	**B.**	Grandparents know about the past.
○	○	**C.**	Children are interested in the past.
○	○	**D.**	Many things have changed over the years

4. When you recycle something, you use it again. Paper and glass can be recycled. Some cities help people recycle. People put used paper, plastic, glass, and cans into bins. The city makes sure that these objects aren't just thrown away but are made into new items. Years ago these things were buried, but they took up too much space.

Fact	Inference		
○	○	**4. A.**	Burying trash takes up too much space.
○	○	**B.**	People now sort their trash.
○	○	**C.**	Many cities now help people recycle.
○	○	**D.**	Recycling saves space.

---

5. Each year during the last week in April, Mr. Mendez began his garden. He planted tomatoes during the second week in May. He weeded the garden as the plants grew. By the middle of summer, the tomatoes were ready to sell. Many people bought them. They liked his red, ripe tomatoes. By Labor Day it was time for Mr. Mendez to pull up all his tomato plants.

Fact	Inference		
○	○	**5. A.**	Mr. Mendez worked hard to grow tomatoes.
○	○	**B.**	The tomatoes were not good after Labor Day.
○	○	**C.**	He weeded the garden as the plants grew.
○	○	**D.**	He sold tomatoes for a very short time.

1. Heavy trucks can destroy roads. To protect the roads, states make truck drivers weigh their cargo. They do this on giant scales at weigh stations along the road. The truck drives onto the scale, and its weight is taken. If the truck is too heavy, it is not allowed to drive any farther.

Fact   Inference

○   ○   **1. A.** Heavy trucks can hurt roads.

○   ○   **B.** States make drivers weigh their cargo.

○   ○   **C.** Trucks must not be overloaded.

○   ○   **D.** Weigh stations have scales.

2. The gym was bright with colored lights. Crepe paper hung from the ceiling, and there was a band playing music. The music was so loud that people couldn't talk to one another. It was crowded in the gym, but no one was playing basketball or wearing gym clothes. All the girls were wearing dresses and flowers. All the boys were wearing suits.

Fact   Inference

○   ○   **2. A.** There was a dance in the gym.

○   ○   **B.** The music was very loud.

○   ○   **C.** Basketball was not being played.

○   ○   **D.** Most people were dancing.

3. What can you do with trash and garbage? You can throw it away, or you can reuse some of it. A jar can be a vase for flowers or a place to store jewelry, money, or food. You can put fruit and vegetable scraps in the garden. You can also save newspapers. They can be made into clean paper.

Fact	Inference		
○	○	**3. A.**	Some things can be used again.
○	○	**B.**	New paper can be made from old.
○	○	**C.**	A jar can be used in several ways.
○	○	**D.**	Not all garbage needs to be thrown away.

4. Most people learn to sail on a small boat. While they are learning, they keep the boat in a protected spot, such as a harbor. First they learn the names of all the parts of the boat. Then they learn how to turn and move the boat with or against the wind. They also learn what to do if the boat turns over. Once people know how to sail a small boat, with practice they can sail a boat of almost any size.

Fact	Inference		
○	○	**4. A.**	People best learn to sail on a small boat.
○	○	**B.**	It is best to learn to sail in a protected spot.
○	○	**C.**	Sailing takes some skill.
○	○	**D.**	Large boats are harder to sail than small boats.

5. Schools need sprinklers. A sprinkler is like a shower. Sprinklers are installed in or near the ceilings. If a fire should start, the heat from the fire quickly melts a lead plug on the sprinkler. Once the plug melts, water rushes out of the showerlike heads. The water sprays out over a wide area.

Fact	Inference		
○	○	**5. A.**	Sprinklers make schools safer.
○	○	**B.**	Schools need sprinklers in case of fire.
○	○	**C.**	Sprinklers have heads like showers.
○	○	**D.**	Sprinklers can put out fires.

1. Airlines didn't have much money to build airports when they first flew planes between countries. Airlines designed airplanes that could land on the water. The bottom of the planes looked like boats. These planes could land anywhere there was water.

Fact	Inference		
○	○	**1. A.**	It didn't cost much to land on water.
○	○	**B.**	Airplanes landed on water.
○	○	**C.**	Airlines didn't have much money to build airports.
○	○	**D.**	Very few planes land on water today.

2. Power lawn mowers make lawn care easy. Years ago people had to push a mower by hand. The push mower had three long blades that were attached to wheels on both sides. As the wheels turned, the blades spun and cut the grass. It took a long time to cut a lawn, especially when the grass was high. You had to be strong to push a mower like this. Today power lawn mowers come in all sizes. Some are so large that a person can ride on them.

Fact	Inference		
○	○	**2. A.**	Power lawn mowers cut grass easily.
○	○	**B.**	It is hard to move a push mower.
○	○	**C.**	People ride on some mowers.
○	○	**D.**	Today mowers come in all sizes.

3. Mammals are animals that feed their young with milk. Pigs are the mammals that have the most babies. A pig can have as many as 34 babies at a time. A mother pig is called a sow. Baby pigs that are less than 10 weeks old are called piglets.

Fact	Inference		
○	○	**3. A.**	Pigs feed their young with milk.
○	○	**B.**	Piglets are very small.
○	○	**C.**	Pigs are mammals.
○	○	**D.**	A pig can have up to 34 babies at a time.

4. The Pony Express carried letters from Missouri to California. Riders rode 10 miles and changed horses. They could put saddles on new horses in two minutes. Each rider had to change his horse seven times a day. The Pony Express was replaced by the telegraph. The telegraph sent messages over wires.

Fact	Inference	
○	○	**4. A.** The Pony Express was slower than the telegraph.
○	○	**B.** Riders changed horses after 10 miles.
○	○	**C.** It was very tiring to be a Pony Express rider.
○	○	**D.** Horses were worn out after 10 miles.

---

5. Parkside Hospital was holding a big bike race. Those who entered would help raise money for the hospital. Robin and Gwen decided to enter the 5-mile race. As the girls reached the end of the race, Gwen rode her bike over a hole in the road. She fell off and landed on the street. Although Robin was in the lead, she stopped to make sure Gwen was okay.

Fact	Inference	
○	○	**5. A.** The race was 5 miles long.
○	○	**B.** Robin and Gwen liked to ride bikes.
○	○	**C.** Gwen fell off her bike.
○	○	**D.** Robin was a helpful person.

1. Hummingbirds are the smallest birds. Some hummingbirds weigh less than a dime. They beat their wings very fast. Their wings beat up to 70 times a second. Because they are so active, they feed about once every 10 or 15 minutes. Hummingbirds are the only birds that can fly backwards.

Fact　　Inference

○　　　○　　**1.** **A.** Hummingbirds are very light.

○　　　○　　**B.** Hummingbirds can fly backwards.

○　　　○　　**C.** Hummingbirds beat their wings fast.

○　　　○　　**D.** Hummingbirds spend a lot of time eating.

2. Many books and movies have been written about the story of Robin Hood. Robin Hood was a folk hero who robbed the rich and gave what he took to the poor. Robin Hood is said to have lived in Sherwood Forest. He lived with a band of merry men. Many people have tried to prove he was a real person. So far no one has been able to show that he really lived.

Fact　　Inference

○　　　○　　**2.** **A.** Robin Hood is a popular story.

○　　　○　　**B.** People admire Robin Hood.

○　　　○　　**C.** Robin Hood cared about the poor.

○　　　○　　**D.** No one can prove that Robin Hood really lived.

3. Have you ever played with a yo-yo? Yo-yos were first used in the Philippines. They were not used as toys. Instead they were used for protection in the jungle. The word *yo-yo* means "to return" in the Philippine language. Today the yo-yo is a favorite toy in many countries.

Fact	Inference		
○	○	**3. A.**	Yo-yos are fun to play with.
○	○	**B.**	Yo-yos protected people from wild animals.
○	○	**C.**	*Yo-yo* means "to return."
○	○	**D.**	Today the yo-yo is a favorite toy.

4. In 1811, David Thompson was exploring the Rockies. He came across a large footprint. It was 14 inches long and 8 inches wide. The footprint was not the print of any known animal. Some people call the creature Bigfoot. More than 750 people say they have seen the hairy creature. It is said to be 8 feet tall and weigh 400 pounds.

Fact	Inference		
○	○	**4. A.**	Bigfoot may live in the Rockies.
○	○	**B.**	The footprint may have belonged to Bigfoot.
○	○	**C.**	More than 750 people say they have seen Bigfoot.
○	○	**D.**	Bigfoot may be 8 feet tall.

5. Hot dogs were named by a newspaper cartoonist from Chicago. One day in 1906, cartoonist Tad Dorgan was at a baseball game. A boy came by selling frankfurters. Dorgan drew a picture of the frankfurters. He made them look like small, long dogs on a bun. Under the cartoon he wrote, "Hot dogs."

Fact	Inference		
○	○	**5. A.**	Hot dogs were first called frankfurters.
○	○	**B.**	Tad Dorgan was a cartoonist.
○	○	**C.**	People liked the new name.
○	○	**D.**	Dorgan's cartoon was printed in the newspaper.

1. Harry Houdini was known as "the escape king." He could escape from iron boxes, straitjackets, and even bank safes. Some of his most exciting acts used water. People were often afraid that Houdini would not escape, but he always got out safely. He was very strong, and he took good care of his body.

Fact	Inference		
○	○	**1. A.**	Houdini took good care of his body.
○	○	**B.**	People were amazed by Houdini's escapes.
○	○	**C.**	Houdini could escape from a bank safe.
○	○	**D.**	People like to watch Houdini's acts.

2. The Taj Mahal is a beautiful building. It is made of snow-white marble. It stands beside a river in Agra, India. The emperor of India had it built for his wife. She died in 1630 at the age of 39. It took 20,000 men to build the Taj Mahal. They worked for more than 22 years. The emperor had planned for a building made of black marble across the river, but it was never built.

Fact	Inference		
○	○	**2. A.**	The Taj Mahal is in India.
○	○	**B.**	The Taj Mahal is made of white marble.
○	○	**C.**	The emperor wanted to honor his wife.
○	○	**D.**	The emperor loved his wife very much.

3. Marcie loved bananas. She loved banana splits, banana pudding, and banana ice cream. Her favorite way to eat a banana was to simply peel it and eat it. One day she had just enjoyed her favorite food while sitting on the front steps of her house. She left the peel on the steps. An hour later her mother came home. As she climbed the steps to the front door, she noticed the peel. But it was too late.

Fact	Inference		
○	○	**3. A.**	Marcie left the peel on the steps.
○	○	**B.**	Marcie's mother slipped on the peel.
○	○	**C.**	Marcie loved bananas.
○	○	**D.**	Marcie's mother was angry.

4. Everyone knows what a tiger is, and everyone has heard of lions. Do you know what a "liger" is? A liger is a cross between a lion and a tiger. The first liger was born in the United States in 1948. It was born at the Hagh Zoo in Salt Lake City, Utah. If you had been there at the time, what would you have named it?

Fact	Inference	
○	○	**4. A.** A liger is a cross between a lion and a tiger.
○	○	**B.** Many people don't know about ligers.
○	○	**C.** Ligers were unusual animals in 1948.
○	○	**D.** Most ligers live in zoos.

---

5. Easter Island is in the South Pacific. More than 600 giant statues stand on the island. They are made of stone. Some are 70 feet tall. Some weigh up to 70 tons. For many years outsiders wondered how the statues were lifted into place. Then Thor Heyerdahl found the answer. He asked some island people to show him their methods. They raised a statue by pushing poles under its head. Thenthey pushed stones under it until it lifted into place.

Fact	Inference	
○	○	**5. A.** The statues were hard to raise upright.
○	○	**B.** Many statues stand on Easter Island.
○	○	**C.** Easter Island is in the South Pacific.
○	○	**D.** The people on Easter Island were quite clever.

1. Do you have to make your bed every day? Of course you don't really make the bed; you just straighten the sheets. The early Romans made beds by putting straw into cloth sacks. The straw then had to be removed every day to dry. People once really did make their beds every day, and that's where we got the saying.

Fact	Inference		
○	○	**1. A.**	The early Romans made beds of straw.
○	○	**B.**	The straw got damp during the night.
○	○	**C.**	Sleeping on damp beds was not comfortable.
○	○	**D.**	Today people don't sleep on straw beds.

2. P. T. Barnum loved to thrill crowds. He knew what would make them happy. No wonder he is known as the father of the modern circus. He started his "Greatest Show on Earth" in the 1870s. He had the huge elephant Jumbo and other strange creatures. He had clowns and singers, bearded ladies, and other odd acts. People flocked to his circus. Barnum's circus is still in business today.

Fact	Inference		
○	○	**2. A.**	Barnum started his circus in the 1870s.
○	○	**B.**	People liked Barnum's circus.
○	○	**C.**	Barnum was a smart businessperson.
○	○	**D.**	People enjoyed seeing bearded ladies.

3. Cows are grass-eating animals. Grass is not easy to chew. Because of this, cows have a special way of making sure they chew it well. They chew a little grass and then swallow it. Then the grass makes its way from the cow's stomach back to its mouth. The cow then chews the grass again. This is called chewing cud.

Fact	Inference	
○	○	**3. A.** Grass is difficult to chew.
○	○	**B.** A cow's stomach helps it chew the grass well.
○	○	**C.** Chewing grass over again is called chewing cud.
○	○	**D.** Grass is an important food for cows.

4. Most people don't like to do chores around the house. Scientists studied this topic. They found that most people don't like washing dishes. They also do not enjoy cleaning the bathroom.

Fact	Inference	
○	○	**4. A.** Scientists asked people about chores.
○	○	**B.** Most people don't like washing dishes.
○	○	**C.** They would rather use a dishwasher.
○	○	**D.** Most people don't like household chores.

5. Dogs are sometimes called "man's best friend," but some dogs are friendlier than others. Some dogs bite many more people than others do. The kind of dog that bites the most is the German police dog. Poodles also often bite people. Sheepdogs, on the other hand, do not bite much at all.

Fact	Inference	
○	○	**5. A.** German police dogs are not good pets.
○	○	**B.** Poodles often bite people.
○	○	**C.** Sheepdogs are friendly.
○	○	**D.** Dogs are called "man's best friend."

1. Have you ever seen a bullfight? A person stands in a large ring and waves a red cape at a bull. Then the bull runs at the cape, and the person scampers out of the way. You might think that the red color of the cape makes the bull angry, but this is not true. In fact the bull is color-blind, so it cannot tell red from other colors. The bull charges at the motion of the cape, not the color of it.

Fact   Inference
○   ○   **1.** **A.** In a bullfight a person stands in a ring.
○   ○   **B.** Red capes are used in bullfights.
○   ○   **C.** Bulls are color-blind.
○   ○   **D.** A bull would charge a green cape.

---

2. Imagine that you are sitting in a wheelchair. You need to get to the third floor of a building. First, you need to avoid the steps in front, so you look for a ramp. To open the heavy door, you look for a button to push. Once inside, you need to avoid the stairway, so you look for an elevator. No problem! Most buildings built today have a special design so that wheelchair users can move around safely.

Fact   Inference
○   ○   **2.** **A.** Wheelchair users go up ramps and elevators.
○   ○   **B.** Most older buildings did not have a special design.
○   ○   **C.** Wheelchair users need to avoid steps.
○   ○   **D.** Many new buildings have a special design.

---

3. Cheryl had never tried to fix her bicycle before. But her bike had a flat tire, and it needed to be fixed. No one else had offered to help, so Cheryl decided to try to fix the flat tire herself.

Fact   Inference
○   ○   **3.** **A.** Cheryl wasn't sure she could fix her bike.
○   ○   **B.** The bike had a flat tire.
○   ○   **C.** Cheryl wanted to ride her bike.
○   ○   **D.** No one else offered to help.

4. Cleopatra lived more than 2,000 years ago. At the age of 18, she became the queen of Egypt. She ruled with her brothers, but both of them died. Cleopatra then became the only ruler of her land. She was not a great queen. She taxed her people heavily. She held control of the throne until her death at the age of 39.

Fact   Inference

○   ○   **4. A.** Cleopatra first ruled with her brothers.
○   ○   **B.** She was the queen of Egypt.
○   ○   **C.** The people of Egypt did not like Cleopatra.
○   ○   **D.** Cleopatra died at age 39.

---

5. The smell of liver made Wally hold his nose, and he thought he would be sick each time he had to taste spinach. Yet there before him sat those two foods, just waiting to be eaten. When his mother left the room, Wally dashed to the window. He scraped his plate clean behind the curtains and hurried back to his seat. When his mother returned, she was surprised at how quickly he had finished his meal. Wally only grinned nervously.

Fact   Inference

○   ○   **5. A.** Wally doesn't like liver or spinach.
○   ○   **B.** Wally's mother was surprised he had finished.
○   ○   **C.** Wally scraped his plate behind the curtains.
○   ○   **D.** Wally was supposed to eat liver and spinach.

Writing Roundup

Read each story. Then read the question that follows it. Write your answers on the lines below each question.

1. A huge wave blasted onto the deck. The few pieces of equipment that hadn't been tied down were washed away. The whistle for help sounded just before another monster of a wave slammed down. This one shattered a fire hose box, and the hose in the box fell and then moved across the deck like a snake.

What is happening?

_____

_____

_____

2. Devin always thought the game looked easy. Now she had a different idea. The ball was very heavy. She found it hard to knock down the pins at the end of the alley.

What game is Devin learning?

_____

_____

_____

3. The captain called out Javier's name. Javier marched to the front of the line. He proudly gave a salute.

What is Javier?

_____

_____

_____

Read the paragraph below. Then answer the questions.

Teresa never misses a workout. Unlike most of the students who use the high school's training gym, Teresa stays away from the weights. She rides the bicycles and runs on the treadmill. She also jumps rope a lot of the time. Teresa does all this with a plan in mind. She expects to run in a marathon race in the future. She wants to stay thin and able to run long distances. Teresa has a fine plan for now, but she still needs a coach's help. She needs someone to give her special facts about training for a marathon.

1. Why doesn't Teresa use weights?

_____

_____

2. Why does Teresa try to stay thin?

_____

_____

3. What kind of person is Teresa?

_____

_____

4. How could a coach help Teresa?

_____

_____

Spelling
Skills

spelling strategies

What can you do when you aren't sure how to spell a word?

Say the word aloud. Make sure you say it correctly. Listen to the sounds in the word. Think about letters and patterns that might spell the sounds.

Look in the Spelling Table on page 265 to find common spellings for sounds in the word.

Think about related words. They may help you spell the word you're not sure of.

discover—cover

Guess the spelling of the word and check it in a dictionary.

Write the word in different ways. Compare the spellings and choose the one that looks correct.

trale (trail) treighl treal

Think about any spelling rules you know that can help you spell the word.

When a singular word ends in s, ch, sh, or x, -es is added to form the plural.

Listen for a common word part, such as a prefix, suffix, or ending.

careful   beginning

Break the word into syllables and think about how each syllable might be spelled.

Sat-ur-day
sur-prise

Create a memory clue to help you remember the spelling of the word.

I hear with my ear

Proofreading Marks

Mark	Meaning	Example
◯	spell correctly	I (liek) dogs.
⊙	add period	They are my favorite kind of pet.
?	add question mark	What kind of pet do you have?
≡	capitalize	My dog's name is scooter.
∧	add	Scooter has brown spots.
ℓ	take out	He likes to to run and play.
¶	indent paragraph	¶I love my dog, Scooter. He is the best pet I have ever had. Every morning he wakes me up with a bark. Every night he sleeps with me.
⟨⟨ ⟩⟩	add quotation marks	You are my best friend, I tell him.

Words with Short a

past	stamp	happen	grass	glad
match	magic	answer	aunt	branch
ask	pass	travel	began	half
snack	laugh	plastic	crack	banana

Say and Listen

Say each spelling word. Listen for the short a sound.

stamp

Think and Sort

Look at the letters in each word. Think about how short a is spelled. Spell each word aloud.

Short a can be shown as /ă/. How many spelling patterns for /ă/ do you see?

1. Write the **eighteen** spelling words that have the *a* pattern, like *glad*.

2. Write the **two** spelling words that have the *au* pattern, like *laugh*.

1. a Words

_____   _____

_____   _____

_____   _____

_____   _____

_____   _____

_____   _____

_____   _____

_____   _____

_____   _____

2. au Words

_____   _____

Definitions

Write the spelling word for each definition.
Use a dictionary if you need to.

1. a sharp snapping sound   _____

2. to come to pass   _____

3. special effects and tricks   _____

4. to go from place to place   _____

5. to set a foot down loudly   _____

6. green plants that people mow   _____

7. a substance made from chemicals   _____

Analogies

An analogy states that two words go together in the same way as two others. Write the spelling word that completes each analogy.

8. *Opened* is to *closed* as _____ is to *ended*.

9. *Bad* is to *good* as *sad* is to _____.

10. *Three* is to *six* as _____ is to *whole*.

11. *Spin* is to *twirl* as *reply* is to _____.

12. *Large* is to *small* as *feast* is to _____.

13. *Vegetable* is to *spinach* as *fruit* is to _____.

14. *Arm* is to *body* as _____ is to *tree*.

15. *Black* is to *white* as *cry* is to _____.

16. *Male* is to *female* as *uncle* is to _____.

17. *Tomorrow* is to *yesterday* as *future* is to _____.

18. *Question* is to _____ as *tell* is to *answer*.

19. *New* is to *old* as *fail* is to _____.

past	stamp	happen	grass	glad
match	magic	answer	aunt	branch
ask	pass	travel	began	half
snack	laugh	plastic	crack	banana

Proofreading

Proofread the news article below. Use proofreading marks to correct five spelling mistakes, three punctuation mistakes, and two missing words. See the chart on page 131 to learn how to use the proofreading marks.

Proofreading Marks

◯ spell correctly

⊙ add period

∧ add

Monroe School Monthly

Weather Safety

When you are outside, be aware of the weather. Watch sky and listen for thunder If you hear loud crak, find shelter right away. A storm can travl fast.

To be safe, never take shelter under a tree bransh. If you hapen to be in a boat, head for shore You will probably be out of danger soon.

Most storms pas quickly

Dictionary Skills

Alphabetical Order

Dictionary words are listed in alphabetical order. Words beginning with *a* come first, then words beginning with *b*, and so on. When the first letter of words is the same, the second letter is used to put the words in alphabetical order. If the first two letters are the same, the third letter is used. Write each group of words in alphabetical order.

1. laugh   glad   stamp

_____   _____   _____

2. plastic   magic   grass

_____   _____   _____

3. began   banana   brick

_____   _____   _____

4. aunt   ask   answer

_____   _____   _____

5. half   have   happy

_____   _____   _____

6. crack   crumb   crisp

_____   _____   _____

Words with Long a

awake	eight	trade	afraid	trail	waist	state
chase	mistake	weight	neighbor	plane	space	shape
paid	plain	waste	taste	wait	break	

Say and Listen

Say each spelling word. Listen for the long a sound.

Think and Sort

Look at the letters in each word. Think about how long a is spelled. Spell each word aloud.

plane

Long a can be shown as /ā/. How many spelling patterns for /ā/ do you see?

1. Write the **ten** spelling words that have the *a*-consonant-*e* pattern, like *plane*.

2. Write the **six** spelling words that have the *ai* pattern, like *paid*.

3. Look at the word *eight*. The spelling pattern for this word is *eigh*. The g and h are silent. Write the **three** spelling words that have the *eigh* pattern.

4. Write the **one** spelling word that has the *ea* pattern.

1. a-consonant-e Words

_____   _____   _____

_____   _____   _____

_____   _____   _____

_____

2. ai Words

_____   _____   _____

_____   _____   _____

3. eigh Words

_____   _____   _____

4. ea Word

_____

Homophones

Homophones are words that sound alike but have different spellings and meanings. Complete each sentence with the correct homophone.

1. The present without a ribbon looked very _____.

2. I would rather take a train than a _____.

3. Don't _____ your time looking for the note.

4. Wear the belt around your _____.

5. Alex checked his _____ on the scale.

6. Would you please _____ for me after school?

Rhymes

Write the spelling word that completes each sentence and rhymes with the underlined word.

7. I like the _____ of tomato <u>paste</u>.

8. Did the dog _____ the <u>lace</u> ribbon?

9. The boys will _____ the cars they <u>made</u>.

10. Rosa carried a <u>pail</u> down the _____.

11. On what <u>date</u> did Florida become a _____?

12. Draw a <u>face</u> in the empty _____.

13. Ms. <u>Cade</u> _____ for everyone's lunch.

14. What is the _____ of a roll of <u>tape</u>?

15. We have _____ pieces of <u>bait</u> left.

16. Are you ready to <u>take</u> a _____ from your work?

17. It was a _____ to keep the baby <u>awake</u>.

18. He was _____ that he had left the bill <u>unpaid</u>.

19. I want to be _____ when it's time to eat the <u>steak</u>.

awake	*mistake*	*waste*	*trail*	*space*
chase	*plain*	*afraid*	*plane*	*break*
paid	*trade*	*neighbor*	*wait*	*state*
eight	*weight*	*taste*	*waist*	*shape*

Proofreading

Proofread the advertisement below. Use proofreading marks to correct five spelling mistakes, three capitalization mistakes, and two unnecessary words.

Proofreading Marks

○ spell correctly
≡ capitalize
ℓ take out

Visit Big Mountain Park

are you planning a visit to our stait?

Be sure to to stop at Big Mountain Park.

Climb the trale to Crystal Falls. Taiste the

clean mountain water. see bears and deer

along the way. Enjoy the wide open spase.

it would be be a misstake to miss this

great place!

Dictionary Skills

Using the Spelling Table

How can you find a word in a dictionary when you are not sure how to spell it? A spelling table can help you find the word. Suppose you are not sure how the long *a* sound in *neighbor* is spelled. You can use a spelling table to find the different spellings for long *a*. First, find the pronunciation symbol for long *a*. Then read the first spelling listed for /ā/, and look up *na* words in a dictionary. Look for each spelling until you find *neighbor*.

Sound	Spellings	Examples
/ā/	a a_e ai ay ea eigh ey	April, chase, plain, day, break, eight, obey

Write each of the following words, spelling the long *a* sound in dark type correctly. Use the above entry for /ā/, from the Spelling Table on page 265, and a dictionary.

1. chas _____

2. awak _____

3. trad _____

4. ralroad _____

5. rotat _____

6. shap _____

7. tral _____

8. lightwat _____

9. acquant _____

10. betra _____

11. sav _____

Words with Short e

again	ready	heavy	breakfast	yesterday
edge	never	friend	fence	desert
bread	echo	health	stretch	sweater
ever	energy	guess	weather	against

Say and Listen

bread

Say each spelling word. Listen for the short e sound.

Think and Sort

Look at the letters in each word. Think about how short e is spelled. Spell each word aloud.

Short e can be shown as /ĕ/. How many spelling patterns for /ĕ/ do you see?

1. Write the **nine** spelling words that have the *e* pattern, like *fence*.
2. Write the **seven** spelling words that have the *ea* pattern, like *ready*.
3. Write the **two** spelling words that have the *ai* pattern, like *again*.
4. Write the **one** spelling word that has the *ie* pattern.
5. Write the **one** spelling word that has the *ue* pattern.

1. e Words

_____   _____   _____

_____   _____   _____

_____   _____   _____

2. ea Words

_____   _____   _____

_____   _____   _____

3. ai Words

_____   _____

4. ie Word   **5. ue Word**

_____   _____

Antonyms

Antonyms are words that have opposite meanings.
Write the spelling word that is an antonym of each word.

1. swamp   _____

2. sickness   _____

3. enemy   _____

4. know   _____

5. lightweight   _____

6. always   _____

7. center   _____

8. for   _____

9. tomorrow   _____

10. unprepared   _____

Common Phrases

Write the spelling word that completes each phrase.

11. again and _____

12. happily _____ after

13. snowy _____

14. _____ and butter

15. skirt and _____

16. jump over the _____

17. bend and _____

18. the _____ of your voice

19. _____ from the sun

again	ready	heavy	breakfast	yesterday
edge	never	friend	fence	desert
bread	echo	health	stretch	sweater
ever	energy	guess	weather	against

Proofreading

Proofread the journal entry below. Use proofreading marks to correct five spelling mistakes, three capitalization mistakes, and two missing words.

Proofreading Marks

◯ spell correctly
≡ capitalize
⋏ add

july 21

Yestarday morning I played tennis my frend Maria. The wether was hot, and we had not eaten much brekfast. we didn't have very much enerjy. I could hardly hit the ball. maria couldn't run very far or very fast.

We will not make the same mistake again. Next time we'll start day with a bigger meal.

Guide Words

Guide words are the two words in dark type at the top of each dictionary page. The first guide word is the first entry word on the page. The second guide word is the last entry word. The other entry words on the page are arranged in alphabetical order between the guide words. When searching for a word in a dictionary, use the guide words to find the correct page.

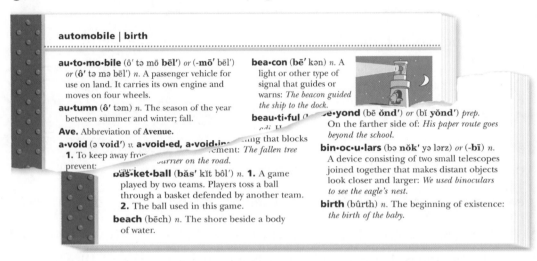

automobile | birth

au·to·mo·bile (ô′ tə mō **bēl′**) *or* (-**mō′** bēl′) *or* (ô′ tə mə bēl′) *n.* A passenger vehicle for use on land. It carries its own engine and moves on four wheels.

au·tumn (ô′ təm) *n.* The season of the year between summer and winter; fall.

Ave. Abbreviation of **Avenue.**

a·void (ə void′) *v.* **a·void·ed, a·void·i**ng that blocks ____ement: *The fallen tree* ____ ____rrier on the road. prevent:

bas·ket·ball (băs′ kĭt bôl′) *n.* **1.** A game played by two teams. Players toss a ball through a basket defended by another team. **2.** The ball used in this game.

beach (bēch) *n.* The shore beside a body of water.

bea·con (bē′ kən) *n.* A light or other type of signal that guides or warns: *The beacon guided the ship to the dock.*

beau·ti·ful ____ ____e·yond (bē ŏnd′) *or* (bĭ yŏnd′) *prep.* On the farther side of: *His paper route goes beyond the school.*

bin·oc·u·lars (bə nŏk′ yə lərz) *or* (-**bī** n.* A device consisting of two small telescopes joined together that makes distant objects look closer and larger: *We used binoculars to see the eagle's nest.*

birth (bûrth) *n.* The beginning of existence: *the birth of the baby.*

Each pair of guide words below is followed by a list of words. Write the list words that are on the same dictionary page as the guide words.

1. after/agree   ace   again   age   afraid

_____   _____

2. straight/sweet   stamp   sweater   stretch   switch

_____   _____

3. head/height   health   help   hamster   heavy

_____   _____

Words with Long e

season	scream	sweep	beach	means	leaf	peace
knee	reason	sweet	seem	speak	treat	please
queen	between	speech	teach	freeze	squeeze	

Say and Listen

Say each spelling word. Listen for the long e sound.

beach

Think and Sort

Look at the letters in each word. Think about how long e is spelled. Spell each word aloud.

Long e can be shown as /ē/. How many spelling patterns for /ē/ do you see?

1. Write the **eleven** spelling words that have the *ea* pattern, like *beach*.

2. Write the **nine** spelling words that have the *ee* pattern, like *sweet*.

1. ea Words

_____   _____

_____   _____

_____   _____

_____   _____

_____   _____

_____

2. ee Words

_____   _____

_____   _____

_____   _____

_____

Classifying

Write the spelling word that belongs in each group.

1. dust, vacuum, _____
2. king, princess, _____
3. trunk, branch, _____
4. ankle, thigh, _____
5. shout, yell, _____
6. among, beside, _____
7. sour, salty, _____
8. shows, intends _____

What's the Answer?

Write the spelling word that answers each question.

9. What word do you use to politely ask for something? _____
10. What word names a part of the year? _____
11. What do you give a good dog? _____
12. What word means the same as *talk*? _____
13. What word means "appear to be"? _____
14. What do you call a public talk? _____
15. Where do people go to have fun in the summer sun? _____
16. What do you do to get juice from an orange? _____
17. What tells why something happens? _____
18. If a lake gets cold, what might it do? _____
19. What word means the opposite of *war*? _____

season	reason	speech	means	treat
knee	between	beach	speak	squeeze
queen	sweep	seem	freeze	peace
scream	sweet	teach	leaf	please

Proofreading

Proofread the letter below. Use proofreading marks to correct five spelling mistakes, three punctuation mistakes, and two missing words.

Proofreading Marks

◯ spell correctly

? add question mark

∧ add

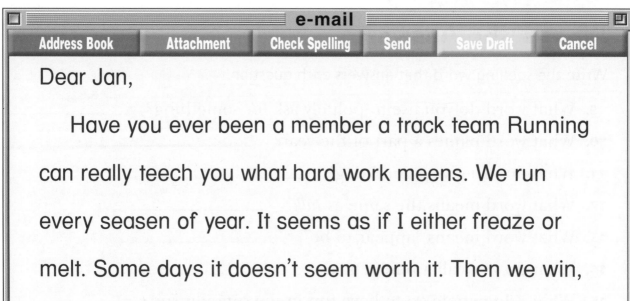

e-mail

Address Book	Attachment	Check Spelling	Send	Save Draft	Cancel

Dear Jan,

   Have you ever been a member a track team Running can really teech you what hard work meens. We run every seasen of year. It seems as if I either freaze or melt. Some days it doesn't seem worth it. Then we win, and I remember the reeson that I joined the team.

   What have you been doing this spring Are you playing tennis again Let me know when you can come for a visit.

Chang

Language Connection

Verbs

A verb is a word that expresses action or being.

> I **ran** across the street.   Ling **is** a good writer.

Write the verb in each group of words.

1. sweep   girl   swan

_____

2. leaf   neat   seem

_____

3. team   scream   queen

_____

4. between   sweet   means

_____

5. speak   peace   plain

_____

6. cheese   squeeze   knee

_____

Months, Days, and Titles

October	Thursday	Dr.	Monday	November
February	December	August	September	Saturday
Friday	July	Sunday	Tuesday	Wednesday
March	May	June	January	April

Say and Listen

Say the spelling words. Listen to the sounds in each word.

Think and Sort

Look at the letters in each word. Spell each word aloud.

A **syllable** is a word part with one vowel sound. *Sun* has one syllable.
Sunny has two syllables: sun-ny.

An **abbreviation** is a shortened form of a word. *Mr.* is an abbreviation for *Mister.*

1. Write the **three** spelling words that have one syllable, like *March.*
2. Write the **nine** spelling words that have two syllables, like *A-pril.*
3. Write the **five** spelling words that have three syllables, like *Sep-tem-ber.*
4. Write the **two** spelling words that have four syllables, like *Jan-u-ar-y.*
5. Write the **one** spelling word that is the abbreviation of *Doctor.*

1. One-syllable Words
_____   _____   _____

2. Two-syllable Words
_____   _____   _____
_____   _____   _____
_____   _____   _____

3. Three-syllable Words
_____   _____   _____
_____   _____

4. Four-syllable Words   5. Abbreviation
_____   _____   _____

Clues

Write the spelling word for each clue.

1. the month to send valentines   _____

2. the first day of the week   _____

3. the day after Monday   _____

4. the last month of the year   _____

5. the first month of autumn   _____

6. the first day of the weekend   _____

7. the month before December   _____

8. the day in the middle of the week   _____

9. the month after March   _____

10. the first day of the school week   _____

11. the month after September   _____

12. the day before Friday   _____

13. the month between July and September   _____

14. a short way to write *Doctor*   _____

Rhymes

Write the spelling word that completes each sentence and rhymes with the underlined word or words.

15. We can <u>play</u> outside in _____.

16. Will the month of _____ be here <u>soon</u>?

17. Kwan visited the Gateway <u>Arch</u> in _____.

18. I gave Dad a <u>new tie</u> in _____.

19. The new <u>highway</u> will be open on _____.

October   Thursday   Dr.   Monday   November
February   December   August   September   Saturday
Friday   July   Sunday   Tuesday   Wednesday
March   May   June   January   April

Proofreading

Proofread the list below. Use proofreading marks to correct five spelling mistakes, three capitalization mistakes, and two unnecessary words.

Proofreading Marks

◯ spell correctly
≡ capitalize
⍭ take out

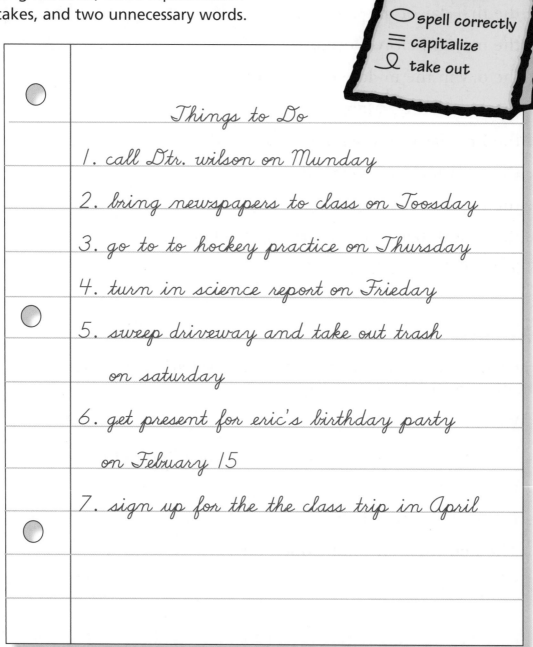

Things to Do

1. call Dtr. wilson on Munday

2. bring newspapers to class on Toosday

3. go to to hockey practice on Thursday

4. turn in science report on Frieday

5. sweep driveway and take out trash
   on saturday

6. get present for eric's birthday party
   on February 15

7. sign up for the the class trip in April

Dictionary Skills

Syllables

A syllable is a word or word part that has one vowel sound. If an entry word in a dictionary has more than one syllable, a dot is used to separate each syllable.

June has one syllable.

> **June** (jo͞on) *n.* The sixth month of the year.

October has three syllables.

> **Oc•to•ber** (ŏk tō′bər) n. The tenth month of the year.

Rewrite each word, using dots or lines to divide it into syllables. Use a dictionary if you need help.

1. January _____

2. February _____

3. April _____

4. July _____

5. August _____

6. September _____

7. November _____

8. December _____

9. Monday _____

10. Wednesday _____

11. Thursday _____

12. Friday _____

13. Saturday _____

unit 1 Review
Lessons 1-5

travel

answer

half

laugh

aunt

Words With Short a

Write the spelling word that completes each sentence.

1. I know the _____ to that question.
2. My dog likes to _____ in our van.
3. My mother's sister is my _____.
4. I saved _____ of my sandwich for later.
5. Grandpa's funny stories make me _____.

mistake

taste

afraid

eight

neighbor

break

Words with Long a

Write the spelling word for each definition. Use a dictionary if you need to.

6. scared _____
7. the number after seven _____
8. a wrong choice _____
9. the sense that recognizes flavor _____
10. someone living nearby _____
11. to split apart _____

LESSON 3

energy

stretch

sweater

against

friend

guess

Words with Short e

Write the spelling word that belongs in each group.

12. pal, buddy, _____

13. grow, lengthen, _____

14. beside, toward, _____

15. power, strength, _____

16. coat, jacket, _____

17. think, suppose, _____

LESSON 4

knee

speech

reason

please

Words with Long e

Write the spelling word that completes each analogy.

18. *When* is to *time* as *why* is to _____.

19. *Question* is to *answer* as _____ is to *thank you*.

20. *Elbow* is to *arm* as _____ is to *leg*.

21. *Notes* is to *music* as *words* is to _____.

LESSON 5

Dr.

Wednesday

February

January

Months, Days, and Titles

Write the spelling word that answers each question.

22. What is the first month of the new year? _____

23. What is the shortest month? _____

24. What day falls in the middle of the week?

_____

25. What is the abbreviation for *Doctor*? _____

More Words with Long e

people	police	evening	piano	ski	angry	sorry
easy	radio	body	copy	city	plenty	secret
every	zebra	family	busy	pizza	hungry	

Say and Listen

Say each spelling word. Listen for the long e sound.

Think and Sort

Look at the letters in each word. Think about how the long e sound is spelled. Spell each word aloud.

Long e can be shown as /ē/. How many spelling patterns for /ē/ do you see?

1. Write the **two** spelling words that have the *e* pattern, like *zebra*.
2. Write the **eleven** spelling words that have the *y* pattern, like *city*.
3. Write the **four** spelling words that have the *i* pattern, like *ski*.
4. Write the **one** spelling word that has the *e*-consonant-*e* pattern.
5. Write the **one** spelling word that has the *eo* pattern.
6. Write the **one** spelling word that has the *i*-consonant-*e* pattern.

1. **e Words**

_____   _____

2. **y Words**

_____   _____   _____

_____   _____   _____

_____   _____   _____

_____   _____

3. **i Words**

_____   _____   _____

_____

4. **e-consonant-e Word**   5. **eo Word**   6. **i-consonant-e Word**

_____   _____   _____

Definitions

Write the spelling word for each definition.

1. equipment used to receive sounds sent over air waves _____

2. something known only to oneself _____

3. government workers who enforce laws _____

4. feeling sadness or pity _____

5. having a lot to do _____

6. to glide across snow or water _____

7. a pie with cheese and tomato sauce _____

8. a striped animal related to the horse _____

9. to make exactly like another _____

10. a center of people and business _____

11. the entire form of a living thing _____

Synonyms

Synonyms are words that have the same or almost the same meaning.
Write the spelling word that is a synonym for each underlined word.

12. Our homework for tomorrow is simple. _____

13. The teacher gave each student a chore. _____

14. Louis is mad about losing his cap. _____

15. It was a lovely night for a walk. _____

16. Many persons were waiting for the bus. _____

17. We have lots of food for supper. _____

18. Jose's relatives had a reunion last summer. _____

19. I'm starving, so let's eat! _____

people	radio	family	ski	plenty
easy	zebra	piano	city	hungry
every	evening	copy	pizza	sorry
police	body	busy	angry	secret

Proofreading

Proofread the ad below. Use proofreading marks to correct five spelling mistakes, three capitalization mistakes, and two unnecessary words.

Proofreading Marks

◯ spell correctly
≡ capitalize
℘ take out

Yard Sale

Famly of seven is having a yard sale! It will be held on saturday, May 7, at 333 Hilly Drive. The house is is eazy to find. Just turn left off Highway 3 at harvey Street. follow the signs at evry street corner. There will be plenty of good stuff and lots of peeple. Come early before we we get too bizzy!

Language Connection

Commas

A series is a list of three or more items.
Use a comma to separate the items in a series.

> Dave has a cat, a dog, and a hamster.

> On our vacation we rode in a car, flew in a plane, and sailed in a boat.

Write the sentences below, adding commas where they are needed.

1. I told the secret to Amy Will and Edward.

_____

2. I love music so much that I play the violin the piano and the flute.

_____

3. At the zoo we saw a zebra an elephant and a lion.

_____

4. I like pizza with cheese peppers and onions.

_____

5. Everyone in my family likes to ski skate and sled.

_____

6. The busy city has plenty of people cars and buses.

_____

7. Rita Jenna Karen and Kim play soccer.

_____

Words with Short i

quick	picture	written	picnic	itch
deliver	middle	bridge	inch	chicken
gym	interesting	guitar	begin	building
different	village	thick	pitch	package

Say and Listen

Say each spelling word. Listen for the short *i* sound.

bridge

Think and Sort

Look at the letters in each word. Think about how short *i* is spelled. Spell each word aloud.

Short *i* can be shown as /ĭ/. How many spelling patterns for /ĭ/ do you see?

1. Write the **two** spelling words that have the *a* pattern, like *package*.
2. Write the **one** spelling word that has the *y* pattern.
3. Write the **fifteen** spelling words that have the *i* pattern, like *pitch*.
4. Write the **two** spelling words that have the *ui* pattern, like *building*.

1. **a** Words

_____   _____

2. **y** Word

_____

3. **i** Words

_____   _____   _____

_____   _____   _____

_____   _____   _____

_____   _____   _____

4. **ui** Words

_____   _____

Antonyms

Write the spelling word that is an antonym of each underlined word.

1. Michael wants to <u>catch</u> the baseball. _____
2. Those two pictures are <u>alike</u>. _____
3. Can we <u>finish</u> reading the story now? _____
4. Yoshi was <u>slow</u> to finish the job. _____
5. The gravy was too <u>thin</u>. _____
6. The movie about whales was very <u>boring</u>. _____
7. I couldn't read the words I had <u>erased</u>. _____
8. The store will <u>receive</u> our new furniture. _____

Classifying

Write the spelling word that belongs in each group.

9. duck, goose, _____
10. foot, yard, _____
11. tunnel, arch, _____
12. beginning, end, _____
13. photo, drawing, _____
14. city, town, _____
15. violin, banjo, _____
16. box, carton, _____
17. tickle, scratch, _____
18. making, constructing, _____
19. cafeteria, classroom, _____

quick	picture	written	picnic	itch
deliver	middle	bridge	inch	chicken
gym	interesting	guitar	begin	building
different	village	thick	pitch	package

Proofreading

Proofread the movie review below. Use proofreading marks to correct five spelling mistakes, three capitalization mistakes, and two punctuation mistakes.

Proofreading Marks

◯ spell correctly

≡ capitalize

? add question mark

Movie Review

A large thik cloud of smoke drops to the earth. The cloud settles on a bridge near a small vilige. It is the middel of the day. people drive their cars over the bridge and through the smoke. Then they disappear! Where do they go Soon the smoke cloud takes the shape of a bilding. firefighters hear voices inside, but no one is quik enough to catch up with it. What is the smoke cloud? Will it return See the movie *Space Visitors* and find out. it's out of this world!

Dictionary Skills

Entry Words

The words listed and explained in a dictionary are called entry words. An entry word in a dictionary is divided into syllables.

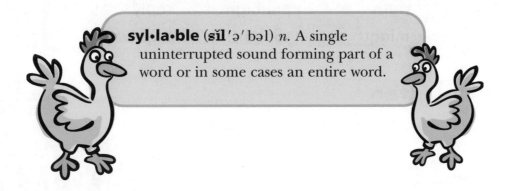

syl•la•ble (sĭl′ə′bəl) *n.* A single uninterrupted sound forming part of a word or in some cases an entire word.

Read the examples of entry words below. Count how many syllables each word has and write the number.

1. chick•en _____

2. pitch _____

3. de•liv•er _____

Find each of the words below in a dictionary. Use dots or lines to write them in syllables.

4. guitar _____

5. picture _____

6. picnic _____

7. written _____

8. begin _____

9. package _____

10. different _____

11. building _____

Words with Long i

night	fight	die	supply	high
dry	flight	spy	lightning	deny
mighty	right	midnight	reply	bright
tie	might	tonight	highway	sight

Say and Listen

Say each spelling word. Listen for the long *i* sound.

Think and Sort

Look at the letters in each word. Think about how long *i* is spelled. Spell each word aloud.

Long *i* can be shown as /ī/. How many spelling patterns for /ī/ do you see?

lightning

1. Look at the word *night*. The spelling pattern for this word is *igh*. The *g* and *h* are silent. Write the **thirteen** spelling words that have the *igh* pattern.

2. Write the **five** spelling words that have the *y* pattern, like *deny*.

3. Write the **two** spelling words that have the *ie* pattern, like *tie*.

1. **igh** Words

_____   _____   _____

_____   _____   _____

_____   _____   _____

_____   _____   _____

_____

2. **y** Words

_____   _____   _____

_____

3. **ie** Words

_____   _____

Analogies

Write the spelling word that completes each analogy.

1. *In* is to *out* as *dim* is to _____.

2. *Left* is to _____ as *up* is to *down*.

3. *Weak* is to *helpless* as *strong* is to _____.

4. *Day* is to *light* as _____ is to *dark*.

5. *Rumble* is to *thunder* as *flash* is to _____.

6. *Down* is to *low* as *up* is to _____.

7. *Ear* is to *hearing* as *eye* is to _____.

8. *Gift* is to *present* as *answer* is to _____.

9. *No* is to *yes* as _____ is to *admit*.

10. *Wet* is to _____ as *hot* is to *cold*.

Definitions

Write the spelling word for each definition. Use a dictionary if you need to.

11. the middle of the night _____

12. to make a bow or a knot _____

13. great strength _____

14. an airplane trip _____

15. to struggle _____

16. to live no more _____

17. this night _____

18. the amount available _____

19. a secret agent _____

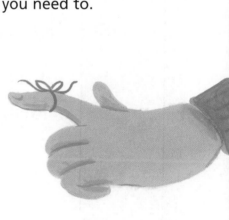

night	fight	die	supply	high
dry	flight	spy	lightning	deny
mighty	right	midnight	reply	bright
tie	might	tonight	highway	sight

Proofreading

Proofread the invitation below. Use proofreading marks to correct five spelling mistakes, three capitalization mistakes, and two unnecessary words.

Proofreading Marks

◯ spell correctly
≡ capitalize
⌒ take out

You Are Invited!

What: a a slumber party

Where: jessica Ramon's house

When: Friday, september 5

Time: 8:00 P.M. until 9:00 A.M. Saturday

Bring: a suply of your favorite games

a sleeping bag to spend the nite

a midnigt movie—a spie or mystery video

Please replie to Mrs. Ramon at 888-4999

by by august 31.

Dictionary Skills

Multiple Meanings

Many words in a dictionary have more than one meaning.
These entries for *bright* and *high* give two or three meanings.

> **bright** (brīt) *adj.* **bright·er, bright·est.**
> **1.** Giving off light in large amounts:
> *the bright sun.* **2.** Smart: *a bright child.*

> **high** (hī) *adj.* **high·er, high·est.**
> **1.** Extending far up; tall: *twenty feet high.*
> **2.** Far above the ground: *a high branch.*
> **3.** Above average: *high grades.*

Write the number of the *bright* definition that goes with each sentence.

1. My dog Baxter is very bright. _____

2. The moon is not very bright tonight. _____

3. The bright light hurt our eyes. _____

4. A bright child can solve problems quickly. _____

5. The cat's bright eyes glowed in the dark. _____

6. Following directions is always a bright idea. _____

Write the number of the *high* definition that goes with each sentence.

7. The sweater was nice, but the price was high. _____

8. The mountain is 15,000 feet high. _____

9. High diving is an Olympic event. _____

10. The car traveled at a high speed. _____

11. Three dollars is a high price for a pencil. _____

More Words with Long i

quiet	giant	smile	twice	child
buy	climb	blind	write	size
life	awhile	slide	surprise	wise
knife	sunshine	beside	behind	iron

Say and Listen

Say each spelling word. Listen for the long *i* sound.

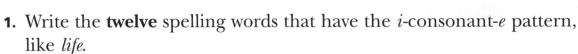

giant

Think and Sort

Look at the letters in each word. Think about how long *i* is spelled. Spell each word aloud.

Long *i* can be shown as /ī/. How many spelling patterns for /ī/ do you see?

1. Write the **twelve** spelling words that have the *i*-consonant-*e* pattern, like *life*.

2. Write the **seven** spelling words that have the *i* pattern, like *child*.

3. Write the **one** spelling word that has the *uy* pattern.

1. **i-consonant-e Words**

_____ _____ _____
_____ _____ _____
_____ _____ _____
_____ _____ _____

2. **i Words**

_____ _____ _____
_____ _____ _____
_____

3. **uy Word**

_____

Definitions

Write the spelling word for each definition.

1. something that happens without warning _____

2. of great size _____

3. the light of the sun _____

4. in back of _____

5. with little or no noise _____

6. next to _____

7. a metal tool used to press wrinkled fabric _____

8. for a brief time _____

9. an instrument used for cutting _____

Rhymes

Write the spelling word that completes each sentence
and rhymes with the underlined word.

10. It's hard to _____ for a long while.

11. What _____ are the pies you baked?

12. She was so nice to call me _____.

13. He had a wife for forty years of his _____.

14. Let's _____ Dad the yellow tie.

15. The _____ had a mild cold.

16. Mike and Ike tried to _____ down the hill.

17. It will take a long time to _____ that mountain.

18. It is _____ not to tell lies.

19. The children were kind to the _____ bird.

quiet	giant	smile	twice	child
buy	climb	blind	write	size
life	awhile	slide	surprise	wise
knife	sunshine	beside	behind	iron

Proofreading

Proofread this paragraph from a report. Use proofreading marks to correct five spelling mistakes, three punctuation mistakes, and two unnecessary words.

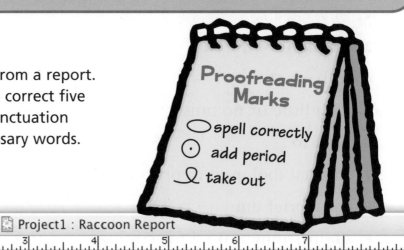

Proofreading Marks

◯ spell correctly
⊙ add period
℥ take out

Project1 : Raccoon Report

Raccoons in the Neighborhood

You probably have a raccoon in your liffe, no matter where you live. A raccoon is a queit, furry animal with a ringed tail It might surprize you some night by your garbage can. It is a wize animal and and can figure out how to get the lid off It looks like a robber because it has a black mask across its eyes. It may run off and clime a tree. It may also sit there looking friendly. Don't think that it will make a a good pet, though It's a wild animal.

100%   Page: 1

Language Connection

Nouns

A noun is a word that names a person, a place, a thing, or an idea.
Look at the nouns below.

child

park

kite

happiness

Write the noun in each group of words.

1. giant   wise   behind

_____

2. knife   over   swam

_____

3. low   iron   before

_____

4. joy   last   twice

_____

5. beside   teach   smile

_____

6. again   child   ran

_____

7. quick   until   sunshine

_____

8. after   at   size

_____

Plural Words

brothers	pennies	buses	inches	stories
families	classes	brushes	branches	foxes
dishes	pockets	rocks	hikes	boxes
trees	cities	babies	peaches	gloves

Say and Listen

Say the spelling words. Listen to the sounds at the end of each word.

Think and Sort

All of the spelling words are plurals. **Plurals** are words that name more than one thing. Look at the spelling words. Think about how each plural was formed. Spell each word aloud.

pennies

1. Most plurals are formed by adding -*s* to the base word. Write the **six** spelling words that are formed by adding -*s*, like *trees*.

2. Some plurals are formed by adding -*es* to the base word. Write the **nine** spelling words that are formed by adding -*es*, like *inches*.

3. If a word ends in a consonant and *y,* the *y* is changed to *i* before -*es* is added. Write the **five** spelling words that are formed by dropping *y* and adding -*ies*, like *cities*.

---

1. -s Plurals

_____   _____   _____

_____   _____   _____

2. -es Plurals

_____   _____   _____

_____   _____   _____

_____   _____   _____

3. -ies Plurals

_____   _____

_____   _____

Classifying

Write the spelling word that belongs in each group.

1. planes, trains, _____

2. villages, towns, _____

3. pebbles, stones, _____

4. fathers, uncles, _____

5. dimes, nickels, _____

6. jars, cans, _____

7. yards, feet, _____

8. dogs, wolves, _____

9. leaves, twigs, _____

10. adults, children, _____

11. tales, legends, _____

What's the Answer?

Write the spelling word that answers each question.

12. What do mothers, fathers, and children belong to? _____

13. On what do apples and oranges grow? _____

14. What holds coins, wallets, and other things? _____

15. What are long walks on foot? _____

16. If it's cold, what do you wear on your hands? _____

17. On what do people serve food? _____

18. What do teachers call groups of students? _____

19. What do you use on your hair and your teeth? _____

brothers	pennies	buses	inches	stories
families	classes	brushes	branches	foxes
dishes	pockets	rocks	hikes	boxes
trees	cities	babies	peaches	gloves

Proofreading

Proofread the newspaper article below. Use proofreading marks to correct five spelling mistakes, three punctuation mistakes, and two missing words.

Proofreading Marks

⬭ spell correctly

⊙ add period

⋀ add

Outdoor Life

Outdoor Fun in the City

by Mark Swift

Many famillys living in citys can't take hiks in the woods They have to visit parks to enjoy nature. Many parks have trees and rockes climb. They also have wild animals such rabbits and squirrels to watch Many animal babyes are born in the spring. It's the perfect season for enjoying park wildlife

Subject of a Sentence

The subject of a sentence is the person or thing that is doing the action or is being talked about. To find the subject, first find the predicate. Then ask yourself who or what does the action in the predicate. The answer is the subject of the sentence. In the sentence below, *marched past the palace* is the predicate, so *The brave soldiers* is the subject of the sentence.

> **The brave soldiers** marched past the palace.

Write the subject of each sentence below.

1. Peaches grow on the tree in my grandmother's front yard.

_____

2. Her older brothers go to high school.

_____

3. Two cardboard boxes tumbled off the shelf.

_____

4. Dance classes begin at three o'clock.

_____

5. My aunt's twin babies look exactly alike.

_____

6. The oak trees lost their leaves in October.

_____

unit 2 Review
Lessons 6-10

secret
family
evening
people
radio
police

More Words with Long e

Write the spelling word for each clue.

1. Your cousins, uncles, and aunts are part of this group. _____
2. This is something you should keep. _____
3. This plays music. _____
4. This time of day happens after sunset. _____
5. All men, women, and children make up this group. _____
6. These people protect our communities. _____

picture
interesting
different
gym
package
building

Words with Short i

Write the spelling word for each definition.

7. a room used for playing sports _____
8. a place with offices where people work _____
9. not the same _____
10. a box or bundle containing something _____
11. holding one's attention _____
12. a photo, painting, or drawing _____

LESSON **8**

lightning

tonight

supply

tie

Words with Long i

Write the spelling word that belongs in each group.

13. rain, thunder, _____

14. coat, shirt, _____

15. today, tomorrow, _____

16. give, provide, _____

LESSON **9**

surprise

quiet

climb

buy

More Words with Long i

Write the spelling word that is a synonym for each underlined word or words.

17. You should be <u>silent</u> during a movie. _____

18. Eva wants to <u>purchase</u> that watch. _____

19. The two boys will <u>move up</u> the playground ladders.
_____

20. Imagine my <u>amazement</u> when I saw you! _____

LESSON **10**

brothers

inches

families

pennies

babies

Plural Words

Write the spelling word that completes each analogy.

21. *Ones* is to *hundreds* as _____ is to *dollars*.

22. *Does* is to *fawns* as *mothers* is to _____.

23. *Meters* is to *centimeters* as *yards* is to _____.

24. *Girls* is to *sisters* as *boys* is to _____.

25. *Dens* is to *lions* as *houses* is to _____.

Words with Short o

hobby	doctor	wallet	watch	swallow
wash	contest	cotton	knock	beyond
model	object	dollar	problem	knot
forgot	o'clock	solve	bottom	hospital

Say and Listen

Say each spelling word. Listen for the short o sound.

dollar

Think and Sort

Look at the letters in each word. Think about how short o is spelled. Spell each word aloud.

Short o can be shown as /ŏ/. How many spelling patterns for /ŏ/ do you see?

1. Write the **sixteen** spelling words that have the *o* pattern, like *solve*.

2. Write the **four** spelling words that have the *a* pattern, like *wash*.

1. o Words

_____   _____

_____   _____

_____   _____

_____   _____

_____   _____

_____   _____

_____   _____

_____   _____

2. a Words

_____   _____

_____   _____

Classifying

Write the spelling word that belongs in each group.

1. sparrow, wren, _____

2. tap, _____, bang

3. clean, scrub, _____

4. see, _____, observe

5. dime, quarter, _____

6. unscramble, answer, _____

7. _____, silk, wool

8. race, game, _____

9. goal, _____, purpose

10. billfold, _____, purse

11. example, _____, copy

12. past, over, _____

What's the Answer?

Write the spelling word that answers each question.

13. Whom do people call when they are sick? _____

14. What is the opposite of *remembered*? _____

15. What word means "of the clock"? _____

16. What can be tied in a rope or cord? _____

17. What is the opposite of *top*? _____

18. Stamp collecting is an example of what? _____

19. What comes before a solution? _____

hobby	doctor	wallet	watch	swallow
wash	contest	cotton	knock	beyond
model	object	dollar	problem	knot
forgot	o'clock	solve	bottom	hospital

Proofreading

Proofread the contest announcement below. Use proofreading marks to correct five spelling mistakes, three capitalization mistakes, and two punctuation mistakes.

Proofreading Marks

◯ spell correctly

≡ capitalize

⊙ add period

Model Plane Contest

Do you build model planes for a hobbie? enter

this contest and win a fifty-dollar prize! You can

also win a new leather walet or a cool wotch.

Fill out the form at the bottom of this page

Bring your completed form and your plane to

the school gym by ten oclock friday morning.

anyone can enter

Dictionary Skills

Parts of Speech

A dictionary lists the part of speech for each entry word. For example, a word may be a noun (*n.*) or a verb (*v.*). Most dictionaries abbreviate the part of speech. Here are some common abbreviations for the parts of speech.

noun **n.**   adjective **adj.**   preposition **prep.**   verb **v.**   adverb **adv.**

Write the following words in alphabetical order. Look up each word in a dictionary and write its part of speech.

forgot   hospital   problem   knock   cotton   dollar   beyond

	Word	Part of Speech
1.	_____	_____
2.	_____	_____
3.	_____	_____
4.	_____	_____
5.	_____	_____
6.	_____	_____
7.	_____	_____

Words with Long o

clothes	obey	coach	only	soap
total	throat	coast	comb	zero
oak	pony	goes	motor	toe
ocean	poem	almost	hotel	program

Say and Listen

Say each spelling word. Listen for the long o sound.

pony

Think and Sort

Look at the letters in each word. Think about how long o is spelled. Spell each word aloud.

Long o can be shown as /ō/. How many spelling patterns for /ō/ do you see?

1. Write the **thirteen** spelling words that have the *o* pattern, like *zero*.

2. Write the **five** spelling words that have the *oa* pattern, like *soap*.

3. Write the **two** spelling words that have the *oe* pattern, like *goes*.

1. **o** Words

_____   _____   _____

_____   _____   _____

_____   _____   _____

_____   _____   _____

_____

2. **oa** Words

_____   _____   _____

_____   _____

3. **oe** Words

_____   _____

Synonyms

Write the spelling word that is a synonym for each underlined word.

1. This <u>shoreline</u> is rocky and steep. _____

2. Wally <u>nearly</u> lost the race. _____

3. You must <u>follow</u> the rules to play. _____

4. The <u>sum</u> was more than fifty dollars. _____

5. Collin <u>travels</u> everywhere by bus. _____

6. The <u>sea</u> here is very blue. _____

7. Ramon had <u>just</u> five dollars left. _____

8. What is your favorite TV <u>show</u>? _____

Clues

Write the spelling word for each clue.

9. People wash with this. _____

10. Ten minus ten equals this. _____

11. This is a place for travelers to stay. _____

12. This is a small horse. _____

13. You can use this to make your hair neat. _____

14. This can get sore when you get a cold. _____

15. This can rhyme. _____

16. This is found on your foot. _____

17. This is a kind of tree. _____

18. This person trains athletes. _____

19. People wear these. _____

clothes	obey	coach	only	soap
total	throat	coast	comb	zero
oak	pony	goes	motor	toe
ocean	poem	almost	hotel	program

Proofreading

Proofread the journal entry below.
Use proofreading marks to correct five
spelling mistakes, three capitalization
mistakes, and two unnecessary words.

Proofreading Marks

◯ spell correctly
≡ capitalize
℟ take out

august 23

Our vacation at the coest has been so much fun.

our hotal room overlooks the ocean. Every morning

i run to to the beach for a swim. Today I stuck only

my toa in the water. It was too cold to swim. If it

doesn't warm up, Dad and I can still combe the the

beach for seashells. Our vacation is allmost

over, but it's been great.

Capital Letters

Use a capital letter to begin a person's first and last names.
Also use a capital letter to begin a title that goes with someone's name.

> **Mrs. Emerick** works in the school cafeteria.
>
> **Barry** and **Judy** both play sports.

The sentences below contain errors in capitalization. Write each sentence correctly.

1. laurie, amber, and keisha climbed to the top of the rope.

_____

_____

2. miss santucci said that the ropes feel as if they've been coated with soap.

_____

_____

3. On Tuesday we have basketball practice with mr. dowling.

_____

_____

4. rebecca and jamal keep track of the points that each team scores.

_____

_____

More Words with Long o

below	broke	own	shadow	slowly
elbow	though	explode	close	tomorrow
froze	knows	hollow	nose	stole
alone	pillow	chose	those	window

Say and Listen

Say each spelling word. Listen for the long o sound.

window

Think and Sort

Look at the letters in each word. Think about how long o is spelled. Spell each word aloud.

Long *o* can be shown as /ō/. How many spelling patterns for /ō/ do you see?

1. Write the **nine** spelling words that have the *o*-consonant-*e* pattern, like *broke*.

2. Write the **ten** spelling words that have the *ow* pattern, like *own*.

3. In the *ough* spelling pattern, the *g* and the *h* are silent. Write the **one** spelling word that has the *ough* pattern.

1. o-consonant-e Words

_____   _____   _____
_____   _____   _____
_____   _____   _____

2. ow Words

_____   _____   _____
_____   _____   _____
_____   _____   _____
_____

3. ough Word

_____

Antonyms

Write the spelling word that is an antonym of each underlined word.

1. The trunk of the oak tree was <u>solid</u>. _____

2. Dad <u>fixed</u> the new window. _____

3. Will you please <u>open</u> the door? _____

4. The car drove <u>quickly</u> past the house. _____

5. Aunt Cleo <u>thawed</u> the turkey. _____

6. Todd's apartment is <u>above</u> Yuri's. _____

7. Let's do the assignment <u>together</u>. _____

Analogies

Write the spelling word that completes each analogy.

8. *Eat* is to *ate* as *steal* is to _____.

9. *Board* is to *hard* as _____ is to *soft*.

10. *Leg* is to *knee* as *arm* is to _____.

11. *Sing* is to *sang* as *choose* is to _____.

12. *Yesterday* is to *past* as _____ is to *future*.

13. *Taste* is to *mouth* as *smell* is to _____.

14. *Says* is to *speaks* as _____ is to *understands*.

15. *Match* is to *burn* as *firecracker* is to _____.

16. *Dark* is to _____ as *smooth* is to *silk*.

17. *Hard* is to *difficult* as *have* is to _____.

18. *This* is to *that* as *these* is to _____.

19. *Also* is to *too* as _____ is to *however*.

below	broke	own	shadow	slowly
elbow	though	explode	close	tomorrow
froze	knows	hollow	nose	stole
alone	pillow	chose	those	window

Proofreading

Proofread this paragraph from the back cover of a book. Use proofreading marks to correct five spelling mistakes, three capitalization mistakes, and two punctuation mistakes.

Proofreading Marks

⬭ spell correctly

≡ capitalize

? add question mark

One night Mario sat at the desk in his room. suddenly he frose. Did something move near the windoe Mario felt as thogh his heart would explode. Then he laughed. It was only his shaddow. Mario laid his head on his pillow and sloly fell asleep. then a loud knock at the front door woke him. who would be visiting at this time of night This book will keep you reading as the mystery unfolds.

Quotation Marks

Place quotation marks around the exact words of a speaker. Sometimes these words are at the end of a sentence. Sometimes they are at the beginning.

> Robin said, **"I'm going to the dentist tomorrow."**
>
> **"Did you hear the fireworks explode?"** asked Raoul.

Rewrite the following sentences, using quotation marks correctly.

1. Bob said, The door to the cellar froze shut.

_____

_____

2. My model car broke! yelled Michael.

_____

_____

3. Is something living in that hollow log? asked Delia.

_____

_____

4. Zak yelled, Look at your shadow on the wall!

_____

_____

5. Stay close together as we hike, said the guide.

_____

_____

6. Randi asked, Is this pillow made of feathers?

_____

_____

Words with Short u

suddenly	touch	does	tough	subject
rough	brush	fudge	country	under
knuckle	couple	hunt	until	jungle
trouble	button	enough	double	hundred

Say and Listen

Say each spelling word. Listen for the short *u* sound.

jungle

Think and Sort

Look at the letters in each word. Think about how short *u* is spelled. Spell each word aloud.

Short *u* can be shown as /ŭ/. How many spelling patterns for /ŭ/ do you see?

1. Write the **eleven** spelling words that have the *u* pattern, like *hunt*.

2. Write the **eight** spelling words that have the *ou* pattern, lie *touch*.

3. Write the **one** spelling word that has the *oe* pattern.

1. **u** Words

_____   _____   _____
_____   _____   _____
_____   _____   _____
_____   _____

2. **ou** Words

_____   _____   _____
_____   _____   _____
_____   _____

3. **oe** Word

_____

Hink Pinks

Hink pinks are pairs of rhyming words that have a funny meaning.
Read each meaning. Write the spelling word that completes each hink pink.

1. grooming the hair in a hurry _____ rush
2. things made out of sandpaper _____ stuff
3. person choosing the best candy _____ judge
4. something that fastens fingers together _____ buckle
5. twins who always cause problems _____ trouble
6. a piece of meat that is hard to chew _____ stuff

What's the Answer?

Write the spelling word that answers each question.

7. Where are you looking when you look below something? _____
8. Which word is a form of *do*? _____
9. What is science or math an example of? _____
10. Which word means "up to the time of"? _____
11. What is Canada? _____
12. How many pennies are in a dollar? _____
13. What can you call two things? _____
14. What is another word for *difficulty*? _____
15. To which sense do fingers belong? _____
16. Which word means "to happen without warning"? _____
17. What do you have when you have all you need? _____
18. Where might you find a monkey? _____

suddenly	touch	does	tough	subject
rough	brush	fudge	country	under
knuckle	couple	hunt	until	jungle
trouble	button	enough	double	hundred

Proofreading

Proofread the e-mail below. Use proofreading marks to correct five spelling mistakes, three capitalization mistakes, and two punctuation mistakes.

Proofreading Marks

⬭ spell correctly

≡ capitalize

? add question mark

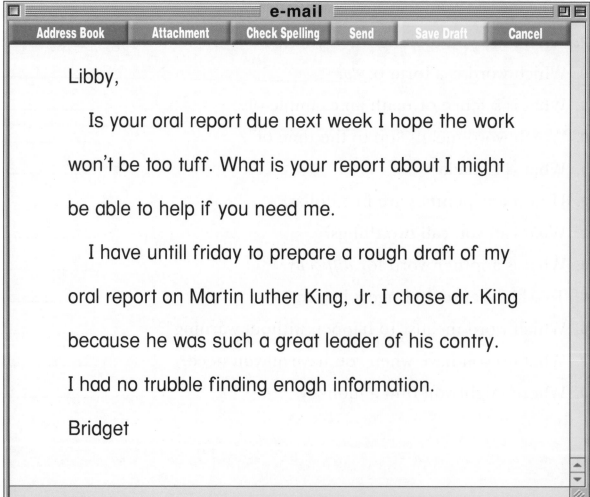

e-mail

Address Book | Attachment | Check Spelling | Send | Save Draft | Cancel

Libby,

Is your oral report due next week I hope the work won't be too tuff. What is your report about I might be able to help if you need me.

I have untill friday to prepare a rough draft of my oral report on Martin luther King, Jr. I chose dr. King because he was such a great leader of his contry.

I had no trubble finding enogh information.

Bridget

Dictionary Skills

Pronunciation

A dictionary lists the pronunciation for most entry words. A pronunciation is written with letters and special symbols. The symbols are a guide to the sounds of the word.

> **e·nough** (ĭ **nŭf** ′) *adj.* Sufficient to satisfy a need: *enough money for the movie.*

Write the following words in alphabetical order. Then look up each word in a dictionary and write its pronunciation beside it.

 couple

 rough

 hundred

 touch

1. _____   _____

2. _____   _____

3. _____   _____

4. _____   _____

Write the spelling word that each pronunciation represents. Then check your answers in a dictionary.

5. /tŭf/ _____

6. /kŭn′ trē/ _____

7. /nŭk′ əl/ _____

8. /sŭb′ jĭkt/ _____

9. /sŭd′n lē/ _____

10. /ĭ nŭf′/ _____

Contractions

that's	doesn't	aren't	I'm	shouldn't
she'd	isn't	we're	hadn't	let's
they've	wouldn't	you'd	haven't	couldn't
weren't	wasn't	don't	didn't	they'll

Say and Listen

Say the spelling words. Listen to the ending sounds.

Think and Sort

All of the spelling words are contractions. A **contraction** is a short way to write two or more words. The words are joined, but one or more letters are left out. An apostrophe (') is used in place of the missing letters. Look at each spelling word. Think about what the second word in the contraction is. Spell each word aloud.

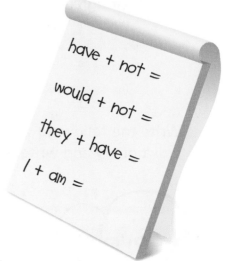

have + not =

would + not =

they + have =

I + am =

1. Write the **twelve** spelling words that are contractions formed with *not*, like *don't*.

2. Solve these contraction puzzles to write **eight** spelling words.

   a. I + am =   **b.** that + is =   **c.** we + are =   **d.** let + us =

   e. they + have =   **f.** you + would =   **g.** she + had =   **h.** they + will =

1. Contractions with **not**

_____   _____   _____

_____   _____   _____

_____   _____   _____

_____   _____   _____

2. Other Contractions

a. _____   b. _____   c. _____

d. _____   e. _____   f. _____

g. _____   h. _____

Rhymes

Write the spelling word that completes each sentence and rhymes with the underlined word.

1. When the bells <u>chime</u>, _____ going home.

2. The team made a <u>save</u>, and now _____ won!

3. She said that _____ <u>need</u> your help.

4. Soon _____ going to move <u>near</u> you.

5. Maybe _____ like to eat Chinese <u>food</u>.

6. After the sun <u>sets</u>, _____ take a walk.

7. Tomorrow _____ pick up the <u>mail</u>.

8. I guess _____ the last of the <u>hats</u>.

9. They _____ going to eat <u>burnt</u> toast.

Trading Places

Write the spelling word that can take the place of the underlined words in each sentence.

10. Wanda <u>did not</u> plan a fancy party.   _____

11. We <u>do not</u> want to argue.   _____

12. This pen <u>does not</u> leak.   _____

13. The bus <u>was not</u> on time today.   _____

14. The students <u>have not</u> eaten lunch yet.   _____

15. I <u>would not</u> try to trick you.   _____

16. You <u>should not</u> forget to brush your teeth.   _____

17. Broccoli <u>is not</u> my favorite vegetable.   _____

18. My parents <u>are not</u> able to go to the meeting.   _____

19. We <u>had not</u> seen the new baby before today.   _____

that's	doesn't	aren't	I'm	shouldn't
she'd	isn't	we're	hadn't	let's
they've	wouldn't	you'd	haven't	couldn't
weren't	wasn't	don't	didn't	they'll

Proofreading

Proofread this paragraph from a tall tale about Pecos Bill. Use proofreading marks to correct five spelling mistakes, three capitalization mistakes, and two punctuation mistakes.

Proofreading Marks

⬭ spell correctly
☰ capitalize
⊙ add period

Pecos Bill Gets Hungry

One day Pecos Bill awoke from a long nap He'd

been asleep for ten years! he was hungry, but he

did'nt have anything to eat. He culdnn't lasso a

bull, because he had lost his lasso. He'd have eaten

snakes, but there werent' any

"I know what I'll do," bill said. "Im going to boil

my boots. i will make boot stew!" And tha'ts

exactly what he did.

Adjectives

An adjective describes a noun or a pronoun
by telling which one, what kind, or how many.

Wouldn't you like a **tall** glass of **cold** lemonade?

The **large glass** pitcher shouldn't ever break.

Write each sentence below, correcting each misspelled word.
Then circle the adjective in each sentence.

1. The video store did'nt have the movie I wanted.

_____

2. Wer'e starting a computer club at school.

_____

3. Becca dosen't want the lead role in the play.

_____

4. Yo'ud better pack your long raincoat.

_____

5. The guide said shed meet us by the iron gate.

_____

LESSON **11**

doctor

dollar

knock

problem

hospital

swallow

watch

Words with Short o

Write the spelling word that completes each analogy.

1. *Ten* is to *dime* as *one hundred* is to

_____.

2. *Chef* is to *cook* as _____ is to *heal.*

3. *Answer* is to *question* as *solve* is to

_____.

4. *Thermometer* is to *temperature* as

_____ is to *time.*

5. *Lion* is to *cat* as _____ is to *bird.*

6. *Tap* is to *window* as _____ is to *door.*

7. *Teacher* is to *school* as *nurse* is to _____.

LESSON **12**

poem

ocean

clothes

throat

goes

Words with Long o

Write the spelling word that belongs in each group.

8. moves, travels, _____

9. outfits, garments, _____

10. verse, rhyme, _____

11. nose, mouth, _____

12. sea, river, _____

LESSON 13 — More Words with Long o

froze

knows

tomorrow

though

Write the spelling word for each clue.

13. If something got very cold, it did this. _____

14. This word sounds like *crow*. _____

15. This word means the same as *understands*.

_____

16. This is the day after today. _____

LESSON 14 — Words with Short u

jungle

suddenly

tough

trouble

does

Write the spelling word for each definition.

17. without warning _____

18. strong _____

19. causes to happen _____

20. land with thick tropical plants _____

21. difficulty _____

LESSON 15 — Contractions

weren't

doesn't

we're

they've

Write the spelling word that completes each sentence.

22. Marco _____ have enough money.

23. I know _____ going to be late.

24. I think _____ all gone home.

25. Why _____ we warned about the storm?

More Words with Short u

wonderful	front	cover	sponge	once
discover	other	month	nothing	become
among	brother	monkey	above	another
blood	money	done	stomach	won

Say and Listen

Say each spelling word. Listen for the short *u* sound.

monkey

Think and Sort

Look at the letters in each word. Think about how short *u* is spelled. Spell each word aloud.

Short *u* can be shown as /ŭ/. How many spelling patterns for /ŭ/ do you see?

1. Write the **sixteen** spelling words that have the *o* pattern, like *front*.

2. Write the **three** spelling words that have the *o*-consonant-*e* pattern, like *become*.

3. Write the **one** spelling word that has the *oo* pattern.

---

1. o Words

_____ _____ _____

_____ _____ _____

_____ _____ _____

_____ _____ _____

_____

2. o-consonant-e Words

_____ _____ _____

3. oo Word

_____

Antonyms

Write the spelling word that is an antonym of each word below.

1. below   _____

2. back   _____

3. unfinished   _____

4. lost   _____

5. horrible   _____

6. something   _____

Clues

Write the spelling word for each clue.

7. A girl is a sister, and a boy is this.   _____

8. Food is digested in this body part.   _____

9. This is one less than twice.   _____

10. This word means "to grow to be."   _____

11. Your heart pumps this through your body.   _____

12. This can soak up water.   _____

13. February is the shortest one.   _____

14. This word means "in the company of."   _____

15. This is a chimpanzee's cousin.   _____

16. This word completes the phrase "some ___ time."   _____

17. People use this to buy things.   _____

18. This means "one more."   _____

19. Do this to hide something.   _____

wonderful	front	cover	sponge	once
discover	other	month	nothing	become
among	brother	monkey	above	another
blood	money	done	stomach	won

Proofreading

Proofread the e-mail message below. Use proofreading marks to correct five spelling mistakes, three punctuation mistakes, and two unnecessary words.

Proofreading Marks

◯ spell correctly

⊙ add period

ℒ take out

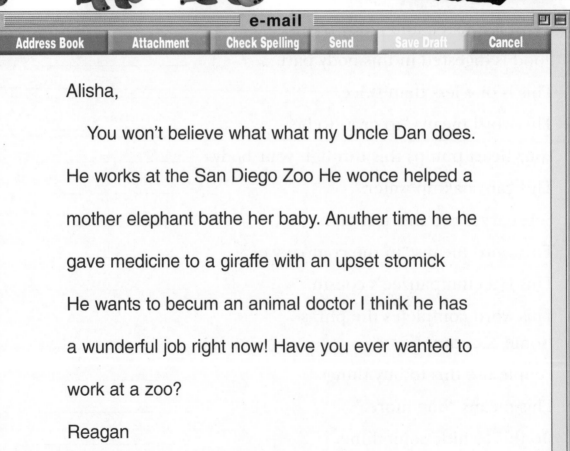

e-mail

| Address Book | Attachment | Check Spelling | Send | Save Draft | Cancel |

Alisha,

You won't believe what what my Uncle Dan does.

He works at the San Diego Zoo He wonce helped a

mother elephant bathe her baby. Anuther time he he

gave medicine to a giraffe with an upset stomick

He wants to becum an animal doctor I think he has

a wunderful job right now! Have you ever wanted to

work at a zoo?

Reagan

Dictionary Skills

Accented Syllables

A dictionary entry for a word usually shows how the word is said. The way a word is said is called its pronunciation. An accent mark (′) tells which syllable is spoken with more stress, or force. In some dictionaries, dark type also indicates the accented syllable.

Study the accent marks in each pair of pronunciations below. Underline the pronunciation that shows the accent mark on the correct syllable. Then write the spelling word.

1. /mŭn ē′/   /**mŭn**′ ē/   _____

2. /nŭth ĭng′/   /**nŭth**′ ĭng/   _____

3. /**brŭ**th′ ər/   /brŭth ər′/   _____

Some words have two accented syllables. The strongest accent is the primary accent: (′). The weaker accent is the secondary accent: (′).

Look at this pronunciation: /**yĕs**′ tər dā′/.

4. Write the syllable with the primary accent.   _____

5. Write the syllable with the secondary accent.   _____

6. Write the word correctly.   _____

Look at this pronunciation: /ăf′ tər **nōōn**′/

7. Write the syllable with the primary accent.   _____

8. Write the syllable with the secondary accent.   _____

9. Write the word correctly.   _____

Words with /ŏŏ/

wool	stood	brook	good-bye	pudding
understood	full	could	pull	yours
cooked	notebook	sugar	wolf	during
should	bush	wooden	would	woman

Say and Listen

Say each spelling word. Listen for the vowel sound you hear in *wool*.

wolf

Think and Sort

Look at the letters in each word. Think about how the vowel sound in *wool* is spelled. Spell each word aloud.

The vowel sound in *wool* can be shown as /ŏŏ/. How many spelling patterns for /ŏŏ/ do you see?

1. Write the **eight** spelling words that have the *oo* pattern, like *wool*.

2. Write the **six** spelling words that have the *u* pattern, like *full*.

3. Write the **four** spelling words that have the *ou* pattern, like *could*.

4. Write the **two** spelling words that have the *o* pattern, like *wolf*.

1. oo Words

_____   _____   _____

_____   _____   _____

_____   _____

2. u Words

_____   _____   _____

_____   _____   _____

3. ou Words

_____   _____   _____

_____

4. o Words

_____   _____

Synonyms

Write the spelling word that is a synonym for each word below.

1. tug _____

2. lady _____

3. while _____

4. stream _____

5. stuffed _____

6. shrub _____

If . . . Then

Write the spelling word that completes each sentence.

7. If you are cold, then put on a _____ sweater.

8. If you want dessert, then ask for cake or _____.

9. If you want to bake, then you may need _____ and flour.

10. If the meat is burnt, then it's been _____ too long.

11. If you need to write, then get a _____ and a pen.

12. If you hear a lone howl, then it might be a _____.

13. If it's not mine, then it may be _____.

14. If no one sat, then everyone _____.

15. If a bench is made from trees, then it's _____.

Rhymes

Use spelling words to complete the following poem.

16. I meant that I was able when I said, "I _____."

17. I meant that I really ought to when I said, "I _____."

18. I meant that I planned to do it when I said, "I _____."

19. I said it very clearly to be sure you _____!

wool	stood	brook	good-bye	pudding
understood	full	could	pull	yours
cooked	notebook	sugar	wolf	during
should	bush	wooden	would	woman

Proofreading

Proofread the book review paragraph below. Use proofreading marks to correct five spelling mistakes, three capitalization mistakes, and two punctuation mistakes.

Proofreading Marks

◯ spell correctly

≡ capitalize

⊙ add period

This book by Caroline lee is about her life as a young womon durring the late 1800s. on summer days she fished in a bruk on the farm In the fall she made maple suger from sap. In the spring she spun yarn from wull. She loved driving a buggy but hated churning butter. lee's book gives readers an interesting look at life in a simpler time

Language Connection

Capitalization

When the words *mother*, *father*, *mom*, and *dad* are used in place of names, they begin with a capital letter. When words such as *aunt*, *uncle*, and *doctor* are used as titles before a name, they begin with a capital letter. These words do not begin with a capital letter when they follow *a*, *an*, *the,* or a possessive word such as *my*, *your*, or *Bob's.*

> My uncle took **M**om and **A**unt **R**osa to the doctor's office.

The following sentences have errors in capitalization and spelling. Write each sentence correctly.

1. my Father cood not fix our broken lawnmower.

_____

2. uncle frank and dad stoud in line for baseball tickets.

_____

3. Danny's Father said gud-bye to dr. dominguez.

_____

4. We took a picture of mom and dad near the wuden bridge.

_____

5. My Aunt asked uncle Mike to share his recipe for bread puding.

_____

Words with /o͞o/ or /yo͞o/

goose	route	soup	two	new	fruit	truth
beautiful	balloon	knew	grew	cartoon	loose	choose
cougar	too	group	through	truly	shoot	

Say and Listen

Say each spelling word. Listen for the vowel sound you hear in *goose* and *beautiful*.

Think and Sort

cougar

The vowel sound in *goose* and *beautiful* can be shown as /o͞o/.
In *beautiful* and some other /o͞o/ words, a *y* is pronounced before the /o͞o/.

Look at the letters in each word. Think about how /o͞o/ or /yo͞o/ is spelled.
Spell each word aloud.

1. Write the **seven** spelling words that have the *oo* pattern, like *goose*.
2. Write the **three** spelling words that have the *ew* pattern, like *new*.
3. Write the **two** spelling words that have the *u* pattern, like *truth*.
4. Write the **five** spelling words that have the *ou* pattern, like *group*.
5. Write the **three** spelling words that have the *ui, o,* or *eau* pattern, like *fruit*.

---

1. oo Words

_____   _____   _____

_____   _____   _____

_____

2. ew Words

_____   _____   _____

3. u Words

_____   _____

4. ou Words

_____   _____   _____

_____   _____

5. ui, o, eau Words

_____   _____   _____

Homophones

Write the spelling word that is a homophone of each word below.

1. chute _____
2. knew _____
3. root _____
4. threw _____
5. two _____

Analogies

Write the spelling word that completes each analogy.

6. *Throw* is to *threw* as *know* is to _____.

7. *One* is to _____ as *A* is to *B*.

8. *Yes* is to *no* as *ugly* is to _____.

9. *Day* is to *night* as _____ is to *lie*.

10. *Bird* is to *flock* as *member* is to _____.

11. *Dirt* is to *flowerpot* as *air* is to _____.

12. *Light* is to *dark* as *tight* is to _____.

13. *Rabbit* is to *fur* as _____ is to *feather*.

14. *Apple* is to _____ as *spinach* is to *vegetable*.

15. *Afraid* is to *frightened* as *really* is to _____.

16. *Fork* is to *spaghetti* as *spoon* is to _____.

17. *Painter* is to *painting* as *cartoonist* is to _____.

18. *Smile* is to *grin* as _____ is to *pick*.

19. *Fly* is to *flew* as *grow* is to _____.

goose	balloon	group	new	loose
beautiful	too	two	cartoon	shoot
cougar	soup	grew	truly	truth
route	knew	through	fruit	choose

Proofreading

Proofread the paragraph below. Use proofreading marks to correct five spelling mistakes, three capitalization mistakes, and two punctuation mistakes.

Proofreading Marks
- ◯ spell correctly
- ≡ capitalize
- ⊙ add period

◯

The Canada Goose

the name of one kind of gouse might lead you

to think that it lives only in canada. The trooth

is that Canada geese live throughout North

America Many of these beootiful birds live close

◯ to people. Some live in parks Others live in ponds

close to neighborhoods. sometimes a groop of

Canada geese chooses to make its home on a

noo golf course!

◯

Dictionary Skills

Homophones

Words that sound the same but have different spellings and meanings are called homophones. If a word is a homophone, some dictionaries list the other homophones at the end of the entry.

> **through** (thro͞o) *prep.* **1.** In one side and out the opposite side of: *through the tunnel.* **2.** Among; in the midst of: *a road through the woods. These sound alike:* **through, threw.**

Use the homophones in the boxes to the right to answer the questions and complete the sentences below. Use a dictionary if you need to.

1. Which word is the opposite of *old*? _____

2. Which word is the past tense of *know*? _____

3. Which word names a number? _____

4. Which word means "also"? _____

5. Even though the quarterback was _____,

   he _____ all the plays.

6. When the other team made _____ points,

   the star player on our team scored points, _____.

Words with /ou/

loud	powerful	cloud	crowded	crown
counter	sour	towel	mouth	tower
somehow	crowd	ours	vowel	noun
hours	growl	south	shower	proud

Say and Listen

Say each spelling word. Listen for the vowel sound you hear in *loud.*

crown

Think and Sort

Look at the letters in each word. Think about how the vowel sound in *loud* is spelled. Spell each word aloud.

The vowel sound in *loud* can be shown as /ou/. How many spelling patterns for /ou/ do you see?

1. Write the **ten** spelling words that have the *ou* pattern, like *loud.*

2. Write the **ten** spelling words that have the *ow* pattern, like *crown.*

1. ou Words

_____   _____
_____   _____
_____   _____
_____   _____

2. ow Words

_____   _____
_____   _____
_____   _____
_____   _____
_____   _____

Classifying

Write the spelling word that belongs in each group.

1. robe, throne, _____

2. seconds, minutes, _____

3. eye, nose, _____

4. group, bunch, _____

5. sweet, salty, _____

6. noisy, booming, _____

7. drizzle, sprinkle, _____

8. bark, snarl, _____

9. east, north, _____

10. mighty, strong, _____

11. yours, theirs, _____

12. full, packed, _____

Partner Words

Complete each sentence by writing the spelling
word that goes with the underlined word.

13. Do you want to sit in a <u>booth</u> or at the _____?

14. <u>Someone</u> somewhere must rescue the princess _____.

15. The castle had a _____ and a <u>moat</u>.

16. I'll get you a _____ and a <u>washcloth</u>.

17. <u>Rain</u> will soon fall from that dark _____.

18. Jamal was <u>pleased</u> with and _____ of his sister's work.

19. You can choose a _____ or a <u>consonant</u>.

loud	powerful	cloud	crowded	crown
counter	sour	towel	mouth	tower
somehow	crowd	ours	vowel	noun
hours	growl	south	shower	proud

Proofreading

Proofread the journal entry below. Use proofreading marks to correct five spelling mistakes, three capitalization mistakes, and two missing words.

Proofreading Marks

◯ spell correctly
≡ capitalize
∧ add

october 21

I think writing amazing. a letter can stand for a

consonant or vowl. A group of letters can form

a word. The word might be a nown. At other

times it might be a verb. When words put

together in the right way, they somhow make

ideas come alive. Ideas are powrful.

i think that anyone would be prowd to be

a writer.

Language Connection

Quotation Marks

Use quotation marks around the exact words of a speaker. Capitalize the first word in the quotation.

> Chester asked, "What letter of the alphabet do you drink?"
> "I drink tea," Lester replied.

Write the following sentences. Use quotation marks and capital letters where needed. Spell the misspelled words correctly.

1. Julie said, a big croud always comes to see our team play.

_____

_____

2. they practice for three howrs each day, said Brian.

_____

_____

3. even when they're behind, they don't throw in the towle, said Chris.

_____

_____

4. let's give them a lowd cheer! shouted Ben.

_____

_____

Words with -ed or -ing

swimming	changed	caused	invited	studied	saving	carrying
asked	pleased	traded	tasted	copied	cried	writing
hoping	beginning	closing	jogging	dried	trying	

Say and Listen

Say the spelling words. Listen for the *-ed* and *-ing* endings.

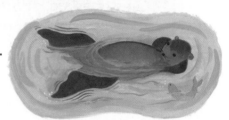

swimming

Think and Sort

A word from which other words are formed is called a **base word**. The spelling of some base words changes when *-ed* or *-ing* is added.

Look at the base word and the ending in each spelling word. Spell each word aloud.

1. Write the **three** spelling words that have no change to the base word, like *asked*.

2. Write the **ten** spelling words formed by dropping the final *e* before *-ed* or *-ing* is added, like *hoping*.

3. Write the **three** spelling words formed by doubling the final consonant before *-ing* is added, like *swimming*.

4. Write the **four** spelling words formed by changing the final *y* to *i* before *-ed* is added, like *studied*.

---

1. No Change to Base Word

_____ _____ _____

2. Final e Dropped

_____ _____ _____

_____ _____ _____

_____ _____ _____

_____

3. Final Consonant Doubled

_____ _____ _____

4. Final y Changed to i

_____ _____ _____

_____

Making Connections

Write the spelling word that goes with each person.

1. a mail carrier   _____

2. a lifeguard   _____

3. a runner   _____

4. a cook   _____

5. an author   _____

6. a baby   _____

7. a student   _____

If . . . Then

Write the spelling word that completes each sentence.

8. If Ramon exchanged baseball cards, then he _____ them.

9. If Carlos is putting money in a bank, then he's _____ it.

10. If Amad wishes for a bicycle, then he's _____ for one.

11. If Mr. Bina is shutting the door, then he's _____ it.

12. If Tyler begged for help, then he _____ for it.

13. If Dad liked the work, then he was _____ with it.

14. If Sarah imitated the star's hairdo, then she _____ it.

15. If Troy asked his friends to a party, then he _____ them.

16. If the sun is coming up, then it is _____ to be seen.

17. If Sam wiped away his tears, then he _____ them.

18. If Lamont is not the same, then he has _____.

19. If heavy rain loosened the mud, then it _____ a mud slide.

swimming	pleased	closing	studied	cried
asked	beginning	invited	copied	trying
hoping	caused	tasted	dried	carrying
changed	traded	jogging	saving	writing

Proofreading

Proofread the magazine article below. Use proofreading marks to correct five spelling mistakes, three capitalization mistakes, and two unnecessary words.

Proofreading Marks

◯ spell correctly

≡ capitalize

✄ take out

Rescue Ray

by Alexa Brown

Early one morning Ray Joseph was joging down Oak street. Suddenly he heard a crying sound high in a tree. Ray wondered what could could make such a sound. Then he saw a fluffy gray kitten.

Ray studied the tree. How would he get up there? meanwhile the kitten cryed louder and louder.

Saveing the kitten was not as hard as Ray thought. Soon a little girl ran up to him. "That's my theo," she said. Ray was pleazed that he had had been able to help.

Language Connection

Predicates

The predicate of a sentence tells what the subject of the sentence is or does.

> The little girl **skipped down the street.**

Write the predicate in each sentence.

1. My cousin Jenny invited me to come to her house last summer.

_____

2. Jenny and I swam in the pool each day.

_____

3. Jenny's brothers and I traded our favorite mystery stories.

_____

A predicate often contains a main verb and a helping verb. In the sentence below, *jogging* is the main verb. *Are* is the helping verb. The predicate begins with the helping verb.

> My friends **are jogging down the sidewalk.**

Write the predicate in each sentence. Circle the helping verb.

4. My famous grandmother is writing a book.

_____

5. Many people are reading her other books.

_____

unit 4 Review
Lessons 16-20

LESSON 16

discover

stomach

wonderful

once

blood

More Words with Short u

Write the spelling word that belongs in each group.

1. realize, notice, _____
2. sweat, tears, _____
3. fantastic, splendid, _____
4. lung, kidney, _____
5. never, twice, _____

LESSON 17

understood

during

sugar

should

woman

Words with /o͝o/

Write the spelling word that completes each analogy.

6. *Sour* is to *lemon* as *sweet* is to _____.
7. *Shall* is to _____ as *will* is to *would*.
8. *Run* is to *ran* as *understand* is to _____.
9. *Boy* is to *man* as *girl* is to _____.
10. *After* is to *following* as *throughout* is to _____.

LESSON 18

loose

truly

knew

through

fruit

two

beautiful

Words with /o͞o/ or /yo͞o/

Write the spelling word for each definition.

11. in one side and out the other _____
12. lovely to look at or listen to _____
13. the number between one and three _____
14. not tight _____
15. really, honestly _____

16. the juicy, seed-bearing part of a plant _____

17. had knowledge of _____

LESSON  19

loud

ours

crowd

Words with /ou/

Write the spelling word for each clue.

18. This develops when many people gather together.

_____

19. People cover their ears because a noise is this.

_____

20. If something belongs to us, it is this. _____

LESSON 20

asked

trying

hoping

beginning

copied

Words with -ed or -ing

Write the spelling word that completes each sentence.

21. "Can you write a better ending for your story?"
_____ Elsa's teacher.

22. "I have been _____ to do that," replied Elsa.

23. "I will read the story again from the _____."

24. Elsa _____ the story for her classmates to read.

25. Everyone was _____ that the ending was happy.

Words with /oi/

coin	destroy	loyal	join	voice
moisture	employ	royal	voyage	noise
enjoy	point	poison	loyalty	soybean
spoil	employer	soil	avoid	choice

Say and Listen

Say each spelling word. Listen for the vowel sound you hear in *coin*.

Think and Sort

Look at the letters in each word. Think about how the vowel sound in *coin* is spelled. Spell each word aloud.

royal

The vowel sound in *coin* can be shown as /oi/. How many spelling patterns for /oi/ do you see?

1. Write the **nine** spelling words that have the *oy* pattern, like *enjoy*.

2. Write the **eleven** spelling words that have the *oi* pattern, like *coin*.

1. oy Words

_____   _____   _____

_____   _____   _____

_____   _____   _____

2. oi Words

_____   _____   _____

_____   _____   _____

_____   _____   _____

_____   _____

Clues

Write the spelling word for each clue.

1. A ship can take you on this. _____

2. This is very harmful to living things. _____

3. You can dig in this. _____

4. Dogs are this to their masters. _____

5. When you can decide between two things, you have this. _____

6. You put this in a parking meter. _____

7. The end of an arrow has this. _____

8. An opera singer uses this. _____

9. People work for this person. _____

10. This plant has nutritious seeds. _____

11. Good friends share this with each other. _____

12. Water adds this to the air. _____

Antonyms

Complete each sentence by writing the spelling word that is an antonym of the underlined word.

13. They had to _____ the old house and build a new one.

14. We can separate or _____ these two wires.

15. Will the rain improve or _____ the crops?

16. Do you dislike your dancing lessons or _____ them?

17. Hector needs silence in order to study, not _____.

18. Will the store fire its workers and _____ new ones?

19. I will meet Laura at the store early and _____ the crowd.

coin	destroy	loyal	join	voice
moisture	employ	royal	voyage	noise
enjoy	point	poison	loyalty	soybean
spoil	employer	soil	avoid	choice

Proofreading

Proofread the letter below. Use proofreading marks to correct five spelling mistakes, three punctuation mistakes, and two unnecessary words.

Proofreading Marks

◯ spell correctly

⊙ add period

♄ take out

2840 Red Hill Avenue

Avon, OH 44011

July 17, 2003

Dear Trina,

Do you enjoi eating tomatoes? We have a great

crop this this year Too much rain can can spoyl the

crop Too little rain can destroi it, too This summer's

rains added just enough moischer to the soyle. I hope

to see you soon!

Your friend, Mark

Dictionary Skills

Parts of Speech

Some words can be used as more than one part of speech. The parts of speech include noun (*n.*), verb (*v.*), adjective (*adj.*), adverb (*adv.*), and preposition (*prep.*). Sometimes the parts of speech are listed within one dictionary entry.

poi·son (**poi′** zən) *n.* Any substance dangerous to life and health: *Bottles containing poison are clearly marked.* —*v.* **poi·soned, poi·son·ing.** To kill or harm with poison

At other times they are listed in two dictionary entries.

soil¹ (soil) *n.* The top layer of the earth's surface in which seeds are planted; dirt.

soil² (soil) *v.* **soiled, soil·ing.** To make or become dirty: *Jarrell soiled his white T-shirt.*

Use *soil* and *poison* to complete the sentences below. Then write *noun* or *verb* after each to tell how it is used in the sentence.

1. Grandma planted flower seeds in the _____.

_____

2. Some everyday cleaners can _____ your plants.

_____

3. Bottles containing _____ should be clearly marked.

_____

4. Don't _____ your clothes by digging in that dirt!

_____

Words with /ô/

pause	strong	cause	coffee	author	daughter	often
already	taught	because	bought	applaud	gone	office
brought	caught	wrong	thought	autumn	offer	

Say and Listen

Say each spelling word. Listen for the vowel sound you hear in *pause*.

autumn

Think and Sort

Look at the letters in each word. Think about how the vowel sound in *pause* is spelled. Spell each word aloud.

The vowel sound in *pause* can be shown as /ô/. How many spelling patterns for /ô/ do you see?

1. Write the **six** spelling words that have the *au* pattern, like *pause*.

2. Write the **seven** spelling words that have the *o* pattern, like *strong*.

3. Write the **three** spelling words that have the *augh* pattern, like *taught*.

4. Write the **three** spelling words that have the *ough* pattern, like *bought*.

5. Write the **one** spelling word that has the *a* pattern.

1. **au** Words

_____   _____   _____

_____   _____   _____

2. **o** Words

_____   _____   _____

_____   _____   _____

_____

3. **augh** Words

_____   _____   _____

4. **ough** Words

_____   _____   _____

5. **a** Word

_____

Classifying

Write the spelling word that belongs in each group.

1. instructed, showed, _____

2. clap, cheer, _____

3. powerful, mighty, _____

4. incorrect, mistaken, _____

5. purchased, paid, _____

6. believed, supposed, _____

7. spring, summer, _____

8. captured, grabbed, _____

9. writer, creator, _____

10. stop, rest, _____

11. parent, son, _____

12. delivered, carried, _____

13. give, present, _____

If . . . Then

Write the spelling word that completes each sentence.

14. If Mary jogs four days a week, then she does it _____.

15. If Kara's cat is not here, then it is _____.

16. If Jon is finished with his work, then he's _____ done.

17. If Mom has a special room for working, then she has an

    _____.

18. If James wins many races, then it's _____ he's a fast runner.

19. If a storm can bend trees, then it might _____ them to fall.

pause	taught	wrong	author	gone
already	caught	coffee	applaud	offer
brought	cause	bought	autumn	often
strong	because	thought	daughter	office

Proofreading

Proofread the note below. Use proofreading marks to correct five spelling mistakes, three capitalization mistakes, and two punctuation mistakes.

Proofreading Marks

◯ spell correctly

≡ capitalize

⊙ add period

August 8

Dear mr. Chang,

My mother and I went to the box ofice on main Street

and baught tickets for the play Sleeping Beauty. We want

to offer you and your daugter two of the tickets She will

enjoy the play becawse she offen reads fairy tales with

me when she comes over May i bring the tickets to

your house tomorrow afternoon?

Keisha

Titles

Underline the titles of books, plays, and movies.

> James and the Giant Peach
>
> The Wizard of Oz

Put quotation marks around the titles of stories, poems, and songs.

> "Hiawatha"   "On Top of Old Smoky"

Capitalize the first, last, and all other important words in a title.

> "Take Me Out to the Ball Game"   The Other Side of the Mountain

Titles are not written correctly in the following sentences, and words are misspelled. Write each sentence correctly.

1. My favorite book, "Harry Potter and the chamber of Secrets," is gonne.

_____

_____

2. Shel Silverstein is the awthor of the poem Recipe for a Hippopotamus Sandwich.

_____

_____

3. Our music teacher tawt us the words to the song city of New Orleans.

_____

_____

More Words with /ô/

lawn	score	dawn	before	important
toward	north	crawl	shore	orbit
straw	water	quart	chorus	report
morning	explore	warm	yawn	popcorn

Say and Listen

Say each spelling word. Listen for the vowel sound you hear in *lawn*.

popcorn

Think and Sort

Look at the letters in each word. Think about how the vowel sound in *lawn* is spelled. Spell each word aloud.

The vowel sound in *lawn* can be shown as /ô/. How many spelling patterns for /ô/ do you see?

1. Write the **five** spelling words that have the *aw* pattern, like *lawn*.

2. Write the **four** spelling words that have the *a* pattern, like *water*.

3. Write the **eleven** spelling words that have the *o* pattern, like *north*.

1. aw Words

_____   _____   _____

_____   _____

2. a Words

_____   _____   _____

_____

3. o Words

_____   _____   _____

_____   _____   _____

_____   _____   _____

_____   _____

Definitions

Write the spelling word for each definition. Use a dictionary if you need to.

1. a snack food made from heating corn _____
2. ground that is covered with grass _____
3. dried stalks of grain used for padding _____
4. having great worth or value _____
5. going in the direction of something _____
6. to open the mouth and take in air when tired _____
7. the path of one heavenly body around another _____
8. the number of points made by a player or a team _____
9. organized oral or written information _____
10. the first appearance of daylight _____

Analogies

Write the spelling word that completes each analogy.

11. *Evening* is to _____ as *night* is to *day*.
12. *After* is to _____ as *up* is to *down*.
13. *South* is to _____ as *east* is to *west*.
14. *Players* are to *team* as *singers* are to _____.
15. *Find* is to *discover* as *search* is to _____.
16. *Creep* is to _____ as *walk* is to *stroll*.
17. *Dry* is to *wet* as *cool* is to _____.
18. *Pint* is to _____ as *foot* is to *yard*.
19. *Desert* is to *sand* as *lake* is to _____.

lawn	score	dawn	before	important
toward	north	crawl	shore	orbit
straw	water	quart	chorus	report
morning	explore	warm	yawn	popcorn

Proofreading

Proofread the newspaper article below. Use proofreading marks to correct five spelling mistakes, three capitalization mistakes, and two missing words.

Proofreading Marks

◯ spell correctly
≡ capitalize
∧ add

The McHenry School Report

Class Trip Big Success

One morning last week, mr. Goodkind took his students to shore along Long Beach. The bus left at doun and headed narth. The students rushed off the bus with a choras of cheers. then they ran tord the water to explore a long stretch of sandy beach. Two students had never been to the beach befour. everyone had great time.

Language Connection

Commas

Use a comma between the city and the state and between the day and the year.

> Tipton, Indiana

> February 29, 2004

In a friendly letter, use a comma after the last word of the greeting and the closing.

> Dear Elliot,

> Your friend,

Add commas where they are needed in the letter below. Also, find the misspelled words and write them correctly on the lines provided.

> 2036 Circle Loop Drive
>
> Richmond VA 23294
>
> June 23 2003
>
> Dear Donna
>
> We're here at the lake, and it's really great. Our cabin is right on the shure. We have a view of the watter from every room.
>
> I plan to eksplore the woods around us tomorrow morening. It has been really waurm here. The weather repourt says the rest of the week will be sunny and hot. What perfect weather for a summer vacation!
>
> Yours truly
>
> Dawn

1. _____   2. _____   3. _____

4. _____   5. _____   6. _____

Words with /är/ or /âr/

sharp	their	heart	stairs	stares
share	where	careful	fair	scarf
they're	smart	square	air	apart
marbles	large	there	fare	alarm

marbles

Say and Listen

The spelling words for this lesson contain the /är/ and /âr/ sounds that you hear in *sharp* and *share.* Say the spelling words. Listen for the /är/ and /âr/ sounds.

Think and Sort

Look at the letters in each word. Think about how the /är/ or /âr/ sounds are spelled. Spell each word aloud. How many spelling patterns for /är/ and /âr/ do you see?

1. The /är/ sounds can be spelled *ar* or *ear.* Write the **eight** /är/ spelling words, like *sharp.* Circle the letters that spell /är/ in each word.

2. The /âr/ sounds can be spelled *are, air, ere, eir,* or *ey're.* Write the **twelve** /âr/ spelling words, like *share.* Circle the letters that spell /âr/ in each word.

1. /är/ Words

_____   _____   _____

_____   _____   _____

_____   _____

2. /âr/ Words

_____   _____   _____

_____   _____   _____

_____   _____   _____

_____   _____   _____

Classifying

Write the spelling word that belongs in each group.

1. wind, breeze, _____

2. thorny, pointed, _____

3. bell, siren, _____

4. hat, gloves, _____

5. bright, clever, _____

6. big, huge, _____

7. separated, in pieces, _____

8. slow, watchful, _____

9. triangle, rectangle, _____

10. give, divide, _____

11. jacks, checkers, _____

12. who, what, _____

Homophones

Complete each sentence with the spelling word that is a homophone of the underlined word.

13. Steven and Jake left _____ shoes over <u>there</u>.

14. The high <u>fare</u> for the plane trip is not _____.

15. Elena <u>stares</u> at the seven flights of _____.

16. The bus _____ to the <u>fair</u> was cheap.

17. <u>They're</u> waiting over _____ by the bench.

18. Today _____ bringing <u>their</u> projects to school.

19. Jess _____ at the ball as it bounces down the <u>stairs</u>.

sharp	their	heart	stairs	stares
share	where	careful	fair	scarf
they're	smart	square	air	apart
marbles	large	there	fare	alarm

Proofreading

Proofread the directions below. Use proofreading marks to correct five spelling mistakes, three capitalization mistakes, and two unnecessary words.

Proofreading Marks

◯ spell correctly

≡ capitalize

ℒ take out

How to Play Hide-and-Seek

Here's how you play hide-and-seek. first, cover

your your eyes with a skarf. Then tell everybody to

hide while you count to fifty. Be carful not to peek.

are you smeart enough to find them? Don't forget to

look under under the stairs. Remember to push larje

bushes apheart. Look until you find someone. then

that person's It and has to find someone.

Dictionary Skills

Pronunciation

A dictionary lists a pronunciation, or sound spelling, for most entry words. Special symbols are used to show the pronunciation. These symbols are listed in the pronunciation key.

stare (stâr) *v.* **stared, star·ing, stares.**
To look at with a steady gaze: *Jasmine stared at the famous movie star. These sound alike:* **stare, stair.**

Pronunciation Key

ă	pat	ŏ	pot	ŭ	cut
ā	pay	ō	toe	ûr	urge
âr	care	ô	paw, for	ə	about,
ä	father	oi	noise		item,
ĕ	pet	ŏŏ	took		edible,
ē	bee	ōō	boot		gallop,
ĭ	pit	ou	out		circus
ī	pie	th	thin	ər	butter
îr	deer	*th*	this		

Write the correct word for each pronunciation. Use a dictionary and the pronunciation key.

1. (wâr) _____

2. (härt) _____

3. (ə **lärm′**) _____

4. (âr) _____

5. (shärp) _____

6. (shâr) _____

7. (skärf) _____

8. (smärt) _____

9. (ə **pärt′**) _____

10. (**mär′** bəls) _____

11. (skwâr) _____

12. (**kâr′** fəl) _____

Plural and Possessive Words

children	cloud's	women's	sheep	wife's
men	women	child's	oxen	knives
shelves	feet	teeth	mice	wives
man's	woman's	children's	geese	men's

Say and Listen

Say each spelling word. Listen to the sounds in each word.

children

Think and Sort

Some of the spelling words are **plural nouns.** They name more than one person, place, or thing. The usual way to form the plural of a noun is to add *-s* or *-es.* The plural nouns in this lesson are not formed in that way. They are called **irregular plurals.**

The other spelling words show ownership. They are called **possessive nouns.** How do all of these words end?

Look at each spelling word. Spell each word aloud.

1. Write the **twelve** spelling words that are plural nouns, like *men.*

2. Write the **eight** spelling words that are possessive nouns, like *man's.*

1. Plural Nouns

_____ _____ _____

_____ _____ _____

_____ _____ _____

_____ _____ _____

2. Possessive Nouns

_____ _____ _____

_____ _____ _____

_____

Analogies

Write the spelling word that completes each analogy.

1. *Horses* are to *hay* as _____ are to *cheese.*
2. *Drawers* are to *dressers* as _____ are to *bookcases.*
3. *Alligators* are to *reptiles* as _____ are to *birds.*
4. *Kittens* are to *cats* as *lambs* are to _____.
5. *Lawnmowers* are to *grass* as _____ are to *food.*
6. *Fingers* are to *hands* as *toes* are to _____.
7. *Floors* are to *mop* as _____ are to *brush.*
8. *Mothers* are to *women* as *fathers* are to _____.
9. *Child* is to *children* as *ox* is to _____.
10. *Gentlemen* are to *men* as *ladies* are to _____.
11. *Ducklings* are to *ducks* as _____ are to *humans.*

Trading Places

Write the possessive word that can be used instead of the underlined words.

12. the shoes <u>belonging to the man</u>   the _____ shoes
13. the toy <u>belonging to the child</u>   the _____ toy
14. the parents <u>of the wife</u>   the _____ parents
15. the shape <u>of the cloud</u>   the _____ shape
16. the dresses <u>belonging to the women</u>   the _____ dresses
17. the books <u>belonging to the children</u>   the _____ books
18. the hands <u>of the men</u>   the _____ hands
19. the face <u>of the woman</u>   the _____ face

children	cloud's	women's	sheep	wife's
men	women	child's	oxen	knives
shelves	feet	teeth	mice	wives
man's	woman's	children's	geese	men's

Proofreading

Proofread the list below. Use proofreading marks to correct five spelling mistakes, three capitalization mistakes, and two unnecessary words.

Proofreading Marks

◯ spell correctly

≡ capitalize

℺ take out

Things to Do

1. Polish mother's knifs, forks, and spoons.

2. Help jacob build a pen for the gooses.

3. Find a mans' suit for for the school play.

4. Wash the kitchen shelfes.

5. Write a report on sheeps for Mr. rice's class.

6. See dr. Keith to to have my teeth cleaned.

Language Connection

Possessive Nouns

An apostrophe is used to show possession, or ownership.
Add 's to a singular noun to make it possessive.

> the boy's hat = the hat that belongs to the boy
>
> the child's toy = the toy that belongs to the child

Add only an apostrophe to a plural noun that ends in s.
Add 's to a plural noun that does not end in s.

> The boys' sleds are red.   The children's sleds are fast.

Complete each sentence with the correct word from the boxes.

1. This _____ car has broken down on the highway.

2. Those two _____ jog every morning along the lake.

3. These _____ gardens are large and beautiful.

4. The _____ all play together every day in the park.

5. Three _____ lunches were missing from the shelf.

6. One _____ jacket sleeve is ripped.

unit 5 review
Lessons 21-25

LESSON 21

loyal

choice

Words with /oi/

Complete each sentence by writing the spelling word that rhymes with the underlined word.

1. If you lose your <u>voice</u>, you have no _____ but to whisper.

2. The prince's _____ dog guarded the <u>royal</u> palace.

LESSON 22

autumn

daughter

wrong

often

bought

already

Words with /ô/

Write the spelling word for each clue.

3. Leaves fall off trees in this season. _____

4. If you are not right, you are this. _____

5. A parent's female child is this. _____

6. This means the same as purchased. _____

7. This means you've done something many times. _____

8. This means something has happened in the past.

_____

dawn

toward

explore

important

More Words with /ô/

Write the spelling word that completes each sentence.

9. The ocean is most beautiful at _____.

10. Kevin walked slowly _____ the frightened puppy.

11. You have an _____ decision to make.

12. Let's _____ those caves today.

marbles

heart

careful

square

stairs

where

their

they're

Words with /är/ or /âr/

Write the spelling word that completes each analogy.

13. *Dinner* is to *supper* as _____ are to *steps*.

14. *Hair* is to *hare* as *wear* is to _____.

15. *Mean* is to *cruel* as _____ is to *watchful*.

16. *Sphere* is to *circle* as *cube* is to _____.

17. *Brain* is to *think* as _____ is to *pump*.

18. *We have* is to *we've* as *they are* is to _____.

19. *Baseball* is to *sport* as _____ are to *game*.

20. *We* is to *our* as *they* is to _____.

geese

oxen

wives

wife's

men's

Plural and Possessive Words

Write the spelling word that belongs in each group.

21. ducks, swans, _____

22. husbands, children, _____

23. husband's, child's, _____

24. women's, children's, _____

25. mules, cows, _____

Words with /ûr/ or /îr/

curve	third	heard	germ	here
hear	dear	squirt	world	circle
clear	circus	early	cheer	earn
learn	skirt	birth	period	dirty

Say and Listen

The spelling words for this lesson contain the /ûr/ or /îr/ sounds that you hear in *curve* and *hear.* Say the spelling words. Listen for the /ûr/ and /îr/ sounds.

Think and Sort

Look at the letters in each word. Think about how the /ûr/ or /îr/ sounds are spelled. Spell each word aloud.

How many spelling patterns for /ûr/ and /îr/ do you see?

1. Write the **fourteen** spelling words that have the /ûr/ sounds, like *curve.* Circle the letters that spell /ûr/ in each word.

2. Write the **six** spelling words that have the /îr/ sounds, like *hear.* Circle the letters that spell /îr/ in each word.

circus

1. /ûr/ Words

_____   _____   _____

_____   _____   _____

_____   _____   _____

_____   _____   _____

_____   _____

2. /îr/ Words

_____   _____   _____

_____   _____   _____

Synonyms

Write the spelling word that is a synonym for each word.

1. bend _____
2. plain _____
3. yell _____
4. soiled _____

Analogies

Write the spelling word that completes each analogy.

5. *Continent* is to _____ as *county* is to *state.*

6. *Ending* is to *death* as *beginning* is to _____.

7. *Too* is to *two* as *deer* is to _____.

8. *Now* is to *then* as _____ is to *there.*

9. *Listened* is to _____ as *story* is to *tale.*

10. *Spend* is to _____ as *give* is to *get.*

11. *Speak* is to *mouth* as _____ is to *ear.*

12. *Door* is to *rectangle* as *plate* is to _____.

13. *Ask* is to *question mark* as *tell* is to _____.

14. *Two* is to *second* as *three* is to _____.

15. *Pour* is to *milk* as _____ is to *toothpaste.*

16. *Blouse* is to *top* as _____ is to *bottom.*

17. *School* is to _____ as *office* is to *work.*

18. *Sad* is to *happy* as *late* is to _____.

19. *Microscope* is to _____ as *telescope* is to *star.*

curve	third	heard	germ	here
hear	dear	squirt	world	circle
clear	circus	early	cheer	earn
learn	skirt	birth	period	dirty

Proofreading

Proofread the e-mail below. Use proofreading marks to correct five spelling mistakes, three capitalization mistakes, and two unnecessary words.

Proofreading Marks

○ spell correctly

≡ capitalize

Ϙ take out

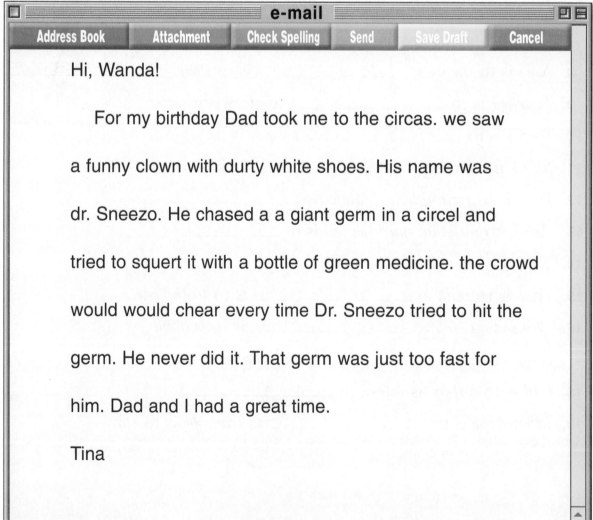

e-mail

| Address Book | Attachment | Check Spelling | Send | Save Draft | Cancel |

Hi, Wanda!

For my birthday Dad took me to the circas. we saw

a funny clown with durty white shoes. His name was

dr. Sneezo. He chased a a giant germ in a circel and

tried to squert it with a bottle of green medicine. the crowd

would would chear every time Dr. Sneezo tried to hit the

germ. He never did it. That germ was just too fast for

him. Dad and I had a great time.

Tina

Language Connection

Plurals

Plurals are words that name more than one thing. Most plurals are formed by adding *-s* or *-es* to the base word.

> To form the plural of most nouns, add *-s*.
>
> cheer + **s** = cheer**s**   circle + **s** = circle**s**
>
> If the noun ends in *s*, *x*, *ch*, *sh*, or *z*, add *-es*.
>
> fox + **es** = fox**es**   bus + **es** = bus**es**

Write the plural form of each word.

1. curve _____   **2.** birth _____

3. circus _____   **4.** brush _____

5. skirt _____   **6.** match _____

7. germ _____   **8.** box _____

9. world _____   **10.** animal_____

11. period _____   **12.** horse _____

13. circle _____   **14.** ax _____

15. branch _____   **16.** dress _____

17. cheer _____   **18.** glass _____

19. inch _____   **20.** buzz _____

Words with /ə/

together	wrinkle	summer	address	purple
animal	calendar	automobile	chapter	tickle
blizzard	special	dinosaur	whether	wander
simple	winter	Canada	whistle	United States of America

Say and Listen

Say the spelling words. Listen for the syllables that are not stressed.

automobile

Think and Sort

Most unstressed syllables have a weak vowel sound called **schwa**. It is shown as /ə/. Some words have one /ə/, and others have more than one.

Look at the letters in each word as you say each word again. Think about how /ə/ is spelled. Spell each word aloud. How many spelling patterns for /ə/ do you see?

1. Write the **fourteen** spelling words that have one /ə/ sound, like *address*. Circle the letter that spells /ə/.

2. Write the **six** spelling words that have more than one /ə/ sound, like *animal*. Circle the letters that spell /ə/.

1. Words with One /ə/

_____ _____ _____

_____ _____ _____

_____ _____ _____

_____ _____ _____

_____ _____

2. Words with More than One /ə/

_____ _____ _____

_____ _____ _____

Classifying

Write the spelling word that belongs in each group.

1. red, blue, _____

2. hurricane, tornado, _____

3. easy, plain, _____

4. crease, crumple, _____

5. name, _____, telephone number

6. roam, stray, _____

7. train, plane, _____

8. beast, creature, _____

Definitions

Write the spelling word for each definition. Use a dictionary if you need to.

9. at the same time _____

10. if _____

11. North American country containing fifty states _____

12. a main division of a book _____

13. the season between fall and spring _____

14. northernmost North American country _____

15. chart showing time by days, weeks, and months _____

16. not usual _____

17. the season between spring and fall _____

18. to touch lightly _____

19. to make a sound by forcing air through the lips _____

together	wrinkle	summer	address	purple
animal	calendar	automobile	chapter	tickle
blizzard	special	dinosaur	whether	wander
simple	winter	Canada	whistle	United States of America

Proofreading

Proofread the list below. Use proofreading marks to correct five spelling mistakes, three capitalization mistakes, and two unnecessary words.

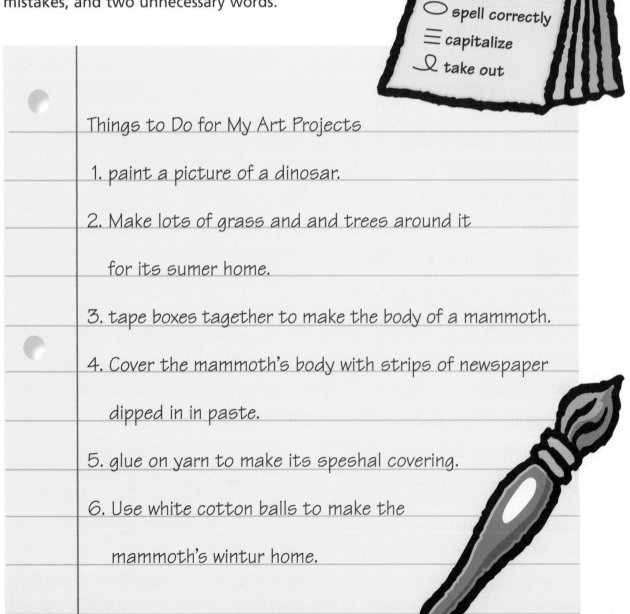

Proofreading Marks

◯ spell correctly
≡ capitalize
ℒ take out

Things to Do for My Art Projects

1. paint a picture of a dinosar.

2. Make lots of grass and and trees around it

    for its sumer home.

3. tape boxes tagether to make the body of a mammoth.

4. Cover the mammoth's body with strips of newspaper

    dipped in in paste.

5. glue on yarn to make its speshal covering.

6. Use white cotton balls to make the

    mammoth's wintur home.

Dictionary Skills

Accent Marks

Special symbols are often used in dictionaries to show the pronunciation of words. The schwa (ə) is a symbol for the weak vowel sound that occurs in unstressed syllables. The accent mark (′) is used to point out syllables that are spoken with more stress, or force. Some dictionaries also use dark type to show accented syllables.

Only one of the pronunciations in each pair below has the accent mark on the correct syllable. Circle the correct pronunciation and write the word. Check your answers in a dictionary.

1. /**blĭz**′ ərd/   /blĭz **ərd**′/
   _____

2. /**ăn**′əməl/   /ăn ə**məl**′/
   _____

3. /wĭs **əl**′/   /**wĭs**′ əl/
   _____

4. /tĭk **əl**′/   /**tĭk**′ əl/
   _____

5. /**sĭm**′ pəl/   /sĭm **pəl**′/
   _____

6. /**rĭng**′ kəl/   /rĭng **kəl**′/
   _____

7. /kăl **ən**′ dər/   /**kăl**′ən dər/
   _____

8. /**sŭm**′ ər/   /sŭm **ər**′/
   _____

9. /pûr **pəl**′/   /**pûr**′ pəl/
   _____

Compound Words

basketball	drugstore	upstairs	anything	downtown
cheeseburger	outside	inside	forever	without
countdown	everybody	nightmare	sometimes	everywhere
newspaper	birthday	afternoon	weekend	railroad

Say and Listen

Say each spelling word. Listen for the two shorter words in each word.

Think and Sort

All of the spelling words are compound words. In a **compound word**, two words are joined to form a new word. For example, *basket + ball = basketball.* Write the spelling word that is formed from each word pair below.

basketball

1. after + noon
2. any + thing
3. for + ever
4. some + times
5. with + out
6. every + body
7. basket + ball
8. count + down
9. in + side
10. out + side
11. night + mare
12. news + paper
13. up + stairs
14. drug + store
15. every + where
16. rail + road
17. week + end
18. birth + day
19. down + town
20. cheese + burger

1. _____
2. _____
3. _____
4. _____
5. _____
6. _____
7. _____
8. _____
9. _____
10. _____
11. _____
12. _____
13. _____
14. _____
15. _____
16. _____
17. _____
18. _____
19. _____
20. _____

Antonyms

Complete each sentence by writing the spelling word that is an antonym of the underlined word.

1. The museum is <u>uptown</u>, but the library is _____.
2. John likes eggs <u>with</u> salt but _____ pepper.
3. I went <u>downstairs</u> as Maria went _____.
4. Customers are _____, but a clerk is <u>nowhere</u> to be found.
5. We couldn't play <u>outside</u>, so we went _____.

Compound Words

Write the spelling word that can be formed by combining two words in each sentence.

6. Have you ever wished for a puppy? _____
7. The count began with ten and went down to zero. _____
8. We shop some of the times that we get together. _____
9. His birth occurred on the last day of June. _____
10. Our collie snatched the ball from the basket. _____
11. Selma wanted cheese on her burger. _____
12. Jill ran out and played on her side of the fence. _____
13. We looked at every part of the frog's body. _____
14. This unusual thing didn't come with any directions. _____
15. A rail fell off the fence and onto the road. _____
16. The pet store sells a special drug to kill fleas. _____
17. Most of the news in our paper is interesting. _____
18. We eat lunch after the clock chimes at noon. _____
19. The end of the week will be here soon. _____

basketball	drugstore	upstairs	anything	downtown
cheeseburger	outside	inside	forever	without
countdown	everybody	nightmare	sometimes	everywhere
newspaper	birthday	afternoon	weekend	railroad

Proofreading

Proofread the journal entry below. Use proofreading marks to correct five spelling mistakes, two capitalization mistakes, and three punctuation mistakes.

Proofreading Marks

◯ spell correctly

= capitalize

⊙ add period

march 10

I went to Jo's party last weakend. There were people everywhere. Everebody sang "Happy Birthday" to Jo Then her mom ran upstares and brought down a large box withowt a top What do you think Jo found inside, asleep on some newspaper? it was a little kitten. Jo had wanted a kitten more than anything else. I'll remember the look on her face fourever

meow

Capital Letters

Geographic names such as names of cities, states, bodies of water, mountains, and streets are capitalized.

> Boston   Utah   Goose Bay
> Swiss Alps   Main Street

The sentences below contain errors in capitalization and spelling. Write each sentence correctly.

1. The <u>Plain Dealer</u> is a noospaper from cleveland, ohio.

_____

2. The rialroad line was built across rollins street.

_____

3. Mr. Diaz spent the aftrnoon fishing on lake erie.

_____

4. We visited niagara falls on my burthday.

_____

5. Would you like to spend the weekind in the rocky mountains?

_____

6. Carly said she wanted to stay in carson city forevr.

_____

Abbreviations

Ave.	F	Hwy.	l	pt.
qt.	in.	gal.	mi.	C
Rd.	St.	yd.	c.	m
cm	ft.	km	Blvd.	Rte.

Say and Listen

Say the spelling word that each abbreviation stands for.

Think and Sort

All of the spelling words are abbreviations. An **abbreviation** is a shortened version of a word. Abbreviations used in street addresses and customary units of measure end with a period. Abbreviations of metric units of measurement and temperature scales do not.

qt.

1. Write the **six** abbreviations used in street addresses, like *Rte.*

2. Write the **twelve** abbreviations for units of measurement, like *qt.*

3. Write the **two** abbreviations for temperature scales, like *C.*

1. Street Addresses

_____ _____ _____

_____ _____ _____

2. Units of Measurement

_____ _____ _____

_____ _____ _____

_____ _____ _____

_____ _____ _____

3. Temperature Scales

_____ _____

Trading Places

Write the abbreviation that can be used instead of the word.

1. Fahrenheit _____
2. gallon _____
3. cup _____
4. yard _____
5. centimeter _____
6. quart _____
7. liter _____
8. Celsius _____
9. pint _____
10. mile _____
11. inch _____
12. kilometer _____
13. foot _____

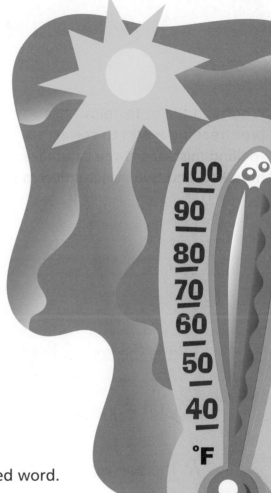

Clues

Write the spelling word for each underlined word.

14. 315 Rose <u>Boulevard</u> _____
15. <u>Route</u> 2, Box 56 _____
16. Box 1010, <u>Highway</u> 47 _____
17. 224 Main <u>Street</u> _____
18. 2067 Green <u>Road</u> _____
19. 1007 Bright <u>Avenue</u> _____

Ave.	F	Hwy.	l	pt.
qt.	in.	gal.	mi.	C
Rd.	St.	yd.	c.	m
cm	ft.	km	Blvd.	Rte.

Proofreading

Proofread the note below. Use proofreading marks to correct six spelling mistakes, three capitalization mistakes, and two punctuation mistakes.

Proofreading Marks

⬭ spell correctly

≡ capitalize

⊙ add period

Kyle,

I have the key to the trunk. You can come by today after school

and get it if you want to Here are the directions to my house.

At the corner of Shady Str. and third Av., turn left and go about

50 ft down the block. go past allen Rd and turn right onto Rte. 7.

Our house is 1 mle down the road. It is white with blue trim.

The key is under a flower pot about 1 yrd from the mailbox

Ryan

Language Connection

End Punctuation

Three different types of punctuation can be used at the end of a sentence. The period (.) is used for a sentence that tells something or gives commands. The question mark (?) is used for a sentence that asks a question. The exclamation point (!) is used for a sentence that shows excitement or strong feeling.

I like this shirt.

Move the car, please.

Where are you going?

Our team is the greatest!

The sentences below have mistakes in end punctuation and spelling. Write each sentence correctly.

1. My family wants to follow Rt 66 on a vacation

_____

2. Can you tell me how to get to Hway. 12

_____

3. The temperature was 106° Fr in the shade

_____

4. Jessica made 2 gall of lemonade

_____

5. Our family drove 100 mil today

_____

6. The store at 632 Rose Av belongs to my dad

_____

Words about the Universe

rotate	Pluto	Saturn	meteor	Neptune	revolve	Mars
gravity	solar system	universe	Earth	comet	Mercury	planets
Jupiter	galaxy	Venus	satellite	Uranus	constellation	

Say and Listen

Say each spelling word. Listen for
the number of syllables in each word.

solar system

Think and Sort

All of the spelling words are terms that people
use to write about the universe. One of the terms is a compound word.

1. Write the **two** spelling words that have one syllable, like *Mars*.
2. Write the **eight** spelling words that have two syllables, like *Sat-urn*.
3. Write the **eight** spelling words that have three syllables, like *Ju-pi-ter*.
4. Write the **one** spelling word that has four syllables.
5. Write the **one** spelling word that is written as two words. Divide each
   word into syllables.

1. One-syllable Words
_____ _____

2. Two-syllable Words
_____ _____ _____
_____ _____ _____
_____ _____

3. Three-syllable Words
_____ _____ _____
_____ _____ _____
_____ _____

4. Four-syllable Word   5. Compound Word
_____   _____

Clues

Write the spelling word for each clue.

1. planet closest to the sun _____

2. seventh planet from the sun _____

3. fourth planet; the "red" one _____

4. eighth planet; named for the Roman sea god _____

5. only planet that can support animal life _____

6. second planet; named for a Roman goddess _____

7. the planet with "rings" _____

8. planet farthest from the sun _____

9. fifth planet from the sun; the largest planet _____

What's the Answer?

Write a spelling word that answers each question.

10. What moves around the sun and has a long tail? _____

11. What falls through space toward Earth? _____

12. What word refers to everything in space? _____

13. What names a communications object that circles Earth? _____

14. The Big Dipper is an example of what? _____

15. Mars, Jupiter, and Venus are examples of what? _____

16. What do planets do as they travel around the sun? _____

17. What keeps us from falling off Earth? _____

18. What does Earth do as it spins on its axis? _____

19. What are the sun and all the planets called as a group? _____

rotate	solar system	Venus	Neptune	Mercury
gravity	galaxy	meteor	comet	constellation
Jupiter	Saturn	Earth	Uranus	Mars
Pluto	universe	satellite	revolve	planets

Proofreading

Proofread the following paragraph from a short story. Use proofreading marks to correct five spelling mistakes, two capitalization mistakes, and three missing words.

Proofreading Marks

◯ spell correctly

≡ capitalize

∧ add

After leaving Erth, Captain diego stopped on Mercurie, venus, and Mars. He had a close call when a metiore almost hit the spaceship. When we last heard from him, he heading for Pluto, at the far edge our solor system. He plans see the whole galaxy, maybe even the uneverse.

Dictionary Skills

Using the Spelling Table

A spelling table can help you find the spelling of a word in a dictionary. Suppose you are not sure how the first vowel sound in *comet* is spelled. You can use a spelling table to find the different spellings for the sound. First, find the pronunciation symbol for the sound. Then read the first spelling listed for /ŏ/, and look up *ca* in a dictionary. Look for each spelling in a dictionary until you find the correct one.

Sound	Spellings	Examples
/ŏ/	o a	d**o**ctor, w**a**sh

Write the correct spelling for each word. Use the Spelling Table on page 265 and a dictionary.

1. klĕnz _____

2. hōst _____

3. pēch _____

4. hôrd _____

5. **lär′** və _____

6. **bûr′** glər _____

7. skwŏd _____

8. bō **kā′** _____

unit 6 review
lessons 26-30

Lesson 26

circle
early
world
germ
clear
here
period
cheer

Words with /ûr/ or /îr/

Write the spelling word that belongs in each group.

1. Earth, globe, _____
2. bug, virus, _____
3. beginning, first, _____
4. square, triangle, _____
5. at this place, in this spot, _____
6. shout, yell, _____
7. comma, hyphen, _____
8. obvious, plain, _____

Lesson 27

whether
special
automobile
animal
wrinkle

Words with /ə/

Write the spelling word that completes each analogy.

9. *Drive* is to _____ as *fly* is to *plane*.
10. *Though* is to *however* as _____ is to *if*.
11. *Garden* is to *flower* as *zoo* is to _____.
12. *Crease* is to _____ as *flat* is to *level*.
13. *Unique* is to *common* as _____ is to *ordinary*.

LESSON 28

without

everywhere

birthday

Compound Words

Write the spelling word that completes each sentence.

14. If you don't have any assignments, you are _____ homework.

15. When something is in all places, it is _____.

16. When you become a year older, you celebrate your _____.

LESSON 29

Blvd.

in.

gal.

cm

F

Abbreviations

Write the spelling word that is the abbreviation for the underlined word in each phrase.

17. 12 <u>inches</u>   _____

18. 98° <u>Fahrenheit</u>   _____

19. 631 River <u>Boulevard</u>   _____

20. 3 <u>gallons</u>   _____

21. 5 <u>centimeters</u>   _____

LESSON 30

Mercury

satellite

gravity

constellation

Words About the Universe

Write the spelling word for each definition.

22. a heavenly body that revolves around a planet

_____

23. the force that causes objects to move toward the center of the Earth _____

24. the planet closest to the sun _____

25. a group of stars with a recognizable shape

_____

commonly misspelled words

about	every	myself	they
above	family	name	they're
across	favorite	nice	though
again	finally	now	through
a lot	first	once	today
always	friend	other	together
another	get	outside	tomorrow
beautiful	getting	party	too
because	goes	people	two
been	guess	play	until
before	happened	please	upon
beginning	have	pretty	very
believe	hear	read	want
birthday	here	really	went
bought	hospital	right	were
buy	house	said	we're
came	into	saw	when
children	it's	scared	where
come	know	school	with
cousin	little	sent	would
didn't	made	some	write
different	make	sometimes	writing
does	many	swimming	wrote
doesn't	might	their	your
enough	morning	there	you're

spelling table

Sound	Spellings	Examples
/ă/	a ai au	match, plaid, laugh
/ā/	a a_e ai ay ea ei eigh ey	April, chase, plain, day, break, reign, eight, obey
/ä/	a	father
/âr/	air are eir ere ey're	fair, share, their, there, they're
/b/	b bb	bus, rabbit
/ch/	ch tch t	child, match, picture
/d/	d dd	dish, address
/ě/	e ea ie ai ue	never, bread, friend, again, guess
/ē/	e e_e ea ee ei eo ey i i_e ie y	zebra, these, please, sweet, deceive, people, key, ski, police, cities, city
/f/	f ff gh	feet, offer, laugh
/g/	g gg	go, jogging
/h/	h wh	hope, who
/ĭ/	i a e ee u ui y	quick, package, secret, been, busy, building, gym
/ī/	i i_e ie igh eye uy y	child, life, die, night, eyesight, buy, dry
/îr/	er ear eer eir ere	period, hear, cheer, weird, here
/j/	j g dg	jog, tragic, edge
/k/	k c ck ch	keep, coast, package, chorus
/ks/	x	axle
/kw/	qu	squeeze
/l/	l ll	life, balloon
/m/	m mb mm	man, comb, swimming

Sound	Spellings	Examples
/n/	n kn nn	nose, knot, beginning
/ng/	n ng	monkey, anything
/ŏ/	o a	doctor, wash
/ō/	o o_e oa oe ow ou ough	zero, those, coach, toe, hollow, boulder, though
/oi/	oi oy	coin, royal
/ô/	o a au augh aw ough	strong, already, cause, taught, shawl, bought
/o͝o/	oo o ou u	wool, wolf, could, full
/o͞o/	oo ew u u_e ue ui o ou	shoot, grew, truly, tune, blue, fruit, two, soup
/ou/	ou ow	ours, towel
/p/	p pp	pay, happen
/r/	r rr wr	reply, hurry, wrinkle
/s/	s ss c	save, pass, fence
/sh/	sh s ce	shape, sugar, ocean
/t/	t tt ed	taste, button, thanked
/th/	th	that
/th/	th	thick
/ŭ/	u o o_e oe oo ou	brush, month, become, does, blood, touch
/ûr/	ur ir er ear ere or our	curve, third, germ, earn, were, world, flourish
/v/	v f	voice, of
/w/	w wh o	win, where, once
/y/	y	yawn
/yo͞o/	u_e ew eau	use, new, beautiful
/z/	z zz s	zebra, blizzard, trees
/ə/	a e i o u	special, often, family, together, surprise

Math
Skills

unit 1
working with whole numbers

Place Value to Thousands

Every **whole number** with four **digits** has a thousands, hundreds, tens, and ones place.

Th	H	T	O	Number
5,	7	4	6	= *5,746*

5 is in the thousands place. Its value is 5,000.	7 is in the hundreds place. Its value is 700.	4 is in the tens place. Its value is 40.	6 is in the ones place. Its value is 6.	
5,000 +	700 +	40 +	6	= 5,746

Write each number.

a
b
c

1. Th H T O
2, 5 6 1 = __2,561__

Th H T O
4, 7 3 9 = _____

Th H T O
6, 2 6 8 = _____

2. Th H T O
8, 0 9 1 = _____

Th H T O
5, 4 7 3 = _____

Th H T O
3, 5 0 2 = _____

3. Th H T O
6, 6 4 8 = _____

Th H T O
9, 7 2 2 = _____

Th H T O
2, 0 5 9 = _____

4. Th H T O
3, 5 4 1 = _____

Th H T O
1, 9 4 3 = _____

Th H T O
5, 5 4 0 = _____

Write each number.

5. 7 thousands   4 hundreds   5 tens   2 ones   = ___*7,452*___

6. 3 thousands   0 hundreds   9 tens   5 ones   = _____

7. 8 thousands   6 hundreds   2 tens   0 ones   = _____

Write the value of each underlined digit.

a
b
c

8. 8,6̲94   ___*600*___   6̲,324 _____   7,90̲4 _____

9. 5,03̲9 _____   7,3̲34 _____   9̲58 _____

10. 8̲,694 _____   6̲,157 _____   8,90̲4 _____

Place Value to Millions

A **place-value chart** can help you understand whole numbers. Each digit in a number has a value based on its place in the number.

The 6 is in the millions place.
Its value is 6 millions or 6,000,000.
The 2 is in the hundred-thousands place.
Its value is 2 hundred thousands or 200,000.
The 3 is in the tens place.
Its value is 3 tens or 30.

hundreds and millions	ten millions	millions	hundred thousands	ten thousands	thousands	hundreds	tens	ones
		6,	2	0	5,	7	3	4

Write each number in the place-value chart.

1. 2,395

2. 418,702

3. 20,091,576

4. 987

5. 13,820

6. 5,482,637

	hundreds and millions	ten millions	millions	hundred thousands	ten thousands	thousands	hundreds	tens	ones
1.						2,	3	9	5
2.									
3.									
4.									
5.									
6.									

Write the place name for the 4 in each number.

	a		b	
7.	251,349	_tens_	1,147,865	
8.	104,361,870		51,428	
9.	1,264		49,617,501	
10.	8,504,976		439,060	

Write the value of the underlined digit.

	a		b	
11.	121,7<u>6</u>4	_7 hundreds or 700_	<u>2</u>83,145,167	
12.	56,34<u>0</u>		2,<u>4</u>01,637	
13.	<u>3</u>,412,906		89<u>2</u>,465,182	
14.	196,3<u>5</u>8		41<u>0</u>,295	

Reading and Writing Numbers

We read and write the number in this place-value chart as: twelve thousand, forty-five.

The digit 1 means 1 ten thousand, or 10,000.
The digit 2 means 2 thousands, or 2,000.
The digit 0 means 0 hundreds, or 0.
The digit 4 means 4 tens, or 40.
The digit 5 means 5 ones, or 5.

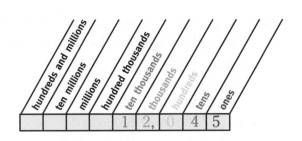

Notice that commas are used to separate the digits into groups of three. This helps make larger numbers easier to read.

Rewrite each number. Insert commas where needed.

	a	b	c
1.	345156 ___345,156___	10105 _____	221689 _____
2.	2970534 _____	369571 _____	50148 _____
3.	17652017 _____	5304602 _____	189360 _____

Write each number using digits. Insert commas where needed.

4. five hundred twenty-nine thousand, thirty-one___529,031___

5. seventy-six thousand, four hundred eleven _____

6. eight million, fifty thousand, two hundred _____

7. two thousand, three hundred seven _____

8. ninety-four thousand, six hundred fifty-five _____

Write each number using words. Insert commas where needed.

9. 23,880 ___twenty-three thousand, eight hundred eighty___

10. 730,604 _____

11. 19,042 _____

12. 5,208,000 _____

Comparing Whole Numbers

To compare two numbers, begin at the left.
Compare the digits in each place.

The symbol < means **is less than**.   *3 < 4*
The symbol > means **is greater than**.   *8 > 6*
The symbol = means **is equal to**.   *7 = 7*

Compare 47 and 29.

4	7	4 > 2, so
2	9	47 > 29.

Compare 123 and 98.

1	2 3	1 > 0, so
0	9 8	123 > 98.

Compare 326 and 351.

3	2	6	The hundreds digits are the same. Compare the tens digits.
3	5	1	

2 < 5, so 326 < 351.

Compare. Write <, >, or =.

	a		b		c
1.	72 ___>___ 27		83 _____ 90		39 _____ 44
	7 2		8 3		3 9
	2 7		9 0		4 4
2.	58 _____ 59		563 _____ 356		721 _____ 712
	5 8		5 6 3		7 2 1
	5 9		3 5 6		7 1 2
3.	619 _____ 640		468 _____ 468		226 _____ 220
4.	893 _____ 98		3,695 _____ 3,659		7,291 _____ 7,921
5.	35 _____ 35		62 _____ 92		100 _____ 99
6.	207 _____ 204		380 _____ 80		174 _____ 474

Problem-Solving Method: Use Logic

Mars and Venus are the closest planets to Earth. The **diameter,** or distance, across one of these three planets is 7,520 miles. The diameters of the other two planets are 4,222 miles and 7,926 miles. Mars is less than 7,000 miles across. Earth is larger than Venus. What are the diameters of Earth, Mars, and Venus?

Understand the problem.

• **What do you want to know?**
the diameters of Earth, Mars, and Venus

• **What information is given?**
The diameters of the three planets are 7,520, 4,222, and 7,926 miles.
Clue 1: Mars is less than 7,000 miles across.
Clue 2: Earth is larger than Venus.

Plan how to solve it.

• **What method can you use?**
You can use logic to find all the possibilities. Then you can organize the information in a table.

	7,520 miles	4,222 miles	7,926 miles
Mars	no	**YES**	no
Venus	**YES**	no	no
Earth	no	no	**YES**

Solve it.

• **How can you use this method to solve the problem?**
Since each planet has one diameter measurement, there can only be one YES in each row and column. Use the clues in the problem to fill out the table.

• **What is the answer?**
The diameter of Earth is 7,926 miles.
The diameter of Mars is 4,222 miles.
The diameter of Venus is 7,520 miles.

Look back and check your answer.

• **Is your answer reasonable?**
Clue 1: Mars is less than 7,000 miles across.
Check: 4,222 < 7,000
Clue 2: Earth is larger than Venus.
Check: 7,926 > 7,520

The answer matches the clues.
The answer is reasonable.

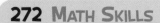

Use logic to solve each problem.

1. The three largest sharks in the world are the great white, basking, and whale shark. Their weights are 7,300 pounds, 46,297 pounds, and 32,000 pounds. Great whites are not the largest. Basking sharks weigh less than 30,000 pounds. How much does a great white shark weigh?

   Clue 1: Great whites are not the largest.

   Clue 2: Basking sharks weigh less than 30,000 pounds.

   great white shark _____

	7,300	46,297	32,000
White			
Basking			
Whale			

2. Wilt Chamberlain, Michael Jordan, and Kareem Abdul-Jabbar scored the most points in the NBA. Their records are 29,277 points, 38,387 points, and 31,419 points. Chamberlain scored more points than Jordan. Abdul-Jabbar scored more than 31,500 points. What are Chamberlain's, Jordan's, and Abdul-Jabbar's scoring records?

   Chamberlain _____

   Jordan _____

   Abdul-Jabbar _____

3. The "Beast," "Shivering Timbers," and "Mean Streak" are the world's longest wooden roller coasters. The longest is 7,400 feet. The other two are 5,384 feet and 5,427 feet long. "Mean Streak" is not the longest. The length of "Shivering Timbers" does not have a 4 in the hundreds place. How long is each roller coaster?

   "Beast" _____

   "Shivering Timbers" _____

   "Mean Streak" _____

Problem Solving

Write each number using words.

1. With a diameter of 88,840 miles, Jupiter is is the largest planet in our solar system.

   Answer _____

   _____

2. *Titanic* was one of the most expensive movies ever made. It cost $250,000,000.

   Answer _____

   _____

Write each number using digits.

3. Most people blink their eyes nine thousand, three hundred sixty-five times a day.

   Answer _____

4. The world's biggest ice cream sundae was made in 1988. It weighed forty-five thousand, one hundred eighty pounds.

   Answer _____

Compare. Write the greater number using digits.

5. A lion can weigh five hundred fifty-one pounds. A tiger can weigh six hundred sixty-one pounds.

   Answer _____

6. The Nile River is four thousand, one hundred forty-five miles long. The Amazon River is four thousand, seven miles long.

   Answer _____

Compare. Write the lesser number using words.

7. The average person in Japan watches 3,285 hours of television each year. The average person in the United States watches 2,555 hours each year.

   Answer _____

   _____

8. Yankee Stadium in New York can seat 55,070 people. Dodger Stadium in California can seat 56,000 people.

   Answer _____

   _____

Addition: Basic Facts

Add two numbers to find a **sum** or total.

Remember,
- adding 3 + 6 is the same as adding 6 + 3.
- adding 4 + 8 is the same as finding the sum of 4 and 8.

Add.

	a	b	c	d
1.	4 + 8 = __12__	6 + 1 = __7__	8 + 5 = __13__	9 + 0 = __9__
2.	7 + 2 = __9__	5 + 5 = __10__	3 + 7 = __10__	2 + 9 = __11__
3.	1 + 3 = __4__	0 + 4 = __4__	6 + 9 = __15__	4 + 3 = __7__
4.	8 + 2 = __10__	4 + 0 = __4__	9 + 4 = __13__	5 + 1 = __6__
5.	3 + 5 = __8__	2 + 6 = __8__	1 + 8 = __9__	4 + 4 = __8__
6.	9 + 7 = __16__	3 + 0 = __3__	5 + 6 = __11__	7 + 8 = __15__

Find the sums.

	a	b	c	d	e	f
7.	4 +6 10	6 +4 10	0 +7 7	4 +5 9	9 +8 17	5 +9 14
8.	6 +7 13	1 +9 10	8 +8 16	2 +4 8	6 +3 9	4 +7 11
9.	5 +2 7	9 +3 12	3 +8 11	7 +5 12	8 +6 14	2 +3 6

Addition

To add larger numbers, start with the digits in the ones place.

Find: 524 + 163

Add the ones.	Add the tens.	Add the hundreds.

H T O
 5 2 4
 +1 6 3
     7
	H T O
	 5 2 4
	 +1 6 3
	   8 7
		H T O
		 5 2 4
		 +1 6 3
		 6 8 7

Add.

	a	b	c	d	e
1.	T O 2 5 + 4 2 9	T O 4 6 + 3 4 9	T O 8 0 + 9 8 9	T O 5 +6 3 6 8	T O 9 2 + 7 99
2.	2 3 +3 4 67	5 3 +4 2 95	3 4 +5 5 89	4 0 +5 0 90	1 6 +7 3 89
3.	1 4 1 +8 2 0 961	4 0 0 +2 5 3 653	4 2 0 +3 0 7 727	3 6 0 +6 0 8 968	5 1 7 +1 6 2 679
4.	1 2 5 + 3 3 158	6 5 4 +2 2 5 879	1 2 +7 4 2 754	2 0 0 + 9 0 290	1 7 +5 4 2 559

Line up the digits. Then find the sums.

	a	b	c

5. 62 + 37 = 99

    62
   +37

234 + 52 = 286

  234
 +52

683 + 106 = 789

6. 74 + 805 = 879

  74
 +805

404 + 91 = 495

16 + 320 = 336

Regrouping in Addition

Add the ones first. **Regroup** when there are ten or more.

Find: 864 + 456

Add the ones. 4 + 6 = 10 ones	Add the tens. 1 + 6 + 5 = 12 tens	Add the hundreds. 1 + 8 + 4 = 13 hundreds
Th|H|T|O Regroup: | | |1 10 ones = |8|6|4 1 ten + |4|5|6 0 ones | | |0	Th|H|T|O Regroup: | |1|1 12 tens = |8|6|4 1 hundred + |4|5|6 2 tens | |2|0	Th|H|T|O Regroup: |1|1| 13 hundreds = |8|6|4 1 thousand + |4|5|6 3 hundreds 1,|3|2|0

Add.

	a	b	c	d	e
1.	T|O 1 3|6 +4|5 8|1	T|O 1 2|9 +3|2 6|1	T|O 1 3|5 +1|9 5|4	T|O 1 4|4 +1|8 6|2	T|O 1 2|6 +2|7 5|3
2.	1 1 4 9 +7 3 1 2 2	5 8 +6 6 1 1 4	7 4 +4 8 1 2 2	8 3 +4 9 1 3 2	4 9 +8 4 1 3 3
3.	1 4 5 7 + 2 8 4 8 5	6 0 8 + 4 9 6 5 7	4 9 +4 9 0 5 3 9	8 5 3 + 3 9 8 9 2	3 6 +3 8 2 4 1 8
4.	1 1 1 9 3 6 +4 8 7 1,4 2 3	7 9 5 +3 2 5 1,1 2 0	9 8 4 +3 2 6 1,2 1 0	1 1 8 2 7 +4 9 6 1,3 2 3	4 7 5 +7 1 5 1,1 9 0

Line up the digits. Then find the sums.

a   b   c

5. 32 + 29 = __61__   734 + 329 = __1,163__   347 + 82 = __429__

$$\begin{array}{r} 32 \\ +29 \\ \hline \end{array}$$

$$\begin{array}{r} 734 \\ +329 \\ \hline 1,163 \end{array}$$

Addition of Three Numbers

To add three numbers, use the same steps as when adding two numbers. Regroup as needed.

Find: 354 + 683 + 95

Add the ones.
Regroup.

Th	H	T	O
		1	
	3	5	4
	6	8	3
+		9	5
			2

Add the tens.
Regroup.

Th	H	T	O
	2	1	
	3	5	4
	6	8	3
+		9	5
		3	2

Add the hundreds.
Regroup.

Th	H	T	O
	2	1	
	3	5	4
	6	8	3
+		9	5
1,	1	3	2

Add.

	a	b	c	d	e
1.	H T O	T O	T O	T O	T O
	1				
	7 5	3 6	9 0	8 7	4 6
	2 0	1 4	8	6 6	9 2
	+ 3 8	+ 8 6	+ 3 5	+ 2	+ 3 8
	1 3 3				

2.	4 9 5	2 7 6	5 6 2	3 3 2	6 3 1
	8 3 0	5 3	1 7 3	4 8 6	2 9 3
	+ 1 8 5	+ 1 9 7	+ 3 4	+ 2 0 0	+ 3 8 0

3.	1 9 2	4 4 0	3 9 3	5 4	5 7 5
	7 0 6	1 7 8	6 4	3 1 7	4 2 8
	+ 5 8	+ 5 0 9	+ 2 7 0	+ 8 0 0	+ 3 5 8

Line up the digits. Then find the sums.

            a   *b*

4. 45 + 29 + 732 = _____   457 + 234 + 158 = _____

       45
       29
   + 732

Subtraction: Basic Facts

Subtract two numbers to find a **difference**.

Remember,
- $7 + 8 = 15$, so $15 - 8 = 7$.
- subtracting $9 - 4$ is the same as finding the difference of 9 and 4.

Subtract.

	a	b	c	d
1.	$15 - 8 = \underline{\quad 7 \quad}$	$8 - 4 = \underline{\qquad}$	$6 - 1 = \underline{\qquad}$	$7 - 0 = \underline{\qquad}$
2.	$11 - 9 = \underline{\qquad}$	$9 - 0 = \underline{\qquad}$	$13 - 5 = \underline{\qquad}$	$10 - 7 = \underline{\qquad}$
3.	$13 - 4 = \underline{\qquad}$	$15 - 9 = \underline{\qquad}$	$8 - 8 = \underline{\qquad}$	$11 - 6 = \underline{\qquad}$
4.	$3 - 0 = \underline{\qquad}$	$7 - 1 = \underline{\qquad}$	$10 - 5 = \underline{\qquad}$	$4 - 4 = \underline{\qquad}$
5.	$14 - 7 = \underline{\qquad}$	$8 - 2 = \underline{\qquad}$	$16 - 7 = \underline{\qquad}$	$8 - 5 = \underline{\qquad}$
6.	$10 - 2 = \underline{\qquad}$	$4 - 3 = \underline{\qquad}$	$9 - 2 = \underline{\qquad}$	$13 - 6 = \underline{\qquad}$

Find the differences.

	a	b	c	d	e	f
7.	$\begin{array}{r} 1\,1 \\ -\ \ 7 \\ \hline 4 \end{array}$	$\begin{array}{r} 9 \\ -3 \\ \hline \end{array}$	$\begin{array}{r} 6 \\ -0 \\ \hline \end{array}$	$\begin{array}{r} 1\,6 \\ -\ \ 8 \\ \hline \end{array}$	$\begin{array}{r} 1\,0 \\ -\ \ 9 \\ \hline \end{array}$	$\begin{array}{r} 1\,3 \\ -\ \ 7 \\ \hline \end{array}$
8.	$\begin{array}{r} 1\,4 \\ -\ \ 9 \\ \hline \end{array}$	$\begin{array}{r} 1\,3 \\ -\ \ 3 \\ \hline \end{array}$	$\begin{array}{r} 1\,7 \\ -\ \ 8 \\ \hline \end{array}$	$\begin{array}{r} 1\,4 \\ -\ \ 6 \\ \hline \end{array}$	$\begin{array}{r} 9 \\ -5 \\ \hline \end{array}$	$\begin{array}{r} 1\,1 \\ -\ \ 8 \\ \hline \end{array}$
9.	$\begin{array}{r} 1\,5 \\ -\ \ 9 \\ \hline \end{array}$	$\begin{array}{r} 8 \\ -1 \\ \hline \end{array}$	$\begin{array}{r} 1\,8 \\ -\ \ 9 \\ \hline \end{array}$	$\begin{array}{r} 5 \\ -4 \\ \hline \end{array}$	$\begin{array}{r} 5 \\ -0 \\ \hline \end{array}$	$\begin{array}{r} 1\,2 \\ -\ \ 6 \\ \hline \end{array}$

Subtraction

To subtract, start with the digits in the ones place.

Find: 587 − 234

	Subtract the ones.	Subtract the tens.	Subtract the hundreds.
	H T O	H T O	H T O
	5 8 7	5 8 7	5 8 7
	− 2 3 4	− 2 3 4	− 2 3 4
	3	5 3	3 5 3

Subtract.

	a	b	c	d	e
1.	T O	T O	T O	T O	T O
	2 9	7 8	4 5	5 9	3 6
	− 6	− 8	− 2	− 7	− 5
	2 3				

2.	8 8	4 9	7 0	3 5	5 7
	− 7 1	− 3 5	− 3 0	− 1 4	− 2 2

3.	7 7 9	9 0 0	8 6 8	4 5 9	9 8 7
	− 3 4 4	− 4 0 0	− 3 3	− 1 2 5	− 7 5 3

4.	8 4 9	8 9 2	7 6 4	2 3 8	6 3 8
	− 5 0 0	− 3 5 1	− 6 1 0	− 1 5	− 2 0 4

Line up the digits. Then find the differences.

	a	b	c

5. 77 − 42 = _____   954 − 630 = _____   375 − 53 = _____

      77
   − 42
   ‾‾‾

6. 485 − 60 = _____   753 − 13 = _____   879 − 21 = _____

Regrouping in Subtraction

Start with the digits in the ones place. Regroup as needed.

Find: 630 − 248

630 has no ones.
Regroup 3 tens 0 ones
as 2 tens 10 ones.
Subtract the ones.

```
  H | T | O
    | 2 | 10
  6 | 3̸ | 0̸
 -2 | 4 | 8
    |   | 2
```

Not enough tens.
Regroup 6 hundreds 2 tens
as 5 hundreds 12 tens.
Subtract the tens.

```
  H | T  | O
     | 12 |
   5 | 2̸  | 10
   6̸ | 3̸  | 0̸
  -2 | 4  | 8
     | 8  | 2
```

Subtract the hundreds.

```
  H | T  | O
     | 12 |
   5 | 2̸  | 10
   6̸ | 3̸  | 0̸
  -2 | 4  | 8
   3 | 8  | 2
```

Subtract.

	a	b	c	d	e
1.	T O 6 13 7̸ 3̸ −3 9 3 4	T O 8 5 −5 9	T O 6 6 −1 8	T O 9 3 −8 5	T O 4 0 −2 7
2.	9 2 −5 9	5 1 −3 2	7 0 −4 7	8 2 − 5	6 3 −2 4
3.	1 1 0 − 3 4	1 5 1 − 7 6	1 2 3 − 4 5	9 2 2 −6 7 4	5 3 0 −2 8 0
4.	7 4 3 −3 6 5	9 2 0 −1 8 8	8 1 8 −4 9 2	6 3 2 −1 5 2	4 7 5 −2 8 6

Line up the digits. Then find the differences.

	a	b	c
5.	96 − 19 = _____ 96 −19	375 − 89 = _____	863 − 675 = _____

Regrouping Twice in Subtraction

Sometimes you may have to regroup twice before you subtract.

Find: 503 − 234

<table>
<tr><td>Not enough ones or tens. Regroup the hundreds.</td><td>Regroup the tens.</td><td>Subtract the ones.</td><td>Subtract the tens.</td><td>Subtract the hundreds.</td></tr>
<tr>
<td>

H | T | O

4 | 10 |

5̶ | 0̶ | 3

− 2 | 3 | 4

</td>
<td>

H | T | O

    9 |

4 | 1̶0̶ | 13

5̶ | 0̶ | 3̶

− 2 | 3 | 4

</td>
<td>

H | T | O

    9 |

4 | 1̶0̶ | 13

5̶ | 0̶ | 3̶

− 2 | 3 | 4

       9

</td>
<td>

H | T | O

    9 |

4 | 1̶0̶ | 13

5̶ | 0̶ | 3̶

− 2 | 3 | 4

   6 | 9

</td>
<td>

H | T | O

    9 |

4 | 1̶0̶ | 13

5̶ | 0̶ | 3̶

− 2 | 3 | 4

2 | 6 | 9

</td>
</tr>
</table>

Subtract.

	a	b	c	d	e
1.	3̶1̶8̶ − 299 = 19 (with regrouping marks 10, 2 0̶ 18)	604 − 459	425 − 237	303 − 64	234 − 178
2.	507 − 149	804 − 326	473 − 86	312 − 235	901 − 357
3.	600 − 124	434 − 265	700 − 570	831 − 75	921 − 738

Line up the digits. Then find the differences.

	a	b	c
4.	301 − 25 = _____	423 − 236 = _____	300 − 142 = _____

    301
−   25

Addition and Subtraction

Sometimes you need to regroup, but sometimes you do not need to regroup.

Find: 612 + 182

No need to regroup.

```
  H | T | O
    |   |
  6 | 1 | 2
+ 1 | 8 | 2
  7 | 9 | 4
```

Find: 612 − 182

Not enough tens.
Regroup the hundreds.

```
     5 | 11 |
  H  | T | O
  6̷  | 1̷ | 2
− 1  | 8 | 2
  4  | 3 | 0
```

Add. Regroup if needed.

	a	b	c	d	e
1.	1 6 2 + 6 5 1 8 1 3	2 7 6 + 1 9 8	3 6 7 + 5 2 6	3 5 6 + 4 3 2	1 5 7 + 2 5 9
2.	3 0 5 + 4 8 2	5 4 9 + 2 6 3	4 6 1 + 3 0 7	8 6 4 + 2 0 9	6 4 2 + 3 5 7

Subtract. Regroup if needed.

	a	b	c	d	e
3.	3 8 9 − 1 4 9 2 4 0	4 0 3 − 1 5 2	9 5 8 − 7 2 4	1 6 4 − 1 5 7	8 4 3 − 6 2 1
4.	5 7 5 − 4 0 8	9 8 0 − 7 3 2	4 9 7 − 1 3 4	8 0 3 − 2 4 6	6 0 0 − 3 9 2

Line up the digits. Then find the sums or differences.

a	b	c
5. 751 + 324 = _____	675 + 587 = _____	308 − 156 = _____

```
  751
+ 324
```

Estimation by Rounding Numbers

Rounded numbers tell **approximately** how many. You can use a number line to help you **round** numbers.

Remember, when a number is halfway, always round the number up.

Round 375 to the nearest ten.

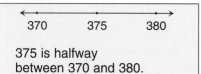

375 is halfway between 370 and 380. So, 375 rounds up to 380.

Round 492 to the nearest hundred.

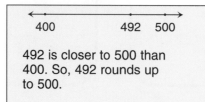

492 is closer to 500 than 400. So, 492 rounds up to 500.

Round 4,120 to the nearest thousand.

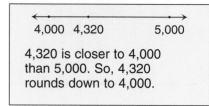

4,320 is closer to 4,000 than 5,000. So, 4,320 rounds down to 4,000.

Round to the nearest ten.

	a	b	c	d
1.	523 _520_	742 _____	258 _____	449 _____
2.	215 _____	869 _____	337 _____	611 _____
3.	876 _____	734 _____	925 _____	862 _____

Round to the nearest hundred.

	a	b	c	d
4.	834 _800_	658 _____	175 _____	717 _____
5.	250 _____	542 _____	326 _____	491 _____
6.	923 _____	789 _____	864 _____	123 _____

Round to the nearest thousand.

	a	b	c	d
7.	1,754 _2,000_	3,958 _____	4,586 _____	9,214 _____
8.	3,621 _____	8,450 _____	6,425 _____	1,642 _____
9.	7,521 _____	1,844 _____	2,453 _____	5,361 _____

Estimation of Sums

To **estimate** a sum, first round each number to the same place value.
Then add the rounded numbers.

Estimate: 64 + 37

Round each number to the same place value. Add.

$$\begin{array}{r} 6\ 4 \rightarrow\ 6\ 0 \\ +3\ 7 \rightarrow +4\ 0 \\ \hline 1\ 0\ 0 \end{array}$$

Estimate: 474 + 127

Round each number to the same place value. Add.

$$\begin{array}{r} 4\ 7\ 4 \rightarrow\ 5\ 0\ 0 \\ +1\ 2\ 7 \rightarrow +1\ 0\ 0 \\ \hline 6\ 0\ 0 \end{array}$$

Estimate the sums.

	a	b	c	d
1.	$\begin{array}{r} 3\ 4 \rightarrow\ 30 \\ +1\ 9 \rightarrow +20 \\ \hline 50 \end{array}$	$\begin{array}{r} 6\ 5 \rightarrow \\ +9\ 2 \rightarrow \\ \hline \end{array}$	$\begin{array}{r} 4\ 9 \rightarrow \\ +6\ 8 \rightarrow \\ \hline \end{array}$	$\begin{array}{r} 5\ 3 \rightarrow \\ +2\ 1 \rightarrow \\ \hline \end{array}$
2.	$\begin{array}{r} 7\ 7 \rightarrow \\ +1\ 4 \rightarrow \\ \hline \end{array}$	$\begin{array}{r} 2\ 9 \rightarrow \\ +6\ 8 \rightarrow \\ \hline \end{array}$	$\begin{array}{r} 5\ 7 \rightarrow \\ +2\ 3 \rightarrow \\ \hline \end{array}$	$\begin{array}{r} 9\ 4 \rightarrow \\ +8\ 1 \rightarrow \\ \hline \end{array}$
3.	$\begin{array}{r} 6\ 3\ 5 \rightarrow \\ +1\ 5\ 4 \rightarrow \\ \hline \end{array}$	$\begin{array}{r} 1\ 7\ 8 \rightarrow \\ +4\ 8\ 2 \rightarrow \\ \hline \end{array}$	$\begin{array}{r} 2\ 9\ 7 \rightarrow \\ +5\ 1\ 4 \rightarrow \\ \hline \end{array}$	$\begin{array}{r} 7\ 8\ 2 \rightarrow \\ +3\ 4\ 1 \rightarrow \\ \hline \end{array}$
4.	$\begin{array}{r} 4\ 1\ 4 \rightarrow \\ +3\ 0\ 8 \rightarrow \\ \hline \end{array}$	$\begin{array}{r} 8\ 5\ 3 \rightarrow \\ +5\ 4\ 6 \rightarrow \\ \hline \end{array}$	$\begin{array}{r} 6\ 7\ 1 \rightarrow \\ +7\ 9\ 3 \rightarrow \\ \hline \end{array}$	$\begin{array}{r} 3\ 2\ 5 \rightarrow \\ +2\ 3\ 0 \rightarrow \\ \hline \end{array}$

Line up the digits. Then estimate the sums.

	a	b	c
5.	$46 + 74 =$ _____	$356 + 198 =$ _____	$518 + 732 =$ _____

$$\begin{array}{r} 46 \rightarrow\ 50 \\ +74 \rightarrow +70 \\ \hline \end{array}$$

Estimation of Differences

To estimate a difference, first round each number to the same place value.
Then subtract the rounded numbers.

Remember, when a number is halfway, always round up.

Estimate: 87 − 19

Round each number to the
same place value. Subtract.

$$
\begin{array}{r}
8\ 7 \rightarrow\ \ 9\ 0 \\
-1\ 9 \rightarrow -2\ 0 \\
\hline
7\ 0
\end{array}
$$

Estimate: 387 − 219

Round each number to the
same place value. Subtract.

$$
\begin{array}{r}
3\ 8\ 7 \rightarrow\ \ 4\ 0\ 0 \\
-2\ 1\ 9 \rightarrow -2\ 0\ 0 \\
\hline
2\ 0\ 0
\end{array}
$$

Estimate the differences.

	a	b	c	d
1.	$\begin{array}{r} 5\ 7 \rightarrow\ \ 60 \\ -3\ 8 \rightarrow -40 \\ \hline 20 \end{array}$	$\begin{array}{r} 5\ 8 \rightarrow \\ -4\ 6 \rightarrow \\ \hline \end{array}$	$\begin{array}{r} 9\ 1 \rightarrow \\ -6\ 2 \rightarrow \\ \hline \end{array}$	$\begin{array}{r} 8\ 3 \rightarrow \\ -6\ 7 \rightarrow \\ \hline \end{array}$
2.	$\begin{array}{r} 7\ 2 \rightarrow \\ -6\ 4 \rightarrow \\ \hline \end{array}$	$\begin{array}{r} 8\ 6 \rightarrow \\ -1\ 5 \rightarrow \\ \hline \end{array}$	$\begin{array}{r} 5\ 3 \rightarrow \\ -\ \ 9 \rightarrow \\ \hline \end{array}$	$\begin{array}{r} 9\ 6 \rightarrow \\ -3\ 3 \rightarrow \\ \hline \end{array}$
3.	$\begin{array}{r} 5\ 4\ 3 \rightarrow \\ -2\ 6\ 4 \rightarrow \\ \hline \end{array}$	$\begin{array}{r} 7\ 5\ 6 \rightarrow \\ -1\ 7\ 9 \rightarrow \\ \hline \end{array}$	$\begin{array}{r} 4\ 3\ 5 \rightarrow \\ -3\ 4\ 8 \rightarrow \\ \hline \end{array}$	$\begin{array}{r} 6\ 4\ 7 \rightarrow \\ -2\ 5\ 3 \rightarrow \\ \hline \end{array}$
4.	$\begin{array}{r} 7\ 3\ 6 \rightarrow \\ -5\ 7\ 6 \rightarrow \\ \hline \end{array}$	$\begin{array}{r} 3\ 5\ 2 \rightarrow \\ -1\ 6\ 4 \rightarrow \\ \hline \end{array}$	$\begin{array}{r} 7\ 4\ 9 \rightarrow \\ -1\ 8\ 5 \rightarrow \\ \hline \end{array}$	$\begin{array}{r} 9\ 1\ 8 \rightarrow \\ -3\ 2\ 9 \rightarrow \\ \hline \end{array}$

Line up the digits. Then estimate the differences.

	a	b	c
5.	92 − 38 = _____	872 − 419 = _____	624 − 336 = _____

$$
\begin{array}{r}
92 \rightarrow\ \ 90 \\
-38 \rightarrow -40 \\
\hline
\end{array}
$$

Problem Solving Method: Identify Extra Information

The tallest building in the United States is the Sears Tower in Chicago, Illinois. It is 1,454 feet tall and has 110 stories. The Empire State Building in New York City has 102 stories. How many more stories does the Sears Tower have than the Empire State Building?

Understand the problem.

- **What do you want to know?**
  how many more stories the Sears Tower has than the Empire State Building

Plan how to solve it.

- **What method can you use?**
  You can identify extra information that is not needed to solve the problem.

Solve it.

- **How can you use this method to solve the problem?**
  Reread the problem. Cross out any unnecessary facts. Then you can focus on the needed facts to solve the problem.

> ~~The tallest building in the United States is the~~ Sears Tower ~~in Chicago, Illinois. It is 1,454 feet tall and~~ has 110 stories. The Empire State Building ~~in New York City~~ has 102 stories. How many more stories does the Sears Tower have than the Empire State Building?

- **What is the answer?**
  110 − 102 = **8**
  The Sears Tower has 8 more stories than the Empire State Building.

Look back and check your answer.

- **Is your answer reasonable?**
  You can check subtraction with addition.

$$\begin{array}{r} 110 \\ -102 \\ \hline 8 \end{array} \qquad \begin{array}{r} 102 \\ +8 \\ \hline 110 \end{array}$$

The sum checks.
The answer is reasonable.

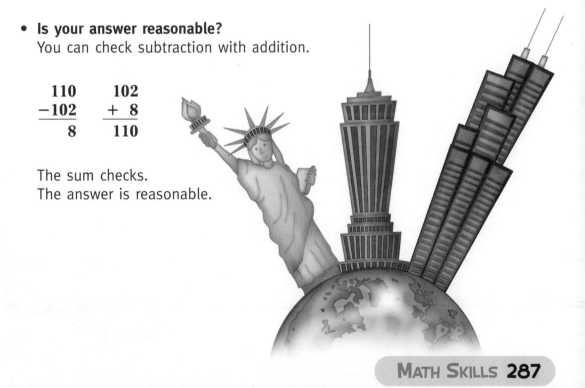

In each problem, cross out the extra information. Then solve the problem.

1. Tyrone drove 512 miles on a two-day trip. He went 55 miles per hour. The first day, he drove 305 miles. How many miles did he drive on the second day?

   Answer _____

2. Vicky worked 25 hours last week and earned $175. This week she worked 28 hours and earned $196. How much money did she earn altogether?

   Answer _____

3. There were 271 events in the 1996 Summer Olympic Games. The United States won 44 gold, 32 silver, and 25 bronze medals. How many medals did the United States win in all?

   Answer _____

4. In a vote for favorite ice-cream flavor, chocolate got 659 votes. Vanilla got 781 votes, and 246 people voted for strawberry. How many more people voted for chocolate than for strawberry?

   Answer _____

5. One Earth year is about 365 days. One year on Mercury is 88 days. On Mars, a year is 687 days. How much shorter is a year on Mercury than on Earth?

   Answer _____

6. A tiger can run 35 miles per hour and sleeps 11 hours a day. A house cat can run 30 miles per hour and sleeps 15 hours a day. How many more hours a day does a house cat sleep than a tiger?

   Answer _____

7. Kelly's web site got 129 hits on Friday and 240 hits on Saturday. Tom's web site got 175 hits on Friday and 192 hits on Saturday. How many hits did their sites get altogether on Friday?

   Answer _____

UNIT 1 Review

Write the place name for the 7 in each number.

	a		*b*
1. 36,712	_____	175,689	_____
2. 1,247,953	_____	17,652,810	_____

Write the value of the underlined digit.

	a		*b*
3. 18,5̲63	_____	1,3̲57,942	_____
4. 9̲46,358	_____	2,587,4̲61	_____

Write each number using digits. Insert commas where needed.

5. nineteen thousand, two hundred six _____

6. four hundred eleven thousand, thirty-five _____

7. two million, six hundred fifty-eight thousand _____

8. seven hundred twenty-three thousand, one hundred four _____

Compare. Write <, >, or =.

	a		*b*		*c*
9. 185	_____ 158	37	_____ 37	78	_____ 780
10. 465	_____ 455	1,274	_____ 1,724	3,690	_____ 3,960

Round to the nearest ten.

	a	*b*	*c*
11. 452	_____	265 _____	139 _____

Round to the nearest hundred.

	a	*b*	*c*
12. 578	_____	364 _____	941 _____

Round to the nearest thousand.

	a	*b*	*c*
13. 5,648	_____	4,250 _____	9,461 _____

Add.

	a	b	c	d	e
14.	5 4 1 +2 3 8	4 1 6 +4 0 2	1 7 4 +3 8 8	5 1 8 + 9 5	9 4 3 + 8 9
15.	3 9 5 +2 8 4	1 9 9 + 6 8	7 5 2 +1 4 9	3 5 4 +4 0 3	8 6 5 +2 3 9

Subtract.

	a	b	c	d	e
16.	7 4 8 − 2 6	3 1 3 −1 0 8	5 1 0 −3 4 6	8 0 1 −5 2 8	4 0 0 −3 1 7
17.	9 8 5 −2 5 4	5 1 6 −2 3 8	6 4 3 − 9 9	7 9 6 −2 8 4	3 0 6 −2 9 8

Estimate the sum or difference.

	a	b	c	d
18.	7 3 → +1 9 →	8 9 8 → +3 5 6 →	8 4 → −3 6 →	9 2 7 → −6 3 2 →
19.	2 8 6 → − 8 9 →	4 5 3 → +1 7 5 →	7 5 0 → −3 2 2 →	4 1 2 → +6 4 5 →

Line up the digits. Then add or subtract.

	a	b
20.	47 + 514 + 56 = _____	304 + 819 + 275 = _____
21.	95 − 47 = _____	508 − 372 = _____
22.	736 − 679 = _____	145 + 536 + 75 = _____

UNIT 1 Review

Use logic to solve each problem.

23. Three of baseball's top run scorers are Babe Ruth, Ty Cobb, and Willie Mays. Their records are 2,062 runs, 2,245 runs, and 2,174 runs. Mays scored the least. Ruth scored less than Cobb. How many runs did each of the three players score?

Babe Ruth _____

Ty Cobb _____

Willie Mays _____

24. The Mississippi, Yukon, and Missouri are the longest rivers in the United States. Their lengths are 2,315 miles, 1,979 miles, and 2,348 miles. The length of the Yukon does not have 3 hundreds. The Missouri is not the longest. What is the length of each river?

Mississippi River _____

Yukon River _____

Missouri River _____

In each problem, cross out the extra information. Then solve the problem.

25. There are 435 representatives and 100 senators in Congress. Sentors serve 6-year terms and representatives serve 2-year terms. How many members are in Congress altogether?

Answer _____

26. A person who weighs 100 pounds on Earth would weigh 254 pounds on Jupiter and 38 pounds on Mars. What is the difference between the weight on Earth and the weight on Mars?

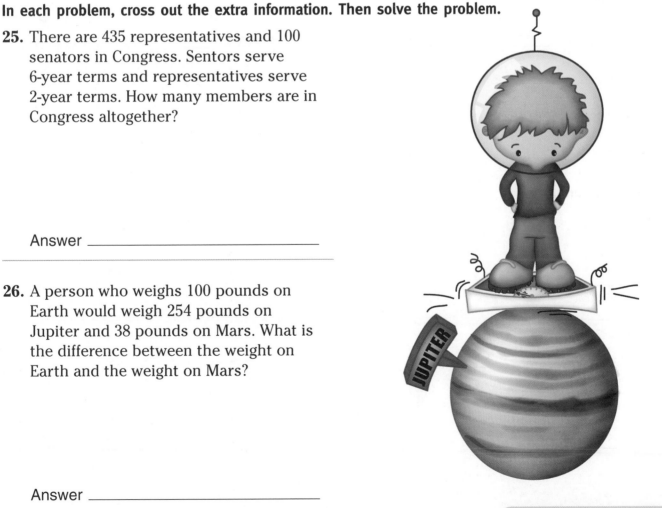

Answer _____

unit 2
multiplication and division facts

Multiplication Facts Through 5

Multiply two numbers to find a **product**.
Multiplication is a short way to do addition.
4 groups of stars with 3 stars in each group
is 12 stars altogether.

We say: 4 times **3** is **12**.
We think: **3 + 3 + 3 + 3 = 12**
We write: **4 × 3 = 12** or 4

$$\begin{array}{r} 4 \\ \times\,3 \\ \hline 12 \end{array}$$

Remember,

- multiplying **4 × 5** is the same as multiplying **5 × 4**.
- multiplying **3 × 2** is the same as finding the product of **3** and **2**.

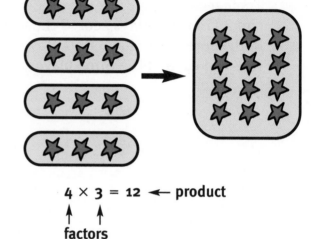

4 × 3 = 12 ← product
↑ ↑
factors

Multiply.

	a	b	c	d
1.	$6 \times 4 = \underline{\quad 24 \quad}$	$7 \times 2 = \underline{\qquad}$	$5 \times 5 = \underline{\qquad}$	$5 \times 3 = \underline{\qquad}$
2.	$3 \times 2 = \underline{\qquad}$	$2 \times 8 = \underline{\qquad}$	$8 \times 3 = \underline{\qquad}$	$0 \times 3 = \underline{\qquad}$
3.	$9 \times 3 = \underline{\qquad}$	$4 \times 4 = \underline{\qquad}$	$1 \times 6 = \underline{\qquad}$	$8 \times 1 = \underline{\qquad}$
4.	$2 \times 2 = \underline{\qquad}$	$2 \times 6 = \underline{\qquad}$	$9 \times 2 = \underline{\qquad}$	$8 \times 5 = \underline{\qquad}$

Find the products.

	a	b	c	d	e	f
5.	$\begin{array}{r} 6 \\ \times\,5 \\ \hline 30 \end{array}$	$\begin{array}{r} 5 \\ \times\,3 \\ \hline \end{array}$	$\begin{array}{r} 7 \\ \times\,2 \\ \hline \end{array}$	$\begin{array}{r} 2 \\ \times\,7 \\ \hline \end{array}$	$\begin{array}{r} 9 \\ \times\,1 \\ \hline \end{array}$	$\begin{array}{r} 6 \\ \times\,2 \\ \hline \end{array}$
6.	$\begin{array}{r} 7 \\ \times\,4 \\ \hline \end{array}$	$\begin{array}{r} 5 \\ \times\,8 \\ \hline \end{array}$	$\begin{array}{r} 3 \\ \times\,9 \\ \hline \end{array}$	$\begin{array}{r} 4 \\ \times\,2 \\ \hline \end{array}$	$\begin{array}{r} 3 \\ \times\,3 \\ \hline \end{array}$	$\begin{array}{r} 8 \\ \times\,4 \\ \hline \end{array}$
7.	$\begin{array}{r} 1 \\ \times\,5 \\ \hline \end{array}$	$\begin{array}{r} 5 \\ \times\,4 \\ \hline \end{array}$	$\begin{array}{r} 6 \\ \times\,3 \\ \hline \end{array}$	$\begin{array}{r} 8 \\ \times\,2 \\ \hline \end{array}$	$\begin{array}{r} 9 \\ \times\,5 \\ \hline \end{array}$	$\begin{array}{r} 4 \\ \times\,0 \\ \hline \end{array}$

Multiplication Facts for 6 and 7

Find: 6 × 7

| 6
×7 | **Say:** 6 times 7 is 42.
Think: 7 + 7 + 7 + 7 + 7 + 7 = 42 | **Write:** 6
× 7
42 or 6 × 7 = 42
or 7 × 6 = 42 |

Multiply.

	a	b	c	d	e	f
1.	1 × 6 6	2 × 6	3 × 6	4 × 6	5 × 6	6 × 6
2.	7 × 6	8 × 6	9 × 6	6 × 5	6 × 3	6 × 4

Find: 7 × 8

| 7
×8 | **Say:** 7 times 8 is 56.
Think: 8 + 8 + 8 + 8 + 8 + 8 + 8 = 56 | **Write:** 7
× 8
56 or 7 × 8 = 56
or 8 × 7 = 56 |

Find the products.

	a	b	c
3.	$7 \times 5 =$ _____	$7 \times 8 =$ _____	$7 \times 7 =$ _____
4.	$7 \times 4 =$ _____	$7 \times 1 =$ _____	$7 \times 6 =$ _____
5.	$7 \times 0 =$ _____	$7 \times 9 =$ _____	$7 \times 3 =$ _____

Multiplication Facts for 8 and 9

Find: 8×9

$\begin{array}{r} 9 \\ \times 8 \\ \hline \end{array}$ **Say:** 8 times 9 is 72.
Think: $9 + 9 + 9 + 9 + 9 + 9 + 9 + 9 = 72$

Write: $\begin{array}{r} 9 \\ \times 8 \\ \hline 72 \end{array}$ or $9 \times 8 = 72$
or $8 \times 9 = 72$

Multiply.

	a	b	c	d	e	f
1.	$\begin{array}{r} 3 \\ \times 8 \\ \hline 24 \end{array}$	$\begin{array}{r} 4 \\ \times 8 \\ \hline \end{array}$	$\begin{array}{r} 1 \\ \times 8 \\ \hline \end{array}$	$\begin{array}{r} 5 \\ \times 8 \\ \hline \end{array}$	$\begin{array}{r} 6 \\ \times 8 \\ \hline \end{array}$	$\begin{array}{r} 2 \\ \times 8 \\ \hline \end{array}$
2.	$\begin{array}{r} 7 \\ \times 8 \\ \hline \end{array}$	$\begin{array}{r} 9 \\ \times 8 \\ \hline \end{array}$	$\begin{array}{r} 0 \\ \times 8 \\ \hline \end{array}$	$\begin{array}{r} 8 \\ \times 5 \\ \hline \end{array}$	$\begin{array}{r} 8 \\ \times 7 \\ \hline \end{array}$	$\begin{array}{r} 8 \\ \times 4 \\ \hline \end{array}$
3.	$\begin{array}{r} 8 \\ \times 3 \\ \hline \end{array}$	$\begin{array}{r} 8 \\ \times 9 \\ \hline \end{array}$	$\begin{array}{r} 8 \\ \times 6 \\ \hline \end{array}$	$\begin{array}{r} 8 \\ \times 8 \\ \hline \end{array}$	$\begin{array}{r} 8 \\ \times 1 \\ \hline \end{array}$	$\begin{array}{r} 8 \\ \times 2 \\ \hline \end{array}$

Find: 9×9

$\begin{array}{r} 9 \\ \times 9 \\ \hline \end{array}$ **Say:** 9 times 9 is 81.
Think: $9 + 9 + 9 + 9 + 9 + 9 + 9 + 9 + 9 = 81$

Write: $\begin{array}{r} 9 \\ \times 9 \\ \hline 81 \end{array}$ or $9 \times 9 = 81$

Find the products.

	a	b	c
4.	$9 \times 5 = \underline{\quad 45 \quad}$	$9 \times 6 = \underline{\quad\quad}$	$9 \times 4 = \underline{\quad\quad}$
5.	$9 \times 1 = \underline{\quad\quad}$	$9 \times 8 = \underline{\quad\quad}$	$9 \times 0 = \underline{\quad\quad}$
6.	$9 \times 9 = \underline{\quad\quad}$	$9 \times 3 = \underline{\quad\quad}$	$9 \times 7 = \underline{\quad\quad}$

Multiplication Table

All the basic multiplication facts are given in the table shown.

×	1	2	3	4	5	6	7	8	9
1	1	2	3	4	5	6	7	8	9
2	2	4	6	8	10	12	14	16	18
3	3	6	9	12	15	18	21	24	27
4	4	8	12	16	20	24	28	32	36
5	5	10	15	20	25	30	35	40	45
6	6	12	18	24	30	36	42	48	54
7	7	14	21	28	35	42	49	56	63
8	8	16	24	32	40	48	56	64	72
9	9	18	27	36	45	54	63	72	81

Use the table to find 3×6.

> 1. Find 3 in the first factor column.
> 2. Find 6 in the top factor row.
> 3. The product is where the column and row meet: $3 \times 6 = 18$

Use the table to find 7×5.

> 1. Find 7 in the first factor column.
> 2. Find 5 in the top factor row.
> 3. The product is where the column and row meet: $7 \times 5 = 35$

Multiply. Use the table if needed.

	a	b	c	d	e	f
1.	2 ×8 16	4 ×3	7 ×1	6 ×2	8 ×9	3 ×7
2.	4 ×8	1 ×8	2 ×2	9 ×7	5 ×8	4 ×5
3.	5 ×7	9 ×6	4 ×2	6 ×6	3 ×2	5 ×9

Find the products. Use the table if needed.

	a	b	c	d
4.	$5 \times 9 = \underline{45}$	$9 \times 2 = \underline{}$	$4 \times 7 = \underline{}$	$4 \times 4 = \underline{}$
5.	$6 \times 9 = \underline{}$	$7 \times 6 = \underline{}$	$8 \times 5 = \underline{}$	$4 \times 6 = \underline{}$

Problem-Solving Method: Make a Model

Anita is making a quilt by sewing squares of fabric together. She wants it to have 6 rows with 8 squares in each row. How many fabric squares does she need to make the quilt?

Understand the problem.

- **What do you want to know?**
  how many fabric squares she needs to make the quilt

- **What information is given?**
  The quilt will have 6 rows of 8 squares.

Plan how to solve it.

- **What method can you use?**
  You can make a model of the quilt.

Solve it.

- **How can you use this method to solve the problem?**
  Use tiles to make a model of the quilt.
  Use one tile for each square of the quilt.
  Then count the tiles.

8

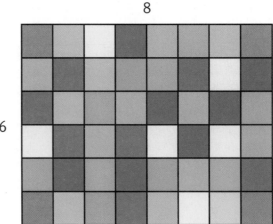

6

- **What is the answer?**
  Anita needs 48 fabric squares to make the quilt.

Look back and check your answer.

- **Is your answer reasonable?**
  You can check your count with multiplication.

  6 rows of 8 squares = 48 squares

  6 × 8 = 48

  The count and the product are the same.
  The answer is reasonable.

Make a model to solve each problem.

1. Kendra put new tiles on her bathroom floor. The floor now has 4 rows with 5 tiles in each row. How many tiles did Kendra use in all?

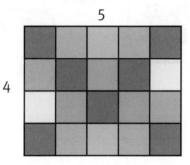

Answer _____

2. Tom needs to replace all the panes of glass in a window. The window has 3 rows with 3 panes in each row. How many panes of glass should Tom buy?

Answer _____

3. Sue cut a pan of lasagna into 6 rows. Each row has 3 servings of lasagna. How many servings of lasagna did she cut?

Answer _____

4. A box of chocolates has 4 rows. Each row has 9 chocolates. How many chocolates are in the box?

Answer _____

5. Tony planted 7 rows of tulips with 8 tulips in each row. How many tulips did Tony plant in his garden?

Answer _____

Division Facts Through 5

Divide two numbers to find a **quotient**.
Division is the opposite of multiplication.

The set of 12 stars is separated into groups
of 3 stars each. There are 4 groups.

We say: 12 divided by 3 is 4.
We think: 3 × 4 = 12, so 12 ÷ 3 = 4.
We write: 12 ÷ 3 = 4 or

$$4 \over 3)\overline{12}$$

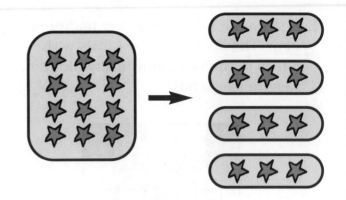

$$\begin{array}{r} 4 \leftarrow \text{quotient} \\ 3)\overline{12} \leftarrow \text{dividend} \\ \uparrow \\ \text{divisor} \end{array}$$

Remember,
* a number divided by itself is 1.
* 20 ÷ 5 is the same as finding the
  quotient of 20 divided by 5.

Divide.

	a	b	c	d
1.	32 ÷ 4 = __8__	12 ÷ 3 = _____	12 ÷ 4 = _____	15 ÷ 3 = _____
2.	35 ÷ 5 = _____	16 ÷ 2 = _____	27 ÷ 3 = _____	4 ÷ 2 = _____
3.	15 ÷ 5 = _____	3 ÷ 3 = _____	20 ÷ 5 = _____	18 ÷ 2 = _____
4.	20 ÷ 4 = _____	24 ÷ 4 = _____	8 ÷ 4 = _____	28 ÷ 4 = _____
5.	7 ÷ 1 = _____	5 ÷ 5 = _____	21 ÷ 3 = _____	40 ÷ 5 = _____

Find the quotients.

	a	b	c	d	e	f
6.	$\overset{6}{5)\overline{30}}$	$3)\overline{24}$	$4)\overline{16}$	$5)\overline{25}$	$4)\overline{4}$	$2)\overline{14}$
7.	$4)\overline{28}$	$2)\overline{4}$	$1)\overline{3}$	$3)\overline{21}$	$4)\overline{36}$	$2)\overline{8}$
8.	$3)\overline{6}$	$2)\overline{12}$	$5)\overline{45}$	$4)\overline{12}$	$2)\overline{2}$	$5)\overline{10}$

Division Facts for 6 and 7

Find: 42 ÷ 6

$6\overline{)42}$ **Say:**   42 divided by 6 is 7.   **Write:** $\dfrac{7}{6\overline{)42}}$ or   42 ÷ 6 = 7
Think: 6 × 7 = 42, so 42 ÷ 6 = 7.

Divide.

	a	b	c	d	e
1.	$6\overline{)18}$ = 3	$6\overline{)36}$	$6\overline{)48}$	$6\overline{)42}$	$6\overline{)6}$
2.	$6\overline{)24}$	$6\overline{)30}$	$6\overline{)12}$	$6\overline{)54}$	$6\overline{)18}$

Find: 42 ÷ 7

$7\overline{)42}$ **Say:**   42 divided by 7 is 6.   **Write:** $\dfrac{6}{7\overline{)42}}$ or   42 ÷ 7 = 6
Think: 7 × 6 = 42, so 42 ÷ 7 = 6.

Find the quotients.

	a	b	c	d
3.	35 ÷ 7 = __5__	28 ÷ 7 = _____	56 ÷ 7 = _____	21 ÷ 7 = _____
4.	49 ÷ 7 = _____	7 ÷ 7 = _____	63 ÷ 7 = _____	14 ÷ 7 = _____

Write two multiplication sentences and two division sentences for the three numbers given.

a	b	c
5. 7, 5, and 35	7, 3, and 21	7, 8, and 56
7 × 5 = 35		
5 × 7 = 35		
35 ÷ 7 = 5		
35 ÷ 5 = 7		

Division Facts for 8 and 9

Find: 64 ÷ 8

> 8)64   **Say:** 64 divided by 8 is 8.   **Write:** $\frac{8}{8)64}$ or $64 \div 8 = 8$
>
>   **Think:** $8 \times 8 = 64$, so $64 \div 8 = 8$.

Divide.

	a	b	c	d	e
1.	$8\overline{)48}$ (6)	$8\overline{)56}$	$8\overline{)72}$	$8\overline{)32}$	$8\overline{)16}$
2.	$8\overline{)8}$	$8\overline{)64}$	$8\overline{)24}$	$8\overline{)40}$	$8\overline{)48}$

Find: 72 ÷ 9

> 9)72   **Say:** 72 divided by 9 is 8.   **Write:** $\frac{8}{9)72}$ or $72 \div 9 = 8$
>
>   **Think:** $9 \times 8 = 72$, so $72 \div 9 = 8$.

Find the quotients.

	a	b	c	d
3.	$45 \div 9 = \underline{\ 5\ }$	$18 \div 9 = \underline{\ \ \ }$	$36 \div 9 = \underline{\ \ \ }$	$81 \div 9 = \underline{\ \ \ }$
4.	$63 \div 9 = \underline{\ \ \ }$	$54 \div 9 = \underline{\ \ \ }$	$27 \div 9 = \underline{\ \ \ }$	$9 \div 9 = \underline{\ \ \ }$

Write two multiplication sentences and two division sentences for the three numbers given.

	a	b	c
5.	5, 9, and 45	6, 9, and 54	3, 9, and 27
	$9 \times 5 = 45$	_____	_____
	$5 \times 9 = 45$	_____	_____
	$45 \div 9 = 5$	_____	_____
	$45 \div 5 = 9$	_____	_____

Problem-Solving Method: Choose an Operation

A total of 63 people signed up to play in the basketball league. There are 7 teams in the league. All the teams have the same number of players. How many people are on each team?

Understand the problem.

- **What do you want to know?**
  how many people are on each team

- **What information is given?**
  63 people signed up, and there are 7 teams.

Plan how to solve it.

- **What method can you use?**
  You can choose the operation needed to solve it.

Unequal Groups	Equal Groups
Add to combine unequal groups.	Multiply to combine equal groups.
Subtract to separate into unequal groups.	Divide to separate into equal groups.

Solve it.

- **How can you use this method to solve the problem?**
  Since you need to separate the total into equal groups, you should divide to find how many will be in each group.

$$63 \div 7 = 9$$

  total number of players   number of teams   number of players on each team

- **What is the answer?**
  There are 9 players on each team.

Look back and check your answer.

- **Is your answer reasonable?**
  You can check division with multiplication.

$$63 \div 7 = 9$$
  Check: $7 \times 9 = 63$

  The product matches the dividend.
  The answer is reasonable.

**Choose an operation to solve each problem.
Then solve the problem.**

1. Lisa used 48 shells to make 6 necklaces. She used the same number of shells for each necklace. How many shells were on each necklace?

   Operation _____

   Answer _____

2. The telephone book has 764 pages. There are 316 yellow pages. The rest are white. How many are white pages?

   Operation _____

   Answer _____

3. Onboard the shuttle *Columbia,* there were 18 mice and 152 rats. How many more rats were onboard than mice?

   Operation _____

   Answer _____

4. Sara bought a pair of sandals for $32 and a belt for $19. How much did she spend altogether?

   Operation _____

   Answer _____

5. We brought 5 bags of rolls to the picnic. There were 6 rolls in each bag. How many rolls did we bring?

   Operation _____

   Answer _____

6. Paul charges $7 per hour for babysitting. How many hours does he have to babysit to earn $28?

   Operation _____

   Answer _____

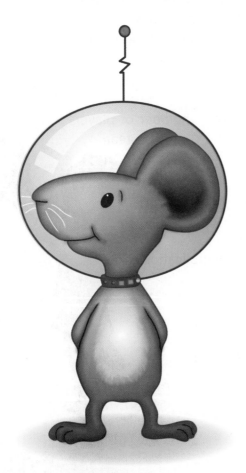

Find each answer.

	a		*b*

1. 4×9 **Say:** _____

$45 \div 5$ **Say:** _____

Think: _____

Think: _____

Write: _____

Write: _____

Multiply.

a	*b*	*c*	*d*
2. $1 \times 8 =$ _____	$2 \times 6 =$ _____	$3 \times 3 =$ _____	$4 \times 7 =$ _____
3. $5 \times 9 =$ _____	$6 \times 4 =$ _____	$7 \times 8 =$ _____	$0 \times 6 =$ _____
4. $8 \times 4 =$ _____	$9 \times 7 =$ _____	$6 \times 3 =$ _____	$8 \times 5 =$ _____
5. $4 \times 4 =$ _____	$5 \times 0 =$ _____	$1 \times 7 =$ _____	$6 \times 7 =$ _____

Find the products.

a	*b*	*c*	*d*	*e*
6. $\begin{array}{r} 1 \\ \times 4 \\ \hline \end{array}$	$\begin{array}{r} 2 \\ \times 3 \\ \hline \end{array}$	$\begin{array}{r} 3 \\ \times 9 \\ \hline \end{array}$	$\begin{array}{r} 4 \\ \times 6 \\ \hline \end{array}$	$\begin{array}{r} 5 \\ \times 4 \\ \hline \end{array}$
7. $\begin{array}{r} 6 \\ \times 6 \\ \hline \end{array}$	$\begin{array}{r} 7 \\ \times 2 \\ \hline \end{array}$	$\begin{array}{r} 8 \\ \times 8 \\ \hline \end{array}$	$\begin{array}{r} 9 \\ \times 0 \\ \hline \end{array}$	$\begin{array}{r} 7 \\ \times 1 \\ \hline \end{array}$
8. $\begin{array}{r} 5 \\ \times 3 \\ \hline \end{array}$	$\begin{array}{r} 9 \\ \times 9 \\ \hline \end{array}$	$\begin{array}{r} 0 \\ \times 3 \\ \hline \end{array}$	$\begin{array}{r} 6 \\ \times 5 \\ \hline \end{array}$	$\begin{array}{r} 8 \\ \times 9 \\ \hline \end{array}$

Divide.

	a	b	c	d
9.	$9 \div 1 =$ _____	$14 \div 2 =$ _____	$24 \div 3 =$ _____	$28 \div 4 =$ _____
10.	$45 \div 5 =$ _____	$36 \div 6 =$ _____	$56 \div 7 =$ _____	$64 \div 8 =$ _____
11.	$72 \div 9 =$ _____	$18 \div 2 =$ _____	$12 \div 3 =$ _____	$32 \div 4 =$ _____
12.	$30 \div 5 =$ _____	$54 \div 6 =$ _____	$49 \div 7 =$ _____	$48 \div 8 =$ _____

Find the quotients.

	a	b	c	d	e
13.	$3\overline{)21}$	$2\overline{)12}$	$5\overline{)20}$	$4\overline{)16}$	$1\overline{)8}$
14.	$6\overline{)42}$	$7\overline{)56}$	$8\overline{)40}$	$9\overline{)81}$	$7\overline{)28}$
15.	$5\overline{)25}$	$4\overline{)16}$	$9\overline{)36}$	$8\overline{)8}$	$6\overline{)24}$
16.	$3\overline{)15}$	$7\overline{)35}$	$9\overline{)54}$	$3\overline{)18}$	$8\overline{)48}$

Write two multiplication sentences and two division sentences for the three numbers given.

	a	b	c
17.	6, 8, and 48	3, 8, and 24	7, 9, and 63
	_____	_____	_____
	_____	_____	_____
	_____	_____	_____
	_____	_____	_____

Make a model to solve each problem.

18. A sheet of postage stamps has 6 rows. Each row has 5 stamps. How many stamps are on 1 sheet?

Answer_____

19. A chessboard has 8 rows with 8 squares in each row. How many squares are on a chessboard?

Answer_____

Choose an operation to solve each problem. Then solve the problem.

20. Donna set the table for 7 people. She put 3 pieces of silverware at each place at the table. How many pieces of silverware did Donna use in all?

Operation_____

Answer_____

21. Most glaciers move about 6 feet a day. How many days does it take a glacier to move 30 feet?

Operation_____

Answer_____

22. In 1998, Randall Cunningham of the Minnesota Vikings completed 259 of his 425 passing attempts. How many of his passes were incomplete?

Operation_____

Answer_____

Multiplying by One-digit Numbers to 5

To multiply by a one-digit number, start with the digits in the ones place.
Then use your basic multiplication facts.

Remember, zero times any number is zero.

Find: 3×20

Multiply the ones. $3 \times 0 = 0$ ones.	Multiply the tens. $3 \times 2 = 60$ tens.
T O 2 **0** × **3** **0**	T O 2 **0** × **3** **6 0**

Find: 4×102

Multiply the ones. $4 \times 2 = 8$ ones.	Multiply the tens. $4 \times 0 = 0$ tens.	Multiply the hundreds. $4 \times 1 = 4$ hundreds.
H T O 1 0 **2** × **4** **8**	H T O 1 **0** 2 × **4** **0** 8	H T O **1** 0 2 × **4** **4 0 8**

Multiply.

	a	b	c	d	e
1.	T O 4 0 × 2 **8 0**	T O 3 0 × 3	T O 1 0 × 5	T O 2 0 × 4	T O 6 0 × 1
2.	T O 1 1 × 5	T O 2 2 × 4	T O 3 2 × 3	T O 5 4 × 1	T O 4 3 × 2
3.	H T O 1 3 0 × 3	H T O 2 1 0 × 4	H T O 1 4 0 × 2	H T O 2 9 0 × 1	H T O 3 3 0 × 3
4.	H T O 3 4 2 × 2	H T O 3 1 1 × 3	H T O 2 4 3 × 2	H T O 1 0 0 × 5	H T O 2 0 2 × 4

Multiply.

	a	*b*	*c*	*d*	*e*
1.	2 0 × 3	1 2 × 4	3 2 × 2	1 0 × 5	4 2 × 2
2.	4 2 1 × 1	3 0 2 × 2	1 2 2 × 3	1 1 3 × 3	1 2 × 2
3.	2 2 × 3	3 1 × 3	4 9 × 1	4 4 × 2	1 0 9 × 1
4.	1 1 0 × 4	2 0 3 × 3	2 1 × 2	2 2 2 × 2	2 3 × 1
5.	1 3 × 2	4 4 2 × 2	3 0 0 × 3	2 1 3 × 3	2 3 × 2

Line up the digits. Then find the products.

	a	*b*	*c*

6.	$99 \times 1 =$ _____
	     99
	    × 1
		$120 \times 4 =$ _____	$100 \times 2 =$ _____

7.	$41 \times 2 =$ _____	$11 \times 5 =$ _____	$31 \times 3 =$ _____

Multiplying by One-digit Numbers with Regrouping

Multiply the ones first. Regroup when there are ten or more.
Remember, one times any number is that number.

Find: 4×37

Multiply the ones.

$4 \times 7 = 28$ ones

H	T	O
	2	
	3	7
×		4
		8

Regroup:

28 ones =
2 tens, 8 ones

Multiply the tens.

$4 \times 3 = 12$ tens

H	T	O
	2	
	3	7
×		4
1	4	8

Add the regrouped tens:

12 tens + 2 tens = 14 tens

Multiply.

       a   b   c   d   e

1.

a.
H	T	O
	1	
	2	8
×		2
	5	6

b.
H	T	O
	1	7
×		3

c.
H	T	O
	2	4
×		4

d.
H	T	O
	1	3
×		5

e.
H	T	O
	3	6
×		2

2.

a.
H	T	O
	5	6
×		3

b.
H	T	O
	2	8
×		4

c.
H	T	O
	6	3
×		5

d.
H	T	O
	3	9
×		4

e.
H	T	O
	4	8
×		5

3.

a.
H	T	O
1	6	7
×		2

b.
H	T	O
2	8	4
×		3

c.
H	T	O
1	7	7
×		5

d.
H	T	O
1	9	5
×		4

e.
H	T	O
2	5	9
×		3

4.

a.
Th	H	T	O
	3	7	8
×			3

b.
Th	H	T	O
	9	9	5
×			2

c.
Th	H	T	O
	2	3	7
×			5

d.
Th	H	T	O
	7	8	9
×			3

e.
Th	H	T	O
	9	7	6
×			4

Multiplying Numbers with Zeros by One-digit Numbers

Find: 5 × 206

Multiply the ones. 5 × 6 = 30 ones Regroup.	Multiply the tens. 5 × 0 = 0 tens Add the regrouped tens.	Multiply the hundreds. 5 × 2 = 10 hundreds Regroup.

Th H T O
     3
  2 0 **6**
×   **5**
      0
	Th H T O
	     3
	  2 **0** 6
	× **5**
	   3 0
		Th H T O
		1 3
		  2 0 6
		× **5**
		1, 0 3 0

Multiply.

          a   *b*   *c*   *d*

1.

H	T	O
	1	
2	0	3
×		4
8	1	2

H	T	O
1	0	9
×		3

H	T	O
4	0	3
×		2

H	T	O
9	0	9
×		1

2.

H	T	O
1	0	8
×		5

H	T	O
2	0	7
×		3

H	T	O
4	0	6
×		2

H	T	O
2	0	5
×		4

3.

Th	H	T	O
	4	0	9
×			3

Th	H	T	O
	7	0	6
×			4

Th	H	T	O
	8	0	9
×			5

Th	H	T	O
	5	0	5
×			2

4.

Th	H	T	O
1,	0	9	2
×			4

Th	H	T	O
1,	0	0	6
×			2

Th	H	T	O
2,	0	4	4
×			3

Th	H	T	O
1,	3	0	0
×			5

Problem-Solving Method: Use Estimation

Giant pandas eat about 35 pounds of bamboo every day. The San Diego Zoo grows its own bamboo crops to feed their 3 pandas. If the zoo can supply 100 pounds of bamboo a day, is it enough to feed the pandas?

Understand the problem.

- **What do you want to know?**
  Is 100 pounds of bamboo enough to feed the pandas each day?

- **What information is given?**
  There are 3 giant pandas in the zoo.
  Each panda eats about 35 pounds of bamboo every day.

Plan how to solve it.

- **What method can you use?**
  Since the problem is not asking for an exact answer, you can use estimation.

Solve it.

- **How can you use this method to solve the problem?**
  Round 35 pounds to 40 pounds and multiply by 3.
  Remember, it is better to overestimate the amount of food needed than to not have enough.

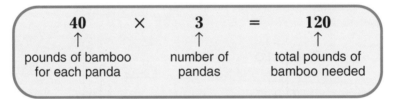

40	×	**3**	=	**120**
↑		↑		↑
pounds of bamboo for each panda		number of pandas		total pounds of bamboo needed

- **What is the answer?**
  No, 100 pounds a day is not enough bamboo to feed 3 pandas.

Look back and check your answer.

- **Is your answer reasonable?**
  You can check your estimate by finding the exact answer.

  Check:
  $$\begin{array}{r} 35 \\ \times\ 3 \\ \hline 105 \text{ pounds} \end{array}$$

  The exact answer shows that 100 pounds is not enough. The estimate is reasonable.

Use estimation to solve each problem.

1. On Saturday, 913 people visited the zoo. On Sunday, 789 people visited the zoo. About how many more people visited the zoo on Saturday than on Sunday?

Answer _____

2. The Ironman triathlon is a three-part race. First, racers swim about 2 miles. Then they bike 112 miles. Finally, they run 26 miles. About how many miles long is the whole race?

Answer _____

3. The world's fastest fish is the sailfish. It can swim 68 miles per hour. About how many miles can a sailfish swim in 3 hours?

Answer _____

4. Super Video sold 385 movies this week. If they sell that much every week, about how many movies will they sell in 4 weeks?

Answer _____

5. Sara charges $29 to mow one lawn. About how much will she earn if she mows 4 lawns?

Answer _____

Multiplying by 6 and 7

Find: 6 × 324

	Multiply the ones.	Multiply the tens.	Multiply the hundreds.
	6 × 4 = 24 ones	6 × 2 = 12 tens	6 × 3 = 18 hundreds
	Regroup.	Add the regrouped tens.	Add the regrouped hundreds.

Multiply the ones.
6 × 4 = 24 ones
Regroup.

Th	H	T	O
		2	
	3	2	4
×			6
			4

Multiply the tens.
6 × 2 = 12 tens
Add the regrouped tens.

Th	H	T	O
	1	2	
	3	2	4
×			6
		4	4

Multiply the hundreds.
6 × 3 = 18 hundreds
Add the regrouped hundreds.

Th	H	T	O
1	1	2	
	3	2	4
×			6
1,	9	4	4

Multiply.

a   **b**   **c**   **d**   **e**

1.

a)
H	T	O
	1	
8	2	
×		6
4	9	2

b)
H	T	O
7	4	
×		6

c)
H	T	O
9	0	
×		6

d)
H	T	O
3	3	
×		6

e)
H	T	O
1	8	
×		6

2.

a)
Th	H	T	O
	8	1	5
×			6

b)
Th	H	T	O
	7	0	3
×			6

c)
Th	H	T	O
	7	2	8
×			7

d)
Th	H	T	O
	2	4	9
×			7

e)
Th	H	T	O
	5	0	0
×			7

3.

a)
TTh	Th	H	T	O
	1,	7	5	2
×				7

b)
TTh	Th	H	T	O
	2,	1	9	3
×				7

c)
TTh	Th	H	T	O
	4,	3	7	6
×				7

d)
TTh	Th	H	T	O
	5,	2	0	0
×				7

e)
TTh	Th	H	T	O
	9,	8	4	0
×				7

Line up the digits. Then find the products.

     a   **b**   **c**

4. 809 × 6 = _____   283 × 6 = _____   745 × 6 = _____

809
× 6

Multiplying by 8 and 9

Find: 8 × 419

Multiply the ones.
8 × 9 = 72 ones
Regroup.

Th	H	T	O
		7	
	4	1	**9**
×			**8**
			2

Multiply the tens.
8 × 1 = 8 tens
Regroup.

Th	H	T	O
	1	7	
	4	**1**	9
×			**8**
		5	2

Multiply the hundreds.
8 × 4 = 32 hundreds
Regroup.

Th	H	T	O
3	1	7	
	4	1	9
×			**8**
3,	3	5	2

Multiply.

	a	b	c	d	e

1.

a)
H	T	O
	4	
	2	6
×		8
2	0	8

b)
H	T	O
	4	8
×		8

c)
H	T	O
	3	9
×		8

d)
H	T	O
	5	0
×		8

e)
H	T	O
	6	7
×		8

2.

a)
Th	H	T	O
	7	2	1
×			8

b)
Th	H	T	O
	6	0	9
×			8

c)
Th	H	T	O
	4	6	8
×			9

d)
Th	H	T	O
	3	0	0
×			9

e)
Th	H	T	O
	7	3	8
×			9

3.

a)
TTh	Th	H	T	O
	3,	8	0	7
×				9

b)
TTh	Th	H	T	O
	2,	9	0	4
×				9

c)
TTh	Th	H	T	O
	4,	1	2	8
×				9

d)
TTh	Th	H	T	O
	9,	0	5	1
×				9

e)
TTh	Th	H	T	O
	1,	4	6	8
×				8

Line up the digits. Then find the products.

	a	b	c

4. $316 \times 8 =$ _____ $803 \times 8 =$ _____ $19 \times 8 =$ _____

316
× 8

Problem-Solving Method: Solve Multi-Step Problems

An average shower uses 37 gallons of water. One washing machine load uses 50 gallons of water. In the last week, Karen took a shower every morning and did 3 loads of laundry. How much water did she use altogether?

Understand the problem.

- **What do you want to know?**
  the total amount of water Karen used

- **What information do you know?**
  One shower uses 37 gallons of water.
  One washing machine load uses 50 gallons of water.
  Karen took 7 showers and did 3 loads of wash.

Plan how to solve it.

- **What method can you use?**
  You can separate the problem into steps.

Solve it.

- **How can you use this method to solve the problem?**
  First find how much water each activity used.
  Then add those amounts to find the total.

Step 1 Showers	Step 2 Laundry	Step 3 Total
37 ← gallons per shower × 7 ← number of showers **259 gallons**	50 ← gallons per load × 3 ← number of loads **150 gallons**	259 ← shower total +150 ← laundry total **409 gallons**

- **What is the answer?**
  Karen used a total of 409 gallons of water.

Look back and check your answer.

- **Is your answer reasonable?**
  You can add to check your multiplication.

  37 + 37 + 37 + 37 + 37 + 37 + 37 + 50 + 50 + 50 = 409

  The answer matches the sum.
  The answer is reasonable.

Separate each problem into steps to solve.

1. Angelo had $100. He bought 6 CDs for $13 each. How much money did he have left?

Answer _____

2. One gram of fat has 9 calories. One egg has 6 grams of fat. How many calories are in 4 eggs?

Answer _____

3. On average, a dragonfly flies 18 miles per hour. A bumblebee flies 11 miles per hour. If both insects fly for 6 hours, how much farther will the dragonfly go?

Answer _____

4. Brenda planted 9 rows of daisies and 8 rows of tulips. She fit 18 flowers in each row. How many flowers did she plant altogether?

Answer _____

5. The average chimpanzee weighs 110 pounds. An orangutan weighs about 55 pounds more than a chimpanzee. A gorilla can weigh 3 times as much as a orangutan. How much does an average gorilla weigh?

Answer _____

Multiply.

	a	b	c	d	e
1.	$\begin{array}{r} 1\ 2 \\ \times\ \ \ 4 \\ \hline \end{array}$	$\begin{array}{r} 2\ 1 \\ \times\ \ \ 3 \\ \hline \end{array}$	$\begin{array}{r} 3\ 0 \\ \times\ \ \ 5 \\ \hline \end{array}$	$\begin{array}{r} 4\ 0\ 4 \\ \times\ \ \ \ \ 2 \\ \hline \end{array}$	$\begin{array}{r} 4\ 3\ 2 \\ \times\ \ \ \ \ 1 \\ \hline \end{array}$
2.	$\begin{array}{r} 7\ 5 \\ \times\ \ \ 6 \\ \hline \end{array}$	$\begin{array}{r} 4\ 2 \\ \times\ \ \ 9 \\ \hline \end{array}$	$\begin{array}{r} 1\ 0\ 3 \\ \times\ \ \ \ \ 7 \\ \hline \end{array}$	$\begin{array}{r} 2\ 0\ 0 \\ \times\ \ \ \ \ 8 \\ \hline \end{array}$	$\begin{array}{r} 4\ 5\ 2 \\ \times\ \ \ \ \ 7 \\ \hline \end{array}$
3.	$\begin{array}{r} 3\ 4\ 2 \\ \times\ \ \ \ \ 3 \\ \hline \end{array}$	$\begin{array}{r} 1\ 2\ 5 \\ \times\ \ \ \ \ 4 \\ \hline \end{array}$	$\begin{array}{r} 1\ 6\ 0 \\ \times\ \ \ \ \ 4 \\ \hline \end{array}$	$\begin{array}{r} 3\ 0\ 6 \\ \times\ \ \ \ \ 5 \\ \hline \end{array}$	$\begin{array}{r} 5\ 4\ 8 \\ \times\ \ \ \ \ 3 \\ \hline \end{array}$
4.	$\begin{array}{r} 2,5\ 9\ 4 \\ \times\ \ \ \ \ \ \ 6 \\ \hline \end{array}$	$\begin{array}{r} 4,3\ 2\ 0 \\ \times\ \ \ \ \ \ \ 8 \\ \hline \end{array}$	$\begin{array}{r} 9\ 5\ 4 \\ \times\ \ \ \ \ \ \ 7 \\ \hline \end{array}$	$\begin{array}{r} 3,0\ 1\ 5 \\ \times\ \ \ \ \ \ \ 9 \\ \hline \end{array}$	$\begin{array}{r} 2,8\ 5\ 7 \\ \times\ \ \ \ \ \ \ 8 \\ \hline \end{array}$

Line up the digits. Then find the products.

a	b	c
5. $20 \times 5 = $ _____	$94 \times 3 = $ _____	$36 \times 8 = $ _____
6. $83 \times 2 = $ _____	$45 \times 8 = $ _____	$104 \times 6 = $ _____
7. $257 \times 7 = $ _____	$1{,}950 \times 2 = $ _____	$2{,}901 \times 4 = $ _____

Use estimation to solve each problem.

8. Leroy has $200 to buy food for the party. If each pizza costs $16, does he have enough money to buy 9 pizzas?

Answer _____

_____

9. The Concord jet cruises at 1,450 miles per hour. About how many miles can it fly in 3 hours?

Answer _____

10. Kendra ordered 500 T-shirts. She needs to deliver 125 T-shirts to each of her 7 stores. Did she order enough?

Answer _____

Separate each problem into steps to solve.

11. The theater seats 176 people. There are 3 shows on Saturday and 2 shows on Sunday. How many more people can see the show on Saturday than on Sunday?

Answer _____

12. Brian has two jobs. He works 20 hours a week at a radio station, where he makes $9 an hour. He also earns $75 a week walking dogs. How much does he make each week altogether?

Answer _____

Dividing Two-digit Numbers by 2, 3, 4, and 5

To divide by a one-digit **divisor,** start with the largest place value of the **dividend.** Then use your division facts. Multiply and subtract.

Remember, you can check your division by multiplying.

Find: 68 ÷ 2

Divide.	Multiply and subtract.		Multiply and subtract.		Check:

Divide.

```
 T O
2)6 8
```

Multiply and subtract.

```
   T O
   3
2)6 8
  -6↓
   0 8
```

6 ÷ 2 = 3
Put a 3 in the tens place. Multiply and subtract. Bring down the 8 ones.

```
  3
2)6
```

Multiply and subtract.

```
   T O
   3 4
2)6 8
  -6↓
   0 8
 __
  -  8
      0
```

8 ÷ 2 = 4
Put a 4 in the ones place. Multiply and subtract.

```
  4
2)8
```

Check:
Multiply divisor and quotient.

```
  34
 × 2
 ___
  68
```

Divide. Check.

a

1.
```
 T O
 2 3
3)6 9
 -6↓
  0 9
 - 9
 ___
   0
```
Check:
```
  23
 × 3
 ___
  69
```

b
```
 T O
2)2 8
```
Check:

c
```
 T O
4)4 4
```
Check:

Set up the problems. Then find the quotients.

a

b

c

2. 242 ÷ 2 = _____   84 ÷ 2 = _____   399 ÷ 3 = _____

```
 2)242
```

Dividing Three-digit Numbers by 2, 3, 4, and 5

To divide, first choose a **trial quotient**. Start with the largest place value in the dividend. Then multiply and subtract.

Find: 208 ÷ 4

Divide.	Multiply and subtract.	Multiply and subtract.	Check:

Divide.

```
  H T O
4)2 0 8
```

2 < 4
4 does not
go into 2.

Move to the next
place value.

```
    5
4)20
```

Multiply and subtract.

```
    5
  H T O
4)2 0 8
 -2 0↓
    0 8
```

```
  5
4)20
```

Multiply and subtract.

```
    5 2
  H T O
4)2 0 8
 -2 0
    0 8
  -   8
      0
```

```
  2
4)8
```

Check:
Multiply divisor and quotient.

```
   52
 × 4
  208
```

Divide. Check.

       a   *b*   *c*

1.
```
    7 1
  H T O
4)2 8 4      Check:
 -2 8↓         71
    0 4       × 4
  -   4       284
      0
```

```
  H T O
2)1 0 8      Check:
```

```
  H T O
5)2 0 5      Check:
```

Set up the problems. Then find the quotients.

             a   *b*   *c*

2. 255 ÷ 5 = _____   120 ÷ 4 = _____   129 ÷ 3 = _____

```
5)255
```

3. 155 ÷ 5 = _____   104 ÷ 2 = _____   216 ÷ 3 = _____

Dividing with Remainders

Sometimes a number cannot be divided into even groups.
Then there is a **remainder**, or an amount left over.

Find: 26 ÷ 5

Divide.	Multiply and subtract.	Write the remainder in the quotient.	Check: Multiply divisor and quotient. Add the remainder.

T|O
 	
5)2 6
 	
2 < 5
5 does not
go into 2.
	T|O
	  5
	5)2 6
	−2 5
	  0 1
	
	5)26 is 5 with a
		T|O
		  5 R 1
		5)2 6
		− 2 5
		  0 1
			5
			  ×5
			  25
			 + 1
			  26

Divide. Check.

       a   *b*   *c*

1. T\|O   Check:
       7 R 1   7
2)1 5   ×2
−1 4   14
  0 1   + 1
            15

      T\|O   Check:
      4)3 5

      T\|O   Check:
      5)3 2

2. H\|T\|O   Check:
    3)1 3 7

    H\|T\|O   Check:
    2)1 1 3

    H\|T\|O   Check:
    4)3 1 9

3. H\|T\|O   Check:
    2)1 0 3

    H\|T\|O   Check:
    3)2 0 9

    H\|T\|O   Check:
    5)6 0 8

Divide. Check.

	a	b	c
1.	4)2 5	5)4 7	3)2 6 1
2.	3)2 4 5	5)1 0 0	7)5 2
3.	4)2 0 6	3)2 2	2)1 1 1
4.	3)1 0 9	2)1 3	4)1 0 4

Set up the problems. Then find the quotients.

	a	b	c
5.	$218 \div 5 =$ _____	$33 \div 4 =$ _____	$201 \div 3 =$ _____
	5)218		
6.	$19 \div 2 =$ _____	$118 \div 3 =$ _____	$304 \div 5 =$ _____

Problem-Solving Method: Use Guess and Check

Anthony's band won $35 in a song contest. When they divided the prize money evenly, they had $2 left over. Each band member got more than $10. How many people are in the band?

Understand the problem.

- **What do you want to know?**
  the number of people in the band

- **What information is given?**
  Clue 1: When they divided $35 evenly, they had $2 left over.
  Clue 2: Each band member got more than $10.

Plan how to solve it.

- **What method can you use?**
  Since there is no clear way to solve the problem, you can guess first and then check your answer.

Solve it.

- **How can you use this method to solve the problem?**
  Guess the number of people in the band. Then divide $35 by your guess to check. Keep guessing and checking until you find a remainder of $2 and a quotient greater than $10.

Guess	5 band members	4 band members	3 band members
Check	$$\begin{array}{r} 7 \\ 5)\overline{35} \\ -35 \\ \hline 0 \end{array}$$	$$\begin{array}{r} 8 \\ 4)\overline{35} \\ -32 \\ \hline 3 \end{array}$$	$$\begin{array}{r} 11\ R\ 2 \\ 3)\overline{35} \\ -3 \\ \hline 05 \\ -3 \\ \hline 2 \end{array}$$
	No remainder Does not check. Keep guessing.	Remainder 3 Does not check. Keep guessing.	Remainder 2, and 11 > 10

- **What is the answer?**
  There are 3 people in the band.

Look back and check your answer.

- **Is your answer reasonable?**
  You can check division with multiplication.

  The multiplication checks and the guess satisfies both clues. The answer is reasonable.

$$\begin{array}{r} 11 \leftarrow \text{money each received} \\ \times\ 3 \leftarrow \text{people in band} \\ \hline 33 \\ +\ 2 \leftarrow \text{money left over} \\ \hline 35 \leftarrow \text{total prize money} \end{array}$$

Guess and check to solve each problem.

1. Will had 47 photographs to put in his album. When he divided them evenly onto 11 pages, he had 3 left over. How many photographs did Will put on each page?

Answer _____

2. Stacey has 4 United States coins. Their total value is 31 cents. What coins does Stacey have? How many of each coin?

Answer _____

3. Jenna is 5 years older than Darius. The sum of their ages is 21 years. How old are Jenna and Darius?

Answer _____

4. The warehouse packed the same number of shirts in 4 boxes. After packing a shipment of 17 shirts, they had 1 left over. How many shirts did they pack in each box?

Answer _____

5. Tickets to the fair cost twice as much for an adult as for a child. Mr. Chin spent $9 on tickets for himself and his son. What is the price of each ticket?

Answer _____

Dividing by 6 and 7

Find: 256 ÷ 6

Divide.

```
  H T O
    4
6)2 5 6
```

2 < 6

6 does not
go into 2.

Multiply and subtract.

```
  H T O
    4
6)2 5 6
 -2 4↓
    1 6
```

6)25 is about 4.

Multiply and subtract.

```
  H  T O
     4 2 R 4
6)2  5 6
 - 2 4
     1 6
   - 1 2
        4
```

6)16 is about 2.

Check:

Multiply divisor
and quotient.

Add the remainder.

```
   42
 ×  6
  252
 +  4
  256
```

Divide. Check.

	a	*b*	*c*	*d*

1.

a
```
  T O
  1 1
6)6 6
 -6↓
  0 6
 -  6
    0
```
```
   11
 × 6
   66
```

b
```
  T O
6)9 2
```

c
```
  T O
7)2 7
```

d
```
  T O
7)4 0
```

2.

a
```
  H T O
6)4 0 0
```

b
```
  H T O
7)5 0 6
```

c
```
  H T O
6)5 4 8
```

d
```
  H T O
7)4 8 7
```

3.

a
```
  Th H T O
7)4, 9 7 9
```

b
```
  Th H T O
6)1, 3 6 4
```

c
```
  Th H T O
7)2, 0 1 7
```

d
```
  Th H T O
7)6, 4 7 5
```

Dividing by 8 and 9

Divide. Check.

	a	*b*	*c*	*d*
1.	8)3 9	8)9 7	9)5 2	9)2 0
2.	8)8 9 8	9)7 0 0	8)4 0 8	9)2 4 3
3.	8)3, 2 8 8	8)1, 1 1 1	9)1, 8 9 9	9)8, 9 0 1

Set up the problems. Then find the quotients.

	a	*b*	*c*
4.	97 ÷ 8 = _____	263 ÷ 9 = _____	7,707 ÷ 8 = _____
	8)97		
5.	8,401 ÷ 9 = _____	496 ÷ 8 = _____	557 ÷ 9 = _____

Problem-Solving Method: Write a Number Sentence

The moon's gravity is one-sixth that of Earth's. This means that an object's Earth weight divided by 6 is its moon weight. If an astronaut weighs 192 pounds on Earth, how much will he weigh on the moon?

Understand the problem.

- **What do you want to know?**
  the astronaut's weight on the moon

- **What information is given?**
  Weight on the moon is the weight on Earth divided by 6.
  The astronaut weighs 192 pounds on Earth.

Plan how to solve it.

- **What method can you use?**
  You can write a number sentence to model the problem.

Solve it.

- **How can you use this method to solve the problem?**
  Since you know his weight on the moon is his Earth weight divided by 6, you can write a division number sentence.

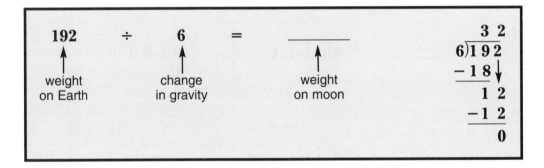

$$192 \div 6 = \underline{\hspace{2cm}}$$

weight on Earth — change in gravity — weight on moon

$$
\begin{array}{r}
3\ 2 \\
6\overline{)1\ 9\ 2} \\
-1\ 8\ \downarrow \\
\hline
1\ 2 \\
-1\ 2 \\
\hline
0
\end{array}
$$

- **What is the answer?**
  The astronaut will weigh 32 pounds on the moon.

Look back and check your answer.

- **Is your answer reasonable?**

You can check division with multiplication.

$$
\begin{array}{r}
32 \\
\times\ 6 \\
\hline
192
\end{array}
$$

32 ← weight on Moon
× 6 ← change in gravity
192 ← weight on Earth

The product matches the dividend.
The answer is reasonable.

Write a number sentence to solve each problem.

1. Between 1969 and 1972, the *Apollo* missions brought back about 840 pounds of lunar rock samples. How much did the rocks weigh on the moon?
(Earth weight ÷ 6 = moon weight)

Answer _____

2. The Brooklyn Bridge in New York is 6,016 feet long. The Golden Gate Bridge in San Francisco is 1,816 feet shorter. How long is the Golden Gate Bridge?

Answer _____

3. Every year, Joel gives the same amount of money to charity. In the past 8 years he has given a total of $1,400. How much money does he give each year?

Answer _____

4. In 1996, Shannon Lucid spent 189 days in space. That is longer than any other female astronaut. How many weeks was she in space?

Answer _____

5. At 8 inches long, the pygmy is the smallest shark in the world. The largest is the whale shark. It can be 75 times as long as a pygmy shark. How long is an average whale shark?

Answer _____

6. The 3,420 new library books are to be shared equally by 9 libraries. How many books will each library get?

Answer _____

Divide. Check.

	a	b	c	d
1.	3)3 6	4)8 4	6)7 9	7)8 5
2.	8)3 7 6	9)4 2 3	2)1 1 6	5)2 0 5
3.	3)7 8	5)7 5	6)3 2 9	7)2 5 0
4.	8)6 9	9)5 3	2)2 7 3	3)1 9 4

Set up the problems. Then find the quotients.

	a	b	c
5.	$96 \div 3 =$ _____	$101 \div 7 =$ _____	$43 \div 4 =$ _____
6.	$680 \div 5 =$ _____	$1,339 \div 9 =$ _____	$5,107 \div 6 =$ _____

Guess and check to solve each problem.

7. Anna had 84 books to place on 9 shelves. She put the same number of books on each shelf. There were 3 books left over. How many books did she put on each shelf?

Answer _____

8. Ryan used 50 apples to make several pies. He put the same number of apples in each pie. He had 1 apple left over. How many pies did he make?

Answer _____

Write a number sentence to solve each problem.

9. Jamal delivers the same number of newspapers every morning. In one week, he delivers 203 newspapers. How many does he deliver each morning?

Answer _____

10. In 8 hours of work, Tyler earns $136. How much does he make each hour?

Answer _____

11. The aquarium has 275 angelfish. The same number of angelfish live in each of the aquarium's 5 tanks. How many angelfish are in each tank?

Answer _____

unit 5
multiplying and Dividing Larger numbers

Multiplying by Tens and Hundreds

To multiply tens, multiply the non-zero numbers. Then write one zero. To multiply hundreds, multiply the non-zero numbers. Then write two zeros.

Find: 30 × 4

Long Way	Short Way
Multiply by 4 ones.	Multiply the non-zero numbers. Write one zero for tens in the product.

$$\begin{array}{r} 4 \rightarrow \\ \times\ 3\ 0 \rightarrow \\ \hline 1\ 2\ 0 \end{array}$$

$$\begin{array}{r} 4 \\ \times 3 \text{ tens} \\ \hline 12 \text{ tens} = 120 \end{array}$$

Find: 3 × 500

Long Way	Short Way
Multiply by 3 ones.	Multiply the non-zero numbers. Write two zeros for hundreds in the product.

$$\begin{array}{r} 5\ 0\ 0 \rightarrow \\ \times\ \quad\ 3 \rightarrow \\ \hline 1,\ 5\ 0\ 0 \end{array}$$

$$\begin{array}{r} 5 \text{ hundreds} \\ \times 3 \\ \hline 15 \text{ hundreds} = 1,500 \end{array}$$

Multiply. Use the short way.

                        a   *b*

1. $\begin{array}{r} 1\ 0 \rightarrow \underline{\ 1\ } \text{ ten} \\ \times\ \ 6 \rightarrow \times\ 6 \\ \hline 6 \text{ tens} = 60 \end{array}$ $\begin{array}{r} 4\ 0 \rightarrow \underline{\quad} \text{ tens} \\ \times\ 8 \rightarrow \times \underline{\quad} \\ \hline \text{tens} = \end{array}$

2. $\begin{array}{r} 3 \rightarrow \underline{\quad} \\ \times 8\ 0 \rightarrow \times \underline{\quad} \text{ tens} \\ \hline \text{tens} = \end{array}$ $\begin{array}{r} 9 \rightarrow \underline{\quad} \\ \times 1\ 0 \rightarrow \times \underline{\quad} \text{ tens} \\ \hline \text{tens} = \end{array}$

3. $\begin{array}{r} 1\ 0\ 0 \rightarrow \underline{\quad} \text{ hundred} \\ \times\ \ 4 \rightarrow \times \underline{\quad} \\ \hline \text{hundreds} = \end{array}$ $\begin{array}{r} 8\ 0\ 0 \rightarrow \underline{\quad} \text{ hundreds} \\ \times\ \ 2 \rightarrow \times \underline{\quad} \\ \hline \text{hundreds} = \end{array}$

4. $\begin{array}{r} 7 \rightarrow \underline{\quad} \\ \times 2\ 0\ 0 \rightarrow \times \underline{\quad} \text{ hundreds} \\ \hline \text{hundreds} = \end{array}$ $\begin{array}{r} 6 \rightarrow \underline{\quad} \\ \times 3\ 0\ 0 \rightarrow \times \underline{\quad} \text{ hundreds} \\ \hline \text{hundreds} = \end{array}$

Multiply. Use the short way.

	a	b	c	d	e
1.	$\begin{array}{r} 3\ 0 \\ \times\ \ 3 \\ \hline \end{array}$	$\begin{array}{r} 5\ 0 \\ \times\ \ 9 \\ \hline \end{array}$	$\begin{array}{r} 7\ 0 \\ \times\ \ 5 \\ \hline \end{array}$	$\begin{array}{r} 8\ 0 \\ \times\ \ 4 \\ \hline \end{array}$	$\begin{array}{r} 9\ 0 \\ \times\ \ 7 \\ \hline \end{array}$
2.	$\begin{array}{r} 9 \\ \times 6\ 0 \\ \hline \end{array}$	$\begin{array}{r} 7 \\ \times 3\ 0 \\ \hline \end{array}$	$\begin{array}{r} 9 \\ \times 8\ 0 \\ \hline \end{array}$	$\begin{array}{r} 3 \\ \times 6\ 0 \\ \hline \end{array}$	$\begin{array}{r} 5 \\ \times 5\ 0 \\ \hline \end{array}$
3.	$\begin{array}{r} 6\ 0\ 0 \\ \times\ \ \ \ 6 \\ \hline \end{array}$	$\begin{array}{r} 7\ 0\ 0 \\ \times\ \ \ \ 8 \\ \hline \end{array}$	$\begin{array}{r} 2\ 0\ 0 \\ \times\ \ \ \ 6 \\ \hline \end{array}$	$\begin{array}{r} 3\ 0\ 0 \\ \times\ \ \ \ 9 \\ \hline \end{array}$	$\begin{array}{r} 8\ 0\ 0 \\ \times\ \ \ \ 4 \\ \hline \end{array}$
4.	$\begin{array}{r} 5 \\ \times 7\ 0\ 0 \\ \hline \end{array}$	$\begin{array}{r} 7 \\ \times 6\ 0\ 0 \\ \hline \end{array}$	$\begin{array}{r} 8 \\ \times 8\ 0\ 0 \\ \hline \end{array}$	$\begin{array}{r} 6 \\ \times 4\ 0\ 0 \\ \hline \end{array}$	$\begin{array}{r} 3 \\ \times 6\ 0\ 0 \\ \hline \end{array}$

Multiply. Use the short way.

	a	b	c
5.	$10 \times 5 =$ _____	$20 \times 3 =$ _____	$10 \times 7 =$ _____
6.	$50 \times 2 =$ _____	$40 \times 6 =$ _____	$70 \times 3 =$ _____
7.	$5 \times 90 =$ _____	$7 \times 50 =$ _____	$8 \times 90 =$ _____
8.	$40 \times 9 =$ _____	$70 \times 7 =$ _____	$80 \times 6 =$ _____
9.	$5 \times 300 =$ _____	$8 \times 600 =$ _____	$9 \times 700 =$ _____
10.	$900 \times 9 =$ _____	$800 \times 9 =$ _____	$500 \times 8 =$ _____

Multiplying Two-digit Numbers by Two-digit Numbers

To multiply two-digit numbers, multiply by the ones first. Then multiply by the tens. Then add these two **partial products**.

Find: 25 × 13

Think of 25 as 2 tens and 5 ones. Multiply by 5 ones.

```
 H | T | O
   | 1 |
   | 1 | 3     Think:   13
 × | 2 | 5            ×  5
   | 6 | 5     ←      65
```

Multiply by 2 tens.

```
 H | T | O
   | 1 |
   | 1 | 3
 × | 2 | 5     Think:   13
   | 6 | 5            × 20
 2 | 6 | 0     ←     260
```
zero place holder

Add the partial products.

```
 H | T | O
   | 1 |
   | 1 | 3
 × | 2 | 5
   | 6 | 5     ←      13 × 5
 +2| 6 | 0     ← +  13 × 20
 3 | 2 | 5     ←     13 × 25
```

Multiply.

| | a | b | c | d |

1.

a)
```
 H | T | O
   | 4 |
   | 1 |
   | 1 | 9
 × | 5 | 2
   | 3 | 8
 +9| 5 | 0
 9 | 8 | 8
```

b)
```
 H | T | O
   | 1 | 8
 × | 5 | 5
```

c)
```
 H | T | O
   | 1 | 4
 × | 3 | 2
```

d)
```
 H | T | O
   | 1 | 6
 × | 1 | 6
```

2.

a)
```
 H | T | O
   | 4 | 5
 × | 1 | 3
```

b)
```
 H | T | O
   | 3 | 7
 × | 4 | 3
```

c)
```
 H | T | O
   | 4 | 4
 × | 1 | 3
```

d)
```
 H | T | O
   | 3 | 8
 × | 1 | 6
```

3.

a)
```
 Th| H | T | O
   |   | 5 | 3
 × |   | 7 | 5
```

b)
```
 Th| H | T | O
   |   | 8 | 9
 × |   | 2 | 4
```

c)
```
 Th| H | T | O
   |   | 4 | 2
 × |   | 8 | 9
```

d)
```
 Th| H | T | O
   |   | 7 | 3
 × |   | 6 | 4
```

Multiply.

	a	*b*	*c*	*d*	*e*
1.	2 8 ×3 3	6 2 ×7 1	2 2 ×5 8	4 9 ×1 6	8 4 ×5 9
2.	2 3 ×9 2	1 8 ×6 6	4 2 ×1 2	3 4 ×2 4	8 1 ×3 7
3.	4 4 ×2 9	3 2 ×1 7	9 4 ×3 5	6 5 ×1 9	4 7 ×2 5

Line up the digits. Then find the products.

	a	*b*	*c*
4.	54 × 46 = _____ 54 ×46	55 × 21 = _____	15 × 39 = _____
5.	36 × 31 = _____	83 × 52 = _____	85 × 11 = _____

Multiplying Three-digit Numbers by Two-digit Numbers

To multiply three-digit numbers by two-digit numbers, multiply by the ones first.
Then multiply by the tens. Then add these two partial products.

Find: 64 × 753

Think of 64 as 6 tens and 4 ones.
Multiply by 4 ones.

TTh	Th	H	T	O
		2	1	
		7	5	3
×			6	4
	3,	0	1	2	← 4 × 753

Multiply by 6 tens.

TTh	Th	H	T	O
		3	1	
		7	5	3
×			6	4
	3,	0	1	2
4	5,	1	8	0	← 60 × 753
zero place holder

Add the partial products.

TTh	Th	H	T	O
		7	5	3
×			6	4
	3,	0	1	2
+4	5,	1	8	0
4	8,	1	9	2

Multiply.

        a   b   c   d

1.

a)
TTh	Th	H	T	O
			1	
			4	
		6	1	9
×			2	5
	3,	0	9	5
+1	2,	3	8	0
1	5,	4	7	5

b)
TTh	Th	H	T	O
		3	2	4
×			8	7

c)
TTh	Th	H	T	O
		1	4	9
×			7	1

d)
TTh	Th	H	T	O
		5	1	7
×			6	6

2.

a)
TTh	Th	H	T	O
		2	4	3
×			4	2

b)
TTh	Th	H	T	O
		3	2	8
×			3	5

c)
TTh	Th	H	T	O
		7	4	5
×			2	3

d)
TTh	Th	H	T	O
		3	6	8
×			5	4

3.

a)
TTh	Th	H	T	O
		9	5	3
×			3	4

b)
TTh	Th	H	T	O
		1	6	3
×			9	2

c)
TTh	Th	H	T	O
		4	2	1
×			5	7

d)
TTh	Th	H	T	O
		7	1	8
×			2	6

Multiply.

	a	b	c	d	e

1.
$\begin{array}{r} 5\ 1\ 6 \\ \times\ \ \ 3\ 9 \\ \hline \end{array}$
$\begin{array}{r} 2\ 7\ 7 \\ \times\ \ \ 5\ 3 \\ \hline \end{array}$
$\begin{array}{r} 3\ 2\ 9 \\ \times\ \ \ 6\ 1 \\ \hline \end{array}$
$\begin{array}{r} 1\ 8\ 7 \\ \times\ \ \ 8\ 4 \\ \hline \end{array}$
$\begin{array}{r} 9\ 1\ 7 \\ \times\ \ \ 2\ 2 \\ \hline \end{array}$

2.
$\begin{array}{r} 4\ 3\ 7 \\ \times\ \ \ 2\ 4 \\ \hline \end{array}$
$\begin{array}{r} 2\ 5\ 6 \\ \times\ \ \ 1\ 8 \\ \hline \end{array}$
$\begin{array}{r} 7\ 0\ 4 \\ \times\ \ \ 3\ 7 \\ \hline \end{array}$
$\begin{array}{r} 1\ 7\ 3 \\ \times\ \ \ 4\ 5 \\ \hline \end{array}$
$\begin{array}{r} 2\ 3\ 1 \\ \times\ \ \ 3\ 6 \\ \hline \end{array}$

3.
$\begin{array}{r} 5\ 3\ 2 \\ \times\ \ \ 4\ 8 \\ \hline \end{array}$
$\begin{array}{r} 1\ 7\ 8 \\ \times\ \ \ 2\ 9 \\ \hline \end{array}$
$\begin{array}{r} 3\ 3\ 7 \\ \times\ \ \ 1\ 3 \\ \hline \end{array}$
$\begin{array}{r} 5\ 4\ 0 \\ \times\ \ \ 5\ 6 \\ \hline \end{array}$
$\begin{array}{r} 3\ 1\ 0 \\ \times\ \ \ 8\ 1 \\ \hline \end{array}$

Line up the digits. Then find the products.

	a	b	c

4. $631 \times 28 =$ _____ $493 \times 55 =$ _____ $127 \times 86 =$ _____

$\begin{array}{r} 631 \\ \times\ 28 \\ \hline \end{array}$

5. $237 \times 44 =$ _____ $905 \times 67 =$ _____

Estimating Products

To estimate products, round each factor.
Then multiply the rounded factors.

Estimate: 35×72

Round each factor to the greatest place value.
Multiply.

$$
\begin{array}{r}
7\,2 \rightarrow \quad 7\,0 \\
\times\ 3\,5 \rightarrow \quad \times\ 4\,0 \\
\hline
2{,}8\,0\,0
\end{array}
\leftarrow \text{2 zeros}
$$
$\leftarrow$ 2 zeros

Estimate: 719×56

Round each factor to the greatest place value.
Multiply.

$$
\begin{array}{r}
7\,1\,9 \rightarrow \quad 7\,0\,0 \\
\times\ 5\,6 \rightarrow \quad \times\ 6\,0 \\
\hline
4\,2{,}0\,0\,0
\end{array}
\leftarrow \text{3 zeros}
$$
$\leftarrow$ 3 zeros

Estimate the products.

	a	b	c	d

1.
a) $\begin{array}{r} 2\,1 \rightarrow\ \ 20 \\ \times 2\,9 \rightarrow \times 30 \\ \hline 600 \end{array}$
b) $\begin{array}{r} 4\,4 \rightarrow \\ \times 3\,2 \rightarrow \\ \hline \end{array}$
c) $\begin{array}{r} 9\,3 \rightarrow \\ \times 1\,4 \rightarrow \\ \hline \end{array}$
d) $\begin{array}{r} 8\,8 \rightarrow \\ \times 4\,3 \rightarrow \\ \hline \end{array}$

2.
a) $\begin{array}{r} 7\,9 \rightarrow \\ \times 2\,8 \rightarrow \\ \hline \end{array}$
b) $\begin{array}{r} 6\,2 \rightarrow \\ \times 6\,1 \rightarrow \\ \hline \end{array}$
c) $\begin{array}{r} 8\,4 \rightarrow \\ \times 2\,6 \rightarrow \\ \hline \end{array}$
d) $\begin{array}{r} 7\,6 \rightarrow \\ \times 5\,1 \rightarrow \\ \hline \end{array}$

3.
a) $\begin{array}{r} 1\,9\,0 \rightarrow \\ \times\ \ 3\,8 \rightarrow \\ \hline \end{array}$
b) $\begin{array}{r} 5\,1\,2 \rightarrow \\ \times\ \ 7\,1 \rightarrow \\ \hline \end{array}$
c) $\begin{array}{r} 6\,6\,4 \rightarrow \\ \times\ \ 5\,8 \rightarrow \\ \hline \end{array}$
d) $\begin{array}{r} 8\,3\,9 \rightarrow \\ \times\ \ 2\,4 \rightarrow \\ \hline \end{array}$

Line up the digits. Then estimate the products.

	a	b	c

4. 34×45 _____
$\begin{array}{r} 34 \rightarrow\ \ 30 \\ \times 45 \rightarrow \times 50 \\ \hline 1{,}500 \end{array}$

56×77 _____

768×91 _____

Estimate the products.

	a	b	c	d

1. $\begin{array}{r} 3\ 7 \to \\ \times 2\ 4 \to \\ \hline \end{array}$ $\begin{array}{r} 5\ 5 \to \\ \times 6\ 8 \to \\ \hline \end{array}$ $\begin{array}{r} 7\ 1 \to \\ \times 1\ 7 \to \\ \hline \end{array}$ $\begin{array}{r} 2\ 3 \to \\ \times 8\ 8 \to \\ \hline \end{array}$

2. $\begin{array}{r} 4\ 2 \to \\ \times 3\ 6 \to \\ \hline \end{array}$ $\begin{array}{r} 8\ 9 \to \\ \times 5\ 4 \to \\ \hline \end{array}$ $\begin{array}{r} 9\ 3 \to \\ \times 6\ 8 \to \\ \hline \end{array}$ $\begin{array}{r} 9\ 9 \to \\ \times 2\ 2 \to \\ \hline \end{array}$

3. $\begin{array}{r} 5\ 4\ 8 \to \\ \times\ \ 4\ 5 \to \\ \hline \end{array}$ $\begin{array}{r} 6\ 3\ 4 \to \\ \times\ \ 5\ 7 \to \\ \hline \end{array}$ $\begin{array}{r} 1\ 7\ 8 \to \\ \times\ \ 8\ 9 \to \\ \hline \end{array}$ $\begin{array}{r} 6\ 0\ 8 \to \\ \times\ \ 9\ 1 \to \\ \hline \end{array}$

4. $\begin{array}{r} 7\ 5\ 9 \to \\ \times\ \ 3\ 8 \to \\ \hline \end{array}$ $\begin{array}{r} 2\ 1\ 4 \to \\ \times\ \ 8\ 1 \to \\ \hline \end{array}$ $\begin{array}{r} 5\ 5\ 4 \to \\ \times\ \ 4\ 7 \to \\ \hline \end{array}$ $\begin{array}{r} 8\ 2\ 7 \to \\ \times\ \ 6\ 9 \to \\ \hline \end{array}$

Line up the digits. Then estimate the products.

	a	b	c

5. 27×14 _____ 36×75 _____ 63×44 _____

$\begin{array}{r} 27 \to \\ \times\ 14 \to \\ \hline \end{array}$

6. 451×36 _____ 742×45 _____ 494×23 _____

Problem-Solving Method: Make a Table

Chris is ordering new equipment for the football league. He needs to buy 84 helmets, 32 footballs, and 100 team shirts. Footballs cost $24 each. The shirts cost $17 each. The helmets cost $39 each. What will be the total cost for the new equipment?

Understand the problem.

- **What do you want to know?**
  the total cost for the new equipment

- **What information is given?**
  the number and price of each item

Plan how to solve it.

- **What method can you use?**
  You can make a table to organize the information.

Solve it.

- **How can you use this method to solve the problem?**
  Find the total cost for each item. Then add these amounts to find the total cost of all the equipment.

NEW EQUIPMENT			
Equipment	**Number**	**Cost of One**	**Total Cost of Each Item**
Helmets	84	$39	84 × $39 = $3,276
Footballs	32	$24	32 × $24 = $768
Shirts	100	$17	100 × $17 = $1,700
Total Cost of All the Equipment:			**$5,783**

- **What is the answer?**
  The total cost of all the new equipment is $5,783.

Look back and check your answer.

- **Is your answer reasonable?**
  You can estimate to check your answer.

Helmets:	80 × $40 = $3,200
Footballs:	30 × $20 = $600
Shirts:	100 × $20 = $2,000
	$5,800

  The estimate is close to the answer.
  The answer is reasonable.

Make a table to solve each problem.

1. On Monday, Sam's Pizza sold 40 large pizzas, 57 mediums, and 35 smalls. A large pizza costs $12. Medium pizzas are $10 each, and small pizzas are $9 each. How much money did Sam's Pizza make on Monday?

Answer _____

2. Anya drove 2 hours to get to the train station. Then she rode the train for 14 hours. She drove about 55 miles per hour. The train traveled at about 80 miles per hour. How many miles did Anya travel altogether?

Answer _____

3. The dining hall has 25 round tables and 40 square tables. Each round table seats 11 people. Each square table seats 16 people. How many people can sit in the dining hall at the same time?

Answer _____

Dividing by 10

To divide by ten, remember that a number divided by one is that number.

Find: 50 ÷ 10

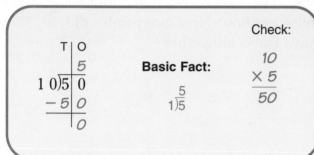

```
      T│O
        5           Basic Fact:        Check:
 1 0)5│0                                10
  -5│0                                × 5
  ───────              5               ────
      │0             1)5                50
```

Find: 263 ÷ 10

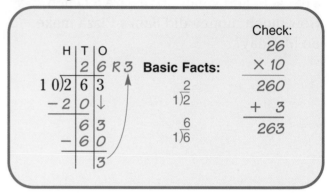

```
     H│T│O
       2│6 R3      Basic Facts:       Check:
 1 0)2│6│3                              26
  -2│0│↓             2               × 10
  ────────         1)2               ─────
     │6│3                              260
    -6│0             6               +  3
  ────────         1)6               ─────
     │ │3                              263
```

Use basic facts to divide. Check.

a   b   c   d

1.

```
      T│O
        4 R8
 1 0)4│8
  -4│0
  ──────
      8
```

```
   T│O
 1 0)7│2
```

```
   T│O
 1 0)8│0
```

```
   T│O
 1 0)5│4
```

2.

```
   T│O
 1 0)9│7
```

```
   T│O
 1 0)1│0
```

```
   T│O
 1 0)6│5
```

```
   T│O
 1 0)2│3
```

3.

```
   H│T│O
 1 0)3│4│0
```

```
   H│T│O
 1 0)1│8│0
```

```
   H│T│O
 1 0)2│0│0
```

```
   H│T│O
 1 0)2│4│0
```

4.

```
   H│T│O
 1 0)6│3│5
```

```
   H│T│O
 1 0)7│2│0
```

```
   H│T│O
 1 0)8│3│4
```

```
   H│T│O
 1 0)6│7│3
```

Dividing by Tens

To divide by tens, use basic division facts to choose a trial quotient.
Then multiply and subtract.

Find: 90 ÷ 30

To divide, use a basic fact.

T	O
	3

$$3\,0\,\overline{)9\,0}$$
$$-9\,0$$
$$0$$

Basic Fact:

$$\frac{3}{3)9}$$

Check:

$$\begin{array}{r} 30 \\ \times\ 3 \\ \hline 90 \end{array}$$

Find: 485 ÷ 60

To divide, use a basic fact.

H	T	O
		8 R5

$$6\,0\,\overline{)4\,8\,5}$$
$$-4\,8\,0$$
$$5$$

Basic Fact:

$$\frac{8}{6)48}$$

Check:

$$\begin{array}{r} 60 \\ \times\ 8 \\ \hline 480 \\ +\ \ 5 \\ \hline 485 \end{array}$$

Divide. Check.

	a	b	c	d
1.	$1\,0\,\overline{)9\,5}$	$3\,0\,\overline{)9\,0}$	$2\,0\,\overline{)6\,2}$	$8\,0\,\overline{)7\,2\,2}$
2.	$5\,0\,\overline{)3\,0\,0}$	$4\,0\,\overline{)2\,8\,3}$	$6\,0\,\overline{)6\,5}$	$7\,0\,\overline{)6,5\,1\,0}$
3.	$7\,0\,\overline{)3\,5\,0}$	$3\,0\,\overline{)1,2\,3\,0}$	$2\,0\,\overline{)2\,5}$	$5\,0\,\overline{)1\,0\,0}$
4.	$3\,0\,\overline{)1\,2\,1}$	$8\,0\,\overline{)1\,6\,0}$	$1\,0\,\overline{)3\,6}$	$9\,0\,\overline{)4,5\,9\,0}$

Set up the problems. Then find the quotients.

	a	b	c
5.	$810 \div 90 = $ _____	$493 \div 70 = $ _____	$120 \div 60 = $ _____

$$90\,\overline{)810}$$

Zeros in Quotients

When you cannot divide, write a zero in the quotient
as a place holder.

Find: 513 ÷ 5

Divide the hundreds.

```
 H | T | O
   1 |   |
5)5 | 1 | 3
 -5 | ↓ |
   0 | 1 |
```
```
  1
5)5
```

Divide the tens.

```
 H | T | O
   1 | 0 |
5)5 | 1 | 3
 -5 | ↓ |
   0 | 1 |
   - | 0 | ↓
     | 1 | 3
```
```
  0
5)1
```

← Write a zero in the
quotient as a place
holder.

1 < 5

Not enough tens.
Bring down the
3 ones.

Divide the ones.

```
 H | T | O
   1 | 0 | 2 R3
5)5 | 1 | 3
 -5 |   |
   0 | 1 |
   - | 0 |
     | 1 | 3
     | -1 | 0
     |    | 3
```
```
   2
5)13
```

Check:

```
   102
 ×   5
   510
 +   3
   513
```

Divide. Check.

          a   b   c   d

1.
```
 H | T | O
   1 | 0 | 2 R2
8)8 | 1 | 8
 -8 | ↓ |
   0 | 1 |
   - | 0 | ↓
     | 1 | 8
   - | 1 | 6
     |   | 2
```

```
 H | T | O
   |   |
3)9 | 2 | 2
```

```
 H | T | O
   |   |
8)8 | 5 | 3
```

```
 H | T | O
   |   |
4)8 | 3 | 3
```

2.
```
 H | T | O
   |   |
7)2 | 8 | 4
```

```
 H | T | O
   |   |
6)4 | 2 | 3
```

```
 H | T | O
   |   |
4)1 | 2 | 1
```

```
 H | T | O
   |   |
9)4 | 5 | 3
```

Divide. Check.

	a	*b*	*c*	*d*
1.	$3\overline{)3\ 0\ 3}$	$9\overline{)9\ 8\ 1}$	$4\overline{)2\ 0\ 3}$	$6\overline{)4\ 8\ 5}$
2.	$5\overline{)3\ 0\ 0}$	$7\overline{)4,9\ 3\ 0}$	$2\overline{)8\ 1\ 9}$	$8\overline{)7\ 2\ 7}$
3.	$9\overline{)2\ 7\ 8}$	$4\overline{)8\ 3\ 6}$	$3\overline{)9\ 1\ 3}$	$2\overline{)1,0\ 0\ 0}$
4.	$6\overline{)1\ 8\ 0}$	$5\overline{)3,5\ 0\ 4}$	$7\overline{)6\ 3\ 0}$	$8\overline{)3,2\ 0\ 8}$

Set up the problems. Then find the quotients.

	a	*b*	*c*
5.	$240 \div 6 =$ _____	$4,510 \div 5 =$ _____	$361 \div 9 =$ _____

$6\overline{)240}$

Trial Quotients: Too Large

When you divide, you may have to try several quotients.

If the product of the trial quotient and the divisor is greater than the dividend, your first trial quotient is too large. Try the number that is 1 less.

Find: 170 ÷ 34

Use rounding to choose a trial quotient.	Try 6 as your trial quotient.	Try 5 as your trial quotient.	Complete the problem.
$3\ 4\overline{)1\ 7\ 3}$ **Think:** 34 rounds to 30. 170 rounds to 200. $\frac{6}{3\overline{)20}}$ So, $\frac{6}{34\overline{)200}}$.	$\begin{array}{r}6\\3\ 4\overline{)1\ 7\ 3}\\-2\ 0\ 4\end{array}$ Since 204 > 173, 6 is too large.	$\begin{array}{r}5\\3\ 4\overline{)1\ 7\ 3}\\-1\ 7\ 0\end{array}$ Since 170 < 173, 5 is correct.	$\begin{array}{r}5\ R3\\3\ 4\overline{)1\ 7\ 3}\\-1\ 7\ 0\\\hline 3\end{array}$

Write *too large* or *correct* for each trial quotient.

	a	b	c
1.	$\begin{array}{r}2\\3\ 1\overline{)6\ 0\ 8}\\-6\ 2\end{array}$ *too large*	$\begin{array}{r}7\\4\ 3\overline{)3\ 2\ 9}\end{array}$ _____	$\begin{array}{r}3\\5\ 3\overline{)1,5\ 7\ 3}\end{array}$ _____
2.	$\begin{array}{r}2\\4\ 2\overline{)8,1\ 9\ 0}\end{array}$ _____	$\begin{array}{r}2\\1\ 2\overline{)2\ 3\ 9}\end{array}$ _____	$\begin{array}{r}5\\7\ 6\overline{)4\ 2\ 1}\end{array}$ _____
3.	$\begin{array}{r}7\\3\ 3\overline{)2,3\ 9\ 5}\end{array}$ _____	$\begin{array}{r}2\\6\ 3\overline{)1,8\ 4\ 6}\end{array}$ _____	$\begin{array}{r}5\\7\ 2\overline{)3,5\ 9\ 8}\end{array}$ _____

Trial Quotients: Too Small

If the difference between the dividend and the product of the trial quotient and divisor is greater than or equal to the divisor, your first trial quotient is too small. Try the number that is 1 greater.

Find: 527 ÷ 17

Use rounding to choose a trial quotient.	Try 2 as your trial quotient.	Try 3 as your trial quotient.	Complete the problem.
$1\ 7\overline{)5\ 2\ 7}$ **Think:** 17 rounds to 20. 527 rounds to 500. $2\overline{)5}$ So, $17\overline{)52}$.	$\begin{array}{r} 2 \\ 1\ 7\overline{)5\ 2\ 7} \\ -3\ 4 \\ \hline 1\ 8 \end{array}$ Since 18 > 17, 2 is too small.	$\begin{array}{r} 3 \\ 1\ 7\overline{)5\ 2\ 7} \\ -5\ 1 \\ \hline 1 \end{array}$ Since 1 < 17, 3 is correct.	$\begin{array}{r} 3\ 1 \\ 1\ 7\overline{)5\ 2\ 7} \\ -5\ 1 \downarrow \\ \hline 1\ 7 \\ -1\ 7 \\ \hline 0 \end{array}$

Write *too small* or *correct* for each trial quotient.

	a	b	c

1.

a.
$$\begin{array}{r} 5 \\ 2\ 8\overline{)1\ 6\ 8} \\ -1\ 4\ 0 \\ \hline 2\ 8 \end{array}$$ *too small*

b.
$$\begin{array}{r} 8 \\ 1\ 2\overline{)9\ 6\ 0} \end{array}$$ _____

c.
$$\begin{array}{r} 4 \\ 1\ 8\overline{)9\ 3\ 0} \end{array}$$ _____

2.

a.
$$\begin{array}{r} 1 \\ 2\ 6\overline{)5,4\ 8\ 6} \end{array}$$ _____

b.
$$\begin{array}{r} 4 \\ 5\ 7\overline{)2,8\ 5\ 9} \end{array}$$ _____

c.
$$\begin{array}{r} 5 \\ 7\ 8\overline{)3\ 9\ 0} \end{array}$$ _____

3.

a.
$$\begin{array}{r} 3 \\ 3\ 9\overline{)1,5\ 6\ 0} \end{array}$$ _____

b.
$$\begin{array}{r} 5 \\ 4\ 6\overline{)2,7\ 6\ 0} \end{array}$$ _____

c.
$$\begin{array}{r} 2 \\ 8\ 3\overline{)1,7\ 4\ 3} \end{array}$$ _____

Two-digit Divisors

To divide by a two-digit divisor, first choose a trial quotient. Then multiply and subtract.

Find: 889 ÷ 34

Choose a trial quotient.	Multiply and subtract.	Multiply and subtract.	Check:

Choose a trial quotient.

```
    H | T | O
3 4)8 | 8 | 9
```

Think:
```
   2
3)8  So, 34)88 is
about 2.
```

Multiply and subtract.

```
        T
    H | 2 | O
3 4)8 | 8 | 9
   -6 | 8 ↓
    2 | 0 | 9
```

Think:
```
    6
3)20  So, 34)209
is about 6.
```

Multiply and subtract.

```
        T | O
    H | 2 | 6  R5
3 4)8 | 8 | 9
   -6 | 8
    2 | 0 | 9
   -2 | 0 | 4
            5
```

Check:
```
   26
  ×34
  884
  + 5
  889
```

Divide.

	a	b	c	d

1.

a.
```
  H | T | O
    | 1 | 3
4 8)6 | 2 | 4
   -4 | 8 ↓
    1 | 4 | 4
   -1 | 4 | 4
            0
```

b.
```
  H | T | O
5 4)9 | 2 | 7
```

c.
```
  H | T | O
2 7)5 | 9 | 8
```

d.
```
  H | T | O
1 8)4 | 7 | 5
```

2.

a.
```
  H | T | O
6 2)2 | 1 | 4
```

b.
```
  H | T | O
8 1)4 | 2 | 8
```

c.
```
  H | T | O
3 5)2 | 8 | 0
```

d.
```
  H | T | O
9 1)8 | 1 | 3
```

3.

a.
```
  Th| H | T | O
4 6)9, | 8 | 6 | 6
```

b.
```
  Th| H | T | O
1 7)5, | 5 | 5 | 1
```

c.
```
  Th| H | T | O
2 3)6, | 4 | 0 | 0
```

d.
```
  Th| H | T | O
1 9)3, | 6 | 9 | 9
```

Divide.

	a	b	c	d

1. $3\ 8 \overline{)2\ 4\ 4}$ $\qquad$ $2\ 8 \overline{)1\ 6\ 8}$ $\qquad$ $1\ 4 \overline{)8\ 1\ 2}$ $\qquad$ $3\ 9 \overline{)5\ 9\ 1}$

2. $5\ 5 \overline{)7\ 8\ 1}$ $\qquad$ $3\ 2 \overline{)6\ 0\ 8}$ $\qquad$ $1\ 9 \overline{)2\ 7\ 0}$ $\qquad$ $1\ 5 \overline{)9\ 3\ 0}$

3. $6\ 3 \overline{)4,8\ 1\ 5}$ $\qquad$ $8\ 3 \overline{)4,6\ 4\ 8}$ $\qquad$ $4\ 2 \overline{)8,1\ 9\ 0}$ $\qquad$ $4\ 4 \overline{)5,5\ 6\ 6}$

4. $7\ 6 \overline{)4,1\ 0\ 4}$ $\qquad$ $9\ 1 \overline{)3,0\ 7\ 6}$ $\qquad$ $6\ 8 \overline{)2,4\ 3\ 9}$ $\qquad$ $8\ 5 \overline{)7,2\ 4\ 0}$

5. $2\ 4 \overline{)4,0\ 0\ 8}$ $\qquad$ $5\ 3 \overline{)1,5\ 8\ 4}$ $\qquad$ $1\ 3 \overline{)1,6\ 7\ 1}$ $\qquad$ $2\ 5 \overline{)7,8\ 5\ 5}$

Set up the problems. Then find the quotients.

	a	b	c

6. $886 \div 74 =$ _____ $\qquad$ $187 \div 22 =$ _____ $\qquad$ $645 \div 49 =$ _____

$74 \overline{)886}$

7. $6,409 \div 37 =$ _____ $\qquad$ $7,298 \div 36 =$ _____ $\qquad$ $7,545 \div 52 =$ _____

Estimating Quotients

To estimate quotients, round the numbers until you are able to use a basic fact.

Estimate: $237 \div 6$

Round the dividend to use a basic fact.
Divide.

$$6\overline{)2\ 3\ 7} \qquad\qquad 237 \div 6$$
$$\downarrow \quad\ \downarrow$$

Think: $24 \div 6 = 4 \qquad 240 \div 6 = 40$

Estimate: $418 \div 72$

Round the dividend and the divisor to use
a basic fact. Divide.

$$7\ 3\overline{)4\ 1\ 8} \qquad\qquad 418 \div 73$$
$$\downarrow \quad\ \downarrow$$

Think: $42 \div 7 = 6 \qquad 420 \div 70 = 6$

Round the dividends to estimate the quotients.

	a	b	c	d

1. $152 \div 4$ $248 \div 5$ $627 \div 7$ $825 \div 9$
$\downarrow \quad \downarrow \qquad\qquad \downarrow \quad \downarrow \qquad\qquad \downarrow \quad \downarrow \qquad\qquad \downarrow \quad \downarrow$
$160 \div 4 = 40$

2. $5{,}432 \div 8$ $2{,}651 \div 3$ $1{,}755 \div 6$ $4{,}859 \div 7$
$\downarrow \quad \downarrow \qquad\qquad \downarrow \quad \downarrow \qquad\qquad \downarrow \quad \downarrow \qquad\qquad \downarrow \quad \downarrow$

Round the dividends and the divisors to estimate the quotients.

	a	b	c	d

3. $345 \div 52$ $183 \div 89$ $778 \div 38$ $845 \div 19$
$\downarrow \quad \downarrow \qquad\qquad \downarrow \quad \downarrow \qquad\qquad \downarrow \quad \downarrow \qquad\qquad \downarrow \quad \downarrow$
$350 \div 50 = 7$

4. $2{,}417 \div 82$ $1{,}212 \div 21$ $3{,}219 \div 39$ $5{,}583 \div 94$
$\downarrow \quad \downarrow \qquad\qquad \downarrow \quad \downarrow \qquad\qquad \downarrow \quad \downarrow \qquad\qquad \downarrow \quad \downarrow$

Round the dividends to estimate the quotients.

         a   *b*   *c*

1. $4\overline{)3\ 5\ 8} \rightarrow 4\overline{)360}$ (90) $3\overline{)2\ 4\ 1} \rightarrow$ $7\overline{)2\ 0\ 7} \rightarrow$

2. $8\overline{)4\ 0\ 2} \rightarrow$ $6\overline{)3\ 6\ 3} \rightarrow$ $5\overline{)3\ 4\ 6} \rightarrow$

3. $2\overline{)1,1\ 3\ 2} \rightarrow$ $4\overline{)2,7\ 1\ 3} \rightarrow$ $9\overline{)5,5\ 3\ 4} \rightarrow$

Round the dividends and the divisors to estimate the quotients.

         a   *b*   *c*

4. $5\ 3\overline{)4\ 6\ 5} \rightarrow 50\overline{)450}$ (90) $3\ 1\overline{)8\ 6\ 6} \rightarrow$ $5\ 8\overline{)2\ 9\ 5} \rightarrow$

5. $2\ 4\overline{)1\ 5\ 8} \rightarrow$ $4\ 3\overline{)8\ 2\ 4} \rightarrow$ $8\ 7\overline{)2\ 7\ 5} \rightarrow$

6. $2\ 8\overline{)6,0\ 1\ 7} \rightarrow$ $9\ 4\overline{)3,4\ 8\ 1} \rightarrow$ $4\ 9\overline{)2,8\ 0\ 7} \rightarrow$

Problem-Solving Method: Complete a Pattern

In 1999, Old Faithful Geyser in Yellowstone National Park had about 56,000 visitors a week. About how many people visited each day?

Understand the problem.

- **What do you want to know?**
  about how many visitors there were each day

- **What information do you know?**
  56,000 people visited each week.
  There are 7 days in a week.

Plan how to solve it.

- **What method can you use?**
  You can find and complete a pattern.

Solve it.

- **How can you use this method to solve the problem?**
  Start with a basic division fact. Then use a pattern of zeros to find 56,000 ÷ 7.

56 ÷ 7 = 8	← Basic Fact
560 ÷ 7 = 80	
5,600 ÷ 7 = 800	
56,000 ÷ 7 = 8,000	← Zero Pattern
↑ ↑	
three zeros three zeros	

- **What is the answer?**
  About 8,000 people visited Old Faithful every day.

Look back and check your answer.

- **Is your answer reasonable?**
  You can check your division with multiplication.

$$\begin{array}{r} 8,000 \\ \times\ \ \ 7 \\ \hline 56,000 \end{array}$$

The product matches the dividend.
The answer is reasonable.

Complete a pattern to solve each problem.

1. The stadium has 48,000 seats. The seats are divided into 80 sections. How many seats are in each section?

48	÷	8	=	6
480	÷	80	=	6
4,800	÷	80	=	60
48,000	÷	80	=	_____

Answer _____

2. The theater collected $2,700 at the box office last night. If they sold 90 tickets, how much did each ticket cost?

27	÷	9	=	3
270	÷	90	=	3
2,700	÷	90	=	_____

Answer _____

3. The average human heart rate is 4,200 beats per hour. About how many times does a human heart beat per minute? (1 hour = 60 minutes)

42	÷	6	=	7
420	÷	60	=	7
4,200	÷	60	=	_____

Answer _____

4. In 1999, the Empire State Building had about 21,000 visitors each week. About how many people visited each day? (1 week = 7 days)

21	÷	7	=	3
210	÷	7	=	30
2,100	÷	7	=	300
21,000	÷	7	=	_____

Answer _____

5. The factory has 40 trucks to deliver 3,600 computers. How many computers will each truck deliver?

36	÷	4	=	_____
360	÷	40	=	_____
3,600	÷	40	=	_____

Answer _____

6. A passenger helicopter can fly 3,000 miles in 10 hours. What is the average speed of the helicopter?

3	÷	1	=	_____
30	÷	10	=	_____
300	÷	10	=	_____
3,000	÷	10	=	_____

Answer _____

Problem Solving

Solve.

1. In 10 hours, Noriko drove her car 520 miles. She drove the same number of miles each hour. How many miles did she travel each hour?

   Answer _____

2. The lodge members collected 840 cans of food. They put 24 cans in each box. How many boxes did they fill?

   Answer _____

3. Dale spends $5,832 each year on rent. He pays the same amount each month. How much are his monthly payments?

   Answer _____

4. Angelo's Bakery sold 4,123 pies in July. How many pies did they sell during an average day? (There are 31 days in July.)

   Answer _____

5. One of the tallest buildings in the world is the Petronas Tower in Malaysia. It is 1,483 feet tall and has 88 stories. Estimate how tall each story is.

   Answer _____

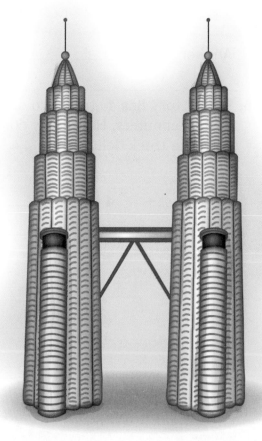

6. Kay has 486 beads. She plans to use 35 beads for each necklace. How many necklaces can she make? How many beads will she have left over?

   Answer _____

UNIT 5 Review

Multiply. Check.

	a	*b*	*c*	*d*
1.	4 0 × 9	7 ×4 0	1 0 0 × 8	6 ×1 0 0
2.	1 7 ×3 4	8 5 ×5 2	4 8 ×2 3	8 9 ×6 7
3.	1 3 5 × 2 4	8 6 2 × 1 9	4 0 3 × 5 8	6 8 3 × 4 1

Set up the problems. Then find the products.

	a	*b*	*c*
4.	37 × 45 = _____	68 × 19 = _____	94 × 56 = _____
5.	394 × 22 = _____	708 × 64 = _____	589 × 37 = _____

Estimate the products.

	a	*b*	*c*	*d*
6.	4 9 → ×2 2 →	5 7 → ×3 8 →	1 8 4 → × 6 7 →	2 6 9 → × 8 3 →

Divide. Check.

	a	b	c	d

7. 1 0)8 5   2 0)6 0 0   3 0)6 9   7 0)5, 6 1 5

8. 9)1 8 1   7)7 7 4   6)1, 2 3 4   8)2, 4 6 4

9. 4 7)2 3 5   2 4)1, 1 7 6   6 3)6, 4 5 0   7 9)4, 9 3 8

Set up the problems. Then find the quotients.

	a	b	c

10. 511 ÷ 36 = _____   614 ÷ 28 = _____   4,368 ÷ 81 = _____

Write _too large_, _too small_, or _correct_ for each trial quotient.

	a	b	c

11.
6
3 4)1 9 5
_____

5
6 5)4, 0 4 1
_____

7
2 9)2, 2 9 5
_____

Estimate the quotients by rounding each number until you can use a basic fact.

	a	b	c	d

12. 637 ÷ 8   4,863 ÷ 7   567 ÷ 74   1,786 ÷ 89
↓   ↓   ↓   ↓   ↓   ↓   ↓   ↓

Make a table to solve each problem.

13. Bill sold 28 large T-shirts, 42 mediums, and 17 smalls. A large T-shirt costs $18. Medium T-shirts are $16 each, and small T-shirts are $12 each. How much money did Bill make for all the T-shirts he sold?

Answer _____

14. Jane bought 13 packs of plates, 25 packs of cups, and 8 packs of napkins. There are 80 plates in each pack, 40 cups in each pack, and 100 napkins in each pack. Which item does she have the most of?

Answer _____

Find and complete a pattern to solve each problem.

15. A frog's heart beats 1,800 times per hour. About how many times does a frog's heart beat per minute?
(1 hour = 60 minutes)

Answer _____

16. In 1999, the London Tower in England got about 49,000 visitors each week. About how many people visited each day?

Answer _____

17. The telethon collected $6,400 yesterday in $80 pledges. How many people pledged $80 each?

Answer _____

unit 6
Time, money, and measurement

Time

A **day** is divided into **hours, minutes,** and **seconds**.
Both of these clocks show the same time of day.

Write: 2:35

Read: 35 minutes after 2
or 25 minutes
before 3

| 1 day = 24 hours |
| 1 hour = 60 minutes |
| 1 minute = 60 seconds |

You can multiply or divide to change units of time.

To change larger units to smaller units, multiply.

8 hours = ___480___ minutes

8 × 60 = 480

total hours × minutes in one hour

To change smaller units to larger units, divide.

180 seconds = ___3___ minutes

180 ÷ 60 = 3

total seconds ÷ seconds in one minute

Write the time shown on each clock.

1.

_____4:45_____   _____   _____   _____

Change the units of time.

a   b

2. 120 minutes = _____ hours   4 minutes = _____ seconds

3. 10 hours = _____ minutes   5 days = _____ hours

4. 144 hours = _____ days   540 seconds = _____ minutes

5. 20 days = _____ hours   half hour = _____ minutes

Calendar

A year is divided into **months, weeks,** and **days**.
The **calendar** below shows the 365 days in the year 2001.

CALENDAR FOR THE YEAR 2001			
JANUARY	**FEBRUARY**	**MARCH**	**APRIL**
S M T W T F S	S M T W T F S	S M T W T F S	S M T W T F S
1 2 3 4 5 6 7 8 9 10 11 12 13 14 15 16 17 18 19 20 21 22 23 24 25 26 27 28 29 30 31	1 2 3 4 5 6 7 8 9 10 11 12 13 14 15 16 17 18 19 20 21 22 23 24 25 26 27 28	1 2 3 4 5 6 7 8 9 10 11 12 13 14 15 16 17 18 19 20 21 22 23 24 25 26 27 28 29 30 31	1 2 3 4 5 6 7 8 9 10 11 12 13 14 15 16 17 18 19 20 21 22 23 24 25 26 27 28 29 30
MAY	**JUNE**	**JULY**	**AUGUST**
S M T W T F S	S M T W T F S	S M T W T F S	S M T W T F S
1 2 3 4 5 6 7 8 9 10 11 12 13 14 15 16 17 18 19 20 21 22 23 24 25 26 27 28 29 30 31	1 2 3 4 5 6 7 8 9 10 11 12 13 14 15 16 17 18 19 20 21 22 23 24 25 26 27 28 29 30	1 2 3 4 5 6 7 8 9 10 11 12 13 14 15 16 17 18 19 20 21 22 23 24 25 26 27 28 29 30 31	1 2 3 4 5 6 7 8 9 10 11 12 13 14 15 16 17 18 19 20 21 22 23 24 25 26 27 28 29 30 31
SEPTEMBER	**OCTOBER**	**NOVEMBER**	**DECEMBER**
S M T W T F S	S M T W T F S	S M T W T F S	S M T W T F S
1 2 3 4 5 6 7 8 9 10 11 12 13 14 15 16 17 18 19 20 21 22 23 24 25 26 27 28 29 30	1 2 3 4 5 6 7 8 9 10 11 12 13 14 15 16 17 18 19 20 21 22 23 24 25 26 27 28 29 30 31	1 2 3 4 5 6 7 8 9 10 11 12 13 14 15 16 17 18 19 20 21 22 23 24 25 26 27 28 29 30	1 2 3 4 5 6 7 8 9 10 11 12 13 14 15 16 17 18 19 20 21 22 23 24 25 26 27 28 29 30 31

> 7 days = 1 week
> 52 weeks = 1 year
> 12 months = 1 year

Use the calendar to write each day and date.

 a *b*

1. 2 days after November 12, 2001

Wednesday, November 14, 2001

5 days before April 1, 2001

2. the third Tuesday in February, 2001

2 weeks after July 4, 2001

3. 1 week before December 5, 2001

3 days after the last Monday in May, 2001

Change the units of time.

 a *b*

4. 7 days = ____168____ hours

48 months = _____ years

5. 3 weeks = _____ days

2 years = _____ days

6. 112 days = _____ weeks

15 years = _____ months

7. 3 years = _____ weeks

84 days = _____ weeks

Elapsed Time

Elapsed time is the amount of time that passes from the start of an event to its end.

These clocks show that 3 hours and 15 minutes elapse between 8:00 and 11:15.

Start   **End**

You can add or subtract elapsed time.

To find when an event ended, add.	To find when an event started, subtract.
Start Time ⟶ 8:00 *8 hr 0 min*	End Time ⟶ 11:15 *11 hr 15 min*
+ Elapsed Time ⟶ *+ 3 hr 15 min*	− Elapsed Time ⟶ *− 3 hr 15 min*
End Time ⟶ 11:15 *11 hr 15 min*	Start Time ⟶ 8:00 *8 hr 0 min*

Tell how much time has elapsed.

              a   *b*

1.   →      

            40 minutes

2.   →      

Find when each event started or ended.

              a   *b*

3. Start: 7:10   *7 hr 10 min*   **End:** 10:30   *10 hr 30 min*

     Elapsed Time: 1 hr 15 min   *+ 1 hr 15 min*   **Elapsed Time:** 3 hr 5 min   *− 3 hr 5 min*

Using a Schedule

A **schedule** is a list or table showing when events happen.

FLIGHT SCHEDULE from CHICAGO, ILLINOIS		
Destination	**Departs**	**Arrives**
New Orleans, Louisiana	7:15	10:45
Houston, Texas	9:00	11:35
Birmingham, Alabama	2:30	4:05
Jackson, Mississippi	3:20	5:35
Kansas City, Missouri	6:00	7:20
Little Rock, Arkansas	8:00	9:35

Use the flight schedule to find each answer.

a   *b*

1. How long is the flight from Chicago to Houston?

   2 hours and 35 minutes
   _____

   How long is the flight from Chicago to Little Rock?

   _____

2. How long is the flight from Chicago to New Orleans?

   _____

   How long is the flight from Chicago to Birmingham?

   _____

3. How long is the flight from Chicago to Jackson?

   _____

   How long is the flight from Chicago to Kansas City?

   _____

4. Which is the shortest flight on the schedule?

   _____

   Which is the longest flight on the schedule?

   _____

5. If it takes 60 minutes to check in for a flight, what time should you arrive at the airport for the flight to Houston?

   _____

   If it takes 30 minutes to drive to the airport, what time should you leave to meet the flight when it arrives in New Orleans?

   _____

Money

To write money amounts, use a **decimal point**, or period, to separate dollars and cents.
A **decimal** is a number less than 1.

These coins are each worth less than 1 dollar.

penny	nickel	dime	quarter	half-dollar
1¢ or $0.01	5¢ or $0.05	10¢ or $0.10	25¢ or $0.25	50¢ or $0.50

These bills are each worth 1 dollar or more.

1 dollar	5 dollars	10 dollars
$1 or $1.00	$5 or $5.00	$10 or $10.00

Answer each question. Remember, 1 dollar = 100 cents.

a

1. 1 dollar = ___100___ pennies
2. 1 dollar = _____ dimes
3. 1 dollar = _____ half-dollars
4. $10.00 = _____ dollars
5. $0.55 = _____ nickels

b

1 dollar = _____ nickels

1 dollar = _____ quarters

$5.00 = _____ dollars

$0.30 = _____ dimes

$1.25 = _____ quarters

Write each money amount using digits.

a

6. two dollars and thirty cents ___$2.30___
7. nine cents _____
8. eighteen dollars _____
9. 3 nickels and 4 pennies _____

b

seven dollars and forty cents _____

ten dollars and sixty-one cents _____

thirteen dollars and two cents _____

2 quarters and 4 dimes _____

Add and Subtract Money

Add and subtract money the same way as whole numbers.
First line up the decimal points. Add or subtract.
Then place the decimal point and **dollar sign** in the answer.

Find: $0.25 + $1.15

Line up the decimal points.	Add. Write your answer in dollars and cents.
$ 0.2 5 + 1.1 5	$0.25 + 1.1 5 $ 1.4 0

Find: $1.00 − $0.25

Line up the decimal points.	Subtract. Write your answer in dollars and cents.
$ 1.0 0 − 0.2 5	0 9 10 $ 1.0 0 − 0.2 5 $ 0.7 5

Add.

	a	b	c	d
1.	$ 0.2 5 + 0.3 1	$ 0.5 4 + 0.2 9	$ 0.2 8 + 1.3 6	$ 1.2 9 + 0.5 2

$0.5 6

2.	$ 2.1 9 + 5.1 4	$ 2.2 6 + 3.1 7	$ 4.2 5 + 3.3 5	$ 2 2.5 0 + 1 4.0 7

Subtract.

	a	b	c	d
3.	$ 0.9 9 − 0.4 5	$ 0.2 7 − 0.1 4	$ 2.6 5 − 1.4 0	$ 2 0.4 8 − 1 0.3 5

$0.5 4

4.	$ 0.7 2 − 0.2 3	$ 0.9 2 − 0.4 7	$ 4.3 5 − 2.4 8	$ 5.5 7 − 2.7 9

Multiply and Divide Money

Multiply and divide money the same as whole numbers.
To multiply, first set up the problem. Multiply or divide.
Then place the decimal point and dollar sign in the answer.

Find: $5.42 × 3

Set up the problem.	Multiply. Write your answer in dollars and cents.
$ 5.4 2 × 3	$ 5.4 2 × 3 $ 1 6.2 6

Find: $2.10 ÷ 3

Set up the problem.	Divide. Write your answer in dollars and cents.	Check.
3)$ 2.1 0	$ 0.7 0 3)$2.1 0 −2.1 0 0	2 $ 0.7 0 × 3 $ 2.1 0

Multiply.

	a	b	c	d
1.	1 $ 2.2 1 × 7 $ 1 5.4 7	$ 2.3 2 × 4	$ 4.5 1 × 5	$ 1.0 6 × 8
2.	$ 1.1 0 × 2 5	$ 2.1 2 × 1 4	$ 1.2 5 × 3 0	$ 2.0 7 × 1 1

Divide.

3.

   4)$ 2.4 8   5)$ 3.5 0   8)$ 4.0 0   6)$ 3.7 2

4.

   9)$ 3.6 0   7)$ 4 2.0 0   6)$ 3 6.1 2   4)$ 0.8 4

Problem-Solving Method: Work Backwards

Maggie had $9.25 left over after going to the State Fair. Admission was $12.50. She spent $18.75 on ride tickets and bought a funnel cake for $2.50. How much money did she take to the fair?

Understand the problem.

- **What do you want to know?**
  how much money Maggie took to the fair

- **What information is given?**
  She spent $12.50 to get in, $18.75 for rides, and $2.50 for food. She had $9.25 left over.

Plan how to solve it.

- **What method can you use?**
  You can work backwards. Work from the amount she had left to find the amount she started with.

Solve it.

- **How can you use this method to solve the problem?**
  Addition is the opposite of subtraction. So, add the amounts she spent to the amount she had left over.

$$
\begin{array}{rl}
\$\ 9.25 & \leftarrow \text{amount left over} \\
12.50 & \leftarrow \text{admission} \\
18.75 & \leftarrow \text{ride tickets} \\
+\ \ 2.50 & \leftarrow \text{funnel cake} \\
\hline
\$43.00 &
\end{array}
$$

- **What is the answer?**
  Maggie took $43.00 to the State Fair.

Look back and check your answer.

- **Is your answer reasonable?**
  You can check by working forwards. Subtract the amounts she spent from the amount she took to the fair.

$$
\begin{array}{r}
\$43.00 \\
-\ \ 12.50 \\
\hline
\$30.50 \\
-\ \ 18.75 \\
\hline
\$11.75 \\
-\ \ 2.50 \\
\hline
\$\ 9.25
\end{array}
$$

The amounts left over match. The answer is reasonable.

Work backwards to solve each problem.

1. Juan had $9.45 left over after going to the movies. He spent $7.50 for his ticket. Then he bought popcorn for $3.75 and a drink for $2.35. How much money did he start with?

Answer _____

2. Craig gave the cashier $50 to pay for 4 CDs. His change was $2.00. How much did each CD cost?

Answer _____

3. Soccer practice ended at 7:00. The team stretched for 10 minutes and practiced for 40 minutes. Then they played a game for 35 minutes. What time did the soccer practice start?

Answer _____

4. Latoya got home from shopping at 4:30. She spent 1 hour and 15 minutes at the mall. Then she did her grocery shopping for 30 minutes. What time did she start shopping?

Answer _____

5. Naomi has $35.00 left over from her paycheck after paying bills. Her rent is $450.00 and her car insurance is $85.25. She spent $46.81 on groceries. How much is her paycheck?

Answer _____

Customary Units

Measure Length

1 foot (ft.) = 12 inches (in.)
1 yard (yd.) = 3 ft.
1 mile (mi.) = 5,280 ft.

One inch is this long.

$\vdash$———— 1 in. ————$\dashv$

This page is about 1 foot long.

A door is about 1 yard wide.

A mile is about the distance you can walk in 20 minutes.

Measure Weight

1 pound (lb.) = 16 ounces (oz.)
1 ton (T.) = 2,000 pounds

A slice of bread weighs about 1 ounce.

A box of cereal weighs about 1 pound.

A truck weighs about 1 ton.

Measure Capacity

1 pint (pt.) = 2 cups (c.)
1 quart (qt.) = 2 pt.
1 gallon (gal.) = 4 qt.

A school milk carton holds 1 cup.

A small container of ice cream holds 1 pint.

A small saucepan holds about 1 quart.

A large jug of milk holds 1 gallon.

Choose the most appropriate unit of measure. Write *in.*, *ft.*, or *mi.*

       a   *b*

1. length of your finger _____*in.*_____ height of a flagpole _____

2. width of a room _____ length of Lake Erie _____

Choose the most appropriate unit of measure. Write *oz.*, *lb.*, or *T.*

       a   *b*

3. weight of a dog _____*lb.*_____ weight of a truckload of coal _____

4. weight of a ship _____ weight of a comb _____

Choose the most appropriate unit of measure. Write *c.*, *pt.*, *qt.*, or *gal.*

       a   *b*

5. capacity of a coffee mug _____*c.*_____ capacity of a bathtub _____

6. capacity of a container of yogurt _____ capacity of a baby bottle _____

Change the units of measure.

	a	*b*	*c*
7.	2 lb. = ___32___ oz.	2,000 lb. = _____ T.	32 oz. = _____ lb.
8.	3 yd. = _____ ft.	5,280 ft. = _____ mi.	6 ft. = _____ in.
9.	4 pt. = _____ qt.	6 c. = _____ pt.	5 gal. = _____ qt.

Metric Units

Measure Length	Measure Weight	Measure Capacity
1 meter (m) = 100 centimeters (cm) 1 kilometer (km) = 1,000 meters	1 kilogram (kg) = 1,000 grams (g)	1 liter (L) = 1,000 milliliters (mL)

One centimeter is this long. $\vdash$ 1 cm $\dashv$

A baseball bat is about 1 meter long.

A kilometer is about the distance you can walk in 15 minutes.

A paper clip weighs about 1 gram.

A dictionary weighs about 1 kilogram.

An eyedropper holds about 1 milliliter.

A large bottle of soda holds 2 liters.

Choose the most appropriate unit of measure. Write *cm*, *m*, or *km*.

	a		b
1. distance between airports	_____km_____	height of a giraffe	_____
2. width of a doorway	_____	length of a toothbrush	_____

Choose the most appropriate unit of measure. Write *g* or *kg*.

	a		b
3. weight of a notebook	_____kg_____	weight of a feather	_____
4. weight of a penny	_____	weight of a football	_____

Choose the most appropriate unit of measure. Write *mL* or *L*.

	a		b
5. capacity of a baby bottle	_____mL_____	capacity of a juice glass	_____
6. capacity of a kitchen sink	_____	capacity of a spoon	_____

Change the units of measure.

	a		b		c
7. 3 L =	_____3,000_____ mL	500 cm =	_____ m	2 kg =	_____ g
8. 4 km =	_____ m	8,000 g =	_____ kg	5 L =	_____ mL
9. 10 m =	_____ cm	6,000 mL =	_____ L	1,000 cm =	_____ m

Comparing Units of Measurement

To compare two measurements, first try to change them to the same unit.

Remember, to change larger units to smaller units, multiply.

Compare: 2 m to 300 cm

> **Think:** 1 m = 100 cm
> 2 m = 2 × 100 = 200 cm
>
> 200 cm _is less than_ 300 cm
>
> 2m ___<___ 300 cm

Compare: 15 qt. to 3 gal.

> **Think:** 1 gal. = 4 qt.
> 3 gal. = 3 × 4 = 12 qt.
>
> 15 qt. _is greater than_ 12 qt.
>
> 15 qt. ___>___ 3 gal.

Compare. Write <, >, or =.

	a	b	c
1.	48 in. __=__ 4 ft.	3,500 g _____ 4 kg	500 mm _____ 5 cm
	1 ft. = 12 in. 4 ft. = 4 × 12 = 48 in.		
2.	3 km _____ 2,000 m	2 T. _____ 4,000 lb.	40,000 mL _____ 40 L
3.	12 ft. _____ 5 yd.	6 pt. _____ 10 c.	5 ft. _____ 600 in.
4.	2 mi. _____ 5,280 ft.	10 m _____ 1,000 cm	7 gal. _____ 30 qt.
5.	3 km _____ 2,000 m	5 T. _____ 500 lb.	8,000 g _____ 80 kg
6.	30 qt. _____ 5 gal.	10 km _____ 10,000 m	40 yd. _____ 120 ft.
7.	6 ft. _____ 100 in.	48 oz. _____ 2 lb.	9 L _____ 9,000 mL

Problem-Solving Method: Use a Graph

Devon is planning a trip to Seattle, Washington sometime between October and February. He found this graph on the Internet. He wants to pick the least rainy time to go. In which month should he go to Seattle?

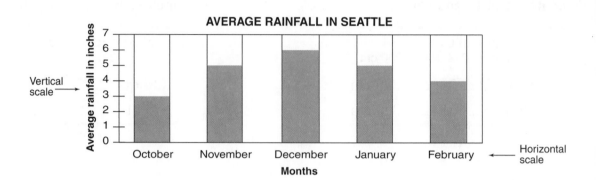

Understand the problem.	•	**What do you want to know?** the least rainy time between October and February to visit Seattle
	•	**What information is given?** a bar graph showing the average monthly rainfall in Seattle
Plan how to solve it.	•	**What method can you use?** You can use the bar graph to compare the data.
Solve it.	•	**How can you use this method to solve the problem?** Compare the lengths of the bars for each month. The month with the shortest bar has the least rainfall.
	•	**What is the answer?** Devon should plan his trip for October.
Look back and check your answer.	•	**Is your answer reasonable?** You can find the number of inches of rain for each month on the vertical scale of the graph and compare.

Oct. = 3 in.
Nov. = 5 in.
Dec. = 6 in.
Jan. = 5 in.
Feb. = 4 in.

October has the least average rainfall, 3 inches.
The answer is reasonable.

Use the graphs to solve each problem.

HEAVIEST LAND MAMMALS

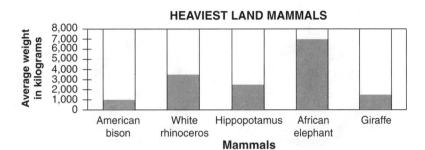

1. Which animal is the heaviest? What is its average weight?

Answer _____

2. Which animal is the lightest? What is its average weight?

Answer _____

3. How much more does a white rhinoceros weigh than a giraffe weighs?

Answer _____

4. A polar bear can weigh 400 kilograms less than the average American bison. How much can a polar bear weigh?

Answer _____

AVERAGE WATER USAGE IN UNITED STATES

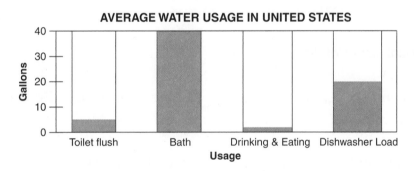

5. Which activity uses the least amount of water? How much water does it use?

Answer _____

6. Which activity uses the greatest amount of water? How much water does it use?

Answer _____

7. How much water would 3 dishwasher loads use?

Answer _____

8. How much water would you use if you took a bath every day for a week?

Answer _____

Write the time shown on each clock.

a	*b*	*c*	*d*

1.

_____   _____   _____   _____

Change the units of time.

2. 5 weeks = _____ days

3. 36 months = _____ years

4. 7 hours = _____ minutes

5. 3 days = _____ hours

Find when each event started or ended.

6. Start: 4:25 **Elapsed Time:** 2 hr 30 min

_____

7. End: 11:00 **Elapsed Time:** 1 hr 45 min

_____

Write each money amount using digits.

a	*b*
8. twenty-five dollars and six cents _____	nine dollars and fifteen cents _____
9. five dollars and ten cents _____	eighty-nine cents _____

Find each answer.

a	*b*	*c*	*d*
10. $ 1 3.4 8 + 5.2 7	$ 2 7.6 3 − 2 4.7 9	$ 2.3 5 × 3 2	4)$ 4.9 6

Compare. Write <, >, or =.

a	*b*
11. 36 in. _____ 2 ft.	5,000 g _____ 5 kg
12. 4 lb. _____ 32 oz.	400 cm _____ 3 m

Change the units of measure.

a   b

13. 3 lb. = _____ oz.   4 T. = _____ lb.

14. 21 ft. = _____ yd.   2 mi. = _____ ft.

15. 8 c. = _____ pt.   10 pt. = _____ qt.

16. 2 L = _____ mL   700 cm = _____ m

Work backwards to solve each problem.

17. Charlie has $11.50 left after paying for his art supplies. He bought a canvas for $38.99 and paintbrushes for $42.70. Then he spent $85.00 on paints. How much money did he start with?

18. Anita has to be at work by 8:30. She needs 45 minutes to get dressed and have breakfast. It takes her 25 minutes to drive to work. What time should she wake up in the morning?

Answer _____

Answer _____

Use the graph to solve each problem.

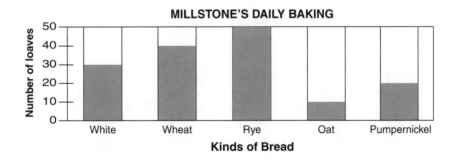

MILLSTONE'S DAILY BAKING

19. Which kind of bread does Millstone bake the greatest number of each day? How many loaves?

20. How many more loaves of white bread than oat bread does Millstone bake?

Answer _____

Answer _____

unit 7
fractions and Geometry

Meaning of Fractions

A **fraction** names a part of a whole. This circle has 4 equal parts.
The purple part is $\frac{1}{4}$ of the circle.

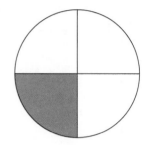

numerator

$\dfrac{1 \text{ — one purple part}}{4 \text{ — four parts in all}}$

Write: $\frac{1}{4}$

Read: one-fourth

denominator

Use the pictures to complete Exercises 1–6.

A	B	C	D	E	F

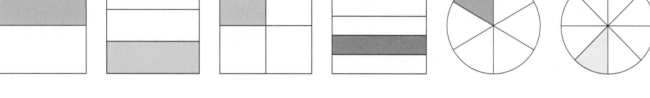

1. Square A has how many equal parts? _____2_____

   The green part is __$\frac{1}{2}$__ or _____one-half_____ of the square.

2. Square B has how many equal parts? _____

   The orange part is _____ or _____ of the square.

3. Square C has how many equal parts? _____

   The blue part is _____ or _____ of the square.

4. Square D has how many equal parts? _____

   The purple part is _____ or _____ of the square.

5. Circle E has how many equal parts? _____

   The pink part is _____ or _____ of the circle.

6. Circle F has how many equal parts? _____

   The yellow part is _____ or _____ of the circle.

Using Fractions

A fraction can name part of a group. Four of the eight cookies are chocolate chip. Or, four-eighths of the cookies are chocolate chip.

$\frac{4}{8}$ of the cookies are chocolate chip.

You can use fractions to find part of a group. To find $\frac{1}{2}$ of 8, divide 8 by 2.

$$8 \div 2 = 4$$

$\frac{1}{2}$ of 8, or 4, of the cookies are chocolate chip.

Find: $\frac{1}{2}$ **of 20**

> To find $\frac{1}{2}$, divide by 2.
> $$20 \div 2 = 10$$
> $$\frac{1}{2} \text{ of } 20 = 10$$

Find: one-fourth of 16

> To find $\frac{1}{4}$, divide by 4.
> $$16 \div 4 = 8$$
> $$\frac{1}{4} \text{ of } 16 = 4$$

Find each number.

a

b

1. To find $\frac{1}{3}$, divide by _____3_____.

To find one-sixth, divide by _____.

2. To find $\frac{1}{8}$, divide by _____.

To find one-tenth, divide by _____.

3. $\frac{1}{4}$ of 20 = _____

One-third of 18 is _____.

4. $\frac{1}{2}$ of 50 = _____

One-sixth of 42 is _____.

5. $\frac{1}{3}$ of 18 = _____

One-half of $1.00 is _____.

6. $\frac{1}{10}$ of $20.00 = _____

One-eighth of $64.00 is _____.

7. $\frac{1}{6}$ of $12.00 = _____

One-fifth of 25 is _____.

Adding Fractions

Like fractions are fractions with the same denominators. To add like fractions, add only the numerators. Then use the same denominator for the sum.

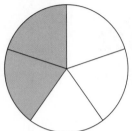

+

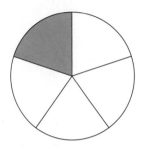

=

2 pink parts	+	1 purple part	=	3 yellow parts
5 parts		5 parts		5 parts

$$\frac{2}{5} \qquad + \qquad \frac{1}{5} \qquad = \qquad \frac{2+1}{5} = \frac{3}{5}$$

Find $\frac{2}{6} + \frac{3}{6}$

$$\frac{2}{6} + \frac{3}{6} \begin{array}{l} \rightarrow \text{ Add the numerators.} \\ \rightarrow \text{ Write the denominator.} \end{array} \rightarrow \frac{2+3}{6} = \frac{5}{6}$$

Add.

	a	*b*	*c*
1.	$\frac{4}{9} + \frac{3}{9} = \underline{\frac{4+3}{9} = \frac{7}{9}}$	$\frac{3}{7} + \frac{3}{7} = \underline{\hspace{2cm}}$	$\frac{2}{8} + \frac{1}{8} = \underline{\hspace{2cm}}$
2.	$\frac{2}{5} + \frac{2}{5} = \underline{\hspace{2cm}}$	$\frac{8}{10} + \frac{1}{10} = \underline{\hspace{2cm}}$	$\frac{3}{9} + \frac{5}{9} = \underline{\hspace{2cm}}$
3.	$\frac{1}{3} + \frac{1}{3} = \underline{\hspace{2cm}}$	$\frac{6}{8} + \frac{1}{8} = \underline{\hspace{2cm}}$	$\frac{3}{7} + \frac{2}{7} = \underline{\hspace{2cm}}$

Find the missing fraction in each number sentence.

	a	*b*
4.	$\frac{2}{9} + \underline{\quad\frac{5}{9}\quad} = \frac{7}{9}$	$\frac{3}{7} + \underline{\hspace{3cm}} = \frac{5}{7}$
5.	$\frac{6}{10} + \underline{\hspace{3cm}} = \frac{9}{10}$	$\frac{1}{6} + \underline{\hspace{3cm}} = \frac{5}{6}$

Subtracting Fractions

To subtract like fractions, subtract only the numerators.
Then use the same denominator for the difference.

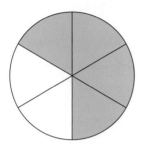   −   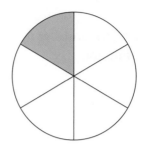   =

$\dfrac{4 \text{ green parts}}{6 \text{ parts}}$	−	$\dfrac{3 \text{ green parts}}{6 \text{ parts}}$	=	$\dfrac{1 \text{ green part}}{6 \text{ parts}}$
$\dfrac{4}{6}$	−	$\dfrac{3}{6}$	=	$\dfrac{4-3}{6} = \dfrac{1}{6}$

Find $\dfrac{6}{10} - \dfrac{3}{10}$

$$\dfrac{6}{10} - \dfrac{3}{10} \quad \rightarrow \begin{array}{l} \text{Subtract the numerators.} \\ \text{Write the denominator.} \end{array} \rightarrow \quad \dfrac{6-3}{10} = \dfrac{3}{10}$$

Subtract.

      a   *b*   *c*

1. $\dfrac{7}{8} - \dfrac{4}{8} = \underline{\dfrac{7-4}{8} = \dfrac{3}{8}}$ $\dfrac{4}{7} - \dfrac{3}{7} = \underline{\qquad}$ $\dfrac{2}{5} - \dfrac{1}{5} = \underline{\qquad}$

2. $\dfrac{6}{7} - \dfrac{5}{7} = \underline{\qquad}$ $\dfrac{8}{10} - \dfrac{1}{10} = \underline{\qquad}$ $\dfrac{6}{9} - \dfrac{5}{9} = \underline{\qquad}$

3. $\dfrac{2}{3} - \dfrac{1}{3} = \underline{\qquad}$ $\dfrac{5}{8} - \dfrac{4}{8} = \underline{\qquad}$ $\dfrac{6}{7} - \dfrac{4}{7} = \underline{\qquad}$

Find the missing fraction in each number sentence.

                        a   *b*

4. $\dfrac{5}{9} - \underline{\dfrac{4}{9}\qquad} = \dfrac{1}{9}$ $\dfrac{6}{7} - \underline{\qquad} = \dfrac{2}{7}$

5. $\dfrac{6}{10} - \underline{\qquad} = \dfrac{3}{10}$ $\dfrac{6}{8} - \underline{\qquad} = \dfrac{5}{8}$

Problem-Solving Method: Make an Organized List

Acme Hardware Store sells three sizes of screws: $\frac{1}{4}$ inch, $\frac{1}{2}$ inch, and $\frac{3}{4}$ inch. All of the screws come in two styles: Phillips head or flat head. How many different kinds of screws does the store sell?

Understand the problem.

- **What do you want to know?**
  how many different kinds of screws they sell

- **What information is given?**
  Sizes: $\frac{1}{4}$ inch, $\frac{1}{2}$ inch, and $\frac{3}{4}$ inch
  Styles: Phillips head or flat head

Plan how to solve it.

- **What method can you use?**
  You can make a list of the different style-size combinations. Then count the combinations.

- **How can you use this method to solve the problem?**
  Start with the first style and list all of its sizes.
  Then do the same thing for the other style.

Style	Size
Phillips head	$\frac{1}{4}$ inch
Phillips head	$\frac{1}{2}$ inch
Phillips head	$\frac{3}{4}$ inch

Style	Size
flat head	$\frac{1}{4}$ inch
flat head	$\frac{1}{2}$ inch
flat head	$\frac{3}{4}$ inch

Solve it.

- **What is the answer?**
  Acme Hardware Store sells 6 different kinds of screws.

Look back and check your answer.

- **Is your answer reasonable?**

You can check by making a tree diagram.

The counts match. The answer is reasonable.

Style	Size	Combination
Phillips head	$\frac{1}{4}$ inch	$\frac{1}{4}$-inch Phillips head
	$\frac{1}{2}$ inch	$\frac{1}{2}$-inch Phillips head
	$\frac{3}{4}$ inch	$\frac{3}{4}$-inch Phillips head
flat head	$\frac{1}{4}$ inch	$\frac{1}{4}$-inch flat head
	$\frac{1}{2}$ inch	$\frac{1}{2}$-inch flat head
	$\frac{3}{4}$ inch	$\frac{3}{4}$-inch flat head

Make an organized list to solve each problem.

1. *City Paper* runs color and black-and-white advertisements. The ads can fill $\frac{1}{2}$, $\frac{1}{4}$, or $\frac{3}{4}$ of a page. Mario's Pizza wants to place an ad. How many different choices do they have?

Answer _____

2. Pop's Ice Cream Shop lets you choose 1 sauce and 1 topping for your sundae. They have hot fudge and caramel syrup. The two toppings are nuts or sprinkles. How many different sundaes can you choose from?

Answer _____

3. Ken has $0.60 in U.S. coins. He only has 1 quarter and no half-dollars or pennies. What are all the possible coin combinations Ken could have?

Answer _____
_____
_____
_____

Plotting Points on a Coordinate Grid

A **point** is an exact location in space. A **coordinate grid** is
a graph with horizontal and vertical lines. To **plot**, or locate,
a point, use an ordered pair. An **ordered pair** is two numbers that
give directions to a point.

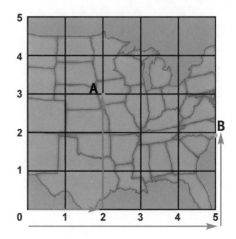

Plot point (2,3).

> 1. Start at 0.
> 2. Move 2 spaces to the right.
> 3. Move 3 spaces up.
> 4. Label your point with a capital letter, *A*.

Name the ordered pair for Point B.

> 1. Start at 0.
> 2. Count how many spaces to the right. (5)
> 3. Count how many spaces up. (2)
> 4. Write the numbers as an ordered pair. (5,2)

Plot each point on the coordinate grid.

	a	b
1.	point *A* (4,3)	point *B* (1,1)
2.	point *C* (3,6)	point *D* (6,7)
3.	point *E* (8,0)	point *F* (8,4)
4.	point *G* (9,2)	point *H* (2,8)

Name the ordered pair for each point.

5. point *L*   _____(2,7)_____

6. point *M*   _____

7. point *N*   _____

8. point *O*   _____

9. point *P*   _____

10. point *Q*   _____

11. point *R*   _____

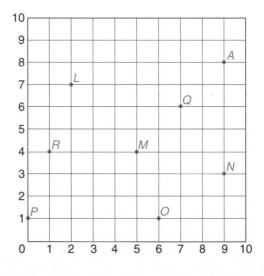

Lines, Rays, and Line Segments

<table>
<tr><td>A line is an endless straight path.</td><td></td><td>Say:
Write:</td><td>line AB or line BA
$\overleftrightarrow{AB}$ or $\overleftrightarrow{BA}$</td></tr>
<tr><td>A line segment is a straight path between two points.</td><td></td><td>Say:

Write:</td><td>line segment RS or
line segment SR
$\overline{RS}$ or $\overline{SR}$</td></tr>
<tr><td>A ray is an endless straight path starting at one point.</td><td></td><td>Say:
Write:</td><td>ray BG
$\overrightarrow{BG}$</td></tr>
</table>

Name each figure. Write *line, line segment,* **or** *ray.*

	a	b	c	d
1.				

line segment

Name each figure using symbols.

	a	b	c	d
2.				

$\overline{PQ}$ or $\overline{QP}$

Use the drawing at right for Exercises 3–6.

3. Name a ray. $\overrightarrow{PB}$ or ray PB

4. Name a line. _____

5. Name a line segment. _____

6. Name a point. _____

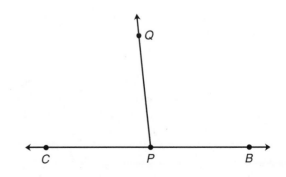

Exploring Angles

An **angle** is two rays with a common endpoint.

Angles are measured in **degrees** (°).

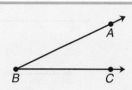

Say: angle *ABC* or angle *CBA*

Write: ∠*ABC* or ∠*CBA*

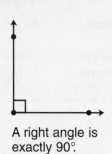

A right angle is exactly 90°.

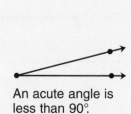

An acute angle is less than 90°.

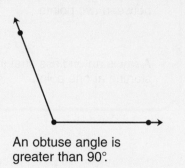

An obtuse angle is greater than 90°.

Name each angle using symbols.

a   *b*   *c*   *d*

1.

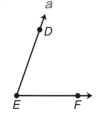   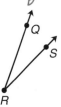   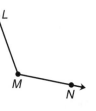   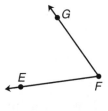

∠ DEF or ∠ FED   _____   _____   _____

Name each angle. Write *right angle*, *acute angle*, or *obtuse angle*.

a   *b*   *c*   *d*

2.

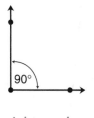      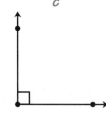   

acute angle   _____   _____   _____

3.

   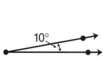   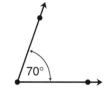

right angle   _____   _____   _____

Perimeter

Perimeter is the distance around a figure.

To find the perimeter of a figure, add the lengths of its sides.

4 in.

6 in.

6 in.
4 in.
6 in.
+ 4 in.
perimeter → *20 in.*

Find the perimeter of each figure.

a

1.

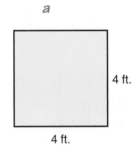

4 ft.

4 ft.

___16 feet___

b

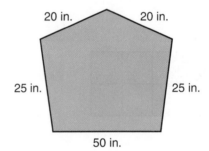

2 yd.

3 yd.

4 yd.

4 yd.

6 yd.

_____

2.

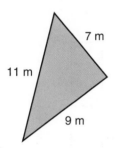

7 m

11 m

9 m

_____

20 in.   20 in.

25 in.   25 in.

50 in.

_____

3.

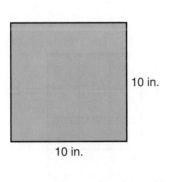

10 in.

10 in.

_____

Area

The **area** of a figure is the number of **square units** that cover its surface.

This is 1 square unit.

Count the number of square units to find the area of a figure.

The area of this figure is 12 square units.

Find the area of each figure.

a

b

1.

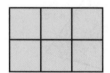

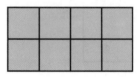

6 square units

_____

2.

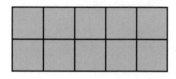

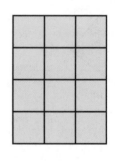

_____   _____

3.

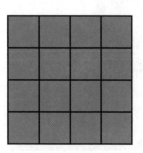

_____   _____

Problem-Solving Method: Use a Formula

Colleen painted a picture that is 6 feet long and 6 feet wide.
How much wood will she need to make a frame?

Understand the problem.
- **What do you want to know?**
  how much wood she needs to make a frame

- **What information is given?**
  The picture is 6 feet long and 6 feet wide.

Plan how to solve it.
- **What method can you use?**
  You can use a formula. Since she wants to know the distance around a figure, she needs a formula for perimeter.

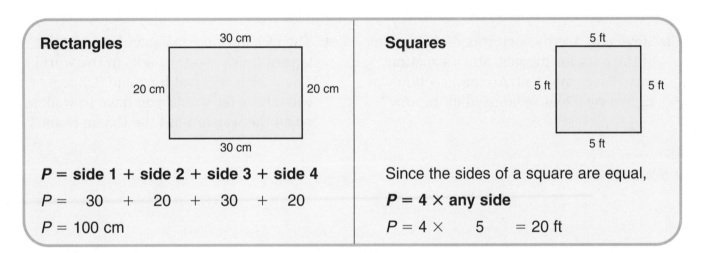

Rectangles

30 cm

20 cm   20 cm

30 cm

P = side 1 + side 2 + side 3 + side 4

P =   30   +   20   +   30   +   20

P = 100 cm

Squares

5 ft

5 ft   5 ft

5 ft

Since the sides of a square are equal,

$P = 4 \times$ any side

$P = 4 \times$ 5   = 20 ft

Solve it.
- **How can you use this method to solve the problem?**
  Since Colleen's picture is a square, she can use the formula for the perimeter of a square.

  P = 4 × any side
  P = 4 × 6
  P = 24 feet

- **What is the answer?**
  Colleen needs 24 feet of wood to make the frame.

Look back and check your answer.
- **Is your answer reasonable?**
  You can check by adding the side lengths.
  The sum matches the answer from the formula.
  The answer is reasonable.

  6 ft
  6 ft
  6 ft
  + 6 ft
  ____
  24 ft

Use a formula to solve each problem.

1. An NBA basketball court is 94 feet long and 50 feet wide. What is the perimeter of the court?

Answer _____

2. Little League baseball diamonds have 60 feet between bases. How far does a player run when she hits a home run?

Answer _____

3. Steve and Aretha each roped-off sections of the park for picnics. Steve's section was 10 feet by 8 feet. Aretha's section was 12 feet by 5 feet. Who used more rope?

Answer _____

4. The Ocean Dome in Japan is one of the largest indoor water parks in the world. The park is 985 feet long and 328 feet wide. How far would you have to walk to go all the way around the Ocean Dome?

Answer _____

5. Raul's vegetable garden measures 15 feet in length and 12 feet in width. How much fencing will he need to surround the garden?

Answer _____

Find each number.

	a		b		c

1. $\frac{1}{5}$ of 20 = _____ $\frac{1}{4}$ of 16 = _____ $\frac{1}{3}$ of 9 = _____

2. $\frac{1}{2}$ of 36 = _____ $\frac{1}{6}$ of 18 = _____ $\frac{1}{7}$ of 21 = _____

Add.

3. $\frac{3}{8} + \frac{4}{8} =$ _____ $\frac{3}{11} + \frac{7}{11} =$ _____ $\frac{1}{4} + \frac{2}{4} =$ _____

4. $\frac{3}{5} + \frac{1}{5} =$ _____ $\frac{2}{9} + \frac{3}{9} =$ _____ $\frac{4}{8} + \frac{3}{8} =$ _____

Subtract.

5. $\frac{3}{4} - \frac{2}{4} =$ _____ $\frac{5}{11} - \frac{3}{11} =$ _____ $\frac{5}{7} - \frac{2}{7} =$ _____

6. $\frac{8}{9} - \frac{4}{9} =$ _____ $\frac{6}{7} - \frac{2}{7} =$ _____ $\frac{4}{5} - \frac{3}{5} =$ _____

Plot each point on the coordinate grid.

7. point A (1,3)

8. point B (0,5)

9. point C (2,0)

10. point D (7,5)

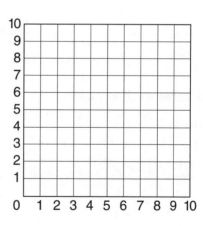

Name each figure using symbols.

	a		b		c		d

11.

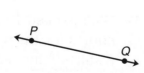

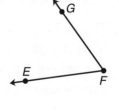

_____   _____   _____   _____

Name each angle. Write *right angle, acute angle,* or *obtuse angle.*

a   b   c   d

12.

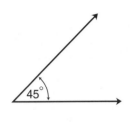 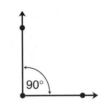 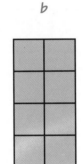 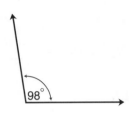

_____ _____ _____ _____

Find the area of each figure.

a   b   c

13.

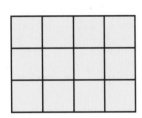 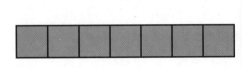

_____ _____ _____

Use a formula to solve each problem.

14. A photograph is 8 inches wide by 10 inches long. How much wood is needed to frame the photo?

15. One side of John's square pool measures 10 meters. What is the perimeter of the pool?

Answer _____

Answer _____

Make an organized list to solve each problem.

16. The cafeteria serves chicken, tuna, and ham sandwiches. They have white, rye, and wheat bread. How many different sandwich choices do they serve?

17. Gina packed 1 pair of jeans and 1 pair of shorts for the weekend. She also brought 3 shirts: blue, white, and green. How many different outfits can she wear?

Answer _____

Answer _____

Common Nouns and Proper Nouns

A **common noun** names any person, place, or thing. It begins with a lowercase letter.

Examples:

inventor   city   month

A **proper noun** names a particular person, place, or thing. Each important word of a proper noun begins with a capital letter.

Examples:

Thomas Alva Edison   Cleveland   August

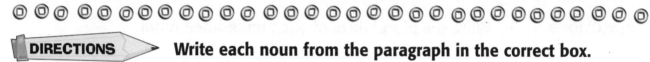

DIRECTIONS   **Write each noun from the paragraph in the correct box. Capitalize all proper nouns.**

Marcos and his parents are planning a long vacation. They will leave dallas, texas, and drive their car to denver. There they will visit some friends named jackson. Then, they will drive across the western states, through utah and nevada. They hope to see some deer as they drive. Then, the family will spend a week in california. Their cousins live on bay view street in san diego. What an exciting trip that will be!

Common Nouns	Proper Nouns
_____	_____
_____	_____
_____	_____
_____	_____
_____	_____
_____	_____
_____	_____
_____	_____

Singular and Plural Nouns

A **singular noun** names one person, one place, or one thing.
Examples:
> dog   house   box

A **plural noun** names more than one person, place, or thing. Make most nouns plural by adding *s* or *es*.
Examples:
> dogs   houses   boxes

DIRECTIONS ▸ Write the plural form of each underlined noun.

1. The <u>kangaroo</u> is native to Australia.

   Singular

2. Everyone knows that kangaroos carry their young in a <u>pouch</u>.

   pural

3. A wallaby is a <u>type</u> of small kangaroo.

   dural

4. It isn't the only unusual <u>animal</u> that lives there.

   Singular

5. Australia is also the home of a huge bird, the <u>emu</u>.

   plural

6. The emu is only a little smaller than an <u>ostrich</u>.

   plural

7. It eats <u>grass</u>, flowers, insects, and almost anything else.

   Singular

8. One very strange <u>mammal</u> from Australia is the platypus.

   Singloor

9. It looks like a combination of a beaver, a duck, and an <u>otter</u>.

   plural

10. Australia's flying <u>fox</u> is not really a fox at all, but a kind of bat.

    Singular

Singular and Plural Nouns, page 2

Remember, a singular noun names one person, place, or thing.
Examples:
> explorer   marsh   sky   monkey

A plural noun names more than one person, place, or thing. Make most nouns plural by adding *s* or *es*. For some nouns ending in *y,* replace the *y* with an *i* and add *es* to form the plural.
Examples:
> explorers   marshes   skies   monkeys

DIRECTIONS ⟩ **Rewrite each sentence by giving the plural form of each noun in ( ).**

1. Many (animal) travel in groups.

_____

2. Monarch (butterfly) travel in swarms of a million or more.

_____

3. Each year these (insect) migrate.

_____

4. Many (bird) also travel in groups.

_____

5. Each autumn, birds flying south for the winter are heard in the (sky).

_____

6. Canadian geese are famous for their long yearly (journey).

_____

7. Many fish hatch in (river).

_____

8. Even people who live in (city) can see migrating animals.

_____

Special Plural Nouns

Some nouns change their spelling in the plural forms.
Other nouns have the same singular and plural forms.
Examples:

Change Spelling	Same Singular and Plural
man—men	salmon
child—children	elk
foot—feet	deer
goose—geese	trout
wolf—wolves	sheep

DIRECTIONS Write the plural form of the noun in ( ).

1. The kindergarten _____ put on a health and safety play for the
   (child)

   rest of the school.

2. The play was written by two _____ whose children are in
   (man)

   the class.

3. A girl in blue _____ played the part of a police officer.
   (pants)

4. The clown wore huge shoes on his _____.
   (foot)

5. Three girls dressed as _____ explained why people should wear
   (mouse)

   seat belts.

6. Two _____ recited a poem about bicycle safety.
   (goose)

7. Several of the boys were dressed as _____.
   (sheep)

8. They told a group of _____ how to be safe while swimming.
   (deer)

9 The boys dressed as _____ were the stars of the show.
   (moose)

10. They sang a song about how to brush _____.
   (tooth)

Singular Possessive Nouns

A **singular possessive noun** shows ownership by one person or thing.
Add an apostrophe (') and *s* to most singular nouns to show
possession.
Examples:

Satoh's dog   the dog's teeth

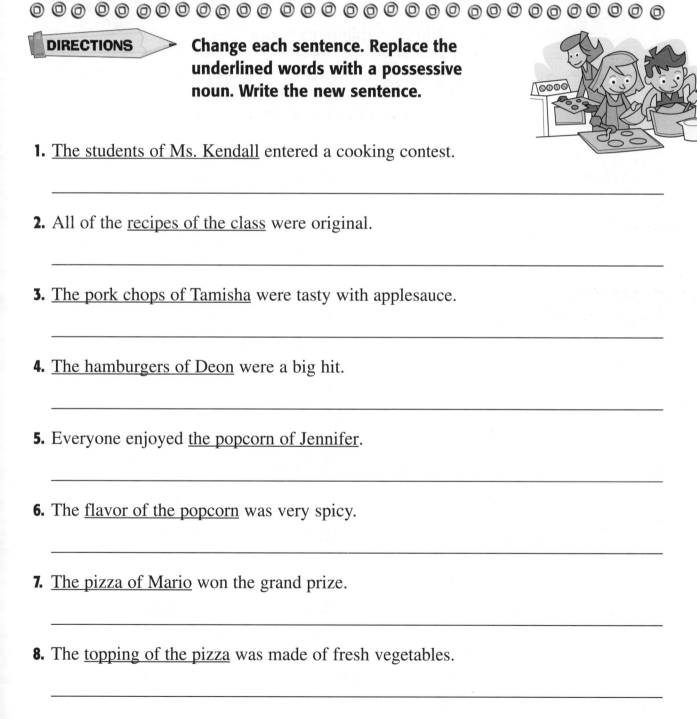

DIRECTIONS   Change each sentence. Replace the
underlined words with a possessive
noun. Write the new sentence.

1. The students of Ms. Kendall entered a cooking contest.

_____

2. All of the recipes of the class were original.

_____

3. The pork chops of Tamisha were tasty with applesauce.

_____

4. The hamburgers of Deon were a big hit.

_____

5. Everyone enjoyed the popcorn of Jennifer.

_____

6. The flavor of the popcorn was very spicy.

_____

7. The pizza of Mario won the grand prize.

_____

8. The topping of the pizza was made of fresh vegetables.

_____

Plural Possessive Nouns

A **plural possessive noun** shows ownership by more than one person or thing.
To form the possessive of a plural noun ending in s or es, add only an apostrophe (').
To form the possessive of a plural noun that does not end in s, add an apostrophe and s ('s).
Examples:

      cars' tires   foxes' home   children's books

DIRECTIONS → Write each group of words in the possessive form.

1. the clothes of the scarecrows

_____

2. the smiles of the pumpkins

_____

3. the hats of the sisters

_____

4. the flavor of the seeds

_____

5. the stems of the plants

_____

6. the costumes of the women

_____

7. the colors of the flowers

_____

8. the shapes of the leaves

_____

9. the games of the children

_____

10. the calves of the moose

_____

11. the wool of the sheep

_____

12. the teachers of the classes

_____

13. the toys of the babies

_____

14. the sounds of the drums

_____

Pronouns

A **pronoun** is a word that takes the place of one or more nouns. Use pronouns to avoid repeating words.
A **singular pronoun** replaces a singular noun. The words *I*, *me*, *you*, *he*, *she*, *him*, *her*, and *it* are singular pronouns. Always capitalize the pronoun *I*.
A **plural pronoun** replaces a plural noun. The words *we*, *you*, *they*, *us*, and *them* are plural pronouns.
Examples:

The traveler thought *he* should go to the city.
He takes the place of *the traveler*.
The campers searched for a place *they* could spend the night.
They takes the place of *the campers*.

DIRECTIONS Circle the pronoun in the second sentence of each pair. Write the noun or nouns it replaced.

1. Tornadoes are frightening storms. They are strong, whirling winds.

_____

2. The funnel reaches down from dark clouds. It may strike Earth.

_____

3. Scientists are studying tornadoes. Exactly why the storms develop is a mystery to them.

_____

4. Kayla watched a tornado strike near her town. "I was afraid of that swirling funnel."

_____

5. The storm didn't hurt Kayla. She was too far away.

_____

6. Grandpa has an underground shelter in the backyard. He calls the shelter a storm cellar.

_____

7. During "tornado weather," Grandpa watches the sky and listens to the radio. Grandma tells him to be careful.

_____

8. Grandpa calls Phil and Brian if a tornado is coming. "You must stay in the cellar until the storm is over."

_____

Pronouns, page 2

Remember, a pronoun is a word that takes the place of one or more nouns.
Use pronouns to avoid repeating words.
A singular pronoun replaces a singular noun. The words *I*, *me*, *you*, *he*, *she*, *him*, *her*, and *it* are singular pronouns. Always capitalize the pronoun *I*.
A plural pronoun replaces a plural noun. The words *we*, *you*, *they*, *us*, and *them* are plural pronouns.

DIRECTIONS > **Read each sentence. Write the pronoun or pronouns in each sentence on the line.**

1. Robin and Paul's garden has many weeds in it.

_____

2. The two of them grow plants.

_____

3. She reads about weeds.

_____

4. He searches through plant catalogs for odd fruits and vegetables.

_____

5. They try to grow them in the garden.

_____

6. "We grow many things," Robin said.

_____

7. "A friend helped us plant popcorn last spring," Paul said.

_____

8. "I will let you try the popcorn later in the afternoon," he said to me.

_____

9. "What are they?" I asked.

_____

10. "They are oxeye daisies, the prettiest weeds in the garden!" she said.

_____

Subject Pronouns

A **subject pronoun** takes the place of one or more nouns in the subject of a sentence. The words *I*, *you*, *he*, *she*, *it*, *we*, and *they* are subject pronouns.
Examples:

He brought a spider to school.
We do not like spiders.
You can hold the spider.

DIRECTIONS ▷ **Read the paragraph below. Circle all the subject pronouns. Write the circled subject pronouns in the first column below. Then, write the word or words each pronoun replaces.**

Sequoia was a member of the Cherokee nation. Sequoia developed a written alphabet for his people. He is also remembered because of the trees that bear his name. Sequoia trees are some of the largest and oldest living things on Earth. They can live for several thousand years! The General Sherman Tree in Sequoia National Park is one of the world's tallest trees. It is 272.4 feet tall.

Subject Pronoun	Word or Words It Replaces
_____	_____
_____	_____
_____	_____

DIRECTIONS ▷ **Imagine that you are a scientist studying sequoia trees. Write a few sentences that you might include in your field notes. Use at least three subject pronouns.**

_____

_____

_____

Object Pronouns

An **object pronoun** follows an action verb, such as *see* or *tell*, or a word
such as *about, at, for, from, near, of, to,* or *with*.
The words *me, you, him, her, it, us,* and *them* are object pronouns.
Examples:

Chan took *it* home.
Dad had a letter for *me*.
My sister heard *you*.

DIRECTIONS Rewrite each sentence. Replace the underlined
words with pronouns.

1. Emilia and Miguel visited the zoo with <u>their aunt</u>.

_____

2. The zoo seemed strange to <u>Emilia and Miguel</u>.

_____

3. There were no cages in <u>the zoo</u>.

_____

4. "I'll show <u>Miguel and Emilia</u> the giraffes first," their aunt told them.

_____

5. An ostrich wandered right up to <u>their car</u>.

_____

6. "The ostrich wanted a closer look at <u>Miguel and me</u>," Emilia laughed.

_____

7. Monkey Island made a good home for <u>monkeys</u>.

_____

8. Emilia asked <u>Miguel</u> to take a picture of the monkeys.

_____

I, Me, We, Us

Use *I* and *we* as subject pronouns.
Use *me* and *us* as object pronouns.
Examples:
    I like to read books.
    We have to read two books this month.
    Dad took *me* to the library.
    The librarian showed *us* the books.

DIRECTIONS **Write the pronoun in ( ) that correctly completes each sentence.**

1. In science class _____ read a story about penguins.
(we, us)

2. Jill and _____ saw the Falkland Islands on a map.
(I, me)

3. The story told _____ about penguins that live there.
(we, us)

4. Our teacher showed Darrell and _____ a picture of some
(I, me)

rockhopper penguins.

5. _____ learned that they may jump into the ocean instead of
(We, Us)

diving in.

6. They looked funny to my friends and _____.
(I, me)

7. The story told _____ about gentoo penguins.
(we, us)

8. _____ found out that penguins lay eggs in a rookery.
(We, Us)

9. The king penguin looked big to Jill and _____.
(I, me)

10. Tony gave a picture of one to _____.
(we, us)

11. _____ read that the adult king penguin can grow three feet tall.
(I, Me)

Possessive Pronouns

A **possessive pronoun** shows ownership. Some possessive pronouns are *my*, *your*, *his*, *her*, *its*, *our*, and *their*.
Examples:
> Skippy is *my* horse.
> He stays in *our* barn.
> Who is *your* pet?

DIRECTIONS ▷ Rewrite each sentence. Replace the underlined words with a possessive pronoun.

1. Jason and Jana visited <u>Abraham Lincoln's</u> birthplace.

_____

2. <u>The park's</u> location is near Hodgenville, Kentucky.

_____

3. <u>Lincoln's</u> birthplace was a small, one-room log cabin.

_____

4. <u>Mr. and Mrs. Lincoln's</u> original cabin has been restored.

_____

5. Only a few of <u>the cabin's</u> original logs are left.

_____

6. <u>Jana's</u> climb up the steps to the cabin left her out of breath.

_____

7. "May I use <u>Jana's</u> camera?" Jason asked Jana.

_____

8. <u>Lincoln's</u> cabin is now part of a beautiful park.

_____

Contractions with Pronouns

A **contraction** is a short way of writing two words together. Some of the letters are left out. An apostrophe (') takes the place of the missing letters. Form some contractions by joining pronouns and verbs.

Examples:

I + would = *I'd*
you + are = *you're*
it + is = *it's*

DIRECTIONS ➤ **Replace the underlined words with a contraction.**

1. I would _____ like to visit the National Air and Space Museum in Washington, D.C.

2. It is _____ full of exhibits of flying machines.

3. I am _____ going there next June with my uncle.

4. He is _____ a pilot in the Air Force.

5. We are _____ going to see all 20 galleries of the museum.

6. I will _____ ask Uncle Roy to show me the Wright brothers' plane.

7. He has _____ seen it several times.

8. "You will _____ think their plane looks really small," Uncle Roy wrote to me.

9. "We will _____ see several spacecraft, too."

10. It's hard to believe they have _____ really been into space.

11. They are _____ part of an exciting exhibit about space flight.

12. At the museum you are _____ even able to see a rock from the moon.

Adjectives

An **adjective** is a word that describes a noun or pronoun. Adjectives can tell how many, what color, or what size or shape. They can also describe how something feels, sounds, tastes, or smells.
Use exact adjectives to paint clear word pictures.
Examples:

    Two birds were in the nest.
    The *blue* ball was in a *big* box.
    The *smooth* soap has a *sweet* smell.

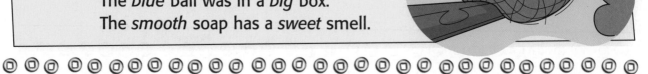

DIRECTIONS ▶ **Read the following paragraph. Underline each adjective.**

The seven families checked the wagons carefully. Were the leather harnesses ready? Two strong oxen would pull each wagon, and many families were bringing several extra oxen. Tomorrow would be the first day of the long journey on the Oregon Trail. In six months, each family would be in a new home in the West.

DIRECTIONS ▶ **Complete the sentences. Write a different adjective on each line.**

1. The children felt _____ about the _____ trip.

2. They expected to see _____ animals, _____ trees, and _____ flowers.

3. Their parents worried about traveling over _____ mountains and through _____, _____ deserts.

4. Families felt _____ about leaving their _____ friends behind.

More Adjectives

Remember to use an adjective to describe a noun or a pronoun.
Use adjectives to give clear and vivid pictures.
Examples:

> *Cold* lemonade tasted good after the *spicy* food.
> I cuddled up by the *blazing* fire on a *starless* night.

DIRECTIONS ➤ **Write a vivid adjective to complete each sentence.**

1. Kerry has a _____ puppy named Button.

2. Button was born on a _____ night in February.

3. Kerry loves to stroke the dog's _____ fur.

4. Button's _____ ways make him fun to watch.

5. He leaps high into the air, chasing
_____ butterflies.

6. He may fall on his chin when he tries to run with his
_____ legs.

7. Button's favorite game is playing school in Kerry's
_____ playhouse.

8. He chews on a _____ shoe while Kerry pretends to be
the teacher.

9. When the weather is warm, Button naps under a _____ tree.

10. At night Kerry tucks him into a _____ basket.

11. "His _____ ears make him so cute," Kerry says.

12. "Nobody could resist those _____ eyes, either."

Predicate Adjectives

An adjective is a word that describes a noun or pronoun. A **predicate adjective** follows a linking verb such as *is*, *seems*, or *looks*. When an adjective follows a linking verb, it can describe the subject of the sentence.
Examples:

That elephant is *huge*.

That snake looks *scary*.

DIRECTIONS Circle each adjective that follows the linking verb. Then, underline the noun or pronoun it describes.

1. Our zoo's old cages were small and dark.

2. A visitor to the zoo was unhappy about this.

3. He was sorry for the animals.

4. Now, new homes for the animals are large and airy.

5. The animals are content in their new zoo homes.

DIRECTIONS Write adjectives to complete each sentence. Underline the noun or pronoun each adjective describes.

6. The zoo's elephant is _____, _____, and _____.

7. Its ears are _____ and _____.

8. Its zoo home is _____ and _____.

9. The nearby monkeys are _____, _____, and _____.

10. During the daytime, they are _____ and _____.

Articles

The words *a*, *an*, and *the* are called **articles**.
Use *a* before a word that begins with a consonant sound.
Use *an* before a word that begins with a vowel sound.
Use *the* before a word that begins with a consonant or a vowel.
Examples:

Have you ever seen *an* owl?
The owl is *a* nocturnal animal.

DIRECTIONS ➤ **Write the article in ( ) that correctly completes each sentence.**

1. Pete wants to be _____ (a, an) sportswriter for

_____ (a, an) newspaper when he grows up.

2. Now he writes stories for _____ (an, the) school paper.

3. "Covering baseball games is _____ (a, the) most fun," Pete says.

4. "Last week I wrote about _____ (a, an) tennis match, too."

5. His teacher says that Pete is _____ (a, an) excellent writer.

6. "His stories make _____ (a, the) readers feel as if they are

watching the game," the teacher says.

7. Pete's mother is _____ (a, an) English teacher.

8. Sometimes she helps him find just _____ (an, the) right words to

use in _____ (a, an) story.

9. It may take him _____ (a, an) hour to write one story.

10. "Sports writing is _____ (a, an) exciting job," says Pete.

11. "It's fun to have _____ (a, an) interview with

_____ (a, an) player."

12. When Pete is _____ (a, an) adult, he would like to work for

_____ (an, the) *New York Times*.

Adjectives That Compare: *er, est*

> Add *er* to most short adjectives to compare two nouns or pronouns.
> Add *est* to most short adjectives to compare more than two nouns or pronouns.
> Change the *y* to *i* before adding *er* or *est* to adjectives that end in a consonant and *y*.
> *Example:*
> This building is *taller* than that one.
> My hair is *curlier* than yours.
> The whale is the *largest* of all animals.

DIRECTIONS ▷ **Write the correct form of the adjective in ( ) to complete each sentence.**

1. Yellowstone is the _____ of all our national parks.
   (old)

2. It is 18 years _____ than Yosemite National Park.
   (old)

3. Tracy thinks it is _____ than Yosemite, too.
   (pretty)

4. "Yellowstone has the _____ scenery I've ever seen," Tracy said.
   (strange)

5. Great Fountain Geyser sometimes shoots water _____ than a
   (high)
   20-story building.

6. "I can't imagine anything _____ than a geyser," said Tracy.
   (strange)

7. Yellowstone Lake is our country's _____ high-altitude lake.
   (large)

8. Its sparkling water seems _____ than a mirror.
   (shiny)

9. "It is the _____ lake I've seen," said Tracy.
   (smooth)

10. Yellowstone has a deep canyon, but the Grand Canyon in Arizona is

    _____.
    (deep)

Adjectives That Compare:
more, most

> Use *more* with some adjectives to compare two nouns or pronouns.
> Use *most* with some adjectives to compare more than two nouns or
> pronouns.
> *Examples:*
> > Diving may be the *most difficult* of all sports.
> > It is *more interesting* to watch than golf.

DIRECTIONS ▷ Write *more* or *most* to complete each sentence.

1. "Making Kites" was one of the _____
   creative classes Jamie had attended.

2. It was _____ fun than the class about clowns.

3. The teacher, Mr. Vargas, was _____ helpful
   than a textbook.

4. The kites the students made were _____
   complex than a simple piece of cloth or plastic.

5. The kite's design took _____ exact measurements than Jamie had
   expected.

6. Of all the students, Jamie was the _____ careful when he cut out
   his kite.

7. Mr. Vargas's kite was _____ unusual than Jamie's.

8. It had the _____ remarkable design in the class.

9. Its butterfly shape was _____ difficult to make than Jamie's
   diamond shape was.

10. Mr. Vargas used the _____ durable kite material he could find.

Special Forms of Adjectives That Compare

Some adjectives have special forms for comparing.
Examples:

Omar has a *good* food puppet.
Chad's puppet is *better* than Omar's.
Teena's celery stalk is the *best* of all the food puppets.

ⓞ ⓞⓞ ⓞⓞ ⓞⓞⓞ ⓞⓞ ⓞ ⓞ ⓞⓞⓞ ⓞⓞ ⓞ ⓞ ⓞⓞ ⓞ ⓞⓞ ⓞⓞ ⓞ ⓞⓞ ⓞ ⓞ ⓞ

Adjective	Comparing Two Things	Comparing More Than Two Things
good	better	best
bad	worse	worst

DIRECTIONS ▷ Read each sentence, and circle the correct word in ( ).

1. Making talking vegetable puppets was the (worstest, worst) idea I ever had.

2. I was much (worse, worst) than my classmates at making puppets.

3. Then, I became (better, gooder) at it.

4. John's carrot looked much (worse, worser) than mine.

5. Suno said her tomato was the (worse, worst) puppet.

6. Her eggplant puppet will look much (better, best).

7. The (best, goodest) puppets are usually not the most realistic.

8. Sasha's new broccoli puppet is (better, best) than his last one because it's brighter.

9. The (bestest, best) part is giving the show.

10. The (worse, worst) part is cleaning up at the end.

Verbs

A **verb** is a word that expresses action or being.
A verb is the main word in the predicate of a sentence. A verb and its subject should agree in number.

Examples:

People all over the world *play* board games.
The game of checkers *is* more than 700 years old.

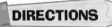 **DIRECTIONS** ➤ **Circle the verb in each sentence.**

1. The French probably invented the game of checkers.

2. Most checkerboards have 64 squares.

3. Chinese checkers probably came from Europe.

4. Nine planets revolve around our Sun.

5. Pluto is the planet farthest from the Sun.

6. It circles the Sun every 248 years.

7. Pluto was unknown to scientists 100 years ago.

8. Percival Lowell estimated the location of the planet in 1915.

9. He never found the planet.

10. In 1930, Clyde Tombaugh studied the sky with a powerful telescope.

11. He took many photographs through the telescope.

12. Three of his photographs showed a distant planet.

Action Verbs

An **action verb** is a word that shows action.
An action verb is the main word in the predicate of a sentence. An action verb tells what the subject of a sentence does or did.
Use strong action verbs to paint clear and vivid pictures.
Examples:
> Sandy *ran* along the path.
> She *jumped* over the sleeping dog.

DIRECTIONS ▷ Write an action verb to complete each sentence.

1. Jets at an air show _____ at top speed.

2. First, they _____ along the ground.

3. Then, they _____ into the air like giant birds.

4. Some pilots _____ stunts at air shows.

5. They _____ their planes upside down in the air.

6. Sometimes sky divers _____ from a plane.

7. They _____ to the ground under colorful parachutes.

8. A daring wing-walker _____ on the wing of a flying plane.

9. She _____ the safety rope tightly.

10. Restored antique planes _____ overhead in formation.

11. On the ground, visitors _____ many types of aircraft.

12. People of all ages _____ an air show.

Main Verbs

Sometimes a simple predicate is made up of two or more verbs. The **main verb** is the most important verb in the predicate. It comes last in a group of verbs.
Examples:
People around the world *have <u>played</u>* board games for years.
We *are <u>learning</u>* games from many countries.

◎◎◎◎◎◎◎◎◎◎◎◎◎◎◎◎◎◎◎◎◎◎◎◎◎◎◎◎◎◎◎◎◎◎

DIRECTIONS **Read each sentence, and write the main verb on the line.**

1. People in India are playing "Snakes and Ladders."

_____

2. They have made a game board with 100 squares.

_____

3. They are throwing dice.

_____

4. Alicia has collected hundreds of coins.

_____

5. Alicia is sorting the coins in her collection.

_____

6. She has received a box of pennies.

_____

7. Alicia's great-grandfather had collected some of the pennies.

_____

8. He had saved a penny from the year 1794.

_____

9. Alicia has added many coins to the collection.

_____

10. She is putting her oldest dime away.

_____

11. She will display it tomorrow at the hobby show.

_____

12. She has won a blue ribbon before.

_____

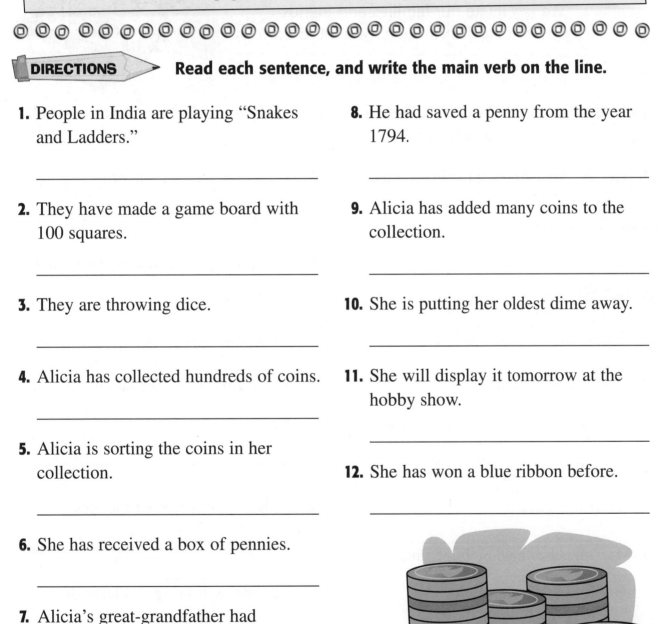

Helping Verbs

A **helping verb** can work with the main verb to tell about an action. The helping verb always comes before the main verb. These words are often used as helping verbs: *am, is, are, was, were, has, have, had,* and *will*. Sometimes another word comes between a main verb and a helping verb. *Examples:*

Our class *is* <u>organizing</u> a large picnic.
We *will* <u>invite</u> our families and friends.
The class *will* certainly <u>have</u> a lot to do.

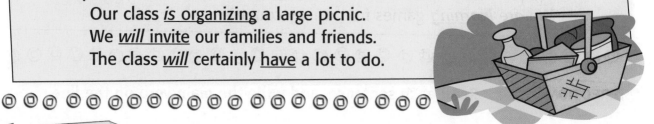

DIRECTIONS In each sentence, circle the helping verb. Then, write the verb it is helping.

1. Mr. and Mrs. Ames have invited us to their farm.

_____

2. We are planning a game.

_____

3. Mrs. Chu is helping us.

_____

4. We will play a game of "Mud Tug."

_____

5. Mr. Ames has made a huge mud puddle near the cornfield.

_____

6. Two teams will tug on a rope.

_____

7. One unlucky team will probably fall into the mud.

_____

8. At first Mrs. Chu had said no to "Mud Tug."

_____

9. She had worried about the mess.

_____

10. Everyone will bring a change of clothes.

_____

Main and Helping Verbs

Remember that the main verb is the most important verb in a sentence. The helping verb works with the main verb to tell about an action. A helping verb often shows when the action in a sentence happens.

DIRECTIONS ▷ **Read the paragraph below. Circle each helping verb. Then, underline the main verb.**

I am reading a book called <u>Planet 945</u>. My brother has read it, too! In the book, some pioneers are settling a new planet. No one has explored the planet yet, so they will have some amazing adventures there. In Chapter 4, two children are looking for a lost dog. They have discovered a ruined city.

DIRECTIONS ▷ **Complete each sentence with a helping verb.**

1. Kim and Ho _____ searching for the lost dog.

2. Kim _____ spotted a gleam between two hills.

3. "I _____ tired," Ho said.

4. "I _____ head for that valley," answered Kim. "You can rest here."

5. Ho _____ napping under a bush when Kim came back.

6. "Come and see. I _____ found the ruins of an old city!" she cried.

DIRECTIONS ▷ **Write two sentences about a weird encounter. Use a helping verb in each sentence.**

_____

_____

Linking Verbs

A **linking verb** connects the subject to a word or words in the predicate. The most common linking verbs are forms of *be*. Some forms of *be* are *am, is, are, was,* and *were*. Use *am, is,* and *are* to show present tense. Use *was* and *were* to show past tense. Some other common linking verbs are *become, feel,* and *seem*.

Examples:

Duane and Aisha *are* in the backyard.
They *seem* happy about something.

◎ ◎◎ ◎◎ ◎◎◎ ◎◎◎ ◎◎◎ ◎◎◎ ◎◎◎ ◎◎◎ ◎◎◎ ◎◎◎ ◎◎◎ ◎◎◎ ◎◎◎

DIRECTIONS ➤ **Write a linking verb to complete each sentence.**

1. One of my favorite novels _____ <u>Caddie Woodlawn</u>.

2. It _____ a book by Carol Ryrie Brink.

3. Caddie, a lively young girl, _____ the main character.

4. She and her family _____ pioneers in Wisconsin in the 1860s.

5. Caddie's life _____ full of adventure.

6. In those days, girls _____ expected to be quiet and stay indoors most of the time.

7. I _____ sure Caddie didn't like to cook and sew all the time.

8. She _____ happiest when she was outdoors, running and playing with her brothers.

9. Caddie's neighbors _____ afraid of the Native Americans who lived across the river.

10. Caddie _____ a friend of theirs.

11. She _____ able to prove that all the people could be friends.

12. I _____ glad that I took the time to read the book.

Action Verbs and Linking Verbs

Remember, verbs that tell what the subject of a sentence does or did are action verbs. Verbs that tell what the subject of a sentence is or is like are called linking verbs.

◎ ◎

DIRECTIONS ➤ **Read the paragraph below. Circle each action verb. Underline each linking verb.**

Last summer my friends and I invented a game called "Quick Changes." In this game we write the names of real or imaginary creatures on slips of paper. Each player takes a slip. For ten minutes, each player is the animal on the slip. For example, I was a seal one morning. I flopped around in the wading pool. I barked. I splashed water at my friends.

DIRECTIONS ➤ **Use a form of the linking verb *be* to complete each sentence.**

1. José and I _____ eager to play the new game.

2. "Oh, boy! I _____ an eagle!" says José.

3. "_____ you ready for your turn?" asks Sara.

4. Maria _____ a bat, hanging from a tree branch.

5. Some of my friends _____ really silly.

6. "This _____ a very strange game!" says José's sister.

DIRECTIONS ➤ **Write two sentences about a game you and your friends enjoy. Use at least one action verb and one linking verb.**

_____

_____

Present-Tense Verbs

A **present-tense verb** tells about actions that are happening now.
Add *s* or *es* to most present-tense verbs when the subject of the
sentence is *he, she, it,* or a singular noun.
Do not add *s* or *es* to a present-tense verb when the
subject is *I, you, we, they,* or a plural noun.
Examples:

  Maria's family *grows* coffee beans.
  She *watches* the harvest.
  The beans *grow* on bushes.

DIRECTIONS Write the present-tense form of the verb in ( ) that correctly
completes each sentence.

1. Dougal Dixon _____ books that stretch the reader's imagination.
(write)

2. In his book <u>The New Dinosaurs</u>, he _____ what dinosaurs might
(imagine)

   be like if they were still alive today.

3. Dixon _____ that dinosaurs would have changed very much
(believe)

   since ancient times.

4. His ideas _____ science and fiction in an exciting way.
(mix)

5. He _____ pictures of the animals that he imagines.
(draw)

6. The long-haired kloon _____ its feet like hands.
(use)

7. A graceful bird called a soar _____ in the ocean with its
(fish)

   long neck.

8. The seal-like plunger _____ fish with its sharp teeth.
(crush)

9. The neck of the lank _____ high into the air like a giraffe's.
(reach)

10. The harridan _____ with wings that fold up when it walks.
(fly)

Past-Tense Verbs

A **past-tense verb** tells about actions that happened in the past.
Add *ed* or *d* to most present-tense verbs to make them show past tense.
You may have to drop an *e*, double a final consonant, or change a *y* to an *i*.
Examples:

Long ago, hunters *hunted* huge mammoths.
These gigantic mammoths *died* long ago.

DIRECTIONS　　　**Write the past-tense form of the verb in ( ).**

1. When Mr. King was a boy, he _____ on a farm.
(live)

2. He and his sisters _____ more than three miles to school.
(hike)

3. They always _____ their lunches.
(carry)

4. "When we were thirsty, we _____ water from a nearby spring,"
(dip)
Mr. King said.

5. "There were no school cafeterias in those days," he _____.
(observe)

6. When Mr. King finished high school, he _____ to the city.
(move)

7. He _____ to become a teacher.
(study)

8. "Even when I began teaching, students still _____ their own
(provide)
lunches," Mr. King told us.

9. In about 1940, the "bring your lunch" system _____.
(change)

10. People _____ because many children were coming to school with
(worry)
nothing to eat.

11. The government _____ food and money for the schools to use to
(supply)
serve hot lunches.

Future-Tense Verbs

A **future-tense verb** shows action that will happen in the future.
To form the future tense of a verb, use the helping verb *will* with the main verb.
Examples:
> Tomorrow we *will visit* my aunt's new restaurant.
> The cook *will make* my favorite tamales for dinner.

DIRECTIONS ➤ Circle the future-tense verb in ( ) to complete each sentence.

1. First, the cook (will steam / steamed) the corn meal.

2. Then, he (chop / will chop) some chicken into pieces.

3. His assistant (will mix / mix) it with herbs and spices.

4. Finally, he (will put / had put) the tamales together.

5. We (will have / having) frijoles, too.

6. Our tour of Parker Ranch (will stretch / stretch) across many miles of the big island of Hawaii.

7. We (learned / will learn) about the history of ranching in the Hawaiian Islands.

8. In the afternoon, we (listening / will listen) to a talk about King Kamehameha the Great.

9. We (will see / saw) the remains of the king's home at Kailua tomorrow morning.

10. After that we (will head / heads) home.

Future-Tense Verbs, page 2

Remember that a future-tense verb shows action that will happen in the future. To form the future tense of a verb, use the helping verb *will* with the main verb.

DIRECTIONS ▷ **Rewrite each sentence. Change the verb to the future tense.**

1. A blanket of cold air settles on the valley.

_____

2. Ms. Asato reads the weather data on her computer.

_____

3. She records a warning on an answering machine.

_____

4. Hundreds of fruit and nut growers call the line.

_____

5. Frost damages young plants and buds on trees.

_____

6. The growers work late into the night.

_____

7. They roll their huge wind machines into the orchards.

_____

8. These giant fans move the air.

_____

9. The movement of the air raises temperatures a few degrees.

_____

10. Wet ground also keeps temperatures higher.

_____

Irregular Verbs

An **irregular verb** is a verb that does not end with *ed* to show past tense. Some irregular verbs show past tense by using a different form of the main verb with *have, has,* or *had.*

Examples:

Present	Past	Past with Helping Verb
do, does	did	(have, has, had) done
come, comes	came	(have, has, had) come
run, runs	ran	(have, has, had) run
go, goes	went	(have, has, had) gone

DIRECTIONS > Write the correct past-tense form of the verb in ( ).

1. Last summer Kara _____ on an exciting raft ride.
(go)

2. She had _____ on several rafting trips before.
(go)

3. She never had _____ a river as swift as this one.
(see)

4. The trip _____ just above a deep canyon.
(begin)

5. "We _____ it would be fun to ride the rapids through the
(think)
canyon," Kara explained.

6. The leader had _____ a life jacket for each person.
(bring)

7. "The leader _____ we should wear our life jackets at all times,"
(say)
Kara pointed out.

8. "We climbed into the raft, and the wild ride _____."
(begin)

9. Excitement _____ Kara's heart pound as the raft plunged through
(make)
the roaring rapids.

10. "The trip was a little scary, but I was glad I _____."
(go)

More Irregular Verbs

Remember that an irregular verb is a verb that does not end with *ed* to show past tense. Some irregular verbs use *n* or *en* when they are combined with *have, has,* or *had.*

DIRECTIONS Add words to complete each sentence. Use the correct form of the verb in ( ).

1. The wind has _____.
(blow)

2. All the leaves have _____.
(fall)

3. My kite _____.
(fly)

4. A shower of acorns _____.
(fall)

5. A busy squirrel _____.
(dig)

6. In the garden, pumpkins have _____.
(grow)

7. Yesterday my friend and I _____.
(ride)

8. We have _____.
(ride)

9. My brother _____.
(write)

10. He has _____.
(write)

11. Our neighbor had _____.
(give)

12. Mom and Dad have _____.
(speak)

Adverbs

An **adverb** is a word that describes a verb.
An adverb may tell how, when, or where an action happens. Many adverbs that tell how end in *ly*.
Vary your sentences by moving the adverbs.
Examples:

> *Today* we visited a zoo.
> We walked through *there slowly*.

DIRECTIONS ▷ Rewrite each sentence to include the adverb in ( ).

1. Kristen visited the Science Museum. (yesterday)

_____

2. She saw an exhibit of holograms. (upstairs)

_____

3. She tried to touch the images. (first)

_____

4. She learned why holograms look so real. (finally)

_____

5. Kristen will go again. (there)

_____

DIRECTIONS ▷ Complete each sentence with an adverb that tells when or where.

6. Look at the fossil exhibit _____.
   (When?)

7. Mammoth bones are displayed _____.
   (Where?)

8. The exhibit opened _____.
   (When?)

9. _____ it will close.
   (When?)

More Adverbs

Remember that an adverb is a word that describes a verb.
Some adverbs tell *how* about a verb. Many adverbs that tell
how end in *ly*.
Use adverbs to make sentences more vivid and exact.
Examples:
   My mother laughed *loudly*.
   We ran *quickly* to the shore.

DIRECTIONS ➤ **Rewrite each sentence. Add an adverb from the box to each sentence to make it more vivid.**

patiently	quickly	impatiently	carefully
calmly	eagerly	tirelessly	surprisingly
promptly	fast	clumsily	enthusiastically

1. Jeff prepared to go snorkeling for the first time.

_____

2. He strapped on his face mask.

_____

3. "You are learning," the instructor said.

_____

4. Jeff plodded across the beach in his fins.

_____

5. He looked through his mask into an underwater world.

_____

6. Brightly colored fish swam in front of his eyes.

_____

7. Jeff snorkeled for several hours.

_____

Adverbs That Compare

To make some one-syllable adverbs show comparison, add *er* or *est*.
To make adverbs that end in *ly* show comparison, use *more* or *most*.
Examples:

Antonio ran *faster* than anyone else did.
I read *more slowly* than my sister does.

DIRECTIONS Write the correct form of the adverb in ( ).

1. Eric and his friends hiked _____ on the steep trail
(more slowly, most slowly)

than on the flat trail.

2. Of all their camping trips, they had planned

this one _____.
(more carefully, most carefully)

3. At first, the trail climbed

_____ upward.
(steadily, most steadily)

4. The group walked _____ in the morning than
(faster, fastest)

in the afternoon.

5. When they reached the camp, John set his backpack down

_____ than Mike did.
(more eagerly, most eagerly)

6. Eric cooked _____ over the campfire than John did.
(more skillfully, most skillfully)

7. Mike cooked _____ of all.
(more skillfully, most skillfully)

8. Steve could set up a tent _____ than Mike could.
(more quickly, most quickly)

9. Eric worked _____ of all the boys.
(more cheerfully, most cheerfully)

10. He _____ accepted the "Outstanding Camper" award.
(proudly, more proudly)

Adverb or Adjective?

Use an adverb to describe a verb. Use an adjective to describe a noun or pronoun.

> **DIRECTIONS** Rewrite each sentence, adding the word in ( ). Write *adverb* or *adjective* to identify the word you added.

1. <u>Ben and Me</u> is a book about Benjamin Franklin.

(humorous) _____

_____

2. The story is told from a mouse's point of view.

(amusingly) _____

_____

3. <u>Johnny Tremain</u> is another story about early America.

(popular) _____

_____

4. It tells about events of the American Revolution.

(exciting) _____

_____

5. Johnny is a silversmith.

(young) _____

_____

6. He helps the patriots fight for independence.

(willingly) _____

_____

Good and Well

Students often have trouble with *good* and *well*.
Use *good* as an adjective.
Use *well* most often as an adverb.
Examples:
　　　Britney did a *good* job on her report.
　　　She writes *well*.

DIRECTIONS ➤ Read each sentence. If *good* or *well* is used correctly, write *correct*. If not, write the sentence correctly.

1. Lake Slo was a well fishing spot.

_____

2. It is a good spot if you're a fish!

_____

3. None of the six of us had well luck.

_____

4. I thought I'd do good because I had my best flies.

_____

5. "What good flies!" said Aunt Sendra.

_____

6. "How did you do that so good?"

_____

7. "Dad taught me to use good materials," I replied.

_____

8. It's not a well idea to be in the hot sun all day without a hat.

_____

9. The hot dogs we ate for dinner were good.

_____

What Is a Sentence?

A **sentence** is a group of words that tells a complete thought. The words in the sentence should be in an order that makes sense. Begin every sentence with a capital letter, and end it with the correct end mark.

Examples:

Cindi's cat has white hair.
Raoul drew pictures of many animals.

DIRECTIONS Read each word group. Write *sentence* if the word group is a sentence. For each word group that is not a sentence, add words to make it a sentence. Then, write the sentence.

1. Sara saw an unusual animal last summer.

_____

2. In an aquarium in Florida.

_____

3. A worker explained that the huge brown animal was a manatee.

_____

4. Manatees live in water, but they are not fish.

_____

5. Looked somewhat like a big, overgrown seal.

_____

6. Seemed to be tame and friendly.

_____

7. Sara watched the manatee take a whole head of lettuce from the worker's hand.

_____

8. Gobbled up the lettuce with a quick gulp.

_____

Parts of a Sentence

A **sentence** is a group of words that expresses a complete thought. Every sentence has two parts. The **subject** is the part about which something is said. The **predicate** tells about the subject.

Subject	Predicate
Multiplication tables	are learned by students.

The **complete subject** is all the words that make up the subject.
My arithmetic homework was not very easy.

The **simple subject** is the key word or words in the complete subject.
The hardest problems had multiplication.

The **complete predicate** is all the words that tell something about the complete subject.
The science class learned how clouds are formed.

The **simple predicate** is the key word or words in the predicate. The simple predicate is an action verb or linking verb together with any helping verbs.
This geography book describes lakes and rivers.

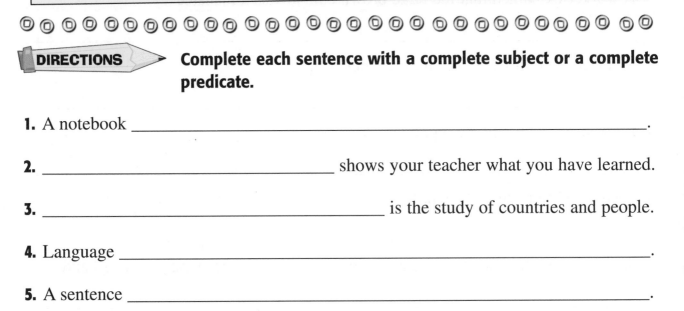

DIRECTIONS Complete each sentence with a complete subject or a complete predicate.

1. A notebook _____.

2. _____ shows your teacher what you have learned.

3. _____ is the study of countries and people.

4. Language _____.

5. A sentence _____.

Subjects and Predicates

Remember that every sentence has a subject that names the person or thing the sentence is about.
Every sentence has a predicate that tells what the subject of the sentence is or does.

DIRECTIONS Write the complete subject of each sentence on the lines below. Underline the complete predicate.

1. Sylvie Martin hears the rain on the roof.

_____

2. The rain is falling softly.

_____

3. The young woman puts on her rain jacket.

_____

4. Her shoes are waterproof.

_____

5. This person walks toward the beach.

_____

6. The streets are quiet today.

_____

7. Sylvie steps carefully over puddles.

_____

8. She hums softly to herself.

_____

9. Her rain jacket keeps her dry.

_____

10. Miss Martin is comfortable in the rain.

_____

Simple Subjects and Complete Subjects

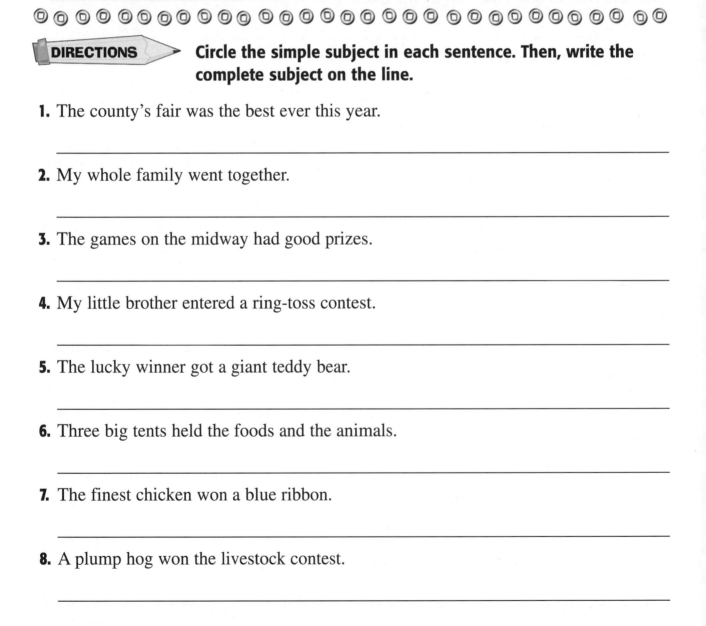

The **simple subject** is the main word or words in the complete subject of a sentence.
The **complete subject** includes all the words that tell whom or what the sentence is about.

Examples:

Many farm <u>children</u> raise pigs for fun. (simple subject)
<u>These proud owners</u> love their unusual pets. (complete subject)

DIRECTIONS   Circle the simple subject in each sentence. Then, write the complete subject on the line.

1. The county's fair was the best ever this year.

_____

2. My whole family went together.

_____

3. The games on the midway had good prizes.

_____

4. My little brother entered a ring-toss contest.

_____

5. The lucky winner got a giant teddy bear.

_____

6. Three big tents held the foods and the animals.

_____

7. The finest chicken won a blue ribbon.

_____

8. A plump hog won the livestock contest.

_____

Compound Subjects

A **compound subject** is two or more subjects joined by *and* or *or*.
These subjects share the same predicate.
Examples:
    A child *or* an adult can ride a bicycle.
    Health *and* fitness are concerns of many bike riders.

> **DIRECTIONS**   Underline the two simple subjects in each sentence.

1. Sun and sand make Hawaii a popular vacation spot.

2. Residents and tourists jam some of the most famous beaches.

3. Peace and quiet can still be found in some places.

4. Molokai and Lanai are less crowded than some other islands.

5. Gorgeous forests and canyons make Kauai a tourist's paradise.

6. Warm weather and tropical breezes lure visitors to Hawaii all year.

> **DIRECTIONS**   Write sentences using the words below in compound subjects.

7. (shops, restaurants) _____

_____

8. (family, I) _____

_____

9. (airplanes, ships) _____

_____

10. (seafood, pineapple) _____

_____

Simple, Complete, and Compound Subjects

Remember that the simple subject is the main word or words in the complete subject of a sentence. The complete subject includes all the words that tell whom or what the sentence is about. A compound subject is two or more subjects joined by *and* or *or*.

DIRECTIONS ▸ Read the paragraph, and underline the complete subject in each sentence. Then, circle the simple subject. If the sentence has a compound subject, circle both simple subjects.

Dogs and humans have lived together happily for thousands of years. Huge hounds and tiny puppies make great pets. They are good company for their owners. Dogs and their owners enjoy playing and exercising together. Dogs help people in special ways. Specially trained dogs work with police officers. Guide dogs lead blind people. Sled dogs can pull heavy loads through the snow. Most dogs and their owners become best friends!

DIRECTIONS ▸ Read each set of sentences below. Write one new sentence that has a compound subject.

1. German shepherds can be excellent watchdogs. Doberman pinschers can be excellent watchdogs.

_____

_____

2. Children often enjoy training dogs. Their parents often enjoy training dogs.

_____

_____

Simple Predicates and Complete Predicates

The **simple predicate** is the main word or words in the complete predicate of a sentence.

The **complete predicate** includes all the words that tell what the subject of the sentence is or does.

To locate the simple predicate, find the key word in the complete predicate.

Examples:

A rescue dog <u>wears</u> bells on its collar. (simple predicate)

Rescue dogs <u>follow the scent of the lost person</u>. (complete predicate)

DIRECTIONS > **Write a simple predicate to complete each sentence. Then, underline the complete predicate.**

1. Visitors to Alaska _____ some of the most beautiful scenery in America.

2. Tall, snowcapped mountains _____ high into the sky.

3. The tallest mountain in North America _____ in central Alaska.

4. Its Native American name, Denali, _____ "the great one."

5. The mountain's official name _____ Mount McKinley.

6. Deep forests _____ much of Alaska.

7. Moose, caribou, mountain sheep, and bears _____ in Alaska's back country.

8. Sometimes a hungry moose _____ into town.

9. A moose at the window _____ a funny but scary sight!

10. Many visitors to Alaska _____ fishing in the clear blue lakes and rushing rivers.

Compound Predicates

A **compound predicate** is two or more predicates that have the same subject.
The simple predicates in a compound predicate are usually joined by *and* or *or*.
Examples:

Bears *chase or injure* sheep sometimes.
Guards *watch and protect* the flocks.

◎◎◎◎◎◎◎◎◎◎◎◎◎◎◎◎◎◎◎◎◎◎◎◎◎◎◎◎◎◎◎◎◎◎

> **DIRECTIONS** Write the two simple predicates in each sentence.

1. Raccoon cubs curl into a ball and sleep cozily in their den.

_____

2. Their mother stays close by and cares for them.

_____

3. Sea lions float in the water and sleep at the same time.

_____

4. Sea otters anchor themselves to seaweed and float on their backs.

_____

5. A leopard sprawls along a limb and relaxes in a tree.

_____

> **DIRECTIONS** Complete each sentence with a compound predicate. You may add other words besides verbs.

6. Little kittens _____.

7. My baby cousin _____.

8. Bear cubs _____.

9. My new puppy _____.

10. Lions at the zoo _____.

Simple, Complete, and Compound Predicates

Remember that the simple predicate is the main word or words in the complete predicate of a sentence. The complete predicate includes all the words that tell what the subject of the sentence is or does. A compound predicate is two or more predicates that have the same subject.

DIRECTIONS Read the paragraph, and underline the complete predicate in each sentence. Then, circle the simple predicate. If the sentence has a compound predicate, circle each simple predicate.

Everyone worked hard on the class play. We formed committees and made plans. The script committee discussed the play for hours. The committee members wrote and rewrote the script many times. The final script sounded terrific! The costumes committee worked hard, too. These committee members collected old-fashioned shirts for the cast members. I volunteered for the sets committee. We sketched many different ideas. We chose the best sketch and turned it into a set. We hammered, sawed, and painted for many days.

DIRECTIONS Read each set of sentences below. For each set, write one new sentence that has a compound predicate.

1. The actors read the script. The actors memorized their lines.

_____

2. Everyone in the audience stood up. Everyone in the audience clapped. Everyone in the audience cheered for us.

_____

_____

Simple and Compound Sentences

A sentence that expresses only one complete thought is a **simple sentence**. A **compound sentence** is made up of two or more simple sentences joined by a word such as *and*, *or*, or *but*. These words are called **conjunctions**. Use a comma (,) before a conjunction that joins two sentences.

Examples:

Cheri sent a poem to a writing contest. (simple sentence)

Three judges liked her poem, *but* two judges did not. (compound sentence)

> **DIRECTIONS** The following paragraph is written with simple sentences only. Rewrite the paragraph by combining at least three pairs of simple sentences to make compound sentences.

Eduardo has always loved the circus. Now he is making plans to become a circus performer. He has taken gymnastics classes. His teacher is impressed with Eduardo's skill. Eduardo also belongs to a drama club. He likes performing in all kinds of plays. Comedies are his favorite. Soon Eduardo will have to decide which skills to develop. He may become a circus acrobat. He may decide to become a circus clown.

_____

_____

_____

_____

_____

_____

_____

_____

Declarative and Interrogative Sentences

Use a **declarative sentence** to make a statement. Begin it with a capital letter and end it with a period (.).
Use an **interrogative sentence** to ask a question. Begin it with a capital letter and end it with a question mark (?).
Examples:

Ricky draws great pictures. (declarative)
What did Ricky draw today? (interrogative)

◎ ◎

 **DIRECTIONS** → **Write each sentence so that it begins and ends correctly. Then, write *declarative* or *interrogative* to tell what kind of sentence it is.**

1. did you know that very few people have been attacked by sharks

_____

_____

2. many types of sharks are not very big

_____

3. one kind is only about as long as your hand

_____

4. how can sharks find food in the dark

_____

5. they use their senses of hearing, smell, and sight

_____

6. some sharks will eat anything

_____

7. have you heard that nails, jewels, and even clothing have been found inside sharks' stomachs

_____

_____

Imperative and Exclamatory Sentences

Use an **imperative sentence** to make a request or give a command. End it with a period (.).
Use an **exclamatory sentence** to express strong feeling. End it with an exclamation point (!).
Begin every sentence with a capital letter.
Examples:
>   Don't be afraid to try new things. (imperative)
>   Watch out for that bus! (exclamatory)

> **DIRECTIONS** Write a period or an exclamation point to end each sentence correctly. After each sentence, write *imperative* or *exclamatory* to tell what kind of sentence it is.

1. Please let me see that magazine article

_____

2. Wow, what a contest the magazine is having

_____

3. Tell me all about it

_____

4. Give me time to read all the rules

_____

5. Oh, it's a poetry contest

_____

6. How much fun it would be to enter

_____

7. Be sure to find out what the prizes are

_____

8. Wow, that's an exciting Grand Prize

_____

9. What a thrill it would be to win a trip to Washington

_____

10. Please help me write a poem about what it means to be a friend

_____

11. Give me some ideas about what to say

_____

12. Oh, I hope our poem wins a prize

_____

Agreement of Subjects and Verbs

The verb of a sentence must agree with the subject in number.
Examples:
The *player hits* the ball.
The other *players chase* after it.

◎◎◎◎◎◎◎◎◎◎◎◎◎◎◎◎◎◎◎◎◎◎◎◎◎◎◎◎◎◎◎◎◎

DIRECTIONS ➤ **Write the verb in ( ) that agrees with the subject.**

1. Breakfast _____ a plate of scrambled eggs and sausage.
(is, are)

2. These foods _____ good on Earth and in space, too.
(taste, tastes)

3. In fact, astronauts _____ just such meals on the space shuttle.
(eat, eats)

4. In the early days of the space program, meals _____ not so tasty.
(was, were)

5. John Glenn _____ unhappy about having to squeeze his food
(was, were)
from tubes.

6. Now astronauts' food _____ better.
(taste, tastes)

7. It _____ easier to eat, too.
(is, are)

8. Foil pouches _____ a great variety of things to eat.
(hold, holds)

9. A meal _____ only about half an hour to prepare on the space
(take, takes)
shuttle.

10. Astronauts _____ careful to eat well-balanced meals.
(is, are)

11. Fruits and vegetables _____ popular on board.
(is, are)

12. I _____ sure I would like to try some space foods.
(am, is)

Agreement of Subject Pronouns with Verbs

The verb of a sentence must agree with the subject pronoun in number.
Examples:
   She knows the answer.
   We know that song.
   I know how to whistle.
   You know the way.

⊙⊙⊙⊙⊙⊙⊙⊙⊙⊙⊙⊙⊙⊙⊙⊙⊙⊙⊙⊙⊙⊙⊙⊙⊙⊙⊙⊙⊙⊙⊙⊙⊙⊙⊙⊙

DIRECTIONS ➤ Write the verb in ( ) that correctly completes each sentence.

1. He _____ that deserts are very dry places.
      (know, knows)

2. We _____ to find nothing but sand there.
      (expect, expects)

3. We _____ many different animals there after all.
      (find, finds)

4. They _____ Matt.
      (surprise, surprises)

5. He _____ a type of lizard called a Gila monster.
      (watch, watches)

6. It _____ slowly, looking for food.
      (move, moves)

7. I _____ at a roadrunner chasing an insect.
      (laugh, laughs)

8. It _____ right by Tammy.
      (speed, speeds)

9. She _____ to look at desert plants.
      (like, likes)

10. Sometimes they _____ colorful blooms.
       (show, shows)

11. She _____ a huge saguaro cactus.
       (admire, admires)

12. It _____ over 50 feet tall.
       (grow, grows)

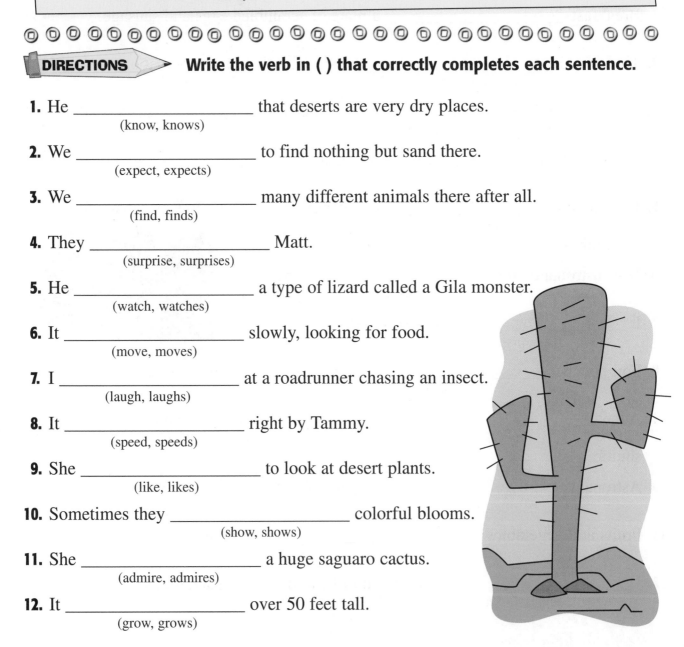

Combining Sentences with the Same Subject

Good writers sometimes combine sentences to make their writing more interesting.

Two short sentences might have the same subject. The writer writes the subject once and then combines the two predicates in the same sentence.

Example:

> Bart *liked macaroni*. Bart *liked cheese*.
>
> Bart liked *macaroni and cheese*.

DIRECTIONS ▶ **Rewrite the paragraph. Combine pairs of sentences that have the same subjects.**

My parents and I went to Washington, D.C., last year. We left on Monday. We drove for three days. I got tired of riding. I was glad when we arrived in Washington. Dad took us to the Capitol. He showed us our senator's office. Mom loves history. She wanted to see the National Museum of American History. I had read about the pandas. I asked to go to the National Zoo to see them. We all admire Abraham Lincoln. We were thrilled to see the Lincoln Memorial. We had a good time in Washington. We learned a lot about our country, too.

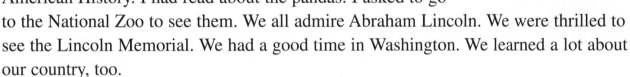

_____

_____

_____

_____

_____

_____

_____

Combining Sentences with the Same Predicate

Good writers often combine short sentences to avoid unnecessary words. Two sentences might have the same predicate. The sentences can be combined by joining the subjects with the word *and*. Be sure that your subjects and verb agree in number.

Example:

    Ann likes to play softball. *Trina* likes to play softball.
    Ann and Trina like to play softball.

DIRECTIONS   **Combine each pair of sentences to make one sentence. Write the new sentence.**

1. Schools should have ramps as well as steps. Libraries should have ramps as well as steps. _____

_____

2. People in wheelchairs find it hard to climb stairs. People on crutches find it hard to climb stairs. _____

_____

3. Libraries should have elevators. Other public buildings should have elevators.

_____

_____

4. Door handles should be placed low. Elevator buttons should be placed low.

_____

_____

5. People in wheelchairs can reach them there. Everyone else can reach them there.

_____

_____

Joining Sentences

Good writers make their writing more interesting by joining sentences that are short and choppy. Sentences that have ideas that go together can be joined with a comma (,) and the word *and*, *but*, or *or*. Be sure the connecting word makes the meaning of the combined sentences clear.

Example:

Raoul may draw a picture of an elephant.

He may draw a lion instead.

Raoul may draw a picture of an elephant, *or* he may draw a lion instead.

◎◎◎◎◎◎◎◎◎◎◎◎◎◎◎◎◎◎◎◎◎◎◎◎◎◎◎◎

DIRECTIONS ➤ **Join each pair of sentences, and write the new sentences.**

1. Many kinds of spiders spin webs. Not all of the webs are alike.

_____

_____

2. A web may be long and narrow. It may be shaped like a triangle.

_____

_____

3. Some webs are like funnels. Others look more like domes.

_____

_____

4. Wolf spiders hide in burrows. Lynx spiders live on trees or bushes.

_____

_____

5. Many lynx spiders are green. They are hard to find on green leaves.

_____

_____

6. Tarantulas are furry. They look fierce.

_____

Joining Sentences to List Words in a Series

A list of three or more materials or items is called a **series**. Short, choppy sentences can be combined into one long, clear sentence with a series.
Example:
> Pet mice can be *black*. They can be *red or silver*.
> Pet mice can be *black, red, or silver*.

◎◎◎◎◎◎◎◎◎◎◎◎◎◎◎◎◎◎◎◎◎◎◎◎◎◎◎◎◎◎

DIRECTIONS ▷ Join each pair of sentences. Write the new sentence.

1. Rey-Ling gave a party. Karen gave a party. Mitch gave a party.

_____

2. They met on Monday to plan the party. They met on Tuesday and Wednesday to plan the party.

_____

_____

3. They invited Tina. They invited Mark. They invited Lee.

_____

4. Each guest received a paper hat. Each guest received a balloon. Each guest received a new pencil.

_____

_____

5. The children played Simon Says. The children played Musical Chairs. The children played Pin the Nose on the Clown.

_____

_____

6. Mitch taught the others a new game. Rey-Ling and Karen taught the others a new game.

_____

7. Tina sang a funny song. Lee sang a funny song. Karen sang a funny song.

_____

Expanding Sentences

A writer can expand short sentences by adding exact details. The details should be colorful words that give the reader an exact picture of how something looks, sounds, or tastes. These details can also tell more about how something moves or feels.

Examples:

Americans chose the eagle as their symbol.

Americans *proudly* chose the *bald* eagle as their *national* symbol.

How to Expand Sentences
1. Look for sentences that do not give a clear picture of your idea.
2. Think of describing words that give a more exact picture.
3. Add these words to your sentences.

DIRECTIONS **Add detail words to these sentences to make them more interesting to read.**

1. The _____ owl has often stood for knowledge.

2. People have thought that the bird's _____ eyes showed wisdom.

3. The _____ bear was a symbol for many warriors.

4. These warriors _____ carried their symbol into battle.

5. The _____ Chinese dragon is another symbol.

6. People often think of the _____ koala bear as the symbol for Australia.

7. This _____ animal is not on Australia's coat of arms.

8. Peace is often symbolized by a _____ dove.

9. Many _____ teams use animals as their mascots.

10. A person wears a costume at _____ games.

Avoiding Sentence Fragments and Run-on Sentences

To avoid writing sentence fragments, make sure each sentence has a subject and a predicate and expresses a complete thought.

To avoid writing run-on sentences, be sure you join two complete sentences with a comma and a linking word. You may also write them as two separate sentences.

DIRECTIONS Rewrite each sentence fragment and run-on sentence. Add words to make the fragments into complete sentences. Change each run-on sentence into a compound sentence or two simple sentences.

1. I went to see a play it was based on the book <u>Charlotte's Web</u>.

_____

_____

2. No adult actors.

_____

3. Played the part of Wilbur the pig.

_____

4. Charlotte was a very smart spider Wilbur was her friend.

_____

_____

5. Wrote words with her web.

_____

6. A girl played the part of Charlotte her costume was black.

_____

_____

7. Looked like a giant spider.

_____

Capital Letters for Proper Nouns

Remember that a proper noun names a particular place, holiday, day of the week, or month.
Capitalize the first letter of each important word in a proper noun.
Examples:

United States   Fourth of July   Wednesday

> **DIRECTIONS** ▶ **Write each sentence correctly. Add capital letters where they are needed.**

1. Americans celebrate independence day on july 4.

_____

2. People in canada celebrate their country's birthday in july, too.

_____

3. It's called dominion day or canada day.

_____

4. On july 1, 1867, canada gained its independence.

_____

5. Two special holidays are celebrated in mexico.

_____

6. Both september 16 and may 5 call for parades and speeches.

_____

7. Next monday, september 3, we will celebrate labor day.

_____

8. Flags will be displayed on cherry street.

_____

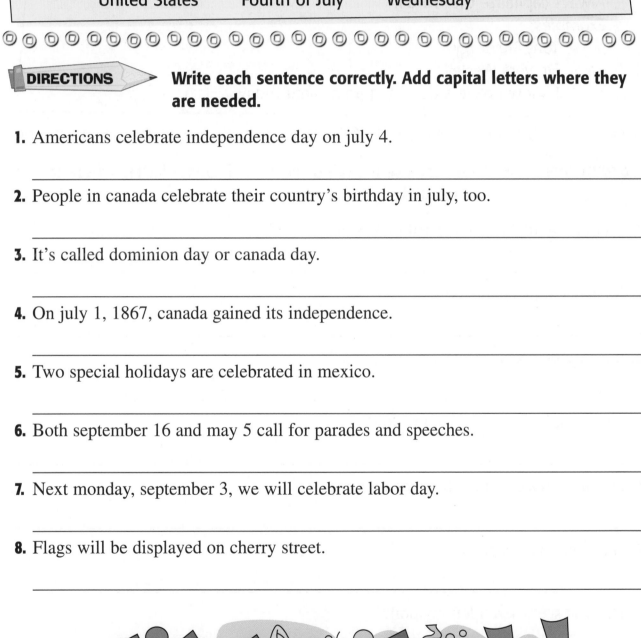

Capital Letters for Names and Titles of People and Pets

Begin each part of the name of a person with a capital letter.
Begin a title of a person, such as *Ms.*, *Mrs.*, *Mr.*, or *Dr.*, with a capital letter.
Always capitalize the word *I*.
Examples:
Tony Treworgy
Dr. Vera Wesley
I know I have a dentist appointment today.

DIRECTIONS Write each sentence correctly. Add capital letters where they are needed.

1. sherman smith has an unusual nickname.

_____

2. Someone took cindi's doll.

_____

3. the only suspect is mr. treworgy.

_____

4. mrs. sample does not have the doll.

_____

5. dr. carter treated a boy the same morning.

_____

6. sherman asked capt. kent for help.

_____

7. Did you see where i left my doll?

_____

8. i cannot believe that i lost it.

_____

Using Capital Letters

Use a capital letter to begin the first word of a sentence.
Use a capital letter to begin the first word, the last word, and all other important words in the title of a book, a story, a magazine article, a poem, a song, or a television show.

Examples:

    Today we solved some arithmetic problems.

    <u>Millions of Cats</u> (book)

    "Numbers and You" (story)

DIRECTIONS   **Read each sentence. Circle the letters that should be capital letters.**

1. school started last week.

2. this year I have a new teacher.

3. her name is Ms. Aarvig.

4. she has given us some interesting arithmetic problems.

5. the problems took a long time to solve.

6. the answers we got were really amazing.

7. One of my favorite books is <u>the amazing number machine</u>.

8. My brother is reading the story "the math magician."

9. My teacher read aloud the article "it all adds up."

10. Have you ever read the poem "crazy eights"?

11. Another good book is <u>math curse</u>.

12. The author also wrote <u>the true story of three little pigs</u>.

Periods

Use a **period (.)** at the end of a declarative or imperative sentence.
Use a period after an abbreviation.
Use a period after an initial.
Use a period after the numeral in a main topic and after the capital letter in a subtopic of an outline.

Examples:

Arithmetic adds up to answers.

U.S.   Tues.   Oct.   Dr.   Mrs.

Jason M. Dawson

   I. How to Master Multiplication
      A. Learn multiplication tables
      B. Practice doing multiplication problems

DIRECTIONS ▷ **Correct each item. Add periods where they are needed.**

1. The new arithmetic books are red and yellow

2. Arithmetic is my first class every morning

3. I have to wake up early to get to class on time

4. Pages full of arithmetic problems are a challenge

5. Mrs Washington is my arithmetic teacher this year

6. Sometimes Dr Carver attends our class

7. Ryan B Right is the smartest boy in my arithmetic class

8. T C Russell won an award at the arithmetic fair

9. I shared my book today with J D Kline

10. I   Arithmetic Every Day
    A   In the classroom
    B   At home
    C   At the store

Abbreviations and Initials

An **abbreviation** is a short way of writing a word or words.
Use capital letters and periods to write most abbreviations.
An **initial** is an abbreviation of a name. The initial is the first letter
of the name.
Use capital letters and periods to write an initial.
Examples:

Doctor = *Dr.*	Avenue = *Ave.*
Tuesday = *Tues.*	January = *Jan.*
Tina Latisha Evers = *T. L. Evers*	

DIRECTIONS → **Rewrite the following items. Use abbreviations and initials whenever possible.**

1. Doctor Jennifer Frances Newsome _____

2. 1623 Plateau Drive _____

3. Thursday, November 10 _____

4. Senator Margaret Jackson _____

5. Captain Marcos Manuel Uribe _____

6. Saturday, September 30 _____

7. 403 Jungle Boulevard _____

8. Tuesday, August 18 _____

DIRECTIONS → **Write each item correctly.**

9. mrs r v Toliver _____

10. 2204 Mountain ave _____

11. wed, apr 27 _____

12. mr a c Hwang _____

Using Commas

Use a **comma (,)** after the words *yes* and *no* when they begin a statement.
Use a comma after time-order words such as *first, next, then,* and *last*.
Use commas to separate three or more words in a series.
Use a comma before the word *and, but,* or *or* when two sentences are combined.
Use a comma to separate a word used in direct address from a sentence.
Use a comma between a quotation and the rest of the sentence.
Examples:

    Yes, the boys should join their father.
    First, the boys must have a plan.
    The boys ran *quickly, silently, and anxiously*.
    Josh felt tired, *but* he continued to run.
    "Andy, I need to rest for a minute."
    "We are almost there," said Andy.

DIRECTIONS ▸ **Read each sentence. Add commas where they are needed.**

1. Yes Mr. and Mrs. Saxby helped the boys.

2. First he told them about the plan.

3. The boys studied letters words and maps.

4. Mr. Saxby talked about Searsville Richmond Washington and Philadelphia.

5. Mr. Saxby had a map but the boys lost it.

6. Mrs. Saxby pasted a label on a jar and she put jelly in it.

7. "Andy you must pretend that this is not yours."

8. "Travel by day" said Mr. Saxby.

Commas in a Series

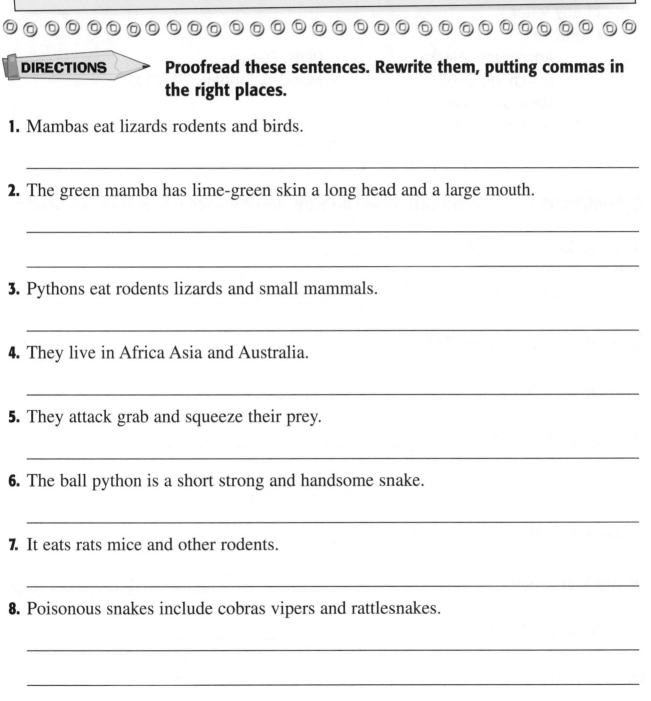

Use a **comma (,)** after each item except the last one in a series of three or more items.
Example:
The green mamba snake is *beautiful, swift, and deadly.*

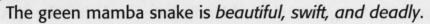

DIRECTIONS ➤ **Proofread these sentences. Rewrite them, putting commas in the right places.**

1. Mambas eat lizards rodents and birds.

_____

2. The green mamba has lime-green skin a long head and a large mouth.

_____

_____

3. Pythons eat rodents lizards and small mammals.

_____

4. They live in Africa Asia and Australia.

_____

5. They attack grab and squeeze their prey.

_____

6. The ball python is a short strong and handsome snake.

_____

7. It eats rats mice and other rodents.

_____

8. Poisonous snakes include cobras vipers and rattlesnakes.

_____

_____

More Uses for Commas

Use a **comma (,)** in an address to separate the city and state or the city and country.
Use a comma between the day and the year.
Use a comma after the greeting of a friendly letter and after the closing of any letter.
Examples:

Anchorage, Alaska	Paris, France
March 19, 2005	Monday, January 27, 2005
Dear Gramma,	
Your granddaughter,	

DIRECTIONS ▷ Write each item correctly. Add commas where they are needed.

1. Lone Star Texas 75668 _____

2. November 15 2005 _____

3. Winter Park Florida 32792 _____

4. August 2 2005 _____

5. Juneau Alaska 99673 _____

6. December 23 2005 _____

7. Dear Aunt Rita _____

8. Sincerely yours _____

9. Dear Mother _____

10. Your friend _____

11. Dear Mika _____

Question Marks and Exclamation Points

> Use a **question mark (?)** at the end of an interrogative sentence.
> Use an **exclamation point (!)** at the end of an exclamatory sentence.
> *Examples:*
> Who stole the roller skates?
> I cannot imagine stealing from a detective!

DIRECTIONS ▷ Finish each sentence with the correct end punctuation mark.

1. Do you enjoy reading mysteries

2. They are also exciting to read

3. Which mystery writers are your favorites

4. Donald Sobol writes terrific mysteries

5. Have you ever read the mystery series about Amy Adams and Hawkeye Collins

6. Nancy Drew mysteries are the greatest

7. How does Nancy solve her mysteries so quickly

8. She is a natural sleuth

9. Would you like to be a detective

10. What case would you like to solve first

11. What a great way to start

12. What is the case

13. How about helping me find my keys

14. What a funny detective you are

Colons and Apostrophes

Use a **colon (:)** between the hour and the minute in the time of day.
Use an **apostrophe (')** to show that one or more letters have been left out in a contraction.
Add an apostrophe and an *s* to singular nouns to show possession.
Add an apostrophe to plural nouns that end in *s* to show possession.
Add an apostrophe and *s* to plural nouns that do not end in *s* to show possession.

Examples:

    2:35 P.M.   7:10 A.M.
    was not = *wasn't*   did not = *didn't*
    Erika's parka   the *cat's* whiskers
    guests' laughter   *boys'* plan
    women's advice   *children's* schoolwork

 **DIRECTIONS** Correct each sentence. Add apostrophes and colons where they are needed.

1. Erika s birthday was on a cold winter day.

2. The children s faces lit up when they saw the snow.

3. The two girls walk home was difficult.

4. Her mother s voice greeted Erika.

5. "We don t have everything for your party."

6. "I ll go with you to the store," Erika replied.

7. "Where s Father?" Erika asked.

8. "We ll look for your father on the way to the store."

9. She added, "Father left at 6 30 this morning."

10. "I left school at 3 15 this afternoon," said Erika.

Contractions with *Not*

A **contraction** is a short way of writing two words together. Some of the
letters are left out. An apostrophe takes the place of the missing letters.
Use verbs and the word *not* to form some contractions.
Examples:
    could + not = *couldn't*   had + not = *hadn't*   will + not = *won't*

DIRECTIONS   Replace the words in ( ) with a contraction. Write the
contraction on the line.

1. Libby _____ ever visited Log Cabin Village before.
        (had not)

2. She _____ believe how small the cabins were.
        (could not)

3. It _____ easy to imagine how a whole family could have
        (was not)
   lived in one.

4. "I _____ understand how they kept warm in the winter," she said.
        (do not)

5. "You just _____ noticed the fireplace," Brad answered.
        (have not)

6. It _____ have been easy to cook over an open fire.
        (must not)

7. "The lives of pioneers _____ easy," Libby remarked.
        (were not)

8. "You _____ imagine that they bought all their clothes at stores,"
        (should not)
   Brad told her.

9. "I just _____ go until I watch the lady in the pioneer costume
        (cannot)
   work her spinning wheel," Libby said.

10. "She _____ stop until she has spun all that wool into yarn."
        (will not)

Direct Quotations and Dialogue

Use a **direct quotation** to tell a speaker's exact words.
Use **quotation marks (" ")** before and after the words a speaker says.
Begin the first word a speaker says with a capital letter. Put
end punctuation before the ending quotation marks. Begin
a new paragraph each time the speaker changes.
Examples:
> Mom asked, "Where have you been?"
> "I went to the library," Ed said.

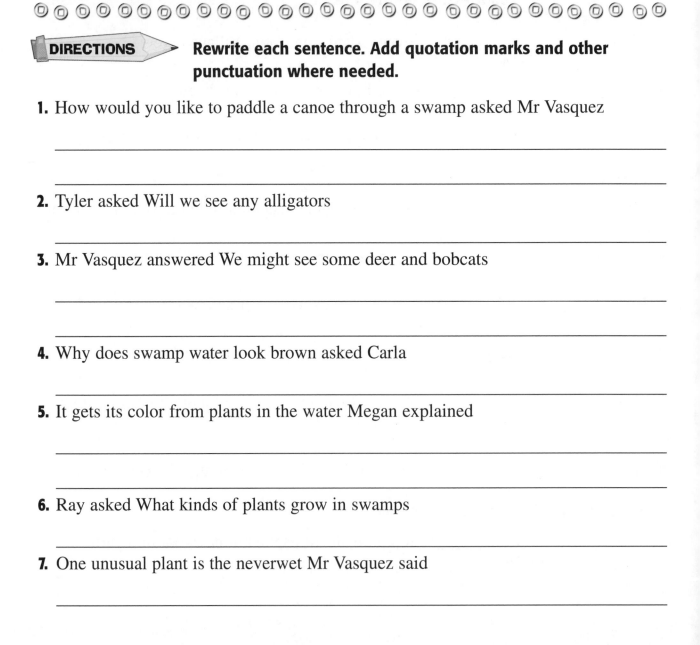

DIRECTIONS Rewrite each sentence. Add quotation marks and other punctuation where needed.

1. How would you like to paddle a canoe through a swamp asked Mr Vasquez

_____

_____

2. Tyler asked Will we see any alligators

_____

3. Mr Vasquez answered We might see some deer and bobcats

_____

_____

4. Why does swamp water look brown asked Carla

_____

5. It gets its color from plants in the water Megan explained

_____

_____

6. Ray asked What kinds of plants grow in swamps

_____

7. One unusual plant is the neverwet Mr Vasquez said

_____

Titles

Underline the title of a book or a television show.
Use quotation marks before and after the title of a story, a poem, or a song.
Begin the first word, last word, and all other important words in a title with a capital letter.
Examples:

<u>My New Kitten</u> (book)
<u>It's a Dog's Life</u> (television show)
"Wind in the Treetops" (story)
"Noses" (poem)

DIRECTIONS ▶ **Complete the sentences correctly. Add quotation marks where they are needed.**

1. Dad is bringing home a puppy today, Trudi said.

2. What kind of puppy will he choose? asked Chris.

3. Trudi said, I asked for a pug.

4. Where is my puppy? Trudi asked.

5. Go into the yard, Trudi, her mother replied.

6. Is it in the yard? Trudi asked eagerly.

7. Trudi wrote a poem called My Puppy.

8. She read a story called Our Dog Digger.

DIRECTIONS ▶ **Read the sentences. Add underlines where they are needed.**

9. Trudi read the book How to Be a Good Master.

10. Then, she watched the television show Lassie.

11. She read The Alphabet Book to her baby brother.

12. Next, she will read A Trip to the Zoo to him.

Compound Words

A **compound word** is formed by putting together two smaller words. The first word in a compound word usually describes the second.
Examples:

play + ground = *playground*
bed + room = *bedroom*

DIRECTIONS Use two words from the box below to make the compound word that is missing in each sentence. Write the compound word.

work	night	over	road	stairs	spreads	up
men	fire	wall	place	rail	bed	paper

My aunt owns a hotel next to an old **(1)**_____ where trains used to run. Long ago, **(2)**_____ who were building the track stayed at the hotel. Now most of the **(3)**_____ guests are tourists. When visitors go **(4)**_____ to the second floor, they find charming, old-fashioned rooms. My aunt has covered the walls of each room with flowered **(5)**_____. Quilted **(6)**_____ decorate the beds and keep guests warm on cool nights. Visitors sit in front of a cozy **(7)**_____ on winter nights and toast marshmallows.

DIRECTIONS Write a sentence with each compound word.

8. watermelon _____

9. roadside _____

10. workshop _____

Synonyms

A **synonym** is a word that has almost the same meaning as another word. When a word has several synonyms, use the one that works best in the sentence.

Examples:

Jobs is a synonym of *tasks*.   End is a synonym of *finish*.

◎◎◎◎◎◎◎◎◎◎◎◎ ◎◎◎◎◎◎◎◎ ◎◎◎ ◎◎◎◎◎◎◎◎ ◎◎◎◎

DIRECTIONS ▷ **Write a synonym for the underlined word in each sentence.**

1. Pioneers had to be very <u>brave</u>.

Synonym: _____

2. Pioneers faced many <u>hardships</u>.

Synonym: _____

3. Thanks to their help, many new cities <u>grew</u>.

Synonym: _____

4. The mountain men played an <u>essential</u> role.

Synonym: _____

5. Mountain men <u>relied</u> on their horses and guns.

Synonym: _____

6. Native Americans often <u>assisted</u> the mountain men.

Synonym: _____

7. <u>Stories</u> of the pioneers live on today.

Synonym: _____

8. They succeeded in finding great <u>opportunities</u>.

Synonym: _____

9. We still read stories of their <u>journeys</u> west.

Synonym: _____

10. You will probably learn about them in your history <u>course</u>.

Synonym: _____

Antonyms

An **antonym** is a word that means the opposite of another word.
When a word has more than one antonym, use the one that expresses
your meaning exactly.
Examples:

> *Hard* is an antonym of *soft*.   *Short* is an antonym of *tall*.

DIRECTIONS ▷ **Complete each sentence by writing an antonym of the word in ( ).**

1. Josh has been reading a very _____ book about inventions.
(boring)

2. He learned that sometimes an invention that seems _____ turns
(great)

out to be important.

3. Early zippers didn't stay _____ very well.
(open)

4. Some jigsaw puzzles were developed to make learning geography

more like _____.
(work)

5. Earmuffs were invented by a teenager whose ears felt _____
(comfortable)

in cold weather.

DIRECTIONS ▷ **Complete each sentence, using an antonym for the underlined
word.**

6. Josh would like to invent a <u>cheap</u> model airplane, but _____

_____

7. He hoped the work would go <u>quickly</u>, but _____

_____

8. Drawing the plans is <u>complicated</u>, but _____

_____

Prefixes

A **prefix** is a letter or group of letters added to the beginning of a base word. A base word is a word to which other word parts may be added. Adding a prefix to a word changes the word's meaning.
Examples:

The prince said he *liked* being in the cave.
He *disliked* the way the kingdom was run.

◎ⓞ◎ⓞ◎ⓞ◎ⓝⓞ◎◎ⓞ◎ⓝⓞ◎ⓞ◎◎ⓝ◎ⓞ◎◎ⓞ◎◎ⓞ◎◎◎ⓞ◎ⓝ◎ⓞ◎◎ⓞ◎◎◎◎

Prefix	Meaning	Example
dis	not	<u>dis</u>like
im	not	<u>im</u>possible
in	not	<u>in</u>active
mis	incorrectly	<u>mis</u>label
non	not	<u>non</u>stop
pre	before	<u>pre</u>pay
re	again	<u>re</u>read
re	back	<u>re</u>pay
un	not	<u>un</u>kind
un	opposite of	<u>un</u>button

DIRECTIONS ▸ **Read each sentence. Add a prefix with the meaning in ( ) to each underlined word. Write the new word on the line. Use the list above to help you.**

1. Tony was <u>fair</u> to keep the doll. _____
(not)

2. He waited <u>patiently</u> for Cindi's reaction. _____
(not)

3. Sherlock <u>planned</u> how he would look for the doll. _____
(before)

4. Tony <u>understood</u> Sherlock's interest in the doll. _____
(incorrectly)

5. Tony <u>covered</u> the doll's hiding place. _____
(opposite of)

6. Sherlock <u>traced</u> Tony's path. _____
(again)

7. She thought he was <u>capable</u> of finding the doll. _____
(not)

Suffixes

A **suffix** is a letter or group of letters added to the ending of a base word. A base word is a word to which other word parts may be added. A suffix changes the meaning of a word.
Examples:
> The tired hik<u>er</u> rested quiet<u>ly</u>.

Suffix	Meaning	Example
al	like, referring to	coas<u>tal</u>
able, ible	able to be	break<u>able</u>, flex<u>ible</u>
er, or	one who	sing<u>er</u>, sail<u>or</u>
ful	full of	help<u>ful</u>
less	without	home<u>less</u>
y	what kind	snow<u>y</u>
ly	how	quick<u>ly</u>
ist	one who does	art<u>ist</u>

 **DIRECTIONS**   Add a suffix from the box to the word in ( ). Write the new word to complete the sentence.

able	er	ful	less	or	y

1. I attended a very _____ concert.
(enjoy)

2. The guest _____ seemed to have a good time.
(conduct)

3. As he conducted, his movements were _____.
(grace)

4. A popular _____ joined the orchestra for one song.
(sing)

5. Another number featured a solo by a famous guitar _____.
(play)

6. The medley of tunes by George Gershwin was peaceful and _____.
(dream)

Homographs

Homographs are words that have the same spelling but different meanings.
Some homographs are pronounced differently.
Examples:

Some animals *live* on land and water.
Live plants are not allowed in this building.

**DIRECTIONS** Write the homograph from the box that completes each sentence. On the line before the sentence, write the number of the definition for the homograph in that sentence.

bass[1]—a kind of fish	bass[2]—a low-pitched sound
slip[1]—a small piece	slip[2]—to slide accidentally
roll[1]—a small piece of bread	roll[2]—to move by turning over and over
wind[1]—moving air	wind[2]—to turn around and around

_____ **1.** Be careful not to _____ on the icy sidewalk.

_____ **2.** The _____ made the kite fly high.

_____ **3.** My baby sister has learned to _____ a ball.

_____ **4.** He wrote his name on a _____ of paper.

_____ **5.** I caught a large _____ at Greenway Lake.

_____ **6.** The paths _____ around the mountain.

_____ **7.** Do you put butter on your _____?

_____ **8.** My brother sings _____ in the choir.

DIRECTIONS Write a sentence that shows one meaning of this homograph: *rock*.

_____

_____

Homophones

Homophones are words that sound alike but are spelled differently and have different meanings.
Example:

Beth did the *right* thing to help her allergy.
Did she *write* a thank-you note to the doctor?

"Please *be* my friend!" Beth begged.
Beth was not allergic to *bee* stings.

DIRECTIONS Complete each sentence correctly. Choose the correct homophone in ( ) and write it in the blank.

1. The dirt road leading to the farm _____ the highway.
(meats, meets)

2. The girl _____ the sign that told her about the puppies.
(red, read)

3. _____ the man sell her a puppy?
(Would, Wood)

4. The girl thought it would be hard to _____ a puppy.
(choose, chews)

5. The girl thought she could _____ her mother.
(hear, here)

6. When she reached the turn, she saw her _____ yellow house.
(pail, pale)

7. Her mother said she _____ nothing about any puppies.
(new, knew)

8. The puppy wagged its _____.
(tail, tale)

9. It would _____ for the girl to come home from school.
(wait, weight)

10. The puppy jumped on her when it _____ its name.
(herd, heard)

Troublesome Words

Use **too** when you mean "more than enough" or "also." Use **to** when you mean "in the direction of." Use **two** when you mean the number.
Examples:

      Washington State is *too* beautiful for words!

      I've never been *to* the Northwest.

      My aunt and uncle went there for *two* weeks.

Use **it's** when you mean "it is." Use **its** when you mean "belonging to it."
Examples:

      It's a good day to carve a totem pole.

      A totem pole has many figures on *its* body.

DIRECTIONS Complete each sentence correctly by writing *to*, *too*, or *two*.

1. Long ago, the Kwakiutl people came

_____ the Northwest.

2. No _____ of their beautiful masks

look alike.

3. The masks were never worn _____

daily events.

4. The masks seem _____ heavy to me.

DIRECTIONS Complete each sentence correctly by writing *it's* or *its*.

5. When I see the log, _____ size surprises me.

6. _____ huge and heavy.

7. Small knots cover _____ surface.

8. I try to carve a bird, but _____ not very good.

Troublesome Words, page 2

Use **your** when you mean "belonging to you." Use **you're** when you mean "you are."
Examples:

> *You're* welcome to join our quilting group.
> Don't forget to bring *your* sketches next week.

Use **their** when you mean "belonging to them." Use **there** when you mean "in that place." Use **they're** when you mean "they are."
Examples:

> *Their* "brains" are really computers.
> I like that little robot over *there*.
> *They're* small, silver, and smart.

DIRECTIONS ▷ Complete each sentence correctly by writing *your* or *you're*.

1. I hear that _____ a good nature artist.

2. Is _____ brother talented, too?

3. Did _____ family teach you how to do this?

4. Allen says _____ making a quilt.

DIRECTIONS ▷ Circle the correct word in ( ) to complete each sentence.

5. Robots are loyal to (they're / their) owners.

6. (Their / They're) good to have nearby.

7. That one over (there / their) has been in the family for years.

8. (Their / They're) the perfect helpers.

9. Robots are worth (their / they're) weight in metal.

Negatives

A **negative** is a word that means "no" or "not."
The words *never, no, nobody, none, not, nothing*, and *nowhere* are negatives.
The negative word *not* is often used in contractions.
Do not use two negatives in the same sentence.
Examples:
Joe had *never* worked in a factory before.
Nobody there knew him.
He *didn't* know at first how hard the work was.

DIRECTIONS ➤ **Write the word in ( ) that makes the sentence correct.**

1. George Washington didn't _____ live in the White House.
(ever, never)

2. The government didn't have _____ special place for the
(any, no)
president to live.

3. There _____ no official home for the president until 1800.
(was, wasn't)

4. The White House wasn't ready for _____ to live in until John
(nobody, anybody)
Adams was president.

5. Even then, the house didn't have _____ rooms that were
(any, no)
completely finished.

6. President Jefferson didn't waste _____ time before improving
(any, no)
the White House.

7. There _____ no terraces at the ends of the building until his time.
(were, weren't)

8. Only a few presidents didn't do _____ to change the White House.
(anything, nothing)

9. There haven't been _____ who were completely satisfied with
(any, none)
the house.

10. The White House doesn't belong to _____ certain president.
(any, no)

Avoiding Wordy Language

Good writers say what they mean in as few words as possible. When you revise, cross out words that don't add to the meaning.
Example:
   Mo made an attempt to jump out of the boat he was in. (wordy)
   Mo tried to jump out of the boat. (better)

DIRECTIONS ▷ **Rewrite the story. Take out the underlined words or replace them with fewer words that mean the same thing.**

Dove was <u>putting on her clothes and getting ready</u> for Wren's party. How <u>puffed up and proud</u> she was of her snowy white dress! It <u>might possibly</u> be the most beautiful outfit <u>of all the birds that had been invited to the party</u>. Dove turned around and around. She admired <u>the reflection of herself</u> in the mirror. "How lovely I look!" she cried. <u>Just about at that time</u> her wing bumped <u>up against</u> a bottle of ink that was sitting on her desk. The <u>little bottle of ink</u> turned over, and splash! Down the front of <u>the white dress that Dove was wearing</u> went an inky black stain.

Moral: Be proud of yourself, but <u>be careful not to be</u> more proud than you should be.

_____

_____

_____

_____

_____

_____

_____

_____

_____

Adding Describing Words to Sentences

Good writers choose describing words to create clear, strong pictures.
Examples:
> The new coin was *shiny* and *bright*.
> The dog's fur was *soft* and *smooth*.

DIRECTIONS ▶ **Replace each word in ( ) with a vivid and exact describing word. Use words from the box, or use other words.**

lovely	silent	fabulous	precious
ear-splitting	frantic	peaceful	colorful
towering	bustling	gentle	glistening

1. The valley was a _____ place.
(quiet)

2. Nestled in the _____ Rockies, it was blanketed with
(high)

_____ snow much of the year.
(shiny)

3. In the summer, green grass and _____ flowers covered the hillsides.
(pretty)

4. Deer grazed there as _____ breezes whispered.
(slow)

5. Then one day, _____ gold was discovered in the
(valuable)

_____ valley.
(nice)

6. Thousands of people rushed to find _____ riches.
(great)

7. Suddenly, Caribou turned into a _____ city.
(busy)

8. The valley was filled with the _____ noise of
(loud)

_____ miners searching for gold.
(eager)

Using Metaphors and Similes

Writers can create vivid word pictures by comparing two things that are not usually thought of as being alike. When *like* or *as* is used to compare two things, the comparison is called a **simile**. A **metaphor** makes a comparison by speaking of one thing as if it were another.
Examples:
> *His feet* smelled *like dead fish.*
> *Paul Bunyan* was as big *as a tree.*
> The *hot room* was an *oven.*

DIRECTIONS Read the paragraph. Then, complete the sentences.

The deep lake was a golden mirror reflecting the setting sun. As a large ball of orange wax slowly melting, the sun slipped below the treetops. Across the water, a row of mountain peaks raised jagged teeth to the sky. Beyond the mountains, the sunset blazed like a pink and orange flame.

1. One metaphor compares the lake to _____.

2. Another metaphor compares mountain peaks to _____.

3. One simile compares the setting sun to _____.

4. Another simile compares the sunset to _____.

DIRECTIONS Complete each metaphor and simile.

5. (metaphor) The white clouds were _____

_____

6. (simile) The warm breeze was like _____

_____

7. (metaphor) The rows of corn were _____

_____

8. (simile) The falling autumn leaves were like

_____

Using Personification

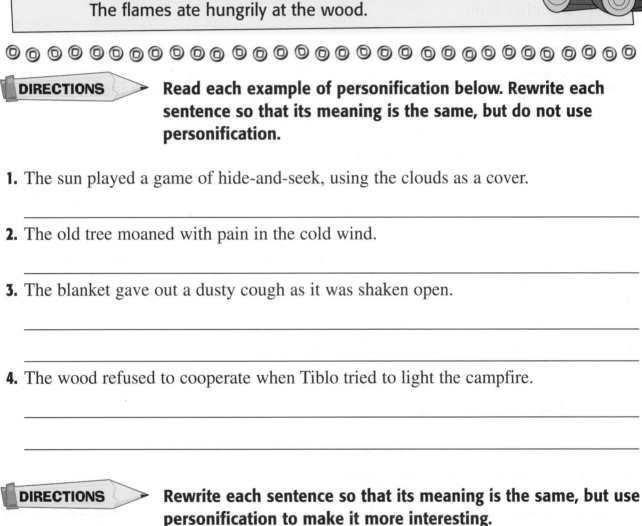

Sometimes a writer will give human characteristics to nonhuman things. Objects, ideas, places, or animals may be given human qualities. They may perform human actions. This kind of language is called **personification**. Personification helps a writer to create an exciting picture in the reader's mind.

Examples:

The clothes on the line danced in the wind.
The flames ate hungrily at the wood.

DIRECTIONS ➤ **Read each example of personification below. Rewrite each sentence so that its meaning is the same, but do not use personification.**

1. The sun played a game of hide-and-seek, using the clouds as a cover.

_____

2. The old tree moaned with pain in the cold wind.

_____

3. The blanket gave out a dusty cough as it was shaken open.

_____

_____

4. The wood refused to cooperate when Tiblo tried to light the campfire.

_____

_____

DIRECTIONS ➤ **Rewrite each sentence so that its meaning is the same, but use personification to make it more interesting.**

5. It was sunny out.

_____

6. There was a small cave among the rocks.

_____

Using Figurative Language

Writers often use **figurative language** to compare unlike things. Figurative language uses figures of speech such as similes, metaphors, and personification. Figurative language gives a meaning that is not exactly that of the words used. Figurative language tries to create a clearer word picture for the reader.

Examples:

Mother Nature

Father Time

DIRECTIONS ➤ Rewrite each statement below. State the same idea, but use a simile, a metaphor, or personification.

1. A heavy rainstorm fell on the mountain.

_____

2. Daffodils blew in the breeze.

_____

3. A bolt of lightning struck the tree.

_____

4. The round, white moon shone brightly overhead.

_____

5. A wolf howled in the forest.

_____

6. A gentle wind blew across the meadow.

_____

7. The building was very tall.

_____

8. Carl ate a big lunch.

_____

Paragraphs

A **paragraph** is a group of sentences that tells about one main idea. The first line of a paragraph is indented. This means the first word is moved in a little from the left margin.

The **topic sentence** expresses the main idea of the paragraph. It tells what all the other sentences in the paragraph are about. The topic sentence is often the first sentence in a paragraph.

The other sentences in a paragraph are **detail sentences**. Detail sentences add information about the topic sentence. They help the reader understand more about the main idea.

Example:

Greenland has a very cold climate. This island is located in the northwest Atlantic Ocean near the Arctic Ocean. More than 85 percent of Greenland is covered with an ice sheet, or glacier. This far north, the ice does not all melt during the summer. The summer sun causes icebergs to break off the ice sheet and to float down the rivers.

How to Write a Paragraph
1. Write a topic sentence that clearly tells the main idea of your paragraph.
2. Indent the first line.
3. Write detail sentences that tell about the main idea.

 **DIRECTIONS** Write three detail sentences for the following topic sentence.

In the summer you can have lots of fun.

_____

_____

_____

Keeping to the Topic

Good writers keep to the point when they give information. A good writer plans a paragraph so that it gives details about one main idea. All the sentences in a paragraph must keep to the topic.

DIRECTIONS On the line below each paragraph, write the sentence that does not belong in the paragraph.

Vehicles called submersibles help scientists explore deep parts of the ocean. Scientists need no special suits for riding in a submersible, since the air pressure inside is the same as at the surface. Some submersibles have mechanical hands for picking up objects on the ocean floor. Scuba divers explore the ocean wearing air tanks.

1. _____

It is true that some rocks can move without any help from humans. Skid marks in the sand in Death Valley show that some big rocks have moved. Death Valley is in California. Scientists believe that rain or freezing temperatures make the desert sand slick enough so that strong winds can push the rocks along the ground.

2. _____

DIRECTIONS Use the facts below to write a paragraph. Leave out the fact that does not support the main idea.

The dingo is a wild dog.
It lives in Australia.
Kangaroos and koalas live in Australia.
Dingoes usually howl instead of bark.
Dingoes can make good pets if they are caught as puppies.

_____

_____

_____

_____

_____

Using Examples

Good writers support their main idea with examples.

DIRECTIONS ▸ **Read the paragraph. Then, answer the questions.**

Good study habits contribute to better grades. Students study more effectively in a quiet room than in a noisy one. When my brother stopped leaving his radio on while he studied, his grades improved from C's to B's. If you want to make better grades, turn off that radio!

1. What is the writer's main idea? _____

_____

2. What example supports the writer's main idea? _____

_____

3. How does the example help the writer's argument? _____

_____

DIRECTIONS ▸ **For each statement, write an example that supports it.**

4. Jumping out of a moving swing can be dangerous. _____

_____

5. A person should always swim with a buddy. _____

_____

6. The library is a good place to spend a rainy afternoon. _____

_____

Narrative

A **narrative** is a story. It tells about real or made-up events. A narrative tells about one main idea. A narrative should have a beginning, a middle, and an end.

Most narratives have **dialogue**. A writer uses dialogue to show how characters speak to one another.

Example:

> It was Halloween night, and Teresa was having a party.
>
> Suddenly, there was a loud crack of thunder, and the room went black.
>
> "What happened?" Amy screamed.
>
> "I don't know," Teresa said.
>
> The lights came on again but not in the living room. Then, Teresa had an idea. She lit all the Halloween candles. Teresa's bright idea saved the party.

How to Write a Story and Dialogue

1. Write an interesting beginning to present the main character and the setting.
2. Tell about a problem that the main character has to solve in the middle. Tell about what happens in order.
3. Write an ending. Tell how the main character solves the problem or meets the challenge.
4. Write a title for your story.
5. Place quotation marks before and after a speaker's exact words.
6. Use a comma to separate a quotation from the rest of the sentence unless a question mark or exclamation point is needed.
7. Begin a new paragraph each time the speaker changes.
8. Be sure the conversation sounds like real people talking. Use words that tell exactly how the character speaks.

Narrative, page 2

DIRECTIONS ▷ **Read the example narrative on page 478. Then, answer the questions.**

1. What is the problem in the narrative?

_____

_____

2. How is the problem solved?

_____

_____

3. Which two characters have dialogue?

_____

_____

DIRECTIONS ▷ **Think about a story that you would like to tell. Use the graphic organizer to plan your narrative.**

WRITING PLAN

Beginning	Middle	End
Characters: Setting:	Problem:	Solution:

Narrative, page 3

Tips for Writing a Narrative:
- Think about an exciting story to tell your reader.
- Create a realistic setting and characters.
- Organize your ideas into a beginning, a middle, and an end.
- Write an interesting introduction that "grabs" your readers.
- Write a believable ending for your story.

DIRECTIONS Think about a story you would like to tell the readers. Use your writing plan as a guide for writing your narrative.

_____

_____

_____

_____

_____

_____

_____

_____

_____

_____

_____

_____

_____

_____

_____

_____

_____

Descriptive Paragraph

In a **descriptive paragraph**, a writer describes a person, place, thing, or event.

A good description lets the reader see, feel, hear, and sometimes taste or smell what is being described.

Example:

> The girl thought her new doll was beautiful. It had a face that had been painted with bright colors. Its eyes looked lifelike. The clothes of the doll were finely stitched. There were beautiful buttons on the jacket, and soft lace was sewn around the hem of the dress. The shoes were as soft as butter to touch.

How to Write a Descriptive Paragraph

1. Write a topic sentence that clearly tells what the paragraph is about.
2. Add detail sentences that give exact information about your topic.
3. Use colorful and lively words to describe the topic. Make an exact picture for the reader with the words you choose.

 **DIRECTIONS** ➤ **Add descriptive words to this paragraph to make it clearer and more interesting to read.**

The girl was worried about her doll. Her _____ brother had wanted to play with the doll. The girl had told him that the doll was too _____ to play with. Now the girl was in school, away from her _____ doll. She had tried to put the doll in a _____ place. But her brother was very _____ and _____. The girl felt _____ thinking of what could happen if her brother found the doll!

Descriptive Paragraph, page 2

DIRECTIONS ▶ Read the example description on page 481. Then, answer the questions.

1. What is the writer describing in the paragraph?

_____

2. What are some words the writer uses that appeal to your senses?

_____

_____

3. What are some descriptions the writer uses to help you imagine the topic?

_____

_____

_____

DIRECTIONS ▶ Think about something that you would like to describe. It could be a thing, a person you know, or something that has happened to you. Write it in the circle. Then, write words on the lines that describe your topic. Use the graphic organizer to plan your descriptive paragraph.

WRITING PLAN

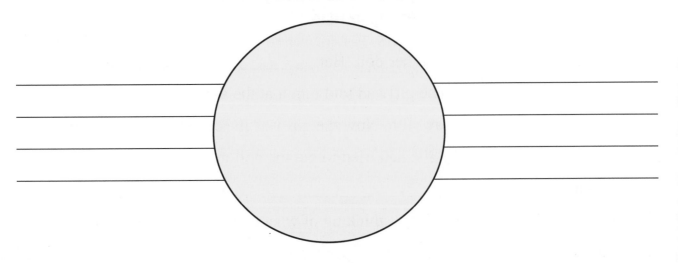

Descriptive Paragraph, page 3

Tips for Writing a Descriptive Paragraph:
- Describe a person, a place, an object, or an event.
- Paint a picture using words.
- Use words that appeal to the reader's senses. Let the reader see, smell, taste, feel, and hear what you are writing about.
- Include a sentence that introduces your topic.
- Write detail sentences that use descriptive words.

DIRECTIONS > **Think about something that you would like to describe. Introduce your topic in your first sentence. Then, use the words that you wrote in the graphic organizer to describe it. Be sure to appeal to the reader's senses.**

_____

_____

_____

_____

_____

_____

_____

_____

_____

_____

_____

_____

_____

_____

Friendly Letter

A person writes to someone he or she knows in a **friendly letter**.
A friendly letter has five parts: a heading, a greeting, a body, a closing, and a signature.
Example:

heading

627 Swan Street
Raleigh, NC 27611
August 14, 2005

greeting — Dear Jason,

body

How is your vacation? I am still selling lemonade. I bought some baseball cards. When you get back, I'll show them to you.

closing — Your friend,

signature — Ben

How to Write a Friendly Letter
1. Write the heading. In the heading, include a comma between the name of the city and the state and between the day of the month and the year.
2. Write the greeting. Capitalize the first letter of each word. End the greeting with a comma.
3. Write a friendly message in the body. Always indent the first line of the body.
4. Write a closing to end the letter. Put a comma after the closing.
5. Sign the letter with your name.

Friendly Letter, page 2

DIRECTIONS Read the example friendly letter on page 484. Then, answer the questions.

1. Who wrote this letter?_____

2. What is the writer's address?

   _____

   _____

3. What is the greeting of this letter?

   _____

4. What is the writer writing about in this letter?

   _____

   _____

Address an Envelope

An envelope is used to send a letter or a note. The receiver's address goes toward the center. The return address is in the upper left corner. Postal abbreviations are used for state names. The ZIP Code goes after the state abbreviation. *Example:*

Geraldine Roberts
8 Maple Drive
Camp Hill, PA 17011 — **return address**

stamp

Joe Canton
15 Talkeetna Road
Nome, AK 99762 — **receiver's name and address**

Friendly Letter, page 3

Tips for Writing a Friendly Letter:
- Think of someone to write to.
- Think of something to write about.
- Write your friendly letter.
- Be sure to include all the parts.
- Fill out the envelope correctly.

heading ______________________________

____

____

greeting ______________________________

body ______________________________

____

____

____

____

____

____

____

____

____

closing ______________________________

signature ______________________________

How-to Paragraph

A **how-to paragraph** gives directions or explains how to do something. Detail sentences in a how-to paragraph use time-order words to show the correct order of the steps.

Example:

How to Recycle Paper at Home

Help save trees by recycling paper at home. First, gather all your old and unwanted newspapers, magazines, and catalogs. Then, separate the newspapers from the glossy paper inserts. The inserts go with magazines and catalogs to be recycled. Next, place each kind of paper in a separate pile. When you have a bundle that is about 10 inches high, tie it up both lengthwise and around the middle with strong string. Finally, store your paper bundles in a dry place until recycling pickup day. If your community doesn't have a pickup, find out where you can take your paper to be recycled.

How to Write a How-to Paragraph

1. Write a topic sentence that tells what you are going to explain.
2. Add a detail sentence that tells what materials are needed.
3. Write detail sentences that tell the steps in the directions.
4. Use time-order words such as *first*, *next*, *then*, and *finally* to show the order of the steps.

How-to Paragraph, page 2

 **DIRECTIONS** Read the example how-to paragraph on page 487. Then, answer the questions.

1. What does this paragraph tell you how to do?

_____

2. What is the first step?

_____

_____

3. What is the final step?

_____

_____

4. What time-order words does the writer use?

_____

 **DIRECTIONS** Think about something you want to tell others how to do. Use this writing plan to help you.

WRITING PLAN

1. What will you tell others how to do?

2. What materials are needed?

3. What steps must the reader follow? Number the steps.

4. What time-order words will you use?

How-to Paragraph, page 3

Tips for Writing a How-to Paragraph:

- Choose one thing to teach someone.
- Think of all the materials that are needed.
- Think of all the steps someone should follow.
- Use time-order words to help the reader follow the steps.

DIRECTIONS **Think about something you want to tell others how to do. Use your writing plan as a guide for writing your how-to paragraph.**

Information Paragraph

An **information paragraph** gives facts about one topic. It has a topic sentence that tells the main idea. Detail sentences give facts about the main idea.

Example:

Where Does All the Paper Go? — title

When paper is recycled, it doesn't just become recycled paper. It is made into many different new products. — topic sentence

Some of these products include boxes for cereal and shoes. Recycled paper can also be used to make egg cartons, paper towels, and tissues. Some recycled paper helps people send messages to friends and family when it becomes greeting cards. Along with other resources, paper waste becomes plaster boards for the walls of homes and tar paper for under roofs. Even our cars may have paper waste in the form of stiffening for doors and sun visors. — detail sentences

How to Write an Information Paragraph
1. Write a topic sentence that tells your main idea.
2. Write at least three detail sentences that give information about your main idea.
3. Think of a title for your information paragraph.

Information Paragraph, page 2

DIRECTIONS > Read the example information paragraph on page 490. Then, answer the questions.

1. What is the main idea of the information paragraph?

_____

_____

2. What are four products made from recycled paper?

_____

_____

3. Write one detail sentence from the paragraph.

_____

_____

_____

DIRECTIONS > Think about a topic you would like to write about. Use this writing plan to help you.

WRITING PLAN

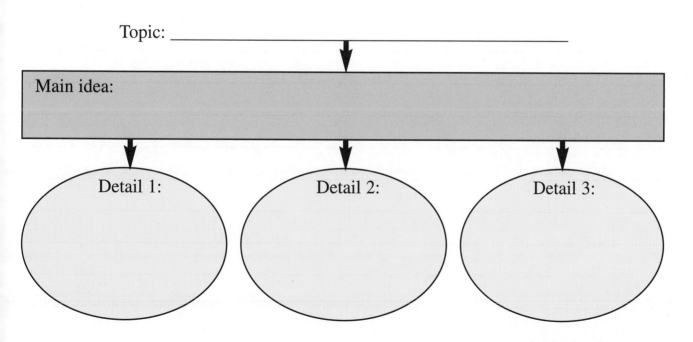

Topic: _____

Main idea:

Detail 1:

Detail 2:

Detail 3:

Information Paragraph, page 3

Tips for Writing an Information Paragraph:
- Choose one topic to write about.
- Write a title for your paragraph.
- Write a topic sentence that tells your main idea.
- Write at least two detail sentences that tell facts about the main idea.
- Make sure your facts are correct.

DIRECTIONS Choose a topic you would like to write about. Use your writing plan as a guide for writing your information paragraph.

_____

_____

_____

_____

_____

_____

_____

_____

_____

_____

_____

_____

_____

_____

_____

_____

_____

_____

Compare and Contrast Paragraph

In a **compare and contrast paragraph**, a writer shows how two people, places, or things are alike or different.

Example:

Colonial Williamsburg and Old Sturbridge Village both show visitors what life was like in the past. Colonial Williamsburg demonstrates life in the 1700s, and Old Sturbridge Village is a recreation of a New England village of about 1830. Both have many shops and other buildings that are open to tourists. Since Williamsburg was an important city in the colony of Virginia, the restored buildings there include the Capitol, the Governor's Palace, and several elegant houses. On the other hand, Old Sturbridge Village gives visitors a taste of life in the country. It includes a farm, a sawmill, and a mill for grinding grain. Popular attractions in both Old Sturbridge Village and Colonial Williamsburg are the demonstrations of crafts that were necessary to life in those times.

How to Write a Compare and Contrast Paragraph
1. Write a topic sentence that names the subjects and tells briefly how they are alike and different.
2. Give examples in the detail sentences that clearly tell how the subjects are alike and different.
3. Write about the likenesses or the differences in the same order you named them in the topic sentence.

Compare and Contrast Paragraph, page 2

 **DIRECTIONS** Read the example compare and contrast paragraph on page 493. Then, answer the questions.

1. What two things are being compared?

_____

_____

2. How are the two things different?

_____

_____

_____

3. How are the two things alike?

_____

_____

_____

DIRECTIONS Choose two things you want to write about. Write them on the lines below. Then, use the Venn diagram to help you plan your writing. List what is true only about A in the A circle. List what is true only about B in the B circle. List what is true about both A and B where the circles overlap.

A = _____   A   B   B = _____

Both

Compare and Contrast Paragraph, page 3

Tips for Writing a Compare and Contrast Paragraph:
- Think about your two subjects.
- Decide how the two subjects are alike and different. Choose at least three important similarities and differences.
- Write a topic sentence that tells how the two subjects are alike and different.
- Explain how the two subjects are alike.
- Explain how the two subjects are different.
- Write about the likenesses or the differences in the same order you named them in the topic sentence.

DIRECTIONS Choose two subjects you would like to compare and contrast. Use your Venn diagram to write your compare and contrast paragraph.

_____

_____

_____

_____

_____

_____

_____

_____

_____

_____

_____

_____

_____

Cause and Effect Paragraph

A cause is an event that makes something else happen. An effect is something that happens as a result of a cause. In a **cause and effect paragraph**, a writer first gives a cause. Then, he or she explains what effect or effects happen because of it. One cause may have several effects. One effect may have several causes.

Example:

> The dog was hungry, so it went looking for a bone. The dog knew there were none in the yard, so it began walking up the street. Soon it was far away from home, and it was not sure where it was! The dog had been sniffing the ground, so it did not watch where it was going. It decided to use its nose to find its way back home again. When the dog got there, the boy was so happy to see it that he gave the dog a big bone!

How to Write a Cause and Effect Paragraph

1. Write a topic sentence that tells what happened. Include the cause.
2. Tell the effects of what happened in the detail sentences. Include any new causes, too.
3. Write the detail sentences in the order in which the effects happened.

Cause and Effect Paragraph, page 2

 **DIRECTIONS** Read the example cause and effect paragraph on page 496. Then, answer the questions.

1. What caused the dog to go looking for a bone?

_____

2. What caused the dog to begin walking up the street?

_____

3. What was the effect of the dog's not watching where it was going?

_____

4. What were the two effects of the dog's getting home safely?

_____

_____

 **DIRECTIONS** Think of something that happened. What caused it to happen? What were the effects? Use the chart to organize your ideas.

WRITING PLAN

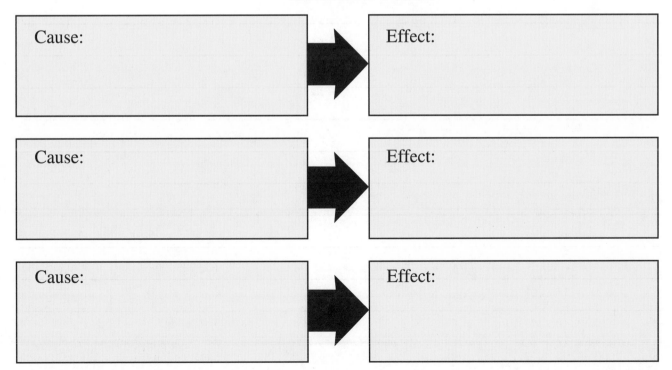

Cause and Effect Paragraph, page 3

Tips for Writing a Cause and Effect Paragraph:
• Think of something that happened. State it in your topic sentence.
• Clearly explain the cause that made something happen.
• Clearly explain the effect that happened because of something else.
• Try to include an end result or effect.

DIRECTIONS Choose an event you would like to write about. Use your writing plan as a guide for writing your cause and effect paragraph.

_____

_____

_____

_____

_____

_____

_____

_____

_____

_____

_____

_____

_____

_____

_____

_____

Book Report

A **book report** tells about the important events in a book. It does not tell the ending. It also gives the writer's opinion of the book. Finally, it says whether others should read the book.

Example:

Go on an Incredible Journey

    <u>The Incredible Journey</u> by Sheila Burnford is an incredible book. It tells the story of a cat, Tao, and two dogs, Bodger and Luath, that set out across 250 miles of Canadian wilderness searching for their way home to the family they love. When the adventure begins, the pets are staying with a friend while the family is away. Due to a mix-up, the pets aren't missed for several weeks when they begin their journey. The pets are chased by wild animals, delayed by people, and challenged by nature. You'll laugh and cry as you journey home with these three animals. They are courageous and true. This book is a must for animal lovers.

- title of report
- title and author of book
- main characters
- setting
- main events of book
- whether others should read it

How to Write a Book Report

1. Tell the title of the book. Underline it.
2. Give the author's name.
3. Tell about the book. Tell the main events. Do not tell the ending.
4. Give your opinion of the book.
5. Think of a title for your report.

Book Report, page 2

DIRECTIONS ⟩ Read the example book report on page 499. Then, answer the questions.

1. What is the title of the book? _____

2. Who wrote the book? _____

3. Who are the main characters in the book?_____

4. Where does the book take place? _____

5. Does the writer of the report think others should read the book? _____

DIRECTIONS ⟩ Think of a book you would like to tell about. Then, use this writing plan to organize your report.

Title of book: _____

Author of book: _____

Main character of book: _____

Setting of book: _____

Main events of book: _____

_____

_____

_____

_____

_____

_____

_____

_____

Should others read this book? _____

Book Report, page 3

DIRECTIONS Choose a book you would like to write about. Use your writing plan as a guide for writing your book report.

_____

_____

_____

_____

_____

_____

_____

_____

_____

_____

_____

_____

_____

_____

_____

_____

_____

Persuasive Paragraph

In a **persuasive paragraph**, a writer tries to make readers agree with his or her opinion.

Example:

> I think students should vote for the lioness as the symbol of our new school. The lioness is intelligent and carries itself with pride. Aren't intelligence and pride in ourselves the qualities we students want to show? Most of all, I think the lioness brings out a feeling of respect in people. People do not usually take advantage of a lioness. By voting for the lioness, we will choose a symbol of intelligence, pride, and respect.

opinion in topic sentence

reasons and facts

strongest reason last

restated opinion or call for action

How to Write a Persuasive Paragraph
1. Write a topic sentence that tells the issue and your opinion about it.
2. Give at least three reasons that will convince your reader to agree with you. Include these reasons in the detail sentences.
3. Explain each reason with one or more examples.
4. Save your strongest reason for last.
5. At the end of your paragraph, tell your feelings again. Ask your reader to feel the same way.

Persuasive Paragraph, page 2

DIRECTIONS > Read the example persuasive paragraph on page 502. Then, answer the questions.

1. What is the writer's main idea in this paragraph?

_____

_____

2. What are two reasons the writer gives to support the main idea?

_____

_____

_____

3. What call for action does the writer have in the last sentence?

_____

_____

DIRECTIONS > Think of something you feel strongly about. Then, use this writing plan to organize your persuasive paragraph.

WRITING PLAN

Main idea: _____

Reason 1: _____

_____

Reason 2: _____

_____

Reason 3 (your strongest reason): _____

_____

Call for action: _____

Persuasive Paragraph, page 3

Tips for Writing a Persuasive Paragraph:
- Choose a topic that you feel strongly about.
- State your opinion in your topic sentence.
- Write good reasons to support your opinion.
- Try to have at least three good reasons.
- Save your strongest reason for last.
- At the end of your paragraph, restate your opinion.
- Tell the reader to take some action.

DIRECTIONS Choose a topic that you have an opinion about. Use your writing plan as a guide for writing your persuasive paragraph.

_____

_____

_____

_____

_____

_____

_____

_____

_____

_____

_____

_____

_____

_____

_____

_____

_____

_____

Writing for a Test

Some kinds of test questions ask you to write. These questions check to see if you can organize your thoughts and express your ideas. They test to see if you can write for a specific purpose and use correct grammar. Here are some tips for writing better on a test.

Before the Test
- Listen carefully to all the directions your teacher or test-giver gives you.
- Read all written directions carefully.
- Ask any questions you have. (You might not be allowed to talk once the test starts.)
- Have several pens or sharpened pencils on hand.
- If you are allowed, read each item on the test before you begin.

During the Test
- Take time to identify your task, audience, and purpose.
- Organize your thoughts before you write.
- Write neatly and clearly.
- Work quietly without disturbing those around you.
- If you need help, raise your hand. Don't call out or get up.

After the Test
- If you finish before time is up, go back and proofread what you have written. Make final corrections.
- Follow directions given at the beginning for what to do at the end of the test. You may have to sit quietly while others finish.

Timed Writing

You have probably taken timed tests before. What are some ways to do well during a timed writing test? Follow these tips to make a timed test go more smoothly:

- Stay calm. Take a deep breath and relax.
- For a writing test, remember to check your task and your purpose. (Unless you are told otherwise, your audience is the person who will read the test.)
- Plan how you will use your time. If this is a writing test, decide how much time you need to spend prewriting, drafting, revising, proofreading, and writing the final draft.
- Use your time wisely once you start writing.
- If you begin to run out of time, decide whether you can combine some steps. Your goal is to finish.

Written Prompts

A written prompt is a statement or a question that asks you to complete a writing task.

- A narrative prompt asks you to tell a story.
- A persuasive prompt asks you to convince the reader.
- An expository prompt asks you to inform or explain.
- A descriptive prompt asks you to describe something.

Picture Prompts

A picture prompt is a statement or question about a picture. It asks you to tell something about the picture. The prompt also tells the purpose for writing.

Using a Dictionary

Each word defined in a dictionary is an **entry word**.

The order of letters from *A* to *Z* is called **alphabetical order**. Entry words in a dictionary are listed in alphabetical order.

There are two **guide words** at the top of every dictionary page. The word on the left is the first entry word on the page. The word on the right is the last entry word. All the other entry words on the page are in alphabetical order between the guide words.

An **entry** is all the information about an entry word.

A **definition** is the meaning of a word. Many words have more than one definition. Each definition is numbered.

A definition is often followed by an **example** that shows how to use the word.

DIRECTIONS → **Use this example dictionary page to answer the questions.**

cherry	chip

cher·ry [cher′ē] *n., pl.* **cher·ries**
  1 A small, round, edible fruit, red, yellow, or nearly black in color, and having a single pit. **2** The tree bearing this fruit. **3** The wood of this tree. **4** A bright red color.

child [chīld] *n., pl.* **chil·dren** [chil′dren] **1** A baby. **2** A young boy or girl. **3** A son or daughter. **4** A person from a certain family.

1. What are the two guide words on this page? _____

2. How many definitions are given for *cherry*? _____

3. What is definition 2 for *child*? _____

4. Which of these words would come before *cherry* in the dictionary: *carrot, corn, cactus, clover*? _____

5. Would the word *chop* be on this page? _____

Using a Dictionary, page 2

A **syllable** is a word part that has only one vowel sound. Each entry word in the dictionary is divided into syllables.

A **pronunciation** follows each entry word. It shows how to say the word and it also shows the number of syllables in the word.

The **pronunciation key** lists the symbol for each sound. It also gives a familiar word in which the sound is heard. A pronunciation key usually appears on every other page of the dictionary.

a	add	i	it	o͝o	took	oi	oil
ā	ace	ī	ice	o͞o	pool	ou	pout
â	care	o	odd	u	up	ng	ring
ä	palm	ō	open	û	burn	th	thin
e	end	ô	order	yo͞o	fuse	th	this
ē	equal					zh	vision

ə = { a in *above*   e in *sicken*   i in *possible*
      o in *melon*   u in *circus*

DIRECTIONS   Read each pronunciation. Circle the word that matches the pronunciation. Tell how many syllables are in the word.

1. pär´ kə   party   parka   _____

2. snō   snow   sun   _____

3. mə · shēn´   matching   machine   _____

4. kâr´ ə · bo͞o   caribou   carbon   _____

5. fä´ th͟ər   feather   father   _____

6. sur · prīz   surplus   surprise   _____

7. līt   light   let   _____

8. (h)wāl   wall   whale   _____

Using a Thesaurus

A **thesaurus** is a book that tells synonyms, words that have nearly the same meaning, and antonyms, words that mean the opposite of a word. Many thesauruses are like dictionaries. The entry words are listed in dark print in alphabetical order. Guide words at the top of the page tell which words can be found on the page. Good writers use a thesaurus to find vivid and exact words.

give	goal

glad *syn* cheerful, happy, jolly, joyful, lighthearted, merry, pleased
ant blue, downcast, glum, sad, unhappy

DIRECTIONS → **Use a thesaurus. Replace each word in ( ) with a synonym or an antonym. Write the new word on the line.**

1. Jared is _____ an excellent football player.
   (really)

2. The other players on his team don't think he is _____ just
   (different)
   because he is deaf.

3. It was _____ for Jared to find a team that would accept
   (hard)
   a deaf player.

4. Jared never became _____ when a team turned him down.
   (angry)

5. Now Coach Taylor is _____ that Jared is playing for the Pioneers.
   (happy)

6. Jared is _____ the star of the game.
   (often)

7. "Jared is the most _____ runner I have ever seen,"
   (exciting)
   Coach Taylor says.

Using an Encyclopedia

An **encyclopedia** is a set of books that contains information on many subjects. Each book in a set is called a volume. Subjects are arranged in alphabetical order in each volume. Volumes are also arranged in alphabetical order.

Some encyclopedias have a separate index. The index lists the number of the volume or volumes in which information about a subject can be found.

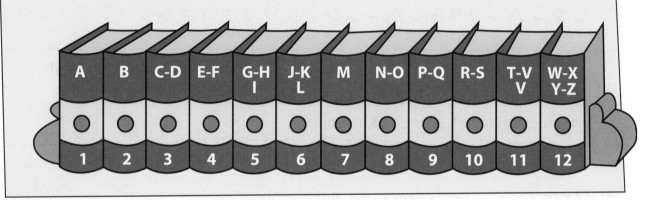

DIRECTIONS Use the example encyclopedia to find the number of the volume in which you would find each of these subjects.

1. Baffin Bay _____

2. Arctic Circle _____

3. penguins _____

4. fur _____

5. North Pole _____

6. kayaks _____

7. Eskimos _____

8. whales _____

9. seals _____

10. ice _____

DIRECTIONS Circle the word or words you would use to find the following information in an encyclopedia.

11. the capital of Greenland

12. animals of the Arctic

13. climate at the South Pole

14. expeditions of Robert E. Peary

15. the average daily temperature in Alaska

Using the Internet

The computer is a powerful research tool. The **Internet**, a system using telephone and cable lines to send signals, helps you to find almost any information in the blink of an eye. You can communicate instantly with other people by sending electronic mail. Some computers let you see the people as you talk. The key to using the computer as a research tool is knowing what keywords to use to start the Internet search. It takes some practice, but you never know what interesting place you can visit or what information you can find. Here are some hints to speed up the search.

How to Use the Internet
1. Make a list of keywords or names.
2. Choose a search engine that has a directory to narrow the topic.
3. Type in two or three keywords.
4. Type in different combinations of keywords until the topic titles focus on the information you need.

Arts and Entertainment	Games	Reference Materials
Cars and Trucks	Health and Fitness	Science
Computers and Internet	Home and Family	Shopping
	News	Sports

 **DIRECTIONS** → **Use the example Internet directory to choose the category you would search for these subjects.**

1. astronaut John Glenn _____

2. first aid _____

3. buying a book _____

4. a musical band _____

5. the weather _____

6. how to add fractions _____

7. which Native American groups lived in your area _____

Parts of a Book

The **title page** tells the name of a book. It gives the name of the author. It also tells the name of the company that published the book.

The **table of contents** comes after the title page. It lists the titles of the chapters, units, stories, or poems in the book. It also lists the page on which each new part begins. Everything in the book is listed in the order in which it appears.

An **index** is a list of all the topics in a book. It is in alphabetical order. It lists the page or pages on which each topic appears.

DIRECTIONS Use the example book parts to answer the questions.

title page	table of contents	index

A Number of Stories
by
Lisa Newton
 	
Brandywine Arts, Inc.
Chicago, Illinois
	Contents
	
	Adding It Up...............1
	Magic Numbers 10
	Time Tells All 17
	Triple Trouble 42
	Millions of Dimes.....58
		Subtraction
		  fractions 58–60, 119
		  whole numbers, 15, 17–20
		Word problems
		  addition, 2–4, 39
		  division, 40–45, 68
		  multiplication, 25–33, 62
		  subtraction, 35–38, 60

1. What is the title of the book? _____

2. Who wrote the book? _____

3. What company published this book? _____

4. What is the first chapter in the book? _____

5. What chapter begins on page 17? _____

6. On what pages would you find facts about fractions? _____

7. What could you learn about on page 39? _____

Reading for Information

Skimming is a quick reading method. When you skim a page in a book, you note its general subject, its divisions, and its major headings.
Scanning is also a quick reading method. When you scan a page, you look for key words.

DIRECTIONS → **Scan the passage to find the answers to the questions below.**

Folk Tales and Fairy Tales

Folk tales and fairy tales are two different kinds of stories. A folk tale tells about the legends and customs of real people. Sometimes America's history is told through the adventures of a folk hero, such as Pecos Bill. However, a fairy tale often takes place in a world of make-believe. "Jack and the Beanstalk," with its giant's castle, is one example of a fairy tale. A character in a fairy tale is often imaginary and sometimes has magical powers. A fairy-tale princess, like Cinderella, has a fairy godmother to grant wishes magically. Even though the two kinds of stories are different, they both always have happy endings.

1. By glancing quickly at the paragraph, how can you tell what it is about?

_____

2. Is "Jack and the Beanstalk" a folk tale or a fairy tale?

_____

3. What is the purpose of a folk tale?

_____

4. Name a fairy-tale princess. _____

5. What are folk characters sometimes based on?

_____

6. Which kind of story has imaginary creatures? _____

7. What kind of ending do folk tales and fairy tales have? _____

Classifying Information

In a research report, good writers limit a topic to one category. They **classify**, or group, details into smaller categories.

ⓄⓄⓄⒹⓄⒹⓄⓄⒹⓄⓄⒹⓄⓄⒹⓄⓄⒹⓄⓄⒹⓄⒹⓄⒹⓄⒹⓄⒹⒹ

DIRECTIONS ➤ Imagine that you are going to write a report about animals. Write each of the words below in the possible categories you may use in your report.

polar bear	cow	boa constrictor	dog	jaguar
arctic fox	walrus	bearded seal	sheep	tiger
goat	reindeer	spider monkey	horse	leopard

1. Jungle Animals

_____

_____

_____

_____

_____

2. Animals of the Arctic

_____

_____

_____

_____

_____

3. Domestic Animals

_____

_____

_____

_____

_____

DIRECTIONS ➤ Identify the category that was used to group each set of items below. Write the name of the category on the line.

4. _____

sandwich

apple

carrot stick

milk

5. _____

crabs

sharks

sunken ships

coral

6. _____

truck

skateboard

wagon

bicycle

Taking Notes

A writer takes good **notes** to remember the facts he or she finds when doing research for a report.
Example:

Royal Symbols by Crystal Wong, pages 15–16
Who has used the dragon as a symbol?
emperors of China
kings of England

How to Take Notes
1. Write a question. Then, find a book to answer the question.
2. List the title of the book, the author, and the page numbers on which you find information.
3. Write only facts you want to include in your report.
4. Write the information in your own words. Write sentences or short groups of words.

DIRECTIONS The items listed below are from the same pages of the book used for the example notes above. Read each note. Tell whether it answers Question A or Question B.

Question A: What things did the dragon stand for?

Question B: What did the dragon look like?

1. symbol of kindness _____
2. beast with long tail _____
3. symbol of fear _____
4. symbol of power _____
5. similar to a dinosaur _____

Summary

A **summary** is a short sentence or paragraph that tells the main facts or ideas in a story or selection. To summarize any writing, you must pay attention to the details. Using the question words *who, what, where, when,* and *why* can help you find the important details to include in a summary. There are some things you leave out of a summary. That is because they are less important than the main idea and the details. They make the story more interesting, but you can summarize the story or selection without them. A summary table can help you organize the information to write a summary.

DIRECTIONS ➤ **Read the paragraph. Then, complete the summary table.**

People who plan to camp should be prepared for some crawly company. Spiders surprise campers by appearing in unusual places. Spiders might be found on early morning canoe trips. They might jump out of boots, drop from trees, or crawl out from under rocks. Spiders crawl into these different spaces looking for a safe place to spin a web to catch food to eat.

Who:	Summary:
What:	
Where:	
When:	
Why:	

Paraphrasing

Paraphrasing means to restate an idea in your own words. For example, you read a paragraph by another writer. How would you tell the information in the paragraph? You should not copy what the other writer has written. Instead, you would tell the information in your own words. When you do, you paraphrase what the other writer has written.

Example: (you read)

Seals are migrating animals. Fur seals from the Pribilof Islands near Alaska migrate every fall. Female and male fur seals migrate to different places. In the fall, female fur seals swim 3,000 miles to southern California. The male fur seals migrate to the Gulf of Alaska. They travel only 400 to 500 miles from their summer homes.

(you paraphrase): Both male and female fur seals in Alaska migrate, but they go to different places when they do.

 **DIRECTIONS** ▷ **Read each paragraph. Then write, in your own words, a sentence or two to tell what the paragraph is about.**

Maureen could hardly believe that she was going to be in fifth grade. She was very excited. But she was nervous, too. The fifth grade was in a different school. The students in her class would be the youngest students in the school. She wondered if the older students would make fun of the younger ones. At the same time, Maureen thought it would be fun to be in a new school. Her stomach was full of butterflies!

1. In your own words, what is this paragraph about?

_____

Maureen discovered that things were not the way she had thought they would be. The new school was large and full of interesting activities. The library was beautiful. The older students were in a different wing. Maureen did not see them often, but when she did, they always smiled at her. Maureen knew that being in the fifth grade was going to be even better than she had imagined.

2. In your own words, what is this paragraph about?

_____

Details

Details are the words and sentences in a paragraph or story that make the selection interesting. They answer the question words *who*, *what*, *where*, *when*, or *why*. Details support the main idea or topic. When taking notes, you should include only details or facts that support the topic of the report or that add interesting information to your writing. A details chart can help you organize the information you read. Then, you can more easily decide which facts should be included in your notes.

DIRECTIONS Read the paragraph. Then, complete the graphic organizer. The first two details have been done for you.

The howler monkeys of South America are very interesting animals. They hardly ever leave the treetops. When they need a drink, they lick damp leaves. The howler monkeys got their name from the noise they make when they are scared. When they sense danger, they make a loud noise that can be heard up to three miles away. Their noise can often scare away what is threatening them.

Topic: How howler monkeys protect themselves	
Question	**Answer**
Who	howler monkey
What	a loud noise
Where	
When	
Why	

Concluding with Details

Sometimes an author may not tell you directly what is happening in a story. You may have to make a **conclusion** based on the facts from the story and on your own experiences or observations. After making a conclusion, though, you may need to change it if additional facts and details are gathered. When taking notes, be sure to note the details. A conclusion must be supported by the details. Using a conclusion flow chart can help you draw the correct conclusion.

How to Draw a Conclusion
1. Read the information carefully.
2. Think about the facts in the resource and your own experiences and observations.
3. Decide what the facts tell you.
4. Change your conclusion if new details show something different.

 **DIRECTIONS** ➤ **Read the paragraph. Then, complete the graphic organizer.**

Tugboats help link the city of Seattle to the sea. The small, strong tugs guide large ships into and out of the harbor. Without the tugs, the big ships could not make the trip safely. To honor the tugs, Seattle holds tugboat races each spring. At that time, the harbor is full of stubby boats splashing in the water like playful whales.

What can you conclude about tugboats?

What details support your conclusion?

1. _____

2. _____

3. _____

Outline

A writer uses an **outline** to organize the information he or she has gathered for a research report.
Example:

> **Royal Dragons**
> I. Symbol of Chinese royalty
>   A. Powerful, kind beast
>   B. Blessed the people
> II. Symbol used by English kings
>   A. Frightening beast
>   B. Represented protection

How to Write an Outline
1. Write a title that tells the subject of your report.
2. Write the main topics. Use a Roman numeral and a period before each topic.
3. Begin each main topic with a capital letter.
4. Write subtopics under each main topic. Use a capital letter followed by a period for each subtopic.

 **DIRECTIONS** ▶ On another piece of paper, organize and write these items in correct outline form.

1. The Falcon
Falcon was symbol of Egyptian King Ramses II
god of the sky
protected the king

2. The Crane
Crane is symbol used in Japan
stands for good luck
used in folk tales

Rough Draft

A writer first puts all of his or her ideas on paper in a **rough draft**.

How to Write a Rough Draft

1. Read your outline and notes. Keep them near you as you write.
2. Follow your outline to write a rough draft. Do not add anything that is not on your outline. Do not leave out anything.
3. Write one paragraph for each Roman numeral in your outline.
4. Write freely. Do not worry about mistakes now.
5. Read over your rough draft. Make notes about changes you want to make.

 **DIRECTIONS** → Choose one of the outlines below. Write a rough draft of a paragraph for this outline. Include one topic sentence and two detail sentences.

Bears as Native American Symbols

I. Bear symbolized protection to some Native Americans
  A. Bear masks worn to protect against enemies
  B. Bears in totem poles protected homes

Bears as Symbols of Sports Teams

I. Bear used as symbol in baseball and football
  A. Football—Chicago Bears
  B. Baseball—Chicago Cubs

_____

_____

_____

_____

_____

Research Report

When a writer makes all the changes in the rough draft, he or she writes the final copy of the **research report**.
Example:

Royal Dragons

Many Chinese emperors used a dragon to represent the royal family. The dragon was considered a powerful, kind creature in Chinese myths. People thought the dragon brought them rain, good crops, and good fortune.

Kings of England also chose the dragon for their symbol. They thought the dragon was a frightening beast that would scare the enemy. Long ago, battle shields of the English army had dragons on them. It was believed that a dragon would protect the carriers of the shields.

How to Write a Research Report
1. Write the title of your report.
2. Write the report from your rough draft and your notes.
3. Make all the changes you marked on your rough draft.
4. Indent the first sentence of each paragraph.

DIRECTIONS ▷ Read the example research report on this page. Then, choose a topic that interests you, and write your own report. Remember to take notes, make an outline, write a rough draft, and then write your report. Save all your notes to turn in with your report. Your report should be at least two paragraphs long and should have a title.

Topic: _____

Sources: _____

_____

_____

_____

_____

Writing Skills

UNIT 1: Personal Narrative

HOW MUCH DO YOU KNOW?

Read the paragraph. Then answer the questions.

My great-uncle Daniel had his seventy-fifth birthday last week. He told us an amazing story at his birthday party.

Daniel's Grandpa Weaver had made bricks many years ago. Daniel and his family were not very interested in bricks. Everyone forgot about Grandpa Weaver's old brick business.

Uncle Daniel and his brothers grew up and moved away. All of them married and had children of their own. Daniel and his wife were schoolteachers for 40 years.

Uncle Daniel and Aunt Ginny built a brick patio in their backyard last summer. Some friends told Uncle Daniel about a place to buy bricks. He and Aunt Ginny drove several miles to look at the bricks. All the bricks lay in a pile near an old house. Uncle Daniel bought several of the bricks. He and Aunt Ginny looked at the bricks in amazement. The name "Weaver" was stamped on them. The bricks had been made by my great-great-grandfather more than 150 years ago!

1. What does the narrative reveal about the writer's great-uncle?

_____

_____

2. What details did the writer use to describe Uncle Daniel and Aunt Ginny?

_____

3. What happens at the end of the narrative?

_____

_____

Analyzing a Personal Narrative

A PERSONAL NARRATIVE

- is written in the first person
- describes an experience important to the writer
- gives details about the experience in time order
- reveals the feelings of the people who took part

Read the narrative. Then answer the questions.

In third grade I never cared much about bicycles. An old two-wheeler with thick tires was fine with me for all the riding I did.

A few days before my tenth birthday, Dad took me shopping. I wanted a skateboard, but he steered me to the bike department. It was there that I saw the beautiful bike. It was a racing bike with pink tires.

I sat on the seat, and it was just my size. I was delighted! To my surprise, Dad wasn't pleased at all. He looked at the price tag and shook his head. "Maybe they'll put it on sale sometime, Sue," he said as we walked away.

On my birthday Dad brought in a huge box. I lifted the lid, and inside was the best surprise I'd ever had: the bike! Dad and I both had tears in our eyes as I hugged him.

1. What do you learn about the writer at the beginning of the narrative?

_____

2. What does the narrative reveal about the writer's father?

_____

3. What happens at the end of the narrative?

_____

4. How do the writer and her father feel about each other?

_____

_____

_____

_____

Visualizing Events and Recalling Feelings

TO CREATE PERSONAL NARRATIVES, GOOD WRITERS

- picture events and remember feelings before beginning to write

- write about events and feelings in an order that makes sense

Read the story. Then answer the questions.

Carlos is sure that if he lives to be a hundred, he will never forget his little sister's eighth birthday. She had opened her presents from Mom and Dad and Grandma, and she was starting to dress her new doll. Then Carlos said, "Wait, Cristina, look!" He handed her the box he had hidden under the table, the box with the gift he had saved for weeks to buy.

The room grew quiet as everyone gathered around. Cristina's eyes were shining with excitement. "Listen!" she whispered. Tiny scratching noises came from the box.

"Open it, Cristina!" Grandma said, smiling.

With trembling fingers, Cristina lifted the lid. "Oh, Carlos! Oh, Carlos!" was all she could say as she snuggled the tiny black kitten to her cheek. Seeing her joy, Carlos thought he had never been so happy.

1. Which details did the writer use to describe things Carlos saw?

_____

_____

_____

2. Which details did the writer use to describe things Carlos heard?

_____

3. Which detail did the writer use to tell how Carlos felt?

_____

_____

Using Vivid Words

> Good writers use vivid words to describe people's feelings.

Rewrite each sentence. Add vivid words or
replace dull words with livelier ones.

1. Last summer my family had a nice vacation.

   _____

   _____

2. The first part of the trip was not good.

   _____

3. It was a 1,000-mile drive.

   _____

4. I was glad when we finally arrived in Colorado Springs.

   _____

   _____

5. One day we took a nice ride to the top of Pikes Peak.

   _____

   _____

6. The view from the top of the mountain was pretty.

   _____

   _____

7. Some small chipmunks took peanuts from our hands.

   _____

   _____

using the Thesaurus

Good writers use a thesaurus to find vivid and exact words.

A. For each sentence, replace the word in parentheses ( ) with a more vivid or exact word from a thesaurus. Be sure the new word makes sense in the sentence.

1. Jared is _____ an excellent
   (really)
   football player.

2. The other players on his team don't think he is

   _____ just because he is deaf.
   (different)

3. It was _____ for Jared to find a team that would accept
   (hard)
   a deaf player.

4. Now Coach Taylor is _____ that Jared is playing for
   (happy)
   the Pioneers.

B. Use a thesaurus to find an antonym, or opposite, of each word. Then write a sentence using the antonym.

5. sad _____

   _____

6. cheer _____

   _____

7. tiresome _____

   _____

Proofreading a Personal Narrative

Proofread the beginning of the personal narrative, paying special attention to spelling. Use the Proofreading Marks to correct at least six errors.

PROOFREADING MARKS	
⬭	spell correctly
⊙	add period
⋏	add comma
?	add question mark
≡	capitalize
/	make lowercase
⤸	take out
⋏	add
∿	switch
¶	indent paragraph
⌄ ⌄	add quotation marks

See the chart on page 643 to learn how to use these marks.

Who could ever fourget the terrible

sandstorm we had last march? It was one of

the most frighetning experiences of my life!

For many months there had been

almost no rain. December, Janurary, and

February had been especially dry. No rain

fell in March, either, but the wind began to

blow furiously. On many days the sky was more brown than blew because the air was so filled with sand. The sand even crept inside hour house. Every morning my bed felt gritty. As I walked to and from school, blowing sand stung my ears, eyes, and cheeks

One afternoon was expecially scary. We all looked anxiously through the classroom windows as the sky grew darker and darker. Our teacher, Mrs. Robertson, tried to tell us a storry, but no one could listen. The wind howled, and we felt sand settle on our desks. Suddenly, everything was as dark as midnite. The electricity had gone off!

Write a Personal Narrative

Write a story about a shark from the shark's point of view. Tell how it feels to be a shark. Be sure to give details about the experience in time order.

_____

_____

_____

_____

_____

_____

_____

_____

_____

_____

_____

Write a Journal Entry

With a friend, make a list of qualities it takes to be a friend.

_____   _____

_____   _____

_____   _____

Use your list to write a journal entry about what it means to be a friend. Give details. Be sure to reveal your feelings. After you have revised and proofread your journal entry, read it aloud to your friend.

_____

_____

_____

_____

_____

_____

Write about an Important Event

Remember, when you write a personal narrative, you are expressing your feelings about an experience that is important to you.

Remember an important event, such as a recent birthday or your first day of school. List details from that day.

_____   _____

_____   _____

_____   _____

_____   _____

Write a personal narrative about that important event. Include the details in your story.

_____

_____

_____

_____

_____

_____

_____

_____

(Continue on your own paper.)

Write a Travel Story

With a friend, discuss places you have traveled in your state or city. Tell about interesting things you did or saw. Choose one place. Write a story telling about your travels. Be sure to give details about the experience in time order.

_____

_____

_____

_____

_____

_____

_____

_____

_____

_____

_____

_____

_____

_____

_____

_____

A Practice Personal Narrative

A FRIEND AT THE RIGHT TIME

I love to tell the story about how I met my best friend. My best friend's name is Tiger. We met at the school fair.

At first, my friend's name surprised me. But I guess it shouldn't have. After all, my name is Sunny. People who know me often wonder how I got that name.

Each year, all the fourth-grade classes hold a school fair. Everyone in fourth grade works at the fair. Some kids get to work inside the booths. Others take care of the little kids who ride the rides. Unfortunately, I got the second job. I don't really like taking care of little kids. My brother is a little kid, and he drives me crazy. But there was one good thing about the job. That's where I met Tiger.

At first, my job at the fair didn't seem so bad. I helped little kids get on the back of a pony. The pony was beautiful and gentle. It didn't seem to mind all those kids half as much as I did. I got tired of telling them to wait their turn. I got tired of hearing them cry for their parents. But more than anything, I got tired of holding their ice cream cones while they rode around. One thing was clear to me. There are problems that come with being older and more responsible.

The day wasn't even half over, and I was already splattered with ice cream. I looked like I had the measles, but the chocolate, vanilla, and strawberry kind. Suddenly, a little boy came screaming into the pony ring. "Oh," I thought, "not another screamer."

The boy grabbed the pony's reins. The pony stopped, and the kid on the pony's back started to fall. The little boy was falling away from me. His eyes were big and filled with tears. He was falling fast.

I stretched over the pony to reach the boy. At the same time, I saw a flash of fur go by my legs.

Tiger grabbed the pony's reins and pulled the pony away from my legs. I caught the boy seconds before we both hit the ground. The boy sat on top of me. He was laughing at the ice cream smeared on my face. "Very funny," I thought to myself. I got up and rubbed my backside. Maybe next time I'll just let the kid fall.

I looked for the pony. It was just a few feet away. Its reins were in Tiger's mouth. Thanks to Tiger's fast action, I saved the little boy. We were both heroes. And Tiger, the fastest dog I've ever known, was my new best friend.

Respond to the Practice Paper

Write your answers to the following questions or directions.

1. What clue tells you why the writer wrote this story? In other words, what is the writer's purpose for writing?

   _____

   _____

2. What is the setting for this story? In other words, where does it happen?

   _____

   _____

3. What did you learn about Sunny from reading this story?

   _____

   _____

4. Write a paragraph to summarize this story. Use these questions to help you write your summary:
   • Who is the story about?
   • What are the main ideas in the story?
   • How does the story end?

   _____

   _____

   _____

   _____

   _____

   _____

Analyze the Practice Paper

Read "A Friend at the Right Time" again. As you read, think about how the writer achieved her purpose for writing. Write your answers to the following questions.

1. How does the writer let you know that this story is a personal narrative?

   _____

   _____

2. In the sixth paragraph, the writer tells the story's problem. What is it?

   _____

   _____

3. What did the writer do to solve her problem?

   _____

   _____

4. What is the purpose of a conclusion in a story?

   _____

   _____

5. How are the first paragraph and the last paragraph in this story alike?

   _____

   _____

Writing Assignment

As people grow and change, they may have many best friends. Think about the best friend in your life now. Think about writing a personal narrative that tells about your best friend. Use examples and details to show why this person is your best friend. Use this writing plan to help you write a first draft on the next page.

Name your friend:

▼

Tell how you and your friend became friends.

▼

Give examples to show why this person is your <u>best</u> friend.

First Draft

TIPS FOR WRITING A PERSONAL NARRATIVE:

- Write from your point of view. Use the words *I*, *me*, and *my* to show your readers that this is your story.

- Think about what you want to tell your reader.

- Organize your ideas into a beginning, middle, and end.

- Write an interesting introduction that "grabs" your readers.

- Write an ending for your story. Write it from your point of view.

Use your writing plan as a guide as you write your first draft of a personal narrative. Include a catchy title.

_____

_____

_____

_____

_____

_____

_____

(Continue on your own paper.)

Revise the Draft

Use the chart below to help you revise your draft. Check YES or NO to answer each question in the chart. If you answer NO, make notes to remind yourself how you can revise, or change, your writing to improve it.

Question	YES ✔	NO ✔	If the answer is NO, what will you do to improve your writing?
Does your story tell about your best friend?			
Do you start your story by introducing your friend?			
Do you describe events in the order they happened?			
Does your conclusion summarize your story in a new way?			
Do you make it clear why this person is your best friend?			
Do you use words such as *I*, *me*, and *my* to tell your story?			
Do you explain how you feel about your best friend?			
Do you include important details?			
Have you corrected mistakes in spelling, grammar, and punctuation?			

Use the notes in your chart and your writing plan to revise your draft.

Writing Report Card

Read your revised draft again or ask someone else to read it. Have the person who reads your paper complete the following Report Card. Revise your paper until you have no less than a Very Good Score for each item.

Title of paper: _____

Purpose of paper: _*This is a personal narrative.*_ _____

Person who scores the paper: _____

Score	Writing Goals
	Does this story tell about something that happened to the writer?
	Does the story have a good beginning, or introduction?
	Are the story's main ideas organized into paragraphs?
	Are there enough details to support each main idea?
	Are the paragraphs organized in a way that makes sense?
	Are there different kinds of sentences that help make the story interesting?
	Does the story have an ending?
	Are the story's grammar, spelling, and punctuation correct?

☺ Excellent Score ☆ Very Good Score + Good Score
✔ Acceptable Score − Needs Improvement

UNIT 2: How-to Writing

HOW MUCH DO YOU KNOW?

Read the paragraph. Rewrite it, putting the steps in the correct order. Then answer the questions.

Homemade peanut butter is easy to make. Spread on bread or crackers and eat! Next, put peanuts in a blender. First, shell the peanuts. Blend them until they are smooth. Last, stir in a little cooking oil and salt.

_____

_____

_____

_____

_____

_____

1. What is the topic sentence of the paragraph?

    _____

    _____

2. What information does the last sentence give?

    _____

    _____

    _____

Analyzing a How-to Paragraph

A HOW-TO PARAGRAPH

- has a topic sentence that tells what the audience will learn to do
- tells what materials are needed
- describes the steps in order

Read the paragraph. Then answer the questions.

"Musical Chairs" is a good game to play with a group of friends. You will need some chairs and a radio or stereo. One person should be in charge of starting and stopping the music. First, count the players and subtract one. Then place that number of chairs in a circle facing outward. Next, the players walk around the circle of chairs as the music plays. When the music stops, each player tries to sit in a chair. The one who is left standing is out of the game. Then, remove one chair from the circle and continue the game. When only one chair is left, the player who gets it wins the game.

1. What is the topic sentence of the paragraph?

    _____

2. What information does the topic sentence give?

    _____

3. What information does the first detail sentence give?

    _____

4. What information do the detail sentences in the middle of the paragraph give?

_____

5. What information does the last sentence give?

_____

Visualizing Steps in a Process

WHEN WRITING A HOW-TO PARAGRAPH, GOOD WRITERS

- make a movie in their heads of the steps in the process
- write directions for the steps in the order in which they happen

Read the steps to make a kite. Then complete the paragraph.

1. Trace the outline of the kite onto a sheet of plastic.
2. Cut out the kite.
3. Glue the frame to the back of the kite.
4. Add a tail and decorations.
5. Attach the kite string.

To make a kite, first _____

Then _____

Next _____

Then _____

The last step is to _____

Writing for an Audience and a Purpose

GOOD WRITERS HELP A READER UNDERSTAND DIRECTIONS BY USING

- clear, exact language
- sentences that are not wordy
- language that suits the audience

Rewrite the following directions so that they would be clear to a group of second-graders. Leave out unnecessary words and information.

Here's how to play "Pin the Nose on the Clown." Everybody always enjoys this game. You will need a drawing of a clown face without a nose, construction paper, some pins, and a blindfold. Cut a circle from the paper for each player to make a colorful nose for the clown. You can make the nose any color you wish. Hang the clown face on a wall, blindfold the first player, and then ask the player to try to pin the nose on the clown. It's funny when someone pins the nose to the clown's ear or hair. Continue the game until everyone has had a turn. The winner is the player who comes the closest to pinning the nose where it really should be.

_____

_____

_____

_____

_____

_____

_____

Combining Sentences with Words in a Series

Good writers combine sentences to avoid repeating words.

Combine each group of sentences to make one sentence.
Write the new sentence.

1. Mei gave a party. Karina gave a party. Martin gave a party.

   _____

2. They met on Wednesday to plan the party. They met on Friday to plan the party.

   _____

3. They invited Tom. They invited Jill. They invited Carlos.

   _____

4. Each guest received a colorful hat. Each guest received a balloon. Each guest received a sparkly pen.

   _____

5. The children played Simon Says. The children played Musical Chairs. The children played Pin the Tail on the Donkey.

   _____

6. Martin taught the others a new game. Mei taught the others a new game.

   _____

7. Tom did a funny dance. Carlos did a funny dance. Karina did a funny dance.

   _____

Proofreading How-to Paragraphs

Proofread the how-to paragraphs, paying special attention to punctuation marks at the end of sentences. Use Proofreading Marks to correct at least six errors.

PROOFREADING MARKS	
⬭	spell correctly
⊙	add period
⋏	add comma
?	add question mark
≡	capitalize
/	make lowercase
ⸯ	take out
⋀	add
∿	switch
¶	indent paragraph
⌄ ⌄	add quotation marks

Do you enjoy collecting large or

unusually pretty leaves then you should

learn to make ink prints of leaves. Making

the prints is fun, and you'll enjoy having

pretty prints of your best leaves

The most important thing for making a leaf print is a leaf that you like.

You also need a piece of felt just a little lareger than your leaf, a smooth

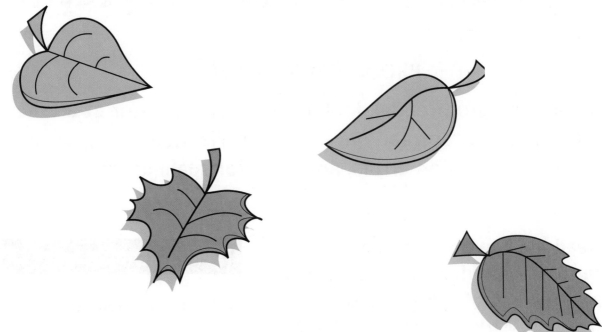

board, a few thick sheets of plain paper, and some ink.

To begin making your leaf print, place the felt on the board Carefully pour the ink onto the felt until the hole piece is damp. With the vein-side down, place your leaf on the felt. Cover it with a sheet of paper, and press down on the leaf. then take away the sheet of paper, pick the leaf up, and put it ink-side down on a clean piece of paper. Cover the leaf with another piece of paper, and press down again When you take away the top paper and the leaf, you'll have your own special leaf print.

Visualize Steps

Think of a sandwich you like. Visualize the ingredients and how you would make it. Then list the materials needed to make the sandwich.

_____   _____

_____   _____

_____   _____

_____   _____

_____   _____

Write a how-to paragraph for making your sandwich.

_____

_____

_____

_____

_____

_____

_____

Game Instructions

Write directions that explain to a group of second-graders how to play one of your favorite games. If you wish, use drawings as well as words to make the directions clear. Revise and proofread your work. If you want, invite a group of second-graders to play the game.

Plan an Invention

With a friend or two, think of something you would like to invent. Draw a picture of your invention. Write a paragraph of instructions for using the invention.

What Do You Know How to Do?

How do you choose a topic for a how-to paragraph? Start by making a list of things you know how to do. Here is a list to get you started. Finish as many of the topic ideas as you can. Think of topics that you really know something about.

1. How to build _____

2. How to cook _____

3. How to fix _____

4. How to make _____

5. How to play _____

Show your list to a friend. Have your friend pick one topic that he or she would like to know about. Write step-by-step instructions for your friend.

_____

_____

_____

_____

_____

_____

A Practice How-to Paper

PAPIER-MÂCHÉ ZOO

Work with friends to make a papier-mâché zoo. It's easy and fun. You don't even need a lot of materials.

There are a few things you'll need to collect before you begin. They include old newspapers, a bucket, glue, water, paper cups, pipe cleaners, tempera paint, and paintbrushes.

The first step is to make the papier-mâché pulp. The pulp is soft and moist. You can shape the pulp by itself or wrap it around cups, pipe cleaners, and other objects. The objects you use depend on the shapes you want to have. When the pulp dries, it hardens. The pulp takes the shape you give it.

Tear old newspapers into small pieces. One-inch pieces work well. Put the pieces in a bucket or a pan. Now make some paste.

To make paste, mix two cups of glue with one cup of water in a cup. Stir the glue and water. Slowly, add this paste to the newspaper pieces. Be sure to add a little paste at a time. Too much paste will make the papier-mâché runny and hard to shape. Squeeze the paste and paper together until the pulp feels like soft clay.

Use reference books to find pictures of animals for your zoo. Twist pipe cleaners together to make the body for each animal.

For example, let's say you want to put a bear in your zoo. To make the bear's body, start with a straight pipe cleaner. Then bend another pipe cleaner in half. Attach it to one end of the straight pipe cleaner. Then bend another pipe cleaner in half. Attach it to the opposite end of the straight pipe cleaner. Use a fourth pipe cleaner to make the bear's head and neck. Bend the pipe cleaner in half. Twist the loose ends around one end of the straight pipe cleaner. Open the closed end of the pipe cleaner to make a head.

Press and squeeze pulp around the legs and body of the bear. Press more pulp around the neck and head. Shape small lumps of pulp to make ears, a nose, and a tail for the bear. Add pulp until the bear is the size you want. Then leave the bear in an open place for two or more days to dry.

When the bear is dry, paint the bear. Use paint to add eyes and a nose. You can glue decorations onto your bear, too.

Together, you and your friends can make a large zoo. You might even want to use papier-mâché pulp to make homes for your animals. Find a large cardboard box. Use pulp to make caves, swimming pools, and other animal homes inside the box. Paint the homes and let them dry. Finally, add your animals and give your zoo a name.

Respond to the Practice Paper

Write your answers to the following questions or directions.

1. What does this how-to paper teach you to do?

   _____

   _____

2. What materials do you need to do this project?

   _____

   _____

3. After you have collected your materials, what is the first thing you should do?

   _____

   _____

4. Why can't the pulp be runny?

   _____

   _____

5. Write a paragraph to describe a papier-mâché animal you would like to make. On a separate piece of paper, draw a picture to go with your paragraph.

   _____

   _____

   _____

   _____

Analyze the Practice Paper

Read "Papier-Mâché Zoo" again. As you read, think about why the writer wrote this paper. Was the writer able to do what he or she planned to do? Write your answers to the following questions.

1. What makes this model an example of a how-to paper?

   _____

   _____

2. What is the first thing the writer tells you to do before you begin to make a papier-mâché zoo?

   _____

   _____

3. Why do you think the writer lists the materials you need for this project?

   _____

   _____

4. Why does the writer use sequence words, such as *first*, *now*, and *then*?

   _____

   _____

5. Read the sixth paragraph again. On a separate piece of paper, draw a picture of the bear's pipe-cleaner body. Do you think the writer did a good job describing the steps?

   _____

   _____

   _____

Writing Assignment

Think about something you want to tell others how to do. Use this writing plan to help you write a first draft on the next page.

Tell what you are explaining to someone.

▼

List the materials someone will need to do this project.

▼

Write the steps someone should follow in order. Number the steps.

▼

Write some sequence words you can use in your paper.

First Draft

TIPS FOR WRITING A HOW-TO PAPER:

- Choose a single topic or project.
- Focus on a plan.
  1. Think of all of the materials someone will need.
  2. Think of all of the steps someone must follow.

- Use sequence words in your directions. A thesaurus will help you find words you need.

Use your writing plan as a guide as you write your first draft of a how-to paper. Include a catchy title.

_____

_____

_____

_____

_____

_____

_____

_____

_____

(Continue on your own paper.)

Revise the Draft

Use the chart below to help you revise your draft. Check YES or NO to answer each question in the chart. If you answer NO, make notes to remind yourself how you can revise, or change, your writing to improve it.

Question	YES ✔	NO ✔	If the answer is NO, what will you do to improve your writing?
Does your paper explain how to do something specific?			
Do you use the first paragraph to introduce the project?			
Do you describe all of the steps someone needs to follow?			
Do you write the steps in the order they should happen?			
Is each step written clearly so that it is easy to follow?			
Do you use sequence words to help make the directions easy to follow?			
Have you corrected mistakes in spelling, grammar, and punctuation?			

Use the notes in your chart and your writing plan to revise your draft.

Writing Report Card

Read your revised draft again or ask someone else to read it. Have the person who reads your paper complete the following Report Card. Revise your paper until you have no less than a Very Good Score for each item.

Title of paper: _____

Purpose of paper: ___*This paper is a how-to paper.*_____

Person who scores the paper: _____

Score	Writing Goals
	Does the paper explain how to do something specific?
	Does the first paragraph explain what the paper will be about?
	Are the steps in order?
	Are there sequence words that make the directions easy to follow?
	Are there enough details for the reader to follow each step?
	Are the story's grammar, spelling, and punctuation correct?

☺ Excellent Score ☆ Very Good Score + Good Score
✔ Acceptable Score − Needs Improvement

UNIT 3: Fable

HOW MUCH DO YOU KNOW?

Read the fable. Then answer the questions.

Dove was in her bedroom dressing for Wren's party. How proud she was of her snowy white dress! It had to be the most beautiful dress at the party. Dove turned around and around, admiring her reflection in the mirror. "How lovely I look!" she cried. Then her wing bumped a bottle of ink that was sitting on the desk. The bottle turned over. Splash! The front of Dove's dress was covered with an inky black stain.

MORAL:
Be proud of yourself, but do not be more proud than you should be.

1. What is the setting of the fable?

   _____

2. What lesson does the fable teach?

   _____

   _____

3. What else might Dove say at the beginning of the story?
   Circle your answer.

   a. "I hope someone at the party will dance with me."

   b. "I know I'll be the most beautiful bird at the party."

   c. "I don't care what I wear to this party."

   d. "I hope this blue dress will fit me."

Analyzing a Fable

A FABLE

- teaches a lesson
- has characters, a setting, and a plot
- ends with a moral

Read the fable. Then answer the questions.

Deep in the outback of Australia lived Emu and Bowerbird. Emu was sad. He could run as swiftly as the wind on his long legs, but try as he might, he could not fly. Bowerbird, too, felt sad. He could soar high and far with his strong wings, but he could not run at all.

"How lucky you are," sighed Emu, "to fly like that!"

Bowerbird was surprised. "You are the lucky one, for see how you run!"

The two birds thought and thought, and at last they agreed upon a fine plan. "I'll teach you," they both said, "and you teach me!"

That is what they did. After many lessons and much practice, Emu became the only bird in his family who could fly. Bowerbird discovered that running was not so difficult after all.

MORAL:
With a little help from a friend, you can do anything.

1. What is the setting of the fable? _____

2. Who are the characters? _____

3. What problem do the characters have? _____

_____

4. How do they solve the problem? _____

_____

5. What lesson does the fable teach? _____

_____

6. What do you think would be a good title for the fable?

_____

Evaluating Ideas to Support a Conclusion

> **TO WRITE A FABLE, GOOD WRITERS**
> - choose a conclusion
> - evaluate possible events and ideas
> - select the facts that best support the conclusion

A. Underline the idea that best supports the conclusion. On the lines write another statement that would help a reader draw that conclusion.

Conclusion: Mrs. Mason will receive the letter today.

1.   (a)   It was almost time for lunch to be served.
     (b)   Mrs. Mason's mailbox is near her steps.
     (c)   Mrs. Mason watched eagerly up the street, looking for the mail carrier.

2. _____

_____

B. Imagine that you are going to write a paragraph based on the conclusion given below. Write *yes* beside each statement you will use to support the conclusion. Write *no* beside each statement that does not support the conclusion.

Conclusion: Yoshiko will take good care of her new puppy.

3. _____ Dogs needs lots of room to run and play.
4. _____ Yoshiko is a very dependable person.
5. _____ A puppy is a lot of trouble.
6. _____ Yoshiko bought a book about pet care.
7. _____ Yoshiko has never had a dog before.
8. _____ Yoshiko takes good care of her other pets.
9. _____ She understands that puppies need love and attention.

Storytelling: Dialogue and Characters

> **GOOD WRITERS CREATE INTERESTING CHARACTERS THROUGH**
> - dialogue, or conversation
> - vivid details

A. Read the paragraph. Then answer the questions.

Libby sat down beside the new girl in her class and smiled. "Hi, I'm Libby," she said. "Want to play with me at recess?"

1. What does the paragraph reveal about the kind of person Libby is?

   _____

2. What details about her actions does the writer use to reveal her character?

   _____

   _____

3. How does the dialogue reveal her character?

   _____

   _____

B. Use the information below to continue the story about Libby. Add details and dialogue to show what the characters are like.

The new girl's name is Allison. She thinks no one will want to play with her because she has to stay in her wheelchair all the time. Libby is sure Allison will have many friends. She suggests that they play catch with the big blue ball.

_____

_____

_____

Avoiding Wordy Language

> ## Good writers say what they mean in as few words as possible.

Rewrite the story. Take out the underlined words or replace them with fewer words that mean the same thing.

    Dove was <u>putting on her clothes and getting ready</u> for Wren's party. How <u>puffed up and proud</u> she was of her snowy white dress! It might possibly be the most beautiful outfit of all <u>the group that had been invited to the party</u>. Dove turned around and around. She admired the <u>reflection of herself in the mirror</u>. "How lovely I look!" she cried. <u>Just about that time</u>, her wing bumped a bottle of ink that was sitting on the desk. The <u>little bottle of ink</u> turned over. Splash! Down the front of <u>the white dress that Dove was wearing</u> went an inky black stain.

MORAL:
Be proud of yourself, but <u>be careful not to be</u> more proud than you should be.

_____

_____

_____

_____

_____

_____

Proofreading a Fable

Proofread the beginning of the fable, paying special attention to quotation marks and commas in dialogue. Use the Proofreading Marks to correct at least seven errors.

PROOFREADING MARKS	
◯	spell correctly
⊙	add period
⋏	add comma
?	add question mark
☰	capitalize
/	make lowercase
℘	take out
∧	add
∿	switch
¶	indent paragraph
⩔ ⩔	add quotation marks

Baby Chick peered through the tall grass at the edge of the pond. His freinds Little Duck and Little Swan splashed happily in the water.

Come on in, Baby Chick!" called Little Duck.

"Yes, added Little Swan. The water's nice and warm today."

Little Duck quacked "Watch me do a trick!" Then he put his head under the water and turned a somersault

Baby Chick sighed. "I wish I could do that" he answered. "Swimming looks like such fun. Look at my feet, though. Yours are webbed, but mine just have little chicken toes

"Don't worry," laughed Little Swan. "I'm sure you can learn to swim anyway. Look at this!" He proudly traced a figure ate in the water.

Read a Fable

Read several fables in library books. Choose a favorite fable. Write a paragraph that tells the setting, characters, and plot of the fable. Then write the moral.

_____

_____

_____

_____

_____

_____

_____

MORAL:

_____

_____

Write a Story Ending

Reread the story of Dove. With a friend, write a story ending that tells what Dove did about the stain on her dress. Revise your work. Use dialogue and vivid details.

Dove was in her bedroom dressing for Wren's party. How proud she was of her snowy white dress! It had to be the most beautiful dress at the party. Dove turned around and around, admiring her reflection in the mirror. "How lovely I look!" she cried. Then her wing bumped a bottle of ink that was sitting on the desk. The bottle turned over. Splash! The front of Dove's dress was covered with an inky black stain.

Write a Fable

Fables usually have animal characters. The animals are often enemies or unlikely companions. Read the pairs of characters in the chart. Add some characters of your own.

With a friend, choose a pair of characters from the chart. Together, write a fable about the characters. Be sure that it ends with a moral.

NATURAL ENEMIES	OPPOSITES
cat and bird wolf and chicken	elephant (big) and ant (small) parrot (brightly colored) and dove (gray)

_____

_____

_____

_____

_____

_____

_____

_____

_____

_____

A Practice Fable

THE ANTS AND THE DOVE

A Fable by Aesop

Ant looked at the seed that lay at her feet. On a spring day, that seed would be easy to carry home. But on a day like today, she might as well try to push a mountain. "My, it's hot," Ant complained softly. "My feet are killing me."

"I agree," said Ant Two. "Sun has been up all morning. Doesn't he have anything better to do? Shine, shine, shine. Goodness, I've had quite enough."

"That's Sun for you. That's his only job. He shines while we work," said Ant.

"Hmmph," said Ant Two. "Even in winter, he shines as though he has nothing better to do. It's not fair, I say. He should have to drag seeds across this dusty meadow at the end of summer."

Ant chuckled. "I'd like to see that," she said. "Imagine that big ball of gas rolling seeds across this field." She got ready to start work again. "Well, we can't stand here all day. It's not getting any cooler, you know. Let's go, shall we?"

"Oh, please, not yet," cried Ant Two. "I can't go on without a drink of water. My antennae tell me there is a river nearby."

Ant dropped her seed again. She waved her antennae. "You're right. I smell it, too. It's coming from that direction," she said as she pointed to a family of trees. "Let's both go."

Ant and Ant Two stepped over and under blades of dry grass. They waved their antennae, searching for signs of hungry lizards. But nothing moved, not even the wind.

The trees stood along the river's bank. They looked like guards outside a castle. The trees threw their shadows across the river, shading it from Sun. Ant and Ant Two stopped to stare. "It's beautiful, isn't it, Ant?"

"Oh, yes. But be careful. Walk softly. The soil is dry. It may spill if you walk heavily."

Ant's warning came too late. Ant Two tumbled down the bank. She plopped into the water and was carried away. "Ant!" she cried behind her. "Help me, please! I can't swim!"

Ant stood on the bank watching her friend float away. "This is terrible," she thought. "What can I do?" She moved quickly along the bank, looking for a twig or vine she could use to rescue her friend.

Downstream, Dove slept quietly at the top of a dusty oak tree. She opened one eye when she heard something slapping the water. The noise traveled with the river. Soon, Dove could see an ant trying to swim. Dove cut a leaf from the tree and let it fall. It landed just as Ant Two floated by. Ant Two jumped aboard, gasping for air. She looked up to see Dove. Dove nodded and closed her eyes.

Ant pulled the leaf and Ant Two from the water. They rested on the bank while Ant Two told her story. Ant Two added lots of details to her story, so Ant listened for a long time. Ant Two was still talking when Ant warned her to be quiet. Ant smelled a human.

The human carried a net. Ant and Ant Two looked at each other. They wiggled their antennae. They smelled danger.

Ant and Ant Two followed the human. He stopped beneath the oak tree where Dove slept quietly. She had not heard the human. Ant and Ant Two looked at each other. They knew what they had to do.

As the human began to throw his net, Ant and Ant Two stung his legs. The human jumped and began scratching fiercely. The noise woke Dove. She glanced to the ground where Ant and Ant Two stood waving. Dove nodded thankfully, opened her wings, and flew away.

Respond to the Practice Paper

Write your answers to the following questions or directions.

1. A fable is a story that teaches a lesson. What is the lesson of this story?

   _____

   _____

2. The animals in fables often act like humans. Name one way the animals in this story act like humans.

   _____

   _____

3. How would you describe the setting for this story?

   _____

   _____

4. Write a paragraph to summarize this story. Use these questions to help you write your summary:
   - What are the main ideas in the story?
   - How does the story end?
   - What lesson does this story teach?

   _____

   _____

   _____

   _____

   _____

   _____

Analyze the Practice Paper

Read the fable "The Ants and the Dove" again. As you read, think about how the writer wrote the story. Answer the following questions or directions.

1. What does the writer do to make this story fun to read?

    _____

    _____

    _____

2. How does the writer make the characters seem human?

    _____

    _____

    _____

3. Name two problems the writer uses to make the story exciting.

    _____

    _____

    _____

4. How does the writer solve these problems?

    _____

    _____

    _____

5. Why is dialogue, or conversation, important to this story?

    _____

    _____

    _____

Writing Assignment

Sometimes stories help us learn about ourselves. They help us think about what we can be or do. Think about writing a fable. What lesson would you like to teach? What animals will you use as characters in your story? It might help you to think about the traits we sometimes give to animals. For example, some people say dogs are faithful or cats are curious. Use this writing plan to help you write a first draft on the next page.

What is the lesson of the fable?

▼

Who are the animal characters?

▼

What problem will the characters have?

▼

How will the characters solve their problem? List what will happen in the story.

First Draft

Use your writing plan as a guide as you write your first draft of a fable. Include a catchy title.

_____

_____

_____

_____

_____

_____

_____

_____

(Continue on your own paper.)

Revise the Draft

Use the chart below to help you revise your draft. Check YES or NO to answer each question in the chart. If you answer NO, make notes to remind yourself how you can revise, or change, your writing to improve it.

Question	YES ✔	NO ✔	If the answer is NO, what will you do to improve your writing?
Does your fable teach a lesson?			
Do your animal characters have human traits?			
Does your fable have a strong beginning?			
Do your characters have a problem?			
Do you describe events in the order they happen?			
Do the characters solve their problem?			
Do you include important details that help the reader imagine the characters and their problem?			
Have you corrected mistakes in spelling, grammar, and punctuation?			

Use the notes in your chart and your writing plan to revise your draft.

Writing Report Card

Read your revised draft again or ask someone else to read it. Have the person who reads your paper complete the following Report Card. Revise your paper until you have no less than a Very Good Score for each item.

Title of paper: _____

Purpose of paper: _*This paper is a fable.*_____

Person who scores the paper: _____

Score	Writing Goals
	Does this story teach a lesson?
	Do the animal characters in this story have human traits?
	Do the characters have a problem they must solve?
	Are events in the story described in the order they happen?
	Are there enough details to describe each event?
	Are there a variety of sentences that make the story interesting?
	Are the story's grammar, spelling, and punctuation correct?

☺ Excellent Score   ☆ Very Good Score   + Good Score
✔ Acceptable Score   − Needs Improvement

UNIT 4: Comparative Writing

HOW MUCH DO YOU KNOW?

Write the number of each sentence below in the correct column to show whether it belongs in a paragraph of comparison or a paragraph of contrast.

1. The Amazon River is the longest in South America, while the Missouri River is the longest in North America.

2. Instead of traveling across plains, the Amazon travels through a rain forest.

3. Both the Amazon and the Missouri give travelers dramatic views of nature.

4. Unlike the Missouri, which flows to a river, the Amazon flows to an ocean.

5. Ships travel on both the Amazon and the Missouri Rivers.

Paragraph of Comparison   **Paragraph of Contrast**

_____   _____

_____   _____

_____   _____

_____   _____

_____   _____

Answer the questions.

6. In the sentences above, which signal word calls attention to details that are alike?

_____

7. Which signal words call attention to details that are different?

_____

Analyzing Paragraphs of Comparison and Contrast

A paragraph of comparison tells how two people, two places, or two things are like each other.

A paragraph of contrast tells how two subjects are different from each other.

A. Write the number of each sentence below in the correct column to show whether it belongs in a paragraph of comparison or a paragraph of contrast.

1. Guatemala and Costa Rica are both Central American nations.
2. Like Guatemala, Costa Rica grows coffee, bananas, and grains.
3. Costa Rica's money is called a colón, but Guatemala's is the quetzal.
4. Unlike Costa Rica, Guatemala has many people who speak Indian languages.
5. The countries have the same national language, Spanish.
6. Instead of bordering Mexico, Costa Rica borders Panama and Nicaragua.

Paragraph of Comparison   **Paragraph of Contrast**

_____   _____

_____   _____

_____   _____

_____   _____

_____   _____

North America

Mexico

Belize

Honduras

Guatemala

Nicaragua

El Salvador

Panama

Costa Rica

South America

B. Answer the questions.

7. In the sentences at left, which signal words call attention to details that are alike?

   _____

8. Which signal words call attention to details that are different?

   _____

Evaluating to Compare and Contrast

WHEN THEY PLAN PARAGRAPHS OF COMPARISON AND CONTRAST, GOOD WRITERS

- evaluate details
- classify details with common features in categories

Read the paragraph. Show how the writer may have classified the information. List each detail from the paragraph in the category in which it belongs.

Colonial Williamsburg and Old Sturbridge Village both show visitors what life was like in the past. Colonial Williamsburg demonstrates life in the 1700s, and Old Sturbridge Village is a re-creation of a New England village of about 1830. Both have many shops and other buildings that are open to

COLONIAL WILLIAMSBURG	BOTH PLACES	OLD STURBRIDGE VILLAGE

tourists. Since Williamsburg was an important city in the colony of Virginia, the restored buildings there include the Capitol, the Governor's Palace, and several elegant houses. On the other hand, Old Sturbridge Village gives visitors a taste of life in the country. It includes a farm, a sawmill, and a mill for grinding grain. Popular attractions in both Old Sturbridge Village and Colonial Williamsburg are the demonstrations of crafts that were necessary to life in those times.

Using Formal and Informal Language

Good writers use formal language to give information.

Rewrite each sentence, replacing informal language with formal language.

1. The Hermitage is a great big house.

_____

2. Andrew Jackson hung out there for 26 years.

_____

3. Jackson's wife gave the okay for the site for the house.

_____

4. Jackson hadn't been elected president yet when he built the house in 1819.

_____

5. The view from the house is pretty nice.

_____

6. You can see swell green hills from up there.

_____

7. A big fire just about ruined the house in 1834.

_____

8. Jackson didn't waste any time rebuilding it.

_____

9. He gave lots of parties and invited a bunch of people.

_____

Adding Describing Words to Sentences

> Good writers choose the right describing words to create clear, strong pictures.

Replace each word in parentheses ( ) with a vivid and exact describing word. Use words from the box.

lovely	frantic	peaceful	colorful	glistening
ear-splitting	towering	bustling	gentle	
silent	fabulous	precious	longed-for	

1. The valley was a _____ place.
   (quiet)

2. Nestled in the _____ Rockies, it was blanketed with
   (high)

   _____ snow much of the year.
   (shiny)

3. In the summer, green grass and _____ flowers covered
   (pretty)

   the hillsides.

4. Deer grazed there as _____ breezes whispered.
   (slow)

5. Then one day, _____ gold was discovered in the
    (valuable)

   _____ valley.
    (nice)

6. Thousands of people rushed to find _____ riches.
    (great)

7. Suddenly, Caribou turned into a _____ city.
    (busy)

8. The valley was filled with the _____ noise of
    (loud)

   _____ miners searching for gold.
    (eager)

9. Before long, all the _____ gold was gone.
    (wanted)

10. Now Caribou is _____ again, only a ghost town.
     (quiet)

Proofreading Paragraphs of Comparison and Contrast

> ## PROOFREADING HINT
>
> To be a good proofreader, look for one type of error at a time. For example, proofread once for capitalization errors, once for punctuation errors, and once for spelling errors.

Proofread the paragraphs of comparison and contrast, paying special attention to capital letters in the names of places. Use the Proofreading Marks to correct at least seven errors.

PROOFREADING MARKS	
⬭	spell correctly
⊙	add period
⋏	add comma
?	add question mark
☰	capitalize
/	make lowercase
℘	take out
∧	add
∿	switch
¶	indent paragraph
⌄ ⌄	add quotation marks

  Texas and New mexico are neighboring

states, and in many weighs they are alike.

Of course, they share a common border.

Both states have large areas of land that

are dry and flat, and both states have

mountains. New Mexico's capital, santa fe,

is not the state's largest city, and Austin, the capital of Texas, is much

smaller than Houston, dallas, or San Antonio.

Although new Mexico and Texas have much in common, they are different in many ways. Some American Indians live in texas, but they make up a much larger portion of the population of New Mexico. The land is also different. Unlike Texas, New mexico has areas of true desert. Also, the rocky Mountains slice through central New Mexico, giving the State large areas of green forests. The mountains of texas, in the area called Big Bend, are much drier and are not forested.

Make a Chart of Comparison and Contrast

Think about your town and a neighboring town. Fill in the chart showing how your town and the neighboring town are alike and how they are different. Then, write a paragraph comparing and contrasting the two places.

HOW THE TOWNS ARE ALIKE	HOW THE TOWNS ARE DIFFERENT

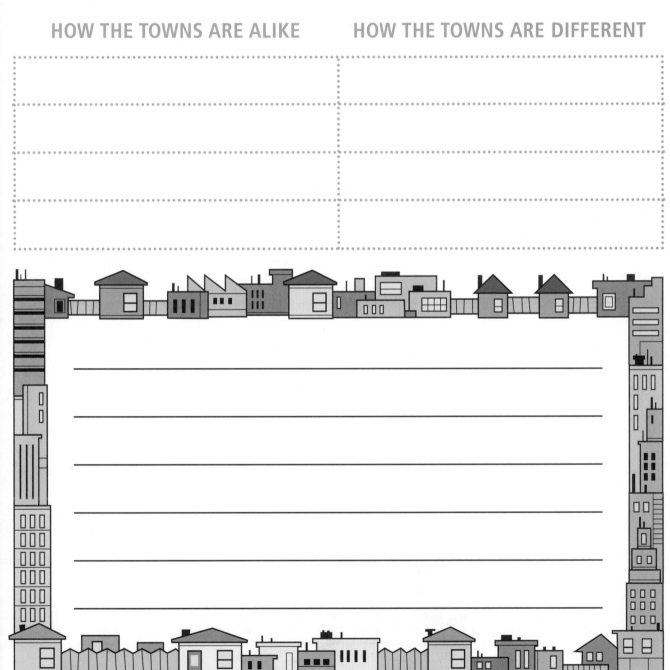

Write from a Set of Topic Ideas

Read the list of paired topic ideas. The two animals or objects in each pair are alike—but not completely. How are they similar? How are they different? Choose one pair and write a paragraph of comparison and contrast.

helicopter, jet	frog, toad	cello, violin
horse, donkey	bicycle, motorcycle	butterfly, moth

_____

_____

_____

_____

_____

_____

_____

Compare and Contrast People

To help find people to compare and contrast, complete the pairs of phrases below. Write the opposite of the underlined word to finish the second phrase in each pair. Then, write a pair of your own. Select one of the pairs. With a friend, write a paragraph to compare and contrast the people.

my <u>aunt</u> and my _____

a popular <u>actor</u> and a popular _____

a <u>sleepy</u> friend and a _____ friend

_____

_____

_____

_____

_____

_____

A Practice Compare-and-Contrast Paper

ALLIGATORS AND CROCODILES

Do you watch adventure movies? You probably know the kind I mean. Somewhere in the world, science experiments go bad. Meat-eating dinosaurs chase humans across the screen. Giant gorillas step on cars and buildings. The animals aren't real, of course, but it's easy to forget that. The fierce-looking animals and the noise keep you waiting to see who will leave the scene alive. For two exciting hours, you forget that you are watching a movie.

Some of the big stars of action movies are life-size reptiles. Alligators and crocodiles are two examples. To some people, they seem like the same animal. It's easy to understand why. In one quick glance, people see long bodies, tough skin, and sharp teeth. But there's more to these reptiles than you might think.

Let's take a closer look at both of these animals. We'll begin with the American Alligator.

When it is grown, the American Alligator is blackish in color. It has a wide, flat snout. When its mouth is closed, the upper jaw hides the teeth in the lower jaw. Teeth in the upper jaw remain visible. Full grown, alligators can be more than 15 feet long and weigh about 500 pounds. When they walk slowly, alligators drag their tails. If they're in a hurry, they can "high walk." That means they walk on their toes. The hind feet and tail leave the ground. This lets alligators run up to 30 miles per hour. They live in and near freshwater lakes, rivers, and swamps. Sometimes, they live in water that's a little saltier than most freshwater.

Now let's look at the American Crocodile. As an adult, it is olive-brown. It has a long, narrow snout. When its mouth is closed, teeth in both jaws remain visible. The fourth tooth on the lower jaw sticks out. American Crocodiles are some of the world's largest crocodiles. Some can grow more than 15 feet long and weigh as much as 450 pounds. They live in freshwater and where saltwater and freshwater meet.

We've talked about how these reptiles look and where they live. Now let's talk about what they eat and where they lay their eggs.

Alligators eat different kinds of foods, including fish, frogs, turtles, snakes, water birds, deer, and other alligators. First, they drown their prey. Then, they use their teeth, slap the prey against the water, or drag the prey around to break it into bite-sized pieces.

Crocodiles eat fish but may also eat any animal that comes too close. They usually drown the prey first and then swallow it whole.

When it's time to mate, the female alligator builds a nest. She uses plants to build mounds that rise out of the water. These mounds are the nests. Each mound can hold about 30 eggs. The eggs hatch in about two months. But baby alligators stay near their mothers a lot longer. Some stay near their mothers for more than two years.

Female crocodiles build nests, too, but not mounds. They dig holes in sand or mud. Then they lay between 30 and 60 eggs. The eggs take about three months to hatch. Baby crocodiles move away from their mothers a few days after birth.

Why do people who make movies use alligators and crocodiles as their models? Maybe it's because these reptiles are large and powerful. Or maybe it's because they have lots of teeth and unusual behaviors. Whatever the reason, alligators and crocodiles are big movie stars.

Respond to the Practice Paper

Which two your answers to the following questions or directions.

1. Which two animals does this paper compare and contrast?

   _____

   _____

2. Summarize the paper by making a chart. Use the chart below to list ways alligators and crocodiles are alike and different.

A COMPARE-AND-CONTRAST CHART FOR ALLIGATORS AND CROCODILES

How Alligators and Crocodiles Are Alike	How Alligators and Crocodiles Are Different

Analyze the Practice Paper

Read "Alligators and Crocodiles" again. As you read, think about how the writer organized information in this paper. Write your answers to the following questions.

1. Most of the time, a writer tells what a paper will be about in the first paragraph. Why do you think this writer begins this paper by talking about action movies?

   _____

   _____

2. How did the writer let you know that this paper was going to be about real alligators and crocodiles?

   _____

   _____

3. First, the writer describes the way alligators and crocodiles look. How does the writer let you know that the main idea is about to change?

   _____

   _____

4. In the fourth paragraph, the writer describes alligators. In the fifth paragraph, the writer describes crocodiles. What does the writer describe in the seventh and eighth paragraphs? Why do you think the writer organized the paper this way?

   _____

   _____

5. Why do you think the writer talks about movies again in the last paragraph?

   _____

   _____

Writing Assignment

When writers compare and contrast two or more things, their main ideas are the important ways that the things are alike and different. Then writers use details to support each main idea. Think about two animals you would like to compare and contrast. Think about writing a paper about them. Use this writing plan to help you write a first draft on page 604.

Choose two animals you want to compare and contrast. Call them Animal A and Animal B.

A = _____   B = _____

Use reference materials such as the encyclopedia to learn more about the animals you chose. Learn about how they look, where they live, and what they eat.

The main ideas are written outside each set of circles below. For each main idea, list what is true only about Animal A in the A circle. List what is true only about Animal B in the B circle. List what is true about both animals where the two circles overlap.

MAIN IDEA:
How they look

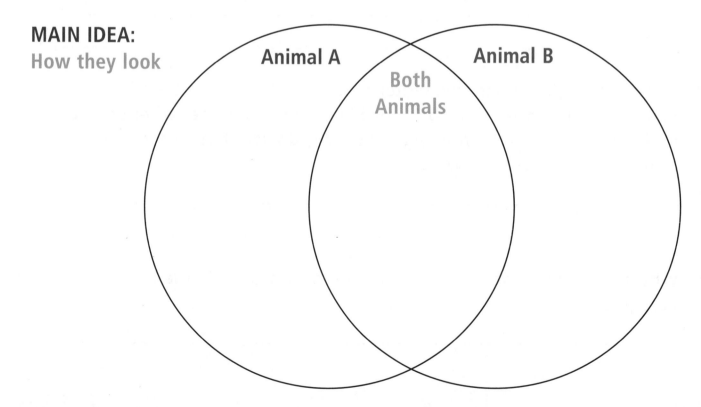

MAIN IDEA:
Where they live

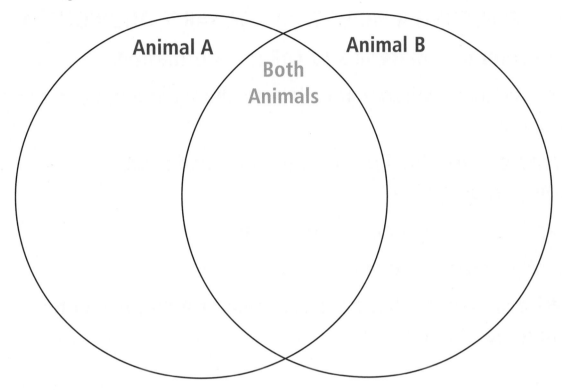

MAIN IDEA:
What they eat

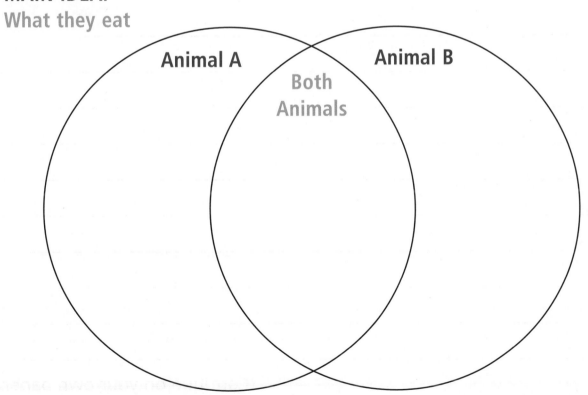

First Draft

Use your writing plan as a guide as you write your first draft of a compare-and-contrast paper. Include a catchy title.

_____

_____

_____

_____

_____

_____

_____

_____

(Continue on your own paper.)

Revise the Draft

Use the chart below to help you revise your draft. Check YES or NO to answer each question in the chart. If you answer NO, make notes to remind yourself how you can revise, or change, your writing to improve it.

Question	YES ✔	NO ✔	If the answer is NO, what will you do to improve your writing?
Do you introduce the animals you will write about in the first paragraph?			
Do you tell how two animals are alike?			
Do you tell how two animals are different?			
Do you have more than one main idea?			
Do you organize the main ideas into paragraphs?			
Do you use details to support each main idea?			
Do you summarize the main ideas of your paper in your conclusion?			
Have you corrected mistakes in spelling, grammar, and punctuation?			

Use the notes in your chart and your writing plan to revise your draft.

Writing Report Card

Read your revised draft again or ask someone else to read it. Have the person who reads your paper complete the following Report Card. Revise your paper until you have no less than a Very Good Score for each item.

Title of paper: _____

Purpose of paper: _This paper tells how two animals are alike and different._

Person who scores the paper: _____

Score	Writing Goals
	Does the first paragraph tell what the paper is about?
	Does the paper tell how two animals are alike?
	Does the paper tell how two animals are different?
	Is there more than one main idea?
	Are the main ideas organized into paragraphs?
	Are there enough details to support each main idea?
	Are the paragraphs in an order that makes sense?
	Does the last paragraph summarize what the paper is about?
	Are the paper's grammar, spelling, and punctuation correct?

☺ Excellent Score   ☆ Very Good Score   + Good Score
✔ Acceptable Score   − Needs Improvement

UNIT 5: Descriptive Writing

HOW MUCH DO YOU KNOW?

Yellowstone National Park has some of the strangest scenery. Great Fountain Geyser sometimes shoots water higher than a twenty-story building. Yellowstone Lake is our country's largest high-altitude lake. Its sparkling water seems shinier than a mirror. The smell of pine trees fills the air. Yellowstone has a deep canyon, but the Grand Canyon in Arizona is deeper. In addition, the park has about 10,000 hot springs with steam rising up to the sky.

1. What is the topic sentence of the paragraph?

    _____

    _____

2. Which detail appeals to the sense of smell?

    _____

    _____

3. Which details could be used to describe the geyser? (Circle all that apply.)

    a. spray of warm water on your face

    b. shoots water as high as the treetops

    c. smell of chocolate syrup

    d. with a hissing sound the water sprays into the air

    e. bright red and purple

Analyzing a Descriptive Paragraph

> **A DESCRIPTIVE PARAGRAPH**
> - has a topic sentence that tells what will be described
> - gives details that appeal to the reader's senses
> - groups details that belong together
> - paints a vivid word picture

Read the descriptive paragraph below. Then answer the questions.

The wintry scene looked like an artist's dream. Horses clip-clopped along on the hard-packed road. Their harness bells jingled. Passengers in their carriages breathed the icy air and snuggled deeper into bright red and purple blankets. The road sloped upward between rows of towering pines. Their branches drooped with snow. Crowning the top of the hill, the castle poked its cold stone towers into the gray sky.

1. Draw a line under the topic sentence of the paragraph.

2. What is the purpose of the topic sentence?

   _____

3. Which details appeal to the sense of hearing?

   _____

4. Which details appeal to the sense of touch?

   _____

5. Which details appeal to the sense of sight?

   _____

6. In what way does the writer group the details?

   _____

Observing Details

IN A DESCRIPTIVE PARAGRAPH, GOOD WRITERS

• group details in a way that makes sense, such as front to back or top to bottom

• organize groups of details in a way that makes sense

Study the groups of details in the chart below. Then use the details to finish writing the paragraph.

OUTSIDE THE HOUSE	ABOVE THE HOUSE	INSIDE THE HOUSE
shadows	crows circling	cold, damp air
broken windows	drooping branches	old, musty smell
overgrown with weeds	dark cloud	cobwebs
		creaking door

Scott approached the old house cautiously. It was half hidden by

_____. The _____ on each side of the

front door told him that no one had lived here in a long time. The flowerbeds were _____ , giving the house a sad and

neglected look. Glancing up, Scott saw _____ around

the crooked chimney. _____ from huge trees brushed the

roof. In the sky, a _____ slipped by. Timidly, Scott pushed

open the door. His face felt the _____ _____ , and his

nose quivered at the _____ . Thick _____ covered

the old furniture. From somewhere overhead, Scott heard a

_____ .

Using Metaphors and Similes

Good writers create vivid word pictures by comparing two things that are not usually thought of as being alike.

Similes use the word *like* or *as* in the comparison. Metaphors do not.

A. Read the paragraph. Then complete the sentences.

The deep lake was a golden mirror reflecting the setting sun. Like a large ball of orange wax slowly melting, the sun slipped below the treetops. Across the water, a row of mountain peaks raised jagged teeth to the sky. Beyond the mountains, the sunset blazed like a pink and orange flame.

1. One metaphor compares _____ to _____.

2. Another metaphor compares _____ to _____.

3. One simile compares _____ to _____.

4. Another simile compares _____ to _____.

B. Complete each metaphor or simile.

5. (metaphor) The white clouds were _____.

6. (simile) The warm breeze was like _____.

7. (metaphor) The rows of corn were _____.

8. (simile) The falling autumn leaves were like_____.

Avoiding Run-on Sentences

> Good writers avoid run-on sentences.

Correct each run-on sentence.

1. Our boat chugged into the bay we saw that the opposite shore was covered by solid ice.

   _____

   _____

2. The mountain of ice was a glacier it rose straight up out of the water.

   _____

   _____

3. I moved out onto the deck an icy wind blistered my face.

   _____

4. Our boat chugged nearer to the wall of ice the wind grew even colder.

   _____

   _____

5. Now I could see jagged pieces of ice floating in the water some had furry passengers.

   _____

   _____

6. The passengers were soft-eyed seals they stared at me without fear.

   _____

7. We drew close to the glacier then we heard a loud rumbling.

   _____

8. A chunk of ice fell from the glacier it dropped into the water.

   _____

Proofreading a Descriptive Paragraph

PROOFREADING HINT

To be a good proofreader, look for one type of error at a time. For example, proofread once for capitalization errors, once for punctuation errors, and once for spelling errors.

Proofread the descriptive paragraph, paying special attention to the agreement of subjects and verbs. Use the Proofreading Marks to correct at least seven errors.

PROOFREADING MARKS	
◯	spell correctly
⊙	add period
⋏	add comma
?	add question mark
≡	capitalize
/	make lowercase
ℰ	take out
∧	add
∿	switch
¶	indent paragraph
⌄ ⌄	add quotation marks

On this sunny day, the crowded beach is as busy as a school playground during recess. Far from the waves, families spreads blankets on the sand and share picnic lunches. A child dig in the sand while his older brother and sister toss a beach ball back and forth. A little nearer the water, huge umbrellas sprout like brightly-colored mushrooms. Men and women stretches out in the shade to read or nap. At the edge of the ocean, a small girl build a sand castle. Her brother look for pretty shells and helps her decorate the castle walls The soft sand and shallow water attract children of all ages. They runs and splash where the water laps the beech. Farther from shore strong swimmers rides the waves. Floating on there backs, they look like playful dolphins. Out where the waves spray white foam, a few surfboards skim across the water. The boards rises and plunge on the waves like crazy elevators.

Writing Metaphors and Similes

Find a picture of a pretty scene in an old magazine. Cut out the picture and paste it in the space below. Under the picture, write some metaphors and similes that describe the picture.

_____

_____

_____

_____

_____

_____

_____

Observe Details

Observe details about your school. Complete the chart by grouping the details according to where they are located.

OUTSIDE THE SCHOOL	ABOVE THE SCHOOL	INSIDE THE SCHOOL

Use the details in the chart to write a descriptive paragraph about your school.

_____

_____

_____

_____

_____

_____

A Practice Descriptive Story

FIRST DAY AT THE BEACH

Miss and Match were puppies. They watched as we put their blue water jug, bowls, food, and towels in the car. Miss and Match knew they were going somewhere special.

We parked in a small lot by the dock. Miss and Match leaped from the back seat. So far, they didn't notice anything unusual. But as soon as their paws touched the sand, the dogs froze. They knew. They had never been here before.

The sand was almost white. The water's color changed all the time. Sometimes it looked blue. Sometimes it looked gray. The sun was yellow, but not summer's sizzling yellow. It was pale. It was a winter sun.

This was the best possible time for a first day at the beach. Winter keeps most people away. Everything seems too cool—the wind, the water, and the sun. Dogs don't mind those things. They wear furry swimsuits all year round.

Miss started digging first. Match followed. When they stopped, both had damp, sandy spots on their noses. Sand as fine as sugar clung to their fur. The dogs shook hard. Ribbons of sand flew around them.

It was hard to convince the dogs to go near the water. There was too much to smell on the beach. The tide had left slippery chains of brown seaweed behind. There were also too many seashells to count. The waves had pounded them into little bits. Pink, white, and yellow scraps littered the beach for miles.

Match finally jumped in the water, but she didn't mean to do it. A clever bird tricked her.

When the dogs ran too close, the seagulls screamed and flew away. The pelicans paid no attention to the noise. They floated peacefully far from the beach. But the sandpipers were different.

The piper that taught Match to swim was smart. It ran up and down the beach like a wind-up toy with a tight spring. Match chased it back and forth. The first time Match got too close, the bird turned quickly. It opened its wings and flew swiftly over the water. Match thought the bird was playing a game, so she followed. Match didn't know that she couldn't run on water.

Suddenly, there was nothing to hold Match up. She started pumping her legs and splashing water. She came back to the beach a lot faster than she left it. The piper returned to the beach, too, flying over Match's head. Match didn't seem to notice.

Match shook hard. Her woolly fur sprayed millions of glittering water drops. She was damp but not discouraged. Her curiosity took her to a new adventure, a blue crab digging a hole in the sand. Match had something more to learn about life at the beach.

Respond to the Practice Paper

Write your answers to the following questions or directions.

1. What does the writer describe?

   _____

   _____

2. What is the first thing the puppies do after they get out of the car?

   _____

   _____

3. How does a bird trick Match into swimming?

   _____

   _____

4. Write a paragraph to summarize this description. Use these questions to help you write your summary:
   - What are the main ideas of this story?
   - What happens first? Second? Third?
   - How does the story end?

   _____

   _____

   _____

   _____

   _____

   _____

   _____

Analyze the Practice Paper

Read "First Day at the Beach" again. As you read, think about why the writer wrote this story. Write your answers to the following questions.

1. How does the writer describe the beach?

   _____

   _____

2. What descriptive words does the writer use to describe the sand?

   _____

   _____

3. Read the seventh paragraph again. Why do you think the writer wrote this paragraph?

   _____

   _____

4. How does the writer describe how the sandpiper runs?

   _____

   _____

5. Why do you think the writer describes the blue crab as a new adventure?

   _____

   _____

Writing Assignment

To describe something or someone, a writer tells what he or she sees, hears, feels, tastes, and smells. The writer also compares things, like a bird to a wind-up toy or a blue crab to an adventure. Think about an experience you would like to describe. Pay special attention to the words and comparisons you choose. Use this writing plan to help you write a first draft on the next page.

What experience would you like to describe? Write the experience in the circle. Write words and comparisons that describe the experience on the lines.

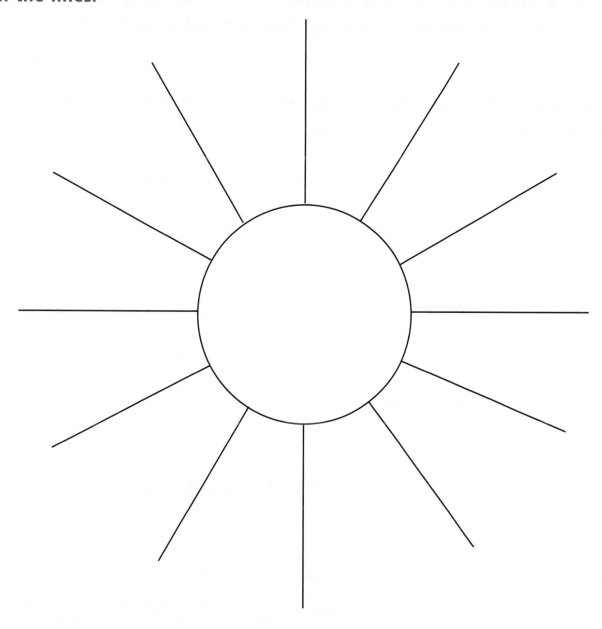

First Draft

Use your writing plan as a guide as you write your first draft of a descriptive story. Include a catchy title.

_____

_____

_____

_____

_____

_____

_____

(Continue on your own paper.)

Revise the Draft

Use the chart below to help you revise your draft. Check YES or NO to answer each question in the chart. If you answer NO, make notes to remind yourself how you can revise, or change, your writing to improve it.

Question	YES ✔	NO ✔	If the answer is NO, what will you do to improve your writing?
Does your story describe a specific experience?			
Do you write using your voice, or special way of expressing yourself?			
Do you use descriptive language, or words that will help your reader see, hear, taste, feel, and smell?			
Do you organize the main ideas of your story into paragraphs?			
Do you use important details to support each main idea?			
Does your story have a beginning, middle, and end?			
Have you corrected mistakes in spelling, grammar, and punctuation?			

Use the notes in your chart and your writing plan to revise your draft.

Writing Report Card

Read your revised draft again or ask someone else to read it. Have the person who reads your paper complete the following Report Card. Revise your paper until you have no less than a Very Good Score for each item.

Title of paper: _____

Purpose of paper: _*This paper is a descriptive story.*_____

Person who scores the paper: _____

Score	Writing Goals
	Does the story describe a specific experience?
	Does the descriptive story have a strong beginning, or introduction?
	Are main ideas in the descriptive story described in the order they happened?
	Are there enough details to support each main idea?
	Is the language descriptive?
	Is there a strong ending, or conclusion?
	Does the story stick to the topic?

☺ Excellent Score   ☆ Very Good Score   + Good Score
✔ Acceptable Score   − Needs Improvement

UNIT 6: Short Report

HOW MUCH DO YOU KNOW?

Read the paragraph below from a short report. Then answer the questions.

     Where does a fish sleep? Animals sleep in a variety of places. Raccoon cubs curl into a ball and sleep cozily in their den. Sea lions float in the water and sleep at the same time. Sea otters anchor themselves to seaweed and float on their backs. A leopard sprawls along a limb and relaxes in a tree.

1. How does the writer make you want to continue reading?

    _____

    _____

2. What is the topic sentence?

    _____

    _____

3. Which of these facts does not support the topic sentence?

    a. A leopard sprawls along a limb and relaxes in a tree.

    b. A raccoon mother stays close by her cubs while they sleep.

    c. Sea lion pups are friendly, cute, and playful.

    d. A swan can sleep while it is floating on a lake.

Analyzing a Short Report

A short report gives facts that the writer learned
by studying or by talking to experts.

Read the paragraphs below from a short
report. Then answer the questions.

    Have you ever heard a dog sing? They may
not actually sing, but dogs, wolves, and coyotes
do make a kind of music. They howl. Why do
they do it?

    Scientists have several different ideas about
why these members of the dog family howl.
They believe that howling is a way for the
animals to communicate. Some scientists think that wolves may howl to call
back members of the pack that have wandered away.

1. What would be a good title for this short report? Why?

    _____

    _____

2. How does the writer make you want to continue reading?

    _____

3. What is the topic sentence of the second paragraph?

    _____

4. What facts does the writer give to support the topic sentence?

    _____

    _____

Classifying Information into Categories

IN A RESEARCH REPORT, GOOD WRITERS

- limit a topic to one category
- group details into smaller categories

A. Imagine that you are going to write a report about animals. Write each of the words below in the three possible categories listed below them that you may use for your report. Use another piece of paper to make your chart.

polar bear	cow	boa constrictor
dog	arctic fox	walrus
jaguar	sheep	tiger
leopard	goat	reindeer
horse	bearded seal	spider monkey

1. JUNGLE ANIMALS   2. ANIMALS OF THE ARCTIC   3. DOMESTIC ANIMALS

B. Identify the category that was used to group each set of items below. Write the name of the category on the line.

4. _____   5. _____   6. _____

sandwich	crabs	truck
apple	sharks	skateboard
carrot stick	sunken ships	wagon
milk	coral	bicycle

Capturing the Reader's Interest

> **GOOD WRITERS**
> - create openings that capture the reader's attention
> - use closings that end what they have written in an interesting way

A. Read the following report openings and answer the questions.

a. Purple urchins are sea animals with stiff spines.

b. What lives in the ocean and looks like a pin cushion? It's a truly amazing sea animal.

1. Which opening is better? _____

2. Why is it a good opening? _____

B. For each of the following sets of facts, write an opening and a closing for a short report.

Moray eels are fish with long bodies. They live in coral reefs. During the day, they hide. At night, they hunt for crabs and other food. Moray eels have sharp teeth and look fierce. Actually, they are quite shy.

3. Opening:

_____

_____

4. Closing:

_____

_____

The octopus lives on the ocean floor. It has eight long arms and uses them to pull itself along from place to place. When an octopus is threatened by an enemy, it squirts an inky liquid into the water. The enemy may attack the ink while the octopus escapes.

5. Opening:

_____

_____

6. Closing:

_____

_____

Combining Two Sentences

> **GOOD WRITERS JOIN**
> - two short, choppy sentences into one long sentence
> - two sentences with a comma and the word *and*, *or*, or *but*

Join each pair of sentences and write the new sentence.

1. Many kinds of spiders spin webs. Not all of the webs are alike.

   _____

   _____

2. A web may be long and narrow. It may be shaped like a triangle.

   _____

   _____

3. Some webs are like funnels. Others look more like domes.

   _____

   _____

4. Wolf spiders hide in burrows. Lynx spiders live on trees or bushes.

   _____

   _____

5. Many lynx spiders are green. They are hard to find on green leaves.

   _____

   _____

6. Tarantulas are furry. They look fierce.

   _____

   _____

Proofreading a Short Report

PROOFREADING HINT

To be a good proofreader, look for one type of error at a time. For example, proofread once for capitalization errors, once for punctuation errors, and once for spelling errors.

Proofread the paragraphs from a short report, paying special attention to commas in compound sentences. Use the Proofreading Marks to correct at least seven errors.

PROOFREADING MARKS	
⬭	spell correctly
⊙	add period
⋏	add comma
?	add question mark
≡	capitalize
/	make lowercase
ꝸ	take out
⋀	add
∿	switch
¶	indent paragraph
⌄ ⌄	add quotation marks

     Mountain gorillas live in the mountain forests of Africa, usually in groups of about ten. At night the gorillas sleep in trees or on the ground and during the day they look for food. They most often eat roots and tree bark but sometimes they find other plants to eat too. Mountain gorillas are shy animals and they are almost always gentle. A group of gorillas may accept a scientist and the scientist might live among them for a while

Mountain gorillas communicate with each other by making sounds. They make barking sounds when they are frightened and gorilla babies sometimes cry. During times of danger, the group leader may roar noisily. this noise often warns enemys away. Happy gorillas may make deep, rumbling noises when they are eating and they make similar sounds when they are resting.

Write an Opening and a Closing

Read an encyclopedia article or another article about a sea creature. Then write an opening and a closing for a short report about the animal. Be sure your opening captures the reader's attention. Use a closing that ends in an interesting way.

_____

_____

_____

_____

_____

_____

_____

_____

_____

_____

_____

_____

Make a Wildlife Guide

Find out about some animals and birds that live in your state.
Have each of your friends choose one animal or bird and write a short
report on it. Everyone in the group can bind their reports into a
booklet that you can share with family and other friends.

A Practice Short Report

THE LOST CITY

The Lost City probably isn't the kind of city you think it is. It isn't lost, either. In fact, it is a busy community sitting near the top of a mountain. The mountain is in the Atlantic Ocean. At one time, it may have been above water. But today, 700 meters (about 2,300 feet) of water cover its top.

The Lost City is a city of mounds, towers, and chimneys. The tallest chimney in the city is 18 stories. The other chimneys are smaller, but they are all made from the same materials. They are made of minerals, such as iron, copper, and sulfur. And there is life in and around these chimneys. Tiny organisms called microbes live there.

Underwater cities like the Lost City are called vent communities. The word *vent* means "opening." Scientists find most vent communities along mid-ocean ridges. Earth's crust is made of plates. Ridges form where these plates spread, or pull apart. As plates spread, ocean water sinks through cracks in the crust. The water moves downward. At the same time, lava, or melted rock, from beneath the crust moves up. It spills out through vents and heats the ocean water. The water picks up minerals from the lava. Eventually, the minerals settle, or drop out of the water. In time, they build odd and sometimes huge shapes.

Very hot water moves through chimneys on its way back to the ocean. Along the way, it meets cooler ocean water. Underwater clouds form where the hot and the cool water meet. These clouds, called smokers, are white or black. Their color depends on the kinds of minerals they hold and their temperature. White smokers are cooler and contain zinc. Black smokers are hotter and contain copper.

Many kinds of animals live near vents. They include large clams, fish, crabs, and worms. The worms are unusual. They make coverings called tubes that protect their bodies. The tubes also give them their name—tubeworms. Some tubeworms grow to be 3 meters (10 feet) long.

Scientists found the first vent community in 1977. At the time, no one knew that communities could survive without energy from the sun. On land, for example, food chains start with the sun. Plants use energy from the sun to make food. Animals get their energy from eating plants. Or they may eat animals. But sunlight doesn't reach the ocean floor. So scientists were surprised to learn that some microbes get their energy from chemicals in the water. These microbes are then food for other living things.

The Lost City is different from other vent communities. First, it is on a mountain, not on the ocean floor. Second, it doesn't have the same kinds of life.

The life around the shapes in the Lost City is different. Microbes live at the vents. But scientists think the crabs and other animals are only visiting. They continue to study life in the Lost City. One day their work may help us understand more about life in unusual places.

Respond to the Practice Paper

Write your answers to the following questions or directions.

1. What is the Lost City?

   _____

   _____

2. How did the Lost City form?

   _____

   _____

3. How are white and black smokers alike?

   _____

   _____

4. How are white and black smokers different?

   _____

   _____

5. How did the tubeworm get its name?

   _____

   _____

6. Write a paragraph to summarize the report.

   _____

   _____

   _____

   _____

Analyze the Practice Paper

Read "The Lost City" again. As you read, think about the main ideas. Pay attention to the details the writer uses to support those main ideas. Write your answers to the following questions or directions.

1. Why do you think the writer introduces the Lost City in the first sentence?

   _____

   _____

2. In the second paragraph, the writer explains what the Lost City looks like and what lives there. Name three other main ideas the writer talks about.

   _____

   _____

3. The writer uses special words, such as *microbes*, *ridges*, and *vents*. How does the writer make it easier for the reader to understand these words?

   _____

   _____

4. Why does the writer include numbers and dates in this report?

   _____

   _____

5. How are the first and last paragraphs alike?

   _____

   _____

   _____

   _____

Writing Assignment

In a short report, writers write about one topic, or subject. They research the topic to find important main ideas. They also find important details that support each main idea. Think about writing a short report about a place you would like to visit. Use this writing plan to help you write a first draft on the next page.

The topic of this paper is:

_____

Main Idea of Paragraph 1: _____

Detail: _____

Detail: _____

Detail: _____

Main Idea of Paragraph 2: _____

Detail: _____

Detail: _____

Detail: _____

Main Idea of Paragraph 3: _____

Detail: _____

Detail: _____

Detail: _____

First Draft

TIPS FOR WRITING A SHORT REPORT:

- Use reference materials to collect information about your subject.

- Take notes about important main ideas.

- Take notes about important details that support each main idea. Introduce the topic, or subject, of your report in the first paragraph.

- Organize the main ideas into separate paragraphs.

- Organize paragraphs in a logical order.

- Summarize your report in the last paragraph.

Use your writing plan as a guide as you write your first draft of a short report. Include a catchy title.

_____

_____

_____

_____

_____

_____

_____

_____

_____

(Continue on your own paper.)

Revise the Draft

Use the chart below to help you revise your draft. Check YES or NO to answer each question in the chart. If you answer NO, make notes to remind yourself how you can revise, or change, your writing to improve it.

Question	YES ✔	NO ✔	If the answer is NO, what will you do to improve your writing?
Do you write about one place in your report?			
Do you introduce the subject of your report in the first paragraph?			
Do you have more than one main idea?			
Do you organize your main ideas into paragraphs?			
Do you support each main idea with important details?			
Do you summarize your report in the last paragraph?			
Have you corrected mistakes in spelling, grammar, and punctuation?			

Use the notes in your chart and your writing plan to revise your draft.

Writing Report Card

Read your revised draft again or ask someone else to read it. Have the person who reads your paper complete the following Report Card. Revise your paper until you have no less than a Very Good Score for each item.

Title of paper: _____

Purpose of paper: _*This paper is a short report.*_____

Person who scores the paper: _____

Score	Writing Goals
	Is this writing an example of a short report?
	Does the report tell about a specific topic, or subject?
	Does the report introduce the topic in the first paragraph?
	Does the report have more than one main idea?
	Are the main ideas organized into paragraphs?
	Does the way the paragraphs are organized make sense?
	Are there details that support each main idea?
	Does the writer summarize the report in the last paragraph?
	Does the writer stick to the topic throughout the report?
	Are the report's grammar, spelling, and punctuation correct?

☺ Excellent Score   ☆ Very Good Score   + Good Score
✔ Acceptable Score   − Needs Improvement

Proofreading Marks

Use the following symbols to help make proofreading faster.

MARK	MEANING	EXAMPLE
⬯	spell correctly	I (liek) dogs. *like*
⊙	add period	They are my favorite kind of pet⊙
⋏	add comma	I also like cats⋏ birds, and bunnies.
?	add question mark	What kind of pet do you have ?
≡	capitalize	My dog's name is scooter. ≡
/	make lowercase	He has Brown spots.
ℰ	take out	He likes to to run and play.
∧	add	He even likes to get ∧ bath. *a*
∿	switch	Afterward he /all\shakes/ over.
¶	indent paragraph	¶ I love my dog, Scooter. He is the best pet I have ever had. Every morning he wakes me with a bark. Every night he sleeps with me.
ˇ ˇ	add quotation marks	ˇYou are my best friend,ˇ I tell him.

Test Prep

GET READY FOR TESTS

WHAT ARE STANDARDIZED TESTS?

You will take many different tests while at school. A standardized test is a special test that your state gives to every student in your grade. These tests are designed to find out how much you know about subjects like reading and math. They may not be fun, but they do not have to be a nightmare. This workbook can help you prepare!

WHAT CAN YOU EXPECT ON A STANDARDIZED TEST?

All standardized tests are different, but they do have some things in common.

- **Multiple-Choice Questions**
  Most of these tests use multiple-choice questions. You have to pick the best answer from four or five choices. You usually indicate your choice on an answer sheet by filling in or darkening a circle next to the correct answer.

- **Time Limits**
  Standardized tests all have time limits. It is best to answer as many questions as possible before you run out of time. But do not let the time limit make you nervous. Use it to help you keep going at a good pace.

- **Short Answers and Essays**
  Some standardized tests have questions that require writing an answer. Sometimes the answer is a word or a sentence. Other times you will write a paragraph or an essay. Always read directions carefully to find out how much writing is required.

HOW CAN THIS BOOK HELP?

Everyone gets a little nervous when taking a test. This book can make test-taking easier by providing helpful tips and practice tests. You will learn strategies that will help you find the best answers. You will also review math, reading, and grammar skills that are commonly needed on standardized tests. Here are some hints for using this book.

- Work in a quiet place. When you take a test at school, the room is very quiet. Try to copy that feeling at home. Sit in a chair at a desk or table, just as you would in school.

- Finish one test at a time. You do not need to finish all of the tests in this book in one session. It is better to complete just one activity at a time. You will learn more if you stop at the end of a practice test to think about the completed questions.

- Ask questions. Talk with a family member or a friend if you find a question you do not understand. These practice tests give you the chance to check your own answers.

- Look for the Test Tips throughout this workbook. They provide hints and ideas to help you find the best answers.

How to Be Test Smart

A test-smart student knows what to do when it is test-taking time. You might not know all of the answers, but you will feel relaxed and focused when you take tests. Your test scores will be accurate. They will provide a snapshot of what you have learned during the school year. Here is how you can become test-smart!

Things You Can Do All Year

The best way to get ready for tests is to pay attention in school every day. Do your homework. Be curious about the world around you. Learning takes place all the time, no matter where you are! When test day rolls around, you will be ready to show what you know. Here are some ways you can become a year-round learner.

- Do your schoolwork. Standardized tests measure how much you have learned. If you keep up with your schoolwork, your test scores will reflect all the things you have learned.

- Practice smart study habits. Most people study best when they work in a quiet, clean area. Keep your study area neat. Make sure you have a calculator, dictionary, paper, and pencils nearby.

- Read, read, read. Make reading an everyday habit. A librarian can suggest enjoyable books. Read the newspaper. Subscribe to a children's magazine. Look for empty times in your schedule when you might read, like on a long drive to a ball game. Carry a book with you if you know you will have to wait somewhere.

- Practice. This book is a great start to help you get ready for test day. It provides practice for all of the important skills on the tests.

How to Do Your Best on Test Day

Your teacher will announce a standardized test day in advance. Follow these tips to help you succeed on the big day.

- Plan a quiet night before a test. Trying to study or memorize facts at this point might make you nervous. Enjoy a relaxing evening instead.

- Go to bed on time. You need to be well rested before the test.

- Eat a balanced breakfast. Your body needs fuel to keep your energy high during a test. Eat foods that provide long-term energy, like eggs, yogurt, or fruit. Skip the sugary cereals—the energy they give does not last very long.

- Wear comfortable clothes. Choose a comfortable outfit that you like.

- Do not worry about the other students or your friends. Everyone works at different speeds. Pay attention to answering the questions in a steady fashion. It does not matter when someone else finishes the test.

- Relax. Take a few deep breaths to help you relax. Hold your pencil comfortably and do not squeeze it. Take a break every so often to wiggle your fingers and stretch your hand.

Here are some hints and strategies to help you feel comfortable with any test. Remember these ideas while taking the tests in this book.

READ THE DIRECTIONS

This sounds obvious. Make sure you read and understand the directions for every test. Never assume that you know what to do. Always read the directions first. They will focus your attention on finding the right answers.

READ THE ANSWERS

Read the answers—ALL the answers—for a multiple-choice question, even if you think the first one is correct. Test writers sometimes include tricky answers that seem right when you first read them.

PREVIEW THE QUESTIONS

Scan each section. This will give you information about the questions. You also can see how many questions there are in the section. Do not spend too much time doing this. A quick glance will provide helpful information without making you nervous.

USE YOUR TIME WISELY

Always follow test rules. On most standardized tests, you can work on only one section at a time. Do not skip ahead or return to another section. If you finish early, go back and check your answers in that section.

- Before the test begins, find out if you can write in the test booklet. If so, add a small circle or star next to those questions that you find difficult. If time allows, come back to these questions before time is up for that section.

- Try not to spend too much time on one question. Skip a difficult question and try to answer it later. Be careful, though! You need to skip that question's number on your answer sheet. When you answer the next question, make sure you carefully fill in or darken the circle for the correct question.

- When finishing a section, look at your answer sheet. Did you answer every question for the section? Erase any extra marks on your answer sheet. Make sure you did not mark two answers for one question.

MAKE AN EDUCATED GUESS

Most standardized tests take away points for wrong answers. It might be wise to skip a question if you have no idea about the answer. Leave the answer blank and move on to the next question. But if you can eliminate one or more of the answers, guessing can be a great strategy. Remember, smart guessing can improve your test scores!

- Read every answer choice.

- Cross out every answer you know is wrong.

- Try rereading or restating the question to find the best answer.

THINK BEFORE YOU SWITCH

When you check your answers, you might be tempted to change one or more of them. In most cases, your first answer is probably the best choice. Ask yourself why you want to make a change. If you have a good reason, pick a new answer. For example, you might have misread the question. If you cannot think of a specific reason, it is probably best to stick with your first answer.

FILL IN THE BLANKS

Fill-in-the-blank questions are found on many tests. The blank is usually in the middle or at the end of a sentence. Use these steps to answer a fill-in-the-blank question.

- Begin with the first answer choice. Try reading the sentence with that word or group of words in place of the blank. Ask yourself, "Does this answer make sense?"

- Then try filling in the blank with each of the other answer choices. Also, use the other words in the sentence as clues to help you decide the correct choice.

- Choose the best answer.

LOOK FOR CLUE WORDS

When you read test questions, watch for *clue words* that provide important information. Here are some words that make a difference.

- NOT: Many questions ask you to find the answer that is not true. These questions can be tricky. Slow down and think about the meaning of the question. Then pick the one answer that is not true.

- ALWAYS, NEVER, ALL, NONE, ONLY: These words limit a statement. They often make a generally true statement into a false one.

- SOMETIMES, SOME, MOST, MANY, OFTEN, GENERALLY: These words make a statement more believable. You will find them in many correct answers.

- BEST, MOST LIKELY, SAME, OPPOSITE, PROBABLY: These words change the meaning of a sentence. You often can use them to eliminate choices.

RESTATE THE QUESTION

Short answer or essay questions require writing an answer. Your response must answer the question. Restate the question to make sure your answer stays on target. For example, if the question is "What is a tornado?" your answer should begin with the words "A tornado is . . ."

Be sure to look for the Test Tips throughout this workbook. They will give you more test-taking strategies and help you with certain subject areas.

SIX READING SKILLS

SKILL 1: DETERMINING WORD MEANINGS

Prefixes and suffixes are parts of some words. A *prefix* appears at the beginning of a word. A *suffix* appears at the end of a word. Both prefixes and suffixes affect the meaning of the word. You can use them to help figure out the meaning of a word.

Phil went to the weight room almost every day after school. The trainer had told him that frequent workouts would <u>strengthen</u> his muscles.

1   In this paragraph, the word <u>strengthen</u> means —

    A make weak.

    B make strong.

    C tire out.

    D energize.

Hint: The suffix "-en" means cause to be.

There are two types of secret codes. In one kind of code, symbols take the place of letters. These symbols can be numbers, words, or even letters. A code book is used to read the message. The other kind of code changes the <u>arrangement</u> of the letters in a word. The letters have to be unscrambled to read the message.

2   In this paragraph, the word <u>arrangement</u> means —

    F face.

    G size.

    H shape.

    J order.

Hint: The suffix "-ment" means the result of.

Maya Lin drew a design for a monument for a contest. Her design won and was built. Thousands of names were carved on two walls of shiny black stone. The names were Americans who had died in the Vietnam War. At first, people thought that the stone was ugly. They <u>disliked</u> it. But then they began to change their minds. They found that they could walk up to the walls. They could touch the names of loved ones.

3   What is the meaning of the word <u>disliked</u>?

_____

_____

_____

_____

_____

_____

Hint: "Dis-" is a prefix. It means the opposite of.

None of the soldiers was prepared for the <u>predawn</u> drill. It seemed as though they had just fallen asleep. The sergeant disagreed and wanted them up, dressed, and ready to obey orders.

4   In this paragraph, the word <u>predawn</u> means —

    A before daybreak.

    B early.

    C difficult.

    D old.

Hint: "Pre-" is a prefix. It means before.

GO ON

Answers

1 Ⓐ Ⓑ Ⓒ Ⓓ   2 Ⓕ Ⓖ Ⓗ Ⓙ   4 Ⓐ Ⓑ Ⓒ Ⓓ

Sometimes you can figure out the meaning of a new or difficult word by using the words around it as clues.

Sand that sits on top of clay in streams is called *quicksand*. The quicksand is <u>saturated</u> with water because the water cannot drain through the clay.

1   In this paragraph, the word <u>saturated</u> means —

A   colored.

B   reached.

C   dried.

D   soaked.

Hint: You get a clue about what <u>saturated</u> means from the words around it.

On the tip of each finger is a pattern of ridges. This pattern is called a *fingerprint*. Each finger has a <u>distinct</u> fingerprint. No two people in the world have the same fingerprints. A person's fingerprints always remain the same.

2   In this paragraph, the word <u>distinct</u> means —

F   one-of-a-kind.

G   silver.

H   smooth.

J   funny.

Hint: You get a clue about what <u>distinct</u> means from the description of fingerprints.

TEST TIP

Notice that many answer choices are either ABCD or FGHJ. This pattern helps make sure you fill in the correct answer for a question.

The rose has been a sign of <u>secrecy</u>. Hundreds of years ago, people wore roses behind their ears. It meant that the people wearing the roses had heard something, but would not tell what they had heard.

3   In this paragraph, the word <u>secrecy</u> means —

A   riddles.

B   silence.

C   talking.

D   sharing.

Hint: You get a clue about what <u>secrecy</u> means by reading the last sentence in the paragraph.

A <u>cavern</u> is a hole in the surface of the earth made by the forces of nature. People like to explore and hide things in these dark rooms and tunnels under the earth.

4   What is another word for <u>cavern</u>?

_____

_____

_____

_____

_____

_____

Hint: You get a clue about what <u>cavern</u> means by reading the entire paragraph.

GO ON➡

Answers

1 Ⓐ Ⓑ Ⓒ Ⓓ   2 Ⓕ Ⓖ Ⓗ Ⓙ   3 Ⓐ Ⓑ Ⓒ Ⓓ

Specialized or technical words are words used in subjects such as science and social studies. You can use all the other information in the text to help figure out the meaning of these words.

Food on the frontier was simple. People ate many things made from flour. Flour was nourishing and did not spoil. Foods made from flour gave people energy to work hard.

1   In this paragraph, the word nourishing means —

A   white.

B   healthful.

C   difficult.

D   expensive.

Hint: Nourishing *is a technical word. You get a clue about what it means by reading the last sentence in the paragraph.*

How do pilots avoid collisions with other planes in the air? The sky is mapped into highways just like the land is. Signals are sent up from control towers to mark these "skyways." It's a pilot's job to listen to the signals.

2   In this paragraph, the word collisions means —

F   birds.

G   crashes.

H   insects.

J   tires.

Hint: Collisions *is a technical word. You get a clue about what it means from the entire paragraph.*

A Venus' flytrap is a plant that consumes bugs. When there are no bugs, this plant will gladly accept bits of cheese!

3   In this paragraph, what does the word consumes mean?

_____

_____

_____

_____

_____

_____

Hint: Consumes *is a technical word. You get a clue about what it means from the sentence after the word.*

TEST TIP

Using information in the text to figure out a word meaning is called using *context clues.* Do not worry if a word is not familiar. In this question type, test writers do not expect you to know the word. They want you to use clues in the sentence or surrounding sentences to find the meaning. Sometimes a nearby word will have a similar meaning. Other times, the ideas before and after the word should help you figure out the answer. Try to connect ideas. Use logic to see which answer choices make sense and which do not.

GO ON

Answers
1 (A) (B) (C) (D)   2 (F) (G) (H) (J)

The sound of a person's voice is <u>determined</u> by the length of his or her vocal cords. Most men have deeper voices than women. That's because men's vocal cords are longer. A tall person often has a deeper voice than a short person.

4 **In this paragraph, the word <u>determined</u> means —**

   A decided.

   B hidden.

   C known.

   D heard.

   Hint: <u>Determined</u> *is a technical term. You get a clue about what it means by reading the entire paragraph.*

Surgeons wore white uniforms until 1914. A doctor thought that the white uniform showed too much blood from <u>surgeries</u>. He wore green instead. Red did not show as much on the green.

5 **In this paragraph, the word <u>surgeries</u> means —**

   F operations.

   G janitors.

   H movies.

   J straps.

   Hint: <u>Surgeries</u> *is a technical word. You get a clue about what it means from the second sentence.*

We all have muscles <u>attached</u> to our outer ears. Some people work hard at moving these muscles. These are the people who can wiggle their ears! Can you do it?

6 **What does the word <u>attached</u> mean in this paragraph?**

   _____

   _____

   _____

   _____

   _____

   Hint: <u>Attached</u> *is a technical word. You get a clue about what it means by reading the entire paragraph.*

TEST TIP

Choose your words carefully when you write a short answer. To answer question 6, you do not need to write a full sentence. Write a word that gives a good definition for the word *attached*. In other short answer questions, you need to write a complete sentence or a paragraph. Read the test directions to find out exactly what to do.

STOP

Answers
4 Ⓐ Ⓑ Ⓒ Ⓓ   5 Ⓕ Ⓖ Ⓗ Ⓙ

Facts or details are important. By noticing and remembering them, you will know what the passage is about.

Starfish of different sizes and colors live in the oceans. Starfish are often yellow, orange, or brown. But they can be bright colors, too. From point to point, a starfish can be as small as a paper clip or as long as a yardstick. Most starfish are shaped like stars, with five arms extending from their bodies. But some starfish, called sunstars, have a dozen arms. Other types have 25 arms.

1   **From point to point, a starfish can be the size of a —**

   A   grain of rice.

   B   car.

   C   yardstick.

   D   door.

Hint: Look at the sentence that starts "From point to point."

Tide pools are nature's aquariums. Ocean water flows inland with the tide. The water carries with it many living creatures. The water collects in hollows in rocks and in small holes in the earth. Tide pools are created when the tide goes out. The creatures stay behind in the pools.

2   **What causes ocean water to flow inland?**

   _____

   _____

   _____

   _____

   _____

Hint: Look for the sentence that talks about the ocean water's flow.

The last two steps in making toys are packaging and advertising them. Toy makers know that children like colorful objects. So they design bright packages for the toys. Writers think of catchy names for the toys. They hope children remember the names when they shop. With these steps completed, the toys are sent to toy stores. There, children decide whether or not a toy becomes a big seller.

3   **Toy makers know that colorful packages —**

   F   are liked by children.

   G   are assembled easily.

   H   are cheap.

   J   last a long time.

Hint: Find the sentence about colorful packages.

Our sun is one hundred times larger than Earth. But it is only a medium-sized star. The brightest, hottest stars are twenty times larger than the sun. They are called blue giants. Red dwarfs are stars that are smaller than our sun. These stars are the most common in the sky.

4   **Compared to Earth, the sun is —**

   A   smaller.

   B   the same size.

   C   ten times larger.

   D   one hundred times larger.

Hint: Look for the sentence that talks about the sun's size.

GO ON

Answers
1 Ⓐ Ⓑ Ⓒ Ⓓ   **3** Ⓕ Ⓖ Ⓗ Ⓙ   **4** Ⓐ Ⓑ Ⓒ Ⓓ

Sometimes it is helpful to arrange events in the order they happened. This may help you to understand a passage better.

In southern India, many people make a living by cutting and hauling wood. They could not do this without the help of trained elephants. Elephants are very smart. They can follow at least fifty different commands called out by the mahouts. A *mahout* is a person who works with elephants.

The mahouts first cut down the tall, heavy trees that grow on the mountains. They take bark from the logs. Next they drill a hole through a tree trunk and put a long, heavy chain through the hole. Then the mahouts tie a short rope to the chain.

Now the elephant takes over. A mahout sits on top of the elephant with his feet behind the elephant's ears. "Lift!" the mahout shouts. The big beast picks up the rope in its trunk and begins to drag the log. The heavy log may weigh as much as three and a half tons. This is about half the elephant's weight.

The elephant drags the log up a steep slope. All the time the mahout commands, "Lift the log over the rock! Walk straight!" The elephant often obeys, but it also thinks on its own. When the animal knows the ground is too slick, it changes direction. When the log gets stuck on a rock, the elephant drops the log, rolls it over, and picks it up again. The elephant does all this without being told.

At the top of the hill, the mahout shouts, "Drop the rope!" The elephant slowly lowers the log onto a huge pile of logs. Another mahout loosens the rope and chain. The animal then carries the mahout down the steep hill again.

The elephant may make this trip as many as thirty times each day. It is as strong as a small truck. But the elephant has what a truck does not have—brain power, common sense, and the ability to follow commands.

1 **When does the elephant drag the log?**

A before the mahout shouts directions

B while the mahout cuts down the tree

C after the elephant picks up the rope

D before the mahout puts the chain through

Hint: Sometimes it helps to write down the steps in order.

2 **When does the elephant take over?**

_____

_____

_____

_____

_____

_____

Hint: Find the paragraph that starts with this.

3 **Which of these happen first when cutting and hauling wood?**

F Mahouts attach chains to logs.

G Mahouts drill holes.

H Mahouts chop down trees.

J Mahouts take the bark from the logs.

Hint: Look at the beginning of the passage.

GO ON

Answers
1 Ⓐ Ⓑ Ⓒ Ⓓ   **3** Ⓕ Ⓖ Ⓗ Ⓙ

Written directions tell you how to do something. Every step is important.

When the wheel fell off their power mower, the Browns had to decide whether it was worth repairing or not. Mr. Brown examined all the wheels carefully. He decided that it was just a matter of time before another wheel fell off. He asked his son, Dave, to drain the oil from the motor. After that, Dave poured the gasoline remaining in the mower back into a gas can. Mrs. Brown shouted at them from the kitchen window, giving them directions. "I don't want the sanitation men to have any problems when they throw that mower into their truck!" she called to them. Dave pulled the old mower to the curb, thinking about the new one he'd be using in the future.

1 **Dave poured the gas from the mower into a gas can before —**

   A he brought it to the curb. .

   B he drained the oil from the mower.

   C his father examined all the wheels.

   D the wheel fell off the mower.

Hint: Find the sentence where Dave pours the gas into the can.

2 **When did Mr. Brown decide the mower wasn't worth fixing?**

_____

_____

_____

_____

_____

_____

_____

Hint: Find the sentence that tells about Mr. Brown's decision.

TEST TIP

Some questions test whether you recognize the *sequence*, or order, of events. Question 2 asks when Mr. Brown made a decision. To find the answer to a sequence question, think about the order in which things happen in the story. Ask yourself:

• What happened first?

• What happened next?

• What happened last?

To answer question 2, begin by restating the question, "Mr. Brown decided the mower wasn't worth fixing when . . ."

GO ON ➤

Answers
1 Ⓐ Ⓑ Ⓒ Ⓓ

The setting of a story lets you know when and where the story is taking place.

Helen Klaben was the only passenger on the small plane that was flying from Alaska to Washington. She stared out the window at the swirling white snowstorm. It was February 4, 1963. Ralph Flores, the pilot of the plane, wasn't sure whether or not they were still on course. He dropped to a lower altitude to see better. He glanced down to change gas tanks. A moment later the plane crashed into some trees.

1   **When did the story take place?**

   A   in the fall

   B   in the winter

   C   in the summer

   D   in the spring

   Hint: Read the third sentence.

2   **Where did the story take place?**

   F   in Alaska

   G   in Washington, D.C.

   H   in the state of Washington

   J   between Alaska and Washington

   Hint: Read the first sentence.

TEST TIP

Be sure to read every answer choice. When you read question 2, you might be tempted to choose answer F because you read the word *Alaska* in the paragraph. But is that really the best answer? Read each choice before making a decision.

In 1892, Chicago city leaders planned a fair. They wanted it to be the greatest fair ever. It would show the newest ideas in science, business, and art. They also wanted to build something grand at the fair. The Eiffel Tower had been built three years before in France. The Chicago leaders wanted something even grander. So they asked people to send in designs.

G. W. Ferris was a young engineer. He heard about the fair. He designed a wheel made of steel. The wheel was 250 feet across. Large cars hung from the end of each spoke. Each car could carry sixty people in a giant circle through the air.

On May 1, 1893, the fair opened. People came from around the world to see the latest inventions. They felt the heat of new electric stoves. They stood in the cool breeze of small fans. They saw a machine that washed dishes.

3   **Where did the fair open?**

   A   Paris, France

   B   Chicago, Illinois

   C   Elgin, Illinois

   D   Frankfurt, Germany

   Hint: Read the first paragraph.

4   **When did the fair open?**

   _____

   _____

   _____

   _____

   Hint: Read the first sentence of the third paragraph.

STOP

Answers

1 Ⓐ Ⓑ Ⓒ Ⓓ   2 Ⓕ Ⓖ Ⓗ Ⓙ   3 Ⓐ Ⓑ Ⓒ Ⓓ

The main idea is the meaning of a piece of writing. Many times, it is written in the passage.

Most teenagers think their bodies have problems. Most girls think they are too fat. Eight out of ten girls go on diets before they are eighteen. Most teenage boys think they are too thin. They try to build up more muscles. Even if teenagers don't exactly think they are ugly, they would still like to make improvements. It takes teenagers a while to learn that their bodies are really all right the way they are.

1   What is the main idea of this selection?

    A   Girls can lose weight.

    B   Teenagers don't like the way they look.

    C   You can improve your looks.

    D   Teenage boys are skinny.

Hint: What does the whole selection talk about?

Fingerprints were not used as records until about 100 years ago. The English government began to keep the prints of its workers and prisoners. Sir Francis Galton made the first large collection of fingerprints. Because of Galton's work, police began to use fingerprints to track down criminals.

2   What is the main idea of this selection?

    F   Fingerprinting was started by the police.

    G   Scotland Yard began about 100 years ago.

    H   Police began to use fingerprints to track down criminals thanks to Sir Francis Galton's work.

    J   Records of fingerprints have been around for hundreds of years.

Hint: What does the whole selection talk about?

Scientists have been studying how people talk to each other. In one study, the scientists asked people about their feelings. Do people talk more about sad and angry feelings? Or do they talk more about happy and proud feelings? Scientists found out that people talk about unhappy feelings twice as much as happy ones.

3   The main idea of this passage is to explain —

    A   how to get over sad and angry feelings.

    B   what scientists have learned about feelings.

    C   which feelings people talk about most often.

    D   how often people brag about feeling unhappy.

Hint: What is the point of the story?

If gum ever sticks on your clothes, don't try to wash them. Otherwise, the gum may never come off. Put an ice cube on the gum. That will harden it, so you can try to scrape it off with a table knife. Try nail polish remover. It can sometimes melt gum. If the gum is from a bubble that burst, try chewing more gum and using it to lift off the stuck pieces.

4   What is the main idea of this passage?

_____

_____

_____

_____

_____

_____

_____

_____

Hint: What does the whole paragraph talk about?

GO ON

Answers

1 Ⓐ Ⓑ Ⓒ Ⓓ   **2** Ⓕ Ⓖ Ⓗ Ⓙ   **3** Ⓐ Ⓑ Ⓒ Ⓓ

Many times the main idea is not given in the text. Sometimes you need to figure it out by putting the facts together.

Look under your kitchen sink. You will see some drain pipes. One pipe is U-shaped. It is called a trap. Harmful gases develop in a sewer line. The curved part of the trap holds a small amount of water. The water closes off the pipe. Then gases can't enter your house and harm you.

1   The main idea of the paragraph is that a trap —

   A   is a straight pipe.

   B   lets harmful gases enter your home.

   C   is not part of the drain pipe.

   D   has a very useful purpose.

Hint: If you put all the facts together, what do they say about the trap?

Electricity moves through wires in houses and buildings. This electrical flow is called a *current*. When a switch is on, the electric current can flow to machines and light fixtures. Then, the electric machines and lights can work. When a switch is off, the electric current doesn't flow. Then, electric machines can't work.

2   What is the main idea in this selection?

   F   If a switch is off, an electric machine will not work.

   G   Switches control electric current.

   H   If a switch is off, an electric machine will work.

   J   Switches are dangerous.

Hint: Read the entire paragraph.

Jackie Cochran was a natural pilot. She often flew in closed-circuit races. Closed circuit means that the course is round. The plane has to be flown with great skill. In 1940, Cochran broke the 2,000-kilometer, closed-circuit world speed record. Then in 1947, she set a new 100-kilometer, closed-circuit speed record. In 1953, she became the first woman to fly faster than the speed of sound.

3   What is the main idea of this passage?

_____

_____

_____

_____

_____

_____

_____

Hint: What does the entire passage talk about?

TEST TIP

When asked to write the main idea of a passage, make sure to tell the key or most important idea. Do not focus on the details. Think about the big meaning.

   To find the main idea of the paragraph for question 3, ask yourself:

• What is this paragraph about?

• What idea connects all of these details?

GO ON

Answers
1 Ⓐ Ⓑ Ⓒ Ⓓ   2 Ⓕ Ⓖ Ⓗ Ⓙ

A good summary contains the main idea of a passage. It is brief, yet it covers the most important points.

Our brain makes our lungs breathe and tells our muscles how to move. We use it to learn and remember. But even though it does so much, our brain weighs only about three pounds. Scientists say we use only a small part of it. They want to know what we do with the rest.

1 What is this passage mostly about?

A We use only a small part of our brain to do many things.

B The brain does not weigh very much.

C People can be smart.

D We use our brain to breathe.

Hint: Which choice sums up the passage?

If you sneeze, you'll almost always hear someone say "Bless you." Some historians think that people started saying "Bless you" over 1,000 years ago in Europe. At that time, the plague was spreading everywhere. One of the first signs of this terrible disease was sneezing. People thought the blessing might keep them from getting sick.

2 What is this selection mostly about?

_____

_____

_____

_____

_____

_____

Hint: Which sentence tells you about the whole passage?

TEST TIP

If a test question asks for a summary, provide a brief description of the main ideas. Your summary might be one or two sentences. It should include the most important ideas and leave out unnecessary details. To answer question 2, ask yourself:

• What does this paragraph tell me about sneezing?

• Which ideas should I include in my summary?

• Which ideas are details I can leave out?

GO ON

Answers

1 Ⓐ Ⓑ Ⓒ Ⓓ

Only about one out of every ten people is left-handed. In ancient times people thought lefties were witches. Not so long ago, people thought they might be crooks. Now scientists have proven that those ideas are not true. In fact, left-handers may be more creative than right-handers.

3 **What is this selection mostly about?**

F People think a lot about right-handed people.

G Left-handed people have been thought about differently over the years.

H Most witches and crooks are left-handed.

J Left-handed people are the most creative kind.

Hint: Which sentence tells you about the whole passage?

TEST TIP

Watch for tricky words. In question 3, you might get left-handed and right-handed mixed up. Reread your answer choice to make sure you have not confused things.

Maybe you have seen flamingos in a zoo. These brightly colored birds with long necks look too pink to be real. Wild flamingos get their bright-pink feathers from the plants and fish they eat. However, in zoos they don't eat the same things that they eat in the wild. They could turn white. To keep this from happening, the zookeepers give these birds a special pill.

4 **What is this story mostly about?**

_____

_____

_____

_____

_____

_____

_____

_____

Hint: What does the whole passage talk about?

TEST TIP

Before taking a test, find out if you can write in the test booklet. If you are allowed to do so, circle important ideas or cross out unnecessary details.

The clue in question 4 is the phrase *mostly about*. This tells you to write a short summary of the most important idea. Circle big ideas in the paragraph. Then write a sentence that tells the main ideas found in the paragraph.

STOP

Answers
3 Ⓕ Ⓖ Ⓗ Ⓙ

Knowing what made something happen or why a character did something will help you to understand what you read.

Sea birds like to flock at an airport in Canada, and often they crash into airplanes. They break glass, damage engines, and cause accidents. Trained falcons can help to keep the sea birds out of the way. The air traffic controller tells the falcon trainer where the flocks of sea birds are. Then the trainer lets a falcon go. The fierce little bird flies very fast. It scares the sea birds away.

1 **When do the sea birds get scared away?**

   A   at the airport in Canada

   B   by the airplanes

   C   when a falcon is let go

   D   when the falcon trainer meets the air traffic controller

   Hint: What happens right before the birds get scared away?

The Aztecs of Mexico played a ball game hundreds of years ago. When a player made a score, people watching had to give the player some of their clothes. The teams tried very hard to win. If a team lost, the team captains had to give up their heads.

2 **What made the team captains give up their heads?**

   F   They wanted more clothes.

   G   They wanted to win.

   H   They were showing off for the people watching.

   J   Their team lost.

   Hint: Something happened right before the team captains had to give up their heads. What was it?

When their enemies chase them, ostriches lie down on the sand. The giant birds stretch their necks out flat on the ground. When they do that, the loose feathers on their bodies look like bushes. But ostriches don't need to hide often. Their strong legs are good for both running and fighting.

3 **What makes ostriches lie down on the sand?**

   _____

   _____

   _____

   _____

   _____

   _____

   _____

   Hint: What happens right before they lie down?

Lots of movies use special effects. Many of these effects are the work of makeup artists. They sometimes use special materials, such as plastic. But often, they use simple things, such as food. When a script calls for fake blood, the artist mixes red food coloring, corn syrup, and peanut butter. This mixture looks real.

4 **What makes the mixture look real?**

   A   The artist uses plastic.

   B   The artist uses only food.

   C   The artist uses red food coloring, corn syrup, and peanut butter.

   D   The artist uses special materials.

   Hint: Certain things were used to make the mixture look real. What were they?

GO ON

Answers

1 Ⓐ Ⓑ Ⓒ Ⓓ   2 Ⓕ Ⓖ Ⓗ Ⓙ   4 Ⓐ Ⓑ Ⓒ Ⓓ

Sneakers were invented more than 100 years ago. They were called "croquet sandals." They cost five times as much as other shoes, so only rich people wore them. Then a company began to make tennis oxfords. Most people could afford these. They were very popular. Soon special sneakers were made for other sports, such as running. Now we have all sorts of sneakers.

5   **What made tennis oxfords popular?**

    F   They were made for running.

    G   Most people could afford them.

    H   They cost five times as much as other shoes.

    J   They were called croquet sandals.

Hint: Something is stated in the selection right before it says they were very popular. What is it?

Ballet dancers often spin around and around, but they don't become dizzy. A dancer's body turns smoothly. But the dancer holds his or her head still and then jerks it around quickly. This way the head is still most of the time, and the dancer does not become dizzy.

6   **Why don't ballet dancers become dizzy?**

    A   They turn their heads smoothly.

    B   Their heads are still most of the time.

    C   Their bodies turn smoothly.

    D   They don't spin around and around much.

Hint: Read the last sentence.

TEST TIP

Tests often ask you to connect ideas. Look back in the paragraph to check that your choice is supported by details in the writing.

The Dead Sea is not really a sea. It is a large lake. The Dead Sea lies between Israel and Jordan. It is the lowest place on Earth. The surface is 1,292 feet below sea level. The water is very salty. It's saltier than ocean water. It is called the Dead Sea because fish can't live in the salty water.

7   **Why is this lake called the Dead Sea?**

_____

_____

_____

_____

_____

_____

_____

Hint: The answer is stated in the passage.

TEST TIP

Restating the question helps you focus your answer to question 7. Begin by writing "This lake is called the Dead Sea because . . ." Then look for the exact reason in the paragraph.

GO ON

Answers
5 Ⓕ Ⓖ Ⓗ Ⓙ   6 Ⓐ Ⓑ Ⓒ Ⓓ

Many times, you can predict, or tell in advance, what is probably going to happen next. You must think about what would make sense if the story were to go on.

Wanda did not get many new clothes. Usually they were handed down from her big sister or older cousins. On her birthday, her mother gave her a beautiful dress handmade from pieces of things she had outgrown. Wanda was very proud of it and wore it to school the next day. But there, the other kids laughed at her and called her new dress a bunch of rags.

1   What is likely to happen next?

    A Wanda will laugh.

    B Wanda will never wear the dress to school again.

    C Wanda will have her mother make dresses for the other girls.

    D Wanda will give the dress to someone else.

Hint: Think about what you would most likely do if you were Wanda.

Mr. Henry's class had been studying birds. The class decided to go bird watching. They walked along a trail in the woods. Suddenly Mr. Henry told them to stop a few minutes. When they were quiet, they could hear a loud pecking sound.

2   What is Mr. Henry most likely to do?

    F point a woodpecker out to the class

    G ask the class to act like woodpeckers

    H leave the woods immediately with the class

    J start to make loud noises

Hint: Think about what the noise is.

It was a hot summer day. Andres and Nicole asked their mom if they could play in the sprinkler. She agreed. As they went outside, she reminded them to turn off the water when they were finished. They ran out to the backyard, turned on the sprinkler, and ran in and out of the sprinkler for about an hour. Then they decided to ride bikes. When they came home, their mother stood at the door with her arms crossed in front of her.

3   What will their mother do next and why?

_____

_____

_____

_____

_____

_____

_____

Hint: Once you figure out why their mother is standing at the door, you will know the answer.

TEST TIP

When a test question asks you to make a prediction, base your prediction on clues in the story. Tell the next logical step or event. To answer question 3, follow the sequence of events. The story contains important details that help you know what will happen next.

GO ON ➡

Answers

1 Ⓐ Ⓑ Ⓒ Ⓓ   2 Ⓕ Ⓖ Ⓗ Ⓙ

Julio had helped his grandfather cut hay all day. It had been another long, hot day, and he was glad to drive the tractor into the cool barn. He walked to the porch, where his grandfather handed him a pitcher of lemonade and a glass.

4 **What will Julio probably do next?**

A take the pitcher and the glass into the house

B pour the lemonade into the glass

C give the pitcher and glass back to his grandfather

D put the pitcher and glass down and go back to the barn

Hint: Think about what you would do.

Monique loved bananas. She loved banana splits, pudding, and ice cream. But her favorite way to eat a banana was simply to peel it and eat it. One day, she had just enjoyed her favorite food while sitting on the front steps of her house. She left the peel on the steps. An hour later, her mother came home and climbed the steps to the house. Monique heard a scream.

5 **What probably happened?**

F Her mother slipped on the peel.

G Her mother realized they needed more bananas.

H Her mother wanted Monique to know she came home.

J Her mother was greeted by a stranger at the front door.

Hint: Which of the choices makes the most sense?

Gabriela helped her father repaint her room. First, they moved all the furniture into the middle of the room and covered it with plastic sheets. Then, they brought in ladders. They spread out old newspapers on the floor. Then, they opened a can of paint and stirred it.

6 **What will Gabriela and her father probably do next?**

_____

_____

_____

_____

_____

_____

_____

Hint: You need to read the entire paragraph and especially the last sentence.

TEST TIP

To answer question 6, think about the *very next* thing that will happen. The test writers want you to explain the next step in this process. You do not need to think about what Gabriela and her father might do the next day or week. Use clue words in the story. Focus on what they did right after they opened the can of paint and stirred it.

Prediction questions can have more than one possible answer. Your answer is correct if it is logical and reasonable.

STOP

Sometimes a passage will have a graph or diagram with it. These are there to help you understand the passage.

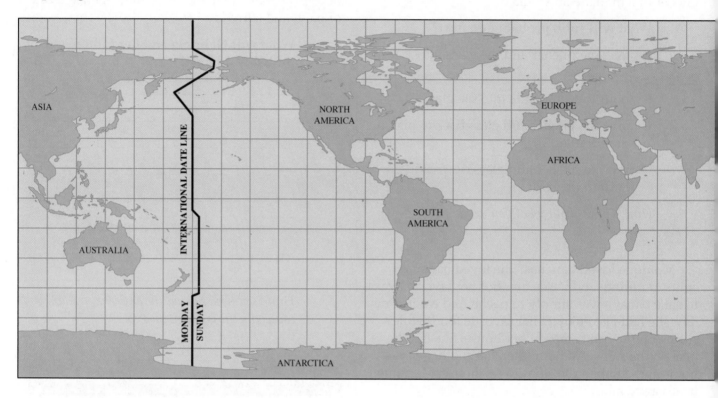

The international date line is a line on a map. It is the ending line for measuring time zones. On one side of the international date line, it is one day. On the other side of the international date line, it is a day later or earlier. The international date line does not always follow a straight line. If it followed a straight line, it would cross land. This would cause problems for the people living in these areas.

1   According to the map, if the international date line were straight, which continent would it go through?

   A   Asia

   B   Africa

   C   Europe

   D   North America

   Hint: Look for each choice on the map and mark it.

2   **What day will it be in North America if it is Tuesday in Asia?**

   _____

   _____

   _____

   _____

   _____

   _____

   _____

   Hint: Look at the map to see where each continent is.

GO ON ➡

Answers
   1 Ⓐ Ⓑ Ⓒ Ⓓ

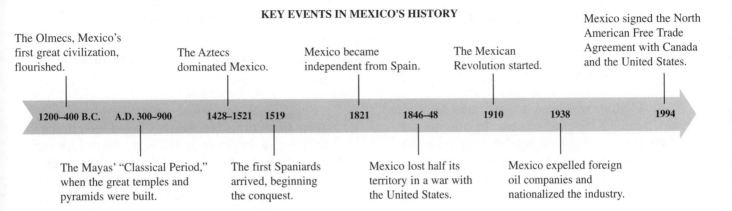

KEY EVENTS IN MEXICO'S HISTORY

The Olmecs, Mexico's first great civilization, flourished.

The Aztecs dominated Mexico.

Mexico became independent from Spain.

The Mexican Revolution started.

Mexico signed the North American Free Trade Agreement with Canada and the United States.

1200–400 B.C.   A.D. 300–900   1428–1521   1519   1821   1846–48   1910   1938   1994

The Mayas' "Classical Period," when the great temples and pyramids were built.

The first Spaniards arrived, beginning the conquest.

Mexico lost half its territory in a war with the United States.

Mexico expelled foreign oil companies and nationalized the industry.

Some of the world's greatest civilizations lived in Mexico. The Olmecs were the earliest culture, and they lasted until 400 B.C. The Mayas were next, and built great temples and pyramids. The Aztecs ruled Mexico until 1521, two years after the arrival of the Spanish invaders. The Aztecs built cities with highly organized societies. Mexico remained under Spanish rule for 300 years.

3   Look at the time line. What year did Mexico gain its independence?

F   400 B.C.

G   1519

H   1521

J   1821

Hint: Check each choice on the time line.

TEST TIP

Notice that the entry lines on the time line indicate important dates. To answer question 3, find the line that shows when Mexico gained its independence. Then find the answer choice that shows that date.

4   Why is Spanish the national language of Mexico?

_____

_____

_____

_____

_____

_____

_____

_____

Hint: Use the time line to help you.

TEST TIP

Question 4 asks you to draw a conclusion based on the time line. *Drawing a conclusion* means gathering information from several sources and making a decision. Read all of the information on the time line to answer the question. Then begin your answer by restating the question: "Spanish is the national language of Mexico because . . ."

GO ON

Answers
3 Ⓕ Ⓖ Ⓗ Ⓙ

A logical conclusion is an ending that makes sense. Many times, it can be proved by the information given in the paragraph.

Lisa Meitner was born in Austria in 1878. She grew up to be a famous scientist. In college, she studied atoms. After college, she began to work with the great scientist Max Planck. Later, she pioneered the splitting of the atom. But Meitner saw the war-like side of her research. She would not help make the atom bomb.

1   The passage suggests that Lisa Meitner —

A   was against using her research for harmful purposes.

B   did not know how to make a bomb.

C   never knew much about atoms.

D   was born in Australia.

Hint: Read the last two sentences.

Where is the safest place to be during a thunderstorm? You might think your house would be the best place. However, you are safer in a car than in a house. If lightning strikes a car, it spreads over the metal and runs through the tires into the ground. Of course, you should not touch metal parts of the car if lightning strikes it.

2   From this passage, you can tell that lightning —

F   does not strike cars.

G   probably won't harm the inside of a car.

H   makes a car run better.

J   does not strike houses.

Hint: Pick the choice that can be proved by what's in the passage.

Reggie Jackson was one of the best baseball players of all time. He always played well in the World Series. In the early 1970s, he played for the Oakland A's. He led the team to victory in three World Series. Then he was traded to the New York Yankees. He led the Yankees into three World Series, too. The Yankees won two of those World Series. In one game, Jackson hit three home runs. Because of this, he became known as "Mr. October."

3   When is the World Series held? Which clue did you use?

_____

_____

_____

_____

_____

Hint: A sentence in the passage will help you answer the question.

TEST TIP

Some tests ask you to explain why you chose or wrote an answer. Notice that question 3 includes two questions. Be sure to answer both parts of this test item.

GO ON

Answers
1 Ⓐ Ⓑ Ⓒ Ⓓ   2 Ⓕ Ⓖ Ⓗ Ⓙ

Do you know about the Seven Wonders of the Ancient World? These structures were built long, long ago. One was the Lighthouse of Pharos in Egypt. It stood over 400 feet tall. Another was the Colossus of Rhodes on an island near Turkey. This bronze statue was almost 200 feet tall. All but one of these wonders have disappeared. You can still see the Great Pyramids in Egypt.

4 **The story suggests that —**

A the Colossus was in Egypt.

B six of the ancient wonders no longer exist.

C the Great Pyramids have disappeared.

D the Colossus was taller than the Lighthouse.

Hint: Pick the choice that can be proved true.

At the age of three, Louis Braille lost his sight. But he did not let this loss stand in his way. As a teenager, he became an accomplished musician. At age 19, Braille began teaching the blind in Paris. One year later, in 1829, he developed a system of printing. The Braille system uses 63 sets of 6 raised dots. This system, often called Braille, is still used today.

5 **The Braille system —**

F is helpful to the deaf.

G is used by everyone today.

H can be read by touch.

J cannot be used by the blind.

Hint: Which choice makes the most sense?

Alfred Wegener looked at a world map. He noticed a strange thing. All the continents looked like jigsaw pieces. All the pieces seemed to fit together. Wegener thought about this idea for a long time. In 1912, he offered a new theory. He claimed that all the continents were once a large land mass. Then, over time, the continents moved apart. Wegener called his theory "continental drift." But other scientists did not accept his ideas until forty years later.

6 **Why did Wegener offer his new theory?**

_____

_____

_____

_____

_____

_____

Hint: Read sentences 7 and 8.

TEST TIP

When a question asks why something happens, look for a cause-and-effect relationship. Think about what caused something else to happen. You can begin your answer by restating the question with the word *because*: "Wegener offered his new theory because . . ."

GO ON ⇒

Answers

4 Ⓐ Ⓑ Ⓒ Ⓓ   **5** Ⓕ Ⓖ Ⓗ Ⓙ

SKILL 5: MAKING INFERENCES AND GENERALIZATIONS

The way a person acts tells you about the character's mood. Other clues may be what is said or how the character responds to what happens in the passage.

In the 1930s, African-American nurses could not care for white soldiers. Mabel Staupers wanted to change this problem. She asked for help from the Red Cross and many nursing groups. Still, Staupers did not succeed. But she kept struggling. Then World War II broke out. As the war got worse, more nurses were needed. By 1945, the armed forces nursing corps were fully integrated. Mabel Staupers had achieved her goal at last.

1 When Mabel Staupers could not care for white soldiers, she probably felt —

    A angry.

    B happy.

    C amused.

    D relieved.

Hint: Think about what she did later.

Tamara ran her finger down the first column on the page. "No, no, no," she repeated over and over. Suddenly her finger stopped on one of the little boxes. "Two rooms with a large kitchen," she read. Then she circled the box of print with her pen and called to her sister, "I think I've finally found something!"

2 You know from this selection that Tamara is —

    F excited.

    G depressed.

    H interested in becoming a newspaper reporter.

    J mad at her sister.

Hint: Read the words Tamara uses to express herself.

Mel studied his son. He wondered what he could say to convince the boy not to take the job. Mel knew the job seemed wonderful to a boy in high school. How could he explain to his son that it was more important to wait until he finished school?

3 How does Mel feel about his son's job offer?

    _____

    _____

    _____

    _____

    _____

    _____

    _____

Hint: Figure out what Mel wants his son to do.

TEST TIP

When making *inferences*, you form ideas that are not directly stated in the text. Base your inferences on clues in the writing. In question 1, the clues tell you about a problem Mabel Staupers wanted to change. You can make an inference about her feelings by thinking about what she did in her life. In question 2, you will find clues in the words and punctuation marks.

GO ON ➡

Answers
1 Ⓐ Ⓑ Ⓒ Ⓓ   **2** Ⓕ Ⓖ Ⓗ Ⓙ

In 1916, a great fire swept through northern Ontario. It left behind 1,000 square miles of burned forests and farmland. Six Canadian towns were burned, too. Bob Foster watched the fire as it neared. Seeing its fury, he lay face down in a potato patch as the fire roared around him. The smoke and heat were awful, but Bob survived the fire unharmed.

4   How did Bob feel after the fire was out?

A   grateful

B   afraid

C   furious

D   great

Hint: Think about how you might feel.

TEST TIP

When you read about characters, it helps to put yourself in their place. To answer question 4, think about how you would feel if you were Bob watching the fire. Put yourself in his place. Your feelings will help you make an accurate inference.

Ken sat with his hands clenching the armrests. The woman in the aisle said, "Please fasten your seat belts." Ken fumbled with the belt. The woman then made sure all the seats were in an upright position. She finished just as the engines began to roar on either side of Ken. He checked to make sure that there was an air sickness bag in the pocket in front of him.

5   How does Ken feel about flying?

_____

_____

_____

_____

_____

_____

_____

Hint: Think about why Ken did all the things he did.

TEST TIP

Forming a mental picture can help you answer many questions. To answer question 5, think about how Ken looks and acts on the airplane. Let the words help you picture what is happening. Then make an inference about how he feels.

STOP

Answers
4 Ⓐ Ⓑ Ⓒ Ⓓ

SKILL 6: RECOGNIZING POINTS OF VIEW, FACTS, AND OPINIONS

It is important to know the difference between fact and opinion. A fact is real and true. An opinion is a feeling or belief. Words that describe are used to offer opinions.

Rubber comes from a rubber tree. White juice, called *latex*, drips out of holes in the tree. Today, latex is used to make many things, such as rubber gloves and paint. People in Mexico were the first to use latex. One thing they did with latex was make shoes. They dipped their feet in the latex and let it dry.

1 **Which of the following is an OPINION based on the passage?**

   A Mexican people made rubber shoes.

   B Rubber comes from a tree.

   C The people in Mexico had good ideas.

   D People dipped their feet in latex.

Hint: Which choice is a feeling or belief?

Power lawn mowers make lawn care easy. Years ago, people had to push a mower by hand. The push mower had three long blades, which were attached to wheels on both sides. As the wheels turned, the blades spun and cut the grass. It took a long time to cut a lawn, especially when the grass was high. You had to be strong to push a mower like that. Today power lawn mowers come in all sizes. Some are so large that a person can ride on them.

2 **Which of these is an OPINION from the passage?**

   F Power lawn mowers make lawn care easier.

   G A push mower has three long blades.

   H You can ride some power mowers.

   J Mowers come in many sizes.

Hint: Which choice is a feeling?

Pocahontas was the daughter of the Native American chief Powatan. She made friends with the English settlers who came to Virginia in the early 1600s. One day, their leader, John Smith, was captured by her tribe. Pocahontas risked her life to save him. She also brought the settlers food to keep them from starving. Later, she married John Smith. She helped keep peace between her tribe and the settlers.

3 **Which of these is a FACT from the passage?**

   A Pocahontas was a fearful person.

   B Pocahontas was of mixed heritage.

   C Pocahontas liked only one of the English settlers.

   D Pocahontas gave food to the settlers.

Hint: Facts are real and true.

TEST TIP

Words printed in capital or uppercase letters in a question are very important. The test writer wants you to focus on those words. The three questions on this page have the words *fact* or *opinion* in them. Remember that facts must be true. Opinions can be feelings or beliefs.

GO ON ➡

Answers

1 Ⓐ Ⓑ Ⓒ Ⓓ   **2** Ⓕ Ⓖ Ⓗ Ⓙ   **3** Ⓐ Ⓑ Ⓒ Ⓓ

Everyone knows what a tiger is. And everyone has heard of lions. But do you know what a liger is? A liger is a cross between a lion and a tiger. In 1948, the first liger was born in the United States. It was born at the Hagh Zoo in Salt Lake City, Utah.

4 **Which of the following is an OPINION based on the passage?**

F A liger is a cross between a tiger and a lion.

G Ligers are more interesting than lions.

H Ligers did not exist before 1948.

J Most ligers live in zoos.

Hint: Which statement is a feeling?

TEST TIP

Read the questions carefully to find out if you are looking for a fact or simply an opinion. To find an *opinion*, look for words that show feelings or beliefs. Opinions tell someone's point of view.

Essie's favorite tree had blown over in a wind storm. She had always loved the graceful weeping willow tree. Her dad suggested that she plant a new one. They went to a tree farm where they picked out a young tree. When they got home, they dug a wide, deep hole and placed the new tree gently into it. Then they watered it thoroughly while covering its roots with dirt.

5 **Which of these is a FACT from the passage?**

A Essie liked willow trees more than oaks.

B Essie's tree was blown over in a storm.

C Essie's dad was glad the tree had blown over.

D It's very hard for two people to plant a tree.

Hint: Which choice is real and true?

TEST TIP

To find a *fact*, look for a statement that is true. Answer choices that describe feelings are not facts. To answer question 5, eliminate all of the statements that you know are opinions. The remaining one is a fact.

STOP

READING COMPREHENSION

Directions: Read each selection carefully. Then read each question. Darken the circle for the correct answer, or write the answer in the space provided.

TRY THIS	More than one answer choice may seem correct. Choose the answer that goes <u>best</u> with the selection.

Sample A

Going to the Store

Ross and Drew went to the store to buy milk. Ross had a dollar in his pocket. He used the dollar to pay for the milk.

What did Ross have in his pocket?

A a dime

B milk

C a dollar

D a map

THINK IT THROUGH	The correct answer is <u>C</u>. The second sentence in the story says that Ross had <u>a dollar</u> in his pocket. The story does not say that Ross had a dime, milk, or a map in his pocket.

STOP

The Butterfly

There are many kinds of butterflies. Some live only for a few weeks. Others live for several months or years. Some butterflies are yellow or green. They look like leaves. They can hide in the trees or in plants. Others have bright colors. All these butterflies help make our world more colorful.

1   From this story you know that —

   A all butterflies live for a long time.

   B there are only a few kinds of butterflies.

   C all butterflies hide in trees.

   D there are many different kinds of butterflies.

2   Why do butterflies hide?

   _____

   _____

   _____

   _____

   _____

   _____

GO ON

Answers
SA (A) (B) (C) (D)   **1** (A) (B) (C) (D)

The Man Behind the Bear

Have you ever heard of Morris Michtom? You may not have heard of him, but you almost certainly have heard about a toy he invented. Michtom and his family came to the United States from Russia. They lived in Brooklyn, New York, where Michtom owned a small candy, novelty, and stationery store.

Michtom greatly admired Theodore Roosevelt, who was the President of the United States at that time. In 1902, Michtom read a newspaper story about Roosevelt. The story told how, during a hunting trip, the President saved a small bear cub from being shot. A cartoon of the event accompanied the story. The cartoon and story gave Michtom an idea for a new toy.

Michtom wrote a letter to President Roosevelt. He asked the President's permission to make and sell a stuffed toy bear cub called the "Teddy Bear." The President wrote back to Michtom and gave his permission. Rose Michtom, Morris' wife, made the first bear for sale with movable arms and legs. It sold quickly, and she made more bears to replace it. Michtom soon formed a new company to produce more of the teddy bears.

Teddy bears became popular all over the United States. Today, many different kinds of stuffed bears are made and sold to both children and adults. Michtom's toy company is still in business today in Brooklyn, New York.

GO ON

3 What is this selection mainly about?

   F Morris Michtom's life in Russia

   G how a toy company is operated

   H how the teddy bear was invented

   J President Roosevelt's hunting trip

4 How did Michtom make a living in Brooklyn?

   A He owned a small store.

   B He wrote newspaper stories.

   C He worked for the President.

   D He owned a toy store.

5 Where did Morris Michtom first get his idea?

_____

_____

_____

_____

_____

_____

6 The toy company started by Michtom—

   F is now owned by the government.

   G closed down when Roosevelt left office.

   H never was very successful.

   J is still in business today.

TEST TIP

Answer one question at a time. Look back at the passage to help you answer each question.

7 Today, teddy bears are—

   A not very popular.

   B bought by many children and adults.

   C hard-to-find items.

   D sold only in Brooklyn.

8 What did Michtom do first after he got his idea?

   F He formed a company.

   G He started selling teddy bears.

   H He read a newspaper story.

   J He wrote to President Roosevelt.

9 Where would this selection most likely be found?

   A in a children's book

   B in a farmer's almanac

   C in a history book

   D in an autobiography

10 What is another good title for this story?

   F "The Beginnings of the Teddy Bear"

   G "Save the Bears"

   H "All about President Theodore Roosevelt"

   J "From Russia to New York"

TEST TIP

Remember that a title gives a general idea about an article. To answer question 10, look for the title that best summarizes the topic of the reading passage.

GO ON

Answers

3 Ⓕ Ⓖ Ⓗ Ⓙ   **6** Ⓕ Ⓖ Ⓗ Ⓙ   **8** Ⓕ Ⓖ Ⓗ Ⓙ   **10** Ⓕ Ⓖ Ⓗ Ⓙ

4 Ⓐ Ⓑ Ⓒ Ⓓ   **7** Ⓐ Ⓑ Ⓒ Ⓓ   **9** Ⓐ Ⓑ Ⓒ Ⓓ

Making Papier-Mâché

Papier-mâché is easy to make and fun to use. If you use your imagination, you can create just about anything you want with papier-mâché. Here's how you make papier-mâché:

1. Gather newspaper, scissors, flour, water, a spoon, and a bowl.
2. Cut or tear the newspaper into strips.
3. Mix a cup of flour and half a cup of water in the bowl until the mixture is smooth.
4. Dip the newspaper into the flour and water mixture until it is completely wet.
5. Then form the wet newspaper into the shape you want. You can make animals, bowls, jewelry, masks, and many other things in this way.
6. Let the wet papier-mâché dry for several days. It will become very hard.
7. Paint the papier-mâché and decorate it with colored paper, feathers, or buttons if you like.

11 Which of these is *not* necessary when making papier-mâché?

A letting the papier-mâché objects dry for several days

B dipping the newspaper strips into the mixture

C using paint and colored paper to decorate the papier-mâché objects

D forming the wet newspaper into a shape

12 Which of the following would *not* be a good choice to make from papier-mâché?

F masks

G jewelry

H bowls

J clothing

13 What is used to make papier-mâché?

A flour, newspaper, and water

B newspaper, salt, and soda

C feathers, buttons, and colored paper

D milk, butter, and eggs

14 How long does it take for the papier-mâché to dry?

_____

_____

_____

_____

_____

_____

_____

_____

GO ON ➡

Brothers

Seth and his big brother Frank were walking along the beach. Frank was home from college for the summer. The boys had time on their hands. As they walked, Seth picked up an oyster shell.

"This reminds me of those great smoked oysters Dad made last fall," said Frank.

"You have always loved oysters," laughed Frank. "Let me tell you what I learned about oysters this year."

Frank picked up an oyster shell and turned it over in his hand. "Did you know that baby oysters do not have shells? They are little, round creatures, about the size of the head of a pin. They swim around by moving tiny hairs on their bodies. When an oyster is one day old, it starts to form a hard shell. In about a week, the shell is fully formed. That is when the oyster finds a rock to attach itself to. It stays there for the rest of its life.

"The oyster shell is really two shells. They are held together by a hinge, which is part of the oyster's body. When the lid of the shell is open, the oyster is in danger. You see, you are not the only one that likes to eat them. Many sea animals love oysters, too.

"The oyster has no eyes or ears. Tiny feelers tell the oyster when it is in danger. When this happens, the shell lid slams shut, keeping the oyster safe inside. Many hungry fish, seals, and otters have been turned away by a tightly shut oyster shell."

"You do know a lot about oysters," said Seth. "What else did you learn?"

"Well," said Frank, "oysters are members of a family called mollusks. Mollusks all have soft bodies without bones. Clams and snails are also members of this family. Other mollusks, such as octopuses and slugs, do not have shells."

"Frank, I hate to cut this walk short," said Seth. "But all your talk about oysters is making me hungry. Let's head home for lunch."

15 About how long does it take for an oyster shell to fully form?

_____

_____

_____

_____

16 Which of these events was happening as the story took place?

F   Frank was arriving home from college.

G   Seth was eating smoked oysters.

H   Seth and Frank were walking.

J   Seth and Frank were fishing.

17 Which words in the story tell that Seth and Frank were in no hurry?

A   …had time on their hands.

B   Let me tell you what I learned…

C   What else…

D   Let's head home…

18 Which statement about baby oysters is *not* true?

F   They are small and round.

G   They are surrounded by a soft shell.

H   They swim by moving tiny hairs.

J   They are about the size of the head of a pin.

GO ON

Wanted: Good Readers!

Tuesday afternoons 3:30–4:00
See Ms. Chung in Room 114.

Are you a good reader? If so, join Reading Talent and volunteer to read books aloud for younger children. We will make cassette recordings of books to be used by kindergarteners and first graders. Make books come alive for beginning readers!

Save the Planet

Wednesday mornings 7:15–7:45 or
Thursday afternoons 3:30–4:00
Choose one or both times.
See Mr. Titan in Room 211.

Help take care of our Earth by picking up litter on the school grounds and managing the school recycling center. If you are Earth-friendly, Earth Patrol is for you!

Food Collection

The last Monday afternoon of each month 3:30–4:30
See Ms. Nethercutt in Room 118.

Help collect and sort food to be distributed to community members in need. Join the food drive to help drive out hunger in your community!

Help Others!

Wednesday afternoons 3:30–5:00
See Ms. Rios in Room 109.

If you enjoy helping others, think about joining Community Outreach. We'll make get-well cards for children in hospitals and write letters to people in military service. We'll spend a good deal of time practicing a musical. At the end of the year, we'll travel to a local nursing home to perform the musical for residents.

GO ON

19 Which group has meetings in the morning?

_____

_____

_____

_____

_____

_____

20 Which group is *not* mentioned in the notices?

A Safety Patrol

B Community Outreach

C Reading Talent

D Earth Patrol

21 Which group has choices for meeting times?

F Community Outreach

G Food Drive

H Earth Patrol

J Reading Talent

22 Which group will take a field trip?

A Reading Talent

B Earth Patrol

C Community Outreach

D Food Drive

23 When does the Food Collection meet?

F every Monday afternoon

G Wednesday mornings

H Tuesday afternoons

J the last Monday afternoon of the month

24 All of the Volunteer Jobs —

A meet once a week.

B provide help to students at school.

C practice a musical.

D have teacher sponsors.

25 Who should you contact if you want to join Earth Patrol?

F Ms. Chung

G Mr. Titan

H Ms. Nethercutt

J Ms. Rios

26 Which of the following is *not* true of "Wanted: Good Readers!"

A Members will record books on tape.

B See Ms. Chung to join.

C The tapes will be used by younger children.

D Members will learn how to read.

TEST TIP

Make sure you pay attention to words in *italics*. In question 26, look for the answer that is not true.

GO ON ➡

Edgardo's Rescue

Edgardo pursued the giant yellow and black butterfly into the field. It was a Tiger Swallowtail, the kind he had been wanting for his collection. What luck to find it so easily! Edgardo was about to swing the butterfly net when his dog Tag started barking loudly at something in the brush. Edgardo looked in that direction, and the butterfly escaped into the sky.

"You worthless dog!" he exclaimed. "What is the matter with you?" Edgardo realized it was his own fault that he had lost the butterfly. He should not have looked away. Still, he wanted to blame somebody.

Suddenly, Edgardo saw what had made Tag bark. A tiny, spotted fawn, no more than a week old, lay nestled in a thicket. It seemed to be *abandoned*, and Edgardo wondered if Tag had chased the mother away. The baby looked very small, alone, and confused.

Then Edgardo remembered something he had read. Mother deer often leave their fawns hidden in the woods for short periods of time while they go off to feed. The doe would probably come back soon. Edgardo grabbed his dog by the collar and told him, "Time to go home, Tag." Tag whined. He wanted to remain right there. Edgardo did, too, in a way. He wanted to be sure the doe would return.

A week later, Edgardo returned to check on the fawn. This time he made sure that Tag stayed behind. First, he looked in the thicket, hoping that the fawn had survived the week. He saw an area of mashed-down brush at the spot where he had first seen the fawn. That revealed to him that the fawn was sleeping there every night, and Edgardo relaxed. The mother had been close by after all. He could stop being concerned and go back to working on his butterfly collection.

27 Why did Edgardo want to stay?

F He wanted to make Tag happy.

G He wanted another chance to catch the butterfly.

H He wanted to make sure that the fawn's mother would return.

J He wanted to hide from his brother.

28 When did Edgardo return?

A later that day

B in a month

C the next day

D a week later

29 What was Edgardo most concerned about?

_____

_____

_____

_____

30 Why did Edgardo lose the Tiger Swallowtail?

F He tripped over the fawn.

G Tag barked and scared the butterfly.

H There was a hole in his net.

J He looked away to see why Tag was barking.

31 In this selection, the word *abandoned* means—

A hungry.　　**C** thirsty.

B tired.　　**D** left behind.

32 Which of these most likely happened after Edgardo went home?

F The doe returned to its fawn.

G Someone took the fawn home.

H Tag found another deer.

J The doe and fawn followed Edgardo home.

STOP

Answers

27 Ⓕ Ⓖ Ⓗ Ⓙ　　**28** Ⓐ Ⓑ Ⓒ Ⓓ　　**30** Ⓕ Ⓖ Ⓗ Ⓙ　　**31** Ⓐ Ⓑ Ⓒ Ⓓ　　**32** Ⓕ Ⓖ Ⓗ Ⓙ

A sample question helps you to understand the type of question you will be asked in the test that follows.

Sample A   **Sports Cover**

Monica likes all kinds of sports. In the fall she plays soccer, and in winter she plays basketball. Spring is the time for baseball. Tennis keeps Monica busy in the summer.

What sport does Monica play in winter?

A   soccer

B   basketball

C   baseball

D   tennis

Directions: Read each selection. Darken the circle for the correct answer to each question, or write your answer in the space provided.

Carmen and Sade's Camping Trip

Carmen and Sade jumped out of the van as soon as it pulled into the campsite. The two friends found a perfect spot under a large pine tree to set up their tent. They drove their tent stakes into the ground. Then, after pulling the tent upright and tightening the ropes, the girls placed their sleeping bags inside. Next, they put their food in a plastic bag and hung it from a tree branch to protect it from wild animals. Finally, they chose a safe place to build a fire. They made sure there were neither low branches nor dry grass or leaves near the campfire. They could not wait to show off their work to the others.

1   The friends placed their tent —

A   next to a lake.

B   under a pine tree.

C   near the bathhouse.

D   far from the road.

2   Why did the campers choose the place for their fire so carefully?

F   They wanted to be warm.

G   They wanted to keep the animals away.

H   They wanted to protect against forest fires.

J   They wanted to be near the other campers.

3   What is the main idea of the story?

A   Building a campfire is easy.

B   Carmen and Sade are friends.

C   Carmen and Sade set up camp.

D   Never leave food in the tent.

4   Why is the food hung from a tree?

_____

_____

_____

_____

GO ON

Answers

SA ⒶⒷⒸⒹ   1 ⒶⒷⒸⒹ   2 ⒻⒼⒽⒿ   3 ⒶⒷⒸⒹ

Learning about Kangaroos

Have you ever heard of "roos"? If you lived in Australia, you would know that this word refers to kangaroos. The kangaroo is the national animal of Australia. Its likeness is found on the money, stamps, and national seal of Australia.

The kangaroo belongs to a family known as marsupials. Most female marsupials have pouches in which their young grow and develop. Some marsupials live in New Guinea and on nearby islands, but many live only in Australia. Kangaroos are the largest marsupials.

There are many different kinds of kangaroos. The most common *species* are the red kangaroo and the gray kangaroo. The red kangaroo is the largest species. It lives in the deserts and dry grasslands of central Australia. Gray kangaroos are smaller than the reds. They live in the forests and grasslands of eastern Australia. Wallabies are smaller than kangaroos, and the smallest of all are rat kangaroos. There are more than a hundred million kangaroos in Australia. That means there are six kangaroos for every person in the country.

Kangaroos live in small groups called mobs. A mob is led by a large male called a boomer. There are usually two or three females and their young in a mob. Often other males challenge the boomer for leadership. He chases them off or fights with them.

Let's follow one female gray kangaroo. Five weeks after mating with the boomer, she gives birth to a tiny baby that isn't even an inch long. This *joey* has no hair and cannot see. Only its forearms are strong and ready to use. Strong arms are important because it has to climb up its mother's stomach and into her pouch. If it falls, it will die. Once inside the pouch, it is safe. It will grow larger and develop hair and a strong tail.

When it is about three months old, the joey will first look out of the pouch. About a month later, it will leave the pouch for the first time. It will eat grass and practice hopping. It will stay close to its mother, and at the first sign of danger, dive back into the pouch headfirst.

Eagles and wild dogs sometimes try to kill young kangaroos. Humans are an even greater enemy. Hunters kill thousands of kangaroos every year. The kangaroos watch for enemies as they eat. Kangaroos have good hearing. Each ear can turn in a half circle. When a kangaroo senses danger, it thumps its tail on the ground. Then the mob hops quickly away. Kangaroos can travel thirty miles an hour when they are frightened.

In some parts of Australia there are kangaroo crossing signs. Kangaroos are not careful when they cross roads, and every year thousands of kangaroos are killed by cars. Generally, the Australian government protects kangaroos by passing laws against killing these native animals.

GO ON

5 In this selection, you can learn—

   F about the height and weight of kangaroos.

   G about the life of a rat kangaroo.

   H why hunters kill kangaroos.

   J about the life of a gray kangaroo.

6 In this selection, the word *joey* means—

   A a baby kangaroo.

   B a large male kangaroo.

   C a young koala bear.

   D a native of Australia.

7 According to the selection, what feature do most female marsupials share?

   F tough skin

   G long legs

   H a pouch

   J white fur

8 Why does a joey stay close to its mother?

_____

_____

_____

_____

_____

_____

9 According to the selection, what is the first thing a newborn kangaroo does?

   A looks out of the pouch

   B climbs into its mother's pouch

   C tumbles out of the pouch

   D opens its eyes

10 In this selection, the word *species* means—

   F an animal that eats only grass.

   G a baby animal.

   H a kind of animal.

   J an enemy.

11 According to the selection, a boomer chases off other males because—

   A he wants to be the leader of the group.

   B there isn't enough food for all of them.

   C he doesn't like company.

   D he is selfish.

12 Where do red kangaroos live?

   F in central Australia

   G only in New Guinea

   H in eastern Australia

   J in western Australia

13 You would probably find this story in a book called—

   A *The Grasslands of Australia.*

   B *Taking Care of Your Pet.*

   C *Unusual Animals.*

   D *Money and Stamps of the World.*

14 If you wanted to know more about kangaroos, you should—

   F travel to Australia.

   G read about them in an encyclopedia.

   H draw pictures of them.

   J visit a pet store.

GO ON

Answers

5 Ⓕ Ⓖ Ⓗ Ⓙ   **7** Ⓕ Ⓖ Ⓗ Ⓙ   **10** Ⓕ Ⓖ Ⓗ Ⓙ   **12** Ⓕ Ⓖ Ⓗ Ⓙ   **14** Ⓕ Ⓖ Ⓗ Ⓙ

6 Ⓐ Ⓑ Ⓒ Ⓓ   **9** Ⓐ Ⓑ Ⓒ Ⓓ   **11** Ⓐ Ⓑ Ⓒ Ⓓ   **13** Ⓐ Ⓑ Ⓒ Ⓓ

Wilderness Adventure

Carla pulled her jacket closer and looked into the campfire. The night was cold and clear, and even though it was too dark to see them, Carla could smell the pine trees that surrounded the campsite. Thousands of stars sparkled like tiny diamonds in the night sky. It was beautiful! Carla couldn't believe she was actually there in the national park. Just that morning when she woke up in her own bed she thought, "Another hot, humid, boring day, just like every other day this summer."

But then she remembered! Today was different. Her favorite aunt and uncle, Tina and Marc, had invited her to join them on a backpacking trip. They picked her up at 8:00 A.M. and drove most of the day to get to the national park. They just had time to pitch their tents, build the fire, and cook dinner before it got dark. Carla went into the forest to gather firewood. Then she helped Tina make hamburger patties. She didn't realize how hungry she was until she smelled them cooking. Everything tasted better when you were outside, she decided.

"Well, it's too dark to do anything else tonight," Uncle Marc said. "We might as well go to bed now so that we can get up at sunrise. I want to get an early start on the trail. Be sure and zip your tent, Carla. You wouldn't want to wake up with a rattlesnake in your sleeping bag!"

Carla couldn't decide if he was teasing or not. She made sure she zipped the tent tight, just in case. She crawled into her sleeping bag and wiggled around, trying to get comfortable. It had been a long day, but she was too excited to sleep. She wished she had brought a flashlight and a book. She wondered what adventures the next day would bring.

Carla woke up to the sounds of pots clanging. She crawled out of her tent and opened her backpack. "Look at this!" she exclaimed in dismay. Some small creature had chewed a hole in her bag of trail mix and eaten the whole thing. "Well, some little field mouse had a great breakfast!" Tina said. "Never mind, I brought plenty of snacks for all of us."

After breakfast, Carla's uncle helped her adjust her backpack. It was heavier than she expected it to be. Then they took off on the trail. The three hikers followed a river for a while; then they crossed it. Carla held her breath as she walked on the narrow log that served as a bridge. She didn't want to fall into the icy water.

The trail led back into the forest. Tina walked in front, and Carla and Marc followed. Suddenly all three heard a terrifying sound—a loud, close rattle. Tina jumped forward. Carla jumped backwards and bumped into her uncle. About a foot to the right of the trail, they saw what was making the sound—a five-foot-long rattlesnake! The snake continued rattling its tail. They noticed something peculiar about the snake. Its mouth was wide open, and it was eating a field mouse. Apparently the snake was in the middle of its lunch.

Marc relaxed as soon as he realized what was happening. He explained that snakes' teeth point inward. It's very difficult for them to spit something out once they have begun eating. The rattlesnake couldn't harm them as long as it had something in its mouth. Tina got her camera. They sat a short distance away and took pictures while they observed the rattlesnake. The snake continued to rattle but didn't move away. Marc told Carla that snakes eat only every ten days or so. It takes them a long time to swallow and digest their *prey*.

After a while, they left the snake and began hiking again. Carla's heart was still beating fast. She decided that Uncle Marc hadn't been teasing when he told her to zip up her tent. He wouldn't have to remind her about that tonight!

GO ON ➤

15 The boxes below show events from the selection.

Carla gathered firewood from the forest.		Carla walked across the narrow log bridge.
1	2	3

Which event belongs in the second box?

A Carla heard a terrifying sound.

B Carla crawled into her sleeping bag.

C Carla watched a rattlesnake eating its prey.

D Carla drove to the national park with her aunt and uncle.

16 At the beginning of the selection Carla feels—

F angry and disappointed.

G worried and nervous.

H excited and happy.

J lonely and sad.

17 What is the last thing Carla did before she went to sleep?

A She wiggled around, trying to get comfortable.

B She zipped up the tent.

C She helped Tina make hamburger patties.

D She went looking for rattlesnakes.

18 Which words in the story show that the evening was cool at the campsite?

F …zip up her tent.

G …pulled her jacket closer…

H …too dark to do anything else…

J …sparkled like tiny diamonds…

19 The word *prey* means—

A a kind of snake.

B a type of backpack.

C an animal hunted for food.

D teeth that point inward.

20 What did the snake most likely do after the three hikers left?

_____

_____

_____

_____

_____

_____

_____

21 What is this story mainly about?

F summer vacations

G the danger of rattlesnakes

H getting along with relatives

J backpacking in a national park

22 Why would Uncle Marc not have to remind Carla to zip up her tent at night?

A The snake had frightened her, and she didn't want another one near her.

B She had a good memory and never forgot anything.

C She knew that no one would remind her, so she told herself to remember.

D She didn't want to make her uncle unhappy.

GO ON ➡

Answers

15 Ⓐ Ⓑ Ⓒ Ⓓ   17 Ⓐ Ⓑ Ⓒ Ⓓ   19 Ⓐ Ⓑ Ⓒ Ⓓ   22 Ⓐ Ⓑ Ⓒ Ⓓ

16 Ⓕ Ⓖ Ⓗ Ⓙ   18 Ⓕ Ⓖ Ⓗ Ⓙ   21 Ⓕ Ⓖ Ⓗ Ⓙ

Come to the Read-Over Friday, May 28! It is sponsored by the fourth-grade teachers to kick off the summer reading program. Principal Jones, Ms. Rodriguez, and Coach Lee will also attend. Let's see how many pages fourth graders can read in one night at a sleep-over party!

Rules and Information

1. You must be a fourth grader at Main Street School to attend.

2. Get a permission slip from Ms. Barker in Room 211. Have your parents complete the slip and return it by Monday, May 24.

3. Report to the gym at 7:30 P.M. on Friday, May 28, dressed in shorts or jeans and a T-shirt to sleep in.

4. Bring a sleeping bag, pillow, and lots of reading material.

6. We will stay up late and read, read, read!

7. In the morning, we'll tally the total number of pages read.

8. Breakfast will be served at 7:00 A.M.

9. Parents must pick up students by 9:00 A.M. on Saturday, May 29.

GO ON ⮞

23 Who can attend the Read-Over?

_____

_____

_____

_____

_____

_____

24 Where will students at the Read-Over spend the night?

F in the principal's office

G in the library

H in Room 211

J in the gym

25 Which of these is *not* important to bring to the Read-Over?

A sleeping bag

B reading material

C flashlight

D pillow

26 When does the Read-Over end?

F 7:30 P.M. on Friday, May 28

G 7:30 A.M. on Friday, May 28

H 7:30 A.M. on Saturday, May 29

J 9:00 A.M. on Saturday, May 29

27 Why are the fourth-grade teachers having a Read-Over?

A to raise money

B to introduce the summer reading program

C to help parents

D to help the librarian

28 What is the last date to turn in permission slips?

F May 12

G May 13

H May 24

J May 5

STOP

Answers
24 Ⓕ Ⓖ Ⓗ Ⓙ   **25** Ⓐ Ⓑ Ⓒ Ⓓ   **26** Ⓕ Ⓖ Ⓗ Ⓙ   **27** Ⓐ Ⓑ Ⓒ Ⓓ   **28** Ⓕ Ⓖ Ⓗ Ⓙ

READING VOCABULARY

UNDERSTANDING WORD MEANINGS

Directions: Darken the circle for the word or words that have the same or almost the same meaning as the underlined word.

TRY THIS	Choose your answers carefully. Some wrong choices may seem correct if you do not think about the meaning of the underlined words.

Sample A

Peculiar means—

A tired   C quick

B hurt   D strange

THINK IT THROUGH	The correct answer is D, strange. Peculiar does not mean "tired," "hurt" or "quick."

STOP

---

1 Immediately means—

A later   C sadly

B slowly   D instantly

2 Mighty means—

F false   H famous

G strong   J soft

3 To challenge is to—

A agree   C plan

B dare   D change

4 Chilly means—

F warm   H cold

G nice   J windy

5 To dangle means to—

A tie   C catch

B cover   D swing

6 To be scared means to be—

F sweaty   H afraid

G tired   J excited

7 To accuse means to—

A honor   C blame

B question   D reward

8 A slogan is a kind of—

F laugh   H answer

G motto   J metal

STOP

Answers
SA Ⓐ Ⓑ Ⓒ Ⓓ   2 Ⓕ Ⓖ Ⓗ Ⓙ   4 Ⓕ Ⓖ Ⓗ Ⓙ   6 Ⓕ Ⓖ Ⓗ Ⓙ   8 Ⓕ Ⓖ Ⓗ Ⓙ
1 Ⓐ Ⓑ Ⓒ Ⓓ   3 Ⓐ Ⓑ Ⓒ Ⓓ   5 Ⓐ Ⓑ Ⓒ Ⓓ   7 Ⓐ Ⓑ Ⓒ Ⓓ

Directions: Darken the circle for the sentence that uses the underlined word in the same way as the sentence in the box.

 TRY THIS | Read the sentence in the box carefully. Decide what the underlined word means. Then find the sentence in which the underlined word has the same meaning.

Sample A

1

> Did you <u>seal</u> the bag tightly?

In which sentence does <u>seal</u> have the same meaning as it does in the sentence above?

A The presidential <u>seal</u> was on the envelope.

B Matt cared for the baby <u>seal</u>.

C Break the <u>seal</u>, and open the trunk.

D We have to <u>seal</u> the cracks in the floor.

THINK IT THROUGH | The correct answer is <u>D</u>. In this sentence and in the sentence in the box, <u>seal</u> means to "make secure or fill in."

 STOP

1

> The bus will <u>drop</u> us at the entrance.

In which sentence does <u>drop</u> have the same meaning as it does in the sentence above?

A There was one <u>drop</u> of medicine left.

B Did the bus <u>drop</u> them off at the corner?

C Business began to <u>drop</u>.

D She was about to <u>drop</u> the plate.

2

> We stood on the <u>bluff</u> looking at the city.

In which sentence does <u>bluff</u> have the same meaning as it does in the sentence above?

F I wanted to call his <u>bluff</u>.

G They built a house on the wooded <u>bluff</u>.

H Can you <u>bluff</u> your way out of trouble?

J Tina recognized the boy's <u>bluff</u>.

3

> Use a hammer to <u>pound</u> the nails.

In which sentence does <u>pound</u> have the same meaning as it does in the sentence above?

A I found my dog at the <u>pound</u>.

B Don't <u>pound</u> your feet on the stairs.

C <u>Pound</u> this stake into the ground.

D This weighs more than one <u>pound</u>.

4

> This is my best <u>lace</u> cover.

In which sentence does <u>lace</u> have the same meaning as it does in the sentence above?

F My boot <u>lace</u> is torn.

G Belgian <u>lace</u> is quite beautiful.

H Would you help Tim <u>lace</u> his boot?

J Next, <u>lace</u> the ribbons together.

STOP

Answers

SA Ⓐ Ⓑ Ⓒ Ⓓ   1 Ⓐ Ⓑ Ⓒ Ⓓ   2 Ⓕ Ⓖ Ⓗ Ⓙ   3 Ⓐ Ⓑ Ⓒ Ⓓ   4 Ⓕ Ⓖ Ⓗ Ⓙ

Directions: Darken the circle for the word or words that give the meaning of the underlined word, or write the answer in the space provided.

TRY THIS

Read the first sentence carefully. Look for clue words in the sentence. Then use each answer choice in place of the underlined word. Remember that the underlined word and your answer must have the same meaning.

Sample A

This <u>specific</u> offer is good for only two weeks. **Specific means—**

A particular   C radio

B cheap   D splendid

THINK IT THROUGH

The correct answer is A. Specific means "particular or exact." The clue words are "good for only two weeks." All four choices could describe the offer, but only particular has the same meaning as <u>specific</u>.

 STOP

---

1   The successful athlete has won <u>numerous</u> track awards during her long career. **Numerous means—**

    A many

    B foreign

    C sport

    D secret

2   This <u>pamphlet</u>, published by an environmental group, describes how we can help protect our world. **Pamphlet means—**

    F contest

    G speaker

    H celebration

    J booklet

3   The newest dance is fun, but it has many <u>complicated</u> steps that are hard to remember. **Complicated means—**

    A short

    B divided

    C difficult

    D slow

4   When we asked directions, the man <u>indicated</u> the correct route on our map. **Indicated means—**

    F drove

    G showed

    H left

    J closed

5   The police captain <u>dispatched</u> a rescue team to search for the lost girl. **Dispatched means—**

    A found

    B sent

    C questioned

    D cheered

6   A family finally moved into the house that has been <u>vacant</u> for six months. **Vacant means—**

_____

_____

_____

_____

_____

 STOP

Answers

SA Ⓐ Ⓑ Ⓒ Ⓓ   2 Ⓕ Ⓖ Ⓗ Ⓙ   4 Ⓕ Ⓖ Ⓗ Ⓙ

1 Ⓐ Ⓑ Ⓒ Ⓓ   3 Ⓐ Ⓑ Ⓒ Ⓓ   5 Ⓐ Ⓑ Ⓒ Ⓓ

Sample A

Drowsy means—

A forgetful

B greedy

C helpless

D sleepy

STOP

For questions 1–8, darken the circle for the word or words that have the same or almost the same meaning as the underlined word.

1 **Coax means—**

A sleep

B hide

C question

D persuade

2 **Mammoth means—**

F dusty

G shiny

H huge

J old

3 **To preserve something is to—**

A borrow it

B sell it

C throw it away

D save it

4 **To burrow means to—**

F escape

G surrender

H multiply

J dig

5 **Anxious means—**

A hopeful

B glad

C worried

D angry

6 **Grave means—**

F silly

G serious

H huge

J broken

7 **A voyage is a kind of—**

A store

B journey

C cage

D dance

8 **To disturb means to—**

F bother

G sneak

H disagree

J ask

Write your answer for the following:

9 What is an **error**?

_____

_____

_____

_____

_____

_____

_____

_____

GO ON

Answers

SA Ⓐ Ⓑ Ⓒ Ⓓ   2 Ⓕ Ⓖ Ⓗ Ⓙ   4 Ⓕ Ⓖ Ⓗ Ⓙ   6 Ⓕ Ⓖ Ⓗ Ⓙ   8 Ⓕ Ⓖ Ⓗ Ⓙ

1 Ⓐ Ⓑ Ⓒ Ⓓ   3 Ⓐ Ⓑ Ⓒ Ⓓ   5 Ⓐ Ⓑ Ⓒ Ⓓ   7 Ⓐ Ⓑ Ⓒ Ⓓ

Sample B

> Omar is in the <u>cast</u> of the school play.

In which sentence does <u>cast</u> have the same meaning as it does in the sentence above?

A   We all signed the <u>cast</u> on Dan's arm.

B   Dad can <u>cast</u> his fishing line a long way.

C   We will <u>cast</u> off at noon on Saturday and return Sunday night.

D   They're planning a party for everyone in the <u>cast</u>.

 STOP

For questions 10–14, darken the circle for the sentence in which the underlined word means the same as it does in the sentence in the box.

10

> We are <u>subject</u> to the laws of our state.

In which sentence does <u>subject</u> have the same meaning as it does in the sentence above?

A   What is the <u>subject</u> of the second sentence?

B   Art is Jennifer's favorite <u>subject</u> in school this year.

C   He was a loyal <u>subject</u> of King Phillip.

D   Everyone is <u>subject</u> to catching a cold right now.

11

> Can you see the ships in the <u>bay</u>?

In which sentence does <u>bay</u> have the same meaning as it does in the sentence above?

F   Fern likes <u>bay</u> windows.

G   Do wolves <u>bay</u> at the moon?

H   Their house faces the <u>bay</u>.

J   The hero holds his enemies at <u>bay</u>.

12

> The stairs had an <u>iron</u> railing.

In which sentence does <u>iron</u> have the same meaning as it does in the sentence above?

A   Do you have to <u>iron</u> this fabric?

B   <u>Iron</u> beams were used in the building.

C   We hope our friends can <u>iron</u> out their differences.

D   Should we buy Mom a new steam <u>iron</u>?

13

> Please <u>raise</u> that window.

In which sentence does <u>raise</u> have the same meaning as it does in the sentence above?

F   Did you <u>raise</u> your hand?

G   I <u>raise</u> peppers, carrots, and peas in my garden.

H   How much money did we <u>raise</u> for the community shelter?

J   There's no need to <u>raise</u> your voice.

14

> This floor is not <u>level</u>.

In which sentence does <u>level</u> have the same meaning as it does in the sentence above?

A   Please hand me the hammer and the <u>level</u>.

B   You should use one <u>level</u> cup of flour for that recipe.

C   The river rose to a <u>level</u> of twenty feet.

D   He reads on a fifth-grade <u>level</u>.

GO ON

Answers

SB Ⓐ Ⓑ Ⓒ Ⓓ   **11** Ⓕ Ⓖ Ⓗ Ⓙ   **13** Ⓕ Ⓖ Ⓗ Ⓙ
10 Ⓐ Ⓑ Ⓒ Ⓓ   **12** Ⓐ Ⓑ Ⓒ Ⓓ   **14** Ⓐ Ⓑ Ⓒ Ⓓ

Sample C

Those three people argue and <u>disagree</u> about everything. <u>Disagree</u> means—

A read

B sing

C quarrel

D plan

STOP

For questions 15–22, darken the circle for the word or words that give the meaning of the underlined word.

15 The military posted a <u>sentry</u> at the king's door to prevent anyone from entering. A <u>sentry</u> is a—

F sign

G crown

H guard

J gate

16 Did you fall asleep and <u>neglect</u> to complete your social studies? <u>Neglect</u> means—

A travel

B fail

C argue

D understand

17 Our newspaper is delivered at 7:00 A.M. <u>daily</u>. <u>Daily</u> means—

F every day

G twice a day

H every week

J once a month

18 He uses bold, <u>vivid</u> colors in his paintings. <u>Vivid</u> means—

A mixed

B soft

C strong

D pale

19 This show has an exciting <u>plot</u> that kept us interested. <u>Plot</u> means—

F hero

G story

H writer

J cast

20 Because conditions were hard, the settlers led a life filled with <u>strife</u>. <u>Strife</u> means—

A vacation

B illness

C struggle

D religion

21 I couldn't <u>budge</u> the heavy rock. <u>Budge</u> means—

F buy

G wash

H paint

J move

22 The newborn horse will probably <u>keel</u> over when it tries to stand. <u>Keel</u> means—

A fall

B scratch

C jump

D run

STOP

Answers

SC (A)(B)(C)(D) 16 (A)(B)(C)(D) 18 (A)(B)(C)(D) 20 (A)(B)(C)(D) 22 (A)(B)(C)(D)

15 (F)(G)(H)(J) 17 (F)(G)(H)(J) 19 (F)(G)(H)(J) 21 (F)(G)(H)(J)

MATH PROBLEM-SOLVING PLAN

THE PROBLEM-SOLVING PLAN

When solving math problems follow these steps:

STEP 1: WHAT IS THE QUESTION/GOAL?

Decide what must be found. This information is usually presented in the form of a question.

STEP 2: FIND THE FACTS

Locate the factual information in three different ways:

A. KEY FACTS are the facts you need to solve the problem.

B. FACTS YOU DON'T NEED are those facts that are not necessary for solving the problem.

C. ARE MORE FACTS NEEDED? Decide if you have enough information to solve the problem.

STEP 3: SELECT A STRATEGY

Decide what strategies you might use, how you will use them, and then estimate what your answer will be. If one strategy does not help solve the problem, try another.

STEP 4: SOLVE

Apply the strategy according to your plan. Use an operation if necessary, and clearly indicate your answer.

STEP 5: DOES YOUR RESPONSE MAKE SENSE?

Check to make sure that your answer makes sense. Use estimation or approximation strategies.

Directions: Use the problem-solving plan to solve this math problem.

PROBLEM/QUESTION:

Jason has $23.00. Does he have enough money to buy a CD for $14.99 and a cassette tape for $9.99?

STEP 1: WHAT IS THE QUESTION/GOAL?

_____

_____

_____

STEP 2: FIND THE FACTS

_____

_____

_____

STEP 3: SELECT A STRATEGY

_____

_____

_____

STEP 4: SOLVE

_____

_____

_____

STEP 5: DOES YOUR RESPONSE MAKE SENSE?

_____

_____

_____

_____

_____

PROBLEM/QUESTION:

Mr. Johnson has 2 twenty-dollar bills. 3 ten-dollar bills, 4 five-dollar bills and 4 one-dollar bills. He wants to buy something which costs $38. How can he pay for it with the exact change?

STEP 1: WHAT IS THE QUESTION/GOAL?

_____

_____

_____

STEP 2: FIND THE FACTS

_____

_____

_____

STEP 3: SELECT A STRATEGY

_____

_____

_____

STEP 4: SOLVE

_____

_____

_____

STEP 5: DOES YOUR RESPONSE MAKE SENSE?

_____

_____

_____

_____

_____

MATH PROBLEM SOLVING

UNDERSTANDING NUMERATION

Directions: Darken the circle for the correct answer, or write in the answer.

> **TRY THIS**
>
> Read each problem carefully. Be sure to think about which numbers stand for hundreds, tens, and ones.

Sample A

What number comes fourth if these numbers are arranged in order from least to greatest?

| 2,345 | 5,423 | 3,254 | 5,234 | 3,542 |

A 5,234   C 3,542

B 5,423   D 2,345

THINK IT THROUGH   The correct answer is A. 2,345 has a 2 in the thousands place and 3,254 has a 3 in the thousands place, as does 3,542. 5,234 comes next, since it has a 5 in the thousands place and a 2 in the hundreds place. The number 5,234 comes fourth.

STOP

---

1 What number means the same as (8 × 1000) + (6 × 100) + (1 × 1)?

A 861   C 8,601

B 80,061   D 8,610

2 Meiko made this chart of some mountain peaks. Which mountain peak is the shortest?

Mountain Peaks

Name	Height (in meters)
Mount Etna	3,390
Mount Blanc	4,807
Mount Fuji	3,776
Mount Cook	3,764

F Mount Etna   H Mount Fuji

G Mount Blanc   J Mount Cook

3 Which words mean 8,902?

A eighty-nine two

B eight thousand nine hundred

C eighty-nine thousand two

D eight thousand nine hundred two

4 The school cafeteria offers hamburgers on the menu on even-numbered days during the school week. How many days were hamburgers offered on the menu this month?

S	M	T	W	T	F	S
					1	2
3	4	5	6	7	8	9
10	11	12	13	14	15	16
17	18	19	20	21	22	23
24	25	26	27	28	29	30

_____

_____

STOP

Answers
SA ⒶⒷⒸⒹ   1 ⒶⒷⒸⒹ   2 ⒻⒼⒽⒿ   3 ⒶⒷⒸⒹ

Directions: Darken the circle for the correct answer, or write in the answer.

TRY THIS

Read the question twice before choosing your answer. Study any pictures given in the problem. Try using all the answer choices back in the problem. Then choose the answer that you think best answers the question.

Sample A

Which expression correctly completes the number sentence?

$$6 + 9 = \boxed{}$$

THINK IT THROUGH
The correct answer is C. Numbers may be reversed in addition. The answer will be the same.

A $9 - 6$ C $9 + 6$

B $15 - 6$ D $15 - 9$

STOP

---

1 What fraction tells how many of the dots are shaded in this figure?

A $\frac{3}{7}$

B $\frac{10}{3}$

C $\frac{3}{8}$

D $\frac{3}{10}$

2 What number makes this number sentence true?

$$\boxed{} \times 1 = 7$$

F 8

G 7

H 6

J 5

TEST TIP

Math problems can be like fill-in-the-blank questions. Try each choice until the number sentence is true.

---

3 Which decimal shows the part of the figure that is shaded?

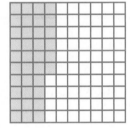

A 0.36   C 0.34

B 0.4   D 0.64

4 What number makes this sentence true?

$$4 + (2 + 3) = (4 + \boxed{}) + 3$$

_____

_____

_____

5 Which number sentence is in the same fact family as $3 \times 8 = 24$?

F $24 - 8 = 16$

G $8 + 3 = 11$

H $6 \times 4 = 24$

J $24 \div 8 = 3$

STOP

Answers
SA Ⓐ Ⓑ Ⓒ Ⓓ   1 Ⓐ Ⓑ Ⓒ Ⓓ   2 Ⓕ Ⓖ Ⓗ Ⓙ   3 Ⓐ Ⓑ Ⓒ Ⓓ   5 Ⓕ Ⓖ Ⓗ Ⓙ

Directions: Darken the circle for the correct answer, or write in the answer

Sample A

Wen is playing a game with the spinner shown here. If it is spun many times, which animal will it probably point to most often?

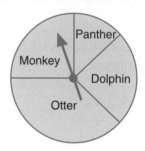

A Dolphin   C Otter

B Panther   D Monkey

STOP

The graph below shows some music recordings produced in 1997. Use it to answer questions 1 and 2.

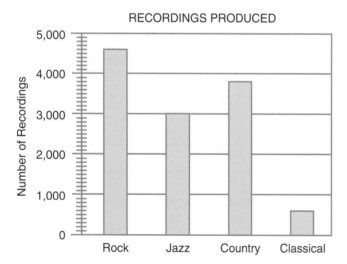

RECORDINGS PRODUCED

1 How many country recordings were produced?

_____

_____

2 How many more rock recordings were produced than jazz recordings?

A 600   C 1,600

B 800   D 4,000

3 The tally chart shows the number of butterflies spotted by four students during one week.

Name	Number of Butterflies				
	M	T	W	T	F
Dawn	I	IIII	III	ℕℲ I	II
Del	III	ℕℲ III	I	I	ℕℲ II
Rafael	IIII	II	ℕℲ	II	III
Kathy	I	ℕℲ I	I	III	I

Who spotted more than 6 butterflies on Tuesday?

F Dawn   H Rafael

G Del   J Kathy

GO ON➡

Answers
SA Ⓐ Ⓑ Ⓒ Ⓓ   2 Ⓐ Ⓑ Ⓒ Ⓓ   3 Ⓕ Ⓖ Ⓗ Ⓙ

The table lists the population of the 6 largest states and the number of members that each state has in the House of Representatives. Study the table. Then use it to answer questions 4 and 5.

State	Population	Representatives
California	29,839,250	52
Florida	13,003,362	23
Illinois	11,466,682	20
New York	18,044,505	31
Pennsylvania	11,964,710	21
Texas	17,059,805	30

4 Which two states combined have the same number of representatives as California?

_____

_____

_____

5 Which state has more than twice as many representatives as Florida?

A California

B New York

C Texas

D Pennsylvania

6 Terry placed these cubes in a bag. The "G" stands for green, and the "R" stands for red. How often would Terry probably pick a red cube if he reached into the bag without looking?

F 1 out of 9 times

G 1 out of 6 times

H 1 out of 4 times

J 1 out of 3 times

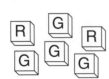

This chart shows the fish tank at a pet store.

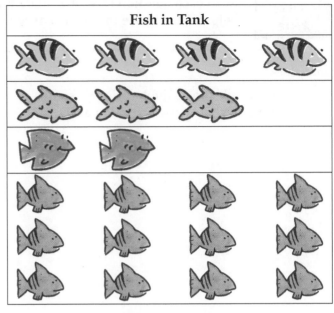

Fish in Tank

7 If the clerk catches a fish in a net, which one will it most likely be?

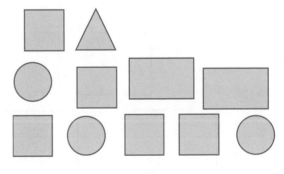

A   C

B   D

8 Minerva put these shapes into a box. If she reaches into the box and picks one shape, which shape will it most likely be?

F a square

G a triangle

H a rectangle

J a circle

Directions: Darken the circle for the correct answer, or write in the answer.

Sample A

The graph shows the location of some shapes. What shape is located at (D, 4)?

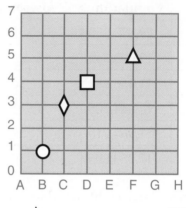

A △   C □

B ○   D ◊

STOP

1   Mona made a card for her mother. If Mona held the card up to a mirror, what would the card look like?

A

C

B

D

2   Which star can be folded on the dotted line so that the two sides match exactly?

F   H

G   J

3   Which names the shape of this traffic sign?

A   octagon

B   hexagon

C   triangle

D   rectangle

GO ON

Answers
SA Ⓐ Ⓑ Ⓒ Ⓓ   1 Ⓐ Ⓑ Ⓒ Ⓓ   2 Ⓕ Ⓖ Ⓗ Ⓙ   3 Ⓐ Ⓑ Ⓒ Ⓓ

4 Which shape has three corners and three sides that are exactly the same?

F

H

G

J

5 What shape is this rug?

_____

_____

_____

6 Ian is part of the flag patrol. Each day he hangs this flag on the pole.

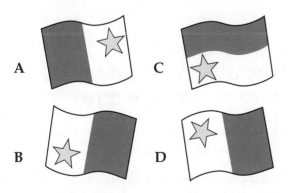

Today he hung the flag upside down by mistake. What did the flag look like?

A

C

B

D

7 Which letter has more than one line of symmetry?

F C   H H

G W   J K

8 Which figure represents a hexagon?

A   C

B   D

9 Each set of pieces below fold to form a three-dimensional shape. Which would form a cube?

F

H

G

J

10 How many corners does this figure have?

_____

_____

_____

_____

TEST TIP

To answer question 6, try to get a mental picture of the problem.

STOP

Answers

4 ⒡ ⒢ ⒣ ⒥   7 ⒡ ⒢ ⒣ ⒥   9 ⒡ ⒢ ⒣ ⒥

6 Ⓐ Ⓑ Ⓒ Ⓓ   8 Ⓐ Ⓑ Ⓒ Ⓓ

Directions: Darken the circle for the correct answer.

TRY THIS — Read each question carefully. Use the objects shown or named to help you answer each question.

Sample A

Which piece of chalk is the shortest?

A (_____) A

B (_____) B

C (___) C

D (_____) D

THINK IT THROUGH — The correct answer in C. Compare each piece of chalk. Piece C is the shortest.

STOP

1   Nancy put some muffins in the oven at the time shown on the clock. They will be ready at 7:20. How many minutes will the muffins take to bake?

   A   35 minutes

   B   20 minutes

   C   15 minutes

   D   10 minutes

2   What is the most likely temperature outside while Gwen shovels snow?

   F   68°F   H   55°F

   G   32°F   J   82°F

3   Which figure has the smallest shaded area?

A   C

B   D

4   Which unit of measurement is best to describe the weight of an egg?

   F   yards   H   inches

   G   liters   J   ounces

TEST TIP

To answer question 3, count squares to compare areas.

GO ON

Answers
SA ⒶⒷⒸⒹ   1 ⒶⒷⒸⒹ   2 ⒻⒼⒽⒿ   3 ⒶⒷⒸⒹ   4 ⒻⒼⒽⒿ

5 Kerry has these coins.

Which group of coins shows the same value?

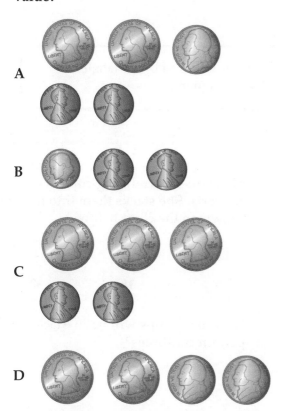

A

B

C

D

6 Danny read a book for 30 minutes. He finished reading at 3:00 P.M. Which clock shows the time that he began reading?

F | 2:30 P.M.

G | 2:15 P.M.

H | 3:15 P.M.

J | 2:45 P.M.

7 Which is most likely to be the length of a bike path?

A 25 yards

B 25 miles

C 25 feet

D 25 pounds

8 Use your centimeter ruler to help you answer this question. How many centimeters long is the trail from the squirrel to the nuts?

F $8\frac{1}{2}$ cm

G $10\frac{3}{4}$ cm

H $12\frac{1}{2}$ cm

J 13 cm

9 Tim looked at the thermometer in the morning to find out the temperature. He looked again at noon.

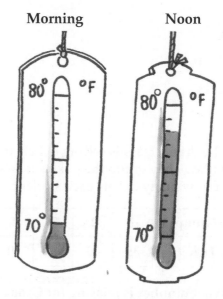

How does the noon temperature reading differ from the morning temperature?

A It is 10° warmer.

B It is 10° cooler.

C It is 8° warmer.

D It is 8° cooler.

Answers

5 Ⓐ Ⓑ Ⓒ Ⓓ   6 Ⓕ Ⓖ Ⓗ Ⓙ   7 Ⓐ Ⓑ Ⓒ Ⓓ   8 Ⓕ Ⓖ Ⓗ Ⓙ   9 Ⓐ Ⓑ Ⓒ Ⓓ

Directions: Darken the circle for the correct answer, or write in the answer.

TRY THIS

Read each question carefully. Look at each answer choice to see which number or figure will answer the question correctly.

Sample A

What comes next in the pattern shown here?

A ☾

B ☐

C △

D ☆

THINK IT THROUGH

The correct answer is <u>B</u>. In this pattern, each star is followed by a triangle, a square, or a moon. The missing shape should be the <u>square</u>.

STOP

---

1 What number completes the pattern in the boxes?

52	47	42		32	27

A 43

B 41

C 37

D 33

2 The drama class is selling tickets to a play. They group the tickets to keep track of how many tickets each student takes.

Group	1	2	3	4	5
Tickets	35	40		50	55

What number is missing for Group 3?

F 41

G 45

H 49

J 56

3 Mrs. Green is counting cups in the cafeteria. She stacks them into the groups shown on the chart below.

Stack	1	2	3	4	5
Cups	8	16	24	32	

How many cups will be in Stack 5 if the pattern continues?

A 33

B 38

C 40

D 48

4 What number completes the pattern in the boxes?

48	55	62		76	83

_____

_____

_____

_____

STOP

Answers
SA Ⓐ Ⓑ Ⓒ Ⓓ   **1** Ⓐ Ⓑ Ⓒ Ⓓ   **2** Ⓕ Ⓖ Ⓗ Ⓙ   **3** Ⓐ Ⓑ Ⓒ Ⓓ

Directions: Darken the circle for the correct answer, or write in the answer.

TRY THIS
Round numbers when you estimate. For some problems, there are no exact answers. Then you should take your best guess. You can check your answer by using the numbers given in the problem.

Sample A

Billy picked 5 baskets of apples in his uncle's orchard. Each basket held *about* 36 apples. Estimate about how many apples Billy picked.

A 100   C 300

B 200   D 500

THINK IT THROUGH
The correct answer is B. 36 is rounded up to 40. Next, multiply 40 × 5 to estimate how many apples Billy picked. The answer is 200.

STOP

1 Mrs. Rogers' Rose Farm had 723 rosebushes. She sold 411 of them. Estimate *about* how many rosebushes Mrs. Rogers had left.

A 100

B 200

C 300

D 400

2 The school store has 29 boxes of pencils. There are 34 pencils in each box. Estimate *about* how many pencils the school store has.

_____

_____

_____

_____

3 Ann keeps her sticker collection in special books. If each book holds 12 stickers, estimate *about* how many books she would need to hold 88 stickers.

F 6

G 8

H 9

J 10

4 The map shows the distances between five cities. Use the map to help you answer this question.

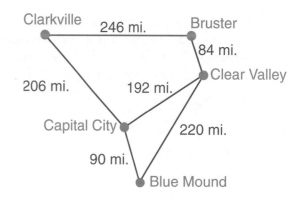

Mr. Tanner wants to drive from Clarkville to Clear Valley using the shortest distance. Estimate *about* how far Mr. Tanner will drive.

A 200 miles

B 300 miles

C 500 miles

D 700 miles

STOP

Answers
SA Ⓐ Ⓑ Ⓒ Ⓓ   1 Ⓐ Ⓑ Ⓒ Ⓓ   3 Ⓕ Ⓖ Ⓗ Ⓙ   4 Ⓐ Ⓑ Ⓒ Ⓓ

Directions: Darken the circle for the correct answer, or write in the answer.

TRY THIS Read each question carefully. Look for information in the problem that will help you solve it. Then choose the correct answer.

Sample A

Gabriela makes decorative pillows as a hobby. She can sew a pillow in 25 minutes. What additional information is needed to find how long it takes Gabriela to sew an entire set of pillows?

A   The length of each pillow

B   The number of pillows in a set

C   The cost of the materials

D   The number of sets Maria has made

THINK IT THROUGH The correct answer is <u>B</u>. Gabriela can sew a pillow in 25 minutes. To find how long it takes her to sew a set of pillows, you must know <u>the number of pillows in a set</u>. This number is multiplied by 25 minutes per pillow.

STOP

---

1 Julio can save $12 a week from his allowance and paper route. Which number sentence shows how to find the amount that he will have saved in 6 weeks?

A $12 \times 6 = \square$

B $12 - 6 = \square$

C $6 + \square = 12$

D $12 \div 6 = \square$

2 Frank likes hamburgers better than hot dogs. He likes peanut butter less than hot dogs. He prefers pizza to hamburgers. Which food is his favorite?

_____

_____

_____

_____

_____

3 What number is inside the triangle, outside the square, and is an even number?

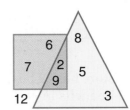

F   3

G   5

H   8

J   12

4 The library placed 8 new videotapes on each shelf of the display case. There are 4 shelves in the case. Which number sentence shows how to find the number of new tapes in the display case?

A $8 \div 4 = \square$

B $8 + 4 = \square$

C $8 - 4 = \square$

D $8 \times 4 = \square$

STOP

Answers

SA Ⓐ Ⓑ Ⓒ Ⓓ   1 Ⓐ Ⓑ Ⓒ Ⓓ   3 Ⓕ Ⓖ Ⓗ Ⓙ   4 Ⓐ Ⓑ Ⓒ Ⓓ

Directions: Darken the circle for the correct answer. Darken the circle for NH (Not Here) if the answer is not given. If no choices are given, write in the answer.

TRY THIS

Study each problem carefully. Decide if you should add, subtract, multiply, or divide. Then work the problem on scratch paper. Be sure to line up the digits. Remember to regroup where necessary.

Sample A

59
× 33

A 19,470
B 3,340
C 1,947
D 334
E NH

THINK IT THROUGH

The correct answer is <u>C</u>. When you multiply 59 by 33, the answer is <u>1,947</u>. You can check this by multiplying 33 by <u>59</u>. You should get the same answer.

STOP

1

$7 \times \square = 49$

A 0
B 6
C 42
D 56
E NH

2

722
− 39

_____

_____

_____

_____

3

$184 + 767 + 302 = \square$

F 1,353
G 1,253
H 1,243
J 1,153
K NH

4

$63 \div 9 =$

A 4
B 5
C 6
D 7
E NH

5

$6\overline{)18}$

F 24
G 12
H 3
J 2
K NH

6

32
× 6

A 192
B 182
C 98
D 38
E NH

STOP

Answers

SA Ⓐ Ⓑ Ⓒ Ⓓ Ⓔ   **3** Ⓕ Ⓖ Ⓗ Ⓙ Ⓚ   **5** Ⓕ Ⓖ Ⓗ Ⓙ Ⓚ
1 Ⓐ Ⓑ Ⓒ Ⓓ Ⓔ   **4** Ⓐ Ⓑ Ⓒ Ⓓ Ⓔ   **6** Ⓐ Ⓑ Ⓒ Ⓓ Ⓔ

Directions: Darken the circle for the correct answer. Darken the circle for NH (Not Here) if the answer is not given.

Read each problem carefully. Decide if you need to round, add, subtract, multiply, or divide the numbers. Think about which numbers stand for ones, tens, and hundreds. Work the problem on scratch paper. Remember to regroup where necessary.

Sample A

Great Meadow Elementary has 1,058 students. *About* how many students are there if the number is rounded to the nearest ten?

A 1,100

B 1,060

C 1,050

D 6,0

E NH

The correct answer is <u>B</u>. When rounding to the nearest 10, look at the number in the ones column. If it is greater than 4, round up. 1,058 is rounded to <u>1,060</u>.

---

1 Wanda has 16 compact disks of rock music and 8 compact disks of country music. How many compact disks does Wanda have altogether?

A 2

B 3

C 8

D 24

E NH

2 It took Sue 45 minutes to do her homework. She spent 22 minutes working math problems and 10 minutes answering science questions. The remaining time she read. How many minutes did Sue read?

F 35

G 32

H 23

J 13

K NH

3 Sam is reading a book with 194 pages. He reads 83 pages.

How many pages does he have left to read?

A 101

B 110

C 111

D 121

E NH

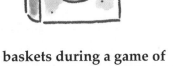

4 Julio makes 8 baskets during a game of basketball. Each basket is worth 2 points.

How many points did Julio score during the game?

F 6

G 10

H 15

J 18

K NH

Answers

SA ⒶⒷ©ⒹⒺ   2 ⒻⒼⒽⒿⓀ   4 ⒻⒼⒽⒿⓀ
1 ⒶⒷ©ⒹⒺ   3 ⒶⒷ©ⒹⒺ

Sample A

43
× 6

A 109
B 248
C 258
D 259
E NH

STOP

Sample B

Sonia used 32 blocks to build a castle. She used 12 rectangles and 15 squares. The other blocks were triangles.

How many triangles did Sonia use to build a castle?

F 27
G 17
H 5
J 3
K NH

STOP

For questions 1–22, darken the circle for the correct answer. Darken the circle for NH (Not Here) if the correct answer is not given, or write in the answer.

1 20)340

A 170
B 120
C 17
D 12
E NH

2 257 × 4

F 1,121
G 1,191
H 1,091
J 1,021
K NH

3 56 ÷ 7 = ☐

A 6
B 7
C 8
D 9
E NH

4 426 − 52

_____

5 5 × 4 = ☐

F 1
G 9
H 15
J 25
K NH

6 5)67

A 14
B 13 R2
C 13
D 11 R4
E NH

7 400 − 139

F 261
G 339
H 371
J 539
K NH

8 50 × 30

A 1,500
B 1,050
C 1,015
D 150
E NH

GO ON

Answers

SA Ⓐ Ⓑ Ⓒ Ⓓ Ⓔ 2 Ⓕ Ⓖ Ⓗ Ⓙ Ⓚ 6 Ⓐ Ⓑ Ⓒ Ⓓ Ⓔ
SB Ⓕ Ⓖ Ⓗ Ⓙ Ⓚ 3 Ⓐ Ⓑ Ⓒ Ⓓ Ⓔ 7 Ⓕ Ⓖ Ⓗ Ⓙ Ⓚ
1 Ⓐ Ⓑ Ⓒ Ⓓ Ⓔ 5 Ⓕ Ⓖ Ⓗ Ⓙ Ⓚ 8 Ⓐ Ⓑ Ⓒ Ⓓ Ⓔ

9

$750 + 228 + 56 = \square$

F 924
G 934
H 1,024
J 1,034
K NH

10 Chou has $10.00. She buys lunch for $5.23, including tax.

How much money will Chou have left?

_____
_____
_____
_____

11 Melissa buys these school supplies.

How much will these three items cost altogether before tax is added?

A $15.08
B $14.08
C $12.98
D $12.08
E NH

12 Coach Reid orders a case of 450 baseball caps. He gives out 231 caps the first week.

How many caps are left?

F 119
G 129
H 219
J 229
K NH

13 A box of popcorn costs 5 tickets at the school fair. Bill buys 7 boxes of popcorn for himself and his 6 cousins.

How many tickets did Bill use to buy the popcorn?

A 12
B 22
C 35
D 40
E NH

14 The librarian ordered 1,236 books last year. *About* how many books were ordered if that number is rounded to the nearest hundred?

F 1,000
G 1,200
H 1,240
J 1,300
K NH

15 Marlon bought a coat for $37.88. *About* how much did Marlon spend if that amount is rounded to the nearest dollar?

A $37.00
B $37.90
C $38.00
D $40.00
E NH

GO ON

16 Mrs. Samuels buys 18 buttons. She has 2 shirts, and she puts the same number of buttons on each shirt.

How many buttons will Mrs. Samuels put on each shirt if she uses all the buttons?

F   6

G   9

H   10

J   12

K   NH

17 Mrs. Maldonado sells 62 calculators in one week. Each calculator costs $4.

How much money did Mrs. Maldonado make selling the calculators?

A $258

B $256

C $248

D $246

E   NH

18 Ed had to pack empty soda bottles for the recycling center. Each box holds 8 bottles.

How many boxes will Ed need to pack 72 bottles?

F   8

G   7

H   6

J   5

K   NH

19 A toy company has 57 wagons that need wheels.

If 4 wheels are put on each wagon, how many wheels will the toy company use?

A   228

B   224

C   208

D   204

E   NH

20 Jim is making a birdhouse. He has a board that is 37 inches long. He cuts a piece that is 7 inches long for the roof.

If Jim cuts the rest of the board into 5 equal pieces to make the sides and floor of the birdhouse, how long will each piece be?

_____

_____

_____

_____

_____

21 Kyra's dog weighs 115 pounds. Her brother's dog weighs 42 pounds. How much heavier is Kyra's dog than her brother's dog?

F   73 pounds

G   83 pounds

H   157 pounds

J   167 pounds

K   NH

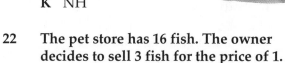

22 The pet store has 16 fish. The owner decides to sell 3 fish for the price of 1.

If people buy 3 fish each time, how many extra fish will be left?

A   0

B   1

C   2

D   3

E   NH

STOP

Answers

16 Ⓕ Ⓖ Ⓗ Ⓙ Ⓚ	18 Ⓕ Ⓖ Ⓗ Ⓙ Ⓚ	21 Ⓕ Ⓖ Ⓗ Ⓙ Ⓚ
17 Ⓐ Ⓑ Ⓒ Ⓓ Ⓔ	19 Ⓐ Ⓑ Ⓒ Ⓓ Ⓔ	22 Ⓐ Ⓑ Ⓒ Ⓓ Ⓔ

Sample A

What number makes the number sentence true?

$$5 + (2 + \square) = (5 + 2) + 6$$

A 2

B 5

C 6

D 7

STOP

For questions 1–36, darken the circle for the correct answer, or write in the answer.

1 A museum recorded the number of people visiting in one week. Which day had the largest number of visitors?

Museum Attendance	
Sunday	4,198
Monday	2,797
Tuesday	2,143
Wednesday	3,033
Thursday	3,419
Friday	3,851
Saturday	4,382

A Sunday

B Thursday

C Friday

D Saturday

2 What number means the same as $(2 \times 1,000) + (7 \times 10) + (8 \times 1)$?

F 278

G 2,078

H 2,708

J 8,680

3 Jamal sold 3,460 raffle tickets. Write this number in words.

_____

_____

_____

4 Which expression will correctly complete the number sentence?

$$4 + 8 = \boxed{}$$

A $12 + 4$

B 8×4

C $8 - 4$

D $8 + 4$

5 Which number has a four in the thousands place and a three in the tens place?

F 4,631

G 3,461

H 4,384

J 2,430

6 Which two numbers make the sentence correct?

$$(3 + \square) + 5 = (\square + 7) + 4$$

A 5 and 2

B 3 and 1

C 2 and 1

D 5 and 3

7 Which number sentence is in the same fact family as $5 \times 4 = 20$?

F $5 + 4 = 9$

G $20 \div 4 = 5$

H $20 - 9 = 11$

J $10 \times 2 = 20$

GO ON

Answers

SA Ⓐ Ⓑ Ⓒ Ⓓ   2 Ⓕ Ⓖ Ⓗ Ⓙ   5 Ⓕ Ⓖ Ⓗ Ⓙ   7 Ⓕ Ⓖ Ⓗ Ⓙ

1 Ⓐ Ⓑ Ⓒ Ⓓ   4 Ⓐ Ⓑ Ⓒ Ⓓ   6 Ⓐ Ⓑ Ⓒ Ⓓ

8 Which mixed number tells what part of the figures are shaded?

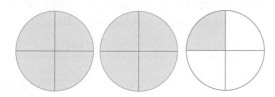

A $2\frac{3}{4}$

B 3

C $2\frac{1}{3}$

D $2\frac{1}{4}$

9 Students in Mrs. Ford's class are reading a book. Mike has read $\frac{2}{7}$ of the book, Ling has read $\frac{5}{6}$ of the book, Dikim has read $\frac{1}{5}$ of the book, and Artez has read $\frac{3}{4}$ of the book. How would these amounts be listed in order from most to least?

F $\frac{5}{6}, \frac{3}{4}, \frac{2}{7}, \frac{1}{5}$

G $\frac{3}{4}, \frac{1}{5}, \frac{5}{6}, \frac{2}{7}$

H $\frac{1}{5}, \frac{2}{7}, \frac{3}{4}, \frac{5}{6}$

J $\frac{5}{6}, \frac{2}{7}, \frac{3}{4}, \frac{1}{5}$

10 Which decimal tells the part of the figure that is shaded?

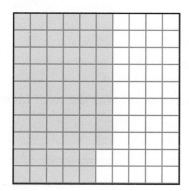

A 0.43

B 0.58

C 0.42

D 0.60

11 Martha records the weight of four puppies.

Puppy	Weight
Red	19.23 pounds
Spot	20.09 pounds
Chico	12.76 pounds
Buster	15.42 pounds

Which dog's weight shows a two in the tenths place?

_____

_____

_____

_____

12 Which figure is $\frac{2}{3}$ shaded?

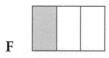

F

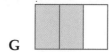

G

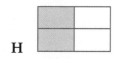

H

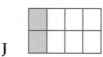

J

13 After picking berries, three children compared the amounts in their buckets. Luis' bucket was $\frac{2}{3}$ full, Elisa's bucket was $\frac{4}{5}$ full, and Lillian's bucket was $\frac{3}{8}$ full. How would the amounts be arranged if they were ordered from least to most?

A $\frac{3}{8}, \frac{4}{5}, \frac{2}{3}$

B $\frac{2}{3}, \frac{3}{8}, \frac{4}{5}$

C $\frac{3}{8}, \frac{2}{3}, \frac{4}{5}$

D $\frac{4}{5}, \frac{2}{3}, \frac{3}{8}$

GO ON

Answers

8 Ⓐ Ⓑ Ⓒ Ⓓ　　**9** Ⓕ Ⓖ Ⓗ Ⓙ　　**10** Ⓐ Ⓑ Ⓒ Ⓓ　　**12** Ⓕ Ⓖ Ⓗ Ⓙ　　**13** Ⓐ Ⓑ Ⓒ Ⓓ

This chart shows the number of days spent in each city by the Smith family on their vacation to Florida. Use the chart to answer questions 14 and 15.

City	Number of Days
Miami	III
Ft. Lauderdale	II
Orlando	NN III
Tampa	IIII
Naples	NN

14 In how many cities did the Smith family spend more than 3 days?

F 2

G 3

H 4

J 5

15 How many more days did the Smith family spend in Orlando than in Naples?

A 3

B 10

C 13

D 14

16 If you spin the spinner many times, which number will the spinner point to most often?

F 1

G 2

H 3

J 4

The graph shows the results of a survey taken at the mall about the desserts most people like. Use the graph to answer questions 17–19.

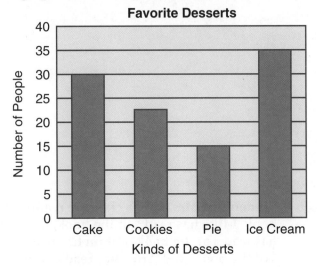

17 How many more people liked ice cream than pie?

A 50

B 40

C 30

D 20

18 What total number of people liked cake?

F 15

G 30

H 35

J 40

19 Which dessert was the least favorite?

_____

_____

_____

_____

GO ON

20 Jessica has these coins.

Which group of coins shows the same value?

A

B

C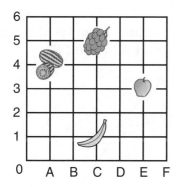

D

21 The graph shows the location of some fruit. What fruit is located at (C, 5)?

F watermelon

G banana

H grapes

J apple

22 Ruth has this bill. She buys the baseball.

How much change will Ruth get back?

A 47¢   C 66¢

B 57¢   D 67¢

23 What shape is the envelope?

_____

_____

24 Look at the angles labeled A, B, and C on the figure shown here.

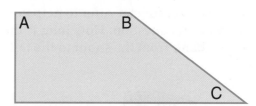

Which angle shown in the answer choices matches the angle for letter B?

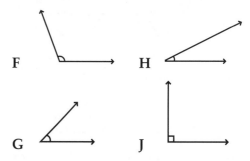

GO ON ➡

Answers
20 Ⓐ Ⓑ Ⓒ Ⓓ   **21** Ⓕ Ⓖ Ⓗ Ⓙ   **22** Ⓐ Ⓑ Ⓒ Ⓓ   **24** Ⓕ Ⓖ Ⓗ Ⓙ

25 The clock shows the time Alex finished mowing the lawn. It took him 50 minutes. At what time did he begin mowing the lawn?

A 2:30

B 3:00

C 3:15

D 4:00

26 Which chain is the longest?

F

G

H

J

27 Use your centimeter ruler to help you answer this question. How long is the piggy bank from the snout to the tail?

_____

_____

_____

_____

28 Mel decided to take a walk in the woods. He looked at the thermometer before he left. Mel looked at the thermometer again when he returned from his walk.

Before   After

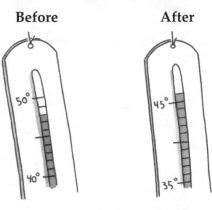

What is the difference in the temperature from the time before and after Mel took his walk?

A 2° warmer   C 12° warmer

B 2° cooler   D 12° cooler

29 What is the missing number that completes the pattern in the boxes?

101	104	107		113	116

F 117   H 112

G 114   J 110

30 Use your inch ruler. What is the distance from point A to point B?

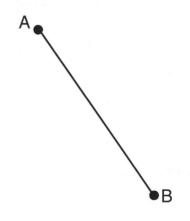

A 1 inch   C 3 inches

B 2 inches   D 4 inches

GO ON ▶

31 The cost of some software is between $60 and $70. The sum of the digits is 18. Which amount could be the price of the software?

F $57.80

G $60.78

H $66.60

J $76.50

32 The population of Alaska in the 1990 census was 525,000. What other information do you need to have to determine how this state's population compares with the population of Hawaii?

A The population of Hawaii in 1990

B The state with the largest population

C The state with the smallest population

D The population of California

33 Which number is greater than 10, less than 15, and is not inside the circle?

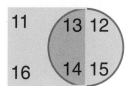

F 11

G 12

H 13

J 16

34 The movie theater has 325 seats. The ticket seller has already sold 186 tickets. Estimate *about* how many seats are left in the theater.

A 100

B 200

C 400

D 500

35 Ms. Fernandez is making a quilt. The chart shows the number of triangles she cuts and groups together to make a square.

Square	1	2	3	4	5
Number of Triangles	12	20	28	36	

How many triangles will be in Square 5 if the pattern continues?

_____

_____

_____

_____

36 Ms. Kwon works in the school cafeteria. She has 138 cartons of milk that need to be stacked on the refrigerator shelf. She can fit 14 cartons in a row. Estimate *about* how many rows of milk cartons Ms. Kwon can make.

F 2

G 10

H 50

J 100

TEST TIP

You can often use rounded numbers to estimate. Question 36 asks how many rows Ms. Kwon can make with 138 milk cartons, placing 14 cartons in each row. Notice that 138 is very close to 140. Since the answer asks you to estimate, you can use 140. Use mental math to divide 140 by 14.

STOP

Answers

31 Ⓕ Ⓖ Ⓗ Ⓙ   **32** Ⓐ Ⓑ Ⓒ Ⓓ   **33** Ⓕ Ⓖ Ⓗ Ⓙ   **34** Ⓐ Ⓑ Ⓒ Ⓓ   **36** Ⓕ Ⓖ Ⓗ Ⓙ

LANGUAGE

Directions: Read each sentence carefully. Then darken the circle for the correct answer to each question, or write in the answer.

TRY THIS
Pretend that you are writing each sentence. Use the rules you have learned for capitalization, punctuation, word usage, and sentence structure to choose the correct answer.

Sample A

> Human beings cannot live on the moon
> **(1)**
> today. For one thing, there is no air or water
> **(2)**
> on the moon. Also, the moon's climate is
> **(3)**
> very extreme. The first time people walked
> **(4)**
> on the moon was in 1969. The days are
> **(5)**
> boiling hot, and the nights are freezing cold.

Which sentence does *not* belong in this paragraph?

A 1

B 2

C 3

D 4

THINK IT THROUGH
The correct answer is D. Choices A, B, and C are about this topic. Choice D, *The first time people walked on the moon was in 1969*, is not about this topic.

Stormy Weather

Loretta is a member of her town's baseball team. She looks forward to her baseball games, but many times the games are canceled because of bad weather. Loretta became interested in what causes storms. So when her class was studying about weather, Loretta was eager to do a report on the subject.

1. Which of these topics should *not* be included in Loretta's report?

A   the causes of rain

B   how the sun affects weather

C   vacation places with good weather

D   how thunderstorms are created

STOP

GO ON

Answers
SA Ⓐ Ⓑ Ⓒ Ⓓ   **1** Ⓐ Ⓑ Ⓒ Ⓓ

Loretta needed to use the dictionary to look up some words to use in her report.

barometer

forecast

sleet

precipitation

2   How can these words be changed so that they are in alphabetical (ABC) order?

F   put <u>barometer</u> after <u>forecast</u>

G   put <u>sleet</u> before <u>forecast</u>

H   put <u>precipitation</u> first

J   put <u>sleet</u> after <u>precipitation</u>

3   Which guide words might mark the page on which Loretta would find the word *hail*?

A   haddock–halibut

B   Halloween–hammer

C   hangar–harbor

D   hardly–harness

TEST TIP

Remember the rules for putting two words in alphabetical, or ABC, order. If the first letters are the same, look at the second letters. If the second letters also are the same, look at the third letters.

Study this Index from a book Loretta found about weather. Then answer questions 4–7.

Index
air pressure, 90–92
clouds
cirrus, 51
cumulus, 52
stratus, 48
hail, 61–63
hurricane, 74–76
lightning, 66–70
rain, 54–64
sleet, 61–64
tornado, 70–72
weather forecasting, 106–108

4   On what pages could Loretta find out how weather is forecast?

_____

_____

_____

_____

_____

_____

5   All of these pages would have information about clouds *except*—

F   48   H   52

G   51   J   90

6   Which page would probably have information about the causes of tornadoes?

A   55   C   71

B   62   D   75

7   Which page would have information about lightning?

F   51   H   71

G   67   J   75

GO ON

Here is a rough draft of the first part of Loretta's report. Read the rough draft carefully. Then answer questions 8–14.

Understanding the Weather

Did you ever notice how much about the weather people talk? That's
(1) **(2)**

probably because much of what we do depends on the weather. A rainy
(3)

day can ruin a picnic. On a cold day a car can have trouble starting
(4)

because of the cold.

To find out what kind of weather you're going to have, you could
(5)

listen to a weather report. The weather report will tell you about a few
(6)

things. One thing it will tell you is the temperature this is how hot or
(7)

cold the air is. Another thing it will tell you is whether there will be
(8)

any precipitation. Such as rain or snow. About the wind is the third
(9) **(10)**

thing that a weather report will tell you. It will tell you how hard the
(11)

wind is blowing. It will tell you from which direction it is coming.
(12)

Knowing what the temperature, the precipitation, and the winds are
(13)

like will give you a good idea about the weather for the day.

GO ON ➡

8 **What is the best way to write sentence 1?**

   A Did you ever notice about the weather how much people talk?

   B Did you ever notice how much people talk about the weather?

   C Did you ever notice how much people about the weather talk?

   D As it is written.

9 **The best way to write sentence 3 is—**

   F By a rainy day, a picnic can be ruined.

   G A picnic by a rainy day can be ruined.

   H A rainy day a picnic can ruin.

   J As it is written.

10 **Which sentence could be added after sentence 4?**

   A About 44,000 storms occur in the world every day.

   B Some parts of the United States have very little rain.

   C A storm can cancel a baseball game.

   D A person who studies the weather is a meteorologist.

11 **Which sentence needlessly repeats a word or group of words?**

   F 4   **H** 8

   G 6   **J** 13

TEST TIP

When looking for a sentence that combines two sentences *without changing their meaning*, select an answer that does not add or change information.

---

12 **What is the best way to write sentence 7?**

   A One thing it will tell you is the temperature, this, is how hot or cold the air is.

   B One thing it will tell you is the temperature. This is how hot or cold the air is.

   C One thing it will tell you is the temperature how hot or cold the air is.

   D As it is written.

13 **Which group of words is not a complete sentence? Write the number of the sentence.**

_____

_____

_____

14 **Which sentence best combines sentences 11 and 12 without changing their meaning?**

   F It will tell you how hard the wind is blowing it will tell you from which direction it is coming.

   G It will tell you how hard the wind is blowing and from which direction it is coming.

   H How hard the wind is blowing and which direction it is from.

   J It will tell you which direction it is coming from it will tell you how hard the wind is blowing.

GO ON ➡

Answers

8 Ⓐ Ⓑ Ⓒ Ⓓ   **10** Ⓐ Ⓑ Ⓒ Ⓓ   **12** Ⓐ Ⓑ Ⓒ Ⓓ

9 Ⓕ Ⓖ Ⓗ Ⓙ   **11** Ⓕ Ⓖ Ⓗ Ⓙ   **14** Ⓕ Ⓖ Ⓗ Ⓙ

Here is the next part of Loretta's rough draft for her report. This part has certain words and phrases underlined. Read the draft carefully. Then answer questions 15–22.

Storms are the violent and dangerous aspects of weather. The kind of
(14)   (15)

storm we see <u>most often is the thunderstorm?</u> A thunderstorm happens
(16)

<u>when theres' a great</u> difference in the temperature between the air close

to the earth and the air higher up. A thunderstorm often happens on a
(17)

hot and muggy summer afternoon. The <u>hot air near the earth</u> is pushed
(18)

up by cooler air around it. Moisture-laden, threatening clouds form, and
(19)

it starts getting darker. Then lightning flashes, <u>thunder rolls and winds</u>
(20)

<u>blow</u>. The storm usually lasts a few minutes. <u>When it was over,</u> the sky
(21)   (22)

usually clears.

Sometimes thunderstorms <u>come with Tornadoes.</u> A tornado is <u>the more</u>
(23)   (24)

<u>violent kind of storm over land.</u> A tornado comes up suddenly. At first it looks
(25)   (26)

like a thick dark cloud coming from a distance. Then <u>an funnel–shaped</u>
(27)

<u>piece</u> dangles down from the cloud. When the funnel touches the ground
(28)

it picks up everything in its path.

GO ON

15 In sentence 15, <u>most often is the thunderstorm?</u> is best written—

    A most often is the thunderstorm.

    B more often is the thunderstorm?

    C most often is the thunderstorm!

    D As it is written.

16 In sentence 16, <u>when there's a great</u> is best written—

    F when theres a great

    G when ther'es a great

    H when there's a great

    J As it is written.

17 In sentence 18, <u>hot air near the earth</u> is best written—

    A hot, air near the earth

    B hot air, near the earth

    C hot, air, near the earth

    D As it is written.

18 In sentence 20, <u>thunder rolls and winds blow</u> is best written—

    F thunder rolls and winds, blow

    G thunder rolls, and winds blow

    H thunder, rolls and winds blow

    J As it is written.

19 In sentence 22, <u>When it was over</u> is best written—

    A When it is over

    B When it has been over

    C When it will be over

    D As it is written.

20 In sentence 23, <u>come with Tornadoes</u> is best written—

    F come with tornadoes

    G comes with tornadoes

    H comes with Tornadoes

    J As it is written.

21 In sentence 24, <u>the more violent kind of storm over land</u> is best written—

    A the much more violent kind of storm over land

    B the more violenter kind of storm over land

    C the most violent kind of storm over land

    D As it is written.

22 In sentence 27, <u>an funnel–shaped piece</u> is best written—

    F a funnel–shaped piece

    G an funnel–shaped piece,

    H an Funnel–Shaped piece

    J As it is written.

STOP

Answers

| **15** Ⓐ Ⓑ Ⓒ Ⓓ | **17** Ⓐ Ⓑ Ⓒ Ⓓ | **19** Ⓐ Ⓑ Ⓒ Ⓓ | **21** Ⓐ Ⓑ Ⓒ Ⓓ |
| **16** Ⓕ Ⓖ Ⓗ Ⓙ | **18** Ⓕ Ⓖ Ⓗ Ⓙ | **20** Ⓕ Ⓖ Ⓗ Ⓙ | **22** Ⓕ Ⓖ Ⓗ Ⓙ |

TEST PREP **725**

Directions: Read each sentence carefully. If one of the words is misspelled, darken the circle for that word. If all the words are spelled correctly, then darken the circle for *No mistake*.

TRY THIS — Read each sentence carefully. If you are not sure of an answer, first decide which answer choices are spelled correctly. Then see if you can recognize the misspelled word from your reading experience.

Sample A

Hakim was <u>absint</u> from <u>class</u> on <u>Tuesday</u>. <u>No mistake</u>
        A   B   C   D

THINK IT THROUGH — The correct answer is A. All of the other words except <u>absint</u> are spelled correctly. <u>Absint</u> is spelled a-b-s-e-n-t.

STOP

1   Meryl was <u>dizzy</u> from <u>spinning</u> <u>around</u> so much. <u>No mistake</u>
              A   B   C   D

2   The <u>storm</u> produced <u>driveing</u> rain and <u>hail</u>. <u>No mistake</u>
            F   G   H   J

3   Birds <u>steak</u> out a <u>territory</u> when they are <u>nesting</u>. <u>No mistake</u>
             A   B   C   D

4   The <u>pair</u> that Beth bought was <u>ripe</u> and <u>sweet</u>. <u>No mistake</u>
            F   G   H   J

5   Mr. Chung <u>traveled</u> a <u>great</u> deal when he was <u>younger</u>. <u>No mistake</u>
                   A   B   C   D

6   Lucia <u>received</u> an <u>imvitation</u> to the <u>birthday</u> party. <u>No mistake</u>
                F   G   H   J

7   There was a <u>livly</u> <u>debate</u> about expanding the park <u>system</u>. <u>No mistake</u>
                     A   B   C   D

8   Roland <u>enjoys</u> eating <u>cereal</u> with <u>blueberrys</u> in it. <u>No mistake</u>
                F   G   H   J

STOP

Answers
SA Ⓐ Ⓑ Ⓒ Ⓓ   2 Ⓕ Ⓖ Ⓗ Ⓙ   4 Ⓕ Ⓖ Ⓗ Ⓙ   6 Ⓕ Ⓖ Ⓗ Ⓙ   8 Ⓕ Ⓖ Ⓗ Ⓙ
1 Ⓐ Ⓑ Ⓒ Ⓓ   3 Ⓐ Ⓑ Ⓒ Ⓓ   5 Ⓐ Ⓑ Ⓒ Ⓓ   7 Ⓐ Ⓑ Ⓒ Ⓓ

Sample A

A Canadian Vacation

    Charley and his family spent a month vacationing in Canada. During that time they visited many places and had an exciting time. Charley wanted to tell his favorite aunt all about the places he visited, so he wrote her a letter.

Charley wants to locate some of the cities in Canada that he visited. He should look in—

A an index.

B an atlas.

C a newspaper.

D a table of contents.

Charley made a concept web to help him write his letter. Study the concept web and use it to answer questions 1 and 2.

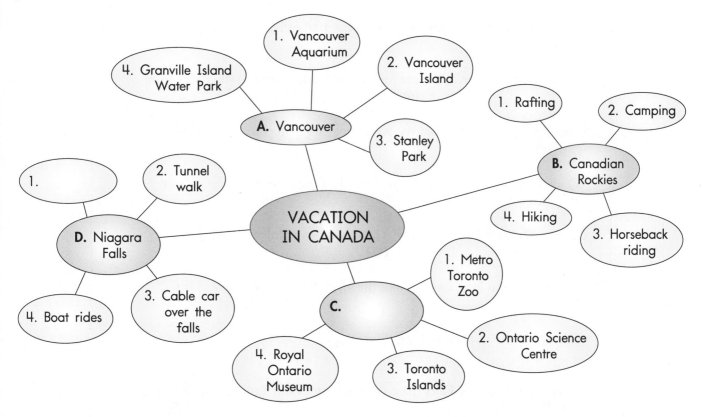

1   **Which of these belongs in circle C?**

    A Toronto

    B Montreal

    C Quebec City

    D Edmonton

2   **Which of these belongs in number 1 around circle D?**

    F Toronto library

    G Niagara Falls nature hikes

    H Montreal harbour cruises

    J Glacier National Park

GO ON

Answers
SA Ⓐ Ⓑ Ⓒ Ⓓ   1 Ⓐ Ⓑ Ⓒ Ⓓ   2 Ⓕ Ⓖ Ⓗ Ⓙ

Here is a rough draft of the first part of Charley's letter. Read the rough draft carefully. Then answer questions 3–10.

July 25

Dear Aunt Cynthia,

I want to tell you about the time we had in Canada that was
(1)

wonderful. We drove more than two thousand miles. We visited many
(2)   (3)

places along the way. My friend went on vacation to Hawaii.
(4)

Niagara Falls was one of my favorite places I can't believe how
(5)

powerful that waterfall is! We took a boat ride. Right to the foot of the
(6)   (7)

Falls. It's a good thing that we were wearing rain coats and rain hats!
(8)

We also took a cable car to view the Falls and viewed the Falls from
(9)

the top. That was quite a view! There is a beautiful park in Niagara
(10)   (11)

Falls. We took a long nature hike through the park. We saw many
(12)   (13)

different kinds of plants along the hike.

We could see the Falls from the balcony of our hotel room. We went
(14)   (15)

swimming every evening in the hotel pool.

GO ON ➤

3 What is the best way to write sentence 1?

   A I want to tell you about Canada and the wonderful time we had in Canada.

   B I want to tell you about the wonderful time we had in Canada.

   C The wonderful time we had in Canada I want to tell you about.

   D As it is written.

4 Which sentence best combines sentences 2 and 3 without changing their meaning?

   F More than two thousand miles, we drove, we visited many places along the way.

   G Drove more than two thousand miles and visited many places along the way.

   H We visited many places along the way and then drove more than two thousand miles.

   J We drove more than two thousand miles and visited many places along the way.

5 Which sentence does not belong in Charley's letter? Write the number.

   _____

   _____

   _____

   _____

   _____

6 Which sentence needlessly repeats a word or a group of words?

   A 2

   B 4

   C 8

   D 9

7 The best way to write sentence 5 is—

   F Niagara Falls was one of my favorite places, I can't believe how powerful that waterfall is!

   G Was one of my favorite places. I can't believe how powerful that waterfall is!

   H Niagara Falls was one of my favorite places. I can't believe how powerful that waterfall is!

   J As it is written.

8 Which group of words is *not* a complete sentence?

   A 3

   B 7

   C 11

   D 14

9 What is the most colorful way to write sentence 13?

   F We saw numerous types of plants on our long hike.

   G We saw a wide variety of interesting plants during our nature hike.

   H We saw lots of different kinds of plants on our hike.

   J As it is written.

10 Which of the following sentences could be added after sentence 15?

   A There are many hotels in Niagara Falls.

   B We sometimes swim in the pool in our park at home.

   C I liked the hotel we stayed at in Niagara Falls.

   D We could have also stayed at a motel.

GO ON

Answers

3 Ⓐ Ⓑ Ⓒ Ⓓ   **6** Ⓐ Ⓑ Ⓒ Ⓓ   **8** Ⓐ Ⓑ Ⓒ Ⓓ   **10** Ⓐ Ⓑ Ⓒ Ⓓ

4 Ⓕ Ⓖ Ⓗ Ⓙ   **7** Ⓕ Ⓖ Ⓗ Ⓙ   **9** Ⓕ Ⓖ Ⓗ Ⓙ

Here is the next part of Charley's rough draft for his letter. This part has certain words and phrases underlined. Read the draft carefully. Then answer questions 11–18.

We had an exciting time <u>in the canadian rockies</u>. This part of
(16)   (17)

Canada has tall mountains, huge waterfalls, and beautiful evergreen

trees. Driving through the mountains was so much fun.
(18)

We did so many things in the mountains. One of the most exciting
(19)   (20)

<u>was River Rafting</u>. A professional rafter took us down the river. It <u>was</u>
         (21)   (22)

<u>funner</u> than a roller coaster ride!

We spent several days camping in a national park. At night we saw
(23)   (24)

thousands of stars in the sky. It was fun to cook marshmallows <u>over a</u>
                                       (25)

<u>open fire</u>. It was also fun to sleep <u>in its tent</u>. During the day we took long
     (26)   (27)

hikes on the mountain trails. We saw many different animals <u>on our hike</u>?
                       (28)

We also got a chance <u>to go horseback riding</u>. It was the first time that
(29)   (30)

I was ever on a horse. The horse I rode was very gentle and easy to ride.
                (31)

Riding a horse was a great way to see the beautiful mountain scenery.
(32)

<u>Your nephew.</u>

Charley

11 In sentence 16, <u>in the canadian rockies</u> is best written—

    F in the Canadian rockies

    G in the Canadian Rockies

    H in the canadian Rockies

    J As it is written.

12 In sentence 20, <u>was River Rafting</u> is best written—

    A was River rafting

    B was river Rafting

    C was river rafting

    D As it is written.

13 In sentence 22, <u>was funner</u> is best written—

    F was most fun

    G was much funner

    H was more fun

    J As it is written.

14 In sentence 25, <u>over a open fire</u> is best written—

    A over an Open fire

    B over a Open fire

    C over an open fire

    D As it is written.

15 In sentence 26, <u>in its tent</u> is best written—

    F in our tent

    G in us tent

    H in it's tent

    J As it is written.

16 In sentence 28, <u>on our hike?</u> is best written—

    A on our hike!

    B on our hike.

    C on their hike?

    D As it is written.

17 In sentence 29, <u>to go horseback riding</u> is best written—

    F to go horseback, riding

    G to go, horseback riding

    H to, go horseback riding

    J As it is written.

18 In the closing, <u>Your nephew.</u> is best written—

    A Your nephew,

    B Your nephew?

    C Your nephew!

    D As it is written.

GO ON

Answers

11	Ⓕ Ⓖ Ⓗ Ⓙ	**13**	Ⓕ Ⓖ Ⓗ Ⓙ	**15**	Ⓕ Ⓖ Ⓗ Ⓙ	**17**	Ⓕ Ⓖ Ⓗ Ⓙ
12	Ⓐ Ⓑ Ⓒ Ⓓ	**14**	Ⓐ Ⓑ Ⓒ Ⓓ	**16**	Ⓐ Ⓑ Ⓒ Ⓓ	**18**	Ⓐ Ⓑ Ⓒ Ⓓ

For questions 19–30, read each sentence carefully. If one of the words is misspelled, darken the circle for that word. If all the words are spelled correctly, then darken the circle for _No mistake_.

19   The dog <u>kept</u> <u>whineing</u> at the <u>kitchen</u> door. <u>No mistake</u>
            F   G   H   J

20   We were <u>starttled</u> by the <u>loud</u> <u>explosion</u>. <u>No mistake</u>
                  A   B   C   D

21   Thomas Edison was the <u>imventor</u> of the <u>light</u> <u>bulb</u>. <u>No mistake</u>
                                F   G   H   J

22   He is a very <u>popular</u> <u>guitar</u> <u>player</u>. <u>No mistake</u>
                      A   B   C   D

23   The <u>heat</u> from the <u>flames</u> was very <u>imtense</u>. <u>No mistake</u>
            F   G   H   J

24   Her <u>abilitys</u> are well <u>above</u> <u>average</u>. <u>No mistake</u>
            A   B   C   D

25   The cat <u>bolted</u> for the <u>aley</u> when the dog <u>barked</u>. <u>No mistake</u>
                  F   G   H   J

26   It is <u>urgent</u> that we <u>return</u> home <u>immediately</u>. <u>No mistake</u>
              A   B   C   D

27   The <u>plane</u> flew <u>threw</u> the <u>clouds</u>. <u>No mistake</u>
            F   G   H   J

28   He <u>recieved</u> the <u>missing</u> package <u>yesterday</u>. <u>No mistake</u>
            A   B   C   D

29   <u>Advertiseing</u> can make your <u>product</u> <u>known</u> to the public. <u>No mistake</u>
        F   G   H   J

30   Gino has <u>missed</u> band <u>practice</u> <u>latly</u>. <u>No mistake</u>
                  A   B   C   D

Answers

19	Ⓕ Ⓖ Ⓗ Ⓙ	22	Ⓐ Ⓑ Ⓒ Ⓓ	25	Ⓕ Ⓖ Ⓗ Ⓙ	28	Ⓐ Ⓑ Ⓒ Ⓓ
20	Ⓐ Ⓑ Ⓒ Ⓓ	23	Ⓕ Ⓖ Ⓗ Ⓙ	26	Ⓐ Ⓑ Ⓒ Ⓓ	29	Ⓕ Ⓖ Ⓗ Ⓙ
21	Ⓕ Ⓖ Ⓗ Ⓙ	24	Ⓐ Ⓑ Ⓒ Ⓓ	27	Ⓕ Ⓖ Ⓗ Ⓙ	30	Ⓐ Ⓑ Ⓒ Ⓓ

READING COMPREHENSION

Use the removable answer sheet on page 763 to record your answers for the practice tests.

Sample A

Early Trains

The first trains in America were very different from modern trains. Horses pulled wagons on wooden rails. During the 1830s, the first steam engines were used. They burned wood for fuel.

What did steam engines use for fuel?

A gas   **C** wood

B water   **D** coal

For questions 1–46, carefully read each selection and the questions that follow. Then darken the circle for the correct answer, or write in the answer.

Learning about King Cobras

King cobras are large, dangerous snakes that live in parts of Asia. These snakes often grow to be 18 feet long. This is the largest of all poisonous snakes in the world. The cobra has loose skin on either side of its neck. When the snake is angry or threatened, it spreads its long ribs and flattens its neck. The skin stands out and makes a *hood*.

King cobras mainly eat other snakes. The cobra has short fangs, but its poison is very strong. Many people have died from being bitten by these snakes.

The king cobra is the only snake that makes a nest. The mother finds a place with many leaves. She pushes the leaves together. Then she lays about 40 eggs. She covers them with more leaves. Then she lies on top of the nest for about two months until the young hatch. The father also stays nearby.

The babies can take care of themselves as soon as they are born. They are about 20 inches long. Even young cobras are very dangerous.

As dangerous as they are, cobras are famous as the partners of snake charmers. The hood creates quite an amazing appearance. During the snake charmer's act, the cobra appears to be affected by the music. Actually, as with all snakes, the cobra cannot hear. Instead, it responds to visual clues. Many snake charmers get a feeling of safety from the fact that cobras can have a rather slow strike.

GO ON➡

1 **In what area of the world do king cobras live?**

   A   Africa

   B   Asia

   C   Iceland

   D   North America

2 **If you saw two king cobras lying on or near a pile of leaves, you might guess that—**

   F   they are tired.

   G   they are hungry.

   H   they are enjoying the sun.

   J   they are protecting their eggs.

3 **In this selection, what does *hood* mean?**

   A   a hat

   B   poison spit by the cobra

   C   skin that stands out from the cobra's neck

   D   a nest

4 **King cobras mainly eat—**

   F   birds' eggs.

   G   leaves and berries.

   H   other snakes.

   J   small animals.

5 **What does the nest of a king cobra look like?**

   A   It is a big pile of leaves.

   B   It is made of branches.

   C   It is hidden high in a tree.

   D   It is made of rocks.

6 **How long are adult king cobras?**

   _____

   _____

   _____

   _____

   _____

7 **Which words from the selection show that a king cobra bite can be deadly?**

   F   …poison is very strong.

   G   …spreads out its ribs…

   H   …responds to visual clues.

   J   …have a rather slow strike.

8 **What is true of king cobras?**

   A   Only the adult snakes are dangerous.

   B   They respond to snake charmers' music.

   C   They strike rapidly.

   D   They are the largest poisonous snakes in the world.

9 **To find out more about king cobras, you should—**

   F   travel to Asia.

   G   read a reference book about snakes.

   H   read a travel book about Asia.

   J   look for snakes in your neighborhood.

10 **What is this selection mainly about?**

   A   what king cobras eat

   B   where king cobras live

   C   what king cobras are like

   D   a kind of dangerous snake

GO ON ➡

The Talking Banana

It was May, and Chris was ready for summer vacation to begin. He didn't want to get up at 6:00 A.M. to catch the bus. He didn't want to do his math homework. And most of all, he didn't want to write. Every Monday, Wednesday, and Friday his class wrote in their journals. Chris had written about a thousand things—spring break, his sister, his bike, even his pet German shepherd, Rusty. He couldn't think of one more thing to write about!

His teacher, Ms. Crain, said there were lots of things to write about. She said, "Write about what you had for breakfast this morning." So Chris wrote, "I had cereal for breakfast." He sat for a long time trying to think of something else to say. Finally, he added, "I put a banana on top of the cereal."

The next time Ms. Crain walked around the room, she read the two sentences. "Oh dear," she said. "I can tell that you need some inspiration. I think I have just what you need." She went back to her desk and pulled out a rectangular box. She opened it and handed Chris a sleek gold pen. Then she whispered, "This is a special pen. It will help you get some ideas."

Chris looked at the pen doubtfully. Slowly, he put it near the paper. The pen wrote, "The banana was from Brazil. It began talking to me." Chris couldn't believe it. He waited for the pen to write more, but it didn't.

Chris wrote that the banana said its name was Joey and that Chris wouldn't believe what had happened to it! Chris and the pen took turns writing the story. For the first time ever, he was sorry when Ms. Crain said writing time was over. Chris read his story aloud the next day. He called it "The Life of a Banana." It read as follows:

The Life of a Banana

Yesterday I had cereal for breakfast. I put a banana on top of the cereal. The banana was from Brazil. It began talking to me. The banana said that its name was Joey and that I wouldn't believe what had happened to it!

Joey told me about being raised on a plantation with millions of other bananas. Joey was as happy as could be, growing in a clump with ten or fifteen other bananas. Joey liked lying in the tropical sun and daydreaming about banana cream pie, banana splits, and other fabulous banana desserts.

All of this came to an end a week ago. A plantation worker suddenly appeared carrying a big knife. He whacked Joey's clump off the banana plant and left it on the ground. Later, another worker picked up the clump and put it with other clumps in a big wooden *crate*. The crate was put onto a truck and taken to a seaport. Joey and hundreds of other bananas were loaded onto a ship that sailed to the United States. Soon my mom was buying Joey and his friends in the supermarket.

Joey said he felt better after we talked. But I still think he was a little disappointed that he didn't end up in a banana cream pie or something more exciting than cereal.

GO ON ➡

11 According to the selection, when does Chris write his story?

    F in July

    G in November

    H in April

    J in May

12 Why didn't Chris want to write in his journal?

_____

_____

_____

_____

_____

_____

13 What did Ms. Crain give to Chris to help him write?

    A a banana

    B a special pen

    C a rectangular box

    D a good grade

14 Why was Chris sorry when Ms. Crain said that writing time was over?

    F He wanted to make a good grade.

    G He did not want to go to science class.

    H He wanted to keep writing.

    J He did not have his math homework finished.

15 In this story, the word *crate* means—

    A supermarket.

    B ship.

    C box.

    D truck.

16 In order to answer number 15, the reader should—

    F reread the first line of each paragraph.

    G reread the last paragraph of the story.

    H look for the word *crate* in the story.

    J reread the title of the story.

17 Where was the banana from?

    A a farm in the Midwest

    B a forest in California

    C a ranch in Central America

    D a plantation in Brazil

18 How do you think Chris will feel when it's time to write in the journal again?

    F bored

    G angry

    H eager

    J sad

19 How can you tell this story was a fantasy?

    A Students wrote in their journals.

    B A banana talked.

    C Bananas were grown on a plantation.

    D A teacher gave a student a pen.

20 If this story continued, what would probably happen next?

    F Someone else would write an interesting story with Ms. Crain's special pen.

    G Chris would talk to a carrot.

    H Chris would do his math homework.

    J Chris' dad would make a banana cream pie.

GO ON➔

Making a Clay Pot

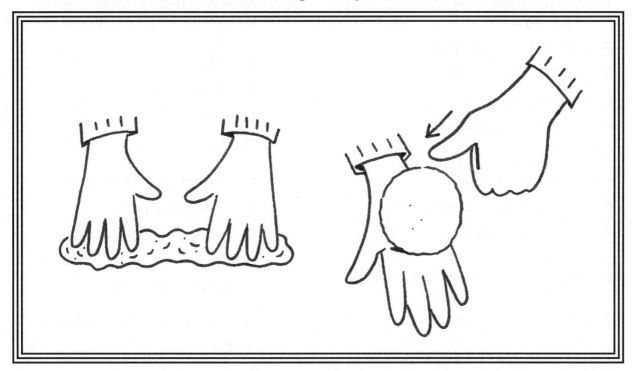

Choose a simple item to create from clay. It might be a pot, bowl, cup, or flower vase. Follow these directions:

1. Take a piece of clay about the size of an apple. Press and squeeze it on a flat surface until there are no lumps or air bubbles.
2. Use both hands to shape the clay into a smooth, round ball.
3. Put the ball of clay in your left hand. With the thumb of your right hand, make an opening in the clay. Press down toward your palm, leaving a half inch of clay at the bottom to make the floor of your pot.
4. Press the clay gently between your thumb and fingers. Turn the pot after each squeeze to make it thin out evenly. Continue until it is as thin as you want it.
5. Cover the pot with plastic so it doesn't dry too quickly and allow it to dry for several days. Take off the plastic and wait several more days.
6. When the pot is completely dry, it is ready to be *fired* in a special oven called a *kiln.* After firing, the pot will keep its shape.

GO ON

21 The first thing you should do when making a clay pot is—

A press and squeeze the clay.

B cover the clay in plastic.

C shape the clay into a ball.

D make the floor of the pot.

22 What is something you should *not* do when making a clay pot?

F remove the lumps from the clay

G squeeze the clay between your thumb and fingers

H shape the clay into a smooth, round ball

J let the pot dry quickly

23 The selection tells about making a clay pot by doing all of the following *except*—

A letting the pot dry.

B firing the pot.

C pressing the clay.

D painting or carving designs.

24 A pot that has been *fired* has been—

F broken.

G covered.

H baked.

J melted.

25 Why should the pot be turned after each squeeze?

_____

_____

_____

_____

_____

_____

26 According to the directions, which of the following is *not* needed to make a pot?

A plastic

B a kiln

C paint

D clay

27 Firing is important because it—

F thins out the pot.

G makes the pot smaller.

H allows the pot to keep its shape.

J adds designs to the pot.

28 You can tell that a kiln is a kind of—

A flat surface.

B clay mixture.

C bowl.

D oven.

29 This selection would probably appear in a book called—

F *Easy Arts and Crafts.*

G *How to Build a Kiln.*

H *The History of Ancient Arts.*

J *The Mystery of Clay Mountain.*

GO ON➡

A Wonderful Woman

"Mama, look over there. Isn't that Jane Addams?" asked Erich.

"Yes, yes, you are correct. That is Jane Addams. I would know her anywhere. She helped me settle into the American way of life when I first moved here from Germany," replied Mrs. Schroeder.

"What do you mean, Mama?" asked Erich.

"When I first came to Chicago in 1890, I could not speak any English. I did not have a job. I am afraid that I did not know anyone either. I was only 19 years old and I was determined to become an American citizen and a successful person in the United States, but it was difficult. I heard about Jane Addams' Hull House from another German immigrant. She told me that I could go to Hull House and learn English and become accustomed to life in the United States," answered Mrs. Schroeder.

"Did you go to Hull House, Mama?" asked Erich.

"I went there as soon as I could. I signed up for an evening class to learn English. The social workers at Hull House were able to get me a job, too. It was not a great job—I stocked shelves at a small local grocery store, but it was a living. The social workers also helped me find a safe place to live. I shared a room in an apartment with two other women about my age. It worked out fine," said Mrs. Schroeder.

"Did you ever talk to Jane Addams?" queried Erich.

"Jane Addams made a point to talk to all the people who came to Hull House. After I finished my English classes, she asked to meet with me. She told me how I could become an American citizen. I took more classes at Hull House. This time I learned about the government of the United States. It was in this class that I met your father. He and I became American citizens in the same naturalization ceremony," explained Mrs. Schroeder.

"Why did Jane Addams help establish Hull House?" wondered Erich. "She knew how to speak English."

"She was a humanitarian. She saw a need for a community center that would help immigrants, young and old alike, keep from becoming *impoverished* and help them become upstanding American citizens. She is my hero," stated Mrs. Schroeder.

HULL House

GO ON ➡

30 According to the selection, why did Mrs. Schroeder come to the United States?

    A She wanted to search for gold.

    B She hoped to learn to speak English.

    C She wanted to find a job in a grocery store.

    D She wanted to become a citizen of the United States.

31 How did Mrs. Schroeder find out about Hull House?

    F Another German immigrant told her.

    G She heard about it while she was still in Germany.

    H She read a newspaper article about Hull House.

    J Jane Addams invited her to come to Hull House.

32 What did Mrs. Schroeder have to do to become a citizen of the United States?

_____

_____

_____

_____

_____

_____

_____

33 Which word best describes Jane Addams?

    A pitiless

    B rash

    C wealthy

    D compassionate

34 In this selection, the word *impoverished* means—

    F affluent.

    G impossible.

    H poor.

    J sent back to the native country.

35 According to the story, Hull House helped immigrants in all of the following ways *except*—

    A finding jobs.

    B finding safe places to live.

    C finding a way back to their native country.

    D learning to speak English.

36 From the story, you can tell that Mrs. Schroeder is—

    F easily frightened.

    G brave and determined.

    H disappointed in the United States.

    J angry with Jane Addams.

37 What would be another good title for this story?

    A "The Life of Erich Schroeder"

    B "Learning at Hull House"

    C "The History of Chicago"

    D "Immigrant Life"

GO ON➡

Visiting Pioneer City

Welcome to Pioneer City! Here you can learn about how the pioneers of the 1800s lived. These buildings are preserved through the efforts of local conservationists. We keep history alive!

The tour begins at the old schoolhouse. Take a look at the slates and inkwells used by the children. Notice that this schoolhouse had two fireplaces to help keep young learners warm!

When you walk out the schoolhouse door, turn right and walk about the length of a city block. You'll come to the storefronts. The first two are closed, but you are invited to go into the General Store. Find out what families stocked up on and what the bargains were back then.

Go directly across the street from the General Store to Minnie's Well. A large group of community members dug the well together.

From the well, go back north toward the schoolhouse. You can peek into the bank, but there is no longer any money there!

Directly beyond the bank is the Rose Hotel. You can go as far as the fancy front desk, but the upstairs is closed. Be sure to flip through the guest registry—one of your relatives might have stayed there.

From the hotel, go back north to the schoolhouse and out to the parking lot. We hope you enjoyed your visit!

GO ON ➡

38 This poster was written in order to—

 F describe pioneer life.

 G congratulate local conservationists.

 H give directions for the tour.

 J raise money for the community.

39 About how far is it from the schoolhouse to the stores?

 A the length of a city block

 B two miles

 C two steps

 D the length of three city blocks

40 To get from the well to the bank, you should—

 F go across the street.

 G go north toward the schoolhouse.

 H turn right and walk about a city block.

 J walk directly behind the well.

41 What is directly beyond the bank?

 _____

 _____

 _____

 _____

 _____

 _____

42 Which of these is not permitted at the Rose Hotel?

 A going upstairs

 B flipping through the guest registry

 C looking at the front desk

 D closing the door

43 What two attractions will you see between the well and returning to the schoolhouse?

 F the bank and the Rose Hotel

 G the bank and the General Store

 H the Rose Hotel and the General Store

 J the library and the hat shop

44 According to the poster, you can see all of the following at Pioneer City *except*—

 A a bank.

 B a schoolhouse.

 C a blacksmith shop.

 D a well.

45 You can tell that the tour is meant to be—

 F led by a tour guide.

 G provided only for historians.

 H a complete picture of pioneer life.

 J self-guided.

46 From the poster, you can tell that local conservationists think it is important to—

 A make good grades.

 B play sports.

 C keep history alive.

 D follow directions.

STOP

Sample A

Terrified means—

A delighted   C frightened

B completed   D puzzled

For questions 1–9, darken the circle for the word or words that have the same or almost the same meaning as the underlined word.

1   To **permit** is to—

A allow

B teach

C measure

D realize

2   To **quit** means the same as to—

F begin

G stop

H continue

J start

3   **Miserable** means—

A joyful

B scared

C unhappy

D confused

4   **Cruel** means the same as—

F little

G mean

H protected

J strange

5   If something is **fragile**, it is—

A very dry

B easily broken

C shiny

D colorful

6   **Frequently** means—

F never

G always

H often

J yearly

7   A **wail** is a kind of—

A cry

B shoe

C tool

D store

8   A **scheme** is a kind of—

F party

G song

H report

J plan

9   **Brisk** means the same as—

A silly

B quick

C difficult

D lonely

GO ON ➡

Sample B

> People are often remembered for their underlined conduct.

In which sentence does underlined conduct have the same meaning as it does in the sentence above?

A I try to conduct myself with the best manners possible.

B What are some objects that can conduct electricity?

C Mr. Green will conduct the orchestra this evening.

D Leticia is proud of her school conduct.

STOP

For questions 10–14, darken the circle for the sentence in which the underlined word means the same as it does in the sentence in the box.

10
> If we can agree on payment, then we have a deal.

In which sentence does deal have the same meaning as it does in the sentence above?

F Kara and Jeff made a deal to trade baseball cards.

G I will deal with them later.

H Is it my turn to deal the cards?

J There is a good deal of work left to be done.

11
> We sat under the shade of a big oak tree.

In which sentence does shade have the same meaning as it does in the sentence above?

A Please pull down the window shade.

B Ramon will use his pencil to shade his map.

C The awning created a spot of shade.

D This is the most beautiful shade of purple.

12
> The judges will grade our performance.

In which sentence does grade have the same meaning as it does in the sentence above?

F My brother is in the seventh grade at St. Paul School.

G Ms. Henning will grade our math tests.

H The truck slowly went up the steep grade.

J We usually try to buy the best grade of eggs.

13
> My cousin is staying in our spare room.

In which sentence does spare have the same meaning as it does in the sentence above?

A The knight decided to spare the dragon.

B We cannot spare the money for the trip.

C I will spare you the time and expense of doing it yourself.

D Please check my spare tire.

14
> The Spanish club will meet for two hours.

In which sentence does meet have the same meaning as it does in the sentence above?

F Our class will meet in the gym.

G Sandra will run in the track meet.

H The newspaper reporter had a deadline to meet.

J I'd like you to meet my grandfather.

GO ON

Sample C

Because it has small parts, that toy is not <u>suitable</u> for a young child. <u>Suitable</u> means—

A neat

B acceptable

C funny

D serious

🛑 STOP

For questions 15–22, darken the circle for the word or words that give the meaning of the underlined word.

15 Our <u>compact</u> camping gear easily fits into the van. <u>Compact</u> means—

A large

B stiff

C compressed

D loose

16 They lived in a <u>remote</u> cabin far back in the woods. <u>Remote</u> means—

F army

G concrete

H manufactured

J distant

17 Most people have to learn how to get along with both friends and <u>foes</u>. <u>Foes</u> means—

A tricks

B enemies

C companions

D families

18 Parent volunteers will <u>transport</u> the team and all its equipment to the game. <u>Transport</u> means—

F move

G make

H send

J receive

19 The clerk was very <u>courteous</u> and helpful. <u>Courteous</u> means—

A stiff

B polite

C sleepy

D fast

20 The hospital has a <u>mobile</u> clinic that comes to schools often. <u>Mobile</u> means—

F special

G safe

H modern

J movable

21 Both work and <u>leisure</u> are important. <u>Leisure</u> means—

A sleep

B free time

C fast food

D friendly

22 Molly said that helping us out wasn't a <u>burden</u>. <u>Burden</u> means—

F gift

G job

H hardship

J pleasure

🛑 STOP

Sample A

What number makes the number sentence true?

$$3 + (2 + \square) = (3 + 2) + 7$$

A 2

B 3

C 5

D 7

STOP

For questions 1–49, darken the circle for the correct answer, or write in the answer.

1 Which expression will correctly complete the number sentence $4 + 6 = \square$?

A $6 + 4$ **C** 6×4

B $10 - 4$ **D** $10 + 4$

2 Mrs. Wilson's students have art class on odd-numbered days during the school week. Use the calendar below to find how many days the students have art class this month.

S	M	T	W	T	F	S
		1	2	3	4	5
6	7	8	9	10	11	12
13	14	15	16	17	18	19
20	21	22	23	24	25	26
27	28	29	30			

F 10   **H** 15

G 11   **J** 30

3

Famous Rivers	
Name	**Length (in miles)**
Amazon	4,000
Congo	2,900
Huang He	2,903
Mekong	2,600
Nile	4,145
Volga	2,194
Yangtze	3,915

Which river is longer than the Congo but shorter than the Yangtze?

A Huang He   **C** Volga

B Nile   **D** Mekong

4 Which number has an eight in the thousands place and a two in the hundreds place?

F 2,845   **H** 8,024

G 6,821   **J** 8,239

5 What number would be placed third if these numbers were arranged in order from least to greatest?

5,291	5,921	4,073	4,628	5,601

A 5,601   **C** 5,291

B 4,628   **D** 5,921

6 What number is expressed by this number sentence?

$$(4 \times 1,000) + (9 \times 100) + (2 \times 1)$$

F 4,920   **H** 4,092

G 4,902   **J** 492

GO ON➡

7 Julie, Jay, Juan, and Cynthia had fun making patterns with their names. They counted the letters in their first names and arranged their names in order from the shortest to the longest name. Which list shows this arrangement?

A Julie, Juan, Jay, Cynthia

B Juan, Julie, Cynthia, Jay

C Cynthia, Julie, Jay, Juan

D Jay, Juan, Julie, Cynthia

8 Write the numeral 2,605 in words.

_____

_____

_____

_____

9 What number makes the number sentence true?

$$1 \times \square = 7$$

_____

_____

_____

_____

10 Julia buys fabric to make pillows. Which list shows the amounts of fabric Julia buys in order from the least amount to the greatest amount?

Fabric	Amount
Yellow calico	$\frac{1}{2}$ yard
Blue chambray	$\frac{2}{3}$ yard
Green cotton	$\frac{1}{5}$ yard
White muslin	$\frac{1}{4}$ yard

F $\frac{1}{5}, \frac{1}{4}, \frac{1}{2}, \frac{2}{3}$ H $\frac{1}{2}, \frac{1}{5}, \frac{2}{3}, \frac{1}{4}$

G $\frac{1}{4}, \frac{2}{3}, \frac{1}{2}, \frac{1}{5}$ J $\frac{1}{2}, \frac{1}{4}, \frac{2}{3}, \frac{1}{5}$

11 Which decimal shows the part of the figure that is shaded?

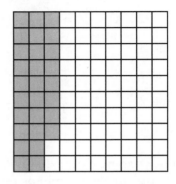

A 0.78   C 0.28

B 0.72   D 0.22

12 Which figure shows $\frac{3}{5}$ shaded?

F   H

G   J

13 Which mixed number tells what part of the figures are shaded?

A $1\frac{3}{4}$ C $1\frac{2}{7}$

B $1\frac{1}{2}$ D $1\frac{5}{7}$

14 Which number sentence is in the same fact family as $10 - 2 = 8$?

F $10 + 2 = 12$ H $8 + 2 = 10$

G $10 \div 2 = 5$ J $8 - 2 = 6$

GO ON➤

15 Which two numbers can be written in the number sentence to make it correct?

$$(2 + 4) + \square = (3 + \square) + 5$$

A   6 and 3

B   7 and 4

C   3 and 2

D   6 and 4

16 Yoshi buys some clothes. The table below shows how much she spends on each item.

Clothing	Amount
Shirt	$21.95
Shorts	$12.50
Shoes	$19.72
Swimsuit	$15.25

Which item has a price with a two in the tenths place?

F   Shirt

G   Shorts

H   Shoes

J   Swimsuit

This chart shows the number of people who want to take classes at the recreation center.

Class	Number of People
Art	⸜⸜ ⸜⸜
Dance	⸜⸜ IIII
Swimming	III
Tennis	⸜⸜ I

17 How many people want to take swimming and tennis classes?

A   3

B   6

C   9

D   10

The table below shows the names and times of some local radio programs. Study the table. Use it to answer questions 18–20.

	9:00-9:30	9:30-10:00	10:00-10:30	10:30-11:00
Station KBJB	Sports	Update News	Green Thumb Hour	
Station KHFB	Golden Oldie Music		Jazz Music	Jazz Music

18 Which program begins at 10:00 and ends at 11:00?

_____

_____

_____

_____

_____

_____

19 Which program begins at 9:00 and ends at 10:00 on station KHFB?

F   "Jazz Music"

G   "Green Thumb Hour"

H   "Update News"

J   "Golden Oldie Music"

20 What time does the program "Sports" end?

A   9:00

B   9:30

C   10:00

D   10:30

GO ON➡

The graph shows how many inches of rain fell in one year in Westwood. Study the graph. Use it to answer questions 21–23.

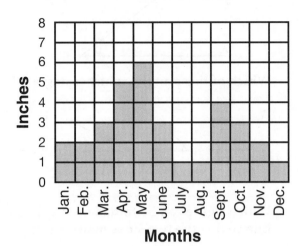

Months

21 How many more inches did it rain in September than in July?

_____

_____

_____

_____

_____

22 How many inches did it rain altogether in April and November?

F   2 inches

G   3 inches

H   5 inches

J   7 inches

23 Which month had 4 inches of rain?

A   February

B   May

C   September

D   November

24 What shape does this picture have?

F   diamond

G   rectangle

H   square

J   oval

25 If Manuel spins the spinner many times, which month will the spinner point to most often?

A   December

B   June

C   May

D   April

26 Ted puts these cards in a box. If he reaches into the box and picks one card without looking, which card will it most likely be?

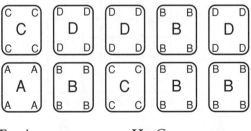

F   A   H   C

G   B   J   D

GO ON➡

27

I have 4 sides that are exactly the same. What am I?

Which figure shown here answers the riddle?

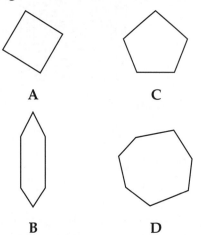

A

C

B

D

28 Liza drew this figure on her paper.

1

What did it look like when she turned it upside down?

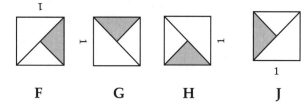

F

G

H

J

29 The graph shows the location of some shapes. What shape is located at (D, 4)?

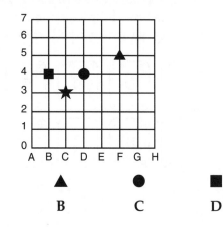

A

B

C

D

30 Look at the angles labeled on the figure shown here.

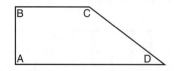

Which of these angles matches angle A?

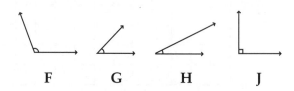

F

G

H

J

31 Which figure can be folded on the dotted line so that the two sides match exactly?

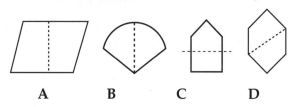

A

B

C

D

32 Trudy has these bills. She buys this toy bear.

$1.49

How much money will Trudy have left?

_____

_____

_____

_____

_____

_____

_____

GO ON

33 What temperature does the picture most likely show?

F 18°F

G 39°F

H 51°F

J 92°F

34 Which unit of measurement is best to describe the height of a building?

A inches

B feet

C pounds

D miles

35 Which figure shows the least area of square units shaded?

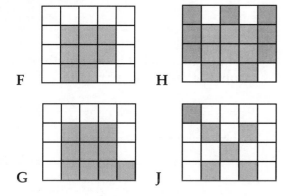

F   H

G   J

36 Which nail is the shortest?

A   B   C   D

37 Samantha has these coins.

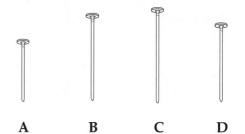

Which group of coins shows the same value?

F

G

H

J

GO ON

38 Julissa played the piano for 35 minutes. She started playing at 3:15. Which of these clocks shows the time that Julissa stopped playing the piano?

A

C

B

D

39 Which unit of measurement is best to measure a window?

  F inches

  G yards

  H cups

  J miles

40 The first thermometer shows the temperature before Tricia played a baseball game. The second thermometer shows the temperature when the game was over.

  Before Game   After Game

  95° °F   95° °F

  90°   90°

  85°   85°

  What is the difference in the temperature after the game than before the game?

  A 5° warmer

  B 5° cooler

  C 10° warmer

  D 10° cooler

41 Use your centimeter ruler. How long is the rocket ship from end to end?

  F 2 centimeters

  G 3 centimeters

  H 4 centimeters

  J 5 centimeters

42 Use your inch ruler to help you answer this question.

  On this map, what is the length of the path from the farm to the bridge?

  _____

  _____

  _____

  _____

43 There are 3 tennis balls in a can. Pat needs 27 tennis balls for tennis camp. Which number sentence shows how to find the number of cans he will need to buy.

  A $27 + 3 = \square$ **C** $27 - 13 = \square$

  B $27 \times 3 = \square$ **D** $27 \div 3 = \square$

GO ON➡

44 A theater seats 285 people. The play now showing has 9 sold-out performances. Estimate how many people all together will see the play.

   F 30   **H** 3,000

   G 300   **J** 30,000

45 How many stars are inside the square and outside the circle?

46 Which two shapes come next in the pattern?

   A □ ▲

   B ▲ △

   C △ □

   D □ △

47 Marco took a box of popsicles to the park. He ate one and gave one to each of 5 friends. What do you need to know to find out how many popsicles Marco has left?

   F how many friends chose grape popsicles

   G how many popsicles were in the box

   H how many boxes of popsicles Marco ate at home

   J how many orange popsicles were in the box

48 Mrs. Sanchez owns a furniture store in Blue Mound. She needs to deliver a chair to a customer in Bruster. She uses the map to find the shortest distance between Blue Mound and Bruster. Estimate *about* how far Mrs. Sanchez will drive one way.

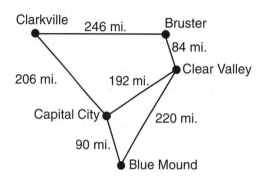

   A 500 miles   **C** 300 miles

   B 400 miles   **D** 200 miles

The shuttle bus at the airport departs from the terminal to the parking garage according to the following schedule.

Shuttle Schedule
9:06 A.M.
9:12 A.M.
9:18 A.M.
9:24 A.M.
9:30 A.M.

49 If the shuttle bus continues this pattern, at what time will the first shuttle depart the terminal after 11:15 A.M.?

   F 11:00 A.M.

   G 11:06 A.M.

   H 11:12 A.M.

   J 11:18 A.M.

STOP

Sample A

$$7\overline{)78}$$

- A 11
- B 10 R1
- C 12
- D 12 R3
- E NH

STOP

For questions 1–15, darken the circle for the correct answer. Darken the circle for NH (Not Here) if the correct answer is not given. If no choices are given, write in the answer.

1

$$\begin{array}{r} 59 \\ \times\ 33 \\ \end{array}$$

- A 334
- B 1,947
- C 3,340
- D 19,470
- E NH

2

$$\begin{array}{r} 721 \\ \times\ 4 \\ \end{array}$$

- F 2,884
- G 2,864
- H 2,184
- J 2,164
- K NH

3

$$5\overline{)75}$$

- A 10
- B 12
- C 15
- D 18
- E NH

4

$$\begin{array}{r} 300 \\ -\ 62 \\ \end{array}$$

- F 362
- G 348
- H 248
- J 238
- K NH

5

$$927 + 32 + 649 = \square$$

- A 1,598
- B 1,608
- C 1,680
- D 1,806
- E NH

6

$$3\overline{)939}$$

- F 323
- G 313
- H 331
- J 13
- K NH

7

$$8 \times 6 = \square$$

- A 2
- B 14
- C 42
- D 48
- E NH

8

$$24 \div 6 = \square$$

_____
_____
_____
_____
_____

9 At work, Al put 129 cans of soup from one box on a shelf. The box held 235 cans. How many cans were left in the box?

- F 102
- G 106
- H 116
- J 114
- K NH

GO ON➡

Sample B

Sharon has 12 carrots. She wants to share them equally with 3 horses.

How many carrots will each horse get?

A 36

B 15

C 5

D 4

E NH

STOP

---

10 There are 11 cats on Josephine's farm. Each cat has 4 kittens. How many kittens are there altogether on the farm?

A 7

B 15

C 44

D 54

E NH

11 Mr. Richards drove 2,531 miles while on vacation. *About* how many miles is that rounded to the nearest hundred?

F 2,500

G 2,530

H 2,600

J 3,000

K NH

12 There are 16 sailboats that will race across the lake. They will sail in groups of 5.

How many extra boats are there?

_____

_____

_____

13 Mrs. Wong is going to paint the living room. She wants to buy these paint supplies.

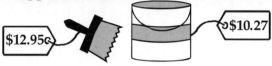

How much will the brush and paint cost before tax?

A $22.22

B $22.53

C $23.22

D $32.53

E NH

14 The students in Ms. Jackson's class took a poll to see which fruit most children liked. Out of 32 students, 15 liked apples the most and 9 liked bananas the most. The rest liked oranges.

How many students liked oranges?

F 6

G 8

H 24

J 27

K NH

15 Fran made 36 bibs to sell at a craft fair. She made 19 bibs from blue fabric and the rest of the bibs from pink fabric. How many bibs were made from pink fabric?

A 16

B 27

C 45

D 55

E NH

STOP

PRACTICE TEST 4

LANGUAGE

Joan's class is learning about different regions of the world. They are learning about forest regions, grassland regions, and desert regions. The students are to locate the regions and determine the kinds of plants and animals that are found there. Joan decided to do a report about deserts. She found information about deserts that surprised her.

Sample A

Joan wants to locate the deserts in North and South America. She should look in—

A   an encyclopedia.

B   an atlas.

C   a newspaper.

D   an index.

STOP

For questions 1–26, darken the circle for the correct answer, or write in the answer.

1   Joan heard that a city in a desert in the United States is concerned about having enough water for people to use. Where could she find more information about this?

A   an atlas

B   a dictionary

C   a history book

D   the *Readers' Guide to Periodical Literature*

2   Which guide words might mark the page on which Joan would find the word *arid*?

F   arm–arose

G   argue–arithmetic

H   around–arrow

J   artery–article

3   Which of these should *not* be included in Joan's report?

A   the definition of a desert

B   where deserts are found

C   the kinds of animals found in a desert

D   where forest regions are found

4   Joan found a book called *Living Things of the Desert*. Where should she look to find a chapter about reptiles in the desert?

F   the table of contents

G   the title page

H   the glossary

J   the index

5   Joan wanted to look up the meaning of some words. She should look in—

A   an atlas.   C   a table of contents.

B   an encyclopedia. D   a dictionary.

GO ON

Here is the Table of Contents from *Deserts,* a book Joan found in the library. Study the Table of Contents carefully. Then answer questions 6–9.

Table of Contents

6 Chapter 5 contains information on all of these *except*—

F insects of the desert.

G the prickly pear cactus.

H the desert rose.

J date palm trees.

7 On which page should Joan start reading to find out how the camel survives in the desert?

A 18

B 22

C 27

D 34

8 Which chapter should Joan read to learn about animals living in the desert?

_____

_____

_____

_____

9 Which chapter would have information about how deserts get water?

F Chapter 2

G Chapter 4

H Chapter 5

J Chapter 7

Before starting her report, Joan looked up several words in the dictionary.

10 The "a" in *locate* sounds most like the vowel sound in—

A sand.

B lake.

C fair.

D large.

Here is a rough draft of the first part of Joan's report. Read the rough draft carefully. Then answer questions 11–16.

A Dry Land

When you think of a desert, what do you think of? You probably
(1)   (2)

think of a place that is hot all the time. Some deserts are hot all the
(3)

time. But there are deserts that are found in cold places. What makes a
(4)   (5)

place a desert is not how hot or cold it is there. What makes it a desert
(6)

is how much rain it gets. A desert is a place. That gets less than 10
(7)   (8)

inches of rain a year.

Because there are no clouds to protect the ground, the days in some
(9)

deserts are warm. At night there are no clouds to keep the heat from
(10)

leaving the ground. The Sahara is a large desert in Africa. So the
(11)   (12)

nights in a desert get very cold. Strong winds can be found in most
(13)

deserts. There are very few plants and trees to slow down the winds.
(14)

So the winds can easily pick up the sand and create sandstorms.
(15)

11 Which sentence best combines sentences 3 and 4 without changing their meaning?

F Although some deserts are hot all the time, there are deserts that are found in cold places.

G Some deserts are hot, there are deserts that are found in cold.

H There are deserts that are found in cold places, some deserts are hot all the time.

J Some deserts are hot all the time, there are deserts that are cold.

12 Which sentence does *not belong* in the second paragraph? Write its number.

_____

_____

_____

_____

13 Which group of words is *not* a complete sentence?

A 8

B 9

C 10

D 11

14 What is the most colorful way to write sentence 12?

F So it can be very cold in the night in a desert.

G So it can often become quite cold in a desert during the night.

H So the nights in a desert can be very cold.

J As it is written.

15 The best way to write sentence 13 is—

A There are strong winds to be found in most deserts.

B Strong winds in most deserts can be found.

C In most deserts can be found strong winds.

D As it is written.

16 Which of these sentences could be added after sentence 15?

F Many kinds of animals live in the world's deserts.

G The Atacama Desert is found in South America.

H What do you think it would be like to live in a desert?

J Sometimes the blowing sand can be so thick that it is hard to see in front of you.

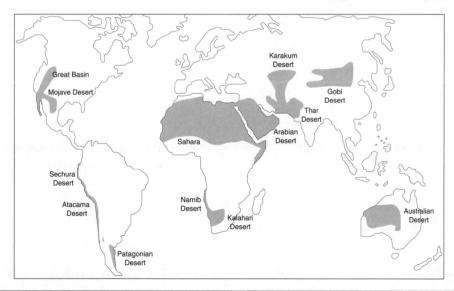

GO ON➡

Here is the next part of Joan's rough draft for her report. This part has certain words and phrases underlined. Read the draft carefully. Then answer questions 17–26.

Camels are important animals of the desert. They is used to carry
(16)   (17)

people and goods through the sunny dry, and windy desert. Camels can
(18)

survive the heat and dryness of the desert.

The camel's body helps the camel live in the desert! The camel has
(19)   (20)

long eyelashes that keep the sand out of its eyes. The camel can keep his
(21)

eyes closed and see well enough through its thin eyelids. The fur in an
(22)

camel's ears also helps to keep sand from getting in. The long legs of a
(23)

camel keep their body higher off the ground, where the air is cool more.

The camel eats tough desert plants. It can go for many days without
(24)   (25)

food. The camels' humps store fat. The camel can use this fat when it
(26)   (27)

does'nt have enough to eat. Although the camel can go for days without
(28)

water, it does need water to live. A camel can drink up to 18 gallons of
(29)

water at one time.

17 In sentence 17, They is used is best written—

A They used

B They are used

C They were used

D As it is written.

18 In sentence 17, the sunny dry, and windy desert is best written—

F the sunny dry and windy desert

G the sunny, dry, and windy, desert

H the sunny, dry, and windy desert

J As it is written.

GO ON➡

19 In sentence 19, <u>live in the desert!</u> is best written—

    A live in the desert.

    B lives in the desert!

    C live in the desert?

    D As it is written.

20 In sentence 21, <u>keep his eyes</u> is best written—

    F keep their eyes

    G keep its eyes

    H keep it eyes

    J As it is written.

21 In sentence 22, <u>an camel's ears</u> is best written—

    A an Camel's ears

    B an camels ears

    C a camel's ears

    D As it is written.

22 In sentence 23, <u>keep their body</u> is best written—

    F keep its body

    G keep them body

    H keep his body

    J As it is written.

23 In sentence 23, <u>air is cool more</u> is best written—

    A air is most cool

    B air is cooler

    C air is more cooler

    D As it is written.

24 In sentence 25, <u>It can go</u> is best written—

    F It gone

    G It went

    H It can went

    J As it is written.

25 In sentence 26, <u>camels' humps</u> is best written—

    A camels humps

    B camel's humps

    C camel humps

    D As it is written.

26 In sentence 27, <u>when it does'nt have enough</u> is best written—

    F when it doesnt' have enough

    G when it doesnt have enough

    H when it doesn't have enough

    J As it is written.

GO ON➡

For questions 27–38, read each sentence carefully. If one of the words is misspelled, darken the circle for that word. If all of the words are spelled correctly, then darken the circle for *No mistake*.

27   Darren and Jamie left immediatly following the concert. No mistake
                           A   B   C   D

28   I would like to exshange this shirt for a larger one. No mistake
                        F   G   H   J

29   Roy received permision to drive his father's car. No mistake
          A   B   C   D

30   Marta and her brothers collect aluminum cans to recycle. No mistake
                    F   G   H   J

31   The messenger was carrying important imformation. No mistake
          A   B   C   D

32   Lin through the pebble into the pond. No mistake
          F   G   H   J

33   It would be a good idea to obtane your tickets before the show. No mistake
                       A   B   C   D

34   The sponge absorbed the water completely. No mistake
          F   G   H   J

35   Manuel was eraseing the chalkboard after class. No mistake
                  A   B   C   D

36   She adjustted the television to get a clear picture. No mistake
          F   G   H   J

37   We climbed over the bolder to reach the entrance to the cave. No mistake
          A   B   C   D

38   During the seventeenth century, Spain had many colonys. No mistake
          F   G   H   J

STOP

762 TEST PREP

Answer Sheet

STUDENT'S NAME

LAST | FIRST | MI

SCHOOL:

TEACHER:

FEMALE ○   MALE ○

BIRTH DATE

MONTH		DAY		YEAR	
Jan ○	⓪	⓪	⓪	⓪	
Feb ○	①	①	①	①	
Mar ○	②	②	②	②	
Apr ○	③	③	③	③	
May ○		④	④	④	
Jun ○		⑤	⑤	⑤	
Jul ○		⑥	⑥	⑥	
Aug ○		⑦	⑦	⑦	
Sep ○		⑧	⑧	⑧	
Oct ○		⑨	⑨	⑨	
Nov ○					
Dec ○					

GRADE ④ ⑤ ⑥ ⑦ ⑧

TEST 1   Reading Comprehension

SA Ⓐ Ⓑ Ⓒ Ⓓ

1 Ⓐ Ⓑ Ⓒ Ⓓ
2 Ⓕ Ⓖ Ⓗ Ⓙ
3 Ⓐ Ⓑ Ⓒ Ⓓ
4 Ⓕ Ⓖ Ⓗ Ⓙ
5 Ⓐ Ⓑ Ⓒ Ⓓ
6 **OPEN ENDED**
7 Ⓕ Ⓖ Ⓗ Ⓙ

8 Ⓐ Ⓑ Ⓒ Ⓓ
9 Ⓕ Ⓖ Ⓗ Ⓙ
10 Ⓐ Ⓑ Ⓒ Ⓓ
11 Ⓕ Ⓖ Ⓗ Ⓙ
12 **OPEN ENDED**
13 Ⓐ Ⓑ Ⓒ Ⓓ
14 Ⓕ Ⓖ Ⓗ Ⓙ
15 Ⓐ Ⓑ Ⓒ Ⓓ

16 Ⓕ Ⓖ Ⓗ Ⓙ
17 Ⓐ Ⓑ Ⓒ Ⓓ
18 Ⓕ Ⓖ Ⓗ Ⓙ
19 Ⓐ Ⓑ Ⓒ Ⓓ
20 Ⓕ Ⓖ Ⓗ Ⓙ
21 Ⓐ Ⓑ Ⓒ Ⓓ
22 Ⓕ Ⓖ Ⓗ Ⓙ
23 Ⓐ Ⓑ Ⓒ Ⓓ

24 Ⓕ Ⓖ Ⓗ Ⓙ
25 **OPEN ENDED**
26 Ⓐ Ⓑ Ⓒ Ⓓ
27 Ⓕ Ⓖ Ⓗ Ⓙ
28 Ⓐ Ⓑ Ⓒ Ⓓ
29 Ⓕ Ⓖ Ⓗ Ⓙ
30 Ⓐ Ⓑ Ⓒ Ⓓ
31 Ⓕ Ⓖ Ⓗ Ⓙ

32 **OPEN ENDED**
33 Ⓐ Ⓑ Ⓒ Ⓓ
34 Ⓕ Ⓖ Ⓗ Ⓙ
35 Ⓐ Ⓑ Ⓒ Ⓓ
36 Ⓕ Ⓖ Ⓗ Ⓙ
37 Ⓐ Ⓑ Ⓒ Ⓓ
38 Ⓕ Ⓖ Ⓗ Ⓙ
39 Ⓐ Ⓑ Ⓒ Ⓓ

40 Ⓕ Ⓖ Ⓗ Ⓙ
41 **OPEN ENDED**
42 Ⓐ Ⓑ Ⓒ Ⓓ
43 Ⓕ Ⓖ Ⓗ Ⓙ
44 Ⓐ Ⓑ Ⓒ Ⓓ
45 Ⓕ Ⓖ Ⓗ Ⓙ
46 Ⓐ Ⓑ Ⓒ Ⓓ

TEST 2   Reading Vocabulary

SA Ⓐ Ⓑ Ⓒ Ⓓ

1 Ⓐ Ⓑ Ⓒ Ⓓ
2 Ⓕ Ⓖ Ⓗ Ⓙ
3 Ⓐ Ⓑ Ⓒ Ⓓ
4 Ⓕ Ⓖ Ⓗ Ⓙ

5 Ⓐ Ⓑ Ⓒ Ⓓ
6 Ⓕ Ⓖ Ⓗ Ⓙ
7 Ⓐ Ⓑ Ⓒ Ⓓ
8 Ⓕ Ⓖ Ⓗ Ⓙ
9 Ⓐ Ⓑ Ⓒ Ⓓ

SB Ⓐ Ⓑ Ⓒ Ⓓ

10 Ⓕ Ⓖ Ⓗ Ⓙ
11 Ⓐ Ⓑ Ⓒ Ⓓ
12 Ⓕ Ⓖ Ⓗ Ⓙ
13 Ⓐ Ⓑ Ⓒ Ⓓ

14 Ⓕ Ⓖ Ⓗ Ⓙ

SC Ⓐ Ⓑ Ⓒ Ⓓ

15 Ⓐ Ⓑ Ⓒ Ⓓ
16 Ⓕ Ⓖ Ⓗ Ⓙ
17 Ⓐ Ⓑ Ⓒ Ⓓ

18 Ⓕ Ⓖ Ⓗ Ⓙ
19 Ⓐ Ⓑ Ⓒ Ⓓ
20 Ⓕ Ⓖ Ⓗ Ⓙ
21 Ⓐ Ⓑ Ⓒ Ⓓ
22 Ⓕ Ⓖ Ⓗ Ⓙ

TEST 3 Part 1: Math Problem Solving

SA (A) (B) (C) (D)

1 (A) (B) (C) (D)	9 OPEN ENDED	18 OPEN ENDED	27 (A) (B) (C) (D)	36 (A) (B) (C) (D)	45 OPEN ENDED
2 (F) (G) (H) (J)	10 (F) (G) (H) (J)	19 (F) (G) (H) (J)	28 (F) (G) (H) (J)	37 (F) (G) (H) (J)	46 (A) (B) (C) (D)
3 (A) (B) (C) (D)	11 (A) (B) (C) (D)	20 (A) (B) (C) (D)	29 (A) (B) (C) (D)	38 (A) (B) (C) (D)	47 (F) (G) (H) (J)
4 (F) (G) (H) (J)	12 (F) (G) (H) (J)	21 OPEN ENDED	30 (F) (G) (H) (J)	39 (F) (G) (H) (J)	48 (A) (B) (C) (D)
5 (A) (B) (C) (D)	13 (A) (B) (C) (D)	22 (F) (G) (H) (J)	31 (A) (B) (C) (D)	40 (A) (B) (C) (D)	49 (F) (G) (H) (J)
6 (F) (G) (H) (J)	14 (F) (G) (H) (J)	23 (A) (B) (C) (D)	32 OPEN ENDED	41 (F) (G) (H) (J)	
7 (A) (B) (C) (D)	15 (A) (B) (C) (D)	24 (F) (G) (H) (J)	33 (F) (G) (H) (J)	42 OPEN ENDED	
8 OPEN ENDED	16 (F) (G) (H) (J)	25 (A) (B) (C) (D)	34 (A) (B) (C) (D)	43 (A) (B) (C) (D)	
	17 (A) (B) (C) (D)	26 (F) (G) (H) (J)	35 (F) (G) (H) (J)	44 (F) (G) (H) (J)	

Part 2: Math Procedures

SA (A) (B) (C) (D) (E)

1 (A) (B) (C) (D) (E)	3 (A) (B) (C) (D) (E)	6 (F) (G) (H) (J) (K)	9 (F) (G) (H) (J) (K)	11 (F) (G) (H) (J) (K)	14 (F) (G) (H) (J) (K)
2 (F) (G) (H) (J) (K)	4 (F) (G) (H) (J) (K)	7 (A) (B) (C) (D) (E)	SB (A) (B) (C) (D) (E)	12 OPEN ENDED	15 (A) (B) (C) (D) (E)
	5 (A) (B) (C) (D) (E)	8 OPEN ENDED	10 (A) (B) (C) (D) (E)	13 (A) (B) (C) (D) (E)	

TEST 4 Language

SA (A) (B) (C) (D)

1 (A) (B) (C) (D)	7 (A) (B) (C) (D)	14 (F) (G) (H) (J)	21 (A) (B) (C) (D)	28 (F) (G) (H) (J)	35 (A) (B) (C) (D)
2 (F) (G) (H) (J)	8 OPEN ENDED	15 (A) (B) (C) (D)	22 (F) (G) (H) (J)	29 (A) (B) (C) (D)	36 (F) (G) (H) (J)
3 (A) (B) (C) (D)	9 (F) (G) (H) (J)	16 (F) (G) (H) (J)	23 (A) (B) (C) (D)	30 (F) (G) (H) (J)	37 (A) (B) (C) (D)
4 (F) (G) (H) (J)	10 (A) (B) (C) (D)	17 (A) (B) (C) (D)	24 (F) (G) (H) (J)	31 (A) (B) (C) (D)	38 (F) (G) (H) (J)
5 (A) (B) (C) (D)	11 (F) (G) (H) (J)	18 (F) (G) (H) (J)	25 (A) (B) (C) (D)	32 (F) (G) (H) (J)	
6 (F) (G) (H) (J)	12 OPEN ENDED	19 (A) (B) (C) (D)	26 (F) (G) (H) (J)	33 (A) (B) (C) (D)	
	13 (A) (B) (C) (D)	20 (F) (G) (H) (J)	27 (A) (B) (C) (D)	34 (F) (G) (H) (J)	

ANSWER KEY

8

ct: The *Titanic* ran into an
berg and sank.

ct: The ship ran into the iceberg
April 14, 1912.

9
A

10-11
C
A
B
D
A
C
D
A
C
. D

12-13
B
A
C
C
C
A
B
C
D

14-15
B
A
C
A
D
B
C
B
A
. A

16-17
B
C
D
D
B
C
C
D
A

18-19
B
A
C
C
D
D
D
A

p. 20-21
1. B
2. C
3. D
4. D
5. C
6. D
7. A
8. D
9. A
10. C

p. 22-23
1. B
2. C
3. B
4. A
5. D
6. A
7. C
8. B
9. D
10. C

p. 24-25
1. B
2. C
3. B
4. A
5. D
6. C
7. D
8. B
9. B
10. C

p. 26
Possible answers include:
1. The earl of Sandwich invented the sandwich.
2. The sandwich was invented in the 1700s.
3. The first sandwich was made of two slices of bread with roast meat in between.

p. 27
Check that you have four facts in your paragraph.

p. 28
2, 1, 3

p. 29
3. C

p. 30-31
1. 2, 1, 3
2. B
3. A
4. B
5. B

p. 32-33
1. 1, 3, 2
2. B
3. B
4. C
5. B

p. 34-35
1. 3, 1, 2
2. A

3. A
4. B
5. A

p. 36-37
1. 3, 1, 2
2. B
3. B
4. B
5. C

p. 38-39
1. 3, 2, 1
2. B
3. A
4. C
5. A

p. 40-41
1. 2, 1, 3
2. C
3. A
4. B
5. A

p. 42-43
1. 1, 3, 2
2. B
3. A
4. C
5. B

p. 44-45
1. 3, 2, 1
2. B
3. A
4. C
5. B

p. 46
Possible answers include:
1. First, two sets of doors close and lock.
2. A set of weights goes down while cables pull the car up.
3. When the car reaches the chosen floor, brakes hold the car in place.
4. The doors open, and people get out.

p. 47
Check that your story is written in sequence.
Check that you have used time order words, such as first, next, and last.

p. 49
2. A
3. B

p. 50-51
1. C
2. B
3. D
4. C
5. A
6. C
7. A
8. D
9. A
10. B
11. B
12. A

13. D
14. B
15. B
16. A

p. 52-53
1. B
2. D
3. B
4. C
5. C
6. D
7. C
8. C
9. A
10. B
11. B
12. D
13. B
14. C
15. B
16. A

p. 54-55
1. C
2. D
3. D
4. B
5. C
6. B
7. B
8. C
9. B
10. C
11. D
12. B
13. B
14. A
15. C
16. B

p. 56-57
1. A
2. D
3. B
4. D
5. A
6. C
7. A
8. C
9. D
10. C
11. A
12. C
13. C
14. A
15. B
16. D

p. 58-59
1. B
2. C
3. B
4. B
5. B
6. B
7. A
8. A

1. D
2. B
3. A
4. C
5. C
6. B
7. A
8. D

p. 62–63
1. C
2. B
3. D
4. B
5. D
6. B
7. A
8. B

p. 64–65
1. B
2. C
3. D
4. C
5. A
6. B
7. C
8. C

p. 66
Possible answers include:
1. umbrella or raincoat
2. head or clothes
3. drum or tuba
4. play or march
5. nails or wood
6. strange or wonderful

p. 67
Possible answers include
1. She dug deeper.
   She ran for help.
2. It was a bag of coins.
   It was a ring she had lost.
3. She would look for the owner.
   She would put it in a safe place.
4. She could walk dogs.
   She could be a pet sitter.
5. She was going on vacation.
   She needed help with her yard.
6. She will water Ms. Fielder's plants.
   She will mow Ms. Fielder's yard.

p. 69
2. The correct answer is D. The paragraph is about the lives of lion cubs. The number of cubs that are born is a detail. The paragraph doesn't really tell how hyenas and leopards hunt. We can tell that they hunt lion cubs because the mother lion wants to keep her cubs safe from them. The paragraph does not tell anything about the weight of cubs at birth.

p. 70–71
1. C
2. A
3. A
4. B
5. B

p. 72–73
1. A
2. B

3. C
4. B
5. A

p 74–75
1. D
2. C
3. D
4. C
5. A

p. 76–77
1. A
2. B
3. A
4. D
5. B

p. 78–79
1. B
2. A
3. C
4. B
5. A

p. 80–81
1. D
2. C
3. A
4. A
5. D

p. 82–83
1. A
2. A
3. A
4. C
5. D

p. 84–85
1. C
2. C
3. D
4. C
5. B

p. 86
Possible answers include:
1. A few rabbits were set free and caused a big problem in Australia.
2. Tom Bradley was an African American man who did a lot for Los Angeles.
3. A Native American actor became famous because of a tear.

p. 87
Check that you have underlined your main idea.
Check that you have used four details in your story.

p. 89
Fall or autumn, Thanksgiving, Fourth of July, Valentine's Day

p. 90–91
1. C
2. A
3. A
4. B
5. C

p. 92–93
1. B
2. C
3. A
4. C
5. D

p. 94–95
1. B
2. B
3. C
4. A
5. D

p. 96–97
1. C
2. C
3. A
4. B
5. B

p. 98–99
1. C
2. B
3. B
4. A
5. A

p. 100–101
1. B
2. B
3. B
4. D
5. D

p. 102–103
1. D
2. B
3. D
4. D
5. C

p. 104–105
1. D
2. D
3. C
4. C
5. D

p. 106
Possible answers include:
1. Jim Thorpe could play many sports.
2. Ms. is the newest title of respect for a woman.
3. Oprah Winfrey did not start out as a star.

p. 107
Possible answers include:
1. Paco's grandfather doesn't live with Paco. He is sharing Paco's room while visiting.
2. Paco and his grandfather probably don't have the same last name. This grandfather is the father of Paco's mother.
3. Texas became a state in 1845. Paco's family moved to Texas in 1847, two years after Texas became a state.
4. Paco's grandfather isn't interested in finding more family in Mexico. He says it seems as if they've always been in Texas.

p. 109

	A	B	C	D
2.	F	I	I	F

p. 110–111

	A	B	C	D
1.	I	I	F	F
2.	I	I	F	F
3.	F	F	I	I
4.	I	F	I	I
5.	F	F	I	I

p. 112–113

	A	B	C	D
1.	F	F	I	D
2.	I	F	I	D
3.	I	F	F	D
4.	F	I	F	D
5.	I	I	F	D

p. 114–115

	A	B	C	D
1.	F	F	I	D
2.	I	F	F	D
3.	F	F	F	D
4.	I	I	I	D
5.	I	I	F	D

p. 116–117

	A	B	C	D
1.	F	F	F	D
2.	I	I	F	D
3.	I	I	F	D
4.	I	F	I	D
5.	F	I	F	D

p. 118–119

	A	B	C	D
1.	F	F	F	D
2.	I	I	I	D
3.	I	I	I	D
4.	I	I	F	D
5.	I	F	I	D

p. 120–121

	A	B	C	D
1.	F	I	F	D
2.	F	F	I	D
3.	F	I	F	D
4.	F	I	I	D
5.	I	F	F	D

p. 122–123

	A	B	C	D
1.	F	I	I	D
2.	F	I	I	D
3.	F	I	F	D
4.	I	F	I	D
5.	I	F	I	D

p. 124–125

	A	B	C	D
1.	F	F	F	D
2.	F	I	F	D
3.	I	F	I	D
4.	F	F	I	D
5.	I	F	F	D

p. 126
Possible answers include:
1. A ship is being hit by a storm.
2. Devin is learning to bowl.
3. Javier is a soldier.

p. 127
Possible answers include:
4. Teresa doesn't think weights he with marathon running.
5. Teresa thinks marathon runners need to be thin.
6. Teresa is dependable, hardworking, and serious.
7. A coach could tell Teresa what she may not know about training for a marathon.

SPELLING SKILLS

p. 132
1. past, match, ask, snack, stamp, magic, pass, happen, answer, travel, plastic, grass, began, crack, glad, branch, half, banana
2. laugh, aunt

p. 133
1. crack
2. happen

magic
travel
stamp
grass
plastic
began
glad
0. half
1. answer
2. snack
3. banana
4. branch
5. laugh
6. aunt
7. past
8. ask
9. pass

134
Spell correctly: crack, travel, branch,
happen, pass
Add period after: thunder, shore,
quickly
Add: the [between "Watch" and
"sky"]; a [between "hear" and
"loud"]

135
glad, laugh, stamp
grass, magic, plastic
banana, began, brick
answer, ask, aunt
half, happy, have
crack, crisp, crumb

136
awake, chase, mistake, trade,
waste, taste, plane, space, state,
shape
paid, plain, afraid, trail, wait, waist
eight, eight, neighbor
break

137
plain
plane
waste
waist
weight
wait
taste
chase
trade
0. trail
1. state
2. space
3. paid
4. shape
5. eight
6. break
7. mistake
8. afraid
9. awake

138
Spell correctly: state, trail, Taste,
space, mistake
Capitalize: Are, See, It
Take out: to, be

139
chase
awake
trade
railroad
rotate
shape

7. trail
8. lightweight
9. acquaint
10. betray
11. save

P. 140
1. edge, ever, never, echo, energy,
fence, stretch, yesterday, desert
2. bread, ready, heavy, health,
breakfast, weather, sweater
3. again, against
4. friend
5. guess

P. 141
1. desert
2. health
3. friend
4. guess
5. heavy
6. never
7. edge
8. against
9. yesterday
10. ready
11. again
12. ever
13. weather
14. bread
15. sweater
16. fence
17. stretch
18. echo
19. energy

P. 142
Spell correctly: Yesterday, friend,
weather, breakfast, energy
Capitalize: July, We, Maria
Add: with [between "tennis" and
"my"]; the/our [between "start"
and "day"]

P. 143
1. again, age
2. sweater, stretch
3. health, heavy

P. 144
1. season, scream, reason, beach,
teach, means, speak, leaf, treat,
peace, please
2. knee, queen, between, sweep,
sweet, speech, seem, freeze,
squeeze

P. 145
1. sweep
2. queen
3. leaf
4. knee
5. scream
6. between
7. sweet
8. means
9. please
10. season
11. treat
12. speak
13. seem
14. speech
15. beach
16. squeeze
17. reason
18. freeze
19. peace

P. 146
Spell correctly: teach, means, season,
freeze, reason
Add question mark after: team,
spring, again
Add: of [between "member" and
"a"]; the [between "of" and
"year"]

P. 147
1. sweep
2. seem
3. scream
4. means
5. speak
6. squeeze

P. 148
1. March, May, June
2. Friday, Thursday, July, August,
Sunday, Monday, Tuesday,
Wednesday, April
3. October, December, September,
November, Saturday
4. February, January
5. Dr.

P. 149
1. February
2. Sunday
3. Tuesday
4. December
5. September
6. Saturday
7. November
8. Wednesday
9. April
10. Monday
11. October
12. Thursday
13. August
14. Dr.
15. May
16. June
17. March
18. July
19. Friday

P. 150
Spell correctly: Dr., Monday,
Tuesday, Friday, February
Capitalize: Wilson, Saturday, Eric's
Take out: to, the

P. 151
1. Jan-u-ar-y
2. Feb-ru-ar-y
3. A-pril
4. Ju-ly
5. Au-gust
6. Sep-tem-ber
7. No-vem-ber
8. De-cem-ber
9. Mon-day
10. Wed-nes-day
11. Thurs-day
12. Fri-day
13. Sat-ur-day

P. 152-153
1. answer
2. travel
3. aunt
4. half
5. laugh
6. afraid
7. eight

8. mistake
9. taste
10. neighbor
11. break
12. friend
13. stretch
14. against
15. energy
16. sweater
17. guess
18. reason
19. please
20. knee
21. speech
22. January
23. February
24. Wednesday
25. Dr.

P. 154
1. zebra, secret
2. easy, every, body, family, copy,
busy, city, angry, plenty, hungry,
sorry
3. radio, piano, ski, pizza
4. evening
5. people
6. police

P. 155
1. radio
2. secret
3. police
4. sorry
5. busy
6. ski
7. pizza
8. zebra
9. copy
10. city
11. body
12. easy
13. every
14. angry
15. evening
16. people
17. plenty
18. family
19. hungry

P. 156
Spell correctly: Family, easy, every,
people, busy
Capitalize: Saturday, Harvey, Follow
Take out: is, we

P. 157
1. I told the secret to Amy, Will,
and Edward.
2. I love music so much that I play
the violin, the piano, and the flute.
3. At the zoo we saw a zebra, an
elephant, and a lion.
4. I like pizza with cheese, peppers,
and onions.
5. Everyone in my family likes to
ski, skate, and sled.
6. The busy city has plenty of
people, cars, and buses.
7. Rita, Jenna, Karen, and Kim play
soccer.

P. 158
1. village, package
2. gym
3. quick, deliver, different, picture,

middle, interesting, written, bridge, thick, picnic, inch, begin, pitch, itch, chicken
4. guitar, building

P. 159
1. pitch
2. different
3. begin
4. quick
5. thick
6. interesting
7. written
8. deliver
9. chicken
10. inch
11. bridge
12. middle
13. picture
14. village
15. guitar
16. package
17. itch
18. building
19. gym

P. 160
Spell correctly: thick, village, middle, building, quick
Capitalize: People, Firefighters, It's
Add question mark after: go, return

P. 161
1. 2
2. 1
3. 3
4. gui-tar
5. pic-ture
6. pic-nic
7. writ-ten
8. be-gin
9. pack-age
10. dif-fer-ent
11. build-ing

P. 162
1. night, mighty, fight, flight, right, might, midnight, tonight, lightning, highway, high, bright, sight
2. dry, spy, supply, reply, deny
3. tie, die

P. 163
1. bright
2. right
3. mighty
4. night
5. lightning
6. high
7. sight
8. reply
9. deny
10. dry
11. midnight
12. tie
13. might
14. flight
15. fight
16. die
17. tonight
18. supply
19. spy

P. 164
Spell correctly: supply, night, midnight, spy, reply
Capitalize: Jessica, September, August
Take out: a, by

P. 165
1. 2
2. 1
3. 1
4. 2
5. 1
6. 2
7. 3
8. 1
9. 2
10. 3
11. 3

P. 166
1. life, knife, awhile, sunshine, smile, slide, beside, twice, write, surprise, size, wise
2. quiet, giant, climb, blind, behind, child, iron
3. buy

P. 167
1. surprise
2. giant
3. sunshine
4. behind
5. quiet
6. beside
7. iron
8. awhile
9. knife
10. smile
11. size
12. twice
13. life
14. buy
15. child
16. slide
17. climb
18. wise
19. blind

P. 168
Spell correctly: life, quiet, surprise, wise, climb
Add period after: tail, off, though
Take out: and, a

P. 169
1. giant
2. knife
3. iron
4. joy
5. smile
6. child
7. sunshine
8. size

P. 170
1. brothers, trees, pockets, rocks, hikes, gloves
2. dishes, classes, buses, brushes, inches, branches, peaches, foxes, boxes
3. families, pennies, cities, babies, stories

P. 171
1. buses
2. cities

3. rocks
4. brothers
5. pennies
6. boxes
7. inches
8. foxes
9. branches
10. babies
11. stories
12. families
13. trees
14. pockets
15. hikes
16. gloves
17. dishes
18. classes
19. brushes

P. 172
Spell correctly: families, cities, hikes, rocks, babies
Add period after: woods, watch, wildlife
Add: to [between "rocks" and "climb"]; as [between "such" and "rabbits"]

P. 173
1. Peaches
2. Her older brothers
3. Two cardboard boxes
4. Dance classes
5. My aunt's twin babies
6. The oak trees

P. 174–175
1. family
2. secret
3. radio
4. evening
5. people
6. police
7. gym
8. building
9. different
10. package
11. interesting
12. picture
13. lightning
14. tie
15. tonight
16. supply
17. quiet
18. buy
19. climb
20. surprise
21. pennies
22. babies
23. inches
24. brothers
25. families

P. 176
1. hobby, model, forgot, doctor, contest, object, o'clock, cotton, dollar, solve, knock, problem, bottom, beyond, knot, hospital
2. wash, wallet, watch, swallow

P. 177
1. swallow
2. knock
3. wash
4. watch
5. dollar
6. solve

7. cotton
8. contest
9. object
10. wallet
11. model
12. beyond
13. doctor
14. forgot
15. o'clock
16. knot
17. bottom
18. hobby
19. problem

P. 178
Spell correctly: hobby, wallet, watch, bottom, o'clock
Capitalize: Enter, Friday, Anyone
Add period after: page, enter

P. 179
1. beyond, preposition
2. cotton, noun
3. dollar, noun
4. forgot, verb
5. hospital, noun
6. knock, verb or noun
7. problem, noun

P. 180
1. clothes, total, ocean, obey, pony, poem, almost, only, comb, motor, hotel, zero, program
2. oak, throat, coach, coast, soap
3. goes, toe

P. 181
1. coast
2. almost
3. obey
4. total
5. goes
6. ocean
7. only
8. program
9. soap
10. zero
11. hotel
12. pony
13. comb
14. throat
15. poem
16. toe
17. oak
18. coach
19. clothes

P. 182
Spell correctly: coast, hotel, toe, comb, almost
Capitalize: August, Our, I
Take out: to, the

P. 183
1. Laurie, Amber, and Keisha climbed to the top of the rope.
2. Miss Santucci said that the rope feel as if they've been coated with soap.
3. On Tuesday we have basketball practice with Mr. Dowling.
4. Rebecca and Jamal keep track of the points that each team scores.

P. 184
1. froze, alone, broke, explode, chose, close, nose, those, stole

below, elbow, knows, pillow,
own, hollow, shadow, slowly,
tomorrow, window
though

185
hollow
broke
close
slowly
froze
below
alone
stole
pillow
). elbow
. chose
2. tomorrow
3. nose
4. knows
5. explode
6. shadow
7. own
8. those
9. though

186
ell correctly: froze, window,
though, shadow, slowly
apitalize: Suddenly, Then, Who
dd question mark after: window,
night

187
Bob said, "The door to the cellar
door froze shut."
"My model car broke!" yelled
Michael.
"Is something living in that
hollow log?" asked Delia.
Zak yelled, "Look at your shadow
on the wall!"
"Stay close together as we hike,"
said the guide.
Randi asked, "Is this pillow made
of feathers?"

188
suddenly, knuckle, brush, button,
fudge, hunt, until, subject, under,
jungle, hundred
rough, trouble, touch, couple,
enough, tough, country, double
does

189
brush
rough
fudge
knuckle
double
tough
under
does
subject
0. until
1. country
2. hundred
3. couple
4. trouble
5. touch
6. suddenly
7. enough
8. jungle

P. 190
Spell correctly: tough, until,
country, trouble, enough
Capitalize: Friday, Luther, Dr.
Add question mark after: week,
about

P. 191
1. couple, kŭp´əl
2. hundred, hŭn´ drĭd
3. rough, rŭf
4. touch, tŭch
5. tough
6. country
7. knuckle
8. subject
9. suddenly
10. enough

P. 192
1. weren't, doesn't, isn't, wouldn't,
wasn't, aren't, don't, hadn't,
haven't, didn't, shouldn't, couldn't
2. a. I'm;
   b. that's;
   c. we're;
   d. let's;
   e. they've;
   f. you'd;
   g. she'd;
   h. they'll

P. 193
1. I'm
2. they've
3. she'd
4. we're
5. you'd
6. let's
7. they'll
8. that's
9. weren't
10. didn't
11. don't
12. doesn't
13. wasn't
14. haven't
15. wouldn't
16. shouldn't
17. isn't
18. aren't
19. hadn't

P. 194
Spell correctly: didn't, couldn't,
weren't, I'm, that's
Capitalize: He, Bill, I
Add period after: nap, any

P. 195
1. The (video) store didn't have the
movie I wanted.
2. We're starting a (computer) club at
school.
3. Becca doesn't want the (lead) role
in the play.
4. You'd better pack your (long)
raincoat.
5. The guide said she'd meet us by
the (iron) gate.

P. 196-197
1. dollar
2. doctor
3. problem
4. watch
5. swallow

6. knock
7. hospital
8. goes
9. clothes
10. poem
11. throat
12. ocean
13. froze
14. though
15. knows
16. tomorrow
17. suddenly
18. tough
19. does
20. jungle
21. trouble
22. doesn't
23. we're
24. they've
25. weren't

P. 198
1. wonderful, discover, among,
front, other, brother, money,
cover, month, monkey, sponge,
nothing, stomach, once, another,
won
2. done, above, become
3. blood

P. 199
1. above
2. front
3. done
4. won
5. wonderful
6. nothing
7. brother
8. stomach
9. once
10. become
11. blood
12. sponge
13. month
14. among
15. monkey
16. other
17. money
18. another
19. cover

P. 200
Spell correctly: once, Another,
stomach, become, wonderful
Add period after: Zoo, stomach,
doctor
Take out: what, he

P. 201
1. underline second pronunciation;
money
2. underline second pronunciation;
nothing
3. underline first pronunciation;
brother
4. yes
5. da
6. yesterday
7. noon
8. af
9. afternoon

P. 202
1. wool, understood, cooked, stood,
notebook, brook, wooden,
good-bye

2. full, bush, sugar, pull, pudding,
during
3. should, could, would, yours
4. wolf, woman

P. 203
1. pull
2. woman
3. during
4. brook
5. full
6. bush
7. wool
8. pudding
9. sugar
10. cooked
11. notebook
12. wolf
13. yours
14. stood
15. wooden
16. could
17. should
18. would
19. understood

P. 204
Spell correctly: woman, during,
brook, sugar, wool
Capitalize: Lee, On, Lee's
Add period after: farm, time

P. 205
1. My father could not fix our
broken lawnmower.
2. Uncle Frank and Dad stood in
line for baseball tickets.
3. Danny's father said good-bye to
Dr. Dominguez.
4. We took a picture of Mom and
Dad near the wooden bridge.
5. My aunt asked Uncle Mike to
share his recipe for bread
pudding.

P. 206
1. goose, balloon, too, cartoon,
loose, shoot, choose
2. knew, grew, new
3. truly, truth
4. cougar, route, soup, group,
through
5. fruit, two, beautiful

P. 207
1. shoot
2. new
3. route
4. through
5. too
6. knew
7. two
8. beautiful
9. truth
10. group
11. balloon
12. loose
13. goose
14. fruit
15. truly
16. soup
17. cartoon
18. choose
19. grew

p. 208
Spell correctly: goose, truth, beautiful, group, new
Capitalize: The, Canada, Sometimes
Add period after: America, parks

p. 209
1. new
2. knew
3. two
4. too
5. new, knew
6. two, too

p. 210
1. loud, counter, hours, sour, cloud, ours, south, mouth, noun, proud
2. somehow, powerful, crowd, growl, towel, crowded, vowel, shower, crown, tower

p. 211
1. crown
2. hours
3. mouth
4. crowd
5. sour
6. loud
7. shower
8. growl
9. south
10. powerful
11. ours
12. crowded
13. counter
14. somehow
15. tower
16. towel
17. cloud
18. proud
19. vowel

p. 212
Spell correctly: vowel, noun, somehow, powerful, proud
Capitalize: October, A, I
Add: is [between "writing" and "amazing"]; are [between "words" and "put"]

p. 213
1. Julie said, "A big crowd always comes to see our team play."
2. "They practice for three hours each day," said Brian.
3. "Even when they're behind, they don't throw in the towel," said Chris.
4. "Let's give them a loud cheer!" shouted Ben.

p. 214
1. asked, trying, carrying
2. hoping, changed, pleased, caused, traded, closing, invited, tasted, saving, writing
3. swimming, beginning, jogging
4. studied, copied, dried, cried

p. 215
1. carrying
2. swimming
3. jogging
4. tasted
5. writing
6. cried
7. studied

8. traded
9. saving
10. hoping
11. closing
12. asked
13. pleased
14. copied
15. invited
16. beginning
17. dried
18. changed
19. caused

p. 216
Spell correctly: jogging, studied, cried, Saving, pleased
Capitalize: Street, Meanwhile, Theo
Take out: could, had

p. 217
1. invited me to come to her house last summer
2. swam in the pool each day
3. traded our favorite mystery stories
4. (is) writing a book
5. (are) reading her other books

p. 218-219
1. discover
2. blood
3. wonderful
4. stomach
5. once
6. sugar
7. should
8. understood
9. woman
10. during
11. through
12. beautiful
13. two
14. loose
15. truly
16. fruit
17. knew
18. crowd
19. loud
20. ours
21. asked
22. trying
23. beginning
24. copied
25. hoping

p. 220
1. enjoy, destroy, employ, employer, loyal, royal, voyage, loyalty, soybean
2. coin, moisture, spoil, point, poison, soil, join, avoid, voice, noise, choice

p. 221
1. voyage
2. poison
3. soil
4. loyal
5. choice
6. coin
7. point
8. voice
9. employer
10. soybean
11. loyalty
12. moisture

13. destroy
14. join
15. spoil
16. enjoy
17. noise
18. employ
19. avoid

p. 222
Spell correctly: enjoy, spoil, destroy, moisture, soil
Add period after: year, crop, too
Take out: this, can

p. 223
1. soil, noun
2. poison, verb
3. poison, noun
4. soil, verb

p. 224
1. pause, cause, because, author, applaud, autumn
2. strong, wrong, coffee, gone, offer, often, office
3. taught, caught, daughter
4. brought, bought, thought
5. already

p. 225
1. taught
2. applaud
3. strong
4. wrong
5. bought
6. thought
7. autumn
8. caught
9. author
10. pause
11. daughter
12. brought
13. offer
14. often
15. gone
16. already
17. office
18. because
19. cause

p. 226
Spell correctly: office, bought, daughter, because, often
Capitalize: Mr., Main, I
Add period after: tickets, over

p. 227
1. My favorite book, <u>Harry Potter and the Chamber of Secrets</u>, is gone
2. Shel Silverstein is the author of the poem "Recipe for a Hippopotamus Sandwich."
3. Our music teacher taught us the words to the song "City of New Orleans."

p. 228
1. lawn, straw, dawn, crawl, yawn
2. toward, water, quart, warm
3. morning, score, north, explore, before, shore, chorus, important, orbit, report, popcorn

p. 229
1. popcorn
2. lawn
3. straw

4. important
5. toward
6. yawn
7. orbit
8. score
9. report
10. dawn
11. morning
12. before
13. north
14. chorus
15. explore
16. crawl
17. warm
18. quart
19. water

p. 230
Spell correctly: dawn, north, choru[s] toward, before
Capitalize: Mr., Then, Everyone
Add: the [between "to" and "shore"]; a [between "had" and "great"]

p. 231
Add comma after: Richmond, 23, Donna, truly
1. shore
2. water
3. explore
4. morning
5. warm
6. report

p. 232
1. sharp, marbles, smart, large, heart, scarf, apart, alarm
2. share, they're, their, where, careful, square, there, stairs, fair, air, fare, stares

p. 233
1. air
2. sharp
3. alarm
4. scarf
5. smart
6. large
7. apart
8. careful
9. square
10. share
11. marbles
12. where
13. their
14. fair
15. stairs
16. fare
17. there
18. they're
19. stares

p. 234
Spell correctly: scarf, careful, smart large, apart
Capitalize: First, Are, Then
Take out: your, under

p. 235
1. where
2. heart
3. alarm
4. air
5. sharp
6. share
7. scarf

smart
apart
0. marbles
1. square
2. careful

236
Children, men, shelves, women, feet, teeth, sheep, oxen, mice, geese, knives, wives
man's, cloud's, woman's, women's, child's, children's, wife's, men's

237
mice
shelves
geese
sheep
knives
feet
teeth
men
oxen
0. women
1. children
2. man's
3. child's
4. wife's
5. cloud's
6. women's
7. children's
8. men's
9. woman's

238
pell correctly: knives, geese, man's, shelves, sheep
apitalize: Jacob, Rice's, Dr.
ake out: for, to

239
woman's
women
women's
children
children's
child's

240-241
choice
loyal
autumn
wrong
daughter
bought
often
already
dawn
0. toward
1. important
2. explore
3. stairs
4. where
5. careful
6. square
7. heart
8. they're
9. marbles
0. their
1. geese
2. wives
3. wife's
4. men's
5. oxen

p. 242
1. curve, learn, third, circus, skirt, heard, squirt, early, birth, germ world, circle, earn, dirty
2. hear, clear, dear, cheer, period, here

p. 243
1. curve
2. clear
3. cheer
4. dirty
5. world
6. birth
7. dear
8. here
9. heard
10. earn
11. hear
12. circle
13. period
14. third
15. squirt
16. skirt
17. learn
18. early
19. germ

p. 244
Spell correctly: circus, dirty, circle, squirt, cheer
Capitalize: We, Dr. The
Take out: a, would

p. 245
1. curves
2. births
3. circuses
4. brushes
5. skirts
6. matches
7. germs
8. boxes
9. worlds
10. animals
11. periods
12. horses
13. circles
14. axes
15. branches
16. dresses
17. cheers
18. glasses
19. inches
20. buzzes

p. 246
1. blizzard, simple, wrinkle, special, winter, summer, dinosaur, address, chapter, whether, whistle, purple, tickle, wander
2. together, animal, calendar, automobile, Canada, United States of America

p. 247
1. purple
2. blizzard
3. simple
4. wrinkle
5. address
6. wander
7. automobile
8. animal
9. together
10. whether

11. United States of America
12. chapter
13. winter
14. Canada
15. calendar
16. special
17. summer
18. tickle
19. whistle

p. 248
Spell correctly: dinosaur, summer, together, special, winter
Capitalize: Paint, Tape, Glue
Take out: and, in

p. 249
1. circle first pronunciation, blizzard
2. circle first pronunciation, animal
3. circle second pronunciation, whistle
4. circle second pronunciation, tickle
5. circle first pronunciation, simple
6. circle first pronunciation, wrinkle
7. circle second pronunciation, calendar
8. circle first pronunciation, summer
9. circle second pronunciation, purple

p. 250
1. afternoon
2. anything
3. forever
4. sometimes
5. without
6. everybody
7. basketball
8. countdown
9. inside
10. outside
11. nightmare
12. newspaper
13. upstairs
14. drugstore
15. everywhere
16. railroad
17. weekend
18. birthday
19. downtown
20. cheeseburger

p. 251
1. downtown
2. without
3. upstairs
4. everywhere
5. inside
6. forever
7. countdown
8. sometimes
9. birthday
10. basketball
11. cheeseburger
12. outside
13. everybody
14. anything
15. railroad
16. drugstore
17. newspaper
18. afternoon
19. weekend

p. 252
Spell correctly: weekend, Everybody, upstairs, without, forever
Capitalize: March, It
Add period after: Jo, top, forever

p. 253
1. The Plain Dealer is a newspaper from Cleveland, Ohio.
2. The railroad line was built across Rollins Street.
3. Mr. Diaz spent the afternoon fishing on Lake Erie.
4. Would you like to spend the weekend in the Rocky Mountains?
5. Carly said she wanted to stay in Carson City forever.

p. 254
1. Ave., Rd., St., Hwy., Blvd., Rte.
2. qt., cm, in., ft., gal., yd, km, l, mi., c., pt., m
3. F. C

p. 255
1. F
2 gal.
3. c.
4. yd.
5. cm
6. qt.
7. l
8. C
9. pt.
10. mi.
11. in.
12. km
13. ft.
14. Blvd.
15. Rte.
16. Hwy.
17. St.
18. Rd.
19. Ave.

p. 256
Spell correctly: St., Ave., ft., Rd., mi., yd.
Capitalize: Third, Go, Allen
Add period after: to, mailbox

p. 257
1. My family wants to follow Rte. 66 on a vacation.
2. Can you tell me how to get to Hwy. 12?
3. The temperature was 106° F in the shade!
4. Jessica made 2 gal. of lemonade.
5. Our family drove 100 mi. today.
6. The store at 632 Rose Ave. belongs to my dad.

p. 258
1. Earth, Mars
2. rotate, Pluto, Saturn, Venus, Neptune, comet, revolve, planets
3. gravity, Jupiter, galaxy, universe, meteor, satellite, Uranus, Mercury
4. constellation
5. so-lar sys-tem

p. 259
1. Mercury
2. Uranus
3. Mars
4. Neptune
5. Earth
6. Venus
7. Saturn
8. Pluto

9. Jupiter
10. comet
11. meteor
12. universe
13. satellite
14. constellation
15. planets
16. revolve
17. gravity
18. rotate
19. solar system

p. 260
Spell correctly: Earth, Mercury, meteor, solar, universe
Capitalize: Diego, Venus
Add: was [between "he" and "heading"], of [between "edge" and "our"], to [between "plans" and "see"]

p. 261
1. cleanse
2. host
3. peach
4. hoard
5. larva
6. burglar
7. squad
8. bouquet

p. 262
1. world
2. germ
3. early
4. circle
5. here
6. cheer
7. period
8. clear
9. automobile
10. whether
11. animal
12. wrinkle
13. special

p. 263
14. without
15. everywhere
16. birthday
17. in.
18. F
19. Blvd.
20. gal.
21. cm
22. satellite
23. gravity
24. Mercury
25. constellation

MATH SKILLS

p. 268

	a	b	c
1.	2,561	4,739	6,268
2.	8,091	5,473	3,502
3.	6,648	9,722	2,059
4.	3,541	1,943	5,540
5.	7,452		
6.	3,095		
7.	8,620		
8.	600	6,000	4
9.	30	300	900
10.	8,000	6,000	4

p. 269

1.					2,	3 9	5
2.		4	1	8,	7	0	2
3.	2	0,	0 9	1,	5	7	6
4.						9 8	7
5.				1	3,	8 2	0
6.		5,	4	8	2,	6 3	7

	a	b
7.	tens	ten thousands
8.	millions	hundreds
9.	ones	ten millions
10.	thousands	hundred thousands
11.	7 hundreds or 700	2 hundred millions or 200,000,000
12.	0 ones or 0	4 hundred thousands or 400,000
13.	3 millions or 3,000,000	9 ten millions or 90,000,000
14.	5 tens or 50	0 thousands or 0

p. 270

	a	b	c
1.	345,156	10,105	221,689
2.	2,970,534	369,571	50,148
3.	17,652,017	5,304,602	189,360
4.	529,031		
5.	76,411		
6.	8,050,200		
7.	2,307		
8.	94,655		

9. twenty-three thousand, eight hundred eighty
10. seven hundred thirty thousand, six hundred four
11. nineteen thousand, forty-two
12. five million, two hundred thousand

p. 271

	a	b	c
1.	>	<	<
2.	<	>	>
3.	<	=	>
4.	>	>	<
5.	=	<	>
6.	>	>	<

p. 273
1. Great white: 32,000 lb.
2. Chamberlain: 31,419 pt.; Jordan: 29,277 pt.; Abdul-Jabbar: 38,387 pt.
3. "Beast": 7,400 ft.; "Shivering Timbers": 5,384 ft.; "Mean Streak": 5,427 ft.

p. 274
1. eighty-eight thousand, eight hundred forty
2. two hundred fifty million
3. 9,365
4. 45,180
5. 661
6. 4,145
7. two thousand, five hundred fifty-five
8. fifty-five thousand, seventy

p. 275

	a	b	c	d
1.	12	7	13	9
2.	9	10	10	11
3.	4	4	15	7
4.	10	4	13	6
5.	8	8	9	8
6.	16	3	11	15

	a	b	c	d	e	f
7.	10	10	7	9	17	14
8.	13	10	16	6	9	11
9.	7	12	11	12	14	5

p. 276

	a	b	c	d	e
1.	29	49	89	68	99
2.	57	95	89	90	89
3.	961	653	727	968	679
4.	158	879	754	290	559
5.	99	286	789		
6.	879	495	336		

p. 277

	a	b	c	d	e
1.	81	61	54	62	53
2.	122	124	122	132	133
3.	485	657	539	892	418
4.	1,423	1,120	1,310	1,323	1,190
5.	61	1,063	429		

p. 278

	a	b	c	d	e
1.	133	136	133	155	176
2.	1,510	526	769	1,018	1,304
3.	956	1,127	727	1,171	1,361
4.	806	849			

p. 279

	a	b	c	d	e	f
1.	7	4	5	7		
2.	2	9	8	3		
3.	9	6	0	5		
4.	3	6	5	0		
5.	7	6	9	3		
6.	8	1	7	7		
7.	4	6	6	8	1	6
8.	5	10	9	8	4	3
9.	6	7	9	1	5	6

p. 280

	a	b	c	d	e
1.	23	70	43	52	31
2.	17	14	40	21	35
3.	435	500	835	334	234
4.	349	541	154	223	434
5.	35	324	322		
6.	425	740	858		

p. 281

	a	b	c	d	e
1.	34	26	48	8	13
2.	33	19	23	77	39
3.	76	75	78	248	250
4.	378	732	326	480	189
5.	77	286	188		

p. 282

	a	b	c	d	e
1.	19	145	188	239	56
2.	358	478	387	77	544
3.	476	169	130	756	183
4.	276	187	158		

p. 283

	a	b	c	d	e
1.	813	474	893	788	41
2.	787	812	768	1,073	99
3.	240	251	234	7	22
4.	167	248	363	557	20
5.	1,075	1,262	152		

p. 284

	a	b	c	d
1.	520	740	260	450
2.	220	870	340	610
3.	880	730	930	860
4.	800	700	200	700
5.	300	500	300	500
6.	900	800	900	100
7.	2,000	4,000	5,000	9,000
8.	4,000	8,000	6,000	2,000
9.	8,000	2,000	2,000	5,000

p. 285

	a	b	c	d
1.	50	160	120	70
2.	90	100	80	170
3.	800	700	800	1,10
4.	700	1,400	1,500	500
5.	120	600	1,200	

p. 286

	a	b	c	d
1.	20	10	30	10
2.	10	70	40	70
3.	200	600	100	30
4.	100	200	500	60
5.	50	500	300	

p. 288
1. Tyrone drove 512 miles on a two day trip. ~~He went 55 miles per hour.~~ The first day, he drove 305 miles. How may miles did he drive on the second day? 207 miles
2. Vicky worked ~~25 hours~~ last week and earned $175. This week she worked 28 hours and earned $196. How much did she earn altogether? $371
3. ~~There were 271 events in the 1996 Summer Olympic Games.~~ The United States won 44 gold, 32 silver, and 25 bronze medals. How many medals did the United States win in all? 101 medals
4. In a vote for favorite ice cream flavor, chocolate got 659 votes. ~~Vanilla got 781 votes, and~~ 246 people voted for strawberry. How many more people voted for chocolate than for strawberry? 413 people
5. One Earth year is about 365 days. One year on Mercury is 88 days. ~~On Mars, a year is 687 days.~~ How much shorter is a year on Mercury than on Earth? 277 days
6. A tiger ~~can run 35 miles per hour and~~ sleeps 11 hours a day. A house cat ~~can run 30 miles per hour and~~ sleeps 15 hours a day. How many more hours does a house cat sleep than a tiger? 4 hours
7. Kelly's web site got 129 hits on Friday and ~~240 hits on Saturday.~~ Tom's web site got 175 hits on

Friday ~~and 192 hits on Saturday~~. How many hits did their sites get altogether on Friday? 304 hits

p. 289

a	b
hundreds thousands	ten thousands millions
5 hundreds or 500	3 hundred thousands or 300,000
4 ten thousands or 40,000	6 tens or 60

19,206
411,035
2,658,000
723,104

	a	b	c
9.	>	=	<
10.	>	<	<
11.	450	270	140
12.	600	400	900
13.	6,000	4,000	9,000

p. 290

	a	b	c	d	e
4.	779	818	562	613	1,032
5.	679	267	901	757	1,104
6.	722	205	164	273	83
7.	731	278	544	512	8
8.	90	1,300	40	300	
9.	200	700	500	1,000	
10.	617	1,398			
11.	48	136			
12.	57	756			

p. 291

3. Ruth: 2,174 runs; Cobb: 2,245 runs; Mays: 2,062 runs
4. Mississippi: 2,348 miles; Yukon: 1,979 miles; Missouri: 2,315 miles
5. There are 100 senators and 435 representatives in Congress. ~~Senators serve 6 year terms and representatives serve 2 year terms.~~ How many members are in Congress altogether? 535 members
6. A person who weighs 100 pounds on Earth would weigh ~~254 pounds on Jupiter and~~ 38 pounds on Mars. What is the difference between the weight on Earth and the weight on Mars? 62 pounds

p. 292

a	b	c	d	e	f
24	14	25	15		
6	16	24	0		
27	16	6	8		
4	12	18	40		
30	15	14	14	9	12
28	40	27	8	9	32
5	20	18	16	45	0

p. 293

a	b	c	d	e	f
6	12	18	24	30	36
42	48	54	30	18	24
35	56	49			
28	7	42			
0	63	21			

P. 294

	a	b	c	d	e	f
1.	24	32	8	40	48	16
2.	56	72	0	40	56	32
3.	24	72	48	64	8	16
4.	45	54	36			
5.	9	72	0			
6.	81	27	63			

P. 295

	a	b	c	d	e	f
1.	16	12	7	12	72	21
2.	32	8	4	63	40	20
3.	35	54	8	36	6	45
4.	45	18	28	16		
5.	54	42	40	24		

P. 297

1. 20 tiles (4 by 5 grid)
2. 9 panes (3 by 3 grid)
3. 18 servings (6 by 3 grid)
4. 36 chocolates (4 by 9 grid)
5. 56 tulips (7 by 8 grid)

P. 298

	a	b	c	d	e	f
1.	8	4	3	5		
2.	7	8	9	2		
3.	3	1	4	9		
4.	5	6	2	7		
5.	7	1	7	8		
6.	6	8	4	5	1	7
7.	7	2	3	7	9	4
8.	2	6	9	3	1	2

P. 299

	a	b	c	d	e
1.	3	6	8	7	1
2.	4	5	2	9	3
3.	5	4	8	3	
4.	7	1	9	2	

5. a: $7 \times 5 = 35, 5 \times 7 = 35, 35 \div 7 = 5, 35 \div 5 = 7$
b: $7 \times 3 = 21, 3 \times 7 = 21, 21 \div 7 = 3, 21 \div 3 = 7$
c: $7 \times 8 = 56, 8 \times 7 = 56, 56 \div 8 = 7, 56 \div 7 = 8$

P. 300

	a	b	c	d	e
1.	6	7	9	4	2
2.	1	8	3	5	6
3.	5	2	4	9	
4.	7	6	3	1	

5. a: $9 \times 5 = 45, 5 \times 9 = 45, 45 \div 9 = 5, 45 \div 5 = 9$
b: $6 \times 9 = 54, 9 \times 6 = 54, 54 \div 9 = 6, 54 \div 6 = 9$
c: $3 \times 9 = 27, 9 \times 3 = 27, 27 \div 9 = 3, 27 \div 3 = 9$

P. 302

1. division 8 shells
2. subtraction 448 pages
3. subtraction 134 rats
4. addition 51 dollars
5. multiplication 30 rolls
6. division 4 hours

P. 303

1. a: 4 times 9 is 36.
$9 + 9 + 9 + 9 = 36$
$4 \times 9 = 36$
b: 45 divided by 5 is 9.
$5 \times 9 = 45$, so
$45 \div 5 = 9$

	a	b	c	d	e
2.	8	12	9	28	
3.	45	24	56	0	
4.	32	63	18	40	
5.	16	0	7	42	
6.	4	6	27	24	20
7.	36	14	64	0	7
8.	15	81	0	30	72

P. 304

	a	b	c	d	e
9.	9	7	8	7	
10.	9	6	8	8	
11.	8	9	4	8	
12.	6	9	7	6	
13.	7	6	4	4	8
14.	7	8	5	9	4
15.	5	4	4	1	4
16.	5	5	6	6	6

17. a: $6 \times 8 = 48, 8 \times 6 = 48, 48 \div 8 = 6, 48 \div 6 = 8$
b: $3 \times 8 = 24, 8 \times 3 = 24, 24 \div 8 = 3, 24 \div 3 = 8$
c: $7 \times 9 = 63, 9 \times 7 = 63, 63 \div 9 = 7, 63 \div 7 = 9$

P. 305

18. 30 stamps (6 by 5 grid)
19. 64 squares (8 by 8 grid)
20. multiplication 21 pieces
21 division 5 days
22. subtraction 166 passes

P. 306

	a	b	c	d	e
1.	80	90	50	80	60
2.	55	88	96	54	86
3.	390	840	280	290	990
4.	684	933	486	500	808

P. 307

	a	b	c	d	e
1.	60	48	64	50	84
2.	421	604	366	339	24
3.	66	93	49	88	109
4.	440	609	42	444	23
5.	26	884	900	639	46
6.	99	480	200		
7.	82	55	93		

P. 308

	a	b	c	d	e
1.	56	51	96	65	72
2.	168	112	315	156	240
3.	334	852	885	780	777
4.	1,134	1,990	1,185	2,367	3,904

P. 309

	a	b	c	d
1.	812	327	806	909
2.	540	621	812	820
3.	1,227	2,824	4,045	1,010
4.	4,368	2,012	6,132	6,500

P. 311

1. about 100 people
2. about 140 miles
3. about 210 miles
4. about 1,600 movies
5. about 120 dollars

P. 312

1. a: 492; b: 492; c: 540; d: 198; e: 108
2. a: 4,890; b: 4,218; c: 5,096; d: 1,743; e: 3,500

3. a: 12,264; b: 15,351; c: 30,632; d: 3,640; e: 68,880
4. a: 4,854; b: 1,698; c: 4,470

P. 313

1. a: 208; b: 384; c: 312; d: 400; e: 536
2. a: 5,768; b: 4,872; c: 4,212; d: 2,700; e: 6,642
3. a: 34,263; b: 26,136; c: 37,152; d: 81,459; e: 11,744
4. a: 2,528; b: 6,424; c: 152

P. 315

1. $22
2. 216 calories
3. 42 miles
4. 306 flowers
5. 495 pounds

P. 316

1. a: 48; b: 63; c: 150; d: 808; e: 432
2. a: 450; b: 378; c: 721; d: 1,600; e: 3,164
3. a: 1,026; b: 500; c: 640; d: 1,530; e: 1,644
4. a: 15,564; b: 34,560; c: 6,678; d: 27,135; e: 22,856
5. a: 100; b: 282; c: 288
6. a: 166; b: 360; c: 624
7. a: 1,799; b: 3,900; c: 11,604

P. 317

8. yes
9. about 4,500 miles
10. no
11. 176 people
12. 255 dollars

P. 318

	a	b	c
1.	23	14	11
2.	121	42	133

P. 319

	a	b	c
1.	71	54	41
2.	51	30	43
3.	31	52	72

P. 320

	a	b	c
1.	7 R1	8 R3	6 R2
2.	45 R2	56 R1	79 R3
3.	51 R1	69 R2	121 R3

P. 321

	a	b	c
1.	6 R1	9 R2	87
2.	81 R2	20	7 R3
3.	51 R2	7 R1	55 R1
4.	36 R1	6 R1	26
5.	43 R3	8 R1	67
6.	9 R1	39 R1	60 R4

P. 323

1. 4 photographs
2. 3 dimes, 1 penny
3. Jenna is 13 years old, Darius is 8 years old
4. 4 shirts
5. Adult is $6, child is $3.

P. 324

	a	b	c	d
1.	11	15 R2	3 R6	5 R5
2.	66 R4	72 R2	91 R2	69 R4
3.	711 R2	227 R2	288 R1	925

p. 325

	a	b	c	d
1.	4 R7	12 R1	5 R7	2 R2
2.	112 R2	77 R7	51	27
3.	411	138 R7	211	989
4.	12 R1	29 R2	963 R3	
5.	933 R4	62	61 R8	

p. 327
1. 140 pounds
2. 4,200 feet
3. $175
4. 27 weeks
5. 600 inches
6. 380 books

p. 328

	a	b	c	d
1.	12	21	13 R1	12 R1
2.	47	47	58	41
3.	26	15	54 R5	35 R5
4.	8 R5	5 R8	136 R1	64 R2
5.	32	14 R3	10 R3	
6.	136	148 R7	851 R1	

p. 329
7. 9 books
8. 7 pies
9. 29 newspapers
10. $17
11. 55 angelfish

p. 330
1. a: 1 ten
    × 6
    6 tens = 60

 b: 4 tens
    × 8
    32 tens = 320

2. a: 3
    × 8
    24 tens = 240

 b: 9
    × 1
    9 tens = 90

3. a: 1 hundred
    × 4
    4 hundreds = 400

 b: 8 hundreds
    × 2
    16 hundreds = 1,600

4. a: 7
    × 2 hundreds
    14 hundreds = 1,400

 b: 6
    × 3 hundreds
    18 hundreds = 1,800

p. 331

	a	b	c	d	e
1.	90	450	350	320	630
2.	540	210	720	180	250
3.	3,600	5,600	1,200	2,700	3,200
4.	3,500	4,200	6,400	2,400	1,800
5.	50	60	70		
6.	100	240	210		
7.	450	350	720		
8.	360	490	480		
9.	1,500	4,800	6,300		
10.	8,100	7,200	4,000		

p. 332

	a	b	c	d
1.	988	990	448	256
2.	585	1,591	572	608
3.	3,975	2,136	3,738	4,672

p. 333

	a	b	c	d	e
1.	924	4,402	1,276	784	4,956
2.	2,116	1,188	504	816	2,997
3.	1,276	544	3,290	1,235	1,175
4.	2,484	1,155	585		
5.	1,116	4,316	935		

p. 334

	a	b	c	d
1.	15,475	28,188	10,579	34,122
2.	10,206	11,480	17,135	19,872
3.	32,402	14,996	23,997	18,668

p. 335
1. a: 20,124; b: 14,681; c: 20,069; d: 15,708; e: 20,174
2. a: 10,488; b: 4,608; c: 26,048; d: 7,785; e: 8,316
3. a: 25,536; b: 5,162; c: 4,381; d: 30,240; e: 25,110
4. a: 17,668; b: 27,115; c: 10,922
5. a: 10,428; b: 60,635

p. 336

	a	b	c	d
1.	600	1,200	900	3,600
2.	2,400	3,600	2,400	4,000
3.	8,000	35,000	42,000	16,000
4.	1,500	4,800	72,000	

p. 337

	a	b	c	d
1.	800	4,200	1,400	1,800
2.	1,600	4,500	6,300	2,000
3.	25,000	36,000	18,000	54,000
4.	32,000	16,000	30,000	56,000
5.	300	3,200	2,400	
6.	20,000	35,000	10,000	

p. 339
1. $1,365
2. 1,230 miles
3. 915 people

p. 340

	a	b	c	d
1.	4 R8	7 R2	8	5 R4
2.	9 R7	1	6 R5	2 R3
3.	34	18	20	24
4.	63 R5	72	83 R4	67 R3

p. 341

	a	b	c	d
1.	9 R5	3	3 R2	9 R2
2.	6	7 R3	1 R5	93
3.	5	41	1 R5	2
4.	4 R1	2	3 R6	51
5.	9	7 R3	2	

p. 342

	a	b	c	d
1.	102 R2	307 R1	106 R5	208 R1
2.	40 R4	70 R3	30 R1	50 R3

p. 343

	a	b	c	d
1.	101	109	50 R3	80 R5
2.	60	704 R2	409 R1	90 R7
3.	30 R8	209	304 R1	500
4.	30	700 R4	90	401
5.	40	902	40 R1	

p. 344

	a	b	c
1.	too large	correct	too large
2.	too large	too large	correct
3.	correct	correct	too large

p. 345

	a	b	c
1.	too small	correct	too small
2.	too small	too small	correct
3.	too small	too small	correct

p. 346

	a	b	c	d
1.	13	17 R9	22 R4	26 R7
2.	3 R28	5 R23	8	8 R85
3.	214 R22	326 R9	278 R6	194 R13

p. 347

	a	b	c	d
1.	6 R16	6	58	15 R6
2.	14 R11	19	14 R4	62
3.	76 R27	56	195	126 R22
4.	54	33 R73	35 R59	85 R15
5.	167	29 R47	128 R7	314 R5
6.	11 R72	8 R11	13 R8	
7.	173 R8	202 R26	145 R5	

p. 348

	a	b	c	d
1.	40	50	90	90
2.	700	900	300	700
3.	7	2	20	40
4.	30	60	80	60

P. 349

	a	b	c
1.	90	80	30
2.	50	60	70
3.	500	700	600
4.	90	30	5
5.	8	20	3
6.	200	40	60

p. 351
1. 600 seats
2. $30
3. 70 times
4. 3,000 people
5. 9; 9; 90 computers
6. 3; 3; 30; 300 mph

p. 352
1. 52 miles
2. 35 boxes
3. $486
4. 133 pies
5. about 20 feet
6. 13 necklaces, 31 left

p. 353

	a	b	c	d
1.	360	280	800	600
2.	578	4,420	1,104	5,963
3.	3,240	16,378	23,374	28,003
4.	1,665	1,292	5,264	
5.	8,668	45,312	21,793	
6.	1,000	2,400	14,000	24,000

p. 354
7. a: 8 R5; b: 30; c: 2 R9; d: 80 R15
8. a: 20 R1; b: 110 R4; c: 205 R4; d: 308
9. a: 5; b: 49; c: 102 R24; d: 62 R40
10. a: 14 R7; b: 21 R26; c: 53 R75
11. a: too large; b: too small; c: correct
12. a: 80; b: 700; c: 8; d: 20

p. 355
13. $1,380
14. plates
15. 30 times
16. 7,000 people
17. 80 people

p. 356

	a	b	c	d
1.	4:45	12:30	8:55	7:0(

	a	b
2.	2 hours	240 second(
3.	600 minutes	120 hours
4.	6 days	9 minutes
5.	480 hours	30 minute(

p. 357
1. a: Wed., Nov. 14, 2001; b: Tues... March 27, 2001
2. a: Tues., Feb. 20, 2001; b: Wed... July 18, 2001
3. a: Wed., Nov. 28, 2001; b: Thurs., May 31, 2001
4. a: 168 hours; b: 4 years
5. a: 21 days; b: 730 days
6. a: 16 weeks; b: 180 months
7. a: 156 weeks; b: 12 weeks

p. 358

	a	b
1.	40 minutes	2 hours
2.	3 hrs 25 mins	5 hrs 5 mi(
3.	8:25	7:25

p. 359

	a	b
1.	2 hrs 35 mins	1 hr 35 mi(
2.	3 hrs 30 mins	1 hr 35 mi(
3.	2 hrs 15 mins	1 hr 20 mi(
4.	Kansas City	New Orlea(
5.	8:00	10:15

p. 360

	a	b
1.	100 pennies	20 nickels
2.	10 dimes	4 quarters
3.	2 half-dollars	5 dollars
4.	10 dollars	3 dimes
5.	11 nickels	5 quarters
6.	$2.30	$7.40
7.	9¢	$10.61
8.	$18.00	$13.02
9.	19¢	90¢

p. 361

	a	b	c	d
1.	$0.56	$0.83	$1.64	$1.81
2.	$7.33	$5.43	$7.60	$36.5
3.	$0.54	$0.13	$1.25	$10.1
4.	$0.49	$0.45	$1.87	$2.78

p. 362

	a	b	c	d
1.	$15.47	$9.28	$22.55	$8.48
2.	$27.50	$29.68	$37.50	$22.7
3.	$0.62	$0.70	$0.50	$0.62
4.	$0.40	$6.00	$6.02	$0.21

p. 364
1. $23.05
2. $12.00
3. 5:35
4. 2:45
5. $617.06

a	b
in.	ft.
ft.	mi.
lb.	T.
T.	oz.
c.	gal.
c. or pt.	c. or pt.

a	b	c
32 oz.	1 T.	2 lb.
9 ft.	1 mi.	72 in.
2 qt.	3 pt.	20 qt.

366

a	b
km	m
m	cm
kg	g
g	kg
mL	mL
L	mL

a	b	c
3,000 mL	5 m	2,000 g
4,000 m	8 kg	5,000 mL
1,000 cm	6 L	10 m

367

a	b	c
=	<	>
>	=	=
<	>	<
>	=	<
>	>	<
>	=	=
<	>	=

369

African elephant, 7,000 kg
American bison, 1,000 kg
2,000 kg
600 kg
drinking & eating, 2 gallons
bath, 40 gallons
60 gallons
280 gallons

370

a	b	c	d
6:35	11:45	2:20	4:05

35 days
3 years
420 mins
72 hours
6:55
9:15
$25.06 $9.15
$5.10 89
10. $18.75 $2.84 $75.20 $1.24
11. > =
12. > >

371

a	b
48 oz.	8,000 lb.
7 yd.	10,560 ft.
4 pt.	5 qt.
2,000 mL	7 m
$178.19	
7:20	
rye, 50 loaves	
20 loaves	

372

2; $\frac{1}{2}$; one-half
3; $\frac{1}{3}$; one-third
4; $\frac{1}{4}$; one-fourth

4. 5; $\frac{1}{5}$; one-fifth
5. 6; $\frac{1}{6}$; one-sixth
6. 8; $\frac{1}{8}$; one-eighth

P. 373

	a	b
1.	3	6
2.	8	10
3.	5	6
4.	25	7
5.	6	50¢
6.	$2.00	$8.00
7.	$2.00	5

P. 374

	a	b	c
1.	$\frac{7}{9}$	$\frac{6}{9}$	$\frac{3}{8}$
2.	$\frac{4}{5}$	$\frac{7}{10}$	$\frac{8}{9}$
3.	$\frac{2}{5}$	$\frac{7}{8}$	$\frac{5}{7}$
4.	$\frac{5}{9}$	$\frac{2}{7}$	
5.	$\frac{3}{10}$	$\frac{4}{6}$	

P. 375

	a	b	c
1.	$\frac{3}{8}$	$\frac{1}{7}$	$\frac{1}{5}$
2.	$\frac{1}{7}$	$\frac{7}{10}$	$\frac{1}{9}$
3.	$\frac{1}{3}$	$\frac{3}{8}$	$\frac{2}{7}$
4.	$\frac{4}{9}$	$\frac{4}{7}$	
5.	$\frac{3}{10}$	$\frac{4}{8}$	$\frac{1}{8}$

P. 377

1. 6 choices
2. 4 combinations:
   1 quarter, 7 nickels
   1 quarter, 5 nickels, 1 dime
   1 quarter, 3 nickels, 2 dimes
   1 quarter, 1 nickel, 3 dimes
3. 4 sundaes

P. 378

5. (2, 7)
6. (5, 4)
7. (9, 3)
8. (6, 1)
9. (0, 1)
10. (7, 6)
11. (1, 4)

P. 379

a
1. line segment
2. $\overline{PQ}$ or $\overline{QP}$

b
1. ray
2. $\overrightarrow{BC}$ or $\overleftrightarrow{CB}$

c
1. line segment
2. $\overline{JK}$

d
1. line
2. $\overleftrightarrow{AB}$ or $\overleftrightarrow{BA}$

Possible Answers:
3. $\overrightarrow{PB}$ or ray PB
4. $\overleftrightarrow{CB}$ or line CB, $\overleftrightarrow{BC}$ or line BC
5. $\overline{CP}$ or $\overline{PC}$ or line segment PQ
6. P or point P, Q or point Q, C or point C, B or point B

P. 380

1. **a:** ∠DEF or ∠FED; **b:** ∠QRS or ∠SRQ; **c:** ∠LMN or ∠NML; **d:** ∠EFG or ∠GFE

2.	acute	obtuse	right	acute
3.	right	acute	acute	obtuse

P. 381

	a	b
1.	16 ft	19 yd
2.	27 m	140 in.
3.	40 in.	

P. 382

	a	b
1.	6 square units	8 square units
2.	10 square units	12 square units
3.	16 square units	20 square units

P. 384

1. 288 ft
2. 240 ft
3. Steve
4. 2,626 ft
5. 54 ft

P. 385

	a	b	c
1.	4	4	3
2.	18	3	3
3.	$\frac{7}{8}$	$\frac{10}{11}$	$\frac{3}{4}$
4.	$\frac{4}{5}$	$\frac{5}{9}$	$\frac{7}{8}$
5.	$\frac{1}{4}$	$\frac{2}{11}$	$\frac{3}{7}$
6.	$\frac{4}{9}$	$\frac{4}{7}$	$\frac{1}{5}$

11. **a:** $\overleftrightarrow{AB}$ or $\overleftrightarrow{BA}$; **b:** $\overrightarrow{PQ}$ or $\overrightarrow{QP}$; **c:** $\overline{LM}$; **d:** ∠EFG or ∠GFE

P. 386

	a	b	c	d
12.	acute angle	obtuse angle	right angle	obtuse angle

13. 12 sq. units 8 sq. units 7 sq. units
14. 36 in.
15. 40 m
16. 9 sandwich choices
17. 6 different outfits

LANGUAGE ARTS

P. 388

Sentences and exact nouns will vary.
1. Tony, family, place, mountains,
2. Tony, boots, clothes, 3. fireplace, corner, room, 4. family, fire, food,
5. person, ranch, Tony, horse,
6. path, place, 7. Tony, dad, things, hike, 8. animals

P. 389

Common nouns: parents, vacation, car, friends, states, deer, family, week, cousins, trip; Proper nouns: Marcos, Dallas, Texas, Denver, Jackson, Utah, Nevada, California, Bay View Street, San Diego

P. 390

1. kangaroos, 2. pouches, 3. types, 4. animals, 5. emus, 6. ostriches, 7. grasses, 8. mammals, 9. otters, 10. foxes

P. 391

1. animals, 2. butterflies, 3. insects, 4. birds, 5. skies, 6. journeys, 7. rivers, 8. cities

P. 392

1. children, 2. men, 3. pants, 4. feet, 5. mice, 6. geese, 7. sheep, 8. deer, 9. moose, 10. teeth

P. 393

1. Ms. Kendall's students entered a cooking contest., 2. All of the class's recipes were original., 3. Tamisha's pork chops were tasty with applesauce., 4. Deon's hamburgers were a big hit., 5. Everyone enjoyed Jennifer's popcorn., 6. The popcorn's flavor was very spicy., 7. Mario's pizza won the grand prize., 8. The pizza's topping was made of fresh vegetables.

P. 394

1. the scarecrows' clothes, 2. the pumpkins' smiles, 3. the sisters' hats, 4. the seeds' flavor, 5. the plants' stems, 6. the women's costumes, 7. the flowers' colors, 8. the leaves' shapes, 9. the children's games, 10. the moose's calves, 11. the sheep's wool, 12. the classes' teachers, 13. the babies' toys, 14. the drums' sounds

P. 395

1. They; tornadoes, 2. It; funnel, 3. them; Scientists, 4. I; Kayla, 5. She; Kayla, 6. He; Grandpa, 7. him; Grandpa, 8. You; Phil, Brian

P. 396

1. it, 2. them, 3. She, 4. He, 5. They, them, 6. We, 7. us, 8. I, you, he, me, 9. they, I, 10. They, she

P. 397

He replaces Sequoia, They replaces sequoia trees, It replaces The General Sherman Tree. Sentences will vary.

P. 398

1. Emilia and Miguel visited the zoo with her., 2. The zoo seemed strange to them., 3. There were no cages in it., 4. "I'll show you the giraffes first," their aunt told them., 5. An ostrich wandered right up to it., 6. "The ostrich wanted a closer look at us," Emilia laughed., 7. Monkey Island made a good home for them., 8. Emilia asked him to take a picture of the monkeys.

p. 399
1. we, 2. I, 3. us, 4. me, 5. We, 6. me, 7. us, 8. We, 9. me, 10. us, 11. I

p. 400
1. Jason and Jana visited his birthplace., 2. Its location is near Hodgenville, Kentucky., 3. His birthplace was a small, one-room log cabin., 4. Their original cabin has been restored., 5. Only a few of its original logs are left., 6. Her climb up the steps to the cabin left her out of breath., 7. "May I use your camera?" Jason asked Jana., 8. His cabin is now part of a beautiful park.

p. 401
1. I'd, 2. It's, 3. I'm, 4. He's, 5. We're, 6. I'll, 7. He's, 8. You'll, 9. We'll, 10. they've, 11. They're, 12. you're

p. 402
Adjectives in paragraph (articles are not listed): seven, leather, Two, strong, each, many, several, extra, first, long, six, each, new; 1.–4. Adjectives will vary.

p. 403
1.–12. Adjectives will vary.

p. 404
1. small, dark; cages, 2. unhappy; visitor, 3. sorry; He, 4. large, airy; homes, 5. content; animals, 6.–10. Adjectives will vary. Nouns or pronouns are listed., 6. elephant, 7. ears, 8. home, 9. monkeys, 10. they

p. 405
1. a, a, 2. the, 3. the, 4. a, 5. an, 6. the, 7. an, 8. the, a, 9. an, 10. an, 11. an, a, 12. an, the

p. 406
1. oldest, 2. older, 3. prettier, 4. strangest, 5. higher, 6. stranger, 7. largest, 8. shinier, 9. smoothest, 10. deeper

p. 407
1. most, 2. more, 3. more, 4. more, 5. more, 6. most, 7. more, 8. most, 9. more, 10. most

p. 408
1. worst, 2. worse, 3. better, 4. worse, 5. worst, 6. better, 7. best, 8. better, 9. best, 10. worst

p. 409
1. invented, 2. have, 3. came, 4. revolve, 5. is, 6. circles, 7. was, 8. estimated, 9. found, 10. studied, 11. took, 12. showed

p. 410
Responses will vary. Be sure each answer is an action verb.

p. 411
1. playing, 2. made, 3. throwing, 4. collected, 5. sorting, 6. received, 7. collected, 8. saved, 9. added, 10. putting, 11. display, 12. won

p. 412
1. have; invited, 2. are; planning, 3. is; helping, 4. will; play, 5. has; made, 6. will; tug, 7. will; fall, 8. had; said, 9. had; worried, 10. will; bring

p. 413
Paragraph: am, reading; has, read; are, settling; has, explored; will, have; are, looking; have, discovered. 1.—6. Helping verbs may vary. Possible responses are given. 1. were, 2. had, 3. am, 4. will, 5. was, 6. have. Sentences will vary.

p. 414
1. is or was, 2. is or was, 3. is or was, 4. were, 5. was, 6. were, 7. am, 8. was, 9. were, 10. was, 11. was, 12. am or was

p. 415
Action verbs: invented, write, takes, flopped, barked, splashed; Linking verbs: is, was. 1. are, 2. am, 3. Are, 4. is, 5. are, 6. is. Sentences will vary.

p. 416
1. writes, 2. imagines, 3. believes, 4. mix, 5. draws, 6. uses, 7. fishes, 8. crushes, 9. reaches, 10. flies

p. 417
1. lived, 2. hiked, 3. carried, 4. dipped, 5. observed, 6. moved, 7. studied, 8. provided, 9. changed, 10. worried, 11. supplied

p. 418
1. will steam, 2. will chop, 3. will mix, 4. will put, 5. will have, 6. will stretch, 7. will learn, 8. will listen, 9. will see, 10. will head

p. 419
1. A blanket of cold air will settle on the valley., 2. Ms. Asato will read the weather data on her computer., 3. She will record a warning on an answering machine., 4. Hundreds of fruit and nut growers will call the line., 5. Frost will damage young plants and buds on trees., 6. The growers will work late into the night., 7. They will roll their huge wind machines into the orchards., 8. These giant fans will move the air., 9. The movement of the air will raise temperatures a few degrees., 10. Wet ground also will keep temperatures higher.

p. 420
1. went, 2. gone, 3. seen, 4. began, 5. thought, 6. brought, 7. said, 8. began, 9. made, 10. went

p. 421
Responses will vary. Be sure each answer contains the verb form shown. 1. blown, 2. fallen, 3. flew, 4. fell, 5. dug, 6. grown, 7. rode, 8. ridden, 9. wrote, 10. written, 11. given, 12. spoken

p. 422
1.–5. Responses will vary. Be sure each sentence includes the adverb in parentheses., 6.–9. Responses will vary. Be sure each answer is an adverb that tells when or where.

p. 423
Responses will vary. Be sure each sentence includes an adverb from the box.

p. 424
1. more slowly, 2. most carefully, 3. steadily, 4. faster, 5. more eagerly, 6. more skillfully, 7. most skillfully, 8. more quickly, 9. most cheerfully, 10. proudly

p. 425
1. Ben and Me is a humorous book about Benjamin Franklin.; adjective, 2. The story is amusingly told from a mouse's point of view.; adverb, 3. Johnny Tremain is another popular story about early America.; adjective, 4. It tells about exciting events of the American Revolution.; adjective, 5. Johnny is a young silversmith.; adjective, 6. He willingly helps the patriots fight for independence.; adverb

p. 426
1. Lake Slo was a good fishing spot., 2. correct, 3. None of the six of us had good luck., 4. I thought I'd do well because I had my best flies., 5. correct, 6. "How did you do that so well?", 7. correct, 8. It's not a good idea to be in the hot sun all day without a hat., 9. correct

p. 427
1. sentence, 2. Accept completed sentence response., 3. sentence, 4. sentence, 5. Accept completed sentence response., 6. Accept completed sentence response., 7. sentence, 8. Accept completed sentence response.

p. 428
Subjects and predicates will vary. Possible responses: 1. helps you remember things, 2. A test, 3. Social studies, 4. is the way we communicate, 5. tells a complete thought

p. 429
1. Sylvie Martin hears the rain on the roof., 2. The rain is falling softly., 3. The young woman puts on her rain jacket., 4. Her shoes are waterproof., 5. This person walks toward the beach., 6. The streets are quiet today., 7. Sylvie steps carefully over puddles., 8. She hums softly to herself., 9. Her rain jacket keeps her dry., 10. Miss Martin is comfortable in the rain.

p. 430
1. fair; The county's fair, 2. family; My whole family, 3. games; The games on the midway, 4. brother; My little brother, 5. winner; The lucky winner, 6. tents; Three big tents, 7. chicken; The finest chicke 8. hog; A plump hog

p. 431
1. Sun, sand, 2. Residents, tourists 3. Peace, quiet, 4. Molokai, Lanai, 5. forests, canyons, 6. weather, breezes, 7.–10. Sentences will vary Be sure each sentence has a compound subject.

p. 432
Paragraph: Dogs and humans, dogs humans; Huge hounds and tiny puppies, hounds, puppies: They; Dogs and their owners, Dogs, owners; Dogs; Specially trained dog dogs; Guide dogs, dogs; Sled dogs, dogs; Most dogs and their owners, dogs, owners. 1.–2. Sentences may vary. 1. German shepherds and Doberman pinschers can be excelle watchdogs., 2. Children and their parents often enjoy training dogs.

p. 433
Simple predicates will vary. Possible responses are included in the complete predicate. 1. see some of the most beautiful scenery in America, 2. reach high into the sky 3. stands in central Alaska, 4. mean "the great one.", 5. is Mount McKinley, 6. cover much of Alaska 7. roam in Alaska's back country, 8 wanders into town, 9. is a funny b scary sight, 10. enjoy fishing in the clear blue lakes and rushing rivers.

p. 434
1. curl, sleep, 2. stays, cares, 3. floa sleep, 4. anchor, float, 5. sprawls, relaxes, 6.–10. Responses will vary. Be sure each sentence has a compound predicate.

p. 435
Paragraph: worked hard on the cla play, worked; formed committees and made plans, formed, made; discussed the play for hours, discussed; wrote and rewrote the script many times, wrote and rewrote; sounded terrific, sounded worked hard, too, worked; collecte old-fashioned shirts for the cast members, collected; volunteered fo the sets committee, volunteered; sketched many different ideas, sketched; chose the best sketch and turned it into a set, chose, turned; hammered, sawed, and painted for many days, hammered, sawed, painted 1. The actors read the scrip and memorized their lines., 2. Everyone in the audience stood up, clapped, and cheered for us.

p. 436
Possible response: Eduardo has always loved the circus, and now h is making plans to become a circus performer. He has taken gymnastic classes, and his teacher is impressec with Eduardo's skill. Eduardo also belongs to a drama club. He likes

rforming in all kinds of plays, but
medies are his favorite. Soon
duardo will have to decide which
lls to develop. He may become a
rcus acrobat, or he may decide to
come a circus clown.

437
Did you know that very few
ople have been attacked by
arks?; interrogative, 2. Many types
sharks are not very big.;
clarative, 3. One kind is only about
long as your hand.; declarative,
How can sharks find food in the
ark?; interrogative, 5. They use
eir senses of hearing, smell, and
ght.; declarative, 6. Some sharks
ll eat anything.; declarative,
Have you heard that nails, jewels,
d even clothing have been found
side sharks' stomachs?;
terrogative

438
.; imperative, 2. !; exclamatory,
.; imperative, 4. .; imperative,
!; exclamatory, 6. !; exclamatory,
; imperative, 8. !; exclamatory,
; exclamatory, 10. .; imperative,
. .; imperative, 12. !; exclamatory

439
is, 2. taste, 3. eat, 4. were, 5. was,
tastes, 7. is, 8. hold, 9. takes,
. are, 11. are, 12. am

440
knows, 2. expect, 3. find,
surprise, 5. watches, 6. moves,
laugh, 8. speeds, 9. likes,
. show, 11. admires, 12. grows

441
ssible response: My parents and I
ent to Washington, D.C., last year.
e left on Monday and drove for
ree days. I got tired of riding and
as glad when we arrived in
ashington. Dad took us to the
apitol and showed us our senator's
fice. Mom loves history and wanted
see the National Museum of
merican History. I had read about
e pandas and asked to go to the
ational Zoo to see them. We all
mire Abraham Lincoln and were
rilled to see the Lincoln
emorial. We had a good time in
ashington and learned a lot about
ur country, too.

442
Schools and libraries should have
mps as well as steps., 2. People in
heelchairs and people on crutches
nd it hard to climb stairs.,
Libraries and other public
uildings should have elevators.,
Door handles and elevator buttons
ould be placed low., 5. People in
heelchairs and everyone else can
ach them there.

443
ntences may vary. Possible
sponses are given. 1. Many kinds
spiders spin webs, but not all of

the webs are alike., 2. A web may be
long and narrow, or it may be
shaped like a triangle., 3. Some
webs are like funnels, but others
look more like domes., 4. Wolf
spiders hide in burrows, but lynx
spiders live on trees or bushes.,
5. Many lynx spiders are green, and
they are hard to find on green
leaves., 6. Tarantulas are furry, and
they look fierce.

P. 444
1. Rey-Ling, Karen, and Mitch gave
a party., 2. They met on Monday,
Tuesday, and Wednesday to plan the
party., 3. They invited Tina, Mark,
and Lee., 4. Each guest received a
paper hat, a balloon, and a new
pencil., 5. The children played
Simon Says, Musical Chairs, and Pin
the Nose on the Clown., 6. Mitch,
Rey-Ling, and Karen taught the
others a new game., 7. Tina, Lee,
and Karen sang a funny song.

P. 445
Answers will vary. Possible responses
are given. 1. wise, 2. yellow,
3. grizzly, 4. bravely, 5. fierce,
6. adorable, 7. cuddly, 8. white,
9. sports, 10. football

P. 446
Possible responses are given. 1. I
went to see a play. It was based on
the book Charlotte's Web., 2. The
play had no adult actors., 3. A boy
played the part of Wilbur the pig.,
4. Charlotte was a very smart spider,
and Wilbur was her friend.,
5. Charlotte wrote words with her
web., 6. A girl played the part of
Charlotte. Her costume was black.,
7. She looked like a giant spider.

P. 447
1. Americans celebrate
Independence Day on July 4.,
2. People in Canada celebrate their
country's birthday in July, too.,
3. It's called Dominion Day or
Canada Day., 4. On July 1, 1867,
Canada gained its independence.,
5. Two special holidays are celebrated
in Mexico., 6. Both September 16
and May 5 call for parades and
speeches., 7. Next Monday,
September 3, we will celebrate
Labor Day., 8. Flags will be
displayed on Cherry Street.

P. 448
1. Sherman Smith has an unusual
nickname., 2. Someone took Cindi's
doll., 3. The only suspect is Mr.
Treworgy., 4. Mrs. Sample does not
have the doll., 5. Dr. Carter treated
a boy the same morning., 6. Sherman
asked Capt. Kent for help., 7. Did
you see where I left my doll?, 8. I
cannot believe that I lost it.

P. 449
1. School started last week., 2. This
year I have a new teacher., 3. Her
name is Ms. Aarvig., 4. She has

given us some interesting arithmetic
problems., 5. The problems took a
long time to solve., 6. The answers
we got were really amazing., 7. One
of my favorite books is The
Amazing Number Machine., 8. My
brother is reading the story "The
Math Magician.", 9. My teacher
read aloud the article "It All Adds
Up.", 10. Have you ever read the
poem "Crazy Eights"?, 11. Another
good book is Math Curse., 12. The
author also wrote The True Story of
the Three Little Pigs.

P. 450
1. The new arithmetic books are red
and yellow., 2. Arithmetic is my first
class every morning., 3. I have to
wake up early to get to class on
time., 4. Pages full of arithmetic
problems are a challenge., 5. Mrs.
Washington is my arithmetic teacher
this year., 6. Sometimes Dr. Carver
attends our class., 7. Ryan B. Right
is the smartest boy in my arithmetic
class., 8. T. C. Russell won an award
at the arithmetic fair., 9. I shared my
book today with J. D. Kline.,
10.
I. Arithmetic Every Day
  A. In the classroom
  B. At home
  C. At the store

P. 451
1. Dr. J. F. Newsome, 2. 1623
Plateau Dr., 3. Thurs., Nov. 10,
4. Sen. M. Jackson, 5. Capt. M. M.
Uribe, 6. Sat., Sept. 30, 7. 403
Jungle Blvd., 8. Tues., Aug. 18,
9. Mrs. R. V. Toliver, 10. 2204
Mountain Ave., 11. Wed., Apr. 27,
12. Mr. A. C. Hwang

P. 452
1. Yes, Mrs. and Mrs. Saxby helped
the boys., 2. First, he told them
about the plan., 3. The boys studied
letters, words, and maps., 4. Mrs.
Saxby talked about Searsville,
Richmond, Washington, and
Philadelphia., 5. Mr. Saxby had a
map, but the boys lost it., 6. Mrs.
Saxby pasted a label on a jar, and
she put jelly in it., 7. "Andy, you
must pretend that this is not
yours.", 8. "Travel by day," said Mr.
Saxby.

P. 453
1. Mambas eat lizards, rodents, and
birds., 2. The green mamba has
lime-green skin, a long head, and a
large mouth., 3. Pythons eat
rodents, lizards, and small
mammals., 4. They live in Africa,
Asia, and Australia., 5. They attack,
grab, and squeeze their prey., 6. The
ball python is a short, strong, and
handsome snake., 7. It eats rats,
mice, and other rodents.,
8. Poisonous snakes include cobras,
vipers, and rattlesnakes.

P. 454
1. Lone Star, Texas 75668,
2. November 15, 2005, 3. Winter
Park, Florida 32792, 4. August 2,
2005, 5. Juneau, Alaska 99673,
6. December 23, 2005, 7. Dear
Aunt Rita, 8. Sincerely yours,
9. Dear Mother, 10. Your friend,
11. Dear Mika,

P. 455
1. ?, 2. !, 3. ?, 4. !, 5. ?, 6. !, 7. ?,
8. !, 9. ?, 10. ?, 11. !, 12. ?, 13. ?,
14. !

P. 456
1. Erika's birthday was on a cold
winter day., 2. The children's faces
lit up when they saw the snow.,
3. The two girls' walk home was
difficult., 4. Her mother's voice
greeted Erika., 5. "We don't have
everything for your party.", 6. "I'll
go with you to the store," Erika
replied., 7. "Where's father?" Erika
asked., 8. "We'll look for your father
on the way to the store.", 9. She
added, "Father left at 6:30 this
morning.", 10. "I left school at
3:15 this afternoon," said Erika.

P. 457
1. hadn't, 2. couldn't, 3. wasn't,
4. don't, 5. haven't, 6. mustn't,
7. weren't, 8. shouldn't, 9. can't,
10. won't

P. 458
1. "How would you like to paddle a
canoe through a swamp?" asked Mr.
Vasquez., 2. Tyler asked, "Will we
see any alligators?", 3. Mr. Vasquez
answered, "We might see some deer
and bobcats.", 4. "Why does swamp
water look brown?" asked Carla.,
5. "It gets its color from plants in
the water," Megan explained.,
6. Ray asked, "What kinds of plants
grow in swamps?", 7. "One unusual
plant is the neverwet," Mr. Vasquez
said.

P. 459
1. "Dad is bringing home a puppy
today," Trudi said., 2. "What kind
of puppy will he choose?" asked
Chris., 3. Trudi said, "I asked for a
pug.", 4. "Where is my puppy?"
Trudi asked., 5. "Go into the yard,
Trudi," her mother replied., 6. "Is it
in the yard?" Trudi asked eagerly.,
7. Trudi wrote a poem called "My
Puppy.", 8. She read a story called
"Our Dog Digger.", 9. Trudi read
the book How to Be a Good
Master., 10. Then, she watched the
television show Lassie., 11. She read
The Alphabet Book to her baby
brother., 12. Next, she will read A
Trip to the Zoo to him.

P. 460
Answers may vary. 1. railroad,
2. workmen, 3. overnight, 4. upstairs,
5. wallpaper, 6. bedspreads,
7. fireplace, 8.–10. Sentences will

vary. Be sure the compound word is correctly written and used.

p. 461
Synonyms may vary. 1. courageous, 2. difficulties, struggles, 3. spread, thrived, 4. key, important, 5. depended, counted, 6. helped, aided, 7. Tales, Legends, 8. chances, jobs, 9. travels, trips, 10. class, book

p. 462
Antonyms may vary. Possible responses are given. 1. interesting, 2. small, 3. closed, 4. play, 5. painful, 6.–8. Responses will vary. Be sure each answer includes an antonym of the underlined word.

p. 463
1. unfair, 2. impatiently, 3. preplanned, 4. misunderstood, 5. uncovered, 6. retraced, 7. incapable

p. 464
1. enjoyable, 2. conductor, 3. graceful, 4. singer, 5. player, 6. dreamy

p. 465
1. slip, 2, 2. wind, 1, 3. roll, 2, 4. slip, 1, 5. bass, 1, 6. wind, 2, 7. roll, 1, 8. bass, 2. Sentences will vary. Be sure that the homograph is used correctly.

p. 466
1. meets, 2. read, 3. Would, 4. choose, 5. hear, 6. pale, 7. knew, 8. tail, 9. wait, 10. heard

p. 467
1. to, 2. two, 3. to, 4. too, 5. its, 6. It's, 7. its, 8. it's

p. 468
1. you're, 2. your, 3. your, 4. you're, 5. their, 6. They're, 7. there, 8. They're, 9. their

p. 469
1. ever, 2. any, 3. was, 4. anybody, 5. any, 6. any, 7. were, 8. anything, 9. any, 10. any

p. 470
Paragraphs may vary.
Dove was dressing for Wren's party. How proud she was of her snowy white dress! It might be the most beautiful outfit at the party. Dove turned around and around. She admired her reflection in the mirror. "How lovely I look!" she cried. Then her wing bumped a bottle of ink that was sitting on her desk. The bottle turned over, and splash! Down the front of Dove's dress went an inky black stain. Moral: Be proud of yourself, but not more proud than you should be.

p. 471
Possible responses are given. Be sure responses are appropriate synonyms. 1. peaceful, 2. towering, glistening, 3. colorful, 4. gentle, 5. precious, lovely, 6. fabulous, 7. bustling, 8. ear-splitting, frantic

p. 472
1. a golden mirror, 2. jagged teeth, 3. a melting ball of wax, 4. a pink and orange flame, 5.–8. Responses will vary. Be sure that similes and metaphors are descriptive.

p. 473
Answers will vary. Possible responses are given. 1. The clouds blocked the sun., 2. The tree creaked as the wind blew against it., 3. Dust came out of the blanket when it was shaken., 4. Tiblo had some trouble getting the fire started., 5. The sun smiled on Earth., 6. A small cave was hiding in the rocks.

p. 474
Answers will vary. Possible responses are given. 1. An army of raindrops attacked the mountaintop., 2. Daffodils danced gracefully to the music of the wind., 3. Lightning struck the tree like a flaming spear., 4. The moon was a bright white balloon floating in the sky., 5. A wolf sang its sad, lonely song to the forest trees., 6. A friendly wind skipped across the sleepy meadow., 7. The building was as tall as a mountain., 8. Carl ate a ton of food for lunch.

p. 475
Detail sentences will vary. Be sure that responses pertain to the topic.

p. 476
1. Scuba divers explore the ocean wearing air tanks., 2. Death Valley is in California; The dingo is a special type of dog. It is a wild dog that lives in Australia. Dingoes usually howl instead of bark. They can make good pets if they are caught as puppies.

p. 477
Answers may vary. 1. Good study habits contribute to better grades., 2. The writer's brother's grades improved from C's to B's when he studied without the radio., 3. It shows that quiet studying improves grades., 4.–6. Responses will vary. Be sure that each answer supports the statement.

p. 479
1. The lights go out at the party., 2. Teresa lights Halloween candles., 3. Amy and Teresa

p 481
Answers will vary.

p. 482
1. a new doll, 2. bright colors, lifelike eyes, finely stitched clothes, beautiful buttons, soft lace, shoes as soft as butter, 3. Answers will vary.

p. 485
1. Ben, 2. 627 Swan Street, Raleigh, NC 27611, 3. Dear Jason, 4. summer vacation

p. 488
1. how to recycle paper at home, 2. gather old and unwanted newspapers, magazines, and catalogs, 3. store the paper bundles in a dry place until pickup day, 4. first, then, next, finally

p. 491
1. When paper is recycled, it doesn't just become recycled paper. It is made into many different new products., 2. Student should name four: cereal boxes, shoe boxes, egg cartons, paper towels, tissues, greeting cards, plaster boards, tar paper, stiffener for car visors and doors, 3. Answers will vary but should be a detail sentence from the paragraph.

p. 494
1. Colonial Williamsburg and Old Sturbridge Village, 2. Colonial Williamsburg shows city life in the 1700s, but Old Sturbridge shows country life in the 1830s. The buildings and locations are different, too., 3. Both show what life was like in the past. Both have many shops and buildings open to tourists. Both have popular demonstrations of crafts.

p. 497
1. It was hungry., 2. It knew there were no bones in the yard., 3. It got lost., 4. The boy was happy, and the dog got a big bone.

p. 500
1. The Incredible Journey., 2. Sheila Burnford, 3. Tao, Bodger, and Luath, 4. in the Canadian wilderness, 5. yes

p. 503
1. Students should vote for the lioness as the symbol of our new school., 2. The lioness is intelligent and carries itself with pride. The lioness brings out a feeling of respect in people., 3. Vote for the lioness to choose a symbol of intelligence, pride, and respect.

p. 507
1. cherry, chip, 2. four, 3. a young boy or girl, 4. carrot, cactus, 5. no

p. 508
1. parka, 2, 2. snow, 1, 3. machine, 2, 4. caribou, 3, 5. father, 2, 6. surprise, 2, 7. light, 1, 8. whale, 1

p. 509
Answers may vary. Be sure answers are appropriate synonyms. 1. actually, 2. unusual, 3. difficult, 4. upset, 5. glad, 6. frequently, 7. thrilling

p. 510
1. 2, 2. 1, 3. 9, 4. 4, 5. 8, 6. 6, 7. 4, 8. 12, 9. 10, 10. 5, 11. Greenland, 12. Arctic, 13. South Pole, 14. Peary, 15. Alaska

p. 511
Answers may vary. 1. Science, 2. Health and Fitness, 3. Shopping, 4. Arts and Entertainment, 5. New 6. Reference Materials, 7. Reference Materials

p. 512
1. A Number of Stories, 2. Lisa Newton, 3. Brandywine Arts, Inc., 4. Adding It Up, 5. Time Tells All, 6. 58–60 and 119, 7. addition word problems

p. 513
1. The title tells what the paragraph is about., 2. fairy tale, 3. to tell legends and customs of real people 4. Cinderella, 5. real people, 6. fair tale, 7. happy

p. 514
1. jaguar, leopard, boa constrictor, tiger, spider monkey, 2. polar bear, arctic fox, bearded seal, walrus, reindeer, 3. dog, horse, cow, sheep, goat, 4.–6. Answers may vary slightly 4. Things in a Lunch Box, 5. Things in the Ocean, 6. Vehicles or Things with wheels

p. 515
1. Question A, 2. Question B, 3. Question A, 4. Question A, 5. Question B

p. 516
Answers may vary. Who: Campers; What: Spiders; Where: In unusual places, such as in canoes and boots; When: At different times; Why: Looking for a safe place to spin a web to catch food; Summary: Spiders spin webs in unusual places to catch food. Campers may be surprised by spiders at any time.

p. 517
Answers will vary. 1. Maureen had conflicting feelings about going into the fifth grade., 2. Maureen found that her fears about the fifth grade were needless.

p. 518
Where: in the treetops; When: if they sense danger; Why: to scare away the threat

p. 519
Answers may vary. Possible responses: Conclusion: I can conclude that tugboats are important to the city of Seattle.; Details: 1. Tugboats guide ships in and out of the harbor., 2. Tugboats help ships move safely. 3. The city of Seattle thinks tugboats should be honored because of their importance.

p. 520
The Falcon
I. Falcon was a symbol of Egyptian King Ramses II
   A. God of the sky
   B. Protected the king

...e Crane
...Crane is symbol used in Japan
  A. Stands for good luck
  B. Used in folk tales

WRITING SKILLS

...nswers to the practice paper
...ercises questions may vary, but
...amples are provided here to give
...ou an idea of how your child may
...spond.

524
...ossible responses:
...He is seventy-five. He was a
...hoolteacher. He is married. He
...ilt a patio. 2. They were
...hoolteachers for 40 years.
...They found bricks made by
...randpa Weaver.

525–526
...ossible responses:
...She doesn't care much about
...kes. 2. He wants his daughter to
...e bikes. He likes to make his
...ughter happy. 3. The writer
...scovers that her father has bought
...r the bike after all as a surprise.
...They love each other.

527–528
...Cristina's shining eyes and
...embling fingers, Grandma's smile,
...ristina's opening her gifts and
...gging the kitten, the tiny black
...ten 2. Grandma's and Cristina's
...ords, the scratching noises from
...e box 3. His happiness at seeing
...w happy he had made his sister

529
...esponses will vary. Be sure that
...ch sentence includes a vivid word.

530
...e sure that words are appropriate
...onyms. Possible responses:
...actually 2. unusual 3. difficult
...glad, 5–7. Responses will vary. Be
...re each sentence uses an antonym.

531–532
                    forget
...Who could ever (fourget) the
...rrible sandstorm we had last
...arch? It was one of the most
...ightening
...ghtening) experiences of my life!

...For many months there had been
                    January
...most no rain. December, (Janurary,)
...d February had been especially
...y. No rain fell in March, either,
...t the wind began to blow furiously.
...n many days the sky was more
         blue
...own than (blew) because the air was
...filled with sand. The sand even

crept inside ^a hour house. Every

morning my bed felt gritty. As I

walked to and from school, blowing

sand stung my ears, eyes, and cheeks ⊙

            especially
One afternoon was (expecially)

scary. We all looked anxiously

through the classroom windows as

the sky grew darker and darker. Our

teacher, Mrs. Robertson, tried to
            story
tell us a (storry) but no one could

listen. The wind howled, and we felt

sand settle on our desks. Suddenly,
                    midnight
everything was as dark as (midnite.)

The electricity had gone off!

P. 539
1. The writer wrote "A Friend at
the Right Time" to explain how she
met her best friend. Sunny tells us at
the very beginning that this is a
story that she loves to tell. 2. This
story takes place at the annual
school fair. 3. Although Sunny says
kids drive her crazy, she takes good
care of them. For instance, she saves
a child when he falls from the pony.
(Look for a clear understanding of
Sunny's character in your child's
answers. Be sure your child includes
details from the narrative to support
his or her understanding.)
4. Summaries will vary. Be sure your
child correctly summarizes the
significant events of the story,
paraphrasing as needed. Summaries
should be organized in a thoughtful
way, with the main ideas and
important details clearly presented.

P. 540
1. Sunny uses words like *I, me,* and
my to show that she is writing about
her own personal experiences. 2. A
little boy is falling off the pony.
Sunny has to catch the boy before
he gets hurt. 3. Tiger, a very fast
dog, actually solved Sunny's
problem. He ran into the pony ring
and led the pony out of the way so
Sunny could catch the little boy.
4. A conclusion brings the story to
an end. It ties up all the loose ends.
5. In the first paragraph, Sunny tells
us that this story is about how she
met her best friend, Tiger. The last
paragraph describes exactly what
Tiger did at the school fair and how
Tiger became Sunny's best friend.

P. 545
    Homemade peanut butter is easy
to make. First, shell the peanuts.

Next, put peanuts in a blender.
Blend them until they are smooth.
Last, stir in a little cooking oil and
salt. Spread on bread or crackers
and eat! 1. Homemade peanut
butter is easy to make.
2. Instructions for eating.

P. 546–547
1. "Musical Chairs" is a good game
to play with a group of friends. 2. It
names the game. 3. It names the
materials needed to play the game.
4. They tell how to play the game.
5. It tells how to decide who wins.

P. 548
Responses will vary. Be sure each
answer lists the steps in correct
order. Trace the outline of the kite
onto a sheet of plastic; cut out the
kite; glue the frame to the back of
the kite; add a tail and decorations;
attach the kite string

P. 549
Possible response:
    Here's how to play Pin the Nose
on the Clown. Draw a large clown
face, but do not draw the nose. Give
each player a pin and a small paper
circle for the nose. Hang the clown
face on a wall. Cover the first
player's eyes with a cloth. The player
tries to pin the nose on the clown.
Keep playing until every player has
had a turn. The winner is the one
who pins the nose closest to the
place where it belongs.

P. 550
1. Mei, Karina, and Martin gave a
party. 2. They met on Wednesday
and Friday to plan the party.
3. They invited Tom, Jill, and
Carlos. 4. Each guest received a
colorful hat, a balloon, and a sparkly
pen. 5. The children played Simon
Says, Musical Chairs, and Pin the
Tail on the Donkey. 6. Martin and
Mei taught the others a new game.
7. Tom, Carlos, and Karina did a
funny dance.

P. 551–552

Do you enjoy collecting large or

unusually pretty leaves ? then you
                       ≡
should learn to make ink prints of

leaves. Making the prints is fun, and

you'll enjoy having pretty prints of

your best leaves ⊙

    The most important thing for

making a leaf print is a leaf that you

like. You also need a piece of felt
                   larger
just a little (lareger) than your leaf, a

smooth board, a few thick sheets of

plain paper, and some ink.

    To begin making your leaf print,

place the felt on the board ⊙ Carefully

pour the ink onto the felt until the
      whole
(hole) piece is damp. With the vein-

side down, place your leaf on the

felt. Cover it with a sheet of paper,

and press down on the leaf. then
                              ≡
take away the sheet of paper, pick the

leaf up, and put it ink-side down on

a clean piece of paper. Cover the leaf

with another piece of paper, and press

down again ⊙ When you take away

the top paper and the leaf, you'll

have your own special leaf print.

P. 559
1. This how-to paper teaches how
to make a papier-mâché zoo. 2. The
materials needed to make a papier-
mâché zoo include old newspapers,
a bucket, glue, water, paper cups,
pipe cleaners, tempera paint, and
paintbrushes. 3. The first step is to
make papier-mâché pulp. 4. If the
papier-mâché pulp is runny, it is too
hard to shape. (Help your child to
recognize this answer as an
important detail. Discuss the
importance of details such as this in
a how-to paper.) 5. Answers will
vary, but look for indications of
understanding, such as a clear
description of an animal and a
corresponding illustration.

P. 560
1. The writer states the purpose of
the paper clearly, lists materials, and
gives clear, step-by-step instructions
and helpful hints and details. 2. The
writer says to collect materials
before beginning the project. 3. The
writer lists the materials so they can
be collected before you start the
project. That way, the project can be
completed without wasting time
finding materials. Plus, some parts
of the papier-mâché process need
quick action. For example, the
newspapers should be torn into
strips before the paste is made so
the paste doesn't harden.
4. Sequence words help the reader
understand the order of the steps.
5. Pictures and answers may vary.
Check pictures to determine if your
child understood the explanation in
the sixth paragraph.

1. Dove's bedroom 2. Be proud of yourself, but do not be more proud than you should be. 3. b

P. 566–567

1. the outback of Australia 2. Emu and Bowerbird 3. Emu wishes he could fly, and Bowerbird wishes he could run. 4. Emu teaches Bowerbird to run, and Bowerbird teaches Emu to fly. 5. With a little help from a friend, you can do anything. 6. Responses will vary.

P. 568

1. c 2. Possible response: Mrs. Mason's son told her the letter was on its way. 3. no 4. yes 5. no 6. yes 7. no 8. yes 9. yes

P. 569

A. 1. She is a friendly person. 2. She sits down beside the new girl and smiles. 3. Introducing herself and inviting the new girl to play shows that she is friendly. B. Responses will vary. Be sure your child uses dialogue.

P. 570

Possible response:

Dove was dressing for Wren's party. How proud she was of her snowy white dress! It might be the most beautiful outfit at the party. Dove turned around and around. She admired her reflection in the mirror. "How lovely I look!" she cried. Then her wing bumped a bottle of ink that was sitting on her desk. The bottle turned over, and splash! Down the front of Dove's dress went an inky black stain. Moral: Be proud of yourself, but not more proud than you should be.

P. 571–572

Baby Chick peered through the tall grass at the edge of the pond. His ~~freinds~~ friends Little Duck and Little Swan splashed happily in the water.

"Come on in, Baby Chick" called Little Duck. "Yes, added Little Swan. "The water's nice and warm today."

Little Duck quacked "Watch me do a trick!" Then he put his head under the water and turned a somersault ⊙

Baby Chick sighed. "I wish I could do that " he answered.

"Swimming looks like such fun. Look at my feet, though. Yours are webbed, but mine just have little chicken toes ⊙"

"Don't worry," laughed Little Swan. "I'm sure you can learn to swim anyway. Look at this!" He proudly traced a figure ~~ate~~ eight in the water.

P. 579

1. Aesop tells this story to teach us that if we are kind to others, they will be kind to us. Dove helped Ant Two. In return, Ant and Ant Two saved Dove's life. 2. Ant, Ant Two, and Dove talk, think, and have feelings, as people do. For example, Ant and Ant Two grow tired and become cranky. They get scared, help each other, and have friendships, as people do. 3. In the beginning of the story, the setting is a big, dusty field. It is the end of summer and hot. In the middle of the story, the setting changes to a beautiful river that is surrounded by trees. The tall trees look like guards around the river. 4. Be sure your child correctly summarizes the significant events of the story, paraphrasing as needed. Summaries should be organized in a thoughtful way, with the main ideas and important details clearly presented.

P. 580

1. Aesop uses talking animals to tell the story. The ants say funny things like, "Imagine that big ball of gas (the Sun) rolling seeds across this field." The animal characters have exciting adventures like tumbling into the river. 2. Aesop shows them making jokes, feeling tired, feeling thirsty, and being scared. He shows them doing brave things and making friends. 3. Ant Two falls into the river. The human tries to catch Dove with a net. 4. Dove drops a leaf into the river and saves Ant Two. Ant and Ant Two sting the human on the legs so Dove can fly to safety. 5. Dialogue adds interest and fun to the story. The ants' conversation helps move the story along. It also shows the characters' feelings and thoughts.

P. 585

Comparison: 3, 5
Contrast: 1, 2, 4
6. both 7. while, instead of, unlike

P. 586–587

Comparison: 1, 2, 5
Contrast: 3, 4, 6
7. both, like, same 8. but, unlike, instead

P. 588–589

Wording may vary.
Colonial Williamsburg: Life in the 1700s. City life. Capitol, Governor's Palace, elegant houses. Both Places: Show what life was like in the past. Many shops and buildings open to tourists. Popular demonstrations of crafts. Old Sturbridge Village: Life in 1830 in a New England village. Country life. Farm, sawmill, mill for grinding grain.

P. 590

Possible responses:
1. The Hermitage is a very large house. 2. It was Andrew Jackson's home for 26 years. 3. Jackson's wife approved the site for the house. 4. Jackson had not yet been elected president when he built the house in 1819. 5. The view from the house is breathtaking. 6. Beautiful green hills can be seen from there. 7. A major fire almost destroyed the house in 1834. 8. Jackson wasted no time in rebuilding. 9. He gave many parties and invited many people.

P. 591–592

Be sure responses are appropriate synonyms. Possible responses:
1. peaceful 2. towering, glistening 3. colorful 4. gentle 5. precious, lovely 6. fabulous 7. bustling 8. earsplitting, frantic 9. longed-for 10. silent

P. 593–594

Texas and New mexico are neighboring states, and in many ~~weighs~~ ways they are alike. Of course, they share a common border. Both states have large areas of land that are dry and flat, and both states have mountains. New Mexico's capital, santa fe, is not the state's largest city, and Austin, the capital of Texas, is much smaller than Houston, dallas, or San Antonio.

Although new Mexico and Texas have much in common, they are different in many ways. Some American Indians live in texas, but they make up a much larger portion of the population of New Mexico. The land is also different. Unlike

Texas, New mexico has areas of tr desert. Also, the rocky Mountains slice through central New Mexico giving the State large areas of gree forests. The mountains of texas, in the area called Big Bend, are muc drier and are not forested.

P. 600

1. This paper compares and contrasts the American Alligator a the American Crocodile. 2. Guide your child in organizing the information in a clear manner. Ho Alligators and Crocodiles Are Alik Both have long bodies, sharp teeth and tough skin.; Both are more th 15 feet long and weigh about 450–500 pounds.; Both live in an near freshwater and where fresh a saltwater meet.; They drown the animals they eat.; Both build nests to lay eggs. How Alligators and Crocodiles Are Different: An adul alligator is nearly black in color an has a wide, flat snout. An adult crocodile is olive-brown and has a long, narrow nose.; Only the uppe teeth are visible when an alligator' mouth is closed, but you can see teeth in both the upper and lower jaws when a crocodile closes its mouth.; Alligators eat many different kinds of food, including fish, frogs, turtles, snakes, birds, deer, and other alligators. Crocodiles generally eat fish, although they may attack and eat other animals if they come too close.; Alligators break their prey into bite-sized pieces. Crocodiles swallow theirs whole.; Alligator mothers build mounds to use as nests. They lay about 30 eggs, which hatch in about two months. Some baby alligators stay near thei mothers for more than two years. Female crocodiles build their nests by digging holes in the sand or mud. They lay about 30 to 60 egg which hatch about three months later. Baby crocodiles leave the ne a few days after birth.

P. 601

1. Talking about action movies in the first paragraph grabs the reade attention. 2. The writer says, "But there's more to these reptiles than you think." Then the writer invite you to take a closer look. 3. The writer uses the sixth paragraph to change the main idea. The writer says, "Now let's talk about what they eat and where they lay their eggs." 4. The seventh paragraph describes what alligators eat. The eighth paragraph tells what crocodiles eat. Talking about

gators and then crocodiles makes
easier for the reader to understand
w the animals are alike and
ferent. 5. In the introduction, the
iter talks about animals in the
ovies. By writing about the movies
ain in the conclusion, the writer
ishes the idea and relates the first
d last paragraphs.

607
Yellowstone National Park has
me of the strangest scenery.
The smell of pine trees fills the
. 3. b, d

608
The wintry scene looked like an
ist's dream. 2. It suggests what
e paragraph is about and sets the
od. 3. The clip-clopping of the
rses; their jingling harness bells
The passengers breathing icy air
d snuggling into blankets; the
d of the stone towers 5. Rows of
vering pines, their branches
ooping with snow; the castle
king its towers into the gray sky;
ght red and purple blankets
The writer begins by telling
out things on the ground and
ves up, ending in the sky.

609–610
rding may vary slightly.
dows; broken windows;
ergrown with weeds; crows
cling; Drooping branches; a dark
ud; cold, damp air; old, musty
ell; cobwebs; creaking door.

611
the lake, a golden mirror
mountain peaks, jagged teeth
the setting sun, a melting ball of
x; 4. the sunset, a pink and
ange flame
6, 7. Responses will vary. Be sure
at similes and metaphors are
scriptive.

612
sure each answer is two
tences or a compound sentence.
ssible responses: 1. Our boat
ugged into the bay. We saw that
e opposite shore was covered by
id ice. 2. The mountain of ice
s a glacier. It rose straight up out
the water. 3. I moved out onto
e deck, and an icy wind blistered
face. 4. Our boat chugged nearer
the wall of ice. The wind grew
en colder. 5. Now I could see
ged pieces of ice floating in the
ter. Some had furry passengers.
The passengers were soft-eyed
ls. They stared at me without
r. 7. We drew close to the glacier.
en we heard a loud rumbling.
A chunk of ice fell from the
cier. It dropped into the water.

p. 613–614

On this sunny day, the crowded
beach is as busy as a school
playground during recess. Far from
the waves, families spreads blankets
on the sand and share picnic lunches.
A child dig^s in the sand while his
older brother and sister toss a beach
ball back and forth. A little nearer
the water, huge umbrellas sprout
like brightly-colored mushrooms.
Men and women stretches out in
the shade to read or nap. At the
edge of the ocean, a small girl build^s
a sand castle. Her brother look^s for
pretty shells and helps her decorate
the castle walls ⊙The soft sand and
shallow water attract children of all
ages. They runs and splash where
the water laps the (beech.) *beach* Farther
from shore ‸ strong swimmers rides
the waves. Floating on (there) *their* backs,
they look like playful dolphins. Out
where the waves spray white foam, a
few surfboards skim across the
water. The boards rises and plunge
on the waves like crazy elevators.

p. 619
1. The writer describes the first time
the two puppies, Miss and Match,
go to the beach. 2. As soon as their
paws touch the sand, the puppies
freeze. 3. A sandpiper runs up and
down the beach. Match chases after
it. Suddenly, the piper turns and
flies out over the water. Match,
without thinking, follows. Match
runs into the water and then swims
back to the beach. 4. Be sure that
your child correctly summarizes the
significant events of the story,
paraphrasing as needed. Main ideas
should be organized logically and
important details presented clearly.

p. 620
1. The writer describes the beach as
always changing. The water changes
from blue to gray. The sand is
almost white. The sun is pale and
weak. The beach is empty and cool
for people but perfect for dogs.
2. The sand is white and fine as
sugar. 3. The writer teases the
reader with information. This makes
the reader curious, so the reader
keeps reading to find out what
happens. 4. The writer compares the
sandpiper to a wind-up toy with a
tight spring. 5. The writer wants the
reader to know that the dogs do
more exciting things at the beach.

p. 625
1. by making you wonder where
animals sleep 2. Animals sleep in a
variety of places. 3. c

p. 626
1. Possible response: Animals That
Make Music 2. by making you
wonder why animals howl
3. Scientists have several different
ideas about why these members of
the dog family howl. 4. They believe
that howling is a way for the animals
to communicate. Some scientists
think that wolves may howl to call
back members of the pack that have
wandered away.

p. 627
Word order in each list may vary.
1. jaguar, leopard, boa constrictor,
tiger, spider monkey, 2. polar bear,
arctic fox, bearded seal, walrus,
reindeer 3. dog, horse, cow, sheep,
goat 4, 5, 6. Responses will vary. Be
sure each answer is a category into
which all the items will fit.

p. 628–629
1. b 2. It gets the reader's attention.
3, 4, 5, 6. Responses will vary. Be
sure that the opening and closing
are suitable.

p. 630
Possible responses:
1. Many kinds of spiders spin webs,
but not all of the webs are alike.
2. A web may be long and narrow,
or it may be shaped like a triangle.
3. Some webs are like funnels, but
others look more like domes.
4. Wolf spiders hide in burrows, but
lynx spiders live on trees or bushes.
5. Many lynx spiders are green, and
they are hard to find on green
leaves. 6. Tarantulas are furry, and
they look fierce.

p.631–632

Mountain gorillas live in the
mountain forests of Africa, usually in
groups of about ten. At night the
gorillas sleep in trees or on the

ground and during the day they
look for food. They most often eat
roots and tree bark ‸ but sometimes
they find other plants to eat ‸ too.
Mountain gorillas are shy animals ‸
and they are almost always gentle. A
group of gorillas may accept a scientist ‸
and the scientist might live among
them for a while ⊙

Mountain gorillas communicate
with each other by making sounds.
They make barking sounds when
they are frightened ‸ and gorilla
babies sometimes cry. During times
of danger, the group leader may
roar noisily. this noise often warns
enemies
(enemys) away. Happy gorillas may
make deep, rumbling noises when
they are eating and they make
similar sounds when they are resting.

p. 637
1. The Lost City is a community
located on top of a mountain under
the Atlantic Ocean. 2. The Lost City
formed when cool ocean water met
hot lava. The water picked up
minerals from the lava. Later, the
minerals settled out and built strange
forms like mounds, towers, and
chimneys. 3. Both black and white
smokers are underwater clouds that
form when very hot water moves
through vents and meets cooler
ocean water. 4. Black smokers are
hotter than white smokers. Also,
black smokers contain copper, while
white smokers contain zinc. 5. The
worms that live near vents make
coverings called tubes to protect
themselves, so they are called
tubeworms. 6. Be sure that your
child identifies the report's main
ideas and includes significant details.

p. 638
1. The first paragraph of a short
report introduces the topic. Because
the topic of this report has such an
interesting, mysterious name, the
writer includes it in the first
sentence to encourage the reader to
keep reading. 2. The other main
ideas in this report are how vent
communities form, how living
things survive in vent communities,

and how the Lost City is different from other vent communities.
3. The writer uses simpler words to define each word that the reader might not know. 4. The writer uses facts like numbers and dates to make the report more accurate. Facts also show the reader that the writer probably used reference materials to find information for the report. 5. The first paragraph introduces the topic of this report. The last paragraph summarizes the topic.

TEST PREP

P. 650
1. B 2. J 3. not liked 4. A

P. 651
1. D 2. F 3. B 4. cave

P. 652-653
1. B 2. G 3. eats 4. A 5. F
6. connected

P. 654
1. C 2. the tide 3. F 4. D

P. 655
1. C 2. after the mahouts tie a short rope to the chain 3. H

P. 656
1. A 2. after he examined all the wheels carefully

P. 657
1. B 2. J 3. B 4. May 1, 1893

P. 658
1. B 2. H 3. C 4. how to remove gum from clothes

P. 659
1. D 2. G 3. Jackie Cochran was a natural pilot.

P. 660-661
1. A 2. why people started saying "Bless you" when someone sneezes 3. G 4. why the feathers on flamingos are bright pink

P. 662-663
1. C 2. J 3. They need to hide from enemies. 4. C 5. G 6. B 7. Fish can't live in such salty water.

P. 664-665
1. B 2. F 3. She will scold Andres and Nicole because they forgot to turn off the water when they were finished. 4. B 5. F 6. Dip a brush into the paint and start painting.

P. 666-667
1. A 2. Monday 3. J 4. Mexico was under Spanish rule for 300 years.

P. 668-669
1. A 2. G 3. October. The clue was in the last sentence that stated that Reggie Jackson was known as Mr. October. 4. B 5. H 6. He thought all the continents were once a large land mass that had drifted apart over time.

P. 670-671
1. A 2. F 3. He feels his son should wait until he finished school to take a job. 4. A 5. He is very nervous about flying.

P. 672-673
1. C 2. F 3. D 4. G 5. B

P. 674-681
SA. C 1. D 2. to escape from their enemies 3. H 4. A 5. by reading a newspaper story about how President Roosevelt saved a small bear cub on a hunting trip 6. J 7. B 8. J 9. A 10. F 11. C 12. J 13. A 14. several days 15. a week 16. H 17. A 18. G 19. Earth Patrol 20. A 21. H 22. C 23. J 24. D 25. G 26. D 27. H 28. D 29. the fawn 30. J 31. D 32. F

P. 682-688
SA. B 1. B 2. H 3. C 4. to protect it from wild animals 5. J 6. A 7. H 8. to stay safe 9. B 10. H 11. A 12. F 13. C 14. G 15. B 16. H 17. A 18. G 19. C 20. continue to swallow its prey 21. J 22. A 23. fourth graders at Main Street school 24. J 25. C 26. J 27. B 28. H

P. 689
SA. D 1. D 2. G 3. B 4. H 5. D 6. H 7. C 8. G

P. 690
SA. D 1. B 2. G 3. C 4. G

P. 691
SA. A 1. A 2. J 3. C 4. G 5. B 6. empty

P. 692-694
SA. D 1. D 2. H 3. D 4. J 5. C 6. G 7. B 8. F 9. a mistake SB. D 10. D 11. H 12. B 13. F 14. B SC. C 15. H 16. B 17. F 18. C 19. G 20. C 21. J 22. A

P. 696
Step 1. To determine if Jason has enough money for both purchases. Step 2. CDs cost $14.99 each. Cassette tapes cost $9.99 each. Jason has $23. Step 3. Estimate the cost of the two items. Step 4. Just under $15 plus just under $10 is just under $25. Jason has only $23, so he does not have enough.
Step 5. Yes, because the actual sum of the prices of each item is greater than $23.

P. 697
Step 1. To use the bills Mr. Johnson has to make exactly $38. Step 2. He has 2 twenties, 3 tens, 4 fives, and 4 ones. Step 3. Try different combinations until you reach the sum of $38. Step 4. 20 + 10 + 5 + 3 = $38; Mr. Johnson can pay with 1 twenty, 1 ten, 1 five, and 3 ones. Step 5. The solution make sense because it adds to $38 using the money available.

P. 698
SA. A 1. C 2. F 3. D 4. 10

P. 699
SA. C 1. D 2. G 3. A 4. 2 5. J

P. 700-701
SA. C 1. 3,800 2. C 3. G 4. New York and Pennsylvania 5. A 6. J 7. D 8. F

P. 702-703
SA. C 1. D 2. H 3. A 4. J 5. rectangle 6. A 7. H 8. B 9. F 10. 5

P. 704-705
SA. C 1. A 2. G 3. B 4. J 5. A 6. F 7. B 8. H 9. C

P. 706
SA. B 1. C 2. G 3. C 4. 69

P. 707
SA. B 1. C 2. 1000 3. G 4. B

P. 708
SA. B 1. A 2. pizza 3. H 4. D

P. 709
SA. C 1. E 2. 683 3. G 4. D 5. H 6. A

P. 710
SA. B 1. D 2. J 3. C 4. K

P. 711-713
SA. C SB. H 1. C 2. K 3. C 4. 374 5. K 6. B 7. F 8. A 9. J 10. $4.77 11. B 12. H 13. C 14. G 15. C 16. G 17. C 18. K 19. A 20. 6 inches 21. F 22. B

P. 714-719
SA. C 1. D 2. G 3. three thousand four hundred sixty 4. D 5. F 6. A 7. G 8. D 9. F 10. B 11. Red 12. G 13. C 14. G 15. A 16. F 17. D 18. G 19. pie 20. D 21. H 22. D 23. square 24. F 25. B 26. F 27. 5 cm 28. B 29. J 30. B 31. H 32. A 33. F 34. A 35. 44 36. G

P. 720-725
SA. D 1. C 2. J 3. A 4. 106–108 5. J 6. C 7. G 8. B 9. J 10. C 11. F 12. B 13. 9 14. G 15. A 16. H 17. D 18. G 19. A 20. F 21. C 22. F

P. 726
SA. A 1. D 2. G 3. A 4. F 5. D 6. G 7. A 8. H

P. 727-732
SA. B 1. A 2. G 3. B 4. J 5. 4 6. D 7. H 8. B 9. G 10. C 11. G 12. C 13. H 14. C 15. F 16. B 17. J 18. A 19. G 20. A 21. F 22. D 23. H 24. A 25. G 26. D 27. G 28. A 29. F 30. C

P. 733-742
SA. C 1. B 2. J 3. C 4. H 5. A 6. 18 feet long 7. F 8. D 9. G 10. C 11. J 12. because he couldn't think of anything to write about 13. B 14. H 15. C 16. H 17. D 18. H 19. B 20. F 21. A 22. J 23. D 24. H 25. to make it thin out evenly 26. C 27. H 28. D 29. F 30. D 31. F 32. She had to take classes at Hull House to learn English and about the American way of life, as well as

about the government of the Uni States. 33. D 34. H 35. C 36. G 37. B 38. H 39. A 40. G 41. the Rose Hotel 42. A 43. F 44. C 45 46. C

P. 743-745
SA. C 1. A 2. G 3. C 4. G 5. B 6. H 7. A 8. J 9. B SB. D 10. F 11. C 12. G 13. D 14. F SC. B 15. C 16. J 17. B 18. F 19. B 20. 21. B 22. H

P. 746-753
SA. D 1. A 2. G 3. A 4. J 5. C 6. 7. D 8. two thousand six hundred five 9. 7 10. F 11. C 12. H 13. D 14. H 15. D 16. J 17. C 18. Gree Thumb Hour 19. J 20. B 21. 3 inches 22. J 23. C 24. G 25. A 26. G 27. A 28. F 29. C 30. J 31. 32. $0.51 33. J 34. B 35. J 36. A 37. J 38. C 39. F 40. A 41. J 42. inches 43. D 44. H 45. 2 46. B 47. G 48. C 49. J

P. 754-755
SA. E 1. B 2. F 3. C 4. J 5. B 6. 7. D 8. 4 9. G SB. D 10. C 11. F 12. 1 13. C 14. G 15. E

P. 756-757
SA. B 1. D 2. G 3. D 4. F 5. D 6. 7. D 8. 6 9. G 10. B 11. F 12. 11 13. A 14. J 15. D 16. J 17. B 18. 19. A 20. G 21. C 22. F 23. B 24. 25. B 26. H 27. A 28. F 29. B 30. 31. C 32. F 33. B 34. J 35. A 36. 37. B 38. H